P9-DOH-984

GENERAL MOTORS
CORSICA/BERETTA
1988-96 REPAIR MANUAL

CHILTON'S™

President	Dean F. Morgantini, S.A.E.
Vice President–Finance	Barry L. Beck
Vice President–Sales	Glenn D. Potere
Executive Editor	Kevin M. G. Maher, A.S.E.
Manager–Consumer Automotive	Richard Schwartz, A.S.E.
Manager–Marine/Recreation	James R. Marotta, A.S.E.
Production Specialists	Brian Hollingsworth, Melinda Possinger
Project Managers	Will Kessler, A.S.E., S.A.E., Thomas A. Mellon, A.S.E., S.A.E., Richard Rivele, Todd W. Stidham, A.S.E., Ron Webb
Editor	Christine L. Sheeky, S.A.E.

CHILTON™ *Automotive Books*

PUBLISHED BY **W. G. NICHOLS, INC.**

Manufactured in USA
© 1998 W. G. Nichols
1020 Andrew Drive
West Chester, PA 19380
ISBN 0-8019-8825-X
Library of Congress Catalog Card No. 97-77879
4567890123 8765432109

www.chiltononline.com

Contents

Contents

7 — DRIVE TRAIN

8 — SUSPENSION AND STEERING

9 — BRAKES

10 — BODY

GLOSSARY

MASTER INDEX

See last page for information on additional titles

SAFETY NOTICE

Proper service and repair procedures are vital to the safe, reliable operation of all motor vehicles, as well as the personal safety of those performing repairs. This manual outlines procedures for servicing and repairing vehicles using safe, effective methods. The procedures contain many NOTES, CAUTIONS and WARNINGS which should be followed, along with standard procedures to eliminate the possibility of personal injury or improper service which could damage the vehicle or compromise its safety.

It is important to note that repair procedures and techniques, tools and parts for servicing motor vehicles, as well as the skill and experience of the individual performing the work vary widely. It is not possible to anticipate all of the conceivable ways or conditions under which vehicles may be serviced, or to provide cautions as to all possible hazards that may result. Standard and accepted safety precautions and equipment should be used when handling toxic or flammable fluids, and safety goggles or other protection should be used during cutting, grinding, chiseling, prying, or any other process that can cause material removal or projectiles.

Some procedures require the use of tools specially designed for a specific purpose. Before substituting another tool or procedure, you must be completely satisfied that neither your personal safety, nor the performance of the vehicle will be endangered.

Although information in this manual is based on industry sources and is complete as possible at the time of publication, the possibility exists that some car manufacturers made later changes which could not be included here. While striving for total accuracy, NP/Chilton cannot assume responsibility for any errors, changes or omissions that may occur in the compilation of this data.

PART NUMBERS

Part numbers listed in this reference are not recommendations by Chilton for any product brand name. They are references that can be used with interchange manuals and aftermarket supplier catalogs to locate each brand supplier's discrete part number.

SPECIAL TOOLS

Special tools are recommended by the vehicle manufacturer to perform their specific job. Use has been kept to a minimum, but where absolutely necessary, they are referred to in the text by the part number of the tool manufacturer. These tools can be purchased, under the appropriate part number, from your local dealer or regional distributor, or an equivalent tool can be purchased locally from a tool supplier or parts outlet. Before substituting any tool for the one recommended, read the SAFETY NOTICE at the top of this page.

ACKNOWLEDGMENTS

Portions of the materials contained herein have been reprinted with the permission of General Motors Corporation, Service Technology Group.

1

GENERAL INFORMATION AND MAINTENANCE

HOW TO USE THIS BOOK

This Chilton's Total Car Care manual, for the Beretta and Corsica, is intended to help you learn more about the inner workings of your vehicle while saving you money on its upkeep and operation.

The beginning of the book will likely be referred to the most, since that is where you will find information for maintenance and tune-up. The other sections deal with the more complex systems of your vehicle. Systems (from engine through brakes) are covered to the extent that the average do-it-yourselfer can attempt. This book will not explain such things as rebuilding a differential because the expertise required and the special tools necessary make this uneconomical. It will, however, give you detailed instructions to help you change your own brake pads and shoes, replace spark plugs, and perform many more jobs that can save you money and help avoid expensive problems.

A secondary purpose of this book is a reference for owners who want to understand their vehicle and/or their mechanics better.

Where to Begin

Before removing any bolts, read through the entire procedure. This will give you the overall view of what tools and supplies will be required. So read ahead and plan ahead. Each operation should be approached logically and all procedures thoroughly understood before attempting any work.

If repair of a component is not considered practical, we tell you how to remove the part and then how to install the new or rebuilt replacement. In this way, you at least save labor costs.

Avoiding Trouble

Many procedures in this book require you to "label and disconnect . . ." a group of lines, hoses or wires. Don't be think you can remember where everything goes—you won't. If you hook up vacuum or fuel lines incorrectly, the vehicle may run poorly, if at all. If you hook up electrical wiring incorrectly, you may instantly learn a very expensive lesson.

You don't need to know the proper name for each hose or line. A piece of masking tape on the hose and a piece on its fitting will allow you to assign your own label. As long as you remember your own code, the lines can be reconnected by matching your tags. Remember that tape will dissolve in gasoline or solvents; if a part is to be washed or cleaned, use another method of identification. A permanent felt-tipped marker or a metal scribe can be very handy for marking metal parts. Remove any tape or paper labels after assembly.

Maintenance or Repair?

Maintenance includes routine inspections, adjustments, and replacement of parts which show signs of normal wear. Maintenance compensates for wear or deterioration. Repair implies that something has broken or is not working. A need for a repair is often caused by lack of maintenance. for example: draining and refilling automatic transmission fluid is maintenance recommended at specific intervals. Failure to do this can shorten the life of the transmission/transaxle, requiring very expensive repairs. While no maintenance program can prevent items from eventually breaking or wearing out, a general rule is true: MAINTENANCE IS CHEAPER THAN REPAIR.

Two basic mechanic's rules should be mentioned here. First, whenever the left side of the vehicle or engine is referred to, it means the driver's side. Conversely, the right side of the vehicle means the passenger's side. Second, screws and bolts are removed by turning counterclockwise, and tightened by turning clockwise unless specifically noted.

Safety is always the most important rule. Constantly be aware of the dangers involved in working on an automobile and take the proper precautions. Please refer to the information in this section regarding SERVICING YOUR VEHICLE SAFELY and the SAFETY NOTICE on the acknowledgment page.

Avoiding the Most Common Mistakes

Pay attention to the instructions provided. There are 3 common mistakes in mechanical work:

1. Incorrect order of assembly, disassembly or adjustment. When taking something apart or putting it together, performing steps in the wrong order usually just costs you extra time; however, it CAN break something. Read the entire procedure before beginning. Perform everything in the order in which the instructions say you should, even if you can't see a reason for it. When you're taking apart something that is very intricate, you might want to draw a picture of how it looks when assembled in order to make sure you get everything back in its proper position. When making adjustments, perform them in the proper order. One adjustment possibly will affect another.

2. Overtorquing (or undertorquing). While it is more common for overtorquing to cause damage, undertorquing may allow a fastener to vibrate loose causing serious damage. Especially when dealing with aluminum parts, pay attention to torque specifications and utilize a torque wrench in assembly. If a torque figure is not available, remember that if you are using the right tool to perform the job, you will probably not have to strain yourself to get a fastener tight enough. The pitch of most threads is so slight that the tension you put on the wrench will be multiplied many times in actual force on what you are tightening.

There are many commercial products available for ensuring that fasteners won't come loose, even if they are not torqued just right (a very common brand is Loctite®). If you're worried about getting something together tight enough to hold, but loose enough to avoid mechanical damage during assembly, one of these products might offer substantial insurance. Before choosing a threadlocking compound, read the label on the package and make sure the product is compatible with the materials, fluids, etc. involved.

3. Crossthreading. This occurs when a part such as a bolt is screwed into a nut or casting at the wrong angle and forced. Crossthreading is more likely to occur if access is difficult. It helps to clean and lubricate fasteners, then to start threading the bolt, spark plug, etc. with your fingers. If you encounter resistance, unscrew the part and start over again at a different angle until it can be inserted and turned several times without much effort. Keep in mind that many parts have tapered threads, so that gentle turning will automatically bring the part you're threading to the proper angle. Don't put a wrench on the part until it's been tightened a couple of turns by hand. If you suddenly encounter resistance, and the part has not seated fully, don't force it. Pull it back out to make sure it's clean and threading properly.

Be sure to take your time and be patient, and always plan ahead. Allow yourself ample time to perform repairs and maintenance.

TOOLS AND EQUIPMENT

♦ **See Figures 1 thru 15**

Without the proper tools and equipment it is impossible to properly service your vehicle. It would be virtually impossible to catalog every tool that you would need to perform all of the operations in this book. It would be unwise for the amateur to rush out and buy an expensive set of tools on the theory that he/she may need one or more of them at some time.

The best approach is to proceed slowly, gathering a good quality set of those tools that are used most frequently. Don't be misled by the low cost of bargain tools. It is far better to spend a little more for better quality. Forged wrenches, 6 or 12-point sockets and fine tooth ratchets are by far preferable to their less expensive counterparts. As any good mechanic can tell you, there are few worse experiences than trying to work on a vehicle with bad tools.

Your monetary savings will be far outweighed by frustration and mangled knuckles.

Begin accumulating those tools that are used most frequently: those associated with routine maintenance and tune-up. In addition to the normal assortment of screwdrivers and pliers, you should have the following tools:

• Wrenches/sockets and combination open end/box end wrenches in sizes ⅛–¾ in. and/or 3mm–19mm ¹³⁄₁₆ in. or ⅝ in. spark plug socket (depending on plug type).

➡**If possible, buy various length socket drive extensions. Universal-joint and wobble extensions can be extremely useful, but be careful when using them, as they can change the amount of torque applied to the socket.**

Fig. 1 All but the most basic procedures will require an assortment of ratchets and sockets

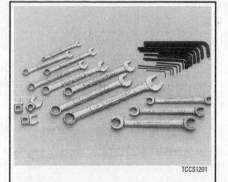

Fig. 2 In addition to ratchets, a good set of wrenches and hex keys will be necessary

Fig. 3 A hydraulic floor jack and a set of jackstands are essential for lifting and supporting the vehicle

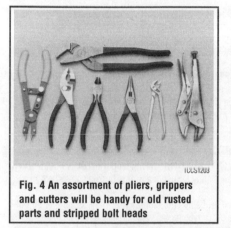

Fig. 4 An assortment of pliers, grippers and cutters will be handy for old rusted parts and stripped bolt heads

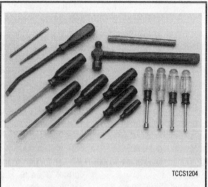

Fig. 5 Various drivers, chisels and prybars are great tools to have in your toolbox

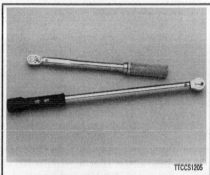

Fig. 6 Many repairs will require the use of a torque wrench to assure the components are properly fastened

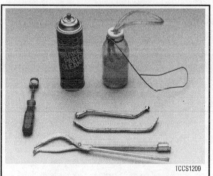

Fig. 7 Although not always necessary, using specialized brake tools will save time

Fig. 8 A few inexpensive lubrication tools will make maintenance easier

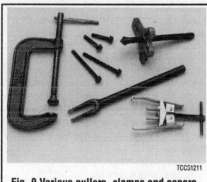

Fig. 9 Various pullers, clamps and separator tools are needed for many larger, more complicated repairs

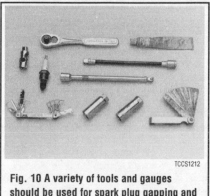

Fig. 10 A variety of tools and gauges should be used for spark plug gapping and installation

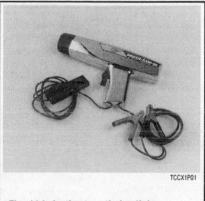

Fig. 11 Inductive type timing light

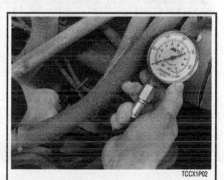

Fig. 12 A screw-in type compression gauge is recommended for compression testing

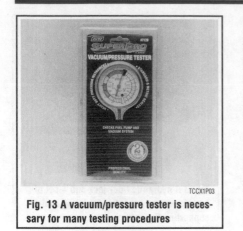

Fig. 13 A vacuum/pressure tester is necessary for many testing procedures

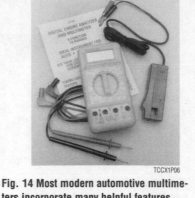

Fig. 14 Most modern automotive multimeters incorporate many helpful features

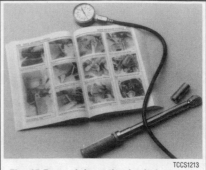

Fig. 15 Proper information is vital, so always have a Chilton Total Car Care manual handy

- Jackstands for support.
- Oil filter wrench.
- Spout or funnel for pouring fluids.
- Grease gun for chassis lubrication (unless your vehicle is not equipped with any grease fittings)
- Hydrometer for checking the battery (unless equipped with a sealed, maintenance-free battery).
- A container for draining oil and other fluids.
- Rags for wiping up the inevitable mess.

In addition to the above items there are several others that are not absolutely necessary, but handy to have around. These include an equivalent oil absorbent gravel, like cat litter, and the usual supply of lubricants, antifreeze and fluids. This is a basic list for routine maintenance, but only your personal needs and desire can accurately determine your list of tools.

After performing a few projects on the vehicle, you'll be amazed at the other tools and non-tools on your workbench. Some useful household items are: a large turkey baster or siphon, empty coffee cans and ice trays (to store parts), a ball of twine, electrical tape for wiring, small rolls of colored tape for tagging lines or hoses, markers and pens, a note pad, golf tees (for plugging vacuum lines), metal coat hangers or a roll of mechanic's wire (to hold things out of the way), dental pick or similar long, pointed probe, a strong magnet, and a small mirror (to see into recesses and under manifolds).

A more advanced set of tools, suitable for tune-up work, can be drawn up easily. While the tools are slightly more sophisticated, they need not be outrageously expensive. There are several inexpensive tach/dwell meters on the market that are every bit as good for the average mechanic as a professional model. Just be sure that it goes to a least 1200–1500 rpm on the tach scale and that it works on 4, 6 and 8-cylinder engines. The key to these purchases is to make them with an eye towards adaptability and wide range. A basic list of tune-up tools could include:

- Tach/dwell meter.
- Spark plug wrench and gapping tool.
- Feeler gauges for valve adjustment.
- Timing light.

The choice of a timing light should be made carefully. A light which works on the DC current supplied by the vehicle's battery is the best choice; it should have a xenon tube for brightness. On any vehicle with an electronic ignition system, a timing light with an inductive pickup that clamps around the No. 1 spark plug cable is preferred.

In addition to these basic tools, there are several other tools and gauges you may find useful. These include:

- Compression gauge. The screw-in type is slower to use, but eliminates the possibility of a faulty reading due to escaping pressure.
- Manifold vacuum gauge.
- 12V test light.
- A combination volt/ohmmeter
- Induction Ammeter. This is used for determining whether or not there is current in a wire. These are handy for use if a wire is broken somewhere in a wiring harness.

As a final note, you will probably find a torque wrench necessary for all but the most basic work. The beam type models are perfectly adequate, although the newer click types (breakaway) are easier to use. The click type torque wrenches tend to be more expensive. Also keep in mind that all types of torque wrenches should be periodically checked and/or recalibrated. You will have to decide for yourself which better fits your pocketbook, and purpose.

Special Tools

Normally, the use of special factory tools is avoided for repair procedures, since these are not readily available for the do-it-yourself mechanic. When it is possible to perform the job with more commonly available tools, it will be pointed out, but occasionally, a special tool was designed to perform a specific function and should be used. Before substituting another tool, you should be convinced that neither your safety nor the performance of the vehicle will be compromised.

Special tools can usually be purchased from an automotive parts store or from your dealer. In some cases special tools may be available directly from the tool manufacturer.

SERVICING YOUR VEHICLE SAFELY

▶ **See Figures 16, 17 and 18**

It is virtually impossible to anticipate all of the hazards involved with automotive maintenance and service, but care and common sense will prevent most accidents.

The rules of safety for mechanics range from "don't smoke around gasoline," to "use the proper tool(s) for the job." The trick to avoiding injuries is to develop safe work habits and to take every possible precaution.

Do's

- Do keep a fire extinguisher and first aid kit handy.
- Do wear safety glasses or goggles when cutting, drilling, grinding or prying, even if you have 20–20 vision. If you wear glasses for the sake of vision, wear safety goggles over your regular glasses.

- Do shield your eyes whenever you work around the battery. Batteries contain sulfuric acid. In case of contact with, flush the area with water or a mixture of water and baking soda, then seek immediate medical attention.
- Do use safety stands (jackstands) for any undervehicle service. Jacks are for raising vehicles; jackstands are for making sure the vehicle stays raised until you want it to come down.
- Do use adequate ventilation when working with any chemicals or hazardous materials. Like carbon monoxide, the asbestos dust resulting from some brake lining wear can be hazardous in sufficient quantities.
- Do disconnect the negative battery cable when working on the electrical system. The secondary ignition system contains EXTREMELY HIGH VOLTAGE. In some cases it can even exceed 50,000 volts.
- Do follow manufacturer's directions whenever working with potentially hazardous materials. Most chemicals and fluids are poisonous.

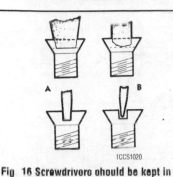

Fig. 16 Screwdrivers should be kept in good condition to prevent injury or damage which could result if the blade slips from the screw

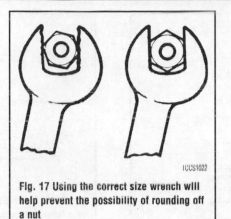

Fig. 17 Using the correct size wrench will help prevent the possibility of rounding off a nut

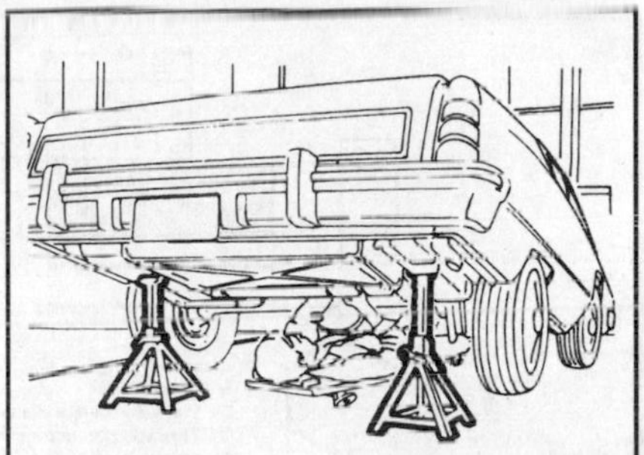

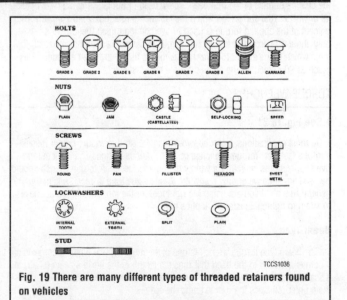

Fig. 18 NEVER work under a vehicle unless it is supported using safety stands (jackstands)

• Do properly maintain your tools. Loose hammerheads, mushroomed punches and chisels, frayed or poorly grounded electrical cords, excessively worn screwdrivers, spread wrenches (open end), cracked sockets, slipping ratchets, or faulty droplight sockets can cause accidents.

• Likewise, keep your tools clean; a greasy wrench can slip off a bolt head, ruining the bolt and often harming your knuckles in the process.

• Do use the proper size and type of tool for the job at hand. Do select a wrench or socket that fits the nut or bolt. The wrench or socket should sit straight, not cocked.

• Do, when possible, pull on a wrench handle rather than push on it, and adjust your stance to prevent a fall.

• Do be sure that adjustable wrenches are tightly closed on the nut or bolt and pulled so that the force is on the side of the fixed jaw.

• Do strike squarely with a hammer; avoid glancing blows.

• Do set the parking brake and block the drive wheels if the work requires a running engine.

Don'ts

• Don't run the engine in a garage or anywhere else without proper ventilation—EVER! Carbon monoxide is poisonous; It takes a long time to leave the human body and you can build up a deadly supply of it in your system by simply breathing in a little at a time. You may not realize you are slowly poisoning yourself. Always use power vents, windows, fans and/or open the garage door.

• Don't work around moving parts while wearing loose clothing. Short sleeves are much safer than long, loose sleeves. Hard-toed shoes with neoprene soles protect your toes and give a better grip on slippery surfaces. Watches and jewelry is not safe working around a vehicle. Long hair should be tied back under a hat or cap.

• Don't use pockets for toolboxes. A fall or bump can drive a screwdriver deep into your body. Even a rag hanging from your back pocket can wrap around a spinning shaft or fan.

• Don't smoke when working around gasoline, cleaning solvent or other flammable material.

• Don't smoke when working around the battery. When the battery is being charged, it gives off explosive hydrogen gas.

• Don't use gasoline to wash your hands; there are excellent soaps available. Gasoline contains dangerous additives which can enter the body through a cut or through your pores. Gasoline also removes all the natural oils from the skin so that bone dry hands will suck up oil and grease.

• Don't service the air conditioning system unless you are equipped with the necessary tools and training. When liquid or compressed gas refrigerant is released to atmospheric pressure it will absorb heat from whatever it contacts. This will chill or freeze anything it touches.

• Don't use screwdrivers for anything other than driving screws! A screwdriver used as a prying tool can snap when you least expect it, causing injuries. At the very least, you'll ruin a good screwdriver.

• Don't use an emergency jack (that little ratchet, scissors, or pantograph jack supplied with the vehicle) for anything other than changing a flat! These jacks are only intended for emergency use out on the road; they are NOT designed as a maintenance tool. If you are serious about maintaining your vehicle yourself, invest in a hydraulic floor jack of at least a 1½ ton capacity, and at least two sturdy jackstands.

FASTENERS, MEASUREMENTS AND CONVERSIONS

Bolts, Nuts and Other Threaded Retainers

▶ See Figures 19 and 20

Although there are a great variety of fasteners found in the modern car or truck, the most commonly used retainer is the threaded fastener (nuts, bolts, screws, studs, etc.). Most threaded retainers may be reused, provided that they are not damaged in use or during the repair. Some retainers (such as stretch bolts or torque prevailing nuts) are designed to deform when tightened or in use and should not be reinstalled.

Whenever possible, we will note any special retainers which should be replaced during a procedure. But you should always inspect the condition of a retainer when it is removed and replace any that show signs of damage. Check all threads for rust or corrosion which can increase the torque necessary to achieve the desired clamp load for which that fastener was originally selected. Additionally, be sure that the driver surface of the fastener has not been compromised by rounding or other damage. In some cases a driver surface may become only partially rounded, allowing the driver to catch in only one direction. In many of these occurrences, a fastener may be installed and tightened, but the driver would not be able to grip and loosen the fastener again.

If you must replace a fastener, whether due to design or damage, you must ALWAYS be sure to use the proper replacement. In all cases, a retainer of the same design, material and strength should be used. Markings on the heads of

Fig. 19 There are many different types of threaded retainers found on vehicles

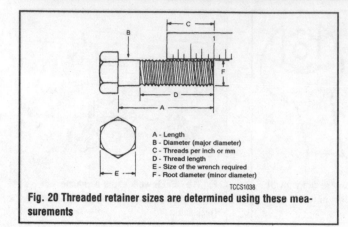

A - Length
B - Diameter (major diameter)
C - Threads per inch or mm
D - Thread length
E - Size of the wrench required
F - Root diameter (minor diameter)

TCCS1038

Fig. 20 Threaded retainer sizes are determined using these measurements

most bolts will help determine the proper strength of the fastener. The same material, thread and pitch must be selected to assure proper installation and safe operation of the vehicle afterwards.

Thread gauges are available to help measure a bolt or stud's thread. Most automotive and hardware stores keep gauges available to help you select the proper size. In a pinch, you can use another nut or bolt for a thread gauge. If the bolt you are replacing is not too badly damaged, you can select a match by finding another bolt which will thread in its place. If you find a nut which threads properly onto the damaged bolt, then use that nut to help select the replacement bolt.

☀ WARNING

Be aware that when you find a bolt with damaged threads, you may also find the nut or drilled hole it was threaded into has also been damaged. If this is the case, you may have to drill and tap the hole, replace the nut or otherwise repair the threads. NEVER try to force a replacement bolt to fit into the damaged threads.

Torque

Torque is defined as the measurement of resistance to turning or rotating. It tends to twist a body about an axis of rotation. A common example of this would be tightening a threaded retainer such as a nut, bolt or screw. Measuring torque is one of the most common ways to help assure that a threaded retainer has been properly fastened.

When tightening a threaded fastener, torque is applied in three distinct areas, the head, the bearing surface and the clamp load. About 50 percent of the measured torque is used in overcoming bearing friction. This is the friction between the bearing surface of the bolt head, screw head or nut face and the base material or washer (the surface on which the fastener is rotating). Approximately 40 percent of the applied torque is used in overcoming thread friction. This leaves only about 10 percent of the applied torque to develop a useful clamp load (the force which holds a joint together). This means that friction can account for as much as 90 percent of the applied torque on a fastener.

TORQUE WRENCHES

♦ See Figure 21

In most applications, a torque wrench can be used to assure proper installation of a fastener. Torque wrenches come in various designs and most automotive supply stores will carry a variety to suit your needs. A torque wrench should be used any time we supply a specific torque value for a fastener. Again, the general rule of "if you are using the right tool for the job, you should not have to strain to tighten a fastener" applies here.

Beam Type

The beam type torque wrench is one of the most popular types. It consists of a pointer attached to the head that runs the length of the flexible beam (shaft) to a scale located near the handle. As the wrench is pulled, the beam bends and the pointer indicates the torque using the scale.

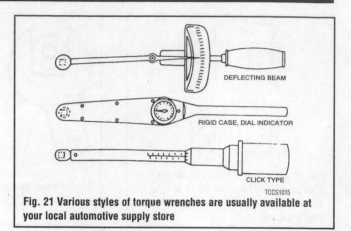

DEFLECTING BEAM

RIGID CASE, DIAL INDICATOR

CLICK TYPE

TCCS1015

Fig. 21 Various styles of torque wrenches are usually available at your local automotive supply store

Click (Breakaway) Type

Another popular design of torque wrench is the click type. To use the click type wrench you pre-adjust it to a torque setting. Once the torque is reached, the wrench has a reflex signaling feature that causes a momentary breakaway of the torque wrench body, sending an impulse to the operator's hand.

Pivot Head Type

♦ See Figure 22

Some torque wrenches (usually of the click type) may be equipped with a pivot head which can allow it to be used in areas of limited access. BUT, it must be used properly. To hold a pivot head wrench, grasp the handle lightly, and as you pull on the handle, it should be floated on the pivot point. If the handle comes in contact with the yoke extension during the process of pulling, there is a very good chance the torque readings will be inaccurate because this could alter the wrench loading point. The design of the handle is usually such as to make it inconvenient to deliberately misuse the wrench.

➡ It should be mentioned that the use of any U-joint, wobble or extension will have an effect on the torque readings, no matter what type of wrench you are using. For the most accurate readings, install the socket directly on the wrench driver. If necessary, straight extensions (which hold a socket directly under the wrench driver) will have the least effect on the torque reading. Avoid any extension that alters the length of the wrench from the handle to the head/driving point (such as a crow's foot). U-joint or wobble extensions can greatly affect the readings; avoid their use at all times.

Rigid Case (Direct Reading)

A rigid case or direct reading torque wrench is equipped with a dial indicator to show torque values. One advantage of these wrenches is that they can be held at any position on the wrench without affecting accuracy. These wrenches are often preferred because they tend to be compact, easy to read and have a great degree of accuracy.

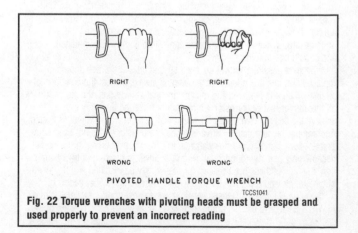

RIGHT

RIGHT

WRONG

WRONG

PIVOTED HANDLE TORQUE WRENCH

TCCS1041

Fig. 22 Torque wrenches with pivoting heads must be grasped and used properly to prevent an incorrect reading

TORQUE ANGLE METERS

Because the frictional characteristics of each fastener or threaded hole will vary, clamp loads which are based strictly on torque will vary as well. In most applications, this variance is not significant enough to cause worry. But, in certain applications, a manufacturer's engineers may determine that more precise clamp loads are necessary (such is the case with many aluminum cylinder heads). In these cases, a torque angle method of installation would be specified. When installing fasteners which are torque angle tightened, a predetermined seating torque and standard torque wrench are usually used first to remove any compliance from the joint. The fastener is then tightened the specified additional portion of a turn measured in degrees. A torque angle gauge (mechanical protractor) is used for these applications.

Standard and Metric Measurements

▶ See Figure 23

Throughout this manual, specifications are given to help you determine the condition of various components on your vehicle, or to assist you in their installation. Some of the most common measurements include length (in. or cm/mm), torque (ft. lbs., inch lbs. or Nm) and pressure (psi, in. Hg, kPa or mm Hg). In most cases, we strive to provide the proper measurement as determined by the manufacturer's engineers.

Though, in some cases, that value may not be conveniently measured with what is available in your toolbox. Luckily, many of the measuring devices which are available today will have two scales so the Standard or Metric measurements may easily be taken. If any of the various measuring tools which are available to you do not contain the same scale as listed in the specifications, use the accompanying conversion factors to determine the proper value.

The conversion factor chart is used by taking the given specification and multiplying it by the necessary conversion factor. For instance, looking at the first line, if you have a measurement in inches such as "free play should be 2 in." but your ruler reads only in millimeters, multiply 2 in. by the conversion factor of 25.4 to get the metric equivalent of 50.8mm. Likewise, if the specification was given only in a Metric measurement, for example in Newton Meters (Nm), then look at the center column first. If the measurement is 100 Nm, multiply it by the conversion factor of 0.730 to get 73.8 ft. lbs.

CONVERSION FACTORS

LENGTH-DISTANCE

Inches (in.)	x 25.4	= Millimeters (mm)	x .0394	= Inches
Feet (ft.)	x .305	= Meters (m)	x 3.281	= Feet
Miles	x 1.609	= Kilometers (km)	x .0621	= Miles

VOLUME

Cubic Inches (in3)	x 16.387	= Cubic Centimeters	x .061	= in3
IMP Pints (IMP pt.)	x .568	= Liters (L)	x 1.76	= IMP pt.
IMP Quarts (IMP qt.)	x 1.137	= Liters (L)	x .88	= IMP qt.
IMP Gallons (IMP gal.)	x 4.546	= Liters (L)	x .22	= IMP gal.
IMP Quarts (IMP qt.)	x 1.201	= US Quarts (US qt.)	x .833	= IMP qt.
IMP Gallons (IMP gal.)	x 1.201	= US Gallons (US gal.)	x .833	= IMP gal.
Fl. Ounces	x 29.573	= Milliliters	x .034	= Ounces
US Pints (US pt.)	x .473	= Liters (L)	x 2.113	= Pints
US Quarts (US qt.)	x .946	= Liters (L)	x 1.057	= Quarts
US Gallons (US gal.)	x 3.785	= Liters (L)	x .264	= Gallons

MASS-WEIGHT

Ounces (oz.)	x 28.35	= Grams (g)	x .035	= Ounces
Pounds (lb.)	x .454	= Kilograms (kg)	x 2.205	= Pounds

PRESSURE

Pounds Per Sq. In. (psi)	x 6.895	= Kilopascals (kPa)	x .145	= psi
Inches of Mercury (Hg)	x .4912	= psi	x 2.036	= Hg
Inches of Mercury (Hg)	x 3.377	= Kilopascals (kPa)	x .2961	= Hg
Inches of Water (H_2O)	x .07355	= Inches of Mercury	x 13.783	= H_2O
Inches of Water (H_2O)	x .03613	= psi	x 27.684	= H_2O
Inches of Water (H_2O)	x .248	= Kilopascals (kPa)	x 4.026	= H_2O

TORQUE

Pounds-Force Inches (in-lb)	x .113	= Newton Meters (N·m)	x 8.85	= in-lb
Pounds-Force Feet (ft-lb)	x 1.356	= Newton Meters (N·m)	x .738	= ft-lb

VELOCITY

Miles Per Hour (MPH)	x 1.609	= Kilometers Per Hour (KPH)	x .621	= MPH

POWER

Horsepower (Hp)	x .745	= Kilowatts	x 1.34	= Horsepower

FUEL CONSUMPTION*

Miles Per Gallon IMP (MPG)	x .354	= Kilometers Per Liter (Km/L)	
Kilometers Per Liter (Km/L)	x 2.352	= IMP MPG	
Miles Per Gallon US (MPG)	x .425	= Kilometers Per Liter (Km/L)	
Kilometers Per Liter (Km/L)	x 2.352	= US MPG	

*It is common to covert from miles per gallon (mpg) to liters/100 kilometers (1/100 km), where mpg (IMP) x l/100 km = 282 and mpg (US) x l/100 km = 235.

TEMPERATURE

Degree Fahrenheit (°F) = (°C x 1.8) + 32
Degree Celsius (°C) = (°F - 32) x .56

TCCS1044

Fig. 23 Standard and metric conversion factors chart

SERIAL NUMBER IDENTIFICATION

Vehicle

▶ See Figure 24

The Vehicle Identification Number (VIN) is a seventeen digit sequence stamped on a plate attached to the left front of the instrument panel, visible through the windshield. This is the legal identification of the vehicle. The eighth digit indicates the engine code and the tenth digit indicates the model year. The engine code (VIN) is specified in all the engine specification charts.

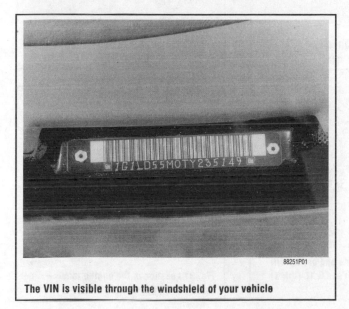

The VIN is visible through the windshield of your vehicle

88251P01

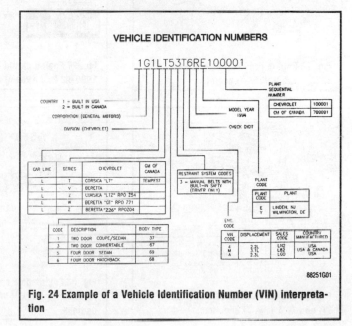

Fig. 24 Example of a Vehicle Identification Number (VIN) interpretation

88251G01

VEHICLE IDENTIFICATION CHART

Engine Code						Model Year	
Code	Liters	Cu. In. (cc)	Cyl.	Fuel Sys.	Eng. Mfg.	Code	Year
1	2.0	121 (2000)	4	TBI	CUS	J	1988
G	2.2	134 (2180)	4	TBI	CUS	K	1989
4	2.2	134 (2180)	4	BFP/SFI	CUS	L	1990
A	2.3	138 (2260)	4	MFI	BOC	M	1991
W	2.8	173 (2837)	6	MFI	CUS	N	1992
T	3.1	195 (3135)	6	MFI	CPC	P	1993
M	3.1	195 (3135)	6	SFI	CPC	R	1994
						S	1995
						T	1996

TBI - Throttle Body Injection

BFP - Bottom Feed Port Injection

MFI - Multi-port Fuel Injection

SFI - Sequential Fuel Injection

CUS - Chevrolet/United States

BOC - Buick/Oldsmobile/Cadillac

CPC - Chevrolet/Pontiac/Canada

88251C01

Engine

♦ See Figures 25 thru 31

The engine code is represented by the eighth character in the VIN and identifies the engine type, displacement, fuel system and manufacturing division.

The engine identification code is either stamped onto the engine block or found on a label affixed to the engine. This code supplies information about the manufacturing plant location and time of manufacture. The locations of the engine code are shown in the accompanying illustrations.

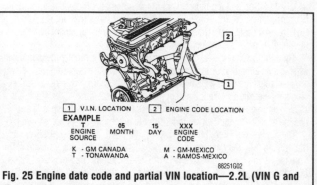

Fig. 25 Engine date code and partial VIN location—2.2L (VIN G and 4) engines

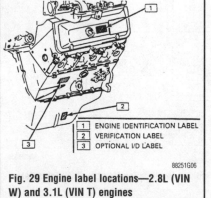

Fig. 26 Engine code label location—1990–92 2.3L (VIN A) engine

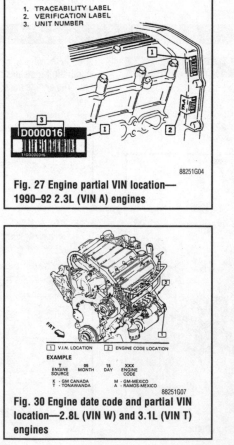

Fig. 27 Engine partial VIN location—1990–92 2.3L (VIN A) engines

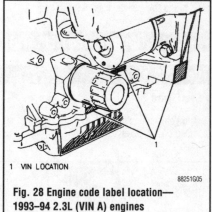

Fig. 28 Engine code label location—1993–94 2.3L (VIN A) engines

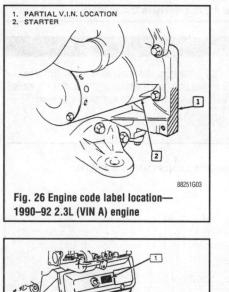

Fig. 29 Engine label locations—2.8L (VIN W) and 3.1L (VIN T) engines

Fig. 30 Engine date code and partial VIN location—2.8L (VIN W) and 3.1L (VIN T) engines

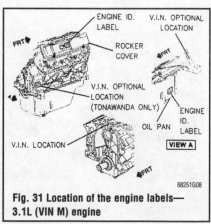

Fig. 31 Location of the engine labels—3.1L (VIN M) engine

GENERAL ENGINE SPECIFICATIONS

Year	Engine ID/VIN	Engine Displacement Liters (cc)	Fuel System Type	Net Horsepower @ rpm	Net Torque @ rpm (ft. lbs.)	Bore x Stroke (in.)	Compression Ratio	Oil Pressure @ rpm
1988	1	2.0L (1991)	TBI	90@5600	108@3200	3.500 x 3.150	9.0:1	63-77@1200
	W	2.8L (2837)	MFI	125@4200	1600@4200	3.503 x 2.990	8.9:1	50-65
1989	1	2.0L (1991)	TBI	90@5600	108@3200	3.500 x 3.150	9.0:1	63-77@1200
	W	2.8L (2837)	MFI	125@4200	1600@4200	3.503 x 2.990	8.9:1	50-65
1990	G	2.2L (2190)	TBI	95@5200	120@3200	3.500 x 3.460	9.0:1	56@3000
	A	2.3L (2260)	MFI	180@6200	160@5200	3.620 x 3.350	10.0:1	15@900
	T	3.1L (3128)	MFI	135@4200	180@3600	3.503 x 3.312	8.8:1	15@1100
1991	G	2.2L (2190)	TBI	110@5200	120@3200	3.500 x 3.460	8.85:1	56@3000
	A	2.3L (2260)	MFI	180@6200	160@5200	3.620 x 3.350	10.0:1	15@900
	T	3.1L (3128)	MFI	140@4200	185@3600	3.503 x 3.312	8.8:1	15@1100
1992	4	2.2L (2190)	BFP	110@5200	120@3200	3.500 x 3.460	8.85:1	56@3000
	A	2.3L (2260)	MFI	180@6200	160@5200	3.620 x 3.350	10.0:1	15@900
	T	3.1L (3128)	MFI	140@4200	185@3600	3.503 x 3.312	8.8:1	15@1100
1993	4	2.2L (2190)	MFI	120@5200	130@4000	3.500 x 3.460	8.85:1	56@3000
	A	2.3L (2260)	MFI	170@6200	150@5200	3.620 x 3.350	10.0:1	15@900
	T	3.1L (3128)	MFI	155@4000	185@4000	3.503 x 3.312	8.8:1	15@1100
1994	4	2.2L (2190)	MFI	120@5200	130@4000	3.500 x 3.460	8.85:1	56@3000
	A	2.3L (2260)	MFI	170@6200	150@5200	3.620 x 3.350	10.0:1	15@900
	M	3.1L (3128)	SFI	155@5200	185@4000	3.504 x 3.307	9.5:1	15@1100
1995	4	2.2L (2190)	SFI	120@5200	130@4000	3.500 x 3.460	8.85:1	56@3000
	M	3.1L (3128)	SFI	155@5200	185@4000	3.504 x 3.307	9.5:1	15@1100
1996	4	2.2L (2190)	SFI	120@5200	130@4000	3.500 x 3.460	8.85:1	56@3000
	M	3.1L (3128)	SFI	155@5200	185@4000	3.504 x 3.307	9.5:1	15@1100

TBI - Throttle Body Injection
MFI - Multi-port Fuel Injection
BFP - Bottom Feed Port Injection
SFI - Sequential Fuel Injection

88251C05

ENGINE IDENTIFICATION

Year	Model	Engine Displacement Liters (cc)	Engine Series (ID/VIN)	Fuel System	No. of Cylinders	Engine Type
1988	Beretta	2.0L (1991)	1	TBI	4	OHV
	Beretta	2.8L (2837)	W	MFI	6	OHV
	Corsica	2.0L (1991)	1	TBI	4	OHV
	Corsica	2.8L (2837)	W	MFI	6	OHV
1989	Beretta	2.0L (1991)	1	TBI	4	OHV
	Beretta	2.8L (2837)	W	MFI	6	OHV
	Corsica	2.0L (1991)	1	TBI	4	OHV
	Corsica	2.8L (2837)	W	MFI	6	OHV
1990	Beretta	2.2L (2190)	G	TBI	4	OHV
	Beretta	2.3L (2260)	A	MFI	4	OHC
	Beretta	3.1L (3128)	T	MFI	6	OHV
	Corsica	2.2L (2190)	G	TBI	4	OHV
	Corsica	3.1L (3128)	T	MFI	6	OHV
1991	Beretta	2.2L (2190)	G	TBI	4	OHV
	Beretta	2.3L (2260)	A	MFI	4	OHC
	Beretta	3.1L (3128)	T	MFI	6	OHV
	Corsica	2.2L (2190)	G	TBI	4	OHV
	Corsica	3.1L (3128)	T	MFI	6	OHV
1992	Beretta	2.2L (2190)	4	BFP	4	OHV
	Beretta	2.3L (2260)	A	MFI	4	OHC
	Beretta	3.1L (3128)	T	MFI	6	OHV
	Corsica	2.2L (2190)	4	BFP	4	OHV
	Corsica	3.1L (3128)	T	MFI	6	OHV
1993	Beretta	2.2L (2190)	4	MFI	4	OHV
	Beretta	2.3L (2260)	A	MFI	4	OHC
	Beretta	3.1L (3128)	T	MFI	6	OHV
	Corsica	2.2L (2190)	4	MFI	4	OHV
	Corsica	3.1L (3128)	T	MFI	6	OHV
1994	Beretta	2.3L (2260)	A	MFI	4	OHC
	Beretta	3.1L (3128)	M	SFI	6	OHV
	Corsica	2.2L (2190)	4	MFI	4	OHV
	Corsica	3.1L (3128)	M	SFI	6	OHV
1995	Beretta	2.2L (2190)	4	MFI	4	OHV
	Beretta	3.1L (3128)	M	SFI	6	OHV
	Corsica	2.2L (2190)	4	MFI	4	OHV
	Corsica	3.1L (3128)	M	SFI	6	OHV
1996	Beretta	2.2L (2190)	4	SFI	4	OHV
	Beretta	3.1L (3128)	M	SFI	6	OHV
	Corsica	2.2L (2190)	4	SFI	4	OHV
	Corsica	3.1L (3128)	M	SFI	6	OHV

TBI - Throttle Body fuel Injection
BFP - Bottom Feed Port Injection
MFI - Multi-port Fuel Injection
SFI - Sequential Fuel Injection
OHV - Overhead Valves
OHC - Overhead Cam

88251C02

Transaxle

♦ **See Figures 32, 33, 34, 35 and 36**

The manual transaxle identification number is stamped on a pad on the forward side of the transaxle case, between the upper and middle transaxle-to-engine mounting bolts or on a paper label attached to the transaxle case. If the label is missing or unreadable, use the service parts information label to determine which transaxle was installed. The automatic transaxle identification number is stamped on the oil flange pad to the right of the oil dipstick, at the rear of the transaxle. The automatic transaxle model code tag is on top of the case, next to the shift lever.

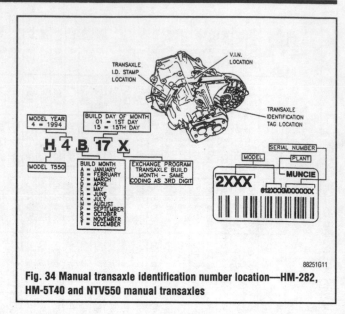

Fig. 34 Manual transaxle identification number location—HM-282, HM-5T40 and NTV550 manual transaxles

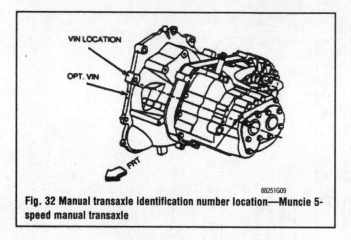

Fig. 32 Manual transaxle identification number location—Muncie 5-speed manual transaxle

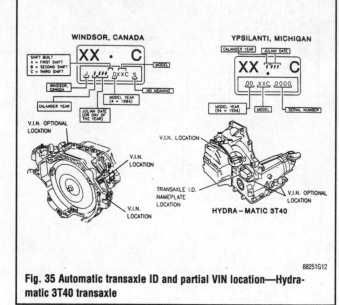

Fig. 35 Automatic transaxle ID and partial VIN location—Hydra-matic 3T40 transaxle

Fig. 33 Isuzu 5-speed manual transaxle ID and partial VIN location

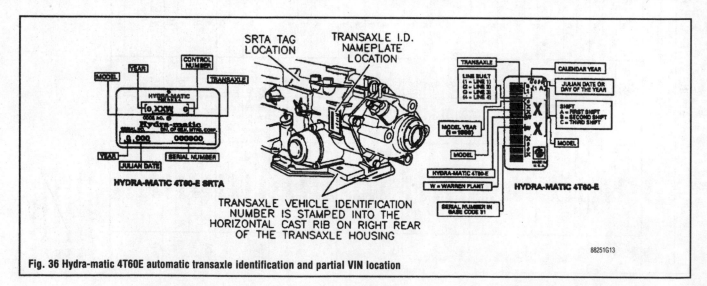

Fig. 36 Hydra-matic 4T60E automatic transaxle identification and partial VIN location

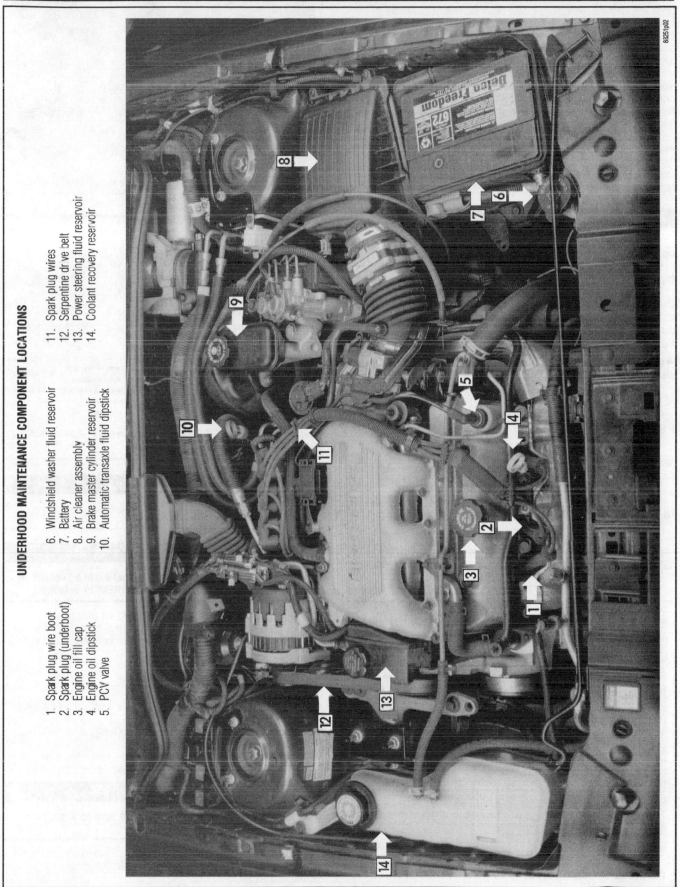

UNDERHOOD MAINTENANCE COMPONENT LOCATIONS

1. Spark plug wire boot
2. Spark plug (underboot)
3. Engine oil fill cap
4. Engine oil dipstick
5. PCV valve
6. Windshield washer fluid reservoir
7. Battery
8. Air cleaner assembly
9. Brake master cylinder reservoir
10. Automatic transaxle fluid dipstick
11. Spark plug wires
12. Serpentine drive belt
13. Power steering fluid reservoir
14. Coolant recovery reservoir

83251p02

Proper maintenance and tune-up is the key to long and trouble-free vehicle life, and the work can yield its own rewards. Studies have shown that a properly tuned and maintained vehicle can achieve better gas mileage than an out-of-tune vehicle. As a conscientious owner and driver, set aside a Saturday morning, say once a month, to check or replace items which could cause major problems later. Keep your own personal log to jot down which services you performed, how much the parts cost you, the date, and the exact odometer reading at the time. Keep all receipts for such items as engine oil and filters, so that they may be referred to in case of related problems or to determine operating expenses. As a do-it-yourselfer, these receipts are the only proof you have that the required maintenance was performed. In the event of a warranty problem, these receipts will be invaluable.

The literature provided with your vehicle when it was originally delivered includes the factory recommended maintenance schedule. If you no longer have this literature, replacement copies are usually available from the dealer. A maintenance schedule is provided later in this section, in case you do not have the factory literature.

Air Cleaner (Element)

All the dust present in the air is kept out of the engine by means of the air cleaner filter element. Proper maintenance is vital, as a clogged element not only restricts the air-flow, and thus the power, but may also cause premature engine wear.

The filter element should be replaced every 30,000 miles or 36 months. Change the filter more often if the car is driven in dry, dusty areas. The condition of the element should be checked periodically; if it appears to be overly dirty or clogged, shake it, if this does not help, the element should be replaced.

➡**The paper element should never be cleaned or soaked with gasoline, cleaning solvent or oil.**

REMOVAL & INSTALLATION

◆ **See Figure 37**

1. Remove either the wing nut, upper cover retaining bolts or release clips from the upper top of the air cleaner and either lift off or separate the upper air cleaner housing or lid.
2. Remove the air cleaner element and replace it with a new one.
3. Wipe the air cleaner housing out using a damp cloth. Check the lid gasket, if equipped, to ensure that it has a tight seal.
   To install:
4. Position the new element in the air cleaner housing.
5. Position the lid or housing cover, then tighten the retaining bolts/nut or fasten the clips.

Remove the air cleaner housing lid using a screwdriver . . .

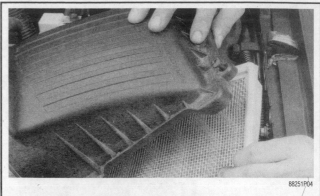

. . . then lift the housing lid up and remove the air cleaner element

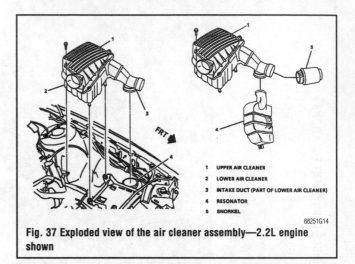

1	UPPER AIR CLEANER
2	LOWER AIR CLEANER
3	INTAKE DUCT (PART OF LOWER AIR CLEANER)
4	RESONATOR
5	SNORKEL

Fig. 37 Exploded view of the air cleaner assembly—2.2L engine shown

Fuel Filter

REMOVAL & INSTALLATION

☀ CAUTION

Never smoke when working around gasoline! Avoid all sources of sparks or ignition. Gasoline vapors are EXTREMELY volatile!

An in-line fuel filter can be found in the fuel feed line attached to the rear crossmember of the vehicle, rear of the fuel tank. There is no service interval for replacing the fuel filter. Only replace the filter if it becomes clogged or restricted.

1988–89 Vehicles

◆ **See Figure 38**

1. Relieve the fuel system pressure. For details regarding this procedure, please refer to Section 5 of this manual.
2. If not already done, disconnect the negative battery cable.
3. Raise and safely support the vehicle.
4. Clean both fuel feed pipe connections and the surrounding areas at the in-line fuel filter with a clean rag to avoid possible contamination of the fuel system.

☀ WARNING

When removing the fuel filter, always use a back-up wrench to disconnect the fuel lines.

5. Using a back-up wrench, remove the fuel line fittings from the fuel filter.
6. Remove the fuel filter mounting screws, then slide the fuel filter out of the mounting bracket.

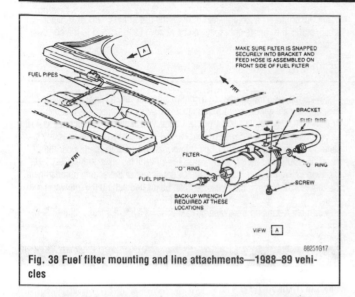

Fig. 38 Fuel filter mounting and line attachments—1988–89 vehicles

7. Remove and discard the fuel line O-rings and replace with new ones during installation.

To install:

8. Install new O-rings to the fuel line fittings.

➡The fuel filter has an arrow indicating fuel flow direction on the side of the case, so be sure to install it correctly in the system, the with arrow facing away from the fuel tank.

9. Connect the fuel lines to the filter.

10. Position the fuel filter in the mounting bracket, in the same position it was originally. Tighten the fuel line fittings to 22 ft. lbs. (30 Nm) using a back-up wrench to avoid twisting the lines.

11. Install the fuel filter mounting bracket screws/bolts and tighten securely.

12. Carefully lower the vehicle. Install or tighten the fuel filler cap.

13. Connnect the negative battery cable, then start the engine and check for leaks.

1990–96 Vehicles

▶ See Figures 39 and 40

➡If your vehicle is equipped with the 3.1L (VIN T) engine, anytime the battery is disconnected, the programmed position of the Idle Air Control (IAC) valve pintle is lost and replaced with a "default" value. The IAC valve pintle can be returned to the proper position by performing an Idle Learn Procedure, which requires the use of a Tech 1® or equivalent scan tool.

1. Relieve the fuel system pressure. For details regarding this procedure, please refer to Section 5 of this manual.

2. If not already done, disconnect the negative battery cable.

3. Raise and safely support the vehicle.

4. Clean both fuel feed pipe connections and the surrounding areas at the in-line fuel filter with a clean rag to avoid possible contamination of the fuel system.

✶✶ WARNING

When removing the fuel filter, always use a back-up wrench to disconnect the fuel lines.

5. Using a back-up wrench, remove the fuel line fittings from the fuel filter.

6. Remove the filter attaching screw and filter.

➡Kinked nylon fuel feed or return lines cannot be straightened and must be replaced.

7. Grasp the filter and one nylon fuel connecting line fitting. Twist the quick connect fitting ¼ turn in each direction to loosen any dirt within the fitting. Repeat for the other nylon fuel connecting line fitting.

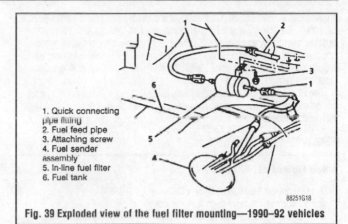

1. Quick connecting pipe fitting
2. Fuel feed pipe
3. Attaching screw
4. Fuel sender assembly
5. In-line fuel filter
6. Fuel tank

Fig. 39 Exploded view of the fuel filter mounting—1990–92 vehicles

1. HOSE, PART OF FUEL SENDER
2. FUEL VAPOR PIPE
3. FUEL RETURN PIPE
4. FUEL FEED PIPE
5. FUEL FEED PIPE NUT 27 N·m (20 LBS. FT.)
6. HOSE, PART OF FUEL SENDER
7. ABS AND FUEL SENDER HARNESS

Fig. 40 Installed position of the fuel filter and lines—1993–96 vehicles

8. Disconnect the quick connect fittings by squeezing the plastic tabs of the male end connector and pulling the connection apart. Repeat for the other fitting and remove the fuel filter.

To install:

9. Remove the protective caps from the ends of the new filter.

10. Install the new plastic connector retainers on the filter inlet and outlet tubes.

11. Apply a few drops of clean engine oil to both tube ends of the filter and O-rings.

12. Push the connectors together to cause the retaining the retaining tabs/fingers to snap into place. Pull on both ends of each connection to make sure they are secure.

13. Install a new O-ring on the fuel filter fitting and tighten to 20 ft. lbs. (27 Nm), using a back-up wrench to avoid twisting or warping the fuel lines..

14. Place the filter, in the same position as it was removed, to the frame with the attaching screw(s).

15. Carefully lower the vehicle.

16. Install or tighten the fuel filler cap, as necessary.

17. Connect the negative battery cable.

18. Turn the ignition switch to the **ON** position for 2 seconds, then turn to the **OFF** position for 10 seconds. Again turn the ignition switch to the **ON** position and check for leaks.

➡For vehicles equipped with the 3.1L engine, the ECM will need to relearn the IAC pintle valve position following the reconnection of the battery.

19. If equipped with the 3.1L engine, perform the idle learn procedure, as follows:

Positive Crankcase Ventilation (PCV) Valve

All engines, except the 2.3L engine, use a Positive Crankcase Ventilation (PCV) valve to regulate crankcase ventilation during various engine running conditions. At high vacuum (idle speed and partial load range) it will open slightly and at low vacuum (full throttle) it will open fully. This causes vapors to be drawn from the crankcase by engine vacuum and then sucked into the combustion chamber where they are dissipated. The crankcase ventilation system used on the 2.3L engine does not use a PCV valve. This system requires no regular scheduled maintenance. Details on all PCV system, including system tests, are given in Section 4.

The PCV valve must be replaced every 30,000 miles and is located in a rubber grommet in the valve cover, connected to the air cleaner housing by a large diameter rubber hose.

REMOVAL & INSTALLATION

▶ **See Figures 41, 42 and 43**

1. Disconnect the hose from the PCV valve.
2. If necessary, remove the retainer or cover.
3. Pull the valve from the rubber grommet in the valve cover.

To install:

4. Press the PCV valve back into the rubber grommet in the valve cover, making sure it is properly seated.
5. If necessary, install the cover or retainer.
6. Connect hose to the PCV valve.

Evaporative Canister

▶ **See Figures 44 and 45**

This system is designed to limit gasoline vapor, which normally escapes from the fuel tank and intake manifold, from discharging into the atmosphere.

Vapor absorption is accomplished through the use of the charcoal canister which stores the vapors until they can be removed and burned in the combustion process.

SERVICING

Check the evaporative emission control system every 15,000 miles. The evaporative canister does not require periodic service. Inspect the fuel vapor lines and the vacuum hoses for proper connections and correct routing, as well as condition. Replace clogged, damaged or deteriorated parts as necessary. Refer to the Vehicle Emission Control Information Label, located under the hood, for routing of the canister hoses. For all vehicles, except the 1996 3.1L, the evaporative canister is located right front corner of the engine compartment. On the 1996 3.1L engine, the canister can be located behind the left wheel well liner.

For more details on the evaporative emissions system, please refer to Section 4.

Battery

PRECAUTIONS

Always use caution when working on or near the battery. Never allow a tool to bridge the gap between the negative and positive battery terminals. Also, be careful not to allow a tool to provide a ground between the positive cable/terminal and any metal component on the vehicle. Either of these conditions will cause a short circuit, leading to sparks and possible personal injury.

88251P05

Disconnect the hose from the PCV valve mounted in the valve cover . . .

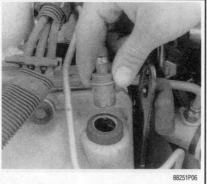

88251P06

. . . then pull the PCV valve out of the grommet in the valve cover

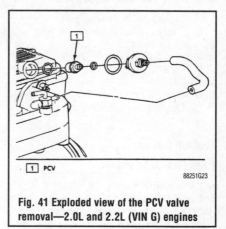

1 PCV

88251G23

Fig. 41 Exploded view of the PCV valve removal—2.0L and 2.2L (VIN G) engines

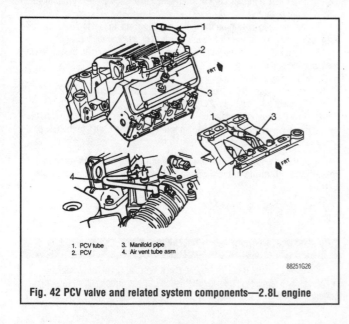

1. PCV tube   3. Manifold pipe
2. PCV   4. Air vent tube asm

88251G26

Fig. 42 PCV valve and related system components—2.8L engine

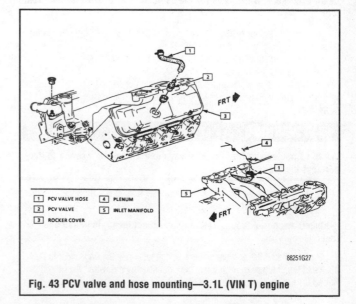

1	PCV VALVE HOSE	4	PLENUM
2	PCV VALVE	5	INLET MANIFOLD
3	ROCKER COVER		

88251G27

Fig. 43 PCV valve and hose mounting—3.1L (VIN T) engine

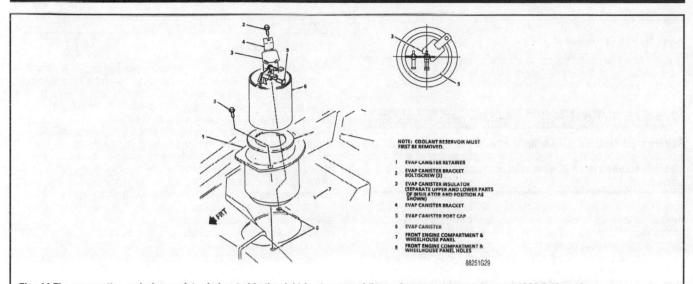

NOTE: COOLANT RESERVOIR MUST
FIRST BE REMOVED.

1 EVAP CANISTER RETAINER
2 EVAP CANISTER BRACKET
  BOLT/SCREW (2)
3 EVAP CANISTER INSULATOR
  (SEPARATE UPPER AND LOWER PARTS
  OF INSULATOR AND POSITION AS
  SHOWN)
4 EVAP CANISTER BRACKET
5 EVAP CANISTER PORT CAP
6 EVAP CANISTER
7 FRONT ENGINE COMPARTMENT &
  WHEELHOUSE PANEL
8 FRONT ENGINE COMPARTMENT &
  WHEELHOUSE PANEL HOLES

88251G29

Fig. 44 The evaporative emission canister is located in the right front corner of the engine compartment—except 1996 3.1L engine

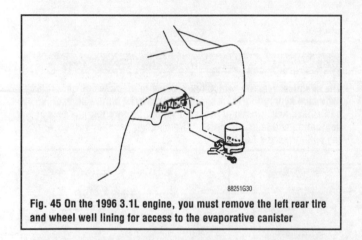

88251G30

Fig. 45 On the 1996 3.1L engine, you must remove the left rear tire and wheel well lining for access to the evaporative canister

Do not smoke or all open flames/sparks near a battery; the gases contained in the battery are very explosive and, if ignited, could cause severe injury or death.

All batteries, regardless of type, should be carefully secured by a battery hold-down device. If not, the terminals or casing may crack from stress during vehicle operation. A battery which is not secured may allow acid to leak, making it discharge faster. The acid can also eat away at components under the hood.

Always inspect the battery case for cracks, leakage and corrosion. A white corrosive substance on the battery case or on nearby components would indicate a leaking or cracked battery. If the battery is cracked, it should be replaced immediately.

GENERAL MAINTENANCE

Always keep the battery cables and terminals free of corrosion. Check and clean these components about once a year.

Keep the top of the battery clean, as a film of dirt can help discharge a battery that is not used for long periods. A solution of baking soda and water may be used for cleaning, but be careful to flush this off with clear water. DO NOT let any of the solution into the filler holes. Baking soda neutralizes battery acid and will de-activate a battery cell.

Batteries in vehicles which are not operated on a regular basis can fall victim to parasitic loads (small current drains which are constantly drawing current from the battery). Normal parasitic loads may drain a battery on a vehicle that is in storage and not used for 6–8 weeks. Vehicles that have additional accessories such as a phone or an alarm system may discharge a battery sooner. If the vehicle is to be stored for longer periods in a secure area and the alarm system is not necessary, the negative battery cable should be disconnected to protect the battery.

Remember that constantly deep cycling a battery (completely discharging and recharging it) will shorten battery life.

BATTERY FLUID

♦ See Figure 46

Check the battery electrolyte level at least once a month, or more often in hot weather or during periods of extended vehicle operation. On non-sealed batteries, the level can be checked either through the case (if translucent) or by removing the cell caps. The electrolyte level in each cell should be kept filled to the split ring inside each cell, or the line marked on the outside of the case.

If the level is low, add only distilled water through the opening until the level is correct. Each cell must be checked and filled individually. Distilled water should be used, because the chemicals and minerals found in most drinking water are harmful to the battery and could significantly shorten its life.

If water is added in freezing weather, the vehicle should be driven several miles to allow the water to mix with the electrolyte. Otherwise, the battery could freeze.

Although some maintenance-free batteries have removable cell caps, the electrolyte condition and level on all sealed maintenance-free batteries must be checked using the built-in hydrometer "eye." The exact type of eye will vary. But, most battery manufacturers, apply a sticker to the battery itself explaining the readings.

➡Although the readings from built-in hydrometers will vary, a green eye usually indicates a properly charged battery with sufficient fluid level. A dark eye is normally an indicator of a battery with sufficient fluid, but which is low in charge. A light or yellow eye usually indicates that electrolyte has dropped below the necessary level. In this last case, sealed batteries with an insufficient electrolyte must usually be discarded.

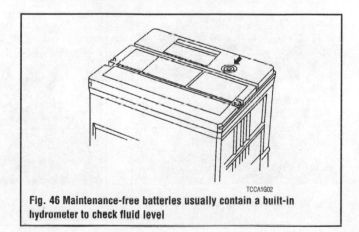

TCCA1G02

Fig. 46 Maintenance-free batteries usually contain a built-in hydrometer to check fluid level

Checking the Specific Gravity

◆ See Figures 47, 48 and 49

A hydrometer is required to check the specific gravity on all batteries that are not maintenance-free. On batteries that are maintenance-free, the specific gravity is checked by observing the built-in hydrometer "eye" on the top of the battery case.

※ CAUTION

Battery electrolyte contains sulfuric acid. If you should splash any on your skin or in your eyes, flush the affected area with plenty of clear water. If it lands in your eyes, get medical help immediately.

The fluid (sulfuric acid solution) contained in the battery cells will tell you many things about the condition of the battery. Because the cell plates must be kept submerged below the fluid level in order to operate, the fluid level is extremely important. And, because the specific gravity of the acid is an indication of electrical charge, testing the fluid can be an aid in determining if the battery must be replaced. A battery in a vehicle with a properly operating charging system should require little maintenance, but careful, periodic inspection should reveal problems before they leave you stranded.

At least once a year, check the specific gravity of the battery. It should be between 1.20 and 1.26 on the gravity scale. Most auto stores carry a variety of inexpensive battery hydrometers. These can be used on any non-sealed battery to test the specific gravity in each cell.

The battery testing hydrometer has a squeeze bulb at one end and a nozzle at the other. Battery electrolyte is sucked into the hydrometer until the float is lifted from its seat. The specific gravity is then read by noting the position of the float. If gravity is low in one or more cells, the battery should be slowly charged and checked again to see if the gravity has come up. Generally, if after charging, the specific gravity between any two cells varies more than 50 points (0.50), the battery should be replaced, as it can no longer produce sufficient voltage to guarantee proper operation.

CABLES

◆ See Figures 50 thru 55

Once a year (or as necessary), the battery terminals and the cable clamps should be cleaned. Loosen the clamps and remove the cables, negative cable first. On top post batteries, the use of a puller specially made for this purpose is recommended. These are inexpensive and available in most parts stores. Side terminal battery cables are secured with a small bolt.

Clean the cable clamps and the battery terminal with a wire brush, until all corrosion, grease, etc., is removed and the metal is shiny. It is especially important to clean the inside of the clamp thoroughly (an old knife is useful here), since a small deposit of oxidation there will prevent a sound connection and inhibit starting or charging. Special tools are available for cleaning these parts, one type for conventional top post batteries and another type for side terminal batteries. It is also a good idea to apply some dielectric grease to the terminal, as this will aid in the prevention of corrosion.

After the clamps and terminals are clean, reinstall the cables, negative cable last; DO NOT hammer the clamps onto battery posts. Tighten the clamps securely, but do not distort them. Give the clamps and terminals a thin external coating of grease after installation, to retard corrosion.

Check the cables at the same time that the terminals are cleaned. If the cable insulation is cracked or broken, or if the ends are frayed, the cable should be replaced with a new cable of the same length and gauge.

CHARGING

※ CAUTION

The chemical reaction which takes place in all batteries generates explosive hydrogen gas. A spark can cause the battery to explode and splash acid. To avoid personal injury, be sure there is proper ventilation and take appropriate fire safety precautions when working with or near a battery.

TCCA1P07

Fig. 47 On non-sealed batteries, the fluid level can be checked by removing the cell caps

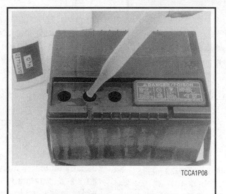

TCCA1P08

Fig. 48 If the fluid level is low, add only distilled water until the level is correct

TCCA1P09

Fig. 49 Check the specific gravity of the battery's electrolyte with a hydrometer

TCCA1P01

Fig. 50 Loosen the battery cable retaining nut . . .

TCCA1P02

Fig. 51 . . . then disconnect the cable from the battery

TCCA1P03

Fig. 52 A wire brush may be used to clean any corrosion or foreign material from the cable

Fig. 53 The wire brush can also be used to remove any corrosion or dirt from the battery terminal

Fig. 54 The battery terminal can also be cleaned using a solution of baking soda and water

Fig. 55 Before connecting the cables, it's a good idea to coat the terminals with a small amount of dielectric grease

A battery should be charged at a slow rate to keep the plates inside from getting too hot. However, if some maintenance-free batteries are allowed to discharge until they are almost "dead," they may have to be charged at a high rate to bring them back to "life." Always follow the charger manufacturer's instructions on charging the battery.

REPLACEMENT

When it becomes necessary to replace the battery, select one with an amperage rating equal to or greater than the battery originally installed. Deterioration and just plain aging of the battery cables, starter motor, and associated wires makes the battery's job harder in successive years. This makes it prudent to install a new battery with a greater capacity than the old.

Belts

All engines are equipped with a single (serpentine belt) to drive all engine accessories with the exception of the power steering pump on the 2.3L engine which is driven by a poly-groove belt. The poly-groove belt is not self adjusting and therefore may require service. The serpentine belt driven accessories are rigidly mounted with belt tension maintained by a spring loaded tensioner assembly. The belt tensioner has the ability to control belt tension over a fairly broad range of belt lengths. However, there are limits to the tensioner's ability to compensate for varying lengths of belts. Poor tension control and/or damage to the tensioner could result with the tensioner operating outside of its range.

INSPECTION

♦ See Figures 56, 57, 58, 59 and 60

Inspect the belts for signs of glazing or cracking. A glazed belt will be perfectly smooth from slippage, while a good belt will have a slight texture of fabric visible. Cracks will usually start at the inner edge of the belt and run outward. All worn or damaged drive belts should be replaced immediately. It is best to replace all drive belts at one time, as a preventive maintenance measure, during this service operation.

1. If fraying of the belt is noticed, check to make sure both the belt and the tensioner assembly are properly aligned and that the belt edges are not in contact with the flanges of the tensioner pulley.

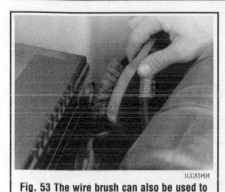

Fig. 56 There are typically 3 types of accessory drive belts found on vehicles today

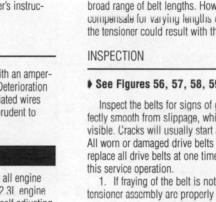

Fig. 57 An example of a healthy drive belt

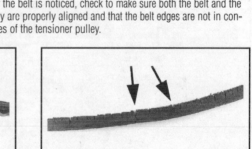

Fig. 58 Deep cracks in this belt will cause flex, building up heat that will eventually lead to belt failure

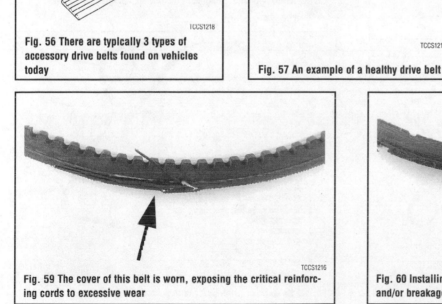

Fig. 59 The cover of this belt is worn, exposing the critical reinforcing cords to excessive wear

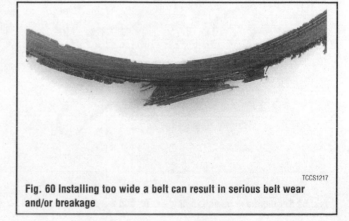

Fig. 60 Installing too wide a belt can result in serious belt wear and/or breakage

2. If, while adjusting belt tension, tensioner runs out of travel, the belt is stretched beyond adjustment and should be replaced.

3. If a whining is heard around the tensioner or idler assemblies, check for possible bearing failure.

➡Routine inspection of the belt may reveal cracks in the belt ribs. These cracks will not impair belt performance and therefore should not be considered a problem requiring belt replacement. However, the belt should be replaced if belt slip occurs or if sections of the belt ribs are missing.

REMOVAL & INSTALLATION

Serpentine Belt

EXCEPT 3.1L (VIN M) ENGINE

◆ See Figures 61, 62, 63 and 64

1. If equipped, remove the belt guard.
2. Rotate the belt tensioner clockwise using a 15mm wrench for 2.0L and 2.2L engines. For 2.8L engines, use a ¾ in. open end wrench to rotate the tensioner. On the 2.3L engine, a serpentine belt is used to drive the alternator and air conditioner compressor. To replace the belt push (rotate) the belt tensioner, using a 13 mm socket. For the 3.1L (VIN T) engine, use a ½ in. breaker bar to rotate the tensioner.
3. Slide the belt from the alternator pulley.
4. Release the tensioner, then remove the serpentine drive belt.

To install:

5. Properly route the serpentine drive belt, as shown in the accompanying figures.
6. Rotate the belt tensioner clockwise, using the proper sized wrench.
7. Slide the belt onto the alternator pulley
8. Release the belt tensioner.
9. If equipped, install the belt guard.

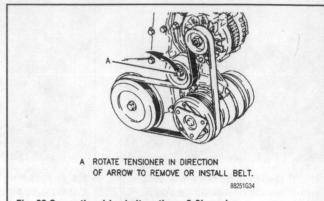

A ROTATE TENSIONER IN DIRECTION OF ARROW TO REMOVE OR INSTALL BELT.

88251G34

Fig. 63 Serpentine drive belt routing—2.3L engine

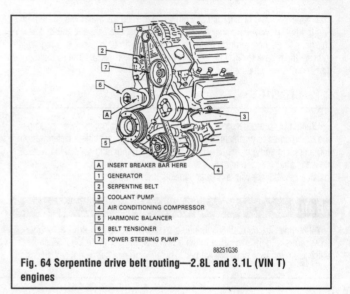

A INSERT BREAKER BAR HERE
1 GENERATOR
2 SERPENTINE BELT
3 COOLANT PUMP
4 AIR CONDITIONING COMPRESSOR
5 HARMONIC BALANCER
6 BELT TENSIONER
7 POWER STEERING PUMP

88251G36

Fig. 64 Serpentine drive belt routing—2.8L and 3.1L (VIN T) engines

3.1L (VIN M) ENGINE

◆ See Figure 65

1. Rotate the belt tensioner using tool J 39914, or equivalent serpentine drive belt tensioner wrench.
2. Remove the belt from the alternator pulley.
3. Carefully support the engine by the oil pan, using a block of wood and a suitable jack.

THE INDICATOR MARK ON THE STATIONARY PORTION OF THE TENSIONER MUST BE WITHIN THE LIMITS OF THE SLOTTED AREA ON THE MOVEABLE PORTION OF THE TENSIONER. ANY READING OUTSIDE THESE LIMITS INDICATES EITHER A FAULTY BELT OR TENSIONER.

A MAXIMUM BELT LENGTH
B NORMAL BELT LENGTH
C MAXIMUM (REPLACE) BELT LENGTH

88251G35

Fig. 61 Serpentine drive belt markings

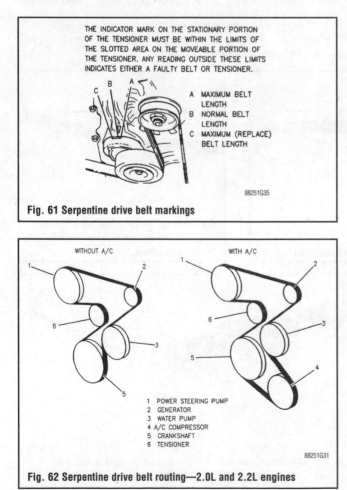

WITHOUT A/C   WITH A/C

1 POWER STEERING PUMP
2 GENERATOR
3 WATER PUMP
4 A/C COMPRESSOR
5 CRANKSHAFT
6 TENSIONER

88251G31

Fig. 62 Serpentine drive belt routing—2.0L and 2.2L engines

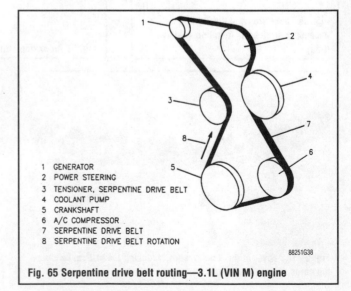

1 GENERATOR
2 POWER STEERING
3 TENSIONER, SERPENTINE DRIVE BELT
4 COOLANT PUMP
5 CRANKSHAFT
6 A/C COMPRESSOR
7 SERPENTINE DRIVE BELT
8 SERPENTINE DRIVE BELT ROTATION

88251G38

Fig. 65 Serpentine drive belt routing—3.1L (VIN M) engine

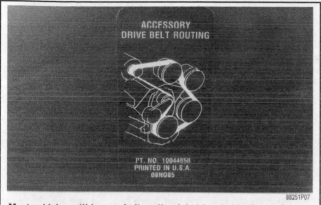

Most vehicles will have a belt routing label located in the engine compartment

4. Remove the engine mount assembly from the engine mount bracket support.
5. Remove the auxiliary bracket.
6. Carefully lower the engine enough to remove the serpentine drive belt.

To install:

7. Rotate the belt tensioner using J 39914, or equivalent.
8. Install the serpentine drive belt, making sure it is properly routed.
9. Install the auxiliary bracket and fasteners. Tighten the fasteners to 37 ft. lbs. (50 Nm).
10. Install the engine mount assembly.
11. Remove the floor jack and block of wood supporting the oil pan.

Poly-Groove Belt

On the 2.3L 4 cyl. engine, the power steering pump is driven by a poly-groove belt and can be replace as follows:
1. Loosen the pump bracket adjustment bolts.

2. Loosen the belt tension adjustment stud.
3. Remove the belt from the vehicle.

To install:

4. Place the belt into position.
5. Set the belt tension by turning the adjustment stud to the following:
- New belt—191 lbs. (850 N)
- Used belt—100 lbs. (450 N)

If installing a new belt, set the belt tension to the new belt specification. Start the engine and run for a minimum of 2 minutes then readjust the belt to the used belt specification.

6. Tighten the pump bracket bolts to 72 ft. lbs. (98 Nm) for the rear bolts and 19 ft. lbs. (26 Nm) for the front bolts.

Hoses

INSPECTION

▶ **See Figures 66, 67, 68 and 69**

Upper and lower radiator hoses along with the heater hoses should be checked for deterioration, leaks and loose hose clamps at least every 15,000 miles (24,000km). It is also wise to check the hoses periodically in early spring and at the beginning of the fall or winter when you are performing other maintenance. A quick visual inspection could discover a weakened hose which might have left you stranded if it had remained unrepaired.

Whenever you are checking the hoses, make sure the engine and cooling system are cold. Visually inspect for cracking, rotting or collapsed hoses, and replace as necessary. Run your hand along the length of the hose. If a weak or swollen spot is noted when squeezing the hose wall, the hose should be replaced.

REMOVAL & INSTALLATION

▶ **See Figures 70 thru 76**

1. Remove the radiator pressure cap.

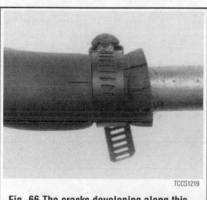

Fig. 66 The cracks developing along this hose are a result of age-related hardening

Fig. 67 A hose clamp that is too tight can cause older hoses to separate and tear on either side of the clamp

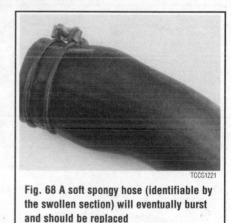

Fig. 68 A soft spongy hose (identifiable by the swollen section) will eventually burst and should be replaced

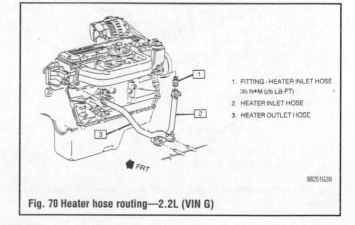

Fig. 69 Hoses are likely to deteriorate from the inside if the cooling system is not periodically flushed

Fig. 70 Heater hose routing—2.2L (VIN G)

1. FITTING - HEATER INLET HOSE 35 N•M (26 LB-FT)
2. HEATER INLET HOSE
3. HEATER OUTLET HOSE

✳✳ CAUTION

Never remove the pressure cap while the engine is running, or personal injury from scalding hot coolant or steam may result. If possible, wait until the engine has cooled to remove the pressure cap. If this is not possible, wrap a thick cloth around the pressure cap and turn it slowly to the stop. Step back while the pressure is released from the cooling system. When you are sure all the pressure has been released, use the cloth to turn and remove the cap.

2. Position a clean container under the radiator and/or engine draincock or plug, then open the drain and allow the cooling system to drain to an appropriate level. For some upper hoses, only a little coolant must be drained. To remove hoses positioned lower on the engine, such as a lower radiator hose, the entire cooling system must be emptied.

✳✳ CAUTION

When draining coolant, keep in mind that cats and dogs are attracted by ethylene glycol antifreeze, and are quite likely to drink any that is left in an uncovered container or in puddles on the ground. This will prove fatal in sufficient quantity. Always drain coolant into a sealable container. Coolant may be reused unless it is contaminated or several years old.

3. Loosen the hose clamps at each end of the hose requiring replacement. Clamps are usually either of the spring tension type (which require pliers to squeeze the tabs and loosen) or of the screw tension type (which require screw or hex drivers to loosen). Pull the clamps back on the hose away from the connection.

4. Twist, pull and slide the hose off the fitting, taking care not to damage the neck of the component from which the hose is being removed.

➥ If the hose is stuck at the connection, do not try to insert a screwdriver or other sharp tool under the hose end in an effort to free it, as the connection and/or hose may become damaged. Heater connections especially may be easily damaged by such a procedure. If the hose is to be replaced, use a single-edged razor blade to make a slice along the portion of the hose which is stuck on the connection, perpendicular to the end of the hose. Do not cut deep so as to damage the connection. The hose can then be peeled from the connection and discarded.

5. Clean both hose mounting connections. Inspect the condition of the hose clamps and replace them, if necessary.
   To install:
6. Dip the ends of the new hose into clean engine coolant to ease installation.
7. Slide the clamps over the replacement hose, then slide the hose ends over the connections into position.
8. Position and secure the clamps at least ¼ in. (6.35mm) from the ends of the hose. Make sure they are located beyond the raised bead of the connector.
9. Close the radiator or engine drains and properly refill the cooling system with the clean drained engine coolant or a suitable mixture of ethylene glycol coolant and water.
10. If available, install a pressure tester and check for leaks. If a pressure tester is not available, run the engine until normal operating temperature is reached (allowing the system to naturally pressurize), then check for leaks.

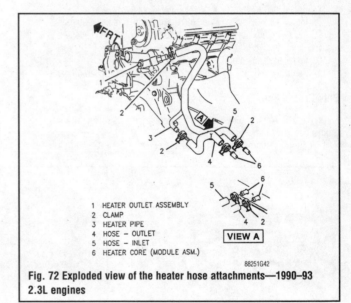

1 HEATER OUTLET ASSEMBLY
2 CLAMP
3 HEATER PIPE
4 HOSE – OUTLET
5 HOSE – INLET
6 HEATER CORE (MODULE ASM.)

88251G42

Fig. 72 Exploded view of the heater hose attachments—1990–93 2.3L engines

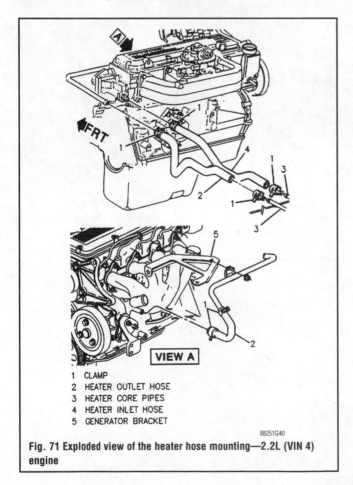

1 CLAMP
2 HEATER OUTLET HOSE
3 HEATER CORE PIPES
4 HEATER INLET HOSE
5 GENERATOR BRACKET

88251G40

Fig. 71 Exploded view of the heater hose mounting—2.2L (VIN 4) engine

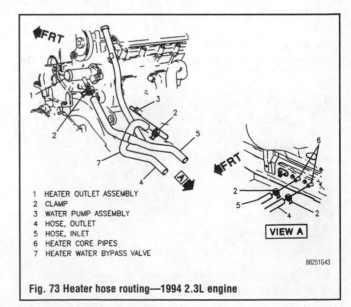

1 HEATER OUTLET ASSEMBLY
2 CLAMP
3 WATER PUMP ASSEMBLY
4 HOSE, OUTLET
5 HOSE, INLET
6 HEATER CORE PIPES
7 HEATER WATER BYPASS VALVE

88251G43

Fig. 73 Heater hose routing—1994 2.3L engine

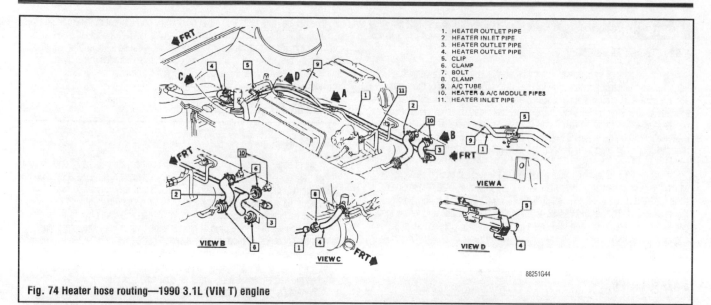

1. HEATER OUTLET PIPE
2. HEATER INLET PIPE
3. HEATER OUTLET PIPE
4. HEATER OUTLET PIPE
5. CLIP
6. CLAMP
7. BOLT
8. CLAMP
9. A/C TUBE
10. HEATER & A/C MODULE PIPES
11. HEATER INLET PIPE

Fig. 74 Heater hose routing—1990 3.1L (VIN T) engine

❄❄ CAUTION

If you are checking for leaks with the system at normal operating temperature, BE EXTREMELY CAREFUL not to touch any moving or hot engine parts. Once temperature has been reached, shut the engine OFF, and check for leaks around the hose fittings and connections which were removed earlier.

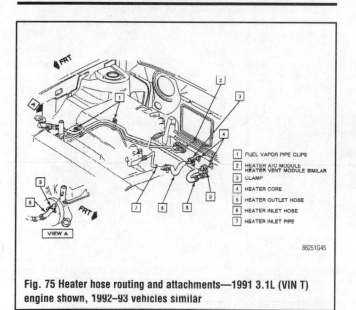

1. FUEL VAPOR PIPE CLIPS
2. HEATER A/C MODULE HEATER VENT MODULE SIMILAR
3. CLAMP
4. HEATER CORE
5. HEATER OUTLET HOSE
6. HEATER INLET HOSE
7. HEATER INLET PIPE

Fig. 75 Heater hose routing and attachments—1991 3.1L (VIN T) engine shown, 1992–93 vehicles similar

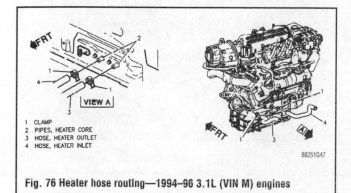

1. CLAMP
2. PIPES, HEATER CORE
3. HOSE, HEATER OUTLET
4. HOSE, HEATER INLET

Fig. 76 Heater hose routing—1994–96 3.1L (VIN M) engines

CV-Boots

INSPECTION

◆ See Figures 77 and 78

The CV (Constant Velocity) boots should be checked for damage each time the oil is changed and any other time the vehicle is raised for service. These boots keep water, grime, dirt and other damaging matter from entering the CV-joints. Any of these could cause early CV-joint failure which can be expensive to repair. Heavy grease thrown around the inside of the front wheel(s) and on the brake caliper/drum can be an indication of a torn boot. Thoroughly check the boots for missing clamps and tears. If the boot is damaged, it should be replaced immediately. Please refer to Section 7 for procedures.

Fig. 77 CV-boots must be inspected periodically for damage

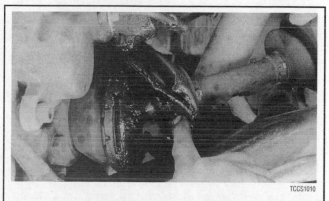

Fig. 78 A torn boot should be replaced immediately

Spark Plugs

▶ **See Figures 79 and 80**

A typical spark plug consists of a metal shell surrounding a ceramic insulator. A metal electrode extends downward through the center of the insulator and protrudes a small distance. Located at the end of the plug and attached to the side of the outer metal shell is the side electrode. The side electrode bends in at a 90° angle so that its tip is just past and parallel to the tip of the center electrode. The distance between these two electrodes (measured in thousandths of an inch or hundredths of a millimeter) is called the spark plug gap.

The spark plug does not produce a spark but instead provides a gap across which the current can arc. The coil produces anywhere from 20,000 to 50,000 volts (depending on the type and application) which travels through the wires to the spark plugs. The current passes along the center electrode and jumps the gap to the side electrode, and in doing so, ignites the air/fuel mixture in the combustion chamber.

SPARK PLUG HEAT RANGE

▶ **See Figure 81**

Spark plug heat range is the ability of the plug to dissipate heat. The longer the insulator (or the farther it extends into the engine), the hotter the plug will operate; the shorter the insulator (the closer the electrode is to the block's cooling passages) the cooler it will operate. A plug that absorbs little heat and remains too cool will quickly accumulate deposits of oil and carbon since it is not hot enough to burn them off. This leads to plug fouling and consequently to misfiring. A plug that absorbs too much heat will have no deposits but, due to the excessive heat, the electrodes will burn away quickly and might possibly lead to pre-ignition or other ignition problems. Pre-ignition takes place when plug tips get so hot that they glow sufficiently to ignite the air/fuel mixture before the actual spark occurs. This early ignition will usually cause a pinging during low speeds and heavy loads.

The general rule of thumb for choosing the correct heat range when picking a spark plug is: if most of your driving is long distance, high speed travel, use a colder plug; if most of your driving is stop and go, use a hotter plug. Original equipment plugs are generally a good compromise between the 2 styles and most people never have the need to change their plugs from the factory-recommended heat range.

REMOVAL & INSTALLATION

Except 2.3L Engine

A set of spark plugs usually requires replacement after about 20,000–30,000 miles (32,000–48,000km), depending on your style of driving. In normal operation plug gap increases about 0.001 in. (0.025mm) for every 2500 miles (4000km). As the gap increases, the plug's voltage requirement also increases. It requires a greater voltage to jump the wider gap and about two to three times as much voltage to fire the plug at high speeds than at idle. The improved air/fuel ratio control of modern fuel injection combined with the higher voltage output of modern ignition systems will often allow an engine to run significantly longer on a set of standard spark plugs, but keep in mind that efficiency will drop as the gap widens (along with fuel economy and power).

When you're removing spark plugs, work on one at a time. Don't start by removing the plug wires all at once, because, unless you number them, they may become mixed up. Take a minute before you begin and number the wires with tape.

1. Disconnect the negative battery cable, and if the vehicle has been run recently, allow the engine to thoroughly cool.

2. Carefully twist the spark plug wire boot to loosen it, then pull upward and remove the boot from the plug. Be sure to pull on the boot and not on the wire, otherwise the connector located inside the boot may become separated.

3. Using compressed air, blow any water or debris from the spark plug well to assure that no harmful contaminants are allowed to enter the combustion chamber when the spark plug is removed. If compressed air is not available, use a rag or a brush to clean the area.

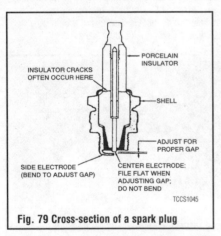

Fig. 79 Cross-section of a spark plug

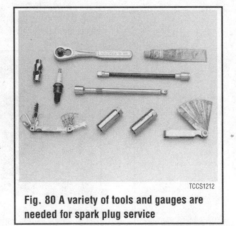

Fig. 80 A variety of tools and gauges are needed for spark plug service

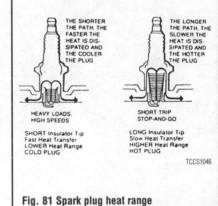

Fig. 81 Spark plug heat range

When disconnecting the spark plug wire from the plug, always pull on the boot, NEVER on the wire itself

Use a ratchet with a spark plug socket to loosen the spark plug . . .

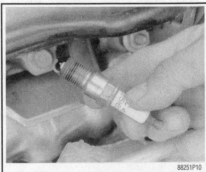

. . . then remove the spark plug from the cylinder head and inspect for wear and/or damage

➡ Remove the spark plugs when the engine is cold, if possible, to prevent damage to the threads. If removal of the plugs is difficult, apply a few drops of penetrating oil or silicone spray to the area around the base of the plug, and allow it a few minutes to work.

4. Using a spark plug socket that is equipped with a rubber insert to properly hold the plug, turn the spark plug counterclockwise to loosen and remove the spark plug from the bore.

✲✲ WARNING

Be sure not to use a flexible extension on the socket. Use of a flexible extension may allow a shear force to be applied to the plug. A shear force could break the plug off in the cylinder head, leading to costly and frustrating repairs.

To install:

5. Inspect the spark plug boot for tears or damage. If a damaged boot is found, the spark plug wire must be replaced.

6. Using a wire feeler gauge, check and adjust the spark plug gap. When using a gauge, the proper size should pass between the electrodes with a slight drag. The next larger size should not be able to pass while the next smaller size should pass freely.

7. Carefully thread the plug into the bore by hand. If resistance is felt before the plug is almost completely threaded, back the plug out and begin threading again. In small, hard to reach areas, an old spark plug wire and boot could be used as a threading tool. The boot will hold the plug while you twist the end of the wire and the wire is supple enough to twist before it would allow the plug to crossthread.

✲✲ WARNING

Do not use the spark plug socket to thread the plugs. Always carefully thread the plug by hand or using an old plug wire to prevent the possibility of crossthreading and damaging the cylinder head bore.

8. Carefully tighten the spark plug. If the plug you are installing is equipped with a crush washer, seat the plug, then tighten about ¼ turn to crush the washer. If you are installing a tapered seat plug, tighten the plug to specifications provided by the vehicle or plug manufacturer.

9. Apply a small amount of silicone dielectric compound to the end of the spark plug lead or inside the spark plug boot to prevent sticking, then install the boot to the spark plug and push until it clicks into place. The click may be felt or heard, then gently pull back on the boot to assure proper contact.

2.3L Engine

♦ See Figures 82 and 83

➡A special tool, J 36011 or equivalent spark plug connector assembly removal tool is required for this procedure.

1. Disconnect the negative battery cable. Make sure the engine is cold.

2. Remove the 4 electronic ignition module retaining bolts and detach the electrical connector.,

3. Remove the electronic ignition module by pulling straight up on the housing.

4. If the connector assembly(s) stick to the spark plugs, free them using tool J 36011 or equivalent spark plug connector removal tool. Use the tool by first twisting, then pulling up on the connector assembly.

5. Use compressed air to remove any debris from around the spark plug area.

6. Using a spark plug socket that is equipped with a rubber insert to properly hold the plug, turn the spark plug counterclockwise to loosen and remove the spark plug from the bore.

✲✲ WARNING

Be sure not to use a flexible extension on the socket. Use of a flexible extension may allow a shear force to be applied to the plug. A shear force could break the plug off in the cylinder head, leading to costly and frustrating repairs.

To install:

7. Inspect the spark plug boot for tears or damage. If a damaged boot is found, the spark plug wire must be replaced.

8. Using a wire feeler gauge, check and adjust the spark plug gap. When using a gauge, the proper size should pass between the electrodes with a slight

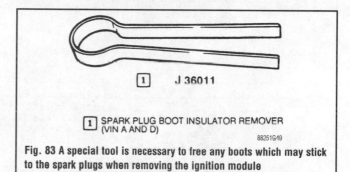

☐1 J 36011

☐1 SPARK PLUG BOOT INSULATOR REMOVER (VIN A AND D)

88251G49

Fig. 83 A special tool is necessary to free any boots which may stick to the spark plugs when removing the ignition module

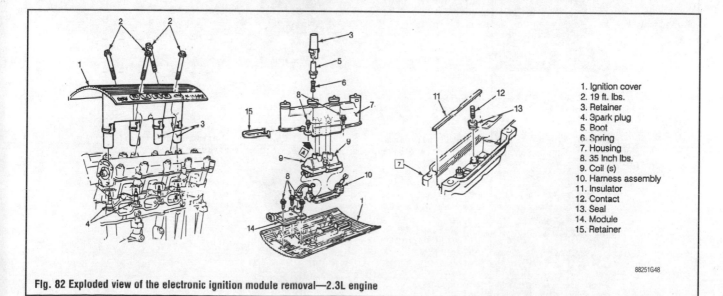

1. Ignition cover
2. 19 ft. lbs.
3. Retainer
4. Spark plug
5. Boot
6. Spring
7. Housing
8. 35 inch lbs.
9. Coil (s)
10. Harness assembly
11. Insulator
12. Contact
13. Seal
14. Module
15. Retainer

88251G48

Fig. 82 Exploded view of the electronic ignition module removal—2.3L engine

drag. The next larger size should not be able to pass while the next smaller size should pass freely.

9. Carefully thread the plug into the bore by hand. If resistance is felt before the plug is almost completely threaded, back the plug out and begin threading again. In small, hard to reach areas, an old spark plug wire and boot could be used as a threading tool. The boot will hold the plug while you twist the end of the wire and the wire is supple enough to twist before it would allow the plug to crossthread.

✳ WARNING

Do not use the spark plug socket to thread the plugs. Always carefully thread the plug by hand or using an old plug wire to prevent the possibility of crossthreading and damaging the cylinder head bore.

10. Carefully tighten the spark plug to 17 ft. lbs. 22 Nm).
11. If any spark plug boots were separated from the module assembly, reinstall them on the module assembly. Check to be sure the spring terminal is inside the boot.

12. Position the module over the spark plugs and push it straight down to fully seat it.
13. Clean off any old lubricant that is found on the module-to-cam housing bolts, then apply a light coat of lubricant no. 1052080, onto the module-to-cam housing bolts.
14. Hand-start the module-to-cam housing bolts, then tighten to 16 ft. lbs. (22 Nm).
15. Attach the electrical connector, then connect the negative battery cable.

INSPECTION & GAPPING

◆ See Figures 84, 85, 86 and 87

Check the plugs for deposits and wear. If they are not going to be replaced, clean the plugs thoroughly. Remember that any kind of deposit will decrease the efficiency of the plug. Plugs can be cleaned on a spark plug cleaning machine, which can sometimes be found in service stations, or you can do an acceptable

A **normally worn** spark plug should have light tan or gray deposits on the firing tip.

A **carbon fouled** plug, identified by soft, sooty, black deposits, may indicate an improperly tuned vehicle. Check the air cleaner, ignition components and engine control system.

This spark plug has been **left in the engine too long**, as evidenced by the extreme gap- Plugs with such an extreme gap can cause misfiring and stumbling accompanied by a noticeable lack of power.

An **oil fouled** spark plug indicates an engine with worn poston rings and/or bad valve seals allowing excessive oil to enter the chamber.

A **physically damaged** spark plug may be evidence of severe detonation in that cylinder. Watch that cylinder carefully between services, as a continued detonation will not only damage the plug, but could also damage the engine.

A **bridged or almost bridged** spark plug, identified by a build-up between the electrodes caused by excessive carbon or oil build-up on the plug.

TCCA1P40

Fig. 84 Inspect the spark plug to determine engine running conditions

Fig. 85 Checking the spark plug gap with a feeler gauge

Fig. 86 Adjusting the spark plug gap

Fig. 87 If the standard plug is in good condition, the electrode may be filed flat—WARNING: do not file platinum plugs

job of cleaning with a stiff brush. If the plugs are cleaned, the electrodes must be filed flat. Use an ignition points file, not an emery board or the like, which will leave deposits. The electrodes must be filed perfectly flat with sharp edges; rounded edges reduce the spark plug voltage by as much as 50%.

Check spark plug gap before installation. The ground electrode (the L-shaped one connected to the body of the plug) must be parallel to the center electrode and the specified size wire gauge (please refer to the Tune-Up Specifications chart for details) must pass between the electrodes with a slight drag.

→NEVER adjust the gap on a used platinum type spark plug.

Always check the gap on new plugs as they are not always set correctly at the factory. Do not use a flat feeler gauge when measuring the gap on a used plug, because the reading may be inaccurate. A round-wire type gapping tool is the best way to check the gap. The correct gauge should pass through the electrode gap with a slight drag. If you're in doubt, try one size smaller and one larger. The smaller gauge should go through easily, while the larger one shouldn't go through at all. Wire gapping tools usually have a bending tool attached. Use that to adjust the side electrode until the proper distance is obtained. Absolutely never attempt to bend the center electrode. Also, be careful not to bend the side electrode too far or too often as it may weaken and break off within the engine, requiring removal of the cylinder head to retrieve it.

Spark Plug Wires

TESTING

♦ See Figure 88

At every tune-up/inspection, visually check the spark plug cables for burns cuts, or breaks in the insulation. Check the boots and the nipples on the distributor cap and/or coil. Replace any damaged wiring.

Fig. 88 Checking individual plug wire resistance with a digital ohmmeter

Every 50,000 miles (80,000 Km) or 60 months, the resistance of the wires should be checked with an ohmmeter. Wires with excessive resistance will cause misfiring, and may make the engine difficult to start in damp weather.

To check resistance, connect one lead of an ohmmeter to an electrode on the ignition coil; connect the other lead to the corresponding spark plug terminal (remove it from the spark plug for this test). Replace any wire which shows a resistance over 30,000 ohms. Generally speaking, it is preferable that resistance be below 25,000 ohms, but 30,000 ohms must be considered the outer limit of acceptability. It should be remembered that resistance is also a function of length; the longer the wire, the greater the resistance. Thus, if the wires on your car are longer than the factory originals, resistance will be higher, quite possibly outside these limits.

Wire length can therefore be used to determine appropriate resistance values.

- 0–15 in. (0–38cm)—3,000–10,000 ohms
- 15–25 in. (38–64cm)—4,000–15,000 ohms
- 25–35 in. (64–89cm)—6,000–20,000 ohms
- Wire over 35 in. (89cm)—25,000 ohms

REMOVAL & INSTALLATION

♦ See Figures 89 thru 95

When installing new wires, replace them one at a time to avoid mix-ups. If it becomes necessary to remove all of the wires from the distributor cap or coil

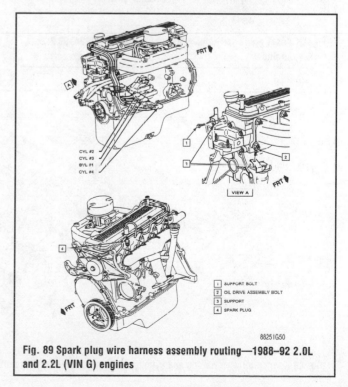

Fig. 89 Spark plug wire harness assembly routing—1988–92 2.0L and 2.2L (VIN G) engines

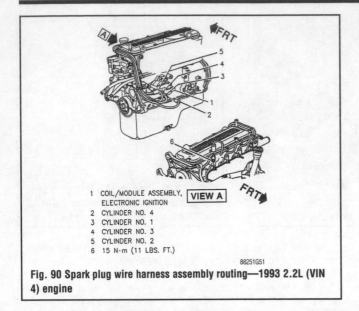

1 COIL/MODULE ASSEMBLY,
  ELECTRONIC IGNITION
2 CYLINDER NO. 4
3 CYLINDER NO. 1
4 CYLINDER NO. 3
5 CYLINDER NO. 2
6 15 N·m (11 LBS. FT.)

VIEW A

88251G51

Fig. 90 Spark plug wire harness assembly routing—1993 2.2L (VIN 4) engine

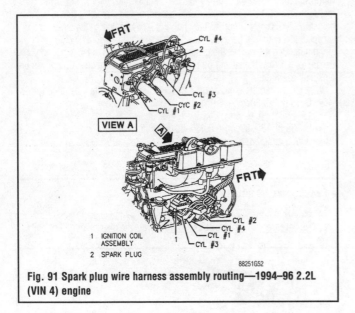

1 IGNITION COIL
  ASSEMBLY
2 SPARK PLUG

VIEW A

88251G52

Fig. 91 Spark plug wire harness assembly routing—1994–96 2.2L (VIN 4) engine

packs at one time, take the time to label the distributor cap/coil pack towers to denote the cylinder number of the wire for that position. When this is done, incorrect positioning of wires can more easily be avoided. Start by replacing the longest one first. Route the wire over the same path as the original and secure in place.

Ignition Timing

GENERAL INFORMATION

All of the vehicles covered by this manual are equipped with distributorless ignition systems. Accordingly, ignition timing is controlled by the Engine/Powertrain Control Module (ECM/PCM) and is not adjustable.

Valve Lash

All off the engines covered by this manual are equipped with hydraulic valve lifters. No adjustments are necessary or possible.

Idle Speed and Mixture Adjustments

All engines covered by this manual utilize an electronic engine control system. No periodic adjustment of the idle speed or mixture is necessary or possible.

On 3.1L engines, anytime the battery is disconnected, the programmed position of the IAC valve pintle is lost. If you are experiencing an incorrect idle with this engine, it may be due to this. Perform the following to "relearn" the idle speed:

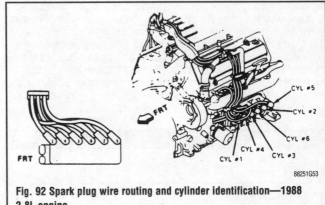

88251G53

Fig. 92 Spark plug wire routing and cylinder identification—1988 2.8L engine

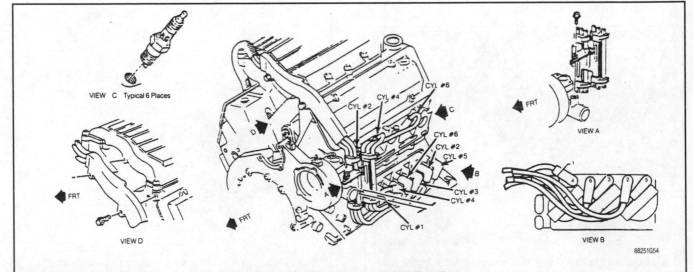

88251G54

Fig. 93 Spark plug wire routing and cylinder identification—1989–90 2.8L and 3.1L (VIN T) engines

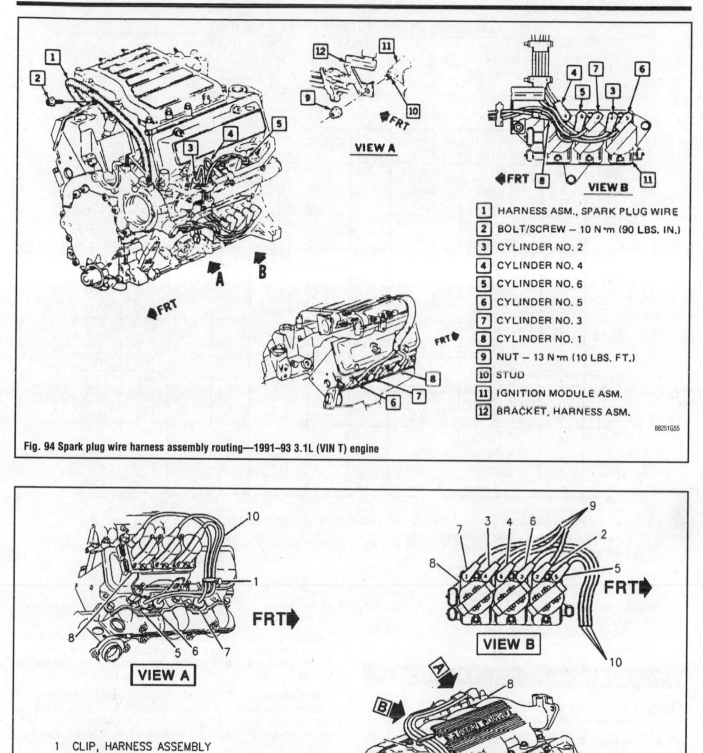

1. HARNESS ASM., SPARK PLUG WIRE
2. BOLT/SCREW — 10 N·m (90 LBS. IN.)
3. CYLINDER NO. 2
4. CYLINDER NO. 4
5. CYLINDER NO. 6
6. CYLINDER NO. 5
7. CYLINDER NO. 3
8. CYLINDER NO. 1
9. NUT — 13 N·m (10 LBS. FT.)
10. STUD
11. IGNITION MODULE ASM.
12. BRACKET, HARNESS ASM.

Fig. 94 Spark plug wire harness assembly routing—1991–93 3.1L (VIN T) engine

1 CLIP, HARNESS ASSEMBLY
2 CYLINDER #2
3 CYLINDER #4
4 CYLINDER #6
5 CYLINDER #5
6 CYLINDER #3
7 CYLINDER #1
8 IGNITION COIL ASSEMBLY
9 LEFT HAND HARNESS ASSEMBLY
10 RIGHT HAND HARNESS ASSEMBLY

Fig. 95 Spark plug wire harness assembly routing—1994–96 3.1L (VIN M) engine

GASOLINE ENGINE TUNE-UP SPECIFICATIONS

Year	Engine ID/VIN	Engine Displacement Liters (cc)	Spark Plugs Gap (in.)	Ignition Timing (deg.) MT	AT	Fuel Pump (psi)	Idle Speed (rpm) MT	AT	Valve Clearance In.	Ex.
1988	1	2.0L (1991)	0.035	①	①	9-13	①	①	HYD	HYD
	W	2.8L (2837)	0.045	①	①	41-47	①	①	HYD	HYD
1989	1	2.0L (1991)	0.035	①	①	9-13	①	①	HYD	HYD
	W	2.8L (2837)	0.045	①	①	41-47	①	①	HYD	HYD
1990	G	2.2L (2190)	0.035	①	①	9-13	①	①	HYD	HYD
	A	2.3L (2260)	0.035	①	①	41-47	①	①	HYD	HYD
	T	3.1L (3128)	0.045	①	①	41-47	①	①	HYD	HYD
1991	G	2.2L (2190)	0.035	①	①	9-13	①	①	HYD	HYD
	A	2.3L (2260)	0.035	①	①	41-47	①	①	HYD	HYD
	T	3.1L (3128)	0.045	①	①	41-47	①	①	HYD	HYD
1992	4	2.2L (2190)	0.045	①	①	41-47	①	①	HYD	HYD
	A	2.3L (2260)	0.035	①	①	41-47	①	①	HYD	HYD
	T	3.1L (3128)	0.045	①	①	41-47	①	①	HYD	HYD
1993	4	2.2L (2190)	0.035	①	①	41-47	①	①	HYD	HYD
	A	2.3L (2260)	0.035	①	①	41-47	①	①	HYD	HYD
	T	3.1L (3128)	0.045	①	①	41-47	①	①	HYD	HYD
1994	4	2.2L (2190)	0.060	①	①	41-47	①	①	HYD	HYD
	A	2.3L (2260)	0.035	①	①	41-47	①	①	HYD	HYD
	M	3.1L (3128)	0.045	①	①	41-47	①	①	HYD	HYD
1995	4	2.2L (2190)	0.060	①	①	41-47	①	①	HYD	HYD
	M	3.1L (3128)	0.060	①	①	41-47	①	①	HYD	HYD
1996	4	2.2L (2190)	0.060	①	①	41-47	①	①	HYD	HYD
	M	3.1L (3128)	0.060	①	①	41-47	①	①	HYD	HYD

NOTE: The Vehicle Emission Control Information Label often reflects specification changes made during production.

The label figures must be used if they differ from those in this chart.

HYD - Hydraulic

① Refer to Vehicle Emission Control Information Label

88251C03

1. Reconnect the battery.
2. Install a Tech 1® scan tool.
3. Select **IAC SYSTEM**, then **IDLE LEARN** in the **MISC TEST** mode.
4. Proceed with the idle learn as directed by the scan tool.

Air Conditioning

SYSTEM SERVICE & REPAIR

➡**It is recommended that the A/C system be serviced by an EPA Section 609 certified automotive technician utilizing a refrigerant recovery/recycling machine.**

The do-it-yourselfer should not service his/her own vehicle's A/C system for many reasons, including legal concerns, personal injury, environmental damage and cost. The following are some of the reasons why you may decide not to service your own vehicle's A/C system.

According to the US Clean Air Act, it is a federal crime to service or repair (involving the refrigerant) a Motor Vehicle Air Conditioning (MVAC) system for money without being EPA certified. It is also illegal to vent R-12 and R-134a refrigerants into the atmosphere. Selling or distributing A/C system refrigerant (in a container which contains less than 20 pounds of refrigerant) to any person who is not EPA 609 certified is also not allowed by law.

State and/or local laws may be more strict than the federal regulations, so be sure to check with your state and/or local authorities for further information. For further federal information on the legality of servicing your A/C system, call the EPA Stratospheric Ozone Hotline.

➡**Federal law dictates that a fine of up to $25,000 may be levelled on people convicted of venting refrigerant into the atmosphere. Additionally, the EPA may pay up to $10,000 for information or services leading to a criminal conviction of the violation of these laws.**

When servicing an A/C system you run the risk of handling or coming in contact with refrigerant, which may result in skin or eye irritation or frostbite. Although low in toxicity (due to chemical stability), inhalation of concentrated refrigerant fumes is dangerous and can result in death; cases of fatal cardiac arrhythmia have been reported in people accidentally subjected to high levels of refrigerant. Some early symptoms include loss of concentration and drowsiness.

➡**Generally, the limit for exposure is lower for R-134a than it is for R-12. Exceptional care must be practiced when handling R-134a.**

Also, refrigerants can decompose at high temperatures (near gas heaters or open flame), which may result in hydrofluoric acid, hydrochloric acid and phosgene (a fatal nerve gas).

R-12 refrigerant can damage the environment because it is a Chlorofluorocarbon (CFC), which has been proven to add to ozone layer depletion, leading to increasing levels of UV radiation. UV radiation has been linked with an increase in skin cancer, suppression of the human immune system, an increase in cataracts, damage to crops, damage to aquatic organisms, an increase in ground-level ozone, and increased global warming.

R-134a refrigerant is a greenhouse gas which, if allowed to vent into the atmosphere, will contribute to global warming (the Greenhouse Effect).

It is usually more economically feasible to have a certified MVAC automotive technician perform A/C system service on your vehicle. Some possible reasons for this are as follows:

• While it is illegal to service an A/C system without the proper equipment, the home mechanic would have to purchase an expensive refrigerant recovery/recycling machine to service his/her own vehicle.

• Since only a certified person may purchase refrigerant—according to the Clean Air Act, there are specific restrictions on selling or distributing A/C system refrigerant—it is legally impossible (unless certified) for the home mechanic to service his/her own vehicle. Procuring refrigerant in an illegal fashion exposes one to the risk of paying a $25,000 fine to the EPA.

R-12 Refrigerant Conversion

If your vehicle still uses R-12 refrigerant, one way to save A/C system costs down the road is to investigate the possibility of having your system converted to R-134a. The older R-12 systems can be easily converted to R-134a refrigerant by a certified automotive technician by installing a few new components and changing the system oil.

The cost of R-12 is steadily rising and will continue to increase, because it is no longer imported or manufactured in the United States. Therefore, it is often possible to have an R-12 system converted to R-134a and recharged for less than it would cost to just charge the system with R-12.

If you are interested in having your system converted, contact local automotive service stations for more details and information.

PREVENTIVE MAINTENANCE

♦ See Figure 96

Although the A/C system should not be serviced by the do-it-yourselfer, preventive maintenance can be practiced and A/C system inspections can be performed to help maintain the efficiency of the vehicle's A/C system. For preventive maintenance, perform the following:

• The easiest and most important preventive maintenance for your A/C system is to be sure that it is used on a regular basis. Running the system for five minutes each month (no matter what the season) will help ensure that the seals and all internal components remain lubricated.

➡ Some newer vehicles automatically operate the A/C system compressor whenever the windshield defroster is activated. When running, the compressor lubricates the A/C system components; therefore, the A/C system would not need to be operated each month.

• In order to prevent heater core freeze-up during A/C operation, it is necessary to maintain proper antifreeze protection. Use a hand-held coolant tester

(hydrometer) to periodically check the condition of the antifreeze in your engine's cooling system.

➡ Antifreeze should not be used longer than the manufacturer specifies.

• For efficient operation of an air conditioned vehicle's cooling system, the radiator cap should have a holding pressure which meets manufacturer's specifications. A cap which fails to hold these pressures should be replaced.

• Any obstruction of or damage to the condenser configuration will restrict air flow which is essential to its efficient operation. It is, therefore, a good rule to keep this unit clean and in proper physical shape.

➡ Bug screens which are mounted in front of the condenser (unless they are original equipment) are regarded as obstructions.

• The condensation drain tube expels any water which accumulates on the bottom of the evaporator housing into the engine compartment. If this tube is obstructed, the air conditioning performance can be restricted and condensation buildup can spill over onto the vehicle's floor.

SYSTEM INSPECTION

Although the A/C system should not be serviced by the do-it-yourselfer, preventive maintenance can be practiced and A/C system inspections can be performed to help maintain the efficiency of the vehicle's A/C system. For A/C system inspection, perform the following:

The easiest and often most important check for the air conditioning system consists of a visual inspection of the system components. Visually inspect the air conditioning system for refrigerant leaks, damaged compressor clutch, abnormal compressor drive belt tension and/or condition, plugged evaporator drain tube, blocked condenser fins, disconnected or broken wires, blown fuses, corroded connections and poor insulation.

A refrigerant leak will usually appear as an oily residue at the leakage point in the system. The oily residue soon picks up dust or dirt particles from the surrounding air and appears greasy. Through time, this will build up and appear to be a heavy dirt impregnated grease.

For a thorough visual and operational inspection, check the following:

• Check the surface of the radiator and condenser for dirt, leaves or other material which might block air flow.

• Check for kinks in hoses and lines. Check the system for leaks.

• Make sure the drive belt is properly tensioned. When the air conditioning is operating, make sure the drive belt is free of noise or slippage.

• Make sure the blower motor operates at all appropriate positions, then check for distribution of the air from all outlets with the blower on **HIGH** or **MAX**.

➡ Keep in mind that under conditions of high humidity, air discharged from the A/C vents may not feel as cold as expected, even if the system is working properly. This is because vaporized moisture in humid air retains heat more effectively than dry air, thereby making humid air more difficult to cool.

• Make sure the air passage selection lever is operating correctly. Start the engine and warm it to normal operating temperature, then make sure the temperature selection lever is operating correctly.

Windshield Wipers

ELEMENT (REFILL) CARE & REPLACEMENT

♦ See Figures 97, 98 and 99

For maximum effectiveness and longest element life, the windshield and wiper blades should be kept clean. Dirt, tree sap, road tar and so on will cause streaking, smearing and blade deterioration if left on the glass. It is advisable to wash the windshield carefully with a commercial glass cleaner at least once a month. Wipe off the rubber blades with the wet rag afterwards. Do not attempt to move wipers across the windshield by hand; damage to the motor and drive mechanism will result.

To inspect and/or replace the wiper blade elements, place the wiper switch in the **LOW** speed position and the ignition switch in the **ACC** position. When the wiper blades are approximately vertical on the windshield, turn the ignition switch to **OFF**.

TCCS1233

Fig. 96 A coolant tester can be used to determine the freezing and boiling levels of the coolant in your vehicle

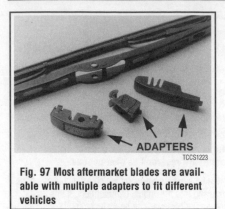

Fig. 97 Most aftermarket blades are available with multiple adapters to fit different vehicles

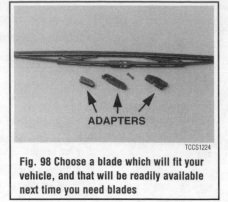

Fig. 98 Choose a blade which will fit your vehicle, and that will be readily available next time you need blades

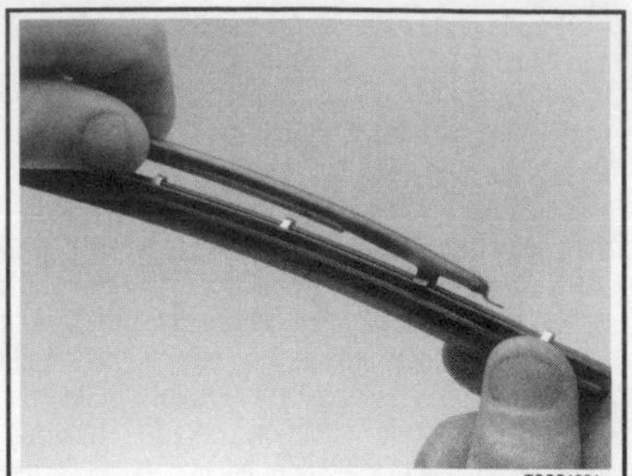

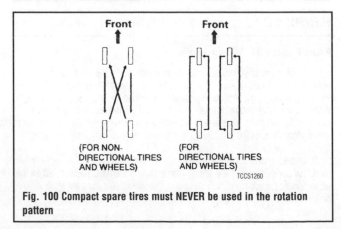

Fig. 99 When installed, be certain the blade is fully inserted into the backing

Examine the wiper blade elements. If they are found to be cracked, broken or torn, they should be replaced immediately. Replacement intervals will vary with usage, although ozone deterioration usually limits element life to about one year. If the wiper pattern is smeared or streaked, or if the blade chatters across the glass, the elements should be replaced. It is easiest and most sensible to replace the elements in pairs.

If your vehicle is equipped with aftermarket blades, there are several different types of refills and your vehicle might have any kind. Aftermarket blades and arms rarely use the exact same type blade or refill as the original equipment.

Regardless of the type of refill used, be sure to follow the part manufacturer's instructions closely. Make sure that all of the frame jaws are engaged as the refill is pushed into place and locked. If the metal blade holder and frame are allowed to touch the glass during wiper operation, the glass will be scratched.

Tires and Wheels

Common sense and good driving habits will afford maximum tire life. Make sure that you don't overload the vehicle or run with incorrect pressure in the tires. Either of these will increase tread wear. Fast starts, sudden stops and sharp cornering are hard on tires and will shorten their useful life span.

➡**For optimum tire life, keep the tires properly inflated, rotate them often and have the wheel alignment checked periodically.**

Inspect your tires frequently. Be especially careful to watch for bubbles in the tread or sidewall, deep cuts or underinflation. Replace any tires with bubbles in the sidewall. If cuts are so deep that they penetrate to the cords, discard the tire. Any cut in the sidewall of a radial tire renders it unsafe. Also look for uneven tread wear patterns that may indicate the front end is out of alignment or that the tires are out of balance.

TIRE ROTATION

▶ **See Figure 100**

Tires must be rotated periodically to equalize wear patterns that vary with a tire's position on the vehicle. Tires will also wear in an uneven way as the front steering/suspension system wears to the point where the alignment should be reset.

Rotating the tires will ensure maximum life for the tires as a set, so you will not have to discard a tire early due to wear on only part of the tread. Regular rotation is required to equalize wear.

When rotating "unidirectional tires," make sure that they always roll in the same direction. This means that a tire used on the left side of the vehicle must not be switched to the right side and vice-versa. Such tires should only be rotated front-to-rear or rear-to-front, while always remaining on the same side of the vehicle. These tires are marked on the sidewall as to the direction of rotation; observe the marks when reinstalling the tire(s).

Some styled or "mag" wheels may have different offsets front to rear. In these cases, the rear wheels must not be used up front and vice-versa. Furthermore, if these wheels are equipped with unidirectional tires, they cannot be rotated unless the tire is remounted for the proper direction of rotation.

➡**The compact or space-saver spare is strictly for emergency use. It must never be included in the tire rotation or placed on the vehicle for everyday use.**

TIRE DESIGN

▶ **See Figure 101**

For maximum satisfaction, tires should be used in sets of four. Mixing of different brands or types (radial, bias-belted, fiberglass belted) should be avoided. In most cases, the vehicle manufacturer has designated a type of tire on which the vehicle will perform best. Your first choice when replacing tires should be to use the same type of tire that the manufacturer recommends.

When radial tires are used, tire sizes and wheel diameters should be selected to maintain ground clearance and tire load capacity equivalent to the original specified tire. Radial tires should always be used in sets of four.

✳✳ CAUTION

Radial tires should never be used on only the front axle.

When selecting tires, pay attention to the original size as marked on the tire. Most tires are described using an industry size code sometimes referred to as P-Metric. This allows the exact identification of the tire specifications, regardless of the manufacturer. If selecting a different tire size or brand, remember to check the installed tire for any sign of interference with the body or suspension while the vehicle is stopping, turning sharply or heavily loaded.

Snow Tires

Good radial tires can produce a big advantage in slippery weather, but in snow, a street radial tire does not have sufficient tread to provide traction and control. The small grooves of a street tire quickly pack with snow and the tire behaves like a billiard ball on a marble floor. The more open, chunky tread of a snow tire will self-clean as the tire turns, providing much better grip on snowy surfaces.

To satisfy municipalities requiring snow tires during weather emergencies, most snow tires carry either an M + S designation after the tire size stamped on the sidewall, or the designation "all-season." In general, no change in tire size is necessary when buying snow tires.

Most manufacturers strongly recommend the use of 4 snow tires on their vehicles for reasons of stability. If snow tires are fitted only to the drive wheels, the opposite end of the vehicle may become very unstable when braking or

Fig. 100 Compact spare tires must NEVER be used in the rotation pattern

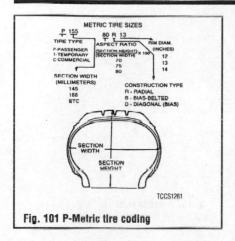

Fig. 101 P-Metric tire coding

Fig. 102 Tires with deep cuts, or cuts which bulge, should be replaced immediately

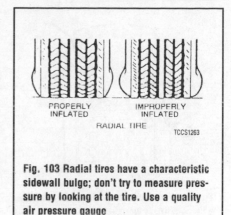

Fig. 103 Radial tires have a characteristic sidewall bulge; don't try to measure pressure by looking at the tire. Use a quality air pressure gauge

turning on slippery surfaces. This instability can lead to unpleasant endings if the driver can't counteract the slide in time.

Note that snow tires, whether 2 or 4, will affect vehicle handling in all non-snow situations. The stiffer, heavier snow tires will noticeably change the turning and braking characteristics of the vehicle. Once the snow tires are installed, you must re-learn the behavior of the vehicle and drive accordingly.

➡Consider buying extra wheels on which to mount the snow tires. Once done, the "snow wheels" can be installed and removed as needed. This eliminates the potential damage to tires or wheels from seasonal removal and installation. Even if your vehicle has styled wheels, see if inexpensive steel wheels are available. Although the look of the vehicle will change, the expensive wheels will be protected from salt, curb hits and pothole damage.

TIRE STORAGE

If they are mounted on wheels, store the tires at proper inflation pressure. All tires should be kept in a cool, dry place. If they are stored in the garage or basement, do not let them stand on a concrete floor; set them on strips of wood, a mat or a large stack of newspaper. Keeping them away from direct moisture is of paramount importance. Tires should not be stored upright, but in a flat position.

INFLATION & INSPECTION

♦ See Figures 102 thru 107

The importance of proper tire inflation cannot be overemphasized. A tire employs air as part of its structure. It is designed around the supporting strength of the air at a specified pressure. For this reason, improper inflation drastically reduces the tire's ability to perform as intended. A tire will lose some air in day-to-day use; having to add a few pounds of air periodically is not necessarily a sign of a leaking tire.

Two items should be a permanent fixture in every glove compartment: an accurate tire pressure gauge and a tread depth gauge. Check the tire pressure (including the spare) regularly with a pocket type gauge. Too often, the gauge

on the end of the air hose at your corner garage is not accurate because it suffers too much abuse. Always check tire pressure when the tires are cold, as pressure increases with temperature. If you must move the vehicle to check the tire inflation, do not drive more than a mile before checking. A cold tire is generally one that has not been driven for more than three hours.

A plate or sticker is normally provided somewhere in the vehicle (door post, hood, tailgate or trunk lid) which shows the proper pressure for the tires. Never counteract excessive pressure build-up by bleeding off air pressure (letting some air out). This will cause the tire to run hotter and wear quicker.

✳✳ CAUTION

Never exceed the maximum tire pressure embossed on the tire! This is the pressure to be used when the tire is at maximum loading, but it is rarely the correct pressure for everyday driving. Consult the owner's manual or the tire pressure sticker for the correct tire pressure.

Once you've maintained the correct tire pressures for several weeks, you'll be familiar with the vehicle's braking and handling personality. Slight adjustments in tire pressures can fine-tune these characteristics, but never change the cold pressure specification by more than 2 psi. A slightly softer tire pressure will give a softer ride but also yield lower fuel mileage. A slightly harder tire will give crisper dry road handling but can cause skidding on wet surfaces. Unless you're fully attuned to the vehicle, stick to the recommended inflation pressures.

All automotive tires have built-in tread wear indicator bars that show up as ½ in. (13mm) wide smooth bands across the tire when ¹⁄₁₆ in. (1.5mm) of tread remains. The appearance of tread wear indicators means that the tires should be replaced. In fact, many states have laws prohibiting the use of tires with less than this amount of tread.

You can check your own tread depth with an inexpensive gauge or by using a Lincoln head penny. Slip the Lincoln penny (with Lincoln's head upside-down) into several tread grooves. If you can see the top of Lincoln's head in 2 adjacent grooves, the tire has less than ¹⁄₁₆ in. (1.5mm) tread left and should be replaced. You can measure snow tires in the same manner by using the "tails" side of the Lincoln penny. If you can see the top of the Lincoln memorial, it's time to replace the snow tire(s).

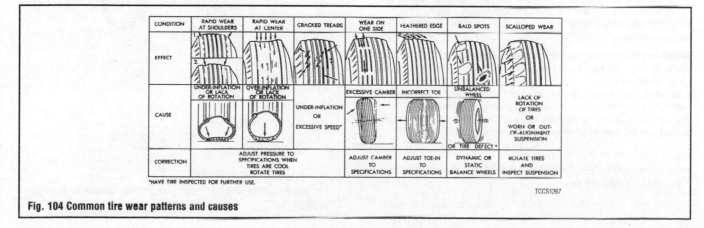

Fig. 104 Common tire wear patterns and causes

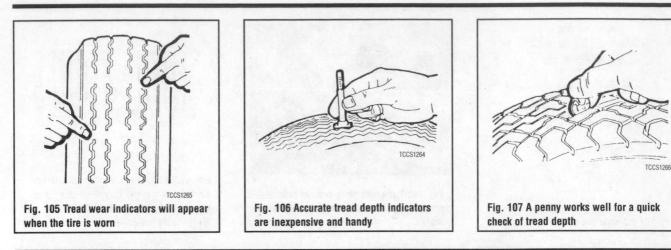

Fig. 105 Tread wear indicators will appear when the tire is worn

Fig. 106 Accurate tread depth indicators are inexpensive and handy

Fig. 107 A penny works well for a quick check of tread depth

FLUIDS AND LUBRICANTS

Used fluids such as engine oil, transmission fluid, antifreeze and brake fluid are hazardous wastes and must be disposed of properly. Before draining any fluids, consult with your local authorities; in many areas waste oil, etc. is being accepted as a part of recycling programs. A number of service stations and auto parts stores are also accepting waste fluids for recycling.

Be sure of the recycling center's policies before draining any fluids, as many will not accept different fluids that have been mixed together.

Fuel and Engine Oil Recommendations

FUEL

➡Some fuel additives contain chemicals that can damage the catalytic converter and/or oxygen sensor. Read all of the labels carefully before using any additive in the engine or fuel system.

All Corsica's and Beretta's are designed to run on unleaded fuel. The use of a leaded fuel in a car requiring unleaded fuel will plug the catalytic converter and render it inoperative. It will also increase exhaust backpressure to the point where engine output will be severely reduced. The minimum octane rating of the unleaded fuel being used must be at least 87, which usually means regular unleaded, but some high performance engines may require higher ratings. Fuel should be selected for the brand and octane which performs best with your engine. Judge a gasoline by its ability to prevent pinging, its engine starting capabilities (cold and hot) and general all weather performance.

As far as the octane rating is concerned, refer to the general engine specifications chart in Section 3 of this manual to find your engine and its compression ratio. If the compression ratio is 9.0:1 or lower, in most cases a regular unleaded grade of gasoline can be used. If the compression ratio is higher than 9.0:1 use a premium grade of unleaded fuel.

The use of a fuel too low in octane (a measure of anti-knock quality) will result in spark knock. Since many factors such as altitude, terrain, air temperature and humidity affect operating efficiency, knocking may result even though the recommended fuel is being used. If persistent knocking occurs, it may be necessary to switch to a higher grade of fuel. Continuous or heavy knocking may result in engine damage.

➡Your engine's fuel requirement can change with time, mainly due to carbon build-up, which will in turn change the compression ratio. If you engine pings, knocks or diesels (runs with the ignition OFF) switch to a higher grade of fuel. Sometimes, just changing brands will cure the problem. If it becomes necessary to retard the timing from the specifications, don't change it more than a few degrees. Retarded timing will reduce power output and fuel mileage, in addition to making the engine run hotter.

OIL

♦ See Figures 108 and 109

The Society Of Automotive Engineer (SAE) grade number indicates the viscosity of the engine oil and thus its ability to lubricate at a given temperature.

The lower the SAE grade number, the lighter the oil; the lower the viscosity, the easier it is to crank the engine in cold weather. Oil viscosities should be chosen from those oils recommended for the lowest anticipated temperatures during the oil change interval. With the proper viscosity, you will be assured of easy cold starting and sufficient engine protection.

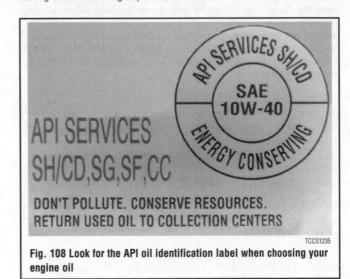

Fig. 108 Look for the API oil identification label when choosing your engine oil

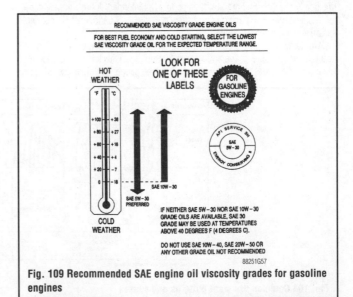

Fig. 109 Recommended SAE engine oil viscosity grades for gasoline engines

Multi-viscosity oils (5W-30, 10W-30 etc.) offer the important advantage of being adaptable to temperature extremes. They allow easy starting at low temperatures, yet they give good protection at high speeds and engine temperatures. This is a decided advantage in changeable climates or in long distance driving.

The American Petroleum Institute (API) designation indicates the classification of engine oil used under certain given operating conditions. Only oil designated for Service SH, or latest superseding oil grade, should be used. Oils of the SH type perform a variety of functions inside the engine in addition to their basic function as a lubricant. Through a balanced system of metallic detergents and polymeric dispersants, the oil prevents the formation of high and low temperature deposits and also keeps sludge and particles of dirt in suspension. Acids, particularly sulfuric acid, as well as other byproducts of combustion, are neutralized. Both the SAE grade number and the API designation can be found on the side of the oil bottle.

Synthetic Oils

There are excellent synthetic and fuel-efficient oils available that, under the right circumstances, can help provide better fuel mileage and better engine protection. However, these advantages come at a price, which can be significantly more than the price per quart of conventional motor oils.

Before pouring any synthetic oils into your car's engine, you should consider the condition of the engine and the type of driving you do. It is also wise to check the vehicle manufacturer's position on synthetic oils.

Generally, it is best to avoid the use of synthetic oil in both brand new and older, high mileage engines. New engines require a proper break-in, and the synthetics are so slippery that they can impede this; most manufacturers recommend that you wait at least 5,000 miles (8,000 km) before switching to a synthetic oil.

Conversely, older engines are looser and tend to lose more oil; synthetics will slip past worn parts more readily than regular oil. If your car already leaks oil, (due to worn parts or bad seals/gaskets), it may leak more with a synthetic inside.

Consider your type of driving. If most of your accumulated mileage is on the highway at higher, steadier speed, a synthetic oil will reduce friction and probably help deliver better fuel mileage. Under such ideal highway conditions, the oil change interval can be extended, as long as the oil filter can operated effectively for the extended life of the oil. If the filter can't do its job for this extended period, dirt and sludge will build up in your engine's crankcase, sump, oil pump and lines, no matter what type of oil is used. If using synthetic oil in this manner, your should continue to change the oil filter at the recommended intervals.

Cars used under harder, stop-and-go, short hop circumstances should always be serviced more frequently, and for these cars synthetic oil may not be a wise investment. Because of the necessary shorter change interval needed for this type of driving, you cannot take advantage of the long recommended change interval of most synthetic oils.

Engine

OIL LEVEL CHECK

Every time you stop for fuel, check the engine oil making sure the engine has fully warmed and the vehicle is parked on a level surface. Because it takes some time for the oil to drain back to the oil pan, you should wait a few minutes before checking your oil. If you are doing this at a fuel stop, first fill the fuel tank, then open the hood and check the oil, but don't get so carried away as to forget to pay for the fuel. Most station attendants won't believe that you forgot.

1. Make sure the car is parked on level ground.

2. When checking the oil level, it is best for the engine to be at normal operating temperature, although checking the oil immediately after stopping will lead to a false reading. Wait a few minutes after turning off the engine to allow the oil to drain back into the crankcase.

3. Open the hood and locate the dipstick which will be in a guide tube mounted in the upper engine block. Pull the dipstick from its tube, wipe it clean (using a clean, lint free rag) and then reinsert it.

4. Pull the dipstick out again and, holding it horizontally, read the oil level. The oil should be between the FULL and ADD marks on the dipstick. The oil is below the ADD mark, add oil of the proper viscosity through the capped opening in the top of the valve cover. See the oil and fuel recommendations listed earlier in this section for the proper viscosity and rating of oil to use.

5. Insert the dipstick and check the oil level again after adding any oil. Approximately one quart of oil will raise the level from the ADD mark to the FULL mark. Be sure not to overfill the crankcase and waste the oil. Excess oil will generally be consumed at an accelerated rate.

✳✳ WARNING

DO NOT overfill the crankcase. It may result in oil-fouled spark plugs, oil leaks cause by oil seal failure or engine damage due to oil foaming.

6. Close the hood.

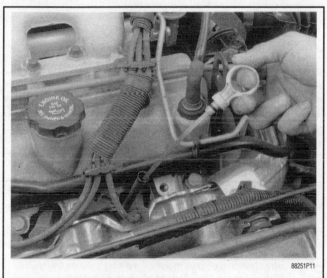

Open the hood and locate the dipstick

88251P11

The oil level should be within the cross-hatched ADD (A) and FULL (B) area of the dipstick

88251P12

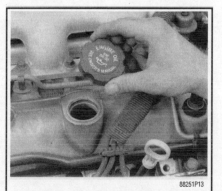

If the oil level is low, remove the fill cap . . .

88251P13

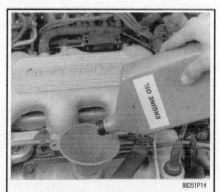

. . . then add the correct amount of oil through the opening in the valve cover

88251P14

OIL AND FILTER CHANGE

▶ See Figure 110

The manufacturer's recommended oil change interval is 7500 miles (12,000 km) under normal operating conditions. We recommend an oil change interval of 3000–3500 miles (4800–5600 km) under normal conditions; more frequently under severe conditions such as when the average trip is less than 4 miles (6 km), the engine is operated for extended periods at idle or low-speed, when towing a trailer or operating is dusty areas.

In addition, we recommend that the filter be replaced EVERY time the oil is changed.

➥Please be considerate of the environment. Dispose of waste oil properly by taking it to a service station, municipal facility or recycling center.

1. Run the engine until it reaches normal operating temperature. The turn the engine **OFF**.
2. Raise and safely support the front of the vehicle using jackstands.

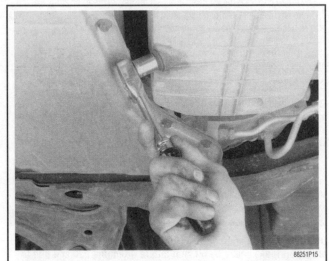

Loosen the drain plug using a proper sized ratchet and socket combination or wrench

3. Slide a drain pan of at least 5 quarts capacity under the oil pan. Wipe the drain plug and surrounding area clean using an old rag.
4. Loosen the drain plug using a ratchet, short extension and socket, or a box-wrench. Turn the plug out by hand, using a rag to shield your fingers from the hot oil. By keeping an inward pressure on the plug as you unscrew it, oil won't escape past the threads and you can remove it without being burned by hot oil.
5. Quickly withdraw the plug and move your hands out of the way, but be careful not to drop the plug into the drain pan, as fishing it out can be an unpleasant mess. Allow the oil to drain completely, then reinstall the drain plug (except on 2.5L engines). Do not overtighten the plug.

➥On some engine, the oil filter is located at the back of the engine. It is impossible to reach from above, and almost as inaccessible from below. On these engines, it may be easiest to remove the right front wheel and tire assembly, then reach through the fender opening to access the oil filter.

6. Move the drain pan under the oil filter. Use a strap-type or cap-type wrench to loosen the oil filter. Cover your hand with a rag, and spin the filter off by hand; turn it slowly. Keep in mind that it's holding about one quart of dirty, hot oil.

➥Be careful when removing the oil filter, because the filter contains about 1 quart of hot, dirty oil.

7. Empty the old oil filter into the drain pan, then properly dispose of the filter.
8. Using a clean shop towel, wipe off the filter adapter on the engine block. Be sure the towel does not leave any lint which could clog an oil passage.
9. Coat the rubber gasket on the new filter with fresh oil. Spin the filter onto the adapter by hand until it contacts the mounting surface. Tighten the filter ¾ to 1 full turn.
10. Carefully lower the vehicle.
11. Refill the crankcase with the correct amount of fresh engine oil. Please refer to the Capacities chart in this section.
12. Check the oil level on the dipstick. It is normal or the level to be a bit above the full mark until the engine is run and the new filter is filled with oil. Start the engine and allow it to idle for a few minutes.

13. Shut off the engine and allow the oil to flow back to the crankcase for a minute, then recheck the oil level. Check around the filter and drain plug for any leaks, and correct as necessary.

When you have finished this job, you will notice that you now possess four or five quarts of dirty oil. The best thing to do is to pour it into plastic jugs, such as milk or old antifreeze containers. Then, locate a service station or automotive parts store where you can pour it into their used oil tank for recycling.

➥Improperly disposing of used motor oil not only pollutes the environment, it violates Federal law. Dispose of waste oil properly.

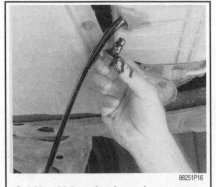

Quickly withdraw the plug and move your hands out of the way

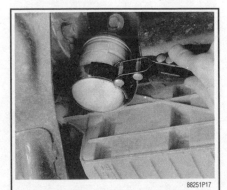

Use a strap-type or cap-type wrench to loosen the oil filter

Fig. 110 Before installing a new oil filter, lightly coat the rubber gasket with clean oil

14. If the oil filter is on so tightly that it collapses under pressure from the wrench, drive a long punch or a nail through it, across the diameter and as close to the base as possible, and use this as a lever to unscrew it. Make sure you are turning it counterclockwise.

15. Clean off the oil filter mounting surface with a rag. Apply a thin film of clean engine oil to the filter gasket.

16. Screw the filter on by hand until the gasket makes contact. Then tighten it by hand an additional ½–¾ turn. Do not overtighten.

17. Remove the filler cap, after wiping the area clean.

18. Add the correct number of quarts of oil specified in the Capacities chart. If you don't have an oil can spout, you will need a funnel. Be certain you do not overfill the engine, which can cause serious damage. Replace the cap.

19. Check the oil level on the dipstick. It is normal for the level to be a bit above the full mark. Start the engine and allow it to idle for a few minutes.

✳✳ CAUTION

Do not run the engine above idle speed until it has built up oil pressure, indicated when the oil light goes out.

Check around the filter and drain plug for any leaks.

20. Shut off the engine, allow the oil to drain for a minute, and check the oil level.

After completing this job, you will have several quarts of filthy oil to dispose of. The best thing to do with it is to funnel it into old plastic milk containers or bleach bottles. Then, you can pour it into a recycling barrel at either your dealer or gas station.

Manual Transaxle

FLUID RECOMMENDATION

According to General Motors, the manual transaxle fluid should be checked every time the oil is changed to make sure the level is full. The manufacturer does not recommends an interval for a manual transaxle fluid change.

The proper fluid for all manual transaxles is Synchromesh® manual transmission oil, GM part No. 12345349 or equivalent. DO NOT use any other fluid as damage may occur.

LEVEL CHECK

◆ See Figures 111, 112 and 113

The fluid level indicator is on the driver's side of the transaxle case above the axle shaft. On 1988 models, the fluid level indicator is in the filler tube on the 4-cylinder engines; on the V6 engines, the fluid level indicator and washer are separate from the filler tube. The filler tube cap must be removed to add fluid on V6 engines. On 1989–96 vehicles, the fluid level indicator and filler plug are one in the same.

➡️**Only check the manual transaxle fluid level with the engine OFF and cold.**

1. Make sure the car is parked on a level surface. The transaxle should be cool to the touch. If it is hot, check the level later, when it has cooled.

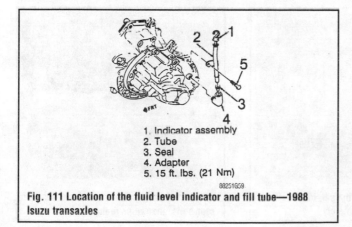

1. Indicator assembly
2. Tube
3. Seal
4. Adapter
5. 15 ft. lbs. (21 Nm)

88251G59

Fig. 111 Location of the fluid level indicator and fill tube—1988 Isuzu transaxles

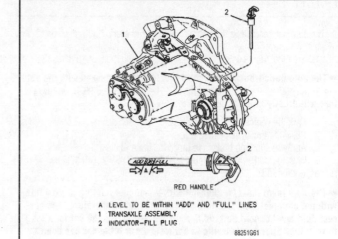

A LEVEL TO BE WITHIN "ADD" AND "FULL" LINES
1 TRANSAXLE ASSEMBLY
2 INDICATOR-FILL PLUG

88251G61

Fig. 112 Location of the fluid level indicator and fill plug mounting—HM-282, 5TM40, NVT550 and NVG-T550 transaxles shown, 1989 Isuzu similar

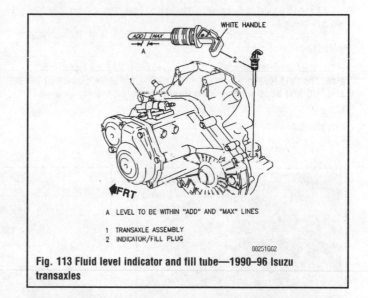

A LEVEL TO BE WITHIN "ADD" AND "MAX" LINES

1 TRANSAXLE ASSEMBLY
2 INDICATOR/FILL PLUG

88251G62

Fig. 113 Fluid level indicator and fill tube—1990–96 Isuzu transaxles

➡️**Oil may appear at the bottom of the dipstick even when the fluid is several pints low.**

2. Remove the fluid level indicator/fill plug and read the fluid level. If the fluid level indicates "Add" or below, use the proper type and amount of fluid to fill the transaxle to the "Full" level.

✳✳ WARNING

The fluid level indicator MUST be seated fully to prevent leakage from occurring at the vent plug when the car is driven.

3. When the level is correct, seat the level indicator and/or filler plug fully.

DRAIN AND REFILL

The fluid in the manual transaxle does not require changing.

Automatic Transaxle

FLUID RECOMMENDATIONS

When adding fluid or refilling the transaxle, use Dexron®IIE or Dexron® III automatic transmission fluid.

LEVEL CHECK

The automatic transaxle fluid should be checked every 7,500 miles or 12 months, whichever comes first.

1. Start the engine and drive the vehicle for a minimum of 15 miles (24 km).

➡**The automatic transmission fluid level must be checked with the vehicle at normal operating temperature; 180–200°F (82–93°C). Temperature will greatly affect transaxle fluid level.**

2. Park the vehicle on a level surface.
3. Place the transaxle gear selector in **P**.
4. Apply the parking brake and block the drive wheels.
5. With the brakes applied, move the shift lever through all the gear ranges, ending in **P**.

➡**The fluid level must be checked with the engine running at slow idle, with the car level, and the fluid at least at room temperature. The correct fluid level cannot be read if you have just driven the car for a long time at high speed, city traffic in hot weather or if the car has been pulling a trailer. In these cases, wait at least 30 minutes for the fluid to cool down.**

6. Pull the dipstick, located at the rear end of the engine, out and wipe with a clean, lint-free rag.
7. Push the dipstick completely into the filler tube, then wait 3 seconds and pull the dipstick out again.
8. Check both sides of the dipstick and read the lower level. The fluid level should be in the crosshatch area.

➡**The fluid level is acceptable if it is anywhere within the crosshatch area. The fluid level does not have to be at the top of the crosshatch area. DO NOT add fluid unless the level is below the crosshatch area.**

9. Inaccurate fluid level readings may result if the fluid is checked immediately after the vehicle has been operated under any or all of the following conditions:

a. In high ambient temperatures above 90°F (32°C).
b. At sustained high speeds.
c. In heavy city traffic during hot weather.
d. As a towing vehicle.
e. In commercial service (taxi or police use).

10. If the vehicle has been operated under these conditions, shut the engine **OFF** and allow the vehicle to cool for 30 minutes. After the cool down period, restart the vehicle and continue from Step 2.

11. If it is determined that the fluid level is low, add only enough fluid to bring the level into the crosshatch area. It generally takes less than a pint. DO NOT overfill the transaxle! If the fluid level is within specifications, simply push the dipstick back into the filler tube completely.

12. After adding fluid, if necessary, recheck the level, making sure it is within the crosshatch area. Turn the engine **OFF**, then unblock the drive wheels.

DRAIN AND REFILL

▶ **See Figure 114**

The car should be driven approximately 15 miles (24 km) to warm the transaxle fluid before the pan is removed.

➡**The fluid should be drained while the transaxle is warm.**

```
✳ WARNING
```

Use only fluid labeled Dexron®IIE or III. Use of other fluids could cause erratic shifting and transaxle damage.

1. Raise and safely support the vehicle with jackstands.
2. Place a suitable drain pan under the transaxle fluid pan.
3. Remove the fluid pan bolts/screws from the front and sides of the pan.
4. Loosen the rear bolts/screws about four turns.

Pull out the dipstick, wipe it clean, then reinsert it in the filler tube

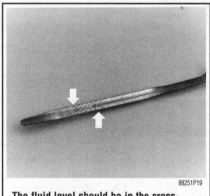

The fluid level should be in the cross-hatched area

Use a funnel to aid in filling the transaxle

Remove the bolts from the front and sides on the fluid pan only

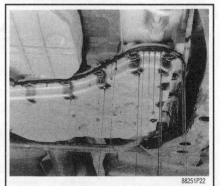

After carefully prying the pan loose, allow the fluid to drain completely

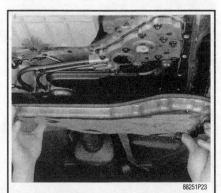

After the fluid has drained, remove the rear bolts, then remove the pan

Remove and discard the gasket. Thoroughly clean the gasket mating surfaces

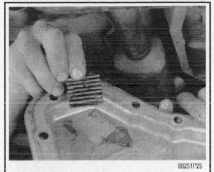

Some vehicles have a magnet in the transaxle pan to collect any loose metal chips or shavings

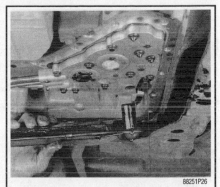

Remove the fluid filter and seal by pulling it straight down from its mounting

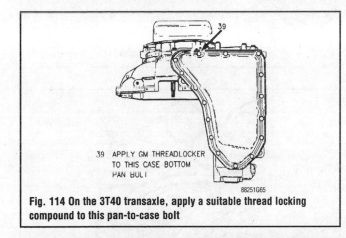

39 APPLY GM THREADLOCKER TO THIS CASE BOTTOM PAN BOLT

Fig. 114 On the 3T40 transaxle, apply a suitable thread locking compound to this pan-to-case bolt

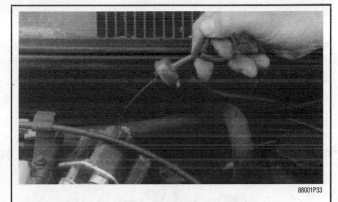

Fig. 115 After filling the transaxle, check the fluid level

✳✳ WARNING

Be careful not to damage the mating surfaces of the oil pan and case. Any damage could result in fluid leaks.

5. Lightly tap the pan with a rubber mallet or carefully pry the fluid pan loose and allow the fluid to drain.

➡ **If the transaxle fluid is dark or has a burnt smell, transaxle damage is indicated. Have the transaxle checked professionally.**

6. Remove the remaining bolts, the pan, and the gasket or RTV sealant. Discard the old gasket. Use a suitable gasket scraper to clean the gasket mating surfaces. If equipped, remove the magnet, or metal chip collector from the transaxle pan.

7. Clean the pan with solvent and dry it thoroughly.

8. Remove the filter and O-ring seal.

To install:

9. Coat the new filter seal with a small amount of Transjel®, part no. J 36850 or equivalent.

10. Install a new transaxle filter and O ring seal, locating the filter against the dipstick stop. Always replace the filter with a new one. Do not attempt to clean the old one!

➡ **For the 3T40 transaxle, it is necessary to use GM Thread Locker part no. 12345382 or equivalent sealant on the specified bolt in the accompanying figure to prevent leaks.**

11. Install a new gasket or RTV sealant. Thoroughly clean and dry all bolts and bolt holes. Install the pan and tighten the bolts in a crisscross manner, starting from the middle and working outward. Tighten the bolts/screws to the following specifications:

a. 440-T4 automatic transaxle: 10 ft. lbs. (13 Nm)
b. THM-125C and 3T40 automatic transaxles: 97 inch lbs. (11 Nm)
c. 4T60 and 4T60E automatic transaxles: 13 ft. lbs. (17 Nm)

12. Carefully lower the vehicle, then add the correct amount of Dexron®III, IIE, or equivalent, transmission fluid. Refer to the Capacities chart for fluid specifications.

13. Follow the fluid check procedure earlier in this section.

14. Check the pan for leaks.

Cooling System

🔹 See Figures 116, 117 and 118

✳✳ CAUTION

Never remove the radiator cap under any conditions while the engine is hot! Failure to follow these instructions could result in damage to the cooling system, engine and/or personal injury. To avoid having scalding hot coolant or steam blow out of the radiator, use extreme care whenever you are removing the radiator cap. Wait until the engine has cooled, then wrap a thick cloth around radiator cap and turn it slowly to the first stop. Step back while the pressure is released from the cooling system. When you are sure the pressure has been released, press down on the radiator cap (still have the cloth in position), turn and remove the cap.

FLUID RECOMMENDATIONS

✳✳ WARNING

For 1996 vehicles, when adding coolant, it is important that you use DEX-COOL®, an orange colored, silicate free coolant meeting GM specifications 6277M. If silicated coolant is added to the system, premature engine, heater core or radiator corrosion may result.

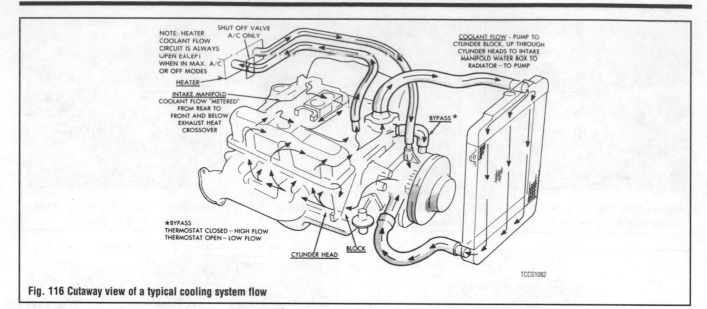

Fig. 116 Cutaway view of a typical cooling system flow

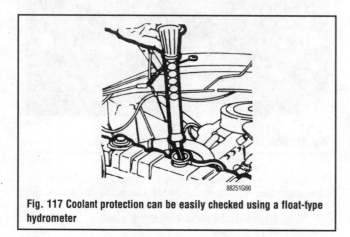

Fig. 117 Coolant protection can be easily checked using a float-type hydrometer

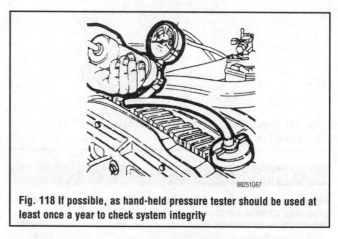

Fig. 118 If possible, as hand-held pressure tester should be used at least once a year to check system integrity

The cooling system should be inspected, flushed and refilled with fresh coolant at least every 30,000 miles (48,000 km) or 24 months. If the coolant is left in the system too long, it loses its ability to prevent rust and corrosion.

When the coolant is being replaced, use a good quality antifreeze that is safe to be used with aluminum cooling system components. The ratio of antifreeze to water should always be a 50/50 mixture. This ratio will ensure the proper balance of cooling ability, corrosion protection and antifreeze protection. At this ratio, the antifreeze protection should be good to –34°F (–37°C). If greater antifreeze protection is needed, the ratio should not exceed 70% antifreeze to 30% water.

LEVEL CHECK

➡ **When checking the coolant level, the radiator cap need not be removed. Simply check the coolant level in the recovery bottle or surge tank.**

Check the coolant level in the recovery bottle or surge tank, usually mounted on the inner fender. With the engine cold, the coolant level should be at the FULL COLD level. With the engine at normal operating temperature, the coolant level should be at the FULL HOT mark. Only add coolant to the recovery bottle or surge tank as necessary to bring the system up to a proper level.

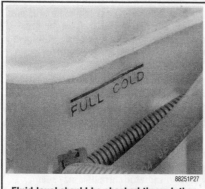

Fluid level should be checked through the recovery bottle

If the coolant level is low, carefully remove the recovery bottle cap . . .

. . . then top off the cooling system using the proper amount and mix of coolant and water

✳✳ CAUTION

Should it be necessary to remove the radiator cap, make sure the system has had time to cool, reducing the internal pressure.

On any vehicle that is not equipped with a coolant recovery bottle or surge tank, the level must be checked by removing the radiator cap. This should only be done when the cooling system has had time to sufficiently cool after the engine has been run. The coolant level should be within 2 in. (51mm) of the base of the radiator filler neck. If necessary, coolant can then be added directly to the radiator.

COOLING SYSTEM INSPECTION

Checking the Radiator Cap Seal

▶ **See Figure 119**

While you are checking the coolant level, check the radiator cap for a worn or cracked gasket. If the cap doesn't seal properly, fluid will be lost and the engine will overheat.

Worn caps should be replaced with a new one.

Checking the Radiator for Debris

▶ **See Figure 120**

Periodically clean any debris; leaves, paper, insects, etc. from the radiator fins. Pick the large pieces off by hand. The smaller pieces can be washed away with water pressure from a hose.

Carefully straighten any bent radiator fins with a pair of needle nose pliers. Be careful, the fins are very soft. Don't wiggle the fins back and forth too much. Straighten them once and try not move them again.

DRAIN AND REFILL

✳✳ CAUTION

When draining the coolant, keep in mind that cats and dogs are attracted by ethylene glycol antifreeze and are quite likely to drink any that is left in an uncovered container or in puddles on the ground. This will prove fatal in sufficient quantity. Always drain the coolant into a sealable container. Coolant should be reused until it is contaminated or several years old. To avoid injuries from scalding fluid and steam, DO NOT remove the radiator cap while the engine and radiator are still hot.

1. Make sure the engine is cool and the vehicle is parked on a level surface, remove the radiator cap by performing the following:
   a. Slowly rotate the cap counterclockwise to the detent.
   b. If any residual pressure is present, WAIT until the hissing stops.

   c. After the hissing noise has ceased, press down on the cap and continue rotating it counterclockwise to remove it.
2. Remove the recovery bottle or surge tank cap.
3. Place a fluid catch pan under the radiator. Open the radiator drain valve, which is located at the bottom of the radiator tank.
4. Remove the thermostat housing cap and thermostat or open the air bleed vent(s), if applicable.
5. Remove the engine block drain plug.
6. Allow the coolant to drain completely from the vehicle.
7. Close the radiator drain valve, then reinstall any block drains which were removed.
8. Using a 50/50 mixture of antifreeze and clean water, fill the radiator to the bottom of the filler neck and the coolant tank to the FULL mark.
9. Install the radiator cap, making sure the arrows line up over the overflow tube leading the reservoir or surge tank. Place the cap back on the recovery bottle or surge tank.
10. Start the engine. Select heat on the climate control panel and turn the temperature valve to full warm. Run the engine until it reaches normal operating temperature. Check to make sure there is hot air flowing from the floor ducts.
11. Check the fluid level in the reservoir or surge tank and add as necessary.

FLUSHING AND CLEANING

1. Refer to the drain and refill procedure in this section, then drain the cooling system.
2. Close the drain valve.

➡ **A flushing solution may be used. Ensure it is safe for use with aluminum cooling system components. Follow the directions on the container.**

3. If using a flushing solution, remove the thermostat. Reinstall the thermostat housing.
4. Add sufficient water to fill the system.
5. Start the engine and run for a few minutes. Drain the system.
6. If using a flushing solution, disconnect the heater hose that connects the cylinder head to the heater core (that end of the hose will clamp to a fitting on the firewall. Connect a water hose to the end of the heater hose that runs to the cylinder head and run water into the system until it begins to flow out of the top of the radiator.
7. Allow the water to flow out of the radiator until it is clear.
8. Reconnect the heater hose.
9. Drain the cooling system.
10. Reinstall the thermostat.
11. Empty the coolant reservoir or surge tank and flush it.
12. Fill the cooling system, using the correct ratio of antifreeze and water, to the bottom of the filler neck. Fill the reservoir or surge tank to the FULL mark.
13. Install the radiator cap, making sure that the arrows align with the overflow tube.

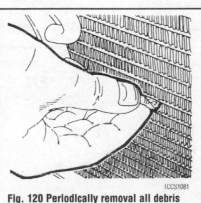

Fig. 119 Be sure the rubber gasket on the radiator cap has a tight seal

Fig. 120 Periodically removal all debris from the radiator fins

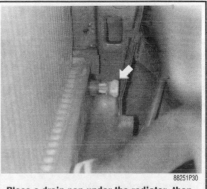

Place a drain pan under the radiator, then open the radiator drain valve

Brake Master Cylinder

FLUID RECOMMENDATIONS

Use only heavy duty brake fluid meeting DOT 3 specifications from a clean, sealed container. Using any other type of fluid may result in severe brake system damage.

✳✳ WARNING

Brake fluid damages paint. It also absorbs moisture from the air; never leave a container or the master cylinder uncovered longer than necessary. All parts in contact with the brake fluid (master cylinder, hoses, plunger assemblies and etc.) must be kept clean, since any contamination of the brake fluid will adversely affect braking performance.

LEVEL CHECK

▶ **See Figure 121**

It should be obvious how important the brake system is to safe operation of your vehicle. The brake fluid is key to the proper operation of your vehicle. Low levels of fluid indicate a need for service (there may be a leak in the system or the brake pads may just be worn and in need of replacement). In any case, the brake fluid level should be inspected at least during every oil change, but more often is desirable. Every time you open the hood is a good time to glance at the master cylinder reservoir.

To check the fluid level on most vehicles covered by this manual, remove the master cylinder reservoir cap and diaphragm (if applicable) and check the level against the markings on the inside of the reservoir.

88251P31

Always follow the fluid specification on the brake master cylinder reservoir cap

When making additions of brake fluid, use only fresh, uncontaminated brake fluid which meets or exceeds DOT-3 standards. Be careful not to spill any brake fluid on painted surfaces, as it will quickly eat the paint. Do not allow the brake fluid container or the master cylinder to remain open any longer than necessary; brake fluid absorbs moisture from the air, reducing the fluid's effectiveness and causing corrosion in the lines.

Clutch Master Cylinder

FLUID RECOMMENDATIONS

Use only hydraulic clutch fluid, part no. 12345347 or equivalent fluid meeting DOT 3 specifications.
NEVER use mineral or paraffin based oil in the clutch hydraulic system. These fluids will damage the rubber parts on the cylinders.

LEVEL CHECK

▶ **See Figure 122**

The clutch system fluid in the master cylinder should be checked every 6 months or 6,000 miles (9,600km).

The clutch master cylinder is mounted to the firewall, next to the brake master cylinder. Check the fluid level on the side of the reservoir. If fluid is required, remove the screw on filler cap and gasket from the master cylinder. Fill the reservoir to the full line in the reservoir with hydraulic clutch fluid or equivalent fluid meeting DOT 3 specifications. Install the filler cap, making sure the gasket is properly seated in the cap. Make sure no dirt enters the system when adding fluid.

If fluid has to be added frequently, the system should be checked for a leak. Check for leaks at the master cylinder, slave cylinder and hose. If a leak is found, replace the component and bleed the system as outlined in Section 7.

Power Steering Pump

FLUID RECOMMENDATIONS

When adding fluid or making a complete fluid change, always use GM P/N 1050017, 1052884, power steering fluid or equivalent. DO NOT use automatic transmission fluid. Failure to use the proper fluid may cause hose and seal damage and fluid leaks.

If you live in an area with a colder climate, you may experience reduced power steering assist upon cold weather starting. This condition is caused by the viscosity of the power steering fluid on vehicles with longer hoses and should not be confused with conditions having similar symptoms. There is a "low temperature climate service fluid" (GM part no. 12345866 or 12345867) available if you fit into this category.

LEVEL CHECK

The power steering fluid level is checked by either looking at the marks on the see-through reservoir or by marks on the fluid level dipstick/reservoir cap, depending upon engine application.

88251P32

Remove the brake master cylinder reservoir cap . . .

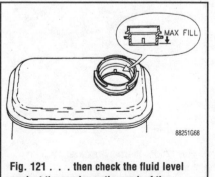
MAX FILL
88251G68

Fig. 121 . . . then check the fluid level against the marks on the neck of the reservoir

88251P33

When adding fluid to the brake master cylinder, use only clean, fresh fluid from a sealed container

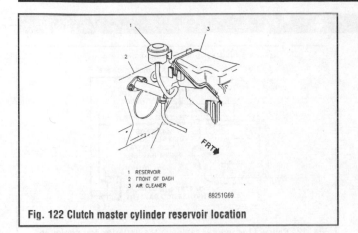

Fig. 122 Clutch master cylinder reservoir location

When the fluid is cool, about 70°F (21°C), the fluid level should be at the full "COLD" or "C" mark. If the fluid is warmed up, to about 170°F (77°C), the fluid level should be at the full "HOT" or "H" mark. If the level is low, add power steering fluid until it is correct. Be careful not to overfill as this will cause fluid loss and seal damage. A large loss in the system may indicate a problem. This should be inspected and repaired at once.

Steering Gear

The rack and pinion steering gear used on the Corsica/Beretta is a sealed unit; no fluid level checks or additions are ever necessary.

Chassis Greasing

▶ See Figure 123

There are only 2 areas which require regular chassis greasing: the lower ball joint fittings and the tie rod end to strut fittings. These parts should be greased every 12 months or 7,500 miles (12,000km.) with an EP grease meeting GM specification 6031M.

If you choose to do this job yourself, you will need to purchase a hand operated grease gun, if you do not own one already, and a long flexible extension hose to reach the various grease fittings. You will also need a cartridge of the appropriate grease.

Press the fitting on the grease gun hose onto the grease fitting on the suspension or steering linkage component. Pump a few shots of grease into the fitting, until the rubber boot on the joint begins to expand, indicating that the joint is full. Remove the gun from the fitting. Be careful not to overfill the joints, which will rupture the rubber boots, allowing the entry of dirt. You can keep the grease fittings clean by covering them with a small square of tin foil.

Body Lubrication and Maintenance

Every 12 months or 7,500 miles (12,000km), the various linkages and hinges on the chassis and body should be lubricated, as follows:

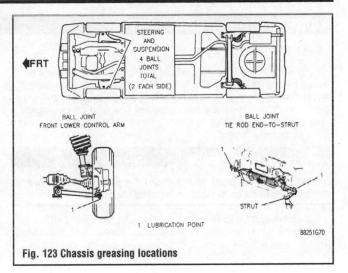

Fig. 123 Chassis greasing locations

TRANSAXLE SHIFT LINKAGE

Lubricate the manual transaxle shift linkage contact points with the EP grease used for chassis greasing, which should meet GM specification 6031M. The automatic transaxle linkage should be lubricated with clean engine oil.

HOOD LATCH AND HINGES

Clean the latch surfaces and apply clean engine oil to the latch pilot bolts and the spring anchor. Use the engine oil to lubricate the hood hinges as well. Use a chassis grease to lubricate all the pivot points in the latch release mechanism.

DOOR HINGES

The gas tank filler door, car door, and rear hatch or trunk lid hinges should be wiped clean and lubricated with clean engine oil. Silicone spray also works well on these parts, but must be applied more often. Use engine oil to lubricate the trunk or hatch lock mechanism and the lock bolt and striker. The door lock cylinders can be lubricated easily with a shot of silicone spray or one of the many dry penetrating lubricants commercially available.

PARKING BRAKE LINKAGE

Use chassis grease on the parking brake cable where it contacts the guides, links, levers, and pulleys. The grease should be a water resistant one for durability under the car.

ACCELERATOR LINKAGE

Lubricate the carburetor stud, carburetor lever, and the accelerator pedal lever at the support inside the car with clean engine oil.

Make sure the cap is clean before removing it; this will prevent dirt from contaminating the system

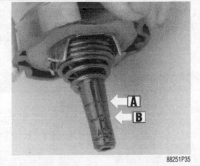

The power steering reservoir cap/dipstick is marked for hot (A) and cold (B) proper fluid levels

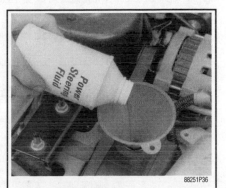

Add power steering fluid through the opening while the cap is removed

UMP STARTING A DEAD BATTERY

♦ See Figure 124

Whenever a vehicle is jump started, precautions must be followed in order to prevent the possibility of personal injury. Remember that batteries contain a small amount of explosive hydrogen gas which is a by-product of battery charging. Sparks should always be avoided when working around batteries, especially when attaching jumper cables. To minimize the possibility of accidental sparks, follow the procedure carefully.

✳✳ CAUTION

NEVER hook the batteries up in a series circuit or the entire electrical system will go up in smoke, including the starter!

Vehicles equipped with a diesel engine may utilize two 12 volt batteries. If so, the batteries are connected in a parallel circuit (positive terminal to positive terminal, negative terminal to negative terminal). Hooking the batteries up in parallel circuit increases battery cranking power without increasing total battery voltage output. Output remains at 12 volts. On the other hand, hooking two 12 volt batteries up in a series circuit (positive terminal to negative terminal, positive terminal to negative terminal) increases total battery output to 24 volts (12 volts plus 12 volts).

ump Starting Precautions

- Be sure that both batteries are of the same voltage. Vehicles covered by this manual and most vehicles on the road today utilize a 12 volt charging system.
- Be sure that both batteries are of the same polarity (have the same terminal, in most cases NEGATIVE grounded).
- Be sure that the vehicles are not touching or a short could occur.
- On serviceable batteries, be sure the vent cap holes are not obstructed.
- Do not smoke or allow sparks anywhere near the batteries.
- In cold weather, make sure the battery electrolyte is not frozen. This can occur more readily in a battery that has been in a state of discharge.
- Do not allow electrolyte to contact your skin or clothing.

ump Starting Procedure

1. Make sure that the voltages of the 2 batteries are the same. Most batteries and charging systems are of the 12 volt variety.
2. Pull the jumping vehicle (with the good battery) into a position so the jumper cables can reach the dead battery and that vehicle's engine. Make sure that the vehicles do NOT touch.
3. Place the transmissions/transaxles of both vehicles in **Neutral** (MT) or **P** (AT), as applicable, then firmly set their parking brakes.

➡ **If necessary for safety reasons, the hazard lights on both vehicles may be operated throughout the entire procedure without significantly increasing the difficulty of jumping the dead battery.**

4. Turn all lights and accessories OFF on both vehicles. Make sure the ignition switches on both vehicles are turned to the **OFF** position.
5. Cover the battery cell caps with a rag, but do not cover the terminals.
6. Make sure the terminals on both batteries are clean and free of corrosion or proper electrical connection will be impeded. If necessary, clean the battery terminals before proceeding.
7. Identify the positive (+) and negative (–) terminals on both batteries.

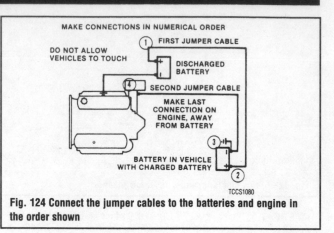

Fig. 124 Connect the jumper cables to the batteries and engine in the order shown

8. Connect the first jumper cable to the positive (+) terminal of the dead battery, then connect the other end of that cable to the positive (+) terminal of the booster (good) battery.
9. Connect one end of the other jumper cable to the negative (–;) terminal on the booster battery and the final cable clamp to an engine bolt head, alternator bracket or other solid, metallic point on the engine with the dead battery. Try to pick a ground on the engine that is positioned away from the battery in order to minimize the possibility of the 2 clamps touching should one loosen during the procedure. DO NOT connect this clamp to the negative (–) terminal of the bad battery.

✳✳ CAUTION

Be very careful to keep the jumper cables away from moving parts (cooling fan, belts, etc.) on both engines.

10. Check to make sure that the cables are routed away from any moving parts, then start the donor vehicle's engine. Run the engine at moderate speed for several minutes to allow the dead battery a chance to receive some initial charge.
11. With the donor vehicle's engine still running slightly above idle, try to start the vehicle with the dead battery. Crank the engine for no more than 10 seconds at a time and let the starter cool for at least 20 seconds between tries. If the vehicle does not start in 3 tries, it is likely that something else is also wrong or that the battery needs additional time to charge.
12. Once the vehicle is started, allow it to run at idle for a few seconds to make sure that it is operating properly.
13. Turn ON the headlights, heater blower and, if equipped, the rear defroster of both vehicles in order to reduce the severity of voltage spikes and subsequent risk of damage to the vehicles' electrical systems when the cables are disconnected. This step is especially important to any vehicle equipped with computer control modules.
14. Carefully disconnect the cables in the reverse order of connection. Start with the negative cable that is attached to the engine ground, then the negative cable on the donor battery. Disconnect the positive cable from the donor battery and finally, disconnect the positive cable from the formerly dead battery. Be careful when disconnecting the cables from the positive terminals not to allow the alligator clips to touch any metal on either vehicle or a short and sparks will occur.

ACKING

Your vehicle was supplied with a jack for emergency road repairs. This jack is fine for changing a flat tire or other short term procedures not requiring you to go beneath the vehicle. If it is used in an emergency situation, carefully follow the instructions provided either with the jack or in your owner's manual. Do not attempt to use the jack on any portions of the vehicle other than specified by the vehicle manufacturer. Always block the diagonally opposite wheel when using a jack.

A more convenient way of jacking is the use of a garage or floor jack. You may use the floor jack to lift the front of the vehicle by positioning the jack under the front side of the vehicle, or you can raise the front of the vehicle by placing a block of wood on the jack and using it to raise the vehicle by the oil pan. When raising the rear of the vehicle, position the jack on the center of the rear axle.

Never place the jack under the radiator, engine or transmission components. Severe and expensive damage will result when the jack is raised. Additionally, never jack under the floorpan or bodywork; the metal will deform.

Whenever you plan to work under the vehicle, you must support it on jackstands or ramps. Never use cinder blocks or stacks of wood to support the vehi-

Be sure the floor jack you use has the proper capacity for the vehicle you are working on

Raise the front of the vehicle using a floor jack, then place jackstands to secure safely

Make sure to properly position the jackstands to ensure maximum stability while working under the vehicle

Raise the rear of the vehicle by placing the floor jack in the center of the rear axle

cle, even if you're only going to be under it for a few minutes. Never crawl under the vehicle when it is supported only by the tire-changing jack or other floor jack.

➡ **Always position a block of wood or small rubber pad on top of the jack or jackstand to protect the lifting point's finish when lifting or supporting the vehicle.**

Small hydraulic, screw, or scissors jacks are satisfactory for raising the vehicle. Drive-on trestles or ramps are also a handy and safe way to both raise and support the vehicle. Be careful though, some ramps may be too steep to drive your vehicle onto without scraping the front bottom panels. Never support the vehicle on any suspension member (unless specifically instructed to do so by a repair manual) or by an underbody panel.

Jacking Precautions

The following safety points cannot be overemphasized:
• Always block the opposite wheel or wheels to keep the vehicle from rolling off the jack.
• When raising the front of the vehicle, firmly apply the parking brake.
• When the drive wheels are to remain on the ground, leave the vehicle in gear to help prevent it from rolling.
• Always use jackstands to support the vehicle when you are working underneath. Place the stands beneath the vehicle's jacking brackets. Before climbing underneath, rock the vehicle a bit to make sure it is firmly supported.

CAPACITIES

Year	Model	Engine ID/VIN	Engine Displacement Liters (cc)	Engine Oil with Filter	Transmission (pts.) 5-Spd	Transmission (pts.) Auto.	Fuel Tank (gal.)	Cooling System (qts.) w/ AC	Cooling System (qts.) wo/ AC
1988	Beretta	1	2.0L (1991)	4.0 ①	5.4	8.0 ②	14.0	9.8	9.6
	Beretta	W	2.8L (2837)	4.0 ①	4.5	8.0 ②	14.0	11.1	11.0
	Corsica	1	2.0L (1991)	4.0 ①	5.4	8.0 ②	14.0	9.8	9.6
	Corsica	W	2.8L (2837)	4.0 ①	4.5	8.0 ②	14.0	11.1	11.0
1989	Beretta	1	2.0L (1991)	4.0 ①	5.4	8.0 ②	14.0	9.8	9.6
	Beretta	W	2.8L (2837)	4.0 ①	4.5	8.0 ②	14.0	11.1	11.0
	Corsica	1	2.0L (1991)	4.0 ①	5.4	8.0 ②	14.0	9.8	9.6
	Corsica	W	2.8L (2837)	4.0 ①	4.5	8.0 ②	14.0	11.1	11.0
1990	Beretta	G	2.2L (2190)	4.0 ①	4.2	14.0 ③	15.6	9.5	9.6
	Beretta	A	2.3L (2260)	4.0 ①	4.2	14.0 ③	15.6	9.5	9.5
	Beretta	T	3.1L (3128)	4.0 ①	4.2	14.0 ③	15.6	④	④
	Corsica	G	2.2L (2190)	4.0 ①	4.2	14.0 ③	15.6	9.5	9.6
	Corsica	T	3.1L (3128)	4.0 ①	4.2	14.0 ③	15.6	④	④
1991	Beretta	G	2.2L (2190)	4.0 ①	4.2	14.0 ③	15.6	9.5	9.6
	Beretta	A	2.3L (2260)	4.0 ①	4.2	14.0 ③	15.6	9.5	9.5
	Beretta	T	3.1L (3128)	4.0 ①	4.2	14.0 ③	15.6	④	④
	Corsica	G	2.2L (2190)	4.0 ①	4.2	14.0 ③	15.6	9.5	9.6
	Corsica	T	3.1L (3128)	4.0 ①	4.2	14.0 ③	15.6	④	④
1992	Beretta	4	2.2L (2190)	4.0 ①	4.0	8.0 ⑤	15.6	9.2	9.2
	Beretta	A	2.3L (2260)	4.0 ①	4.0	8.0 ⑤	15.6	10.3	10.3
	Beretta	T	3.1L (3128)	4.0 ①	4.0	8.0 ⑤	15.6	13.1	13.1
	Corsica	4	2.2L (2190)	4.0 ①	4.0	8.0 ⑤	15.6	9.2	9.2
	Corsica	T	3.1L (3128)	4.0 ①	4.0	8.0 ⑤	15.6	13.1	13.1
1993	Beretta	4	2.2L (2190)	4.0 ①	4.0	8.0 ⑤	15.6	9.5	9.5
	Beretta	A	2.3L (2260)	4.0 ①	4.0	8.0 ⑤	15.6	9.5	9.5
	Beretta	T	3.1L (3128)	4.0 ①	4.0	8.0 ⑤	15.6	14.2	14.2
	Corsica	4	2.2L (2190)	4.0 ①	4.0	8.0 ⑤	15.6	9.5	9.5
	Corsica	T	3.1L (3128)	4.0 ①	4.0	8.0 ⑤	15.6	14.2	14.2
1994	Beretta	A	2.3L (2260)	4.0 ①	4.0	⑥	15.2	10.4	10.4
	Beretta	M	3.1L (3128)	4.0 ①	4.0	⑥	15.2	13.1	13.1
	Corsica	4	2.2L (2190)	4.0 ①	4.0	⑥	15.2	10.7	10.7
	Corsica	M	3.1L (3128)	4.0 ①	4.0	⑥	15.2	13.1	13.1
1995	Beretta	4	2.2L (2190)	4.0 ①	4.0	⑥	15.2	10.7	10.7
	Beretta	M	3.1L (3128)	4.0 ①	4.0	⑥	15.2	13.1	13.1
	Corsica	4	2.2L (2190)	4.0 ①	4.0	⑥	15.2	10.7	10.7
	Corsica	M	3.1L (3128)	4.0 ①	4.0	⑥	15.2	13.1	13.1
1996	Beretta	4	2.2L (2190)	4.0 ①	4.0	⑥	15.2	10.7	10.7
	Beretta	M	3.1L (3128)	4.0 ①	4.0	⑥	15.2	13.1	13.1
	Corsica	4	2.2L (2190)	4.0 ①	4.0	⑥	15.2	10.7	10.7
	Corsica	M	3.1L (3128)	4.0 ①	4.0	⑥	15.2	13.1	13.1

NOTE: All capacities are approximate. Add fluid gradually and check to be sure a proper fluid level is obtained

① Figure shown is without filter change. When replacing the filter, add oil as necessary to obtain proper fluid level

② Figure shown is for pan removal. For overhaul use 12.0 pts.

③ Figure shown is for pan removal. For overhaul use 18.0 pts.

④ With automatic transmission use 12.4 qts. - with manual transmission use 11.8 qts.

⑤ Figure shown is for pan removal. For overhaul use 12.0 pts.

⑥ 3T40 automatic transaxle - pan removal: 8 pts., overhaul: 14 pts.
  4T60E automatic transaxle - pan removal: 12 pts., overhaul: 16 pts.

Maintenance Intervals—Schedule I

FOLLOW SCHEDULE I IF THE CAR IS MAINLY OPERATED UNDER ONE OR MORE OF THE FOLLOWING CONDITIONS: WHEN MOST TRIPS ARE LESS THAN 4 MILES (6 KILOMETERS).
WHEN MOST TRIPS ARE LESS THAN 10 MILES (16 KILOMETERS) AND OUTSIDE TEMPERATURE REMAINS BELOW FREEZING.
WHEN MOST TRIPS INCLUDE EXTENDED IDLING AND/OR FREQUENT LOW-SPEED OPERATION AS IN STOP-AND-GO TRAFFIC. TOWING A TRAILER.** OPERATING IN DUSTY AREAS.

SCHEDULE I SHOULD ALSO BE FOLLOWED IF THE CAR IS USED FOR DELIVERY SERVICE, POLICE, TAXI OR OTHER COMMERCIAL APPLICATION.

THE SERVICE SHOWN IN THIS SCHEDULE UP TO 60,000 MILES (100,000 KM) ARE TO BE PERFORMED AFTER 60,000 MILES (100,00 KM) AT THE SAME INTERVALS.

TO BE SERVICED	WHEN TO PREFORM MILES (KILOMETERS) OR MONTHS WHICHEVER OCCURS FIRST	MILES (000): 3 / KM: 5	6 / 10	9 / 15	12 / 20	15 / 25	18 / 30	21 / 35	24 / 40	27 / 45	30 / 50	33 / 55	36 / 60	39 / 65	42 / 70	45 / 75	48 / 80	51 / 85	54 / 90	57 / 95	60 / 100
ENGINE OIL & OIL FILTER CHANGE #	EVERY 3,000 (5000 KM) OR 3 MOS.	•	•	•	•	•	•	•	•	•	•	•	•	•	•	•	•	•	•	•	•
CHASSIS LUBRICATION	EVERY OTHER OIL CHANGE		•		•		•		•		•		•		•		•		•		•
SERVICE TO BE PERFORMED AT LEAST TWICE A YEAR (SEE EXPLANATION)																					
SERVICE TO BE PERFORMED AT LEAST ONCE A YEAR (SEE EXPLANATION)																					
THROTTLE BODY MOUNT BOLT TORQUE (SOME MODELS) *	AT 6,000 MI (10,000 KM) ONLY		•																		
TIRE & WHEEL INSP. AND ROTATION	AT 6,000 MI. (10,000 KM) AND THEN EVERY 12,000 MI. (20,000 KM)		•				•				•				•				•		
ENGINE ACCESSORY DRIVE BELT(S) INSP.*	EVERY 30,000 MI. (50,000 KM) OR 24 MOS.										•										•
COOLING SYSTEM SERVICE *	SEE EXPLANATION FOR SERVICE INTERVAL																				
TRANSMISSION/TRANSAXLE SERVICE	SEE EXPLANATION FOR SERVICE INTERVAL																				
SPARK PLUG REPLACEMENT	4 CYL: 100,000 MI. (160,900 KM) / 6 CYL: 30,000 MI. (50,000 KM)										•										•
SPARK PLUG WIRE INSP. (SOME MODELS) *	EVERY 30,000 MI. (50,000 KM)										•										•
EGR SYSTEM INSP. * ††	EVERY 30,000 MI. (50,000 KM) OR 36 MOS.										•										•
AIR CLEANER & PVC INLET FILTER ELEMENT REPLACEMENT *	EVERY 30,000 MI. (50,000 KM) OR 36 MOS.										•										•
FUEL TANK, CAP, & LINES INSP. * ††	EVERY 30,000 MI. (50,000 KM)										•										•

FOOTNOTES:

* AN EMISSION CONTROL SERVICE

** TRAILERING IS NOT RECOMMENDED FOR SOME MODELS. SEE THE OWNERS MANUAL FOR COMPLETE DETAILS.

†† THE U.S. ENVIRONMENTAL PROTECTION AGENCY OR CALIFORNIA AIR RESOURCES BOARD HAS DETERMINED THAT THE FAILURE TO PERFORM THIS MAINTENANCE ITEM WILL NOT NULLIFY THE EMISSION WARRANTY OR LIMIT RECALL LIABILITY PRIOR TO THE COMPLETION OF VEHICLE USEFUL LIFE. GENERAL MOTORS, HOWEVER, URGES THAT ALL RECOMMENDED MAINTENANCE SERVICES BE PERFORMED AT THE INDICATED INTERVALS AND THE MAINTENANCE BE RECORDED IN SECTION C OF THE OWNER'S MAINTENANCE SCHEDULE.

Maintenance Intervals—Schedule II

+ FOLLOW SCHEDULE II ONLY IF NONE OF THE DRIVING CONDITIONS SPECIFIED IN SCHEDULE I APPLY.

THE SERVICES SHOWN IN THIS SCHEDULE UP TO 60,000 MILES (100,000 KM) ARE TO BE PERFORMED AFTER 60,000 MILES (100,000 KM) AT THE SAME INTERVALS.

TO BE SERVICED	WHEN TO PERFORM — MILES (KILOMETERS) OR MONTHS WHICHEVER OCCURS FIRST	MILES (000): 7.5 / KM: 12.5	15 / 25	22.5 / 37.5	30 / 50	37.5 / 62.5	45 / 75	52.5 / 87.5	60 / 100
ENGINE OIL CHANGE ■, PLUS OTHER REQUIRED SERVICES (SEE EXPLANATION)	EVERY 7,500 MI. (12,500 KM) OR 12 MONTHS	●	●	●	●	●	●	●	●
OIL FILTER CHANGE *			●		●		●		●
CHASSIS LUBRICATION	EVERY 7,500 MI. (12,500) OR 12 MOS.	●	●	●	●	●	●	●	●
SERVICES TO BE PERFORMED AT LEAST TWICE A YEAR (SEE EXPLANATION)									
SERVICES TO BE PERFORMED AT LEAST ONCE A YEAR (SEE EXPLANATION)									
THROTTLE BODY MOUNT BOLT TORQUE (SOME MODELS)	AT 7,500 MI. (12,500 KM) ONLY	●							
TIRE & WHEEL INSP. AND ROTATION	AT 7,500 MI. (12,500 KM) AND THEN EVERY 15,000 MI. (25,000 KM)	●		●		●		●	
ENGINE ACCESSORY DRIVE BELT(S) INSP. ■	30,000 MI. (50,000 KM) OR 24 MOS.				●				●
COOLING SYSTEM SERVICE ■	SEE EXPLANATION FOR SERVICE INTERVAL				●				●
TRANSMISSION/TRANSAXLE SERVICE									
SPARK PLUG REPLACEMENT *	4 CYL: 100,000 MI. (160,900 KM) 6 CYL: 30,000 MI. (50,000 KM)				●				●
SPARK PLUG WIRE INSP. (SOME MODELS) *	EVERY 30,000 MI. (50,000 KM)				●				●
EGR SYSTEM INSP. * ††	EVERY 30,000 MI. (50,000 KM) OR 36 MOS.				●				●
AIR CLEANER & PCV INLET FILTER ELEMENT REPT. *					●				●
FUEL TANK, CAP & LINES INSP. * ††	EVERY 30,000 MI. (50,000 KM)				●				●

†† THE U.S. ENVIRONMENTAL PROTECTION AGENCY OR CALIFORNIA AIR RESOURCES BOARD HAS DETERMINED THAT THE FAILURE TO PERFORM THIS MAINTENANCE ITEM WILL NOT NULLIFY THE EMISSION WARRANTY OR LIMIT RECALL LIABILITY PRIOR TO THE COMPLETION OF VEHICLE USEFUL LIFE. GENERAL MOTORS, HOWEVER, URGES THAT ALL RECOMMENDED MAINTENANCE SERVICES BE PERFORMED AT THE INDICATED INTERVALS AND THE MAINTENANCE

FOOTNOTES:

■ AN EMISSION CONTROL SERVICE

88251C06

ENGLISH TO METRIC CONVERSION: MASS (WEIGHT)

Current **mass** measurement is expressed in pounds and ounces (lbs. & ozs.). The metric unit of mass (or weight) is the kilogram (kg). Even although this table does not show conversion of masses (weights) larger than 15 lbs, it is easy to calculate larger units by following the data immediately below.

To convert ounces (oz.) to grams (g): multiply th number of ozs. by 28
To convert grams (g) to ounces (oz.): multiply the number of grams by .035

To convert pounds (lbs.) to kilograms (kg): multiply the number of lbs. by .45
To convert kilograms (kg) to pounds (lbs.): multiply the number of kilograms by 2.2

lbs	kg	lbs	kg	oz	kg	oz	kg
0.1	0.04	0.9	0.41	0.1	0.003	0.9	0.024
0.2	0.09	1	0.4	0.2	0.005	1	0.03
0.3	0.14	2	0.9	0.3	0.008	2	0.06
0.4	0.18	3	1.4	0.4	0.011	3	0.08
0.5	0.23	4	1.8	0.5	0.014	4	0.11
0.6	0.27	5	2.3	0.6	0.017	5	0.14
0.7	0.32	10	4.5	0.7	0.020	10	0.28
0.8	0.36	15	6.8	0.8	0.023	15	0.42

ENGLISH TO METRIC CONVERSION: TEMPERATURE

To convert Fahrenheit (°F) to Celsius (°C): take number of °F and subtract 32; multiply result by 5; divide result by 9

To convert Celsius (°C) to Fahrenheit (°F): take number of °C and multiply by 9; divide result by 5; add 32 to total

Fahrenheit (F)		Celsius (C)		Fahrenheit (F)		Celsius (C)		Fahrenheit (F)		Celsius (C)	
°F	°C	°C	°F	°F	°C	°C	°F	°F	°C	°C	°F
−40	−40	−38	−36.4	80	26.7	18	64.4	215	101.7	80	170
−35	−37.2	−36	−32.8	85	29.4	20	68	220	104.4	85	185
−30	−34.4	−34	−29.2	90	32.2	22	71.6	225	107.2	90	194
−25	−31.7	−32	−25.6	95	35.0	24	75.2	230	110.0	95	202
−20	−28.9	−30	−22	100	37.8	26	78.8	235	112.8	100	212
−15	−26.1	−28	−18.4	105	40.6	28	82.4	240	115.6	105	221
−10	−23.3	−26	−14.8	110	43.3	30	86	245	118.3	110	230
−5	−20.6	−24	−11.2	115	46.1	32	89.6	250	121.1	115	239
0	−17.8	−22	−7.6	120	48.9	34	93.2	255	123.9	120	248
1	−17.2	−20	−4	125	51.7	36	96.8	260	126.6	125	257
2	−16.7	−18	−0.4	130	54.4	38	100.4	265	129.4	130	266
3	−16.1	−16	3.2	135	57.2	40	104	270	132.2	135	275
4	−15.6	−14	6.8	140	60.0	42	107.6	275	135.0	140	284
5	−15.0	−12	10.4	145	62.8	44	112.2	280	137.8	145	293
10	−12.2	−10	14	150	65.6	46	114.8	285	140.6	150	302
15	−9.4	−8	17.6	155	68.3	48	118.4	290	143.3	155	311
20	−6.7	−6	21.2	160	71.1	50	122	295	146.1	160	320
25	−3.9	−4	24.8	165	73.9	52	125.6	300	148.9	165	329
30	−1.1	−2	28.4	170	76.7	54	129.2	305	151.7	170	338
35	1.7	0	32	175	79.4	56	132.8	310	154.4	175	347
40	4.4	2	35.6	180	82.2	58	136.4	315	157.2	180	356
45	7.2	4	39.2	185	85.0	60	140	320	160.0	185	365
50	10.0	6	42.8	190	87.8	62	143.6	325	162.8	190	374
55	12.8	8	46.4	195	90.6	64	147.2	330	165.6	195	383
60	15.6	10	50	200	93.3	66	150.8	335	168.3	200	392
65	18.3	12	53.6	205	96.1	68	154.4	340	171.1	205	401
70	21.1	14	57.2	210	98.9	70	158	345	173.9	210	410
75	23.9	16	60.8	212	100.0	75	167	350	176.7	215	414

TCCS1C01

ENGLISH TO METRIC CONVERSION: LENGTH

To convert inches (ins.) to millimeters (mm): multiply number of inches by 25.4

To convert millimeters (mm) to inches (ins.): multiply number of millimeters by .04

Inches		Decimals	Milli-meters	Inches to millimeters		Inches		Decimals	Milli-meters	Inches to millimeters	
				inches	mm					inches	mm
	1/64	0.051625	0.3969	0.0001	0.00254		33/64	0.515625	13.0969	0.6	15.24
	1/32	0.03125	0.7937	0.0002	0.00508	17/32		0.53125	13.4937	0.7	17.78
	3/64	0.046875	1.1906	0.0003	0.00762		35/64	0.546875	13.8906	0.8	20.32
1/16		0.0625	1.5875	0.0004	0.01016	9/16		0.5625	14.2875	0.9	22.86
	5/64	0.078125	1.9844	0.0005	0.01270		37/64	0.578125	14.6844	1	25.4
	3/32	0.09375	2.3812	0.0006	0.01524	19/32		0.59375	15.0812	2	50.8
	7/64	0.109375	2.7781	0.0007	0.01778		39/64	0.609375	15.4781	3	76.2
1/8		0.125	3.1750	0.0008	0.02032	5/8		0.625	15.8750	4	101.6
	9/64	0.140625	3.5719	0.0009	0.02286		41/64	0.640625	16.2719	5	127.0
	5/32	0.15625	3.9687	0.001	0.0254	21/32		0.65625	16.6687	6	152.4
	11/64	0.171875	4.3656	0.002	0.0508		43/64	0.671875	17.0656	7	177.8
3/16		0.1875	4.7625	0.003	0.0762	11/16		0.6875	17.4625	8	203.2
	13/64	0.203125	5.1594	0.004	0.1016		45/64	0.703125	17.8594	9	228.6
	7/32	0.21875	5.5562	0.005	0.1270	23/32		0.71875	18.2562	10	254.0
	15/64	0.234375	5.9531	0.006	0.1524		47/64	0.734375	18.6531	11	279.4
1/4		0.25	6.3500	0.007	0.1778	3/4		0.75	19.0500	12	304.8
	17/64	0.265625	6.7469	0.008	0.2032		49/64	0.765625	19.4469	13	330.2
	9/32	0.28125	7.1437	0.009	0.2286	25/32		0.78125	19.8437	14	355.6
	19/64	0.296875	7.5406	0.01	0.254		51/64	0.796875	20.2406	15	381.0
5/16		0.3125	7.9375	0.02	0.508	13/16		0.8125	20.6375	16	406.4
	21/64	0.328125	8.3344	0.03	0.762		53/64	0.828125	21.0344	17	431.8
	11/32	0.34375	8.7312	0.04	1.016	27/32		0.84375	21.4312	18	457.2
	23/64	0.359375	9.1281	0.05	1.270		55/64	0.859375	21.8281	19	482.6
3/8		0.375	9.5250	0.06	1.524	7/8		0.875	22.2250	20	508.0
	25/64	0.390625	9.9219	0.07	1.778		57/64	0.890625	22.6219	21	533.4
	13/32	0.40625	10.3187	0.08	2.032	29/32		0.90625	23.0187	22	558.8
	27/64	0.421875	10.7156	0.09	2.286		59/64	0.921875	23.4156	23	584.2
7/16		0.4375	11.1125	0.1	2.54	15/16		0.9375	23.8125	24	609.6
	29/64	0.453125	11.5094	0.2	5.08		61/64	0.953125	24.2094	25	635.0
	15/32	0.46875	11.9062	0.3	7.62	31/32		0.96875	24.6062	26	660.4
	31/64	0.484375	12.3031	0.4	10.16		63/64	0.984375	25.0031	27	690.6
1/2		0.5	12.7000	0.5	12.70						

ENGLISH TO METRIC CONVERSION: TORQUE

To convert foot-pounds (ft. lbs.) to Newton-meters: multiply the number of ft. lbs. by 1.3

To convert inch-pounds (in. lbs.) to Newton-meters: multiply the number of in. lbs. by .11

in lbs	N·m	in lbs	N·m	in lbs	N·m	in lbs	N·m	in lbs	N·m
0.1	0.01	1	0.11	10	1.13	19	2.15	28	3.16
0.2	0.02	2	0.23	11	1.24	20	2.26	29	3.28
0.3	0.03	3	0.34	12	1.36	21	2.37	30	3.39
0.4	0.04	4	0.45	13	1.47	22	2.49	31	3.50
0.5	0.06	5	0.56	14	1.58	23	2.60	32	3.62
0.6	0.07	6	0.68	15	1.70	24	2.71	33	3.73
0.7	0.08	7	0.78	16	1.81	25	2.82	34	3.84
0.8	0.09	8	0.90	17	1.92	26	2.94	35	3.95
0.9	0.10	9	1.02	18	2.03	27	3.05	36	4.0

TCCS1C02

ENGLISH TO METRIC CONVERSION: TORQUE

Torque is now expressed as either foot-pounds (ft./lbs.) or inch-pounds (in./lbs.). The metric measurement unit for torque is the Newton-meter (Nm). This unit—the Nm—will be used for all SI metric torque references, both the present ft./lbs. and in./lbs.

ft lbs	N-m	ft lbs	N-m	ft lbs	N-m	ft lbs	N-m
0.1	0.1	33	44.7	74	100.3	115	155.9
0.2	0.3	34	46.1	75	101.7	116	157.3
0.3	0.4	35	47.4	76	103.0	117	158.6
0.4	0.5	36	48.8	77	104.4	118	160.0
0.5	0.7	37	50.7	78	105.8	119	161.3
0.6	0.8	38	51.5	79	107.1	120	162.7
0.7	1.0	39	52.9	80	108.5	121	164.0
0.8	1.1	40	54.2	81	109.8	122	165.4
0.9	1.2	41	55.6	82	111.2	123	166.8
1	1.3	42	56.9	83	112.5	124	168.1
2	2.7	43	58.3	84	113.9	125	169.5
3	4.1	44	59.7	85	115.2	126	170.8
4	5.4	45	61.0	86	116.6	127	172.2
5	6.8	46	62.4	87	118.0	128	173.5
6	8.1	47	63.7	88	119.3	129	174.9
7	9.5	48	65.1	89	120.7	130	176.2
8	10.8	49	66.4	90	122.0	131	177.6
9	12.2	50	67.8	91	123.4	132	179.0
10	13.6	51	69.2	92	124.7	133	180.3
11	14.9	52	70.5	93	126.1	134	181.7
12	16.3	53	71.9	94	127.4	135	183.0
13	17.6	54	73.2	95	128.8	136	184.4
14	18.9	55	74.6	96	130.2	137	185.7
15	20.3	56	75.9	97	131.5	138	187.1
16	21.7	57	77.3	98	132.9	139	188.5
17	23.0	58	78.6	99	134.2	140	189.8
18	24.4	59	80.0	100	135.6	141	191.2
19	25.8	60	81.4	101	136.9	142	192.5
20	27.1	61	82.7	102	138.3	143	193.9
21	28.5	62	84.1	103	139.6	144	195.2
22	29.8	63	85.4	104	141.0	145	196.6
23	31.2	64	86.8	105	142.4	146	198.0
24	32.5	65	88.1	106	143.7	147	199.3
25	33.9	66	89.5	107	145.1	148	200.7
26	35.2	67	90.8	108	146.4	149	202.0
27	36.6	68	92.2	109	147.8	150	203.4
28	38.0	69	93.6	110	149.1	151	204.7
29	39.3	70	94.9	111	150.5	152	206.1
30	40.7	71	96.3	112	151.8	153	207.4
31	42.0	72	97.6	113	153.2	154	208.8
32	43.4	73	99.0	114	154.6	155	210.2

TCC31C03

ENGLISH TO METRIC CONVERSION: FORCE

Force is presently measured in pounds (lbs.). This type of measurement is used to measure spring pressure, specifically how many pounds it takes to compress a spring. Our present force unit (the pound) will be replaced in SI metric measurements by the Newton (N). This term will eventually see use in specifications for electric motor brush spring pressures, valve spring pressures, etc.

To convert pounds (lbs.) to Newton (N): multiply the number of lbs. by 4.45

lbs	N	lbs	N	lbs	N	oz	N
0.01	0.04	21	93.4	59	262.4	1	0.3
0.02	0.09	22	97.9	60	266.9	2	0.6
0.03	0.13	23	102.3	61	271.3	3	0.8
0.04	0.18	24	106.8	62	275.8	4	1.1
0.05	0.22	25	111.2	63	280.2	5	1.4
0.06	0.27	26	115.6	64	284.6	6	1.7
0.07	0.31	27	120.1	65	289.1	7	2.0
0.08	0.36	28	124.6	66	293.6	8	2.2
0.09	0.40	29	129.0	67	298.0	9	2.5
0.1	0.4	30	133.4	68	302.5	10	2.8
0.2	0.9	31	137.9	69	306.9	11	3.1
0.3	1.3	32	142.3	70	311.4	12	3.3
0.4	1.8	33	146.8	71	315.8	13	3.6
0.5	2.2	34	151.2	72	320.3	14	3.9
0.6	2.7	35	155.7	73	324.7	15	4.2
0.7	3.1	36	160.1	74	329.2	16	4.4
0.8	3.6	37	164.6	75	333.6	17	4.7
0.9	4.0	38	169.0	76	338.1	18	5.0
1	4.4	39	173.5	77	342.5	19	5.3
2	8.9	40	177.9	78	347.0	20	5.6
3	13.4	41	182.4	79	351.4	21	5.8
4	17.8	42	186.8	80	355.9	22	6.1
5	22.2	43	191.3	81	360.3	23	6.4
6	26.7	44	195.7	82	364.8	24	6.7
7	31.1	45	200.2	83	369.2	25	7.0
8	35.6	46	204.6	84	373.6	26	7.2
9	40.0	47	209.1	85	378.1	27	7.5
10	44.5	48	213.5	86	382.6	28	7.8
11	48.9	49	218.0	87	387.0	29	8.1
12	53.4	50	224.4	88	391.4	30	8.3
13	57.8	51	226.9	89	395.9	31	8.6
14	62.3	52	231.3	90	400.3	32	8.9
15	66.7	53	235.8	91	404.8	33	9.2
16	71.2	54	240.2	92	409.2	34	9.4
17	75.6	55	244.6	93	413.7	35	9.7
18	80.1	56	249.1	94	418.1	36	10.0
19	84.5	57	253.6	95	422.6	37	10.3
20	89.0	58	258.0	96	427.0	38	10.6

TCCS1C04

ENGLISH TO METRIC CONVERSION: LIQUID CAPACITY

Liquid or fluid capacity is presently expressed as pints, quarts or gallons, or a combination of all of these. In the metric system the liter (l) will become the basic unit. Fractions of a liter would be expressed as deciliters, centiliters, or most frequently (and commonly) as milliliters.

To convert pints (pts.) to liters (l): multiply the number of pints by .47
To convert liters (l) to pints (pts.): multiply the number of liters by 2.1
To convert quarts (qts.) to liters (l): multiply the number of quarts by .95

To convert liters (l) to quarts (qts.): multiply the number of liters by 1.06
To convert gallons (gals.) to liters (l): multiply the number of gallons by 3.8
To convert liters (l) to gallons (gals.): multiply the number of liters by .26

gals	liters	qts	liters	pts	liters
0.1	0.38	0.1	0.10	0.1	0.05
0.2	0.76	0.2	0.19	0.2	0.10
0.3	1.1	0.3	0.28	0.3	0.14
0.4	1.5	0.4	0.38	0.4	0.19
0.5	1.9	0.5	0.47	0.5	0.24
0.6	2.3	0.6	0.57	0.6	0.28
0.7	2.6	0.7	0.66	0.7	0.33
0.8	3.0	0.8	0.76	0.8	0.38
0.9	3.4	0.9	0.85	0.9	0.43
1	3.8	1	1.0	1	0.5
2	7.6	2	1.9	2	1.0
3	11.4	3	2.8	3	1.4
4	15.1	4	3.8	4	1.9
5	18.9	5	4.7	5	2.4
6	22.7	6	5.7	6	2.8
7	26.5	7	6.6	7	3.3
8	30.3	8	7.6	8	3.8
9	34.1	9	8.5	9	4.3
10	37.8	10	9.5	10	4.7
11	41.6	11	10.4	11	5.2
12	45.4	12	11.4	12	5.7
13	49.2	13	12.3	13	6.2
14	53.0	14	13.2	14	6.6
15	56.8	15	14.2	15	7.1
16	60.6	16	15.1	16	7.6
17	64.3	17	16.1	17	8.0
18	68.1	18	17.0	18	8.5
19	71.9	19	18.0	19	9.0
20	75.7	20	18.9	20	9.5
21	79.5	21	19.9	21	9.9
22	83.2	22	20.8	22	10.4
23	87.0	23	21.8	23	10.9
24	90.8	24	22.7	24	11.4
25	94.6	25	23.6	25	11.8
26	98.4	26	24.6	26	12.3
27	102.2	27	25.5	27	12.8
28	106.0	28	26.5	28	13.2
29	110.0	29	27.4	29	13.7
30	113.5	30	28.4	30	14.2

TCCS1C05

ENGLISH TO METRIC CONVERSION: PRESSURE

The basic unit of pressure measurement used today is expressed as pounds per square inch (psi). The metric unit for psi will be the kilopascal (kPa). This will apply to either fluid pressure or air pressure, and will be frequently seen in tire pressure readings, oil pressure specifications, fuel pump pressure, etc.

To convert pounds per square inch (psi) to kilopascals (kPa): multiply the number of psi by 6.89

Psi	kPa	Psi	kPa	Psi	kPa	Psi	kPa
0.1	0.7	37	255.1	82	565.4	127	875.6
0.2	1.4	38	262.0	83	572.3	128	882.5
0.3	2.1	39	268.9	84	579.2	129	889.4
0.4	2.8	40	275.8	85	586.0	130	896.3
0.5	3.4	41	282.7	86	592.9	131	903.2
0.6	4.1	42	289.6	87	599.8	132	910.1
0.7	4.8	43	296.5	88	606.7	133	917.0
0.8	5.5	44	303.4	89	613.6	134	923.9
0.9	6.2	45	310.3	90	620.5	135	930.8
1	6.9	46	317.2	91	627.4	136	937.7
2	13.8	47	324.0	92	634.3	137	944.6
3	20.7	48	331.0	93	641.2	138	951.5
4	27.6	49	337.8	94	648.1	139	958.4
5	34.5	50	344.7	95	655.0	140	965.2
6	41.4	51	351.6	96	661.9	141	972.2
7	48.3	52	358.5	97	668.8	142	979.0
8	55.2	53	365.4	98	675.7	143	985.9
9	62.1	54	372.3	99	682.6	144	992.8
10	69.0	55	379.2	100	689.5	145	999.7
11	75.8	56	386.1	101	696.4	146	1006.6
12	82.7	57	393.0	102	703.3	147	1013.5
13	89.6	58	399.9	103	710.2	148	1020.4
14	96.5	59	406.8	104	717.0	149	1027.3
15	103.4	60	413.7	105	723.9	150	1034.2
16	110.3	61	420.6	106	730.8	151	1041.1
17	117.2	62	427.5	107	737.7	152	1048.0
18	124.1	63	434.4	108	744.6	153	1054.9
19	131.0	64	441.3	109	751.5	154	1061.8
20	137.9	65	448.2	110	758.4	155	1068.7
21	144.8	66	455.0	111	765.3	156	1075.6
22	151.7	67	461.9	112	772.2	157	1082.5
23	158.6	68	468.8	113	779.1	158	1089.4
24	165.5	69	475.7	114	786.0	159	1096.3
25	172.4	70	482.6	115	792.9	160	1103.2
26	179.3	71	489.5	116	799.8	161	1110.0
27	186.2	72	496.4	117	806.7	162	1116.9
28	193.0	73	503.3	118	813.6	163	1123.8
29	200.0	74	510.2	119	820.5	164	1130.7
30	206.8	75	517.1	120	827.4	165	1137.6
31	213.7	76	524.0	121	834.3	166	1144.5
32	220.6	77	530.9	122	841.2	167	1151.4
33	227.5	78	537.8	123	848.0	168	1158.3
34	234.4	79	544.7	124	854.9	169	1165.2
35	241.3	80	551.6	125	861.8	170	1172.1
36	248.2	81	558.5	126	868.7	171	1179.0

TCCS1C06

2

ENGINE
ELECTRICAL

DIRECT IGNITION SYSTEM (DIS)

➡️**For information on general electrical system testing, please refer to Section 6.**

General Information

Vehicles which are equipped with the 2.0L, 2.2L, 2.8L and 3.1L engines utilize the Direct Ignition System (DIS). this system is called the Electronic Ignition (EI) system in later model years. This system features a distributorless ignition. The DIS/EI system consists of two separate ignition coils on 4-cylinder engines or 3 separate coils on V6 engines, and Ignition Control Module (ICM), and a secondary conductor housing which is mounted to an aluminum cover plate. The system also consists of on or two Crankshaft Position (CKP) sensors, crankshaft reluctor ring, related connecting wires and the Electronic Spark Timing (EST) or Ignition Control (IC) portion of the Electronic Control Module (ECM). A Camshaft Position (CMP) sensor may also be incorporated on some engines.

➡️**When the term Electronic Control Module (ECM) is used in this manual, it refers to the engine control computer; regardless if the term Powertrain Control Module (PCM) or Electronic Control Module (ECM) is used.**

The DIS/EI ignition system uses a magnetic crankshaft sensor (mounted remotely from the ignition module) and a reluctor to determine crankshaft position and engine speed. The reluctor is a special wheel cast into the crankshaft with several machined slots. A specific slot on the reluctor wheel is used to generate a sync pulse.

The camshaft sensor, used on some engines, provides a cam signal to identify correct firing sequence. The crankshaft sensor signal triggers each coil at the proper time.

The ECM uses the EST circuit to control spark advance and ignition dwell, when the ignition system is operating in the EST/IC mode.

The Electronic Spark Control (ESC) system is used to control spark knock and enable maximum spark advance to improve driveability and fuel economy. This system consists of a knock sensor and ESC module. The computer control module (ECM/PCM) monitors the ESC signal to determine when engine detonation occurs.

SYSTEM COMPONENTS

Crankshaft Position (CKP) Sensor

▶ **See Figure 1**

The Crankshaft Position (CKP) sensor is mounted remotely, next to the Ignition Control Module (ICM) on the 2.0L and 2.2L engines. The sensor is

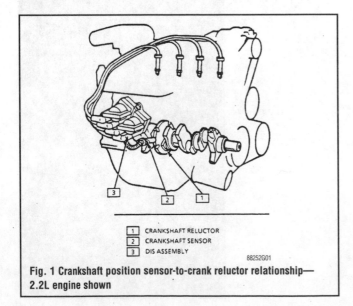

1	CRANKSHAFT RELUCTOR
2	CRANKSHAFT SENSOR
3	DIS ASSEMBLY

88252G01

Fig. 1 Crankshaft position sensor-to-crank reluctor relationship— 2.2L engine shown

mounted remotely, on the opposite side of the engine from the module on the 2.8L and 3.1L engines located toward the bottom of the rear (right side) of the engine block on V6 engines. It is used to determine crankshaft position and engine speed.

Ignition Coils

▶ **See Figure 2**

The ignition coil assemblies are mounted inside the module assembly housing. Each coil distributes the spark for two plugs simultaneously.

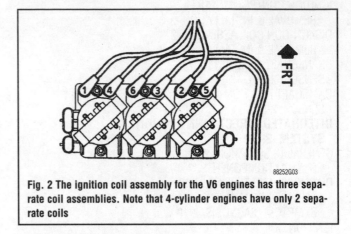

88252G03

Fig. 2 The ignition coil assembly for the V6 engines has three separate coil assemblies. Note that 4-cylinder engines have only 2 separate coils

Electronic Spark Timing (EST)/Ignition Control (IC) System

The EST system, used on 1988–93 models, includes the following circuits: These systems include the following circuits:
• Reference circuit (CKT 430)—provides the ECM with rpm and crankshaft position information from the IDI module. The IDI module receives this signal from the crank sensor.
• Bypass signal (CKT 424)—above 700 rpm, the ECM applies 5 volts to this circuit to switch spark timing control from the IDI module to the ECM.
• EST/IC signal (CKT 423)—reference signal is sent to the ECM via the DIS module during cranking. Under 600 rpm, the IDI module controls the ignition timing. Above 600 rpm, the ECM applies 5 volts to the bypass line to switch the timing to the ECM control.
• Reference ground circuit (CKT 453)—this wire is grounded through the module and insures that the ground circuit has no voltage drop between the ignition module and the ECM which could affect performance.

Ignition Control (IC)

The IC system, used on 1994–96 models, includes the following circuits:

2.2L ENGINE

• Ignition control A & B (CKTs 423 & 406)—The PCM sends the Ignition Control (IC) pulses to the ICM on these circuits. These signals are similar to the 7X reference pules square wave except that the PCM uses sensor inputs to determine the pulse timing to control spark advance. When the PCM receives the 7X signal, it will determine which pair of cylinders will be fired (1 & 4 or 2 & 3). It will tell the ICM which cylinder pair will be fired via CKTs 423 or 406.

3.1L ENGINE

• 3X Reference high (CKT 430)—The CKP sensor generates a signal to the ICM, resulting in a reference pulse which is sent to the PCM. The PCM uses this signal to determine crankshaft position, engine speed and injector pulse width. The engine will not start or run if this circuit is open or grounded.
• 3X Reference low (CKT 453)—This wire is grounded through the module and insures that the ground circuit has no voltage drop between the ICM and the PCM which may affect engine performance.
• Ignition control bypass (CKT 424)—During initial cranking, the PCM will look for synchronizing pulses from the camshaft and 3X crankshaft position sensor indicating the position of the no. 1 piston and intake valve. 5 volts are

applied to the bypass circuit the instant these signals are received by the PCM. This generally occurs within 1 or 2 revolutions of the crankshaft. An open our grounded bypass circuit will set a diagnostic trouble code and the engine will run at base timing. A small amount of advance is built into the ignition control module to enhance performance.

• Ignition control (CKT 423)—The PCM uses this circuit to trigger the electronic ignition control module. The PCM uses the crankshaft reference signal to base its calculation of the amount of spark advance needed under present engine conditions.

• 24X reference signal—Additional to the electronic ignition system is the 24X crankshaft position sensor. Its function is to smooth idle quality and provide improved low speed driveability.

Diagnosis and Testing

SERVICE PRECAUTIONS

☼ CAUTION

The ignition coil's secondary voltage output capabilities can exceed 40,000 volts. Avoid body contact with the DIS high voltage secondary components when the engine is running, or personal injury may result.

➡ To avoid damage to the computer control module or other ignition system components, do not use electrical test equipment such as battery or AC powered voltmeter, ohmmeter, etc. or any type of tester other than specified.

• When performing electrical tests on the system, use a high impedance multimeter or quality digital voltmeter (DVM). Use of a 12 volt test light is not recommended.

• To prevent electrostatic discharge damage, when working with the ECM, do not touch the connector pins or soldered components on the circuit board.

• When handling a PROM, CAL-PAK or MEM-CAL, do not touch the component leads. Also, do not remove the integrated circuit from the carrier.

• When performing electrical tests on the system, use a high impedance multimeter, digital voltmeter (DVM) J-34029-A or equivalent.

• Never pierce a high tension lead or boot for any testing purpose; otherwise, future problems are guaranteed.

• Leave new components and modules in the shipping package until ready to install them.

• Never disconnect any electrical connection with the ignition switch **ON** unless instructed to do so in a test.

SYMPTOM DIAGNOSIS

◆ See Figures 3 thru 20

The ECM uses information from the MAP and coolant sensors, in addition to rpm to calculate spark advance as follows:
1. Low MAP output voltage—more spark advance
2. Cold engine—more spark advance
3. High MAP output voltage—less spark advance
4. Hot engine—less spark advance
Therefore, briefly, detonation could be caused by low MAP output or high resistance in the coolant sensor circuit. And poor performance could be caused by high MAP output or low resistance in the coolant sensor circuit.

To diagnose what may be an ignition-related problem, first check for codes, as described in Section 4. If codes, exist, refer to the corresponding diagnostic charts in Section 4. Otherwise, the following charts may be helpful.

Ignition Coil

TESTING

1. Remove the ignition coil(s).
2. Using an ohmmeter, check the resistance between the primary terminals on the underside of the coil. The resistance should be 0.50–0.90 ohms.

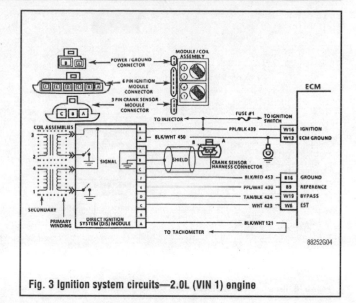

Fig. 3 Ignition system circuits—2.0L (VIN 1) engine

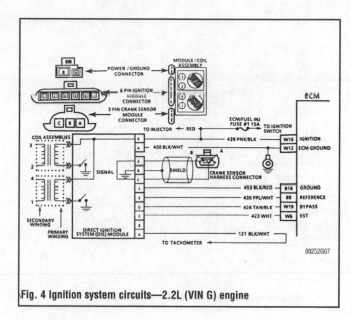

Fig. 4 Ignition system circuits—2.2L (VIN G) engine

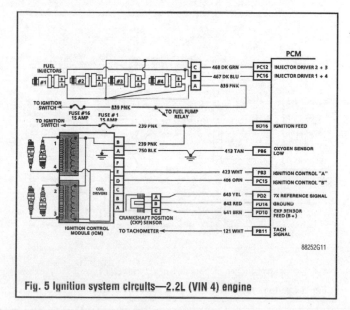

Fig. 5 Ignition system circuits—2.2L (VIN 4) engine

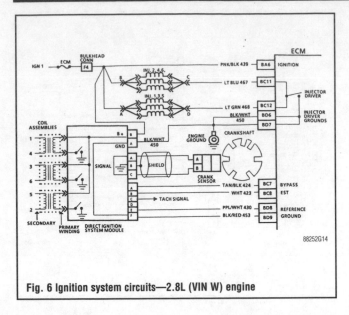

Fig. 6 Ignition system circuits—2.8L (VIN W) engine

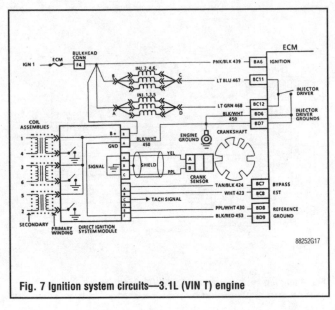

Fig. 7 Ignition system circuits—3.1L (VIN T) engine

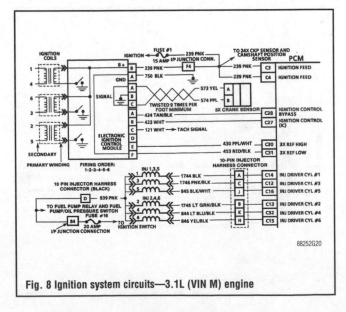

Fig. 8 Ignition system circuits—3.1L (VIN M) engine

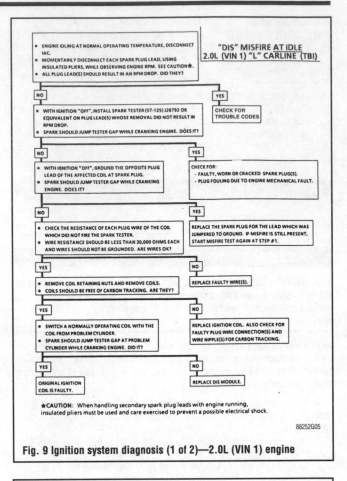

Fig. 9 Ignition system diagnosis (1 of 2)—2.0L (VIN 1) engine

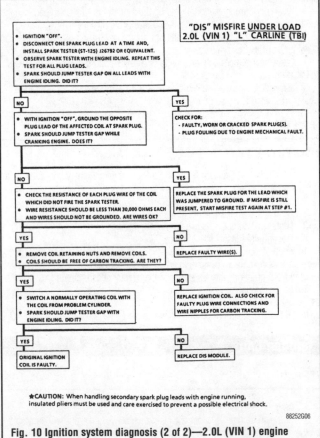

Fig. 10 Ignition system diagnosis (2 of 2)—2.0L (VIN 1) engine

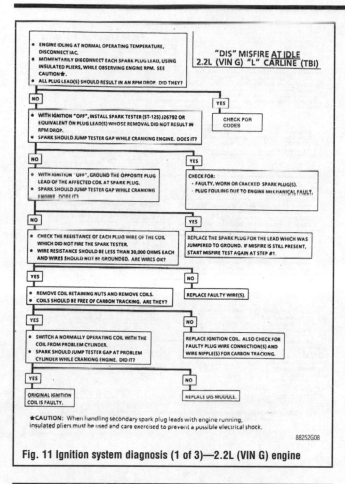

Fig. 11 Ignition system diagnosis (1 of 3)—2.2L (VIN G) engine

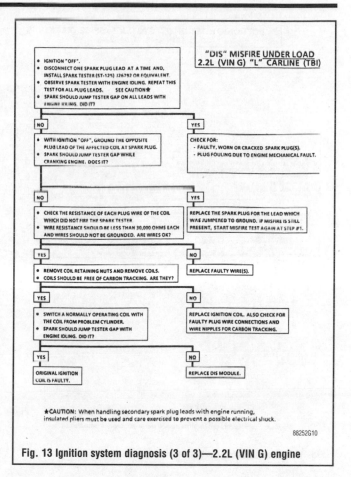

Fig. 13 Ignition system diagnosis (3 of 3)—2.2L (VIN G) engine

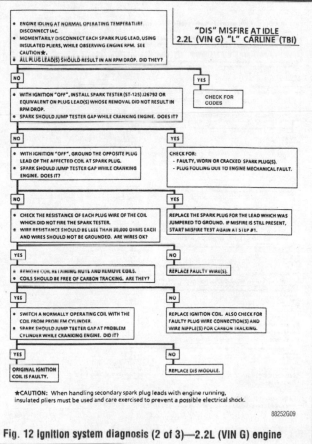

Fig. 12 Ignition system diagnosis (2 of 3)—2.2L (VIN G) engine

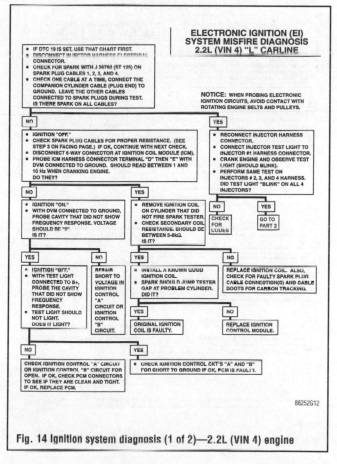

Fig. 14 Ignition system diagnosis (1 of 2)—2.2L (VIN 4) engine

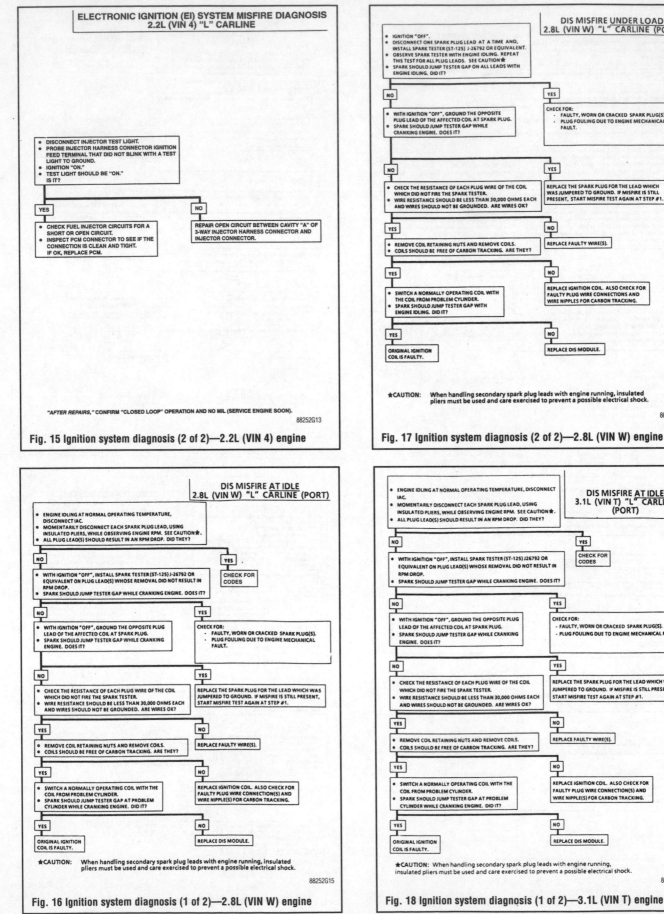

**ELECTRONIC IGNITION (EI) SYSTEM MISFIRE DIAGNOSIS
2.2L (VIN 4) "L" CARLINE**

- DISCONNECT INJECTOR TEST LIGHT.
- PROBE INJECTOR HARNESS CONNECTOR IGNITION FEED TERMINAL THAT DID NOT BLINK WITH A TEST LIGHT TO GROUND.
- IGNITION "ON."
- TEST LIGHT SHOULD BE "ON."
  IS IT?

YES
- CHECK FUEL INJECTOR CIRCUITS FOR A SHORT OR OPEN CIRCUIT.
- INSPECT PCM CONNECTOR TO SEE IF THE CONNECTION IS CLEAN AND TIGHT. IF OK, REPLACE PCM.

NO
REPAIR OPEN CIRCUIT BETWEEN CAVITY "A" OF 3-WAY INJECTOR HARNESS CONNECTOR AND INJECTOR CONNECTOR.

"AFTER REPAIRS," CONFIRM "CLOSED LOOP" OPERATION AND NO MIL (SERVICE ENGINE SOON).

88252G13

Fig. 15 Ignition system diagnosis (2 of 2)—2.2L (VIN 4) engine

---

**DIS MISFIRE UNDER LOAD
2.8L (VIN W) "L" CARLINE (PORT)**

- IGNITION "OFF".
- DISCONNECT ONE SPARK PLUG LEAD AT A TIME AND, INSTALL SPARK TESTER (ST-125) J-26792 OR EQUIVALENT. OBSERVE SPARK TESTER WITH ENGINE IDLING. REPEAT THIS TEST FOR ALL PLUG LEADS. SEE CAUTION★
- SPARK SHOULD JUMP TESTER GAP ON ALL LEADS WITH ENGINE IDLING. DID IT?

NO
- WITH IGNITION "OFF", GROUND THE OPPOSITE PLUG LEAD OF THE AFFECTED COIL AT SPARK PLUG.
- SPARK SHOULD JUMP TESTER GAP WHILE CRANKING ENGINE. DOES IT?

YES
CHECK FOR:
- FAULTY, WORN OR CRACKED SPARK PLUG(S).
- PLUG FOULING DUE TO ENGINE MECHANICAL FAULT.

NO
- CHECK THE RESISTANCE OF EACH PLUG WIRE OF THE COIL WHICH DID NOT FIRE THE SPARK TESTER.
- WIRE RESISTANCE SHOULD BE LESS THAN 30,000 OHMS EACH AND WIRES SHOULD NOT BE GROUNDED. ARE WIRES OK?

YES
REPLACE THE SPARK PLUG FOR THE LEAD WHICH WAS JUMPERED TO GROUND. IF MISFIRE IS STILL PRESENT, START MISFIRE TEST AGAIN AT STEP #1.

YES
- REMOVE COIL RETAINING NUTS AND REMOVE COILS.
- COILS SHOULD BE FREE OF CARBON TRACKING. ARE THEY?

NO
REPLACE FAULTY WIRE(S).

YES
- SWITCH A NORMALLY OPERATING COIL WITH THE COIL FROM PROBLEM CYLINDER.
- SPARK SHOULD JUMP TESTER GAP WITH ENGINE IDLING. DID IT?

NO
REPLACE IGNITION COIL. ALSO CHECK FOR FAULTY PLUG WIRE CONNECTIONS AND WIRE NIPPLES FOR CARBON TRACKING.

YES
ORIGINAL IGNITION COIL IS FAULTY.

NO
REPLACE DIS MODULE.

★CAUTION: When handling secondary spark plug leads with engine running, insulated pliers must be used and care exercised to prevent a possible electrical shock.

88252G16

Fig. 17 Ignition system diagnosis (2 of 2)—2.8L (VIN W) engine

---

**DIS MISFIRE AT IDLE
2.8L (VIN W) "L" CARLINE (PORT)**

- ENGINE IDLING AT NORMAL OPERATING TEMPERATURE, DISCONNECT IAC.
- MOMENTARILY DISCONNECT EACH SPARK PLUG LEAD, USING INSULATED PLIERS, WHILE OBSERVING ENGINE RPM. SEE CAUTION★.
- ALL PLUG LEAD(S) SHOULD RESULT IN AN RPM DROP. DID THEY?

NO
- WITH IGNITION "OFF", INSTALL SPARK TESTER (ST-125) J-26792 OR EQUIVALENT ON PLUG LEAD(S) WHOSE REMOVAL DID NOT RESULT IN RPM DROP.
- SPARK SHOULD JUMP TESTER GAP WHILE CRANKING ENGINE. DOES IT?

YES
CHECK FOR CODES

NO
- WITH IGNITION "OFF", GROUND THE OPPOSITE PLUG LEAD OF THE AFFECTED COIL AT SPARK PLUG.
- SPARK SHOULD JUMP TESTER GAP WHILE CRANKING ENGINE. DOES IT?

YES
CHECK FOR:
- FAULTY, WORN OR CRACKED SPARK PLUG(S).
- PLUG FOULING DUE TO ENGINE MECHANICAL FAULT.

NO
- CHECK THE RESISTANCE OF EACH PLUG WIRE OF THE COIL WHICH DID NOT FIRE THE SPARK TESTER.
- WIRE RESISTANCE SHOULD BE LESS THAN 30,000 OHMS EACH AND WIRES SHOULD NOT BE GROUNDED. ARE WIRES OK?

YES
REPLACE THE SPARK PLUG FOR THE LEAD WHICH WAS JUMPERED TO GROUND. IF MISFIRE IS STILL PRESENT, START MISFIRE TEST AGAIN AT STEP #1.

YES
- REMOVE COIL RETAINING NUTS AND REMOVE COILS.
- COILS SHOULD BE FREE OF CARBON TRACKING. ARE THEY?

NO
REPLACE FAULTY WIRE(S).

YES
- SWITCH A NORMALLY OPERATING COIL WITH THE COIL FROM PROBLEM CYLINDER.
- SPARK SHOULD JUMP TESTER GAP AT PROBLEM CYLINDER WHILE CRANKING ENGINE. DID IT?

NO
REPLACE IGNITION COIL. ALSO CHECK FOR FAULTY PLUG WIRE CONNECTION(S) AND WIRE NIPPLE(S) FOR CARBON TRACKING.

YES
ORIGINAL IGNITION COIL IS FAULTY.

NO
REPLACE DIS MODULE.

★CAUTION: When handling secondary spark plug leads with engine running, insulated pliers must be used and care exercised to prevent a possible electrical shock.

88252G15

Fig. 16 Ignition system diagnosis (1 of 2)—2.8L (VIN W) engine

---

**DIS MISFIRE AT IDLE
3.1L (VIN T) "L" CARLINE (PORT)**

- ENGINE IDLING AT NORMAL OPERATING TEMPERATURE, DISCONNECT IAC.
- MOMENTARILY DISCONNECT EACH SPARK PLUG LEAD, USING INSULATED PLIERS, WHILE OBSERVING ENGINE RPM. SEE CAUTION★.
- ALL PLUG LEAD(S) SHOULD RESULT IN AN RPM DROP. DID THEY?

NO
- WITH IGNITION "OFF", INSTALL SPARK TESTER (ST-125) J26792 OR EQUIVALENT ON PLUG LEAD(S) WHOSE REMOVAL DID NOT RESULT IN RPM DROP.
- SPARK SHOULD JUMP TESTER GAP WHILE CRANKING ENGINE. DOES IT?

YES
CHECK FOR CODES

NO
- WITH IGNITION "OFF", GROUND THE OPPOSITE PLUG LEAD OF THE AFFECTED COIL AT SPARK PLUG.
- SPARK SHOULD JUMP TESTER GAP WHILE CRANKING ENGINE. DOES IT?

YES
CHECK FOR:
- FAULTY, WORN OR CRACKED SPARK PLUG(S).
- PLUG FOULING DUE TO ENGINE MECHANICAL FAULT.

NO
- CHECK THE RESISTANCE OF EACH PLUG WIRE OF THE COIL WHICH DID NOT FIRE THE SPARK TESTER.
- WIRE RESISTANCE SHOULD BE LESS THAN 30,000 OHMS EACH AND WIRES SHOULD NOT BE GROUNDED. ARE WIRES OK?

YES
REPLACE THE SPARK PLUG FOR THE LEAD WHICH WAS JUMPERED TO GROUND. IF MISFIRE IS STILL PRESENT, START MISFIRE TEST AGAIN AT STEP #1.

YES
- REMOVE COIL RETAINING NUTS AND REMOVE COILS.
- COILS SHOULD BE FREE OF CARBON TRACKING. ARE THEY?

NO
REPLACE FAULTY WIRE(S).

YES
- SWITCH A NORMALLY OPERATING COIL WITH THE COIL FROM PROBLEM CYLINDER.
- SPARK SHOULD JUMP TESTER GAP AT PROBLEM CYLINDER WHILE CRANKING ENGINE. DID IT?

NO
REPLACE IGNITION COIL. ALSO CHECK FOR FAULTY PLUG WIRE CONNECTION(S) AND WIRE NIPPLE(S) FOR CARBON TRACKING.

YES
ORIGINAL IGNITION COIL IS FAULTY.

NO
REPLACE DIS MODULE.

★CAUTION: When handling secondary spark plug leads with engine running, insulated pliers must be used and care exercised to prevent a possible electrical shock.

88252G18

Fig. 18 Ignition system diagnosis (1 of 2)—3.1L (VIN T) engine

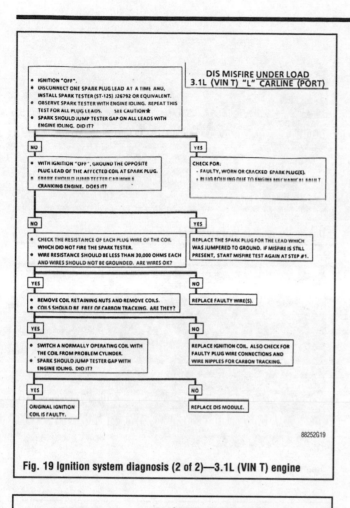

Fig. 19 Ignition system diagnosis (2 of 2)—3.1L (VIN T) engine

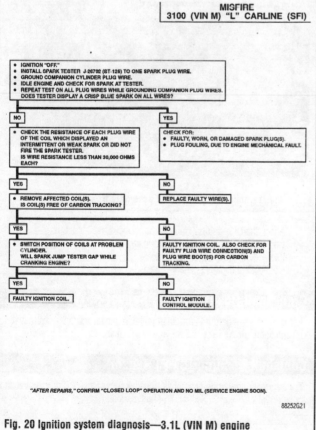

Fig. 20 Ignition system diagnosis—3.1L (VIN M) engine

3. Check the resistance between the secondary terminals. It should be 5000–10,000 ohms.
4. If the coil failed either test, replace the coil.

REMOVAL & INSTALLATION

▶ **See Figures 21 and 22**

1. Disconnect the negative battery cable.
2. If necessary for access, raise and safely support the vehicle.
3. Tag and disconnect the spark plug wires from the ignition coil.

➥When removing the coil be careful not to bend the module prongs.

4. Remove the coil attaching screws, then remove the ignition coils from the module.

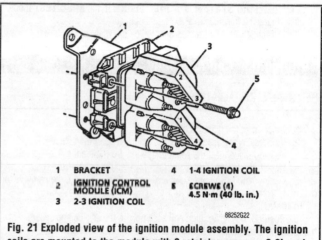

1	**BRACKET**	**4**	**1-4 IGNITION COIL**
2	**IGNITION CONTROL MODULE (ICM)**	**5**	**SCREWS (4)** 4.5 N·m (40 lb. in.)
3	**2-3 IGNITION COIL**		

Fig. 21 Exploded view of the ignition module assembly. The ignition coils are mounted to the module with 2 retaining screws—2.0L and 2.2L engines

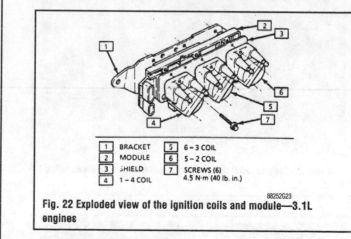

1	**BRACKET**	**5**	**6 – 3 COIL**
2	**MODULE**	**6**	**5 – 2 COIL**
3	**SHIELD**	**7**	**SCREWS (6)** 4.5 N·m (40 lb. in.)
4	**1 – 4 COIL**		

Fig. 22 Exploded view of the ignition coils and module—3.1L engines

To install:

5. Position the coil to the module and secure with the retaining screws. Tighten the screws to 40 inch lbs. (4.5 Nm).
6. Connect the spark plugs, as tagged during removal.
7. If raised, carefully lower the vehicle.
8. Connect the negative battery cable.
9. If equipped with the 3.1L engine, perform the idle learn procedure to allow the ECM/PCM memory to be updated with the correct IAC valve pintle position and provide for a stable idle speed.
    a. Install a Tech 1®, or equivalent scan tool.
    b. Turn the ignition to the **ON** position, engine not running.
    c. Select **IAC SYSTEM**, then **IDLE LEARN** in the **MISC TEST** mode.
    d. Place the transaxle in **P** or **N**, as applicable.
    e. Proceed with idle learn as directed by the scan tool.

Ignition Control Module

REMOVAL & INSTALLATION

1. Disconnect the negative battery cable.
2. If necessary for access, raise and safely support the vehicle.
3. Remove the DIS/ignition coil assembly from the engine.
4. Remove the coils from the assembly.
5. Remove the module from the assembly plate.
6. Installation is the reverse of the removal procedure.
7. If equipped with the 3.1L engine, perform the idle learn procedure to allow the ECM/PCM memory to be updated with the correct IAC valve pintle position and provide for a stable idle speed.
   a. Install a Tech 1®, or equivalent scan tool.
   b. Turn the ignition to the **ON** position, engine not running.
   c. Select **IAC SYSTEM**, then **IDLE LEARN** in the **MISC TEST** mode.
   d. Place the transaxle in **P** or **N**, as applicable.
   e. Proceed with idle learn as directed by the scan tool.

DIS/Ignition Coil Assembly

REMOVAL & INSTALLATION

1. Disconnect the negative battery cable.
2. If necessary for access, raise and safely support the vehicle.
3. Tag and disconnect the spark plug wires from the coils.
4. Detach the DIS/ignition coil assembly electrical connector(s).
5. Remove the DIS/ignition coil assembly attaching bolts, then remove the assembly from the vehicle.

To install:

6. Position the DIS/ignition coil assembly to the engine and secure with the retaining bolts. Tighten the bolts to 15–22 ft. lbs. (20–30 Nm).

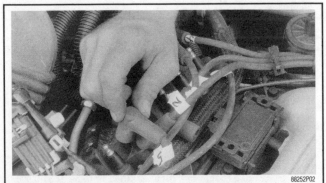

You can use tape to label the spark plug wires before disconnecting them

Grasp the boot (see arrow), then detach the spark plug wires from the ignition coil assembly

Unplug the ignition coil electrical connector

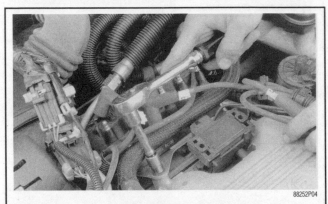

Remove the ignition coil assembly retaining bolts . . .

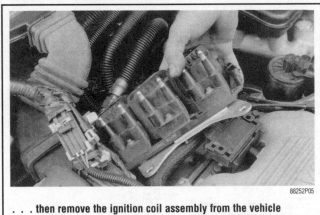

. . . then remove the ignition coil assembly from the vehicle

7. Attach the DIS/ignition coil assembly electrical connector(s).
8. Connect the spark plug wires to the coils, as tagged during removal.
9. If raised, carefully lower the vehicle.
10. Connect the negative battery cable.

Crankshaft Position (CKP) Sensor

For information regarding crankshaft position sensor testing and removal and installation, please refer to Section 4 of this manual.

Camshaft Position (CMP) Sensor

For information regarding camshaft position sensor testing and removal and installation, please refer to Section 4 of this manual.

INTEGRATED DIRECT IGNITION (IDI) SYSTEM

General Description

♦ See Figure 23

Vehicles with the 2.3L engine are equipped with the Integrated Direct Ignition (IDI) system, or Electronic Ignition (EI) system, as is was called in later model years. This system features a distributorless ignition. The IDI system consists of two separate ignition coils, an ignition module and a secondary conductor housing mounted to an aluminum cover plate. The system also consists of a crankshaft sensor, connecting wires and the Electronic Spark Timing (EST), or Ignition Control (IC) portion of the Electronic Control Module (ECM).

→ **When the term Electronic Control Module (ECM) is used in this manual, it refers to the engine control computer; regardless, if the term Powertrain Control Module (PCM) or Electronic Control Module (ECM) is used.**

The IDI ignition system uses a magnetic crankshaft sensor, mounted remotely from the ignition module, and a reluctor to determine crankshaft position and engine speed. The reluctor is a special wheel cast into the crankshaft, with 7 slots machined into it. Six of the slots are equally spaced 60 degrees apart and the seventh slot is spaced 10 degrees from 1 of the other slots. This seventh slot is used to generate a sync-pulse.

The ECM uses the EST circuit to control spark advance and ignition dwell, when the ignition system is operating in the EST mode.

To control spark knock and to use maximum spark advance to improve driveability and fuel economy, an Electronic Spark Control (ESC) system is used. This system consists of a knock sensor and an ESC module. The ECM monitors the ESC signal to determine when engine detonation occurs.

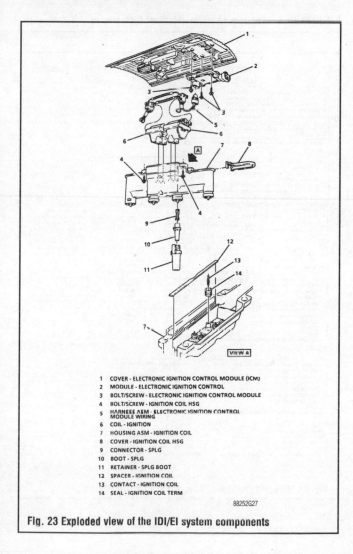

1 COVER - ELECTRONIC IGNITION CONTROL MODULE (ICM)
2 MODULE - ELECTRONIC IGNITION CONTROL
3 BOLT/SCREW - ELECTRONIC IGNITION CONTROL MODULE
4 BOLT/SCREW - IGNITION COIL HSG
5 HARNESS ASM - ELECTRONIC IGNITION CONTROL MODULE WIRING
6 COIL - IGNITION
7 HOUSING ASM - IGNITION COIL
8 COVER - IGNITION COIL HSG
9 CONNECTOR - SPLG
10 BOOT - SPLG
11 RETAINER - SPLG BOOT
12 SPACER - IGNITION COIL
13 CONTACT - IGNITION COIL
14 SEAL - IGNITION COIL TERM

88252G27

Fig. 23 Exploded view of the IDI/EI system components

SYSTEM COMPONENTS

Crankshaft Sensor

♦ See Figure 24

The crankshaft sensor, mounted remotely from the ignition module on an aluminum cover plate, is used to determine crankshaft position and engine speed.

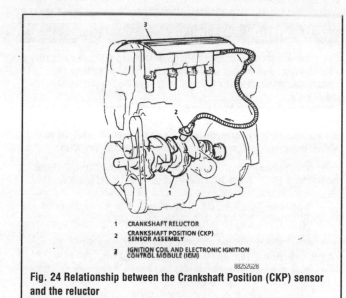

1 CRANKSHAFT RELUCTOR
2 CRANKSHAFT POSITION (CKP) SENSOR ASSEMBLY
3 IGNITION COIL AND ELECTRONIC IGNITION CONTROL MODULE (ICM)

88252G28

Fig. 24 Relationship between the Crankshaft Position (CKP) sensor and the reluctor

Ignition Coil

The ignition coil assemblies are mounted inside the ignition module housing. Each coil distributes the spark for two plugs simultaneously.

Electronic Spark Timing (EST)

The EST system, used on 1990–92 vehicles, is basically the same EST to ECM circuit uses on the distributor type ignition systems with EST. This system includes the following circuits:

• Reference circuit (CKT 430)— provides the ECM with rpm and crankshaft position information from the IDI module. The IDI module receives this signal from the crank sensor.

• Bypass signal (CKT 424)— above 700 rpm, the ECM applies 5 volts to this circuit to switch spark timing control from the IDI module to the ECM.

• EST signal (CKT 423)—reference signal is sent to the ECM via the DIS module during cranking. Under 700 rpm, the IDI module controls the ignition timing. Above 700 rpm, the ECM applies 5 volts to the bypass line to switch the timing to the ECM control.

• Reference ground circuit (CKT 453)—this wire is grounded through the module and insures that the ground circuit has no voltage drop between the ignition module and the ECM which could affect performance.

Ignition Control (IC)

The IC system, used on 1993–94 vehicles, is basically the same EST to ECM circuit uses on the distributor type ignition systems with EST. This system includes the following circuits:

• 7X reference circuit (CKT 483)—provides the ECM with rpm and crankshaft position information from the IDI module. The IDI module receives this signal from the crank sensor.

• Reference low (CKT 453)—this wire is grounded through the Ignition Control Module (ICM) and insures that the ground circuit has no voltage drop between the ICM and the PCM which could affect performance.

• Ignition control 1 & 2 (CKTs 423 & 485)—the ignition control pulse is sent to the ICM on these circuits by the ECM. Similar to the 7X reference pulse square wave except that the PCM uses sensor inputs to determine the pulse timing to control spark advance.

ESC/Knock Sensor

The ESC/Knock sensor, mounted in the engine block near the cylinders, detects abnormal vibration (spark knock) in the engine.

Diagnosis and Testing

SERVICE PRECAUTIONS

> **✳✳ CAUTION**
>
> **The ignition coil's secondary voltage output capabilities can exceed 40,000 volts. Avoid body contact with the IDI high voltage secondary components when the engine is running, or personal injury may result.**

➡️**To avoid damage to the ECM or other ignition system components, do not use electrical test equipment such as battery or AC powered voltmeter, ohmmeter, etc. or any type of tester other than specified.**

• When performing electrical tests on the system, use a high impedance multimeter, digital voltmeter (DVM) J-34029-A or equivalent. Use of a 12 volt test light is not recommended.
• To prevent Electrostatic Discharge damage, when working with the ECM, do not touch the connector pins or soldered components on the circuit board.
• When handling a PROM, CAL-PAK or MEM-CAL, do not touch the component leads. Also, do not remove the integrated circuit from the carrier.
• Never pierce a high tension lead or boot for any testing purpose; otherwise, future problems are guaranteed.
• Leave new components and modules in the shipping package until ready to install them.
• Never detach any electrical connection with the ignition switch **ON** unless instructed to do so in a test.

SYMPTOM DIAGNOSIS

◆ **See Figures 25 thru 30**

The ECM uses information from the MAP and coolant sensors, in addition to rpm to calculate spark advance as follows:
1. Low MAP output voltage—more spark advance
2. Cold engine—more spark advance

3. High MAP output voltage—less spark advance
4. Hot engine—less spark advance

Therefore, detonation could be caused by low MAP output or high resistance in the coolant sensor circuit. And poor performance could be caused by high MAP output or low resistance in the coolant sensor circuit.

To diagnose what may be an ignition-related problem, first check for codes, as described in Section 4. If codes, exist, refer to the corresponding diagnostic information in Section 4. Otherwise, the accompanying charts may be helpful.

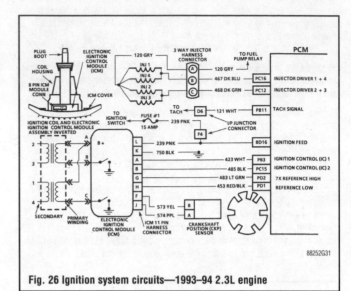

Fig. 26 Ignition system circuits—1993–94 2.3L engine

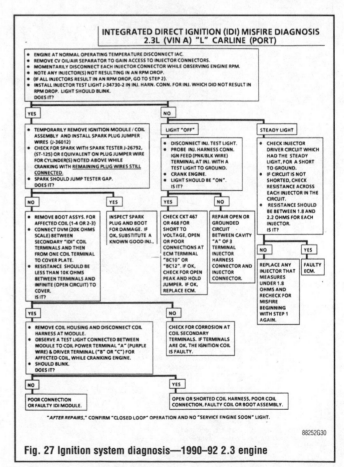

Fig. 27 Ignition system diagnosis—1990–92 2.3 engine

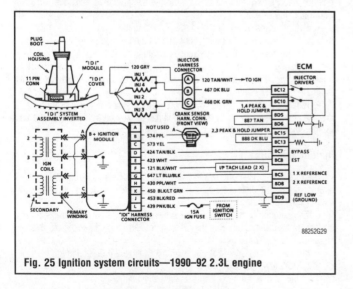

Fig. 25 Ignition system circuits—1990–92 2.3L engine

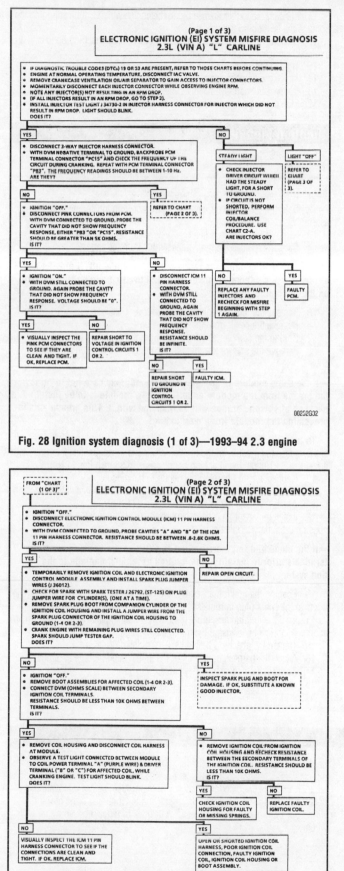

(Page 1 of 3)
ELECTRONIC IGNITION (EI) SYSTEM MISFIRE DIAGNOSIS
2.3L (VIN A) "L" CARLINE

- IF DIAGNOSTIC TROUBLE CODES (DTCs) 19 OR 53 ARE PRESENT, REFER TO THOSE CHARTS BEFORE CONTINUING.
- ENGINE AT NORMAL OPERATING TEMPERATURE, DISCONNECT IAC VALVE.
- REMOVE CRANKCASE VENTILATION OIL/AIR SEPARATOR TO GAIN ACCESS TO INJECTOR CONNECTORS.
- MOMENTARILY DISCONNECT EACH INJECTOR CONNECTOR WHILE OBSERVING ENGINE RPM.
- NOTE ANY INJECTOR(S) NOT RESULTING IN AN RPM DROP.
- (IF ALL INJECTORS RESULT IN AN RPM DROP, GO TO STEP 2).
- INSTALL INJECTOR TEST LIGHT J 34730-2 IN INJECTOR HARNESS CONNECTOR FOR INJECTOR WHICH DID NOT RESULT IN RPM DROP. LIGHT SHOULD BLINK.
  DOES IT?

YES →
- DISCONNECT 3-WAY INJECTOR HARNESS CONNECTOR.
- WITH DVM NEGATIVE TERMINAL TO GROUND, BACKPROBE PCM TERMINAL CONNECTOR "PC15" AND CHECK THE FREQUENCY OF THE CIRCUIT DURING CRANKING. REPEAT WITH PCM TERMINAL CONNECTOR "PB3". THE FREQUENCY READINGS SHOULD BE BETWEEN 1-10 Hz. ARE THEY?

NO →
- STEADY LIGHT
- CHECK INJECTOR DRIVER CIRCUIT WHICH HAD THE STEADY LIGHT, FOR A SHORT TO GROUND.
- IF CIRCUIT IS NOT SHORTED, PERFORM INJECTOR COIL/BALANCE PROCEDURE. USE CHART C2-A. ARE INJECTORS OK?

LIGHT "OFF" → REFER TO CHART (PAGE 3 OF 3).

NO →
- IGNITION "OFF."
- DISCONNECT PINK CONNECTORS FROM PCM. WITH DVM CONNECTED TO GROUND, PROBE THE CAVITY THAT DID NOT SHOW FREQUENCY RESPONSE, EITHER "PB3" OR "PC15". RESISTANCE SHOULD BE GREATER THAN 5K OHMS. IS IT?

YES → REFER TO CHART (PAGE 2 OF 3).

YES →
- IGNITION "ON."
- WITH DVM STILL CONNECTED TO GROUND. AGAIN PROBE THE CAVITY THAT DID NOT SHOW FREQUENCY RESPONSE. VOLTAGE SHOULD BE "0". IS IT?

NO →
- DISCONNECT ICM 11 PIN HARNESS CONNECTOR.
- WITH DVM STILL CONNECTED TO GROUND, AGAIN PROBE THE CAVITY THAT DID NOT SHOW FREQUENCY RESPONSE. RESISTANCE SHOULD BE INFINITE. IS IT?

NO → REPLACE ANY FAULTY INJECTORS AND RECHECK FOR MISFIRE BEGINNING WITH STEP 1 AGAIN.

YES → FAULTY PCM.

YES →
- VISUALLY INSPECT THE PINK PCM CONNECTORS TO SEE IF THEY ARE CLEAN AND TIGHT. IF OK, REPLACE PCM.

NO → REPAIR SHORT TO VOLTAGE IN IGNITION CONTROL CIRCUITS 1 OR 2.

NO → REPAIR SHORT TO GROUND IN IGNITION CONTROL CIRCUITS 1 OR 2.

YES → FAULTY ICM.

00252G32

Fig. 28 Ignition system diagnosis (1 of 3)—1993–94 2.3 engine

---

(Page 3 of 3)
ELECTRONIC IGNITION (EI) SYSTEM MISFIRE DIAGNOSIS
2.3L (VIN A) "L" CARLINE

FROM CHART PAGE 1 OF 3.
- DISCONNECT PAIRED INJECTOR ON CKT (1 & 4 OR 2 & 3).
- OBSERVE INJECTOR TEST LIGHT.
- TEST LIGHT SHOULD BE BLINKING. IS IT?

LIGHT "OFF" →
- DISCONNECT INJECTOR TEST LIGHT.
- PROBE INJECTOR HARNESS CONNECTOR IGNITION FEED (GRY WIRE) TERMINAL AT INJECTOR WITH A TEST LIGHT TO GROUND.
- CRANK ENGINE.
- TEST LIGHT SHOULD BE "ON" WHILE CRANKING. IS IT?

BLINKING LIGHT → PERFORM INJECTOR COIL/BALANCE TEST PROCEDURE.

YES →
CHECK CKT 467 OR 468 FOR SHORT TO VOLTAGE, OPEN OR VISUALLY INSPECT PINK C-D PCM CONNECTOR TO SEE IF THE CONNECTION IS CLEAN AND TIGHT. IF OK, REPLACE PCM.

NO →
REPAIR OPEN OR GROUNDED CIRCUIT BETWEEN CAVITY "A" OF 3-WAY INJECTOR HARNESS CONNECTOR AND INJECTOR CONNECTOR.

88252G34

Fig. 30 Ignition system diagnosis (3 of 3)—1993–94 2.3L engine

---

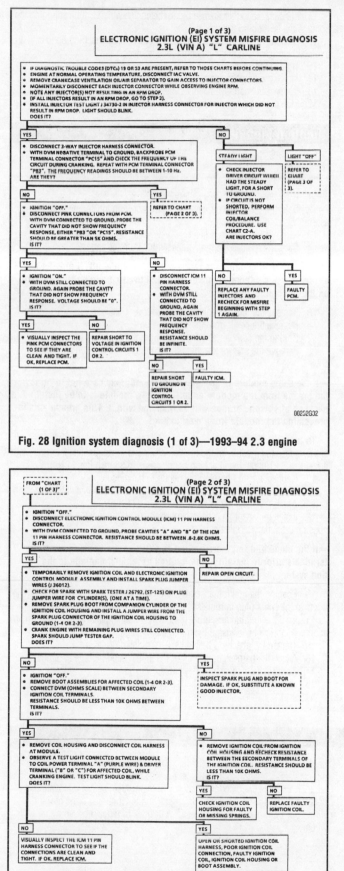

(Page 2 of 3)
ELECTRONIC IGNITION (EI) SYSTEM MISFIRE DIAGNOSIS
2.3L (VIN A) "L" CARLINE

FROM "CHART (1 OF 3)"

- IGNITION "OFF."
- DISCONNECT ELECTRONIC IGNITION CONTROL MODULE (ICM) 11 PIN HARNESS CONNECTOR.
- WITH DVM CONNECTED TO GROUND, PROBE CAVITIES "A" AND "B" OF THE ICM 11 PIN HARNESS CONNECTOR. RESISTANCE SHOULD BE BETWEEN .6-2.6K OHMS. IS IT?

YES →
- TEMPORARILY REMOVE IGNITION COIL AND ELECTRONIC IGNITION CONTROL MODULE ASSEMBLY AND INSTALL SPARK PLUG JUMPER WIRES (J 36012).
- CHECK FOR SPARK WITH SPARK TESTER J 26792. (ST-125) ON PLUG JUMPER WIRE FOR CYLINDER(S), (ONE AT A TIME).
- REMOVE SPARK PLUG BOOT FROM COMPANION CYLINDER OF THE IGNITION COIL HOUSING AND INSTALL A JUMPER WIRE FROM THE SPARK PLUG CONNECTOR OF THE IGNITION COIL HOUSING TO GROUND (1-4 OR 2-3).
- CRANK ENGINE WITH REMAINING PLUG WIRES STILL CONNECTED. SPARK SHOULD JUMP TESTER GAP. DOES IT?

NO → REPAIR OPEN CIRCUIT.

NO →
- IGNITION "OFF."
- REMOVE BOOT ASSEMBLIES FOR AFFECTED COIL (1-4 OR 2-3).
- CONNECT DVM (OHMS SCALE) BETWEEN SECONDARY IGNITION COIL TERMINALS. RESISTANCE SHOULD BE LESS THAN 10K OHMS BETWEEN TERMINALS. IS IT?

YES → INSPECT SPARK PLUG AND BOOT FOR DAMAGE. IF OK, SUBSTITUTE A KNOWN GOOD INJECTOR.

YES →
- REMOVE COIL HOUSING AND DISCONNECT COIL HARNESS AT MODULE.
- OBSERVE A TEST LIGHT CONNECTED BETWEEN MODULE TO COIL POWER TERMINAL "A" (PURPLE WIRE) & DRIVER TERMINAL ("B" OR "C") FOR AFFECTED COIL, WHILE CRANKING ENGINE. TEST LIGHT SHOULD BLINK. DOES IT?

NO →
- REMOVE IGNITION COIL FROM IGNITION COIL HOUSING AND RECHECK RESISTANCE BETWEEN THE SECONDARY TERMINALS OF THE IGNITION COIL. RESISTANCE SHOULD BE LESS THAN 10K OHMS. IS IT?

YES → CHECK IGNITION COIL HOUSING FOR FAULTY OR MISSING SPRINGS.

NO → REPLACE FAULTY IGNITION COIL.

NO → VISUALLY INSPECT THE ICM 11 PIN HARNESS CONNECTOR TO SEE IF THE CONNECTIONS ARE CLEAN AND TIGHT. IF OK, REPLACE ICM.

YES → OPEN OR SHORTED IGNITION COIL HARNESS, POOR IGNITION COIL CONNECTION, FAULTY IGNITION COIL, IGNITION COIL HOUSING OR BOOT ASSEMBLY.

"AFTER REPAIRS," CONFIRM "CLOSED LOOP" OPERATION AND NO MIL (SERVICE ENGINE SOON).

88252G33

Fig. 29 Ignition system diagnosis (2 of 3)—1993–94 2.3L engine

---

Ignition Coil and Module Assembly

REMOVAL & INSTALLATION

◆ See Figure 31

1. Disconnect the negative battery cable.
2. Detach the 11-pin (1990–92 vehicles), or 8-pin (1993–94 vehicles) harness connector from the coil and module assembly.
3. Remove the 4 ignition assembly-to-camshaft housing attaching bolts.

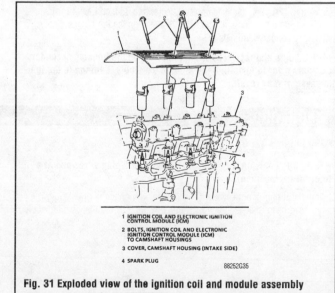

1 IGNITION COIL AND ELECTRONIC IGNITION CONTROL MODULE (ICM)
2 BOLTS, IGNITION COIL AND ELECTRONIC IGNITION CONTROL MODULE (ICM) TO CAMSHAFT HOUSINGS
3 COVER, CAMSHAFT HOUSING (INTAKE SIDE)
4 SPARK PLUG

88252G35

Fig. 31 Exploded view of the ignition coil and module assembly

4. Carefully remove the ignition coil and module assembly from the engine.

➡️ **If the spark plug boots stick to the plugs, use tool J 36011, or equivalent, to remove the boots by first twisting, then pulling up on the retainers.**

To install:

5. Install the spark plug boots and retainers on the ignition assembly housing secondary terminals.

➡️ **If the boots and retainers are not in place on the housing secondary terminals prior to installing the ignition assembly, damage to the ignition system may result.**

6. Position the ignition assembly to the engine while carefully aligning the boots to the spark plug terminals.
7. Coat the ignition assembly-to-camshaft housing attaching bolts with 1052080 or equivalent lubricant and install them into the housing.
8. Tighten the attaching bolts to 16–19 ft. lbs. (22–26 Nm).
9. Attach the harness connector to the ignition coil module assembly.
10. Connect the negative battery cable.
11. Start the engine check for proper operation and performance.

Ignition Coil

REMOVAL & INSTALLATION

1. Disconnect the negative battery cable.
2. Detach the 8 or 11-pin harness connector, as applicable, from the coil and module assembly.
3. Remove the ignition assembly-to-camshaft housing attaching bolts.
4. Carefully remove the ignition assembly from the engine.

➡️ **If the spark plug boots present a problem coming off, it may be necessary to use a special removal tool, first twisting and pulling upward on the retainers.**

5. Remove the ignition coil housing-to-cover bolts/screws.
6. Remove the cover from the coil housing.
7. Detach the ignition coil harness connectors from the coil pack assembly.
8. Carefully lift the coil pack out and remove the contacts and seals from the housing.

To install:

9. Install new coil seals into the coil housing.
10. Install the coil contacts to the coil housing and retain with petroleum jelly.
11. Place the coil pack into the housing and connect the harness connectors.
12. Assemble the cover to the coil housing and install the attaching bolts/screws. Tighten the attaching bolts/screws to 35 inch lbs. (4 Nm).
13. Install the spark plug boots and retainers on the ignition assembly housing secondary terminals.

➡️ **If the boots and retainers are not in place on the housing secondary terminals prior to installing the ignition assembly, damage to the ignition system may result.**

14. Position the ignition assembly to the engine while carefully aligning the boots to the spark plug terminals.
15. Coat the ignition assembly-to-camshaft housing attaching bolts with an approved lubricant and install them into the housing.
16. Tighten the attaching bolts to 16–19 ft. lbs. (22–26 Nm).
17. Attach the harness connector to the ignition coil module assembly.
18. Connect the negative battery cable.
19. Start the engine and check for proper operation and performance.

Ignition Module

REMOVAL & INSTALLATION

1. Disconnect the negative battery cable.
2. Detach the 8 or 11-pin harness connector from the coil and module assembly.
3. Remove the ignition assembly-to-camshaft housing attaching bolts.
4. Carefully remove the ignition assembly from the engine.

➡️ **If the spark plug boots present a problem coming off, it may be necessary to use a special removal tool, first twisting and pulling upward on the retainers.**

5. Remove the ignition coil housing-to-cover bolts/screws.
6. Remove the cover from the coil housing.
7. Unplug the coil harness connector from the module.
8. Remove the screws attaching the module to the ignition assembly cover.

➡️ **If the same module is going to be replaced, take care not to remove the grease from the module or coil. If a new module is to be installed, a package of silicone grease will be included with it. This grease aids in preventing the module from overheating.**

To install:

9. Place the module on the ignition cover and install the attaching bolts/screws. Tighten the attaching bolts/screws to 35 inch lbs. (4 Nm).
10. Connect the coil harness connector to the module.
11. Assemble the module cover to the coil housing and install the attaching bolts. Tighten the attaching bolts to 35 inch lbs. (4 Nm).
12. Install the spark plug boots and retainers on the ignition assembly housing secondary terminals.

➡️ **If the boots and retainers are not in place on the housing secondary terminals prior to installing the ignition assembly, damage to the ignition system may result.**

13. Position the ignition assembly to the engine while carefully aligning the boots to the spark plug terminals.
14. Coat the ignition assembly-to-camshaft housing attaching bolts with an approved lubricant and install them into the housing.
15. Tighten the attaching bolts to 16–19 ft. lbs. (22–26 Nm).
16. Attach the harness connector to the ignition coil module assembly.
17. Connect the negative battery cable.
18. Start the engine and check for proper operation and performance.

FIRING ORDERS

▶ **See Figures 32, 33 and 34**

➡️ **To avoid confusion, remove and tag the spark plug wires one at a time, for replacement.**

If a distributor is not keyed for installation with only one orientation, it could have been removed previously and rewired. The resultant wiring would hold the correct firing order, but could change the relative placement of the plug towers in relation to the engine. For this reason it is imperative that you label all wires before disconnecting any of them. Also, before removal, compare the current wiring with the accompanying illustrations. If the current wiring does not match, make notes in your book to reflect how your engine is wired.

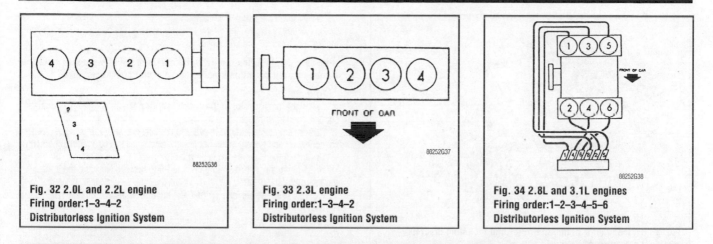

Fig. 32 2.0L and 2.2L engine
Firing order:1–3–4–2
Distributorless Ignition System

Fig. 33 2.3L engine
Firing order:1–3–4–2
Distributorless Ignition System

Fig. 34 2.8L and 3.1L engines
Firing order:1–2–3–4–5–6
Distributorless Ignition System

CHARGING SYSTEM

ALTERNATOR PRECAUTIONS

Observing these precautions will ensure safe handling of the electrical system components, and will avoid damage to the vehicle's electrical system:

• Be absolutely sure of the polarity of a booster battery before making connections. Connect the cables positive to positive, and negative to negative. Connect positive cables first and then make the last connection to ground on the body of the booster vehicle so that arcing cannot ignite hydrogen gas that may have accumulated near the battery. Even momentary connection of a booster battery with the polarity reversed will damage alternator diodes.

• Disconnect both vehicle battery cables before attempting to charge a battery.

• Never ground the alternator or generator output or battery terminal. Be cautious when using metal tools around a battery to avoid creating a short circuit between the terminals.

• Never ground the field circuit between the alternator and regulator.

• Never run an alternator or generator without load unless the field circuit is disconnected.

• Never attempt to polarize an alternator.

• Keep the regulator cover in place when taking voltage and current limiter readings.

• Use insulated tools when adjusting the regulator.

• Whenever DC generator-to-regulator wires have been disconnected, the generator must be repolarized. To do this with an externally grounded, light duty generator, momentarily place a jumper wires between the battery terminal and the generator terminal of the regulator. With an internally grounded heavy duty unit, disconnect the wire to the regulator field terminal and touch the regulator battery terminal with it.

CHARGING SYSTEM TROUBLESHOOTING

There are many possible ways in which the charging system can malfunction. Often the source of a problem is difficult to diagnose, requiring special equipment and a good deal of experience. This is usually not the case, however, where the charging system fails completely and causes the dash board warning light to come on or the battery to become dead. To troubleshoot a complete system failure only two pieces of equipment are needed: a test light, to determine that current is reaching a certain point; and a current indicator (voltmeter), to determine the direction of the current flow and its measurement in Volts.

This test works under three assumptions:
1. The battery is known to be good and fully charged.
2. The alternator belt is in good condition and adjusted to the proper tension.
3. All connections in the system are clean and tight.

➥In order for the current indicator to give a valid reading, the car must be equipped with battery cables which are of the same gauge size and quality as original equipment battery cables.

4. For vehicles without charge indicator lamp, go to step 7.
5. With the switch **ON**, engine stopped, the lamp should be on. If not, detach the harness at the alternator and ground the **L** terminal.

• If the lamp lights, replace or repair the alternator.
• If the lamp does not light, locate the open circuit between the grounding lead and the ignition switch. Lamp may be open.
6. With the switch on and the engine running at moderate speed, the lamp should be off. If not, detach the wiring harness at the alternator.
• If the lamp goes off, replace or repair the alternator.
• If the lamp stays on, check for a grounded **L** terminal in the wiring harness.
7. Battery undercharged or overcharged.
• Detach the wiring harness connector from the alternator.
• With the switch on, engine not running, connect the voltmeter from ground to the **L** terminal.
• A zero reading indicates an open circuit between the terminal and the battery. Correct as required.
• Reconnect the harness connector to the alternator and run the engine at moderate speed.
• Measure the voltage across the battery. If above 16V, replace or repair alternator
8. Turn on the accessories, load the battery with a carbon pile (variable rheostat that controls the flow of electric current) to obtain maximum amperage. Maintain voltage at 13V or below.
• If within 15 amperes of rated output, the alternator is OK.
• If not within 15 amperes of rated output, replace or repair alternator.

REMOVAL & INSTALLATION

2.0 and 2.2L Engines

▶ See Figure 35

1. Disconnect the negative battery cable.

❊❊ CAUTION

Failure to disconnect the negative cable may result in injury from the positive battery lead at the alternator, and may short the alternator and regulator during the removal process.

2. Remove the serpentine drive belt from the alternator.
3. For 1990–92 vehicles remove the 3 bolts from the alternator brace (including bolt from the alternator to the brace).
4. For 1993–96 vehicles, remove the 2 bolts from the alternator brace (including bolt from the alternator to the brace).
5. For 1988–90 vehicles, remove the two alternator mounting bolts.
6. For 1991–96 vehicles, perform the following:
   a. Remove the upper bracket nut from the exhaust manifold.
   b. Remove the upper bracket bolt.
   c. Remove the upper bracket with the heat shield.
7. Detach the alternator electrical connections.
8. Remove the alternator from the vehicle.
9. Installation is the reverse of the removal procedure. Note the following tightening specifications:

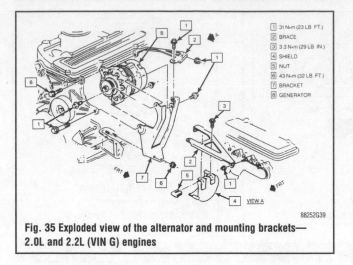

```
1  31 N·m (23 LB. FT.)
2  BRACE
3  3.3 N·m (29 LB. IN.)
4  SHIELD
5  NUT
6  43 N·m (32 LB. FT.)
7  BRACKET
8  GENERATOR
```

Fig. 35 Exploded view of the alternator and mounting brackets— 2.0L and 2.2L (VIN G) engines

- Battery lead nut: 65 inch lbs. (7.5 Nm)
- Rear alternator mounting bolt: 22 ft. lbs. (30 Nm)
- Upper bracket bolt and nut (1988–92 vehicles): 22 ft. lbs. (30 Nm)
- Bracket nuts (1993–96 vehicles): 32 ft. lbs. (43 Nm)
- Upper alternator mounting bolts: 22 ft. lbs. (30 Nm)
- Lower alternator mounting bolt and nut: 33–37 ft. lbs. (45–50 Nm)

2.3L Engine

♦ See Figure 36

1. Disconnect the negative battery cable.
2. Remove the serpentine drive belt.

☀ CAUTION

When rotating the serpentine belt tensioner, be sure to use tool J 37059 or a tight fitting 13mm wrench at least 24 in. (610mm) long to avoid personal injury.

3. Remove the coolant and washer reservoir attaching screws.
4. Detach the washer fluid pump electrical connector, then and position the reservoir aside.
5. If equipped, remove the A/C line rail clip.
6. If equipped, disconnect the 2 vacuum lines at the front of the engine and remove vacuum harness attaching bracket.
7. Remove the alternator mounting bolts.
8. Reposition the alternator to access the wiring, then tag and detach the alternator electrical connections and battery lead.

9. Position the harness out of the way.
10. Carefully remove the alternator from between the mounting bracket and the A/C compressor and condenser hoses.

➡ Be very careful when removing or installing the alternator as not to damage the air conditioner compressor and/or condenser hoses.

To install:
11. Place the alternator in the vehicle, between the air conditioner compressor and condenser hoses.
12. Position the alternator in order to connect the wiring. Attach the electrical connector and battery lead. Tighten the battery lead to 65 inch lbs. (7.5 Nm).
13. Install the alternator mounting bolts.
14. Tighten the rear mounting bolts to 20 ft. lbs. (26 Nm) and the front mounting bolt to 37–40 ft. lbs. (50–54 Nm).
15. For 1990–91 vehicles, tighten the upper front mounting bolt to 19 ft. lbs. (26 Nm).
16. Install the remaining components in the reverse of the removal procedure.
17. Connect the negative battery cable, then start the engine and perform a charging system test.

2.8L and 3.1L Engines

♦ See Figure 37

1. Disconnect the negative battery cable.
2. Remove the serpentine drive belt.
3. If accessible at this time, detach the alternator electrical connector.
4. Remove the three alternator mounting bolts.
5. For 1995–96 vehicles, detach the alternator air intake connector.
6. Label and detach the remaining electrical connector(s) from the back of the alternator.
7. Remove the alternator from the vehicle.
8. Installtion is the reverse of the removal procedure. Note the following tightening specifications:
- Battery lead nut: 65 inch lbs. (7.5 Nm)
- Rear stud and bolt: 18 ft. lbs. (25 Nm)
- Front bolt: 18 ft. lbs. (25 Nm)
- Rear bolt to support to 37 ft. lbs. (50 Nm)
9. Connect the negative battery cable, then start the engine and perform a charging system test.

Regulator

A solid state regulator is mounted within the alternator. All regulator components are enclosed in a solid mold. The regulator is non-adjustable and requires no maintenance. A solid state regulator is mounted within the alternator. All regulator components are enclosed in a solid mold. The regulator is non-adjustable and requires no maintenance.

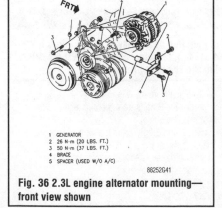

```
1  GENERATOR
2  26 N·m (20 LBS. FT.)
3  50 N·m (37 LBS. FT.)
4  BRACE
5  SPACER (USED W/O A/C)
```

Fig. 36 2.3L engine alternator mounting— front view shown

Remove the serpentine drive belt from the alternator

Unplug the alternator electrical connector

Remove the alternator mounting bolts

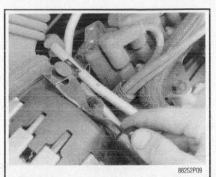

To remove the air intake connector, use a suitable tool (see arrow) to unfasten the retainers . . .

. . . then pull the air intake connector from the back of the alternator

Unfasten the retaining nut securing the BAT cable to the alternator . . .

. . . then detach the remaining connector(s) and remove the alternator from the vehicle

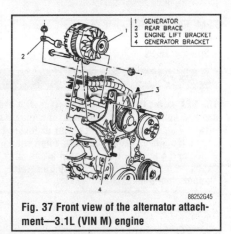

1	GENERATOR
2	REAR BRACE
3	ENGINE LIFT BRACKET
4	GENERATOR BRACKET

Fig. 37 Front view of the alternator attachment—3.1L (VIN M) engine

STARTING SYSTEM

Starter

TESTING

▶ **See Figure 38**

1. Make the connections as shown in the accompanying figure.
2. Close the switch and compare the RPM, current and voltage readings with the following values.

• 2.0L engine: No load test @ 10 volts—50–75 amps, RPM at drive pinion—6,000–11,900 rpm
• 1990 2.2L engine: No load test @ 10 volts—50–75 amps, RPM at drive pinion—6,000–11,900 rpm

• 1991 2.2L engine: No load test @ 10 volts—55–85 amps, RPM at drive pinion—7,500–12,000 rpm
• 1992 2.2L engine: No load test @ 10 volts—45–75 amps, RPM at drive pinion—6,000–11,000 rpm
• 1993 2.2L engine: No load test @ 10 volts—52–76 amps, RPM at drive pinion—6,000–12,000 rpm
• 1994–95 2.2L engine: No load test @ 10 volts—45–75 amps, RPM at drive pinion—6,000–11,000 rpm
• 1996 2.2L engine: No load test @ 10 volts—50–75 amps, RPM at drive pinion—6,000–12,000 rpm
• 1990 2.3L engine: No load test @ 10 volts—50–75 amps, RPM at drive pinion—6,000–11,900 rpm
• 1991–93 2.3L engine: No load test @ 10 volts—52–76 amps, RPM at drive pinion—6,000–12,000 rpm
• 1994 2.3L engine: No load test @ 10 volts—50–75 amps, RPM at drive pinion—6,000–12,000 rpm
• 2.8L engine: No load test @ 10 volts—50–75 amps, RPM at drive pinion—6,000–11,900 rpm
• 1990 3.1L engine: No load test @ 10 volts—50–75 amps, RPM at drive pinion—6,000–11,900 rpm
• 1991–95 3.1L engine: No load test @ 10 volts—45–75 amps, RPM at drive pinion—6,000–11,000 rpm
• 1996 3.1L engine: No load test @ 10 volts—50–75 amps, RPM at drive pinion—6,000–12,000 rpm

3. Rated current draw and no load speed indicates normal condition of the starter motor.
4. Low free speed and high current draw indicates:
• Too much friction. Tight, dirty, or worn bushings, bent armature shaft allowing armature to drag.
• Shorted armature. This can be further checked on a growler after disassembly.
• Grounded armature or fields. Check further after assembly.

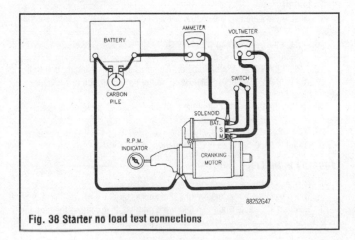

Fig. 38 Starter no load test connections

5. Failure to operate with high current draw indicates:
- A direct ground in the terminal or fields.
- "Frozen" bearings.

6. Failure to operate with low or no current draw indicates:
- Open solenoid windings.
- Open field circuit. This can be checked after disassembly by inspecting internal connections and tracing the circuit with a test lamp.
- Open armature coils. Inspect the commutator for badly burned bar after disassembly.
- Broken brush springs, worn brushes, high insulation between the commutator bars of other causes which would prevent good contact between the brushes and commutator.

7. Low no-load speed and low current draw indicates:
- High internal resistance due to poor connections, defective leads, dirty commutator and causes listed under Step 6.

8. High free speed and high current drain usually indicate shorted fields. If shorted fields are suspected, replace the field and frame assembly. Also check for shorted armature using a growler.

REMOVAL & INSTALLATION

♦ **See Figure 39**

☀ CAUTION

The EPA warns that prolonged contact with used engine oil may cause a number of skin disorders, including cancer! You should make every effort to minimize your exposure to used engine oil. Protective gloves should be worn when changing the oil. Wash your hands and any other exposed skin areas as soon as possible after exposure to used engine oil. Soap and water, or waterless hand cleaner should be used.

2.0L and 2.2L Engines

1988 VEHICLES

1. Disconnect the negative battery cable at the battery.
2. Raise and support the car safely.
3. Remove the solenoid wires and the battery cable.
4. Remove the rear motor support bracket.
5. Remove the air conditioning compressor support rod (if so equipped).
6. Remove the two starter-to-engine bolts, and allow the starter to drop down. Note the location and number of any shims (if used). Remove the starter.
7. Installation is the reverse of removal. Torque the 2 mounting bolts to 26–37 ft. lbs. (30–50 Nm).

1989–96 VEHICLES

1. Disconnect the negative battery cable from the battery.
2. Raise and safely support the vehicle.
3. For 1995–96 vehicles equipped with manual transaxles, remove the bending brace.
4. Remove the solenoid wires and the battery cable from the starter.
5. If equipped, remove the wiring clamp from the support bracket.

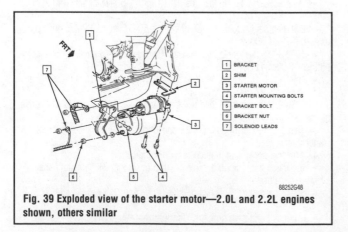

1	BRACKET
2	SHIM
3	STARTER MOTOR
4	STARTER MOUNTING BOLTS
5	BRACKET BOLT
6	BRACKET NUT
7	SOLENOID LEADS

88252G48

Fig. 39 Exploded view of the starter motor—2.0L and 2.2L engines shown, others similar

6. Remove the support bracket-to-engine bolt.
7. Remove the 2 bolts from the starter motor.
8. Remove the starter motor and shims, if equipped.
9. Installation is the reverse of the removal procedure. Tighten the starter mounting bolts to 32 ft. lbs. (43 Nm) and the ssupport bracket bolt to 24 ft. lbs. (32 Nm). Tighten the wiring clamp-to-support bracket bolt to 106 inch lbs. (12 Nm).

2.3L Engine

1990 VEHICLES

1. Disconnect the negative battery cable.
2. Detach the electrical connector from the cooling fan.
3. Remove the cooling fan mounting bolts and remove the fan assembly.

➡**You can use a 15mm socket with a 6 inch extension to remove the brace-to-starter bolt.**

4. Remove the intake manifold-to-engine brace bolts and remove the brace from the engine.
5. Remove the starter mounting bolts.
6. Carefully lift the starter away from the engine with the solenoid harness attached to it.
7. When the starter is clear, detach the solenoid harness connections and lift the starter up and out toward the front of the vehicle.
To install:
8. Attach the solenoid harness connections to the starter, while supporting the starter toward the mounting position.
9. Rotate the starter so the solenoid faces the engine at a slight angle to clear the bottom of the intake manifold.
10. Position the starter to the engine and install the mounting bolts. Tighten the bolts to 32 ft. lbs. (43 Nm).
11. Install the intake manifold-to-engine brace and the attaching bolts.
12. Install the cooling fan and attaching bolts. Tighten bolts to 89 inch lbs. (10 Nm). Attach the cooling fan electrical connector.
13. Connect the negative battery cable, then crank the engine and check for proper starter operation.

1991 VEHICLES

1. Disconnect the negative battery cable.
2. Remove the serpentine drive belt.
3. Remove the coolant reservoir.
4. Unfasten the A/C rail line clip.
5. Remove the alternator, as outlined in this section.
6. Remove the dipstick, bolt and oil filler tube.
7. Remove the alternator bracket.
8. Remove the air cleaner assembly.
9. Remove the upper transaxle-to-starter mounting bolt.
10. Remove the oil filter.
11. Remove the lower starter mounting bolt.
12. Position the starter for access to the solenoid wiring.
13. Disconnect the electrical wiring.
14. Remove the starter from the vehicle, routing through the front of the engine between the intake manifold and engine block.
To install:
15. Install the starter by lowering it between the intake manifold and engine block.
16. Attach the starter electrical connectors.
17. Position the starter to the engine.
18. Install the starter mounting bolts. Tighten the lower mounting bolt to 46 ft. lbs. (63 Nm) and the upper transaxle-to-starter mounting bolt to 71 ft. lbs. (96 Nm).
19. Install the remaining components in the reverse of the removal procedure.
20. Connect the negative battery cable.
21. Refill the engine oil as necessary and check for leaks.

1992–94 VEHICLES

1. Disconnect the negative battery cable.
2. Disconnect the air induction tubing, as necessary.
3. Position a suitable drain pan under the oil filter, then remove the oil filter.

4. Remove the starter mounting bolts.

5. Position the starter to access the wiring, then disconnect the electrical wiring.

6. Remove the starter from the vehicle.

7. Installation is the reverse of the removal procedure. Tighten the mounting bolts to 74 ft lbs. (100 Nm).

2.8L and 3.1L Engines

1988–89 VEHICLES

1. Disconnect the negative battery cable from the battery.
2. Raise and support the car safely.
3. Remove the solenoid wires and the battery cable from the starter.
4. For 1989 vehicles, place a drain pan under the engine oil pan and remove the oil filter.
5. Remove the 2 starter motor to engine bolts and remove the starter. Note the location and number of any shims (if used).
6. Installation is the reverse of removal. Tighten the 2 retaining bolts to 32 ft. lbs. (43 Nm).

1990 VEHICLES

1. Disconnect the negative battery cable.
2. Remove the air cleaner assembly, as required.
3. Raise and safely support the vehicle.

➡If equipped with an oil cooler, remove the oil filter and position the hose next to the starter to the side.

4. Remove the air conditioning compressor brace attaching nuts and remove the brace from the engine, as required.
5. Remove flywheel inspection cover bolts and remove the inspection cover, as required.
6. Remove the starter attaching bolts.
7. Carefully lower the starter and remove the shims. Note the number and position of any shims.
8. Detach the electrical wiring connections at the starter.
9. Installation is the reverse of the removal procedure. Tighten the starter mounting bolts to 32 ft. lbs. (43 Nm).
10. Connect the negative battery cable, then crank the engine and check the starter operation.

1991–96 VEHICLES

1. Disconnect the negative battery cable at the battery.
2. Raise and support the car safely.
3. Remove the starter motor-to-engine bolt(s).
4. If necessary, remove the retaining bolts, then remove the flywheel dust cover.
5. Remove the remaining starter-to-engine bolt(s).
6. Partially lower the starter to access the wiring.

7. Support the starter, then disconnect the electrical leads.
8. Remove the starter from the vehicle. Note the location and number of any shims (if used).

To install:

9. Support the starter motor and attach the electrical leads.
10. Raise the starter into installed position and install the starter-to-engine bolt(s). Tighten to 32 ft. lbs. (43 Nm).
11. If removed, install the flywheel dust cover and secure with the retaining bolts.
12. Tighten the remaining starter mounting bolt(s) to 32 ft. lbs. (43 Nm).
13. Carefully lower the vehicle, then connect the negative battery cable.

Remove the accessible starter mounting bolts

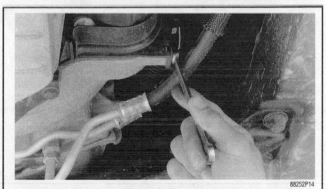

On some vehicles it may be necessary to unfasten the flywheel dust cover retaining bolts . . .

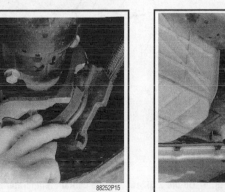

. . . then remove the flywheel dust cover from the starter

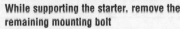

While supporting the starter, remove the remaining mounting bolt

Partially lower the starter, detach the wiring, then remove the starter motor from the vehicle

SENDING UNITS

➡This section describes the operating principles of sending units, warning lights and gauges. Sensors which provide information to the Electronic Control Module (ECM) are covered in Section 4 of this manual.

Instrument panels contain a number of indicating devices (gauges and warning lights). These devices are composed of two separate components. One is the sending unit, mounted on the engine or other remote part of the vehicle, and the other is the actual gauge or light in the instrument panel.

Several types of sending units exist, however most can be characterized as being either a pressure type or a resistance type. Pressure type sending units convert liquid pressure into an electrical signal which is sent to the gauge. Resistance type sending units are most often used to measure temperature and use variable resistance to control the current flow back to the indicating device. Both types of sending units are connected in series by a wire to the battery (through the ignition switch). When the ignition is turned **ON**, current flows from the battery through the indicating device and on to the sending unit.

Low Coolant Sensor

OPERATION

The low coolant sensor activates a light in the instrument cluster when the coolant in the radiator goes below a certain level. The sensor is mounted on the radiator's right side tank.

REMOVAL & INSTALLATION

▶ **See Figure 40**

1. Disconnect the negative battery cable.
2. Partially drain the radiator, into a suitable container, to a level below the sensor.
3. Detach the electrical connector from the sensor.
4. Remove the sensor. To unlock the sensor, lift one leg of the snap clip from its locked position and pull outward with a slight twisting motion. Remove and discard the O-ring.
   To install:
5. Lubricate a new O-ring seal with clean coolant.
6. Place the snap clip leg in the place.
7. Install the sensor. Attach the electrical connector to the sensor.
8. Fill the radiator to the proper level with coolant.
9. Connect the negative battery cable.

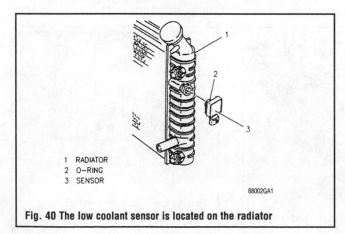

1 RADIATOR
2 O-RING
3 SENSOR

88002GA1

Fig. 40 The low coolant sensor is located on the radiator

Coolant Temperature Sensor

OPERATION

The coolant temperature sensor changes resistance as the coolant temperature increases and decreases.

TESTING

1. Remove the temperature sender from the engine.
2. Position the water temperature sending unit in such a way that the metal shaft (opposite end from the electrical connectors) is situated in a pot of water. Make sure that the electrical connector is not submerged and that only the tip of the sending unit's body is in the water.
3. Heat the pot of water at a medium rate. While the water is warming, continue to measure the resistance of the terminal and the metal body of the sending unit:
   a. As the water warms up, the resistance exhibited by the ohmmeter goes down in a steady manner: the sending unit is good.
   b. As the water warms up, the resistance does not change or changes in erratic jumps: the sender is bad, replace it with a new one.
4. Install the good or new sending unit into the engine, then connect the negative battery cable.

REMOVAL & INSTALLATION

▶ **See Figure 41**

1. Disconnect the negative battery cable.
2. Properly drain the engine coolant into a suitable container.
3. Disconnect the sensor electrical lead and unscrew the sensor. The coolant sensor can be found on the front, left side of the engine block, visible through, or below, the manifold, or threaded into the thermostat housing or water outlet.
   To install:
4. Install the sensor and tighten it to 17 ft. lbs. (23 Nm).
5. Connect the sensor electrical lead.
6. Connect the battery cable and fill the engine with the proper type and amount of coolant.

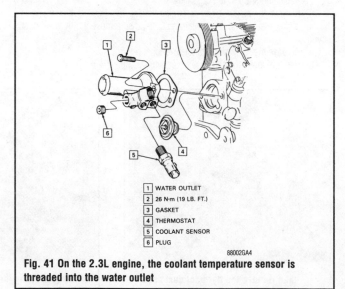

1 WATER OUTLET
2 26 N·m (19 LB. FT.)
3 GASKET
4 THERMOSTAT
5 COOLANT SENSOR
6 PLUG

88002GA4

Fig. 41 On the 2.3L engine, the coolant temperature sensor is threaded into the water outlet

Oil Level Sensor

OPERATION

The low oil level sensor activates a light in the instrument cluster when the oil level in the pan goes below a certain level. The sensor is mounted on the oil pan.

REMOVAL & INSTALLATION

♦ See Figure 42

1. Disconnect the negative battery cable.
2. Raise and safely support the vehicle.
3. Position a suitable drain pan under the sensor.
4. Detach the sensor connector harness.
5. Drain the engine oil into a suitable container.
6. Remove the oil level sensor.

To Install:

7. Install the oil level sensor and tighten it to 89 inch lbs. (10 Nm).
8. Attach the sensor harness connector.
9. Carefully lower the vehicle.
10. Add the correct type and amount of engine oil to the crankcase, then connect the negative battery cable.

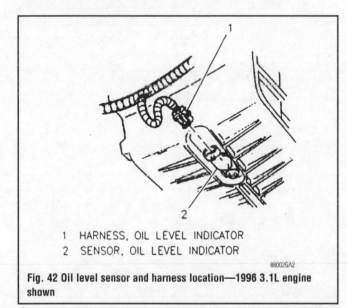

1 HARNESS, OIL LEVEL INDICATOR
2 SENSOR, OIL LEVEL INDICATOR

88002GA2

Fig. 42 Oil level sensor and harness location—1996 3.1L engine shown

Oil Pressure Sender

OPERATION

The oil pressure sender relays to the dash gauge the oil pressure in the engine.

TESTING

1. To test the normally closed oil lamp circuit, disengage the locking connector and measure the resistance between the switch terminal (terminal for the wire to the warning lamp) and the metal housing. The ohmmeter should read 0 ohms.
2. To test the sending unit, measure the resistance between the sending unit terminal and the metal housing. The ohmmeter should read an open circuit (infinite resistance).
3. Start the engine.

4. Once again, test each terminal against the metal housing:
   a. The oil switch terminal-to-housing circuit should read an open circuit if there is oil pressure present.
   b. The sending unit-to-housing circuit should read between 15–80 ohms, depending on the engine speed, oil temperature and oil viscosity.
5. To test the oil pressure sender only, rev the engine and watch the ohms reading, which should fluctuate slightly (within the range of 15–80 ohms) as rpm increases.
6. If the above results were not obtained, replace the sending unit/switch with a new one.

REMOVAL & INSTALLATION

♦ See Figures 43, 44 and 45

1. Remove the air cleaner assembly.
2. Disconnect the negative battery cable.
3. Raise and safely support the vehicle.
4. Position a suitable drain pan under the switch.
5. If the vehicle is equipped with a gauge package (large sensor assem-

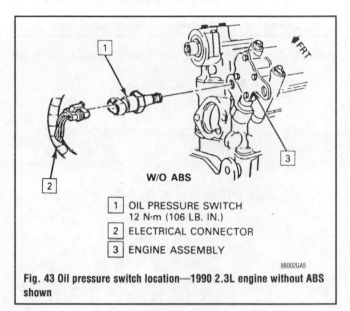

W/O ABS

1	OIL PRESSURE SWITCH 12 N·m (106 LB. IN.)
2	ELECTRICAL CONNECTOR
3	ENGINE ASSEMBLY

88002GA5

Fig. 43 Oil pressure switch location—1990 2.3L engine without ABS shown

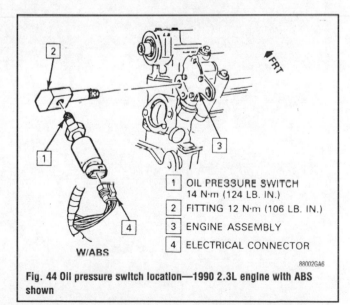

W/ABS

1	OIL PRESSURE SWITCH 14 N·m (124 LB. IN.)
2	FITTING 12 N·m (106 LB. IN.)
3	ENGINE ASSEMBLY
4	ELECTRICAL CONNECTOR

88002GA6

Fig. 44 Oil pressure switch location—1990 2.3L engine with ABS shown

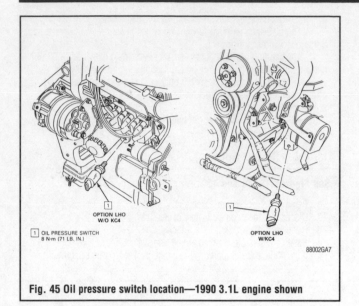

Fig. 45 Oil pressure switch location—1990 3.1L engine shown

bly) and does not have and oil cooler, drain the engine oil, then remove the oil filter.

6. Detach the sensor electrical connector.
7. Remove the sensor.

To install:

8. Coat the first two or three threads with sealer. Install the sensor and tighten until snug. Engage the electrical lead.
9. If removed, install the oil filter.
10. Carefully lower the vehicle.
11. Connect the negative battery cable and fill the engine with oil.

Fan Switch

OPERATION

The fan circuit contains the auxiliary fan, coolant temperature sensor and a relay. When the sensor reaches a predetermined temperature, it closes the circuit to the relay. This energizes the relay sending 12 volts to the fan. When the temperature decreases below the set point of the sensor, the circuit opens and the voltage is no longer applied to the fan.

REMOVAL & INSTALLATION

1. Disconnect the negative battery cable.
2. Disconnect the sensor electrical lead and unscrew the sensor.

To install:

3. Install the sensor or relay and connect the electrical lead.
4. Connect the battery cable.

3

ENGINE AND ENGINE OVERHAUL

ENGINE MECHANICAL

2.0L (VIN 1) ENGINE SPECIFICATIONS

Description	English	Metric
Type	Inline Overhead Valve (OHV)	
Displacement	122 cu. in.	2.0L (2000cc)
Number of Cylinders	4	
Bore	3.500 in.	88.9mm
Stroke	3.150 in.	80mm
Compression ratio	9.0:1	
Pistons and rings		
Ring gap		
1st compression ring	0.010-0.020 in.	0.254-0.508mm
2nd compression ring	0.010-0.020 in.	0.254-0.508mm
Oil ring	0.010-0.050in.	0.254-1.270mm
Ring side clearance		
1st compression ring	0.001-0.003 in.	0.025-0.076mm
2nd compression ring	0.001-0.003 in.	0.025-0.076mm
Oil ring	0.0080 in.	0.2032mm
Piston Clearance	0.0010-0.0022 in.	0.0254-0.0059mm
Camshaft		
Journal diameter	1.867-1.869 in.	47.42-47.47mm
Bearing clearance	0.001-0.004 in.	0.025-0.102mm
Elevation		
Intake	0.260 in.	6.604mm
Exhaust	0.260 in.	6.604mm
Crankshaft and connecting rods		
Crankshaft		
Main bearing journal diameter (all)	2.4945-2.4954 in.	63.36-63.38mm
Main bearing oil clearance	0.0006-0.0019 in.	0.015-0.048mm
Crankshaft end-play	0.002-0.008 in.	0.051-0.203mm
Thrust	On no. 1	
Connecting rod		
Journal diameter	1.9983-1.9994 in.	50.76-50.78mm
Oil clearance	0.0010-0.0030 in.	0.0254-0.0762mm
Side clearance	0.0040-0.0150 in.	0.102-0.381mm
Valves and valve springs		
Face angle	46°	
Seat angle	45°	
Spring test pressure (with valve open)	176-188 lbs. @ 1.33 in.	782-835N @ 33.78mm
Spring installed height (with valve open)	1.60 in.	40.64mm
Stem-to-guide clearance		
Intake	0.0011-0.0026 in.	0.028-0.066mm
Exhaust	0.0014-0.0030 in.	0.035-0.076mm

88253C01

2.2L (VIN G and 4) ENGINE SPECIFICATIONS

Description	English	Metric
Type	Inline Overhead Valve (OHV)	
Displacement	134.2 cu. in.	2.2L (2,200cc)
Number of Cylinders	4	
Bore	3.50 in.	89mm
Stroke	3.46 in.	88mm
Compression ratio	8.85:1	
Cylinder bore		
Diameter	3.5036-3.5043 in.	88.991-89.009mm
Out-of-round (max.)	0.0005 in.	0.013mm
Taper (max.)	0.0005 in.	0.013mm
Taper-thrust side (max.)	0.001 in.	0.02mm
Pistons		
Clearance to bore	0.0007-0.0017 in.	0.015-0.045mm
Piston rings		
End-gap		
Compression ring	0.010-0.020 in.	0.25-0.50mm
Oil ring	0.010-0.050 in.	0.25-1.27mm
Groove Clearance		
Top compression ring	0.0019-0.0027 in.	0.05-0.07mm
Second compression ring	0.0019-0.0082 in.	0.05-0.21mm
Piston Pin		
Diameter	0.8000-0.8002 in.	20.320-20.325mm
Fit in piston	0.0004-0.0009 in.	0.010-0.022mm
Press fit in rod	0.00098-0.0017 in.	0.025-0.045mm
Camshaft		
Lift		
Intake		
1988-93 engines	0.259 in.	6.60mm
1994-96 engines	0.288 in.	7.309mm
Exhaust		
1988-93 engines	0.259 in.	6.60mm
1994-96 engine	0.288 in.	7.307mm
Journal diameter	1.867-1.869 in.	47.44-47.49mm
Journal clearance	0.001-0.0039 in.	0.026-0.101mm
Crankshaft and connecting rods		
Main journal diameter (all)	2.4945-2.4954 in.	63.360-63.384mm
Taper (max.)	0.00019 in.	0.005mm
Out of round (max.)	0.00019 in.	0.005mm
Main bearing clearance (all)	0.0006-0.0019 in.	0.015-0.047mm
Crankshaft end-play	0.002-0.007 in.	0.0511-0.1780mm
Connecting rod bearing journal diameter	1.9983-1.9994 in.	50.758-50.784mm
Journal clearance	0.00019 in.	0.005mm
Out of round (max.)	0.00019 in.	0.005mm
Rod bearing clearance	0.00098-0.0031 in.	0.025-0.079mm
Rod side clearance	0.0039-0.0149 in.	0.10-0.38mm
Valves and valve springs		
Lifter type	Hydraulic	
Face angle	45 degrees	
Seat angle	46 degrees	
Seat runout	0.002 in.	0.05mm
Face runout (max. all)	0.0012 in.	0.03mm
Seat width		
Intake valves	0.049-0.059 in.	1.25-1.50mm
Exhaust valves	0.063-0.075 in.	1.60-1.90mm

88253C02

2.2L (VIN G and 4) ENGINE SPECIFICATIONS

Description	English	Metric
Valve margin	0.031 (min.)	0.08mm (min.)
Stem-to-guide clearance		
Intake valves		
1988-93 Vehicles	0.001-0.0026 in.	0.028-0.066mm
1994-96 Vehicles	0.0010-0.0027 in.	0.025-0.069mm
Exhaust valves		
1988-93 Vehicles	0.0014-0.0031 in.	0.035-0.081mm
1994-96 Vehicles	0.0014-0.0031in.	0.035-0.081mm
Valve spring free length		
1988-93 Engines	2.06 in.	52.3mm
1994-96 Engines	1.95 in.	49.5mm
Valve spring preload		
Closed		
1988-93 Engines	100-110 lbs. @ 1.51 in.	446-488 N @ 40.9mm
1994-96 Engines	75-81 lbs. @ 1.71 in.	332-362 N @ 43.43mm
Open		
1988-93 Engines	208-222 lbs. @ 1.22 in.	925-987 N @ 30.9mm
1994-96 Engines	220-236 lbs. @ 1.278 in.	979-1049 N @ 32.47mm
Oil Pump		
Pressure @ 3000 rpm	56 psi @ 65 degrees F	384 kPa @ 65 degrees C
Gear lash	0.004-0.008 in.	0.094-0.195mm
Gear pocket		
Depth	1.195-1.198 in.	30.35-30.43mm
Diameter	1.503-1.506 in.	38.1B-38.25mm
Gear length		
Drive gear	1.199-1.200 in.	30.45-30.48mm
Idler	1.199-1.200 in.	30.45-30.48mm
Gear diameter		
Drive gear	1.496-1.500 in.	38.05-38.10mm
Idler	1.498-1.500 in.	38.05-38.10mm
Side clearance		
Drive gear	0.0015-0.0040 in.	0.033-0.102mm
Idler	0.0015-0.0004 in.	0.033-0.102mm
Gear end clearance	0.002-0.006 in.	0.08-0.10mm
Valve-to-bore clearance	0.0015-0.0035 in.	0.038-0.089mm

88253C03

2.3L (VIN A) ENGINE SPECIFICATIONS

Description	English	Metric
Type	Inline Overhead Cam (OHC)	
Displacement	'138 cu. in.	2.3L (2261cc)
Number of Cylinders	4	
Bore	3.62 in.	92mm
Stroke	3.35 in.	85mm
Compression ratio	10.0:1	
Cylinder bore		
Diameter	3.2617-3.6223 in.	91.992-92.008mm
Out-of-round (max.)	0.0004 in.	0.010mm
Taper (max.) - top to 4.173 in. (106mm) down	0.0003 in.	0.008mm
Runout - rear face of block to crank, center line (max.)	0.002 in.	0.05mm
Flatness (max.)	0.008 in.	0.203mm
Cylinder head		
Flatness (max.)	0.008 in.	0.203mm
Volume	1.5825-1.6501 oz.	46.8-48.8cc
Runout	0.0196 in.	0.05mm
Diameter		
Intake	.3412 in.	34.066mm
Exhaust	.1436 in.	29.048mm
Valve guide ID	0.2762-0.2772 in.	7.015-7.041mm
Valve stem-to-valve guide clearance		
Intake	0.000984-0.00271 in	0.025-0.069mm
Exhaust	0.00149-0.00319 in.	0.038-0.081mm
Pistons		
Clearance in bore	0.0017-0.0020 in.	0.019-0.051mm
Compression height	1.256-1.264 in.	31.9-32.1mm
Piston diameter at 70° F (21°C)	3.6293-3.6210 in.	91.957-91.973mm
Piston pin bore ID at 70°F (21°C)	0.8664-0.8666 in.	22.008-22.012mm
Weight less pin and rings	14.8130-14.8172 in.	414-426g
Ring groove width		
Top compression	0.061-0.062 in.	1.55-1.57mm
Second compression	0.0598-0.0606 in.	1.52-1.54mm
Oil	0.1185-0.1193 in.	3.01-3.03mm
Piston rings		
Compression ring width (both)	0.05708-0.05827 in.	1.450-1.480mm
Compression ring gap		
Top ring	0.0138-0.0236 in.	0.35-0.60mm
2nd ring	0.0157-0.0256 in.	0.40-0.65mm
Compression ring side clearance in groove		
Top ring	0.0027-0.0047 in.	0.070-0.120mm
Second ring	0.00157-0.00315 in.	0.040-0.080mm
Oil ring width	0.01957-0.02060 in.	0.497-0.523mm
Oil ring gap	0.0157-0.0551 in.	0.40-1.40mm
Piston Pin		
Diameter	0.8659-0.8661 in.	21.995-22.000mm
Pin-to-piston clearance @ 70°F (21°C)	0.00031-0.00066 in.	0.008-0.017mm
Pin-to-rod clearance	0.00027-0.00122 in.	0.007-0.031mm
Weight	4.0207 oz.	114g
End-play on floating pin	0.00-0.0236 in.	0.0-0.6mm

88253C04

2.3L (VIN A) ENGINE SPECIFICATIONS

Description	English	Metric
Camshaft		
Lobe lift		
Intake	0.410 in.	10.414mm
Exhaust	0.410 in.	10.414mm
Journal Diameter		
No. 1	1.5720-1.5728 in.	39.93-39.95mm
Nos. 2-5	1.3751-1.3760 in.	34.93-34.95mm
Journal clearance	0.0019-0.0043 in.	0.050-0.0110mm
End-play clearance	0.0009-0.0088 in.	0.025-0.225mm
Lobe taper - on diameter in 0.5512 in. (14.0mm)	0.0018-0.0033 in.	0.046-0.083mm
Camshaft housing		
Lifter bore ID	1.3775-1.3787 in.	34.989-35.019mm
Lifter bore OD	1.3763-1.3770 in.	34.959-34.975mm
Lifter-to-bore clearance	0.0006-0.0024 in.	0.014-0.060mm
Lip seal bore ID	1.9675-1.9695 in.	49.975-50.025mm
Lip seal OD	1.9740-1.9830 in.	50.140-50.370mm
Cam carrier flatness	0.002 in.	0.05mm
Bottom - max. within 3.937 in. (100.0mm)	0.001 in.	0.025mm
Crankshaft and connecting rods		
Main bearing journal diameter (all)	2.0470-2.0480 in.	51.996-52.020mm
Width - main, thrust bearing journal (no. 3), including fillets	1.0959-1.0989 in.	27.837-27.913mm
Out-of-round (max.)	0.0005 in.	0.0127mm
Taper	0.0005 in.	0.0127mm
Clearance	0.0005-0.0023 in.	0.013-0.058mm
Crankshaft end-play	0.0034-0.0095 in.	0.087-0.243mm
Rod bearing journal		
Diameter	1.8887-1.8897 in.	47.975-48.00mm
Out-of-round	0.0005 in.	0.0127mm
Taper	0.0005 in.	0.0127mm
Clearance	0.0005-0.0020 in.	0.013-0.053mm
Rod side clearance	0.0059-0.0177 in.	0.150-0.450mm
Width	1.0925-1.1024 in.	27.75-28.00m
Runout of crankshaft at flywheel range (max.)	0.00098 in.	0.025mm
Runout of crankshaft (max.)	0.00098 in.	0.025mm
Clearance to crankshaft position sensor	0.0303-0.0697 in.	0.77-1.77mm
Connecting rod		
Small end ID	0.8664-0.8672 in.	22.007-22.027mm
Large end	2.0144-2.0154 in.	51.167-51.193mm
Connecting rod width		
Small end	0.8662-0.8700 in.	21.900-22.100mm
Large end	1.0846-1.0866 in.	27.550-27.600mm
Connecting rod weight - large end (in same engine)	0.0705 oz.	all within 2g
Connecting rod clearance to piston pin	0.00027-0.0122 in.	0.007-0.031mm
Rod assembly center-to-center distance	5.8051-5.8090 in.	147.45-147.55mm
Oil pump drive		
Oil pump drive gear	3.2621-.32632 in.	82.859-82.887mm
Crankshaft OD	3.2681-3.2672 in.	83.012-82.988mm
Oil pump drive gear to crankshaft	0.03333-0.00601 in.	0.101-0.153mm
Flywheel		
Fit	0.00000-0.0005 in.	0.000-0.013mm
Flange runout (max.)	0.00120 in.	0.03mm
Stroke of crank	3.3366-3.3504	84.9-85.1mm
OD of seal diameter on crank	3.2210-3.2299 in.	81.96-82.04mm
Runout of seal surface	0.0012 in.	0.03mm

88253C05

2.3L (VIN A) ENGINE SPECIFICATIONS

Description	English	Metric
Balancer hub ID to crank snout		
OD crank	1.2992-1.3004 in.	33.00-33.03mm
ID balancer	1.2992-1.3004 in.	33.00-33.03mm
Timing gear fit to crankshaft snout	1.3004-1.3016 in.	33.03-33.06mm
Valves and springs		
Valve lifter clearance in bore		
Valve installed height	0.9840-1.0040 in.	25.00-25.50mm
From top of stem to top of cam housing mounting sur		
Valve tip above spring retainer	0.0394-0.0787 in.	1.00-2.00mm
Intake		
Face angle		44°
Seat angle		45°
Head diameter	1.4318-1.4421 in.	36.37-36.63mm
Stem diameter	0.2751-2-0.27445 in.	6.990-6.972mm
Overall length	4.3300 in.	109.994mm
Stem-to-guide clearance	0.00'-0-0.0027 in.	0.025-0.069mm
Valve seat width	0.0370-0.0748 in.	0.94-1.90mm
Valve seat margin (min.)	0.0098 in.	0.25mm
Valve face runout	0.0015 in.	0.038mm
Valve tip-to-groove	0.1190-0.1367 in.	3.023-3.473mm
Exhaust		
Face angle		44.5°
Seat angle		45°
Head diameter	1.2350-1.2453 in.	31.37-31.63mm
Stem diameter	0.2740-.02747 in.	6.959-6.977mm
Overall length	4.3103 in.	109.482mm
Stem-to-guide clearance	0.0015-0.0032 in.	0.038-0.081mm
Valve seat width	0.0037-0.0748 in.	0.094-1.90mm
Valve seat margin (min.)	0.0098 in.	0.25mm
Valve face runout	0.0015 in.	0.038mm
Valve tip-to-groove	0.1190-0.1367 in.	3.023-3.473mm
Valve spring pressure		
Load @ 1.4370 in. (36.5mm) - closed	71-79 lbs.	314-353N
Load @ 1.0433 in. (26.08mm) - open	193-207 lbs.	857-922 N

88253C06

3.1L (VIN T and M) ENGINE SPECIFICATIONS

Description	English	Metric
Type	V6 Overhead valve (OHV)	
Displacement	189 cu. in.	3.1L (3100cc)
Number of Cylinders	6	6
Bore	3.530 in.	89mm
Stroke	3.3122 in.	84mm
Compression ratio	8.8:1	
Cylinder bore		
Diameter	3.5046-3.5053 in.	89.016-89.034mm
Out-of-round (max.)	0.0005 in.	0.013mm
Taper production thrust (max.)		
1990-93 engines	0.0006 in.	0.014mm
1994-96 engines	0.0008 in.	0.020mm
Piston clearance		
1990-93 engines	0.00093-0.00222 in.	0.0235-0.0565mm
1994-96 engines	0.0013-0.0027 in.	0.032-0.068mm
Piston diameter - gauged on skirt of 12mm below centerline		
1994-96 engines	3.5026-3.5033 in.	88.984-88.996mm
Piston pin bore		
1994-96 engines	0.9059-0.9061 in.	23.009-23.016mm
Piston rings		
Compression ring		
Groove clearance		
1st	0.002-0.0035 in.	0.05-0.09mm
2nd	0.002-0.0035 in.	0.05-0.09mm
Gap (at gauge diameter)		
1st	0.010-0.020 in.	0.25-0.50mm
2nd	0.020-0.028 in.	0.50-0.71mm
Oil ring		
Groove clearance (max.)	0.008 in.	0.20mm
Gap (segment at gauge diameter)	0.0100-0.0300 in.	0.25-0.75mm
Piston Pin		
Diameter	0.9052-0.9054 in.	22.9915-22.9964mm
Clearance		
1990-93 engines	0.0004-0.0006 in.	0.0096-0.0215mm
1994-96 engines	0.0005-0.0010 in.	0.0126-0.0245mm
Fit in rod - press	0.00065-0.0013 in.	0.0165-0.046mm
Camshaft		
Lobe lift		
1990-93 engines		
Intake	0.2626 in.	6.67mm
Exhaust	0.2732 in.	6.94mm
1994-96 engines		
Intake	0.2727 in.	6.9263mm
Exhaust	0.2727 in.	6.9263mm
Journal Diameter		
1990-93 engines	1.8678-1.8815 in.	47.44-47.79mm
1994-96 Engine	1.868-1.869 in.	47.45-47.48mm
Camshaft bearing bore diameter		
1994-96 engines		
Front and rear	2.009-2.011 in.	51.030-51.080mm
Middle # 2 and #3	1.999-2.001 in.	50.770-50.820mm
Bearing inside diameter	1.870-1.871 in.	47.516-47.541mm
Journal clearance	0.001-0.004 in.	0.026-0.101mm

88253C08

2.8L (VIN W) ENGINE SPECIFICATIONS

Description	English	Metric
Type	V6 Overhead Valve (OHV)	
Displacement	171 cu. in.	2.8L (2800cc)
Number of Cylinders	6	
Bore	3.503 in.	89mm
Stroke	2.990 in.	76mm
Compression ratio	8.9:1	
Pistons and rings		
Ring gap		
1st compression ring	0.010-0.020 in.	0.254-0.508mm
2nd compression ring	0.010-0.020 in.	0.254-0.508mm
Oil ring	0.020-0.055 in.	0.508-1.397mm
Ring side clearance		
1st compression ring	0.001-0.003 in.	0.025-0.076mm
2nd compression ring	0.001-0.003 in.	0.025-0.076mm
Oil ring	0.0080 in.	0.2032mm
Piston Clearance	0.0010-0.0029	0.0254-0.0736mm
Camshaft		
Journal diameter	1.867-1.881 in.	47.42-47.78mm
Bearing clearance	0.001-0.004 in.	0.0254-0.1016mm
Elevation		
Intake	0.262 in.	6.655mm
Exhaust	0.273 in.	6.934mm
Crankshaft and connecting rods		
Crankshaft		
Main bearing journal diameter (all)	2.6473-2.6483 in.	67.24-67.27mm
Main bearing oil clearance	0.0016-0.0019	0.0406-0.0482mm
Crankshaft end-play	0.002-0.008 in.	0.0508-0.2032mm
Thrust	On no. 4	
Connecting rod		
Journal diameter	1.9983-1.9993 in.	50.76-50.78mm
Oil clearance	0.0010-0.0030 in.	0.0250-0.0762mm
Side clearance	0.0060-0.0170 in.	0.1524-0.4318mm
Valves and valve springs		
Face angle	46°	
Seat angle	45°	
Spring test pressure (with valve open)	215 lbs. @ 1.29 in.	955N @ 32.77mm
Spring installed height (with valve open)	1.70 in.	43.18mm
Stem-to-guide clearance		
Intake	0.0010-0.0027 in.	0.025-0.068mm
Exhaust	0.0010-0.0027 in.	0.025-0.068mm

88253C07

3.1L (VIN T and M) ENGINE SPECIFICATIONS

Description	English	Metric
Crankshaft and connecting rods		
Main journal diameter (all)	2.6473-2.6483 in.	67.241-67.265mm
Taper (max.)	0.0002 in.	0.005mm
Out-of-round (max.)	0.0002 in.	0.005mm
Flange runout (max.)	0.0005-00.0010 in.	0.0126-0.0245mm
Main bearing bore diameter		
1994-96 engines	2.8407-2.8412 in.	72.155-72.168mm
Main bearing inner diameter		
1994-96 engines	2.6492-2.62502 in.	67.289-67..316mm
Main bearing clearance	0.0012-0.0030 in.	0.032-0.077mm
Main thrust bearing clearance	0.0012-0.0030 in.	0.032-0.077mm
Crankshaft end-play and build paper clearance (distortion and wear not included)	0.0024-0.0083 in.	0.06-0.21mm
Crankpin		
Diameter	1.9983-1.9994 in.	50.758-50.784mm
Taper (max.)	0.0002 in.	0.005mm
Out-of-round (max.)	0.0002 in.	0.005mm
Rod bearing bore diameter		
1994-96 engines	2.124-2.125 in.	53.962-53.984mm
Rod inside bearing diameter	2.000-2.002 in.	50.812-50.850mm
Rod bearing clearance	0.0011-0.0037 in.	0.028-0.086mm
Rod side clearance (distortion and wear not included)	0.014-0.027 in.	0.36-0.68mm
Oil Pump (cast iron body)		
Gear lash	0.0037-0.0077 in.	0.094-0.195mm
Gear pocket		
Depth		
1990-93 engines	1.202-1.205 in.	30.53-30.61mm
1994-96 engines	1.202-1.204 in.	30.52-30.58mm
Diameter		
1990-93 engines	1.504-1.506 in.	38.202-38.252mm
1994-96 engines	1.503-1.505 in.	38.176-38.226mm
Gear		
Length	1.199-1.200 in.	30.45-30.48mm
Diameter	1.498-1.500 in.	38.05-38.10mm
Side clearance		
1990-93 engines	0.003-0.004 in.	0.08-0.10mm
1994-96 engines	0.001-0.003 in.	0.038-0.088mm
End clearance		
1990-93 engines	0.002-0.006 in.	0.050-0.152mm
1994-96 engines	0.002-0.005 in.	0.040-0.125mm
Valve-to-bore clearance	0.0015-0.0035 in.	0.038-0.089mm
Valves and valve springs		
Valve lifter	Hydraulic	
Rocker arm ratio		
1990-93 engines	1.50:1	
1994-96 engines	1.60:1	
Face angle	45°	
Seat angle		
1990-93 engines	46°	
1994-96 engines	45°	
Seat runout (max.)	0.001 in.	0.025mm

88253C09

3.1L (VIN T and M) ENGINE SPECIFICATIONS

Description	English	Metric
Seat width		
Intake	0.061-0.073 in.	1.55-1.85mm
Exhaust	0.067-0.079 in.	1.70-2.00mm
Valve Margin (min.)		
1994-96 engines		
Intake	0.083 in.	2.10mm
Exhaust	0.106 in.	2.70mm
Stem clearance	0.001-0.0027 in.	0.026-0.068mm
Valve spring		
Free length		
1990-93 engines	1.91 in.	48.5mm
1994-96 engines	1.89 in.	48.01mm
Load - closed		
1990-93 engines	90 lbs. @ 1.701 in.	400N @ 43mm
1994-96 engines	80bs. @ 1.170 in.	356N @ 43mm
Load - open		
1990-93 engines	215 lbs. @ 1.291 in.	956N @ 33mm
1994-96 engines	250 lbs. @ 1.239 in.	1111N @ 31.5mm
Installed height		
1990-93 engines	1.5748 in.	40mm
1994-96 engines	1.710 in.	43mm
Approximate # of coils		
1990-93 engines	4	
1994-96 engines	6.55	

88253C10

Engine

REMOVAL & INSTALLATION

✳✳ CAUTION

When draining the coolant, keep in mind that cats and dogs are attracted by ethylene glycol antifreeze, and are quite likely to drink any that is left in an uncovered container or in puddles on the ground. This will prove fatal in sufficient quantity. Always drain the coolant into a sealable container. Coolant should be reused unless it is contaminated or several years old.

In the process of removing the engine, you will come across a number of steps which call for the removal of a separate component or system, such as "disconnect the exhaust system" or "remove the radiator." In most instances, a detailed removal procedure can be found elsewhere in this manual.

It is virtually impossible to list each individual wire and hose which must be disconnected, simply because so many different model and engine combinations have been manufactured. Careful observation and common sense are the best possible approaches to any repair procedure.

Removal and installation of the engine can be made easier if you follow these basic points:

- If you have to drain any of the fluids, use a suitable container.
- Always tag any wires or hoses and, if possible, the components they came from before disconnecting them.
- Because there are so many bolts and fasteners involved, store and label the retainers from components separately in muffin pans, jars or coffee cans. This will prevent confusion during installation.
- After unbolting the transmission or transaxle, always make sure it is properly supported.
- If it is necessary to disconnect the air conditioning system, have this service performed by a qualified technician using a recovery/recycling station. If the system does not have to be disconnected, unbolt the compressor and set it aside.
- When unbolting the engine mounts, always make sure the engine is properly supported. When removing the engine, make sure that any lifting devices are properly attached to the engine. It is recommended that if your engine is supplied with lifting hooks, your lifting apparatus be attached to them.
- Lift the engine from its compartment slowly, checking that no hoses, wires or other components are still connected.
- After the engine is clear of the compartment, place it on an engine stand or workbench.
- After the engine has been removed, you can perform a partial or full teardown of the engine using the procedures outlined in this manual.

2.0L Engine

1. Disconnect the negative, then the positive battery cables from the battery. Remove the battery from the vehicle.
2. Position a clean drain pan under the radiator, open the drain cock and drain the cooling system. Remove the air intake hose.
3. From the throttle body, disconnect the T.V. and accelerator cables. Unplug the ECM electrical harness connector from the engine.
4. Tag and disconnect all vacuum hoses (not a part of the engine assembly), the upper/lower radiator hoses and the heater hoses from the engine.
5. Remove the heat shield from the exhaust manifold. Label and disconnect the engine wiring harness from the firewall.
6. Disconnect the windshield washer hoses and the bottle.
7. Rotate the tensioner pulley (to reduce the belt tension) and remove the serpentine drive belt.
8. Disconnect and plug the fuel hoses.
9. Raise and safely support the front of the vehicle.
10. Position a suitable drain pan under the oil pan, then drain the engine oil.
11. Remove the right-side inner fender splash shield.
12. Unfasten the A/C compressor-to-bracket bolts and position the compressor aside (so it will not interfere with the engine removal); DO NOT disconnect the refrigerant lines.
13. Remove the flywheel splash shield. Label and disconnect electrical wires from the starter.

14. Remove the front starter brace, the starter-to-engine bolts and the starter.
15. If equipped with an automatic transaxle, remove the torque converter-to-flywheel bolts and push the converter back into the transaxle.
16. Remove the crankshaft pulley-to-crankshaft bolt. Use Crankshaft Pulley Hub Remover tool No. J-24420 or equivalent, to press the pulley from the crankshaft.
17. Position a drain pan under the oil filter, then remove the filter.
18. Remove the engine-to-transaxle support bracket. Disconnect the right-rear engine mount.
19. Remove the exhaust pipe-to-exhaust manifold bolts, then disconnect the exhaust pipe from the center hanger and loosen the muffler hanger.
20. Remove the T.V. and shift cable bracket. Remove the two lower engine-to-transaxle bolts.
21. Carefully lower the vehicle. From the intake manifold, remove the T.V. and accelerator cable bracket.
22. Remove the right-front engine mount nuts. Tag and unplug the electrical connectors. Remove the alternator-to-bracket bolts and the alternator.
23. Remove the master cylinder-to-booster nuts, move the master cylinder and support it out of the way; DO NOT disconnect the brake lines.
24. Install a suitable vertical lifting to the engine and lift it slightly.
25. Remove the right-front engine mount bracket. Remove the remaining engine-to-transaxle bolts.
26. Remove the power steering pump-to-engine bolts and position the pump aside; DO NOT disconnect the high pressure hoses.
27. Carefully lift and remove the engine from the vehicle.
28. Install the engine using the reverse of the removal procedure. Make sure to tighten all retainers securely, or to the specifications provided.
29. Connect the right rear motor mount. If the rear engine mount bracket is removed, the following procedure should be used to ensure proper engine mount bracket locations:
    a. Loosely install the engine mount bracket.
    b. Raise the engine and transaxle.
    c. Tighten the engine mount nuts and bolts to the specifications shown.
30. Fill the cooling system, then connect the negative battery cable.

2.2L Engine

➡The following procedure is for the engine and transaxle assembly.

1. If equipped with A/C, take the vehicle to a reputable repair shop to have the system discharged.
2. Disconnect the battery, then drain the cooling system.
3. Relieve the fuel system pressure.
4. Disconnect the hood lamp wiring, if so equipped and remove the hood.
5. Disconnect the throttle body intake duct.
6. Remove the rear sight shields.
7. Disconnect the upper radiator hose.
8. Detach the brake booster vacuum hose.
9. Disconnect the alternator top brace and wiring.
10. Tag and detach the upper engine harness from the engine.
11. Disconnect the A/C compressor-to-condenser and accumulator lines.
12. Raise and support the vehicle safely.
13. Remove the left splash shield.
14. Disconnect the exhaust system.
15. Tag and disconnect the lower engine wiring.
16. Remove the flywheel inspection cover.
17. Remove the front wheels.
18. Disconnect the lower radiator hose.
19. Disconnect the heater hoses from the heater core.
20. Remove the brake calipers from the steering knuckle and wire up out of the way as outlined in Section 9.
21. Disconnect the tie rods from the struts.
22. Carefully lower the vehicle.
23. Remove the clutch slave cylinder.
24. With the fuel system pressure released, place an absorbent shop towel around the connections and disconnect the fuel lines.
25. Disconnect the transaxle linkage at the transaxle.
26. Disconnect the accelerator cables from the TBI unit.
27. Disconnect the cruise control cables from the TBI unit.
28. Disconnect the throttle valve cables from the TBI, on vehicles equipped with an automatic transaxle.
29. Disconnect the automatic transaxle cooling lines.

30. Disconnect the power steering hoses from the power steering pump.
31. Remove the center suspension support bolts.
32. Align Engine/Transaxle Frame Handler tool No. J 36295 under the suspension supports, engine and transaxle; lower vehicle to dolly and add support under the engine.
33. Safely support the rear of the vehicle.
34. Disconnect the upper transaxle mount.
35. Remove the upper strut bolts and nuts.
36. Disconnect the front engine mount.
37. Disconnect the rear engine mount.
38. Remove the 4 rear suspension support bolts.
39. Remove the 4 front suspension support bolts and wire the bolt holes together to prevent axle separation.
40. Raise the vehicle and remove the engine and transaxle assembly on tool No. J 36295.

To install:

41. Carefully lower the vehicle and install the engine and transaxle assembly using tool No. J 36295.
42. Install the suspension supports bolts and tighten to 65 ft. lbs. (88 Nm) for the front and rear suspension supports and 66 ft. lbs. (89 Nm) for the center suspension support.
43. Install the transaxle mount but do not tighten.
44. Install the rear engine mount but do not tighten.
45. Install the front engine mount but do not tighten.
46. Tighten the manual transaxle mounting bolts as follows:
   a. Front transaxle strut-to-body bolts-to 40 ft. lbs. (54 Nm).
   b. Rear transaxle mount-to-body bolts to 23 ft. lbs. (31 Nm).
47. Tighten the automatic transaxle mount bolts to 22 ft. lbs. (30 Nm).
48. Tighten the front and rear engine mount bolts.

➡**All engine mount bolts that have been removed must be cleaned and a new thread locking compound applied to the threads before reinstallation.**

49. Installation of the remaining components is the reverse of removal.
50. Check and adjust the wheel alignment.
51. Install the hood and connect the positive, then the negative battery cables.
52. Have the A/C system recharged at a reputable repair facility.

2.3L Engine

1. If equipped with A/C, take the vehicle to a reputable repair shop to have the system discharged.
2. Disconnect the negative battery cable. Drain the cooling system and remove the air cleaner assembly.
3. Remove the air cleaner assembly.
4. Disconnect the heater hoses.
5. Disconnect the upper radiator hose.
6. Disconnect the coolant fan.
7. Raise and safely support the vehicle.
8. Remove the front tire and wheel assemblies.
9. Remove the oil filter.
10. Disconnect the compressor/condenser hose assembly.
11. Disconnect and tag all vacuum lines and electrical connections.
12. Disconnect the negative battery cable from the block.
13. Disconnect the shift cable from the bracket assembly and power brake hose.
14. Disconnect the throttle cable and bracket.
15. Remove the power steering bracket with the pump and lines attached.
16. Disconnect the oil/air separator.
17. Relieve the fuel system pressure as outlined in Section 5 and disconnect the fuel lines.
18. Disconnect the clutch actuator.
19. Disconnect the engine oil cooler lines at the adapter.
20. Remove the exhaust manifold heat shield.
21. Remove the exhaust manifold.
22. Remove the front engine mount nut.
23. Disconnect the lower radiator hose and heater hose.
24. Install engine support J 28467 or equivalent, disconnect the vacuum lines and pull the vacuum harness back through the front lift bracket.
25. Remove the left and right splash shields.

26. Separate the ball joints from the steering knuckles.
27. Support the suspension support, crossmember and stabilizer shaft with a suitable holding fixture and remove the suspension support retaining bolts.
28. Remove the suspension support, crossmember and stabilizer shaft as an assembly.
29. Install drive axle boot protectors J 34754 or equivalent, and remove the drive axles from the transaxle.
30. Position a suitable support below the engine and lower the car onto the support.
31. Remove the engine mount strut and transaxle brackets.
32. Mark the threads on the support fixture hooks so that the setting can be duplicated when reinstalling the engine. Remove the engine support fixture.
33. Raise the vehicle slowly off the engine and transaxle assembly.

To install:

➡**Make certain the correct bolts are installed in their correct positions.**

34. Position the engine and transaxle assembly under the engine compartment and slowly lower the vehicle over the assembly until the transaxle is indexed and install the bolt.
35. Install the engine support fixture J 28467–A or equivalent and adjust to the previous setting.
36. Raise the vehicle off of the support fixture.
37. Install the engine mount strut and transaxle brackets.
38. Install drive axle boot protectors J 34754 or equivalent, and install the drive axles to the transaxle.
39. Install the suspension support, crossmember and stabilizer shaft as an assembly. Install and tighten the rear bolts first to 66 ft. lbs. (89 Nm), then the front bolts to 65 ft. lbs. (88 Nm).
40. Install the ball joint nuts.
41. Install the left and right splash shields.
42. Connect the lower radiator hose and heater hose.
43. Install the front engine mount nut.
44. Carefully lower the vehicle.
45. Remove the engine support fixture J 28467–A or equivalent.
46. Install the remaining components in the reverse of the removal procedure. Make sure all components are tightened securely, and connectors properly attached.
47. Fill the cooling system, oil crankcase and connect the battery.

2.8L and 3.1L Engine

1. Relieve the fuel pressure. Disconnect the negative, then the positive battery cables. Remove the battery from the vehicle.
2. Remove the air cleaner, the air inlet hose and the Mass Air Flow (MAF) sensor.
3. Position a clean drain pan under the radiator, open the drain cock and drain the cooling system. Remove the exhaust manifold crossover assembly bolts and separate the assembly from the exhaust manifolds.
4. Remove the serpentine belt tensioner and the drive belt. Remove the power steering pump-to-bracket bolts and support the pump aside.
5. Disconnect the radiator hose from the engine.
6. Disconnect the TV and accelerator cables from the throttle valve bracket on the plenum.
7. Detach the electrical connectors. Remove the alternator-to-bracket bolts and the alternator. Label and disconnect the electrical wiring harness from the engine.
8. Disconnect and plug the fuel hoses. Remove the coolant overflow and bypass hoses from the engine.
9. From the charcoal canister, disconnect the purge hose. Label and disconnect all the necessary vacuum hoses.
10. Using a engine holding fixture tool, support the engine.
11. Raise and safely support the vehicle.
12. Remove the right inner fender splash shield. Remove the crankshaft pulley-to-crankshaft bolt. Using a wheel puller, press the crankshaft pulley from the crankshaft.
13. Remove the flywheel cover. Label and disconnect the starter wires. Remove the starter-to-engine bolts and the starter.
14. Disconnect the wires from the oil pressure sending unit.
15. Remove the air conditioning compressor-to-bracket bolts and the bracket-to-engine bolts. Support the compressor so it will not interfere with the engine; do not disconnect the refrigerant lines.

16. Disconnect the exhaust pipe from the rear of the exhaust manifold.

17. If equipped with an automatic transaxle, remove the torque converter-to-flywheel bolts and push the converter into the transaxle.

18. Remove the front and rear engine mount bolts along with the mount brackets.

19. Remove the intermediate shaft bracket from the engine.

20. Disconnect the shifter cable from the transaxle.

21. Remove the lower engine-to-transaxle bolts and lower the vehicle.

22. Disconnect the heater hoses from the engine.

23. Using an vertical engine lift, install it to the engine and lift it slightly. Remove the engine holding fixture. Using a floor jack, support the transaxle.

24. Remove the upper engine-to-transaxle bolts. Remove the front engine mount bolts and transaxle mounting bracket.

25. Remove the engine from the vehicle.

To install:

26. Secure the engine on a engine suitable lifting device.

27. Carefully lower the engine into the vehicle, aligning it to the transaxle.

28. Install the upper engine-to-transaxle bolts. Tighten bolts to 55 ft. lbs. (75 Nm).

29. Install the transaxle mount bracket and front engine mount attaching bolts. Tighten the bolts to 65 ft. lbs. (88 Nm).

30. Using a floor jack, support the transaxle and remove the engine lifting device from the engine.

31. Install the lower engine-to-transaxle bolts.

32. Install the remaining components in the reverse of the removal procedure.

33. Close the radiator drain cock and refill the cooling system.

34. Install the battery and secure it in place. Connect the battery cables (the negative cable last).

35. Start the engine, allow it to reach normal operating temperatures and check for leaks.

Rocker Arm (Valve) Cover

REMOVAL & INSTALLATION

✳✳ CAUTION

When draining the coolant, keep in mind that cats and dogs are attracted by ethylene glycol antifreeze, and are quite likely to drink any that is left in an uncovered container or in puddles on the ground. This will prove fatal in sufficient quantity. Always drain the coolant into a sealable container. Coolant should be reused unless it is contaminated or several years old.

2.0L and 2.2L Engines

▶ See Figure 1

1. Disconnect the negative battery cable.

2. Disconnect the air intake hose from the throttle body and air cleaner.

3. For 1994–96 vehicles, remove the cruise, throttle and T.V. cable bracket.

4. Disconnect the crankcase ventilation hose(s).

5. Unfasten the rocker arm (valve) cover bolts, then remove the cover. Remove and discard the gasket.

6. Clean the sealing surfaces of the head and the cover using a suitable degreaser.

To install:

7. Position a new gasket, then install the rocker arm (valve) cover. Tighten the retaining bolts to 89 inch lbs. (10 Nm).

8. Connect the crankcase ventilation hose(s).

9. For 1994–96 vehicles, install the cruise, throttle and T.V. cable bracket.

10. Connect the air intake hose to the throttle body and air cleaner

11. Connect the negative battery cable. Start the engine and check for leaks.

2.3L Engine

The camshaft housing covers and cylinder head are retained by the same bolts. When the bolts are removed to service the camshaft cover, the cylinder head gasket MUST be replaced also. Refer to the Cylinder Head removal procedure for details.

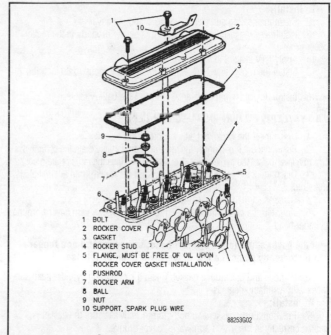

1 BOLT
2 ROCKER COVER
3 GASKET
4 ROCKER STUD
5 FLANGE, MUST BE FREE OF OIL UPON ROCKER COVER GASKET INSTALLATION.
6 PUSHROD
7 ROCKER ARM
8 BALL
9 NUT
10 SUPPORT, SPARK PLUG WIRE

88253G02

Fig. 1 Rocker arm (valve) cover mounting—2.0L and 2.2L engines

2.8L and 3.1L Engines

FRONT COVER—1988 VEHICLES

1. Disconnect the negative battery cable.

2. Remove the bracket tube at the cover.

3. Remove the plug wire guide.

4. Disconnect the heater hose at the filler neck.

5. Remove the cover bolts and remove the cover.

6. If the cover adheres to the cylinder head, lightly tap the end of the cover with a soft rubber mallet or palm of the hand.

✳✳ WARNING

Do not distort or scratch the sealing flange.

To install:

7. Clean the sealing surfaces of the head and the cover.

8. Install a new gasket and make sure it is seated properly in the rocker cover groove.

9. Apply RTV sealant in the notch.

10. Install the rocker cover and tighten the retaining bolts to 6–9 ft. lbs. (8–12 Nm).

11. Install the remaining parts and reconnect the battery cable.

FRONT (LEFT) COVER—1989–93 VEHICLES

1. Disconnect the negative battery cable.

2. Remove the air cleaner assembly

3. Position a suitable drain pan under the radiator, then drain the engine coolant.

4. Remove the ignition wire clamps from the coolant tube.

5. Disconnect the coolant tube mount at the head.

6. Disconnect the coolant tube at each end.

7. Disconnect the coolant tube at the water pump and remove the tube.

8. Remove the tube from the rocker cover to air inlet.

9. Remove the ignition wire guide.

10. Remove the cover bolts and remove the cover.

11. If the cover adheres to the cylinder head, lightly tap the end of the cover with a soft rubber mallet or palm of the hand.

✳✳ WARNING

Do not distort or scratch the sealing flange.

To install:

12. Clean the sealing surfaces of the head and the cover.

13. Install a new gasket and make sure it is seated properly in the rocker cover groove.

14. Apply RTV sealant in the notch.

15. Install the rocker cover and tighten the retaining bolts to 89 inch lbs. (10 Nm).

16. Install the remaining parts and reconnect the battery cable.

FRONT (LEFT) COVER—1994–96 VEHICLES

1. Disconnect the negative battery cable.

2. Position a drain pan under the radiator, then partially drain the cooling system to a level below the bypass pipe. Don't forget to close the radiator drain cock.

3. Disconnect the coolant bypass pipe from the water pump and exhaust manifold.

4. Disconnect the PCV valve from the rocker arm (valve) cover.

5. Unfasten the retaining bolts, then remove the rocker arm cover from the cylinder head.

➡**If the cover sticks to the cylinder head, use your palm or a rubber mallet to gently bump the end of the cover to break it loose.**

6. Remove and discard the gasket. Clean the cover and cylinder head surfaces with a suitable degreaser.

To install:

7. Position a new gasket and bolt grommets. Make sure the gasket is seated correctly in the rocker arm (valve) cover groove.

8. Apply RTV sealer 1052917, or equivalent to the notch shown in the accompanying figure.

9. Position the rocker arm cover in place and secure with the retaining fasteners, finger-tight. Tighten the fasteners to 89 inch lbs. (10 Nm).

10. Connect the PCV valve to the rocker arm cover.

11. Attach the coolant bypass pipe to the water pump and manifold.

12. Add the proper type and amount of coolant to bring up to the correct level.

13. Connect the negative battery cable, then start the vehicle, check for leaks and inspect the coolant level. Add coolant if necessary.

REAR (RIGHT) COVER—1988–93 VEHICLE

1. Disconnect the negative battery cable.

2. Remove the air cleaner assembly.

3. Position a drain pan under the radiator, then drain the cooling system. Don't forget to close the radiator drain cock.

4. Tag and disconnect the vacuum hoses from the intake plenum.

5. Disconnect the airflow tube.

6. Disconnect the EGR tube from the crossover pipe.

7. Remove the spark plug wire guide.

8. Detach the spark plug wire harness from the plenum and plugs.

9. Disconnect the coolant hoses from the throttle base.

10. Tag and detach any wiring from the plenum in order to remove the rocker arm cover.

11. Disconnect the throttle, T.V. and cruise control (if equipped) cables.

12. Remove the bracket from the right side of the plenum.

13. Disconnect the brake booster vacuum supply from the plenum.

14. Remove the serpentine drive belt.

15. Disconnect the exhaust pipe from the crossover.

16. Unbolt the alternator and position it aside.

17. Disconnect the PCV valve from the rocker arm (valve) cover.

18. Unfasten the retaining bolts, then remove the rocker arm cover from the cylinder head. Remove and discard the gasket.

➡**If the cover sticks to the cylinder head, lightly tap the end of the cover with a soft rubber mallet or the palm of your hand. Be careful not to not distort or scratch the sealing flange.**

19. Clean the sealing surfaces of the head and the cover with a suitable degreaser.

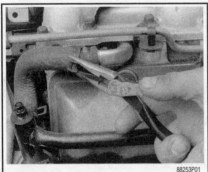

Unfasten the retaining clamp and disconnect the coolant bypass pipe from the manifold

Unfasten the coolant bypass pipe retaining bolts . . .

. . . then remove the bypass pipe from the vehicle

Unfasten the rocker arm (valve) cover retaining bolts . . .

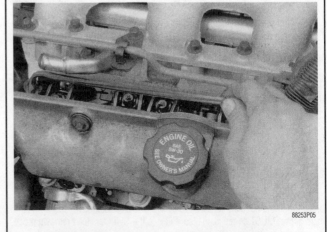

. . . then remove the rocker arm cover from the vehicle

To install:

20. Position a new gasket and bolt grommets. Make sure the gasket is seated correctly in the rocker arm (valve) cover groove.

21. Apply RTV sealer 1052917, or equivalent to the notch shown in the accompanying figure.

22. Position the rocker arm cover in place and secure with the retaining fastener finger-tight. Tighten the fasteners to 89 inch lbs. (10 Nm).

23. Connect the PCV valve to the valve cover.

24. Install the remaining components in the reverse of the removal procedure. Make sure all components are tightened securely and connected properly.

25. Add the proper type and amount of coolant to bring up to the correct level.

26. Connect the negative battery cable, then start the vehicle, check for leaks and inspect the coolant level. Add coolant if necessary.

REAR (RIGHT) COVER—1994–96 VEHICLE

1. Disconnect the negative battery cable.

2. Detach the rear spark plug wire harness from the upper intake manifold and spark plugs.

3. Disconnect the brake booster vacuum supply from the upper intake manifold.

4. Remove the serpentine drive belt.

5. Remove the alternator and position it aside.

6. Remove the electronic ignition coil and module assembly and remove the EVAP canister purge solenoid.

7. Unfasten the retaining bolts, then remove the rocker arm (valve) cover from the cylinder head.

➡ **If the cover sticks to the cylinder head, use your palm or a rubber mallet to gently bump the end of the cover to break it loose.**

8. Remove and discard the gasket. Clean the cover and cylinder head surfaces with a suitable degreaser.

To install:

9. Position a new gasket and bolt grommets. Make sure the gasket is seated correctly in the rocker arm (valve) cover groove.

10. Apply RTV sealer 1052917, or equivalent to the notch shown in the accompanying figure.

11. Position the rocker arm cover in place and secure with the retaining fasteners, finger-tight. Tighten the fasteners to 89 inch lbs. (10 Nm).

12. Install the remaining components and connect the negative batter cable. Start the engine and check for leaks.

Rocker Arms and Pushrods

REMOVAL & INSTALLATION

2.0L and 2.2L Engines

1. Disconnect the negative battery cable.

2. Remove the rocker arm (valve) cover.

➡ **Be sure to keep the components in order for installation purposes.**

3. Remove the rocker arm nuts, then remove the rocker arm(s) and ball(s).

4. Remove the pushrods.

To install:

5. Coat the bearing surfaces of the rocker arms and the rocker arm balls with Molykote® or its equivalent.

6. Install the pushrods, making sure they seat in their lifters.

7. Install the rocker arm(s) and ball(s). Apply Dri-Slide Moly lubricant 1052948 or equivalent to the threads of the stud(s), then install the nuts.

8. Tighten the rocker arm nuts to 7–11 ft. lbs. (10–15 Nm) for 1988 vehicles, to 14 ft. lbs. (20 Nm) for 1989–92 vehicles and to 22 ft. lbs. (30 Nm). for 1993–96 vehicles.

9. Install the rocker arm (valve) cover.

10. Connect the negative battery cable.

2.8L and 3.1L V6 Engine

1988 VEHICLES

1. Disconnect the negative battery cable.

2. Remove the rocker arm (valve) cover(s).

3. Remove the rocker arm nuts, rocker arm balls, rocker arms, push rod guides and push rods and place in a rack so that they may be reinstalled in the same location.

To install:

4. Coat the bearing surfaces of the rocker arms and the rocker arm balls with Molykote® or its equivalent.

5. Install the pushrods making sure that they seat properly in the lifter.

6. Install the pushrod guides, rocker arms, pivot balls and nuts.

7. Tighten the rocker arm nuts to 18 ft. lbs. (25 Nm).

8. Connect the negative battery cable.

1989–96 VEHICLES

▶ **See Figure 2**

1. Disconnect the negative battery cable.

2. Remove the rocker arm (valve) cover(s).

3. Unfasten and remove the rocker arm nuts or bolts depending upon vehicle year.

4. Remove the rocker arm pivot balls, rocker arms and push rods and place in a rack so that they may be reinstalled in the same location.

To install:

➡ **Intake pushrods are marked orange, red or yellow (depending upon the year of the vehicle) and are 6 in. (152mm) long. Exhaust pushrods are marked blue or green (depending upon the year of the vehicle) and are 6⅜ in. (162mm) long.**

5. Coat the bearing surfaces of the rocker arms and the rocker arm balls with Molykote® or its equivalent.

6. Install the pushrods, in their original locations, making sure that they seat properly in the lifter.

7. Install the pushrods, rocker arms, pivot balls and nuts.

8. Either tighten the rocker arm nuts to 18 ft. lbs. (25 Nm) or tighten the rocker arm bolts to 89 inch lbs. (10 Nm), plus an additional 30 degree rotation.

Remove the rocker arm retaining bolts

Remove the rocker arm assembly

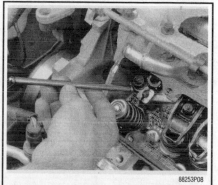

Remove the pushrod by pulling it straight up, out of the cylinder head

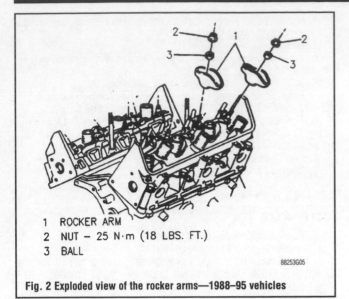

1 ROCKER ARM
2 NUT – 25 N·m (18 LBS. FT.)
3 BALL

88253G05

Fig. 2 Exploded view of the rocker arms—1988–95 vehicles

Installed view of the rocker arms (A), bolts (B) valve springs (C) and related valve train components

9. Install the rocker arm (valve) cover(s).
10. Connect the negative battery cable.

VALVE LASH ADJUSTMENT

➡️The following adjustment procedure should be used on 2.8L and 3.1L engines when reconditioning a valve seat, and a new adjustable rocker arm stud has been installed.

1. Install the rocker arms, balls and nuts. Tighten the rocker arm nuts until all lash is eliminated.
2. Adjust the valves when the lifter is on the base circle of a camshaft lobe:
     a. Crank the engine until the mark on the crankshaft pulley lines up with the **0** mark on the timing tab. Make sure that the engine is in the No. 1 firing position. Place your fingers on the No. 1 rocker arms as the mark on the crank pulley comes near the **0** mark. If the valves are not moving, the engine is in the No. 1 firing position. If the valves move, the engine is in the No. 4 firing position; rotate the engine 1 complete revolution and it will be in the No. 1 position.
     b. When the engine is in the No. 1 firing position, adjust the following valves:
- Exhaust—1,2,3
- Intake—1,5,6

     c. Back the adjusting nut out until lash can be felt at the pushrod, then turn the nut until all lash is removed (this can be determined by rotating the pushrod while turning the adjusting nut). When all lash has been removed, turn the nut in 1½ additional turns, this will center the lifter plunger.
     d. Crank the engine 1 complete revolution until the timing tab and the **0** mark are again in alignment. Now the engine is in the No. 4 firing position. Adjust the following valves:
- Exhaust—4,5,6
- Intake—2,3,4

Thermostat

REMOVAL & INSTALLATION

❊❊ CAUTION

When draining the coolant, keep in mind that cats and dogs are attracted by ethylene glycol antifreeze, and are quite likely to drink any that is left in an uncovered container or in puddles on the ground. This will prove fatal in sufficient quantity. Always drain the coolant into a sealable container. Coolant should be reused unless it is contaminated or several years old.

2.0L and 2.2L Engines

▶ See Figure 3

The thermostat is located inside a housing on the back of the cylinder head. It is not necessary to remove the radiator hose from the thermostat housing when removing the thermostat.
1. Disconnect the negative battery cable.
2. Position a drain pan under the radiator, then partially drain the coolant to a level below the thermostat. Don't forget to close the radiator drain cock.
3. Remove the air cleaner.
4. On some models it may be necessary to disconnect the AIR pipe from the upper check valve and remove the bracket from the water outlet.
5. If necessary, disconnect the electrical lead.
6. Remove the 3 thermostat housing retaining nuts, pulling the housing away, then remove the thermostat. Thoroughly clean the mating surfaces.
To install:
7. Place a thin bead of sealant in the thermostat housing groove.
8. Position the thermostat in the housing. Install the housing assembly and secure with the retaining nuts. Tighten the nuts to 89 inch lbs. (10 Nm).

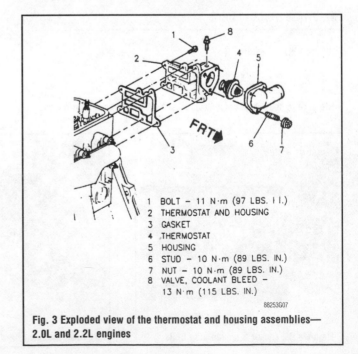

1 BOLT – 11 N·m (97 LBS. I I.)
2 THERMOSTAT AND HOUSING
3 GASKET
4 THERMOSTAT
5 HOUSING
6 STUD – 10 N·m (89 LBS. IN.)
7 NUT – 10 N·m (89 LBS. IN.)
8 VALVE, COOLANT BLEED – 13 N·m (115 LBS. IN.)

88253G07

Fig. 3 Exploded view of the thermostat and housing assemblies— 2.0L and 2.2L engines

→Poor heater output and slow warm-up is often caused by a thermostat stuck in the open position; occasionally one sticks shut causing immediate overheating. Do not attempt to correct a chronic overheating condition by permanently removing the thermostat. Thermostat flow restriction is designed into the system; without it, localized overheating (due to coolant turbulence) may occur, causing expensive troubles.

9. Install the remaining components, then fill the engine cooling system with the proper type and amount of coolant.

10. Connect the negative battery cable, then start the engine and check for leaks. Check the coolant level and add if necessary.

2.3L Engine

1990–93 VEHICLES

▶ See Figure 4

1. Disconnect the negative battery cable.
2. Position a drain pan under the radiator, then partially drain the coolant to a level below the thermostat. Don't forget to close the radiator drain cock.
3. Remove the upper radiator hose from the thermostat water outlet and position it aside.
4. Disconnect the heater and throttle body coolant hoses from the thermostat housing.
5. Detach the electrical connector from the coolant temperature sensor.
6. Remove the 2 thermostat housing attaching bolts.
7. Remove the thermostat housing and thermostat. Remove and discard the gasket.

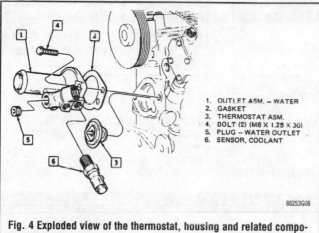

1. OUTLET ASM. – WATER
2. GASKET
3. THERMOSTAT ASM.
4. BOLT (2) (M8 X 1.25 X 30)
5. PLUG – WATER OUTLET
6. SENSOR, COOLANT

88253G08

Fig. 4 Exploded view of the thermostat, housing and related components—1990–93 2.3L engines

To install:

8. Throughly clean the mating surfaces of the engine and thermostat.
9. Install the thermostat, gasket and housing, being careful not to allow the thermostat to slip out of position.
10. Install the attaching bolts and tighten to 19 ft. lbs. (26 Nm).
11. Install the remaining components, then refill and bleed the cooling system. Start the engine, allow it to reach normal operating temperature and check for leaks.
12. Allow time for the thermostat to open, recheck the coolant level and top off, as required.

1994 VEHICLES

▶ See Figure 5

1. Disconnect the negative battery cable.
2. Position a drain pan under the radiator, then partially drain the coolant to a level below the thermostat. Don't forget to close the radiator drain cock.
3. Remove the thermostat bolt which is accessible through the exhaust manifold.
4. Raise and safely support the vehicle.
5. Remove the radiator outlet pipe stud.

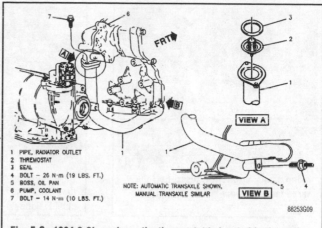

1. PIPE, RADIATOR OUTLET
2. THERMOSTAT
3. SEAL
4. BOLT – 26 N·m (19 LBS. FT.)
5. BOSS, OIL PAN
6. PUMP, COOLANT
7. BOLT – 14 N·m (10 LBS. FT.)

NOTE: AUTOMATIC TRANSAXLE SHOWN, MANUAL TRANSAXLE SIMILAR

VIEW A
VIEW B
FRT

88253G09

Fig. 5 On 1994 2.3L engines, the thermostat is located in the radiator outlet pipe

6. Remove the second thermostat mounting bolt, then remove the thermostat from the vehicle.
7. Thoroughly clean the gasket mating surfaces.

To install:

8. Position the thermostat in the outlet pipe.
9. Install the gasket and radiator outlet pipe. Tighten the bolt to the specification shown in the accompanying figure.
10. Carefully lower the vehicle.
11. Install the thermostat bolt that is accessible through the exhaust manifold and tighten to the specifications shown in the accompanying figure.
12. Fill the cooling to the proper level with the correct type of coolant.
13. Start the engine, allow it to warm to normal operating temperatures and check for leaks.

2.8L and 3.1L Engines

▶ See Figure 6

1. Disconnect the negative battery cable.
2. Position a drain pan under the radiator, then partially drain the coolant to a level below the thermostat. Don't forget to close the radiator drain cock.
3. Some models with cruise control have a vacuum modulator attached to the thermostat housing with a bracket. If your vehicle is equipped as such, remove the bracket from the housing.
4. For 1993 vehicles, disconnect the crankcase vent tube.
5. For 1994–96 vehicles, perform the following:
   a. Disconnect the air inlet tube from the throttle body.
   b. Detach the surge tank line from the thermostat housing.

88253P10

Unfasten the retaining clamp bolt, then disconnect the air inlet tube from the throttle body

Using a back-up wrench, disconnect the surge tank line from the thermostat housing

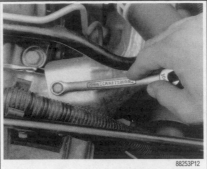

On some vehicles you may have to remove the heat shield bolt and reposition the shield slightly

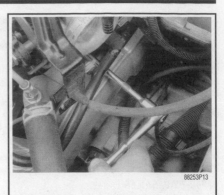

Unfasten the water outlet retaining bolts . . .

. . . then remove the water outlet (with the hose attached, if not replacing the outlet)

Remove the thermostat . . .

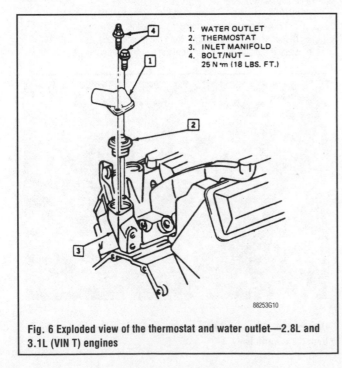

. . . then inspect the thermostat seal and replace if necessary

6. If may be necessary to remove the exhaust manifold heat shield bolt and reposition the heat shield in order to remove the outlet.

7. If replacing the water outlet, disconnect the upper hose from the outlet.

8. Unfasten the 2 retaining bolts, then remove the outlet. Remove the thermostat.

9. Remove and discard the gasket, then thoroughly clean the gasket mating surfaces.

To install:

10. Install the thermostat, position a new gasket, then install the thermostat housing. Install the 2 retaining bolts and tighten to 18 ft. lbs. (25 Nm).

11. Install the remaining components, then fill the engine cooling system with the proper type and amount of coolant.

12. Connect the negative battery cable, then start the engine and check for leaks. Check the coolant level and add if necessary.

Intake Manifold

REMOVAL & INSTALLATION

✳✳ CAUTION

When draining the coolant, keep in mind that cats and dogs are attracted by ethylene glycol antifreeze, and are quite likely to drink any that is left in an uncovered container or in puddles on the ground. This will prove fatal in sufficient quantity. Always drain the coolant into a sealable container. Coolant should be reused unless it is contaminated or several years old.

2.0L and 2.2L Engine

1988–91 VEHICLES

▶ See Figure 7

1. Properly relieve the fuel system pressure, as outlined in Section 5 of this manual.

2. If not already done, disconnect the negative battery cable.

3. Place a suitable container under the radiator, then drain the cooling system.

4. Remove the air cleaner assembly.

5. Tag and disconnect all necessary vacuum lines and wires.

---

1. WATER OUTLET
2. THERMOSTAT
3. INLET MANIFOLD
4. BOLT/NUT — 25 N·m (18 LBS. FT.)

Fig. 6 Exploded view of the thermostat and water outlet—2.8L and 3.1L (VIN T) engines

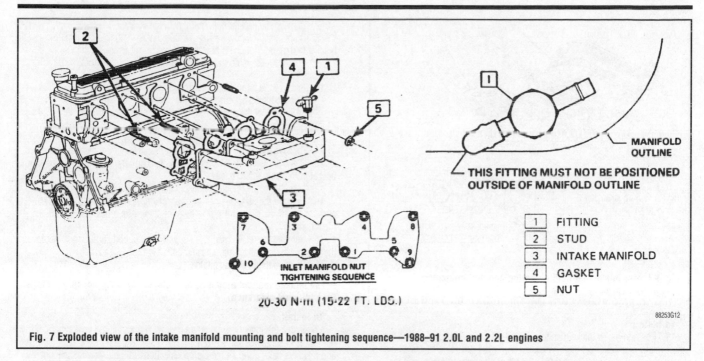

Fig. 7 Exploded view of the intake manifold mounting and bolt tightening sequence—1988–91 2.0L and 2.2L engines

6. Disconnect the fuel lines at the TBI unit. Disconnect the TBI linkage, then remove the TBI unit.

7. Remove the serpentine drive bolt.

8. Remove the power steering pump-to-bracket bolts, then position the pump out of the way; DO NOT disconnect the pressure hoses.

9. Raise and safely support the front of the vehicle.

10. Disconnect the T.V. and accelerator cables, then remove the cable bracket.

11. Position the drain pan, then disconnect the heater hose from the bottom of the intake manifold.

12. Unfasten the intake manifold lower mounting bolts/nuts, then carefully lower the vehicle.

13. Remove the upper intake manifold-to-cylinder head nuts/bolts, then remove the intake manifold from the vehicle.

14. Remove and discard the gasket. Use a suitable gasket to carefully and thoroughly clean the mating surfaces on the manifold and cylinder head.

To install:

15. Position a new intake manifold gasket on the cylinder. Place the intake manifold over the new gasket, then install the retaining bolts/nuts. Tighten the intake manifold-to-cylinder heads bolts, in the sequence shown in the accompanying figure, to 15–22 ft. lbs. (20–30 Nm).

16. The remainder of installation is the reverse of the removal procedure.

17. Fill the engine cooling system with the proper type and amount of coolant.

1992–93 VEHICLES

♦ See Figures 8 and 9

1. Relieve the fuel system pressure, as outlined in Section 5 of this manual.

2. If not already done, disconnect the negative battery cable.

3. Remove the air intake duct.

4. Position a suitable drain pan under the radiator, then drain the cooling system.

5. Tag and disconnect all necessary vacuum lines and wires.

6. Disconnect the throttle linkage.

7. For 1994–96 vehicles, remove the serpentine drive belt.

8. Unbolt the power steering pump, then position it aside without disconnecting the fluid lines.

9. For 1994–96 vehicles, remove the transaxle fluid level indicator and fill tube.

10. For 1994–96 vehicles, detach the electrical connectors from the following components:
   a. MAP sensor
   b. EGR solenoid valve

c. Idle Air Control (IAC) valve
d. Throttle Position (TP) sensor
e. Fuel injector wire harness

11. Remove the MAP sensor and EGR solenoid valve.

12. Remove the upper intake manifold assembly.

13. Remove the EGR valve injector.

14. Remove the fuel injector retainer bracket, regulator and injectors.

15. Disconnect the accelerator and T.V. cables, then remove the cable bracket.

16. For 1992–93 vehicles, perform the following
   a. Raise the vehicle and support it safely.
   b. Remove the 6 intake manifold lower mounting nuts
   c. Carefully lower the vehicle.
   d. Unfasten the lower intake manifold upper mounting nuts, then remove the manifold.

17. For 1994–96 vehicles, perform the following:
   a. Remove the EGR valve pipe.
   b. Remove the lower intake manifold-to-cylinder head retaining nuts and studs, then remove the lower intake manifold from the vehicle.

18. Remove and discard the gasket. Use a suitable gasket to carefully and thoroughly clean the mating surfaces on the manifold and cylinder head.

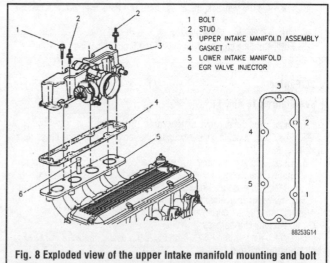

Fig. 8 Exploded view of the upper intake manifold mounting and bolt tightening sequence—1993–96 2.2L engines

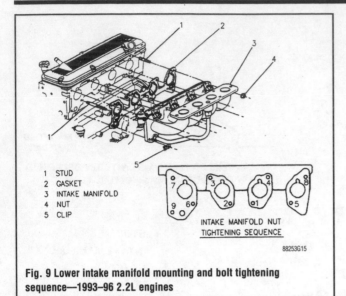

1 STUD
2 GASKET
3 INTAKE MANIFOLD
4 NUT
5 CLIP

INTAKE MANIFOLD NUT
TIGHTENING SEQUENCE

88253G15

Fig. 9 Lower intake manifold mounting and bolt tightening sequence—1993–96 2.2L engines

To install:

19. Position a new intake manifold gasket on the cylinder, then place the lower intake manifold over the new gasket. For 1994–96 vehicles, install the retaining nuts and studs. Tighten the studs to 89 inch lbs. (10 Nm) and the nuts, in sequence, to 24 ft. lbs. (33 Nm).

20. For 1994–96 vehicles, install the EGR valve pipe.

21. Connect the fuel lines.

22. Install the fuel injectors, regulator and injector retainer bracket and tighten the retaining bolts to 22 inch lbs. (3.5 Nm).

23. Install the cable bracket, then connect the accelerator and T.V. cables.

24. For 1992–93 vehicles, perform the following:
  a. Raise the vehicle and support it safely.
  b. Tighten the lower intake manifold nuts in the proper sequence to 22 ft. lbs. (30 Nm).
  c. Carefully lower the vehicle.

25. Install the EGR valve injector so that the port is facing directly towards the throttle body.

26. Install the upper intake manifold assembly. Tighten the upper intake manifold nuts in the proper sequence to 22 ft. lbs. (30 Nm).

27. Install the MAP sensor and EGR solenoid valve.

28. For 1994–96 vehicles, install the serpentine drive belt.

29. Install the accelerator cable bracket and throttle linkage. Tighten the cable bracket bolts to 18 ft. lbs. (25 Nm).

30. Connect the vacuum lines and wires as tagged during removal.

31. Attach the air intake duct.

32. Position the power steering pump and secure with retaining bolts.

33. For 1994–96 vehicles, install the transaxle fluid level indicator and fill tube.

34. Connect the negative battery cable.

35. Fill the engine cooling system with the proper type and amount of coolant.

2.3L Engine

▶ See Figures 10 and 11

1. Disconnect the negative battery cable.

2. Position a suitable container under the radiator, then drain the cooling system.

3. Detach the vacuum hose and electrical connector from the MAP sensor.

4. Unplug the electrical connectors from the following components:
  a. Manifold Absolute Pressure (MAP) sensor.
  b. Intake Air Temperature (IAT) sensor.
  c. EVAP canister purge solenoid.
  d. Fuel injector harness.

5. Detach the vacuum hoses from the fuel pressure regulator and EVAP canister purge solenoid.

6. Disconnect the throttle body-to-air cleaner duct.

7. Remove the accelerator control cable bracket.

8. Disconnect the power brake vacuum hose, including the retaining bracket to the power steering bracket and position it aside.

9. For 1990–92 vehicles, disconnect the coolant lines from the throttle body.

10. Remove the oil/air separator (crankcase ventilation system), as follows:
  a. Leave the hoses attached to the separator.
  b. Disconnect the hoses from the oil fill, chain cover intake duct and intake manifold.
  c. Remove the oil/air separator as an assembly.

11. Remove the oil fill cap and oil level dipstick.

12. Remove the oil fill tube bolt/screw, then pull the oil fill tube upward to unseat from block and remove.

13. Disconnect the injector harness connector.

14. Remove the fill tube from the top, rotating as necessary to gain clearance for the oil/air separator nipple between the intake tubes and fuel rail electrical harness.

15. Remove the intake manifold support bracket bolts and/or nut. Remove the intake manifold attaching nuts and bolts.

16. Remove the intake manifold.

➡The intake manifold mounting hole closest to chain housing is slotted for additional clearance.

To install:

17. Install the intake manifold and gasket. Tightening the intake manifold bolts/nuts in sequence and to 18 ft. lbs. (25 Nm). Tighten intake manifold brace and retainers hand tight. Tighten to specifications in the following sequence:
  a. Nut to stud bolt: 18 ft. lbs. (25 Nm).
  b. Bolt to intake manifold: 40 ft. lbs. (55 Nm).
  c. Bolt to cylinder block: 40 ft. lbs. (55 Nm).

18. Lubricate a new oil fill tube ring seal with engine oil. Install the tube between No. 1 and 2 intake tubes. Rotate as necessary to gain clearance for oil/air separator nipple on fill tube.

19. Locate the oil fill tube in its cylinder block opening. Align the fill tube so it is approximately in its installed position. Place the palm of the hand over the oil fill opening and press straight down to seat fill tube and seal into cylinder block.

20. Install oil/air separator assembly, it may be necessary to lubricate the hoses for ease of assembly.

21. Using a new gasket, install the throttle body to the intake manifold.

22. Attach the injector harness connector.

23. Install the oil fill cap and oil level dipstick.

24. Connect the power brake vacuum hose.

25. Install the throttle cable bracket.

26. Connect the throttle body to air cleaner duct.

27. Install the cooling fan shroud, vacuum hose and electrical connector to the MAP sensor.

28. Connect the negative battery cable.

2.8L and 3.1L (VIN T) Engines

▶ See Figure 12

1. Properly relieve the fuel system pressure, as outlined in Section 5 of this manual.

2. If not already done, disconnect the negative battery cable.

3. Position a suitable drain pan under the radiator, then drain the cooling system.

4. Disconnect the T.V. and accelerator cables from the plenum.

5. Remove the throttle body-to-plenum bolts and the throttle body. Remove the EGR valve.

6. Remove the plenum-to-intake manifold bolts and the plenum. Disconnect and plug the fuel lines and return pipes at the fuel rail.

7. Remove the serpentine drive belt.

8. Remove the power steering pump-to-bracket bolts and support the pump out of the way; but DO NOT disconnect the pressure hoses.

9. Remove the alternator-to-bracket bolts and support the alternator out of the way.

10. Loosen the alternator bracket. From the throttle body, disconnect the idle air vacuum hose.

11. Label and disconnect the electrical connectors from the fuel injectors. Remove the fuel rail.

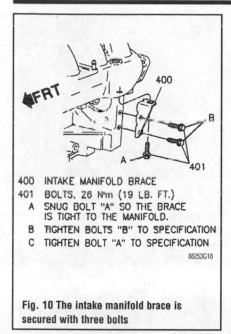

400 INTAKE MANIFOLD BRACE
401 BOLTS, 28 N·m (19 LB. FT.)
A SNUG BOLT "A" SO THE BRACE IS TIGHT TO THE MANIFOLD.
B TIGHTEN BOLTS "B" TO SPECIFICATION
C TIGHTEN BOLT "A" TO SPECIFICATION

88253G18

Fig. 10 The intake manifold brace is secured with three bolts

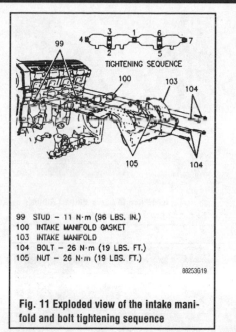

TIGHTENING SEQUENCE

99 STUD – 11 N·m (96 LBS. IN.)
100 INTAKE MANIFOLD GASKET
103 INTAKE MANIFOLD
104 BOLT – 26 N·m (19 LBS. FT.)
105 NUT – 26 N·m (19 LBS. FT.)

88253G19

Fig. 11 Exploded view of the intake manifold and bolt tightening sequence

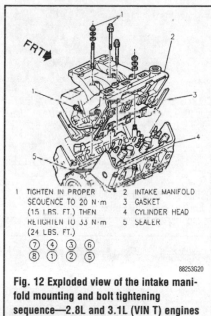

1 TIGHTEN IN PROPER SEQUENCE TO 20 N·m (15 LBS. FT.) THEN RETIGHTEN TO 33 N·m (24 LBS. FT.)
2 INTAKE MANIFOLD
3 GASKET
4 CYLINDER HEAD
5 SEALER

⑦ ④ ③ ⑥
⑧ ① ② ⑤

88253G20

Fig. 12 Exploded view of the intake manifold mounting and bolt tightening sequence—2.8L and 3.1L (VIN T) engines

12. Remove the breather tube. Disconnect the runners.
13. Remove both rocker arm cover-to-cylinder head bolts and the covers. Remove the radiator hose from the thermostat housing.
14. Label and unplug the electrical connectors from the coolant temperature sensor and oil pressure sending unit. Remove the coolant sensor.
15. Remove the bypass hose from the filler neck and cylinder head.
16. Unfasten the intake manifold-to-cylinder head bolts, then remove the intake manifold from the vehicle. Remove and discard the gaskets.
17. Loosen the rocker arm nuts, turn them 90° and remove the pushrods; be sure to keep the components in order for installation purposes.
18. Using a suitable gasket scraper and degreaser, carefully and thoroughly clean all gasket mounting surfaces.

To install:
19. Use new gaskets and place a $\frac{1}{16}$in. (5mm) bead of RTV sealant on the ridges of the manifold.
20. Install the pushrods in their original positions, then tighten the rocker arm nuts to 18 ft. lbs. (25 Nm).
21. Install the intake manifold and tighten (following the torquing sequence) the intake manifold-to-cylinder head bolts to 15 ft. lbs. (20 Nm) and retighten to 24 ft. lbs. (33 Nm).
22. Attach the heater inlet pipe.
23. Install the coolant sensor, then connect the wires to the coolant sensor and oil sending unit.
24. Install the radiator hose at the thermostat outlet.
25. Fill the cooling system.
26. Install the rocker arm cover, then attach the breather tube.
27. Install the fuel rail.

28. Attach the wires at the injectors.
29. Connect the idle air vacuum hose to the throttle body.
30. Install the alternator bracket and the alternator.
31. Install the power steering pump.
32. Install the serpentine belt.
33. Install the fuel inlet and return lines at the fuel rail.
34. Install the plenum.
35. Install the EGR valve.
36. Attach the throttle body to the plenum.
37. Install the accelerator and T.V. cable bracket at the plenum.
38. Connect the negative battery cable, then start the vehicle and check for leaks.
39. Check the cooling system level, and top off as necessary.

3.1L (VIN M) Engine

♦ **See Figure 13**

1. Properly relieve the fuel system pressure, as outlined in Section 5 of this manual.
2. If not already done, disconnect the negative battery cable.
3. Remove the top half of the air cleaner assembly and the throttle body duct.
4. Place a suitable container under the radiator, then drain the cooling system.
5. Remove the EGR pipe from the exhaust manifold.
6. Remove the serpentine drive belt.
7. Disconnect brake vacuum pipe from the plenum.

88253P83

Unfasten the retaining bolts, then remove the MAP sensor

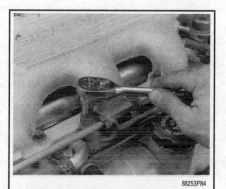

88253P84

Remove the upper intake manifold (plenum) retaining bolts . . .

88253P85

. . . then remove the upper manifold from the engine

Unfasten the top engine mount-to-mount bracket retaining bolts . . .

. . . then remove the side engine mount-to-mount bracket retaining bolts . . .

. . . and remove the engine mount bracket from the vehicle

Remove the engine mount retaining bolts . . .

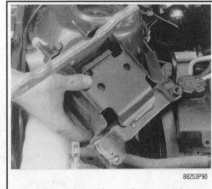

. . . then remove the engine mount from the vehicle

Remove the power steering pump and pulley mounting bolts . . .

. . . then remove the power steering pump and position aside with the fluid lines attached

Remove the retaining bolts, then remove the valve covers from the vehicle

8. Remove the power steering lines from the alternator bracket, then remove the alternator.

9. Tag and disconnect the spark plug wires from the plugs, then detach the harness from the plenum.

10. At the same time, remove the electronic ignition coil and module assembly and the EVAP canister purge solenoid.

11. Tag and detach the upper engine wiring harness connectors from the following components:
   a. Throttle Position (TP) sensor.
   b. Idle Air Control (IAC) valve.
   c. Injector harness.
   d. Engine Coolant Temperature (ECT) sensor.
   e. Manifold Absolute Pressure (MAP) sensor.
   f. Camshaft Position (CMP) sensor.

12. Label and disconnect the vacuum lines from the vacuum modulator, fuel pressure regulator and PCV valve.

13. Remove the MAP sensor.

14. Remove the retaining bolts, then remove the upper intake manifold.

15. Disconnect the fuel lines from the fuel rail, then remove them from the bracket.

16. Install tool J 38467-A or equivalent engine support fixture.

17. Remove the right engine mount.

18. Unfasten the power steering pump mounting bolts, then position the pump aside. DO NOT disconnect the fluid lines.

19. Disconnect the coolant inlet pipe from the coolant outlet housing.

20. Detach the coolant bypass at the water pump and cylinder head.

21. Disconnect the radiator hose from the coolant outlet housing, then remove the coolant outlet housing.

22. Remove both rocker arm (valve) covers.

23. Remove the lower intake manifold mounting bolts, making sure to keep the washers on the center bolts in their original positions. Remove the lower intake manifold from the vehicle.

24. Loosen the rocker arms, then remove the pushrods. Keep the pushrods organized, so they can be installed in their original positions.

25. Remove and discard the intake manifold gasket. Thoroughly clean the gasket mating surfaces with a suitable degreaser.

To install:

26. Place a 2–3mm bead of RTV sealer on each ridge where the front and rear of the intake manifold contact the block, then position a new intake manifold gasket.

Remove the lower intake manifold mounting bolts then remove the lower intake manifold from the vehicle

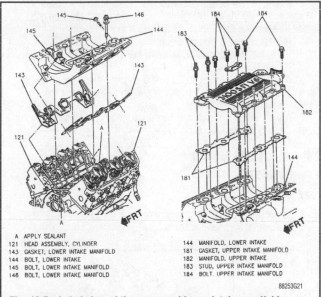

A APPLY SEALANT
121 HEAD ASSEMBLY, CYLINDER
143 GASKET, LOWER INTAKE MANIFOLD
144 BOLT, LOWER INTAKE
145 BOLT, LOWER INTAKE MANIFOLD
146 BOLT, LOWER INTAKE MANIFOLD

144 MANIFOLD, LOWER INTAKE
181 GASKET, UPPER INTAKE MANIFOLD
182 MANIFOLD, UPPER INTAKE
183 STUD, UPPER INTAKE MANIFOLD
184 BOLT, UPPER INTAKE MANIFOLD

88253G21

Fig. 13 Exploded view of the upper and lower intake manifolds— 3.1L (VIN M) engines

➡️Intake pushrods are 5¾ inches long and marked red, and exhaust pushrods are 6 inches long and marked blue.

27. Coat the ends of the pushrods with prelube 1052356 or equivalent. Install the pushrods in their original locations, making sure they are properly seated in the lifters.

28. Install the rocker arms nuts and tighten to 18 ft. lbs. (24 Nm).

29. Coat the threads of the lower intake manifold bolts with sealant 12345739 or equivalent. Position the lower intake manifold and secure with the retaining bolts. Tighten the bolts 115 inch lbs. (13 Nm).

30. Install the front rocker arm (valve) cover.

31. Install the coolant outlet housing. Connect the radiator hose to the thermostat housing.

32. Attach the coolant inlet pipe to the thermostat housing. Attach the coolant bypass pipe to the water pump and cylinder head.

33. Position the power steering pump, then secure with the retaining bolts.

34. Install the serpentine drive belt, loosely, due to the trap design.

35. Install the right engine mount, then remove the engine support fixture.

36. Attach the fuel lines to the fuel rail and bracket.

37. Install the upper intake manifold and tighten the retaining bolts to 18 ft. lbs. (25 Nm).

38. Install the MAP sensor.

39. Connect the vacuum lines to the PCV valve, fuel pressure regulator and vacuum modulator, as tagged during removal.

40. The remainder of installation is the reverse of the removal procedure. Attach all electrical connectors as tagged during removal.

41. Fill the cooling system to the correct level with the proper type and amount of coolant.

42. Connect the negative battery cable, then start the engine and check for leaks.

Exhaust Manifold

REMOVAL & INSTALLATION

2.0L and 2.2L Engine

▶ See Figure 14

1. Disconnect the negative battery cable.

2. Disconnect the oxygen sensor wire.

3. Remove the serpentine belt.

4. Remove the alternator-to-bracket bolts and support the alternator (with the wires attached) out of the way.

5. Raise and support the front of the vehicle.

6. Disconnect the exhaust pipe-to-exhaust manifold bolts and separate the pipe from the manifold, then carefully lower the vehicle.

7. Remove the oil fill tube.

8. For 1993–96 vehicles, remove the heater outlet hose assembly nut from the exhaust manifold.

9. Remove the exhaust manifold retaining nuts/bolts.

10. Remove the exhaust manifold from the exhaust pipe flange and the manifold from the vehicle.

For access to the pushrods (A), loosen the rocker arm (B) retaining bolt s (C) . . .

. . . then remove the pushrods and place them in a suitable holder to keep them in order

Remove the intake manifold gasket and replace with a new one during installation

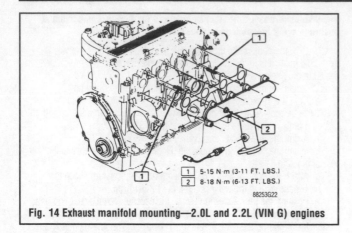

1	5-15 N·m (3-11 FT. LBS.)
2	8-18 N·m (6-13 FT. LBS.)

88253G22

Fig. 14 Exhaust manifold mounting—2.0L and 2.2L (VIN G) engines

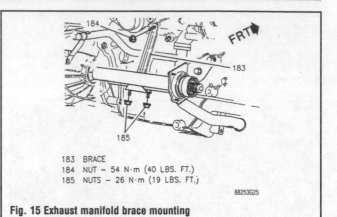

183	BRACE
184	NUT – 54 N·m (40 LBS. FT.)
185	NUTS – 26 N·m (19 LBS. FT.)

88253G25

Fig. 15 Exhaust manifold brace mounting

11. Remove and discard the gasket. Using a gasket scraper, thoroughly clean the gasket mounting surfaces.

To install:

12. Position a new exhaust manifold gasket, then install the manifold and secure using the retaining nuts/bolts.

13. Tighten the exhaust manifold-to-cylinder head nuts to 3–11 ft. lbs. (5–15 Nm) for 1988–90 vehicles, and 115 inch lbs. (13 Nm) for 1991–96 vehicles. Tighten the bolts to 6–13 ft. lbs. (8–18 Nm) for 1988–90 vehicles, and studs to 89 inch lbs. (10 Nm) for 1991–92 vehicles.

14. If removed, install the heater outlet hose assembly nut and tighten to 18 ft. lbs. (25 Nm).

15. The remainder of installation is the reverse of the removal procedure.

16. Connect the negative battery cable, then start the engine and check for leaks.

2.3L Engine

♦ See Figures 15, 16 and 17

1. Disconnect the negative battery cable.
2. Detach the oxygen sensor connector.
3. Remove the upper exhaust manifold heat shield.
4. Raise and safely support the vehicle.
5. Remove exhaust manifold brace-to-manifold bolt.
6. Remove the exhaust manifold-to-exhaust pipe spring loaded nuts by breaking each nut loose gradually, then remove the nuts.
7. Pull down and back on the exhaust pipe to disengage it from the exhaust manifold bolts.
8. Carefully lower the vehicle.
9. Unfasten the exhaust manifold-to-cylinder head attaching nuts, then remove the exhaust manifold.

10. Remove the lower exhaust manifold heat shield, seals and gaskets. Discard the gaskets, then thoroughly clean all of the gasket sealing surfaces.

To install:

11. If installing a new exhaust manifold, transfer following components to the new manifold:

    a. Oxygen sensor (coat the threads of the sensor with a suitable anti-seize compound).
    b. Bolt and nuts.
    c. Lower heat shield.
    d. Exhaust manifold studs.

12. Position a new exhaust manifold gasket, then install the exhaust manifold and secure with the exhaust manifold-to-cylinder head attaching nuts. Tighten, in sequence, to 27–31 ft. lbs. (37–42 Nm).

13. Raise and safely support the vehicle.

14. Install the exhaust manifold brace-to-manifold bolt.

15. Connect the exhaust pipe to the exhaust manifold flange.

16. Install the manifold to exhaust pipe bolts to the exhaust pipe flange. Tighten to 22 ft. lbs. (30 Nm). Turn the nuts evenly to prevent binding.

17. Carefully lower the vehicle.

18. Install the upper heat shield, then attach the oxygen sensor connector.

19. Connect the negative battery cable.

2.8L and 3.1L (VIN T) Engines

♦ See Figure 18

LEFT SIDE

1. Disconnect the negative battery cable.
2. Remove the air cleaner assembly.

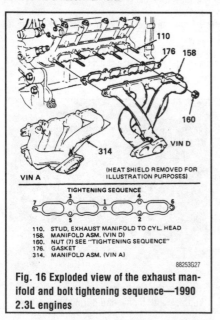

110.	STUD, EXHAUST MANIFOLD TO CYL. HEAD
158.	MANIFOLD ASM. (VIN D)
160.	NUT (7) SEE "TIGHTENING SEQUENCE"
176.	GASKET
314.	MANIFOLD ASM. (VIN A)

88253G27

Fig. 16 Exploded view of the exhaust manifold and bolt tightening sequence—1990 2.3L engines

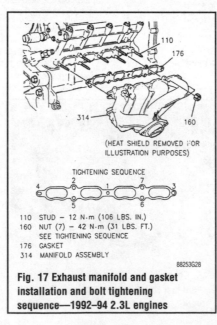

110	STUD – 12 N·m (106 LBS. IN.)	
160	NUT (7) – 42 N·m (31 LBS. FT.)	
	SEE TIGHTENING SEQUENCE	
176	GASKET	
314	MANIFOLD ASSEMBLY	

88253G28

Fig. 17 Exhaust manifold and gasket installation and bolt tightening sequence—1992–94 2.3L engines

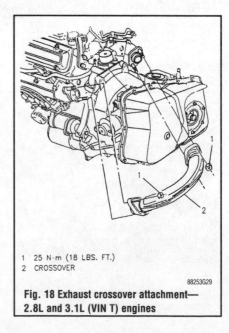

1	25 N·m (18 LBS. FT.)
2	CROSSOVER

88253G29

Fig. 18 Exhaust crossover attachment—2.8L and 3.1L (VIN T) engines

3. Remove the coolant fan.
4. Remove the heat shield.
5. Disconnect the exhaust crossover pipe from the manifold.
6. Unfasten the exhaust manifold-to-cylinder bolts, then remove the manifold from the vehicle.
7. Remove and discard the gaskets. Thoroughly clean the gasket mating surfaces.

To install:

8. Position a new gasket, then install the exhaust manifold. Loosely install the exhaust manifold-to-cylinder head bolts.
9. Attach the exhaust crossover pipe to the manifold.
10. Tighten the exhaust manifold-to-cylinder head bolts to 22–30 ft lbs. (30–40 Nm) for 1988 vehicles, or to 18–21 ft. lbs. (25–28 Nm) for 1989–93 vehicles.
11. Tighten the crossover bolts to 18 ft. lbs. (25 Nm).
12. Install the heat shield and tighten the retaining nuts to 89 inch lbs. (10 Nm).
13. Install the coolant fan and the air cleaner assembly.
14. Connect the negative battery cable, then start the engine and check for exhaust leaks.

RIGHT SIDE

1. Remove the air cleaner assembly.
2. Disconnect the negative battery cable.
3. Raise and safely support the vehicle.
4. Disconnect the exhaust pipe at the crossover.
5. Carefully lower the vehicle.
6. Remove the heat shield.
7. Disconnect the crossover at the manifold.
8. Disconnect the accelerator and T.V. cables, then remove the cable bracket from the plenum.
9. Remove the oxygen sensor.
10. Unfasten the exhaust manifold bolts, then remove the exhaust manifold from the vehicle. Remove and discard the gasket. Thoroughly clean the gasket mating surfaces.

To install:

11. Position a new exhaust manifold gasket, then install the exhaust manifold. Loosely install the manifold retaining bolts.
12. Attach the crossover to the manifold.
13. Tighten the exhaust manifold-to-cylinder head bolts to 14–22 ft. lbs. (20–30 Nm) for 1988 vehicles and 18–21 ft. lbs. (25–28 Nm) for 1989–93 vehicles. Tighten the crossover pipe bolts to 18 ft. lbs. (25 Nm).
14. Install the remaining components in the reverse of the removal procedure.
15. Connect the negative battery cable, then install the air cleaner assembly.
16. Start the engine and check for leaks.

3.1L VIN (M) Engines

♦ See Figure 19

LEFT SIDE

1. Disconnect the negative battery cable.
2. Remove the top half of the air cleaner assembly and throttle cable duct.
3. Place a suitable drain pan under the radiator, then partially drain the cooling system.
4. Disconnect the radiator hose from the thermostat housing.
5. Disconnect the coolant bypass pipe from the water pump and exhaust manifold.
6. Remove the exhaust crossover heat shield, then disconnect the crossover pipe from the manifold.
7. Tag and disconnect the spark plug wires from the plugs.
8. Remove the exhaust manifold head shield.
9. Unfasten the exhaust manifold retaining nuts, then remove the manifold from the vehicle.
10. Remove and discard the gasket, then thoroughly clean the mating surfaces.

To install:

11. Position a new exhaust manifold gasket, then install the manifold. Loosely install all of the manifold retaining nuts, then tighten them to 12 ft. lbs. (16 Nm).
12. Install the exhaust manifold heat shield, then tighten the retaining nuts to 89 inch lbs. (10 Nm).

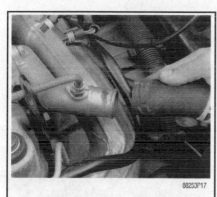

Disconnect the radiator hose from the thermostat housing

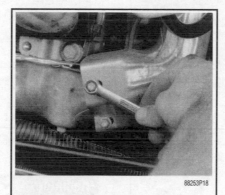

Unfasten the crossover heat shield retaining bolts . . .

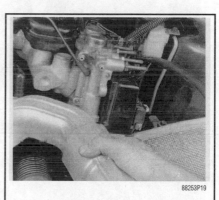

. . . then remove the heat shield from the crossover pipe

Remove the crossover pipe-to-manifold retaining bolts

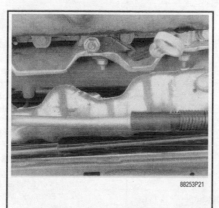

Remove the exhaust manifold heat shield

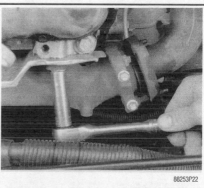

Unfasten the exhaust manifold retaining nuts . . .

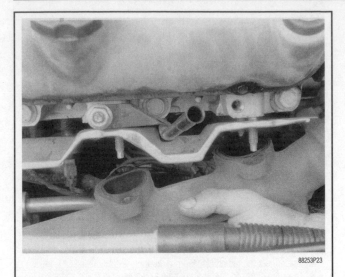

. . . then remove the exhaust manifold from the vehicle

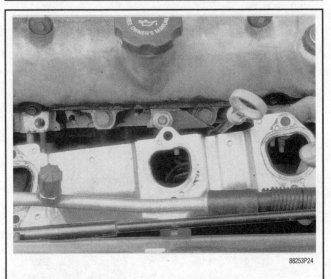

Remove and discard the exhaust manifold gasket

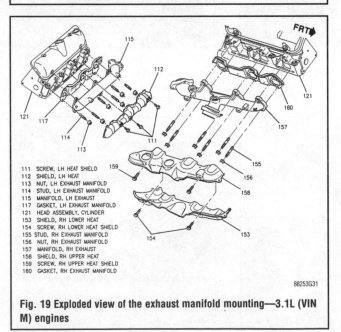

111 SCREW, LH HEAT SHIELD
112 SHIELD, LH HEAT
113 NUT, LH EXHAUST MANIFOLD
114 STUD, LH EXHAUST MANIFOLD
115 MANIFOLD, LH EXHAUST
117 GASKET, LH EXHAUST MANIFOLD
121 HEAD ASSEMBLY, CYLINDER
153 SHIELD, RH LOWER HEAT
154 SCREW, RH LOWER HEAT SHIELD
155 STUD, RH EXHAUST MANIFOLD
156 NUT, RH EXHAUST MANIFOLD
157 MANIFOLD, RH EXHAUST
158 SHIELD, RH UPPER HEAT
159 SCREW, RH UPPER HEAT SHIELD
160 GASKET, RH EXHAUST MANIFOLD

Fig. 19 Exploded view of the exhaust manifold mounting—3.1L (VIN M) engines

13. Fasten the exhaust crossover pipe to the manifold, then install the crossover pipe heat shield.

14. Connect the spark plug wires to the plugs, as tagged during removal.

15. Attach the coolant bypass pipe to the water pump and exhaust manifold.

16. Connect the radiator hose to the coolant outlet housing.

17. Install the top half of the air cleaner and throttle body duct.

18. Connect the negative battery cable, then start the engine and check for exhaust leaks.

RIGHT SIDE

1. Disconnect the negative battery cable.

2. Remove the top half of the air cleaner assembly and throttle cable duct.

3. Remove the exhaust crossover heat shield, then disconnect the crossover from the exhaust manifold.

4. Remove the heated oxygen sensor.

5. Disconnect the EGR pipe from the exhaust manifold.

6. Raise and safely support the vehicle.

7. Remove the transaxle oil fill tube and dipstick assembly.

8. Disconnect the exhaust pipe from the manifold.

9. Detach the exhaust pipe from the converter flange, then support the converter with a suitable piece of wire.

10. Remove the converter heat shield from the body.

11. Remove the exhaust manifold heat shield.

12. Unfasten the exhaust manifold nuts, then remove the exhaust manifold from underneath the vehicle.

13. Remove and discard the gasket, then thoroughly clean the mating surfaces.

To install:

14. Position a new exhaust manifold gasket, then install the manifold. Loosely install the heat shield and the manifold retaining nuts

15. Tighten the exhaust manifold mounting nuts and tighten them to 12 ft. lbs. (16 Nm).

16. Install the manifold heat shield nuts and tighten to 89 inch lbs. (10 Nm).

17. Fasten the converter heat shield to the body.

18. Connect the exhaust pipe to the converter flange and the exhaust pipe to the exhaust manifold.

19. Install the transaxle oil fill tube and dipstick assembly.

20. Carefully lower the vehicle.

21. Install the heated oxygen sensor.

22. Attach the crossover pipe to the exhaust manifolds. Install the crossover heat shield.

23. Connect the EGR pipe to the exhaust manifold.

24. Install the top half of the air cleaner assembly and throttle body duct.

25. Connect the negative battery cable, then start the engine and check for exhaust leaks

Radiator

REMOVAL & INSTALLATION

✳ CAUTION

When draining the coolant, keep in mind that cats and dogs are attracted by ethylene glycol antifreeze, and are quite likely to drink any that is left in an uncovered container or in puddles on the ground. This will prove fatal in sufficient quantity. Always drain the coolant into a sealable container. Coolant should be reused unless it is contaminated or several years old.

1. Disconnect the negative battery cable. For 3.1L (VIN T) engines, remove the battery from the vehicle.

2. Position a suitable drain pan under the radiator, then drain the cooling system.

3. Remove the air intake duct or air cleaner assembly, as applicable.

4. If equipped with an automatic transaxle, disconnect the upper transaxle cooler line.

5. Disconnect the upper radiator hose.

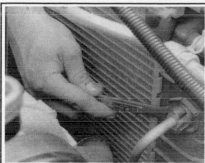

On vehicles equipped with automatic transaxles, disconnect the upper transaxle cooler line

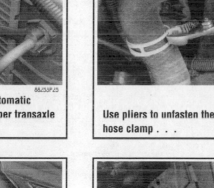

Use pliers to unfasten the lower radiator hose clamp . . .

. . . then disconnect the lower hose from the radiator

If your vehicle has A/C, remove the condenser line clip, then remove the condenser-to-radiator bolts

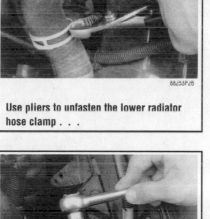

Remove the radiator retaining bolts . . .

. . . then lift the radiator up and out of the engine compartment

6. If equipped with an automatic transaxle, disconnect the lower transaxle cooler line.

7. If necessary for access to the upper fan bolt, unclip and reposition the A/C line.

8. Detach the cooling fan electrical connector and retaining bolt(s), then remove the cooling fan.

9. Remove the splash guard located below the lower radiator hose.

10. Disconnect the lower radiator hose from the radiator.

11. If equipped with A/C, remove the condenser line clip, then remove the condenser-to-radiator bolts.

12. Disconnect the coolant surge tank hose.

13. Unfasten the radiator retaining bolts, then lift the radiator up and out of the vehicle.

To install:

14. Place the radiator in its mounting position, then secure with the retaining bolts. Tighten the bolts to 89 inch lbs. (10 Nm).

15. The remainder of installation is the reverse of the removal procedure.

16. If equipped with a 3.1L (VIN T) engine, install the battery and connect the positive, then the negative battery cables.

17. If not already done, connect the negative battery cable. Fill the cooling system with the proper type and quantity of coolant, then start the engine, let it warm up, and check for leaks. Check the coolant level and add, if necessary.

Electric Cooling Fan

❊❊❊ CAUTION

To avoid personal injury, always keep your hands, tools and clothing away from the cooling fan. The fan is electric and may come on at any time, even when the engine is not running.

REMOVAL & INSTALLATION

1988–93 Vehicles

EXCEPT 2.3L ENGINES

▶ See Figure 20

1. Remove the air cleaner assembly.
2. For 2.0L and 2.2L engines, disconnect the negative battery cables.

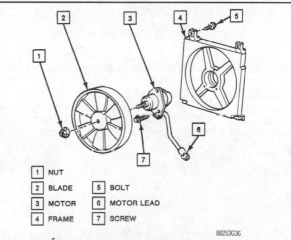

1	NUT	4	FRAME
2	BLADE	5	BOLT
3	MOTOR	6	MOTOR LEAD
		7	SCREW

Fig. 20 The electric fans can usually be disassembled so you can order a specific part that may be faulty—3.1L (VIN T) shown, other engines similar

3. For 2.8L and 3.1L engines, disconnect the negative, then the positive battery cables, then remove the battery from the vehicle.

4. Remove the air cleaner housing and bracket assembly.

5. Detach the fan electrical connector.

6. If necessary for access to the upper fan bolt, unclip and reposition the A/C line.

7. Disconnect the electrical harness clip or A/C line clip, as applicable.

8. Unfasten the fan frame attaching bolts, then remove the fan assembly from the vehicle.

To install:

9. Install the fan in the vehicle and secure with the retaining bolts. Tighten the bolts to 89 inch lbs. (10 Nm).

10. The remainder of installation is the reverse of the removal procedure.

11. Either connect the negative battery cable or install the battery, then connect the positive, then the negative battery cables, as applicable.

12. Start the engine and check for proper fan operation, making sure the fan is moving the air in the proper direction.

2.3L ENGINES

▶ **See Figure 21**

1. Disconnect the negative battery cable.

2. If necessary for access, remove the air intake duct assembly.

3. Detach the wiring harness from the motor and fan frame.

4. Remove the bolt and rubber insulator.

5. Remove the fan assembly from the radiator support. On 1992–93 engine, the fan must be removed from the bottom of the vehicle.

6. Installation is the reverse of the removal procedure. Tighten the retaining bolt to 89 inch lbs. (10 Nm).

7. Connect the negative battery cable, then start the vehicle and check for proper fan operation, making sure the fan is moving the air in the proper direction.

1994–96 Vehicles

2.2L, 2.3L AND 1996 3.1L ENGINES

1. Disconnect the negative battery cable.

2. If necessary for access to the upper fan bolt, unclip and reposition the A/C line.

3. Remove the cooling fan mounting bolt.

4. Detach the electrical connector, then remove the cooling fan from the vehicle.

5. Installation is the reverse of the removal procedure.

6. Connect the negative battery cable, then start the engine and check for proper fan operation, making sure the fan is moving the air in the proper direction.

1994–95 3.1L ENGINES

1. Disconnect the negative battery cable.

2. Remove the air intake duct.

3. Place a suitable drain pan under the radiator, then drain the cooling system.

4. Remove the cooling fan mounting bolt.

5. Detach the fan electrical connector.

6. Disconnect the radiator inlet hose from the radiator.

7. Remove the radiator mounting bolt.

8. Pull the windshield washer fluid bottle fill tube from the bottle.

9. Remove the vacuum tank and vacuum tank bracket.

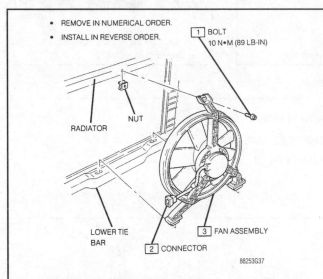

Fig. 21 Exploded view of the electric fan attachment—2.3L engine

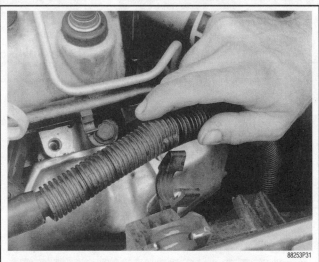

You may have to unclip and reposition the A/C line in order to get to the upper fan bolt

Remove the cooling fan mounting bolt

Detach the cooling fan electrical connector . . .

. . . then remove the cooling fan from the vehicle

10. Remove the cooling fan by sliding the fan leg into the area left from the vacuum tank.

11. Installation is the reverse of the removal procedure.

12. Connect the negative battery cable, then start the engine and check for proper fan operation, making sure the fan is moving the air in the proper direction.

Water Pump

REMOVAL & INSTALLATION

✳✳ CAUTION

When draining the coolant, keep in mind that cats and dogs are attracted by ethylene glycol antifreeze, and are quite likely to drink any that is left in an uncovered container or in puddles on the ground. This will prove fatal in sufficient quantity. Always drain the coolant into a sealable container. Coolant should be reused unless it is contaminated or several years old.

2.0L and 2.2L Engines

♦ See Figure 22

1. Disconnect the negative battery cable.
2. Position a suitable drain pan under the radiator, then drain the cooling system.
3. For 2.2L (VIN 4) engines, loosen the water pump pulley bolts.
4. Remove the serpentine drive belt.
5. For 2.0L and 2.2L (VIN G) engines, unfasten the water pump pulley retaining bolts, then remove the pulley.
6. For 2.0L and 2.2L (VIN G) engines, perform the following:
   a. Remove the alternator attaching bolts, then remove the alternator bracket and heat shield.
   b. Detach the wiring, then remove the alternator from the vehicle.
7. Remove the alternator side bracket.
8. Unfasten the water pump attaching bolts, then remove the pump from the vehicle.
9. Remove and discard the gasket, then thoroughly clean the gasket mating surfaces.

To install:

10. Position a new water pump gasket, then install the water pump. Tighten the retaining bolts to 18–22 ft. lbs. (25–30 Nm).
11. Install the water pump pulley and tighten the bolts to 22 ft. lbs. (30 Nm).
12. If removed, install the alternator side bracket and alternator. Attach the wiring, then install the heat shield and bracket.

13. Install the serpentine drive belt.
14. Fill the cooling system with the proper amount and type of coolant.
15. Connect the negative battery cable, then start the engine and inspect for leaks. Check the coolant level, and add if necessary.

2.3L Engine

♦ See Figure 23

1. Disconnect the negative battery cable.
2. Position a suitable clean container under the radiator, then drain the engine coolant into it for reuse. For more complete draining, disconnect the heater hose from the thermostat housing.
3. Detach the oxygen sensor connector.
4. Remove the upper and lower exhaust manifold heat shield attaching bolts, then remove the shields.
5. Remove the exhaust manifold brace-to-manifold attaching bolt.
6. Break the exhaust pipe-to-manifold spring nuts/bolts loose
7. Raise and safely support the vehicle.
8. Remove the bolts from the exhaust flange using a 7/32 in. (5.5mm) socket and 1 bolt rotate clockwise first.

➡**Rotating the bolt clockwise is necessary to relieve the spring pressure from 1st bolt prior to removing the 2nd bolt otherwise the exhaust pipe will twist and bind the bolt as it is removed.**

9. Thread the bolt with least pressure on it out 4 turns.
10. Move the other bolt and turn it all the way out of the exhaust pipe flange.
11. Return to the 1st bolt and rotate it the rest of the way out.
12. Pull the exhaust pipe back from the exhaust manifold.
13. Disconnect the radiator outlet pipe from the oil pan and transaxle. The exhaust manifold brace will have to be removed. Leave the lower radiator hose attached and pull down on the radiator outlet pipe to disengage it from the water pump. Let the radiator outlet pump hang.
14. Carefully lower the vehicle.
15. Remove the exhaust manifold-to-cylinder head attaching nuts, then remove the exhaust manifold, seals and gaskets.
16. Remove the water pump cover-to-engine attaching bolts.
17. Unfasten the water pump-to-timing chain housing attaching nuts.
18. Remove the water pump and cover assembly from the engine.
19. Remove the water pump cover-to-radiator pump assembly. Clean all mating surfaces thoroughly and use new gaskets.

To install:

➡**Before installing the water pump it is important to first read over the entire procedure. Pay special attention to the tightening sequence, to avoid part damage and to insure proper sealing.**

20. Position the water pump cover to the radiator pump assembly and install the attaching bolts. Do not tighten.
21. Lubricate the splines of the radiator pump drive with the an approved chassis grease and install the pump and cover assembly.
22. Install the pump cover-to-engine attaching bolts, hand-tight.
23. Install the timing chain housing nuts, hand-tight.

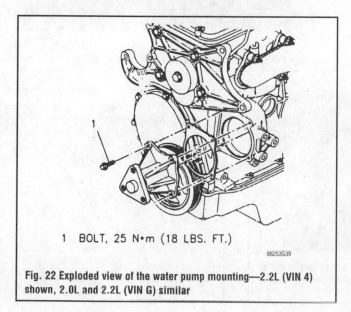

1 BOLT, 25 N•m (18 LBS. FT.)

88253G39

Fig. 22 Exploded view of the water pump mounting—2.2L (VIN 4) shown, 2.0L and 2.2L (VIN G) similar

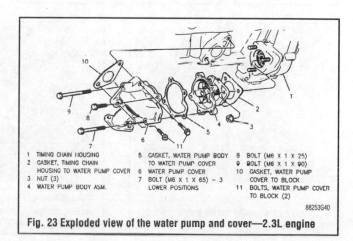

1 TIMING CHAIN HOUSING	5 GASKET, WATER PUMP BODY TO WATER PUMP COVER	8 BOLT (M6 X 1 X 25)
2 GASKET, TIMING CHAIN HOUSING TO WATER PUMP COVER	6 WATER PUMP COVER	9 BOLT (M6 X 1 X 90)
3 NUT (3)	7 BOLT (M6 X 1 X 65) – 3 LOWER POSITIONS	10 GASKET, WATER PUMP COVER TO BLOCK
4 WATER PUMP BODY ASM.		11 BOLTS, WATER PUMP COVER TO BLOCK (2)

88253G40

Fig. 23 Exploded view of the water pump and cover—2.3L engine

24. Lubricate the O-ring on the radiator outlet pipe with a solution of antifreeze and slide the pipe into the radiator pump cover. Install the attaching bolts hand-tight.

25. Tighten the bolts and nuts in following order:
   a. Pump assembly-to-timing chain housing nuts: 19 ft. lbs. (26 Nm).
   b. Water pump-to-pump cover assembly: 106 inch lbs. (12 Nm).
   c. Water pump cover-to-engine (tighten the bottom bolt first): 19 ft. lbs. (26 Nm).
   d. Radiator outlet pipe assembly-to-pump cover: 125 ft. lbs. (14 Nm).

26. Position new gasket, then install the exhaust manifold. Install the exhaust manifold-to-cylinder head attaching nuts and tighten, in sequence, to 22 ft. lbs. (30 Nm).

27. Raise and safely support the vehicle.

28. Seat the exhaust manifold bolts into the exhaust pipe flange.

29. Using a 7/32 in. (5.5mm) socket, start both bolts. Rotate the bolts counterclockwise. Turn both bolts in evenly to avoid cocking the exhaust pipe and binding the bolts. Turn the bolts in until fully seated.

30. Attach the radiator outlet pipe to the transaxle and the oil pan, then install the exhaust manifold brace.

31. Carefully lower the vehicle.

32. Install the exhaust manifold brace-to-manifold attaching bolt.

33. Using a 13mm wrench, tighten the exhaust pipe-to-manifold nuts to 22 ft. lbs. (30 Nm).

34. Install the lower heat shields.

35. Attach the electrical connector to the oxygen sensor.

36. Connect the negative battery cable.

37. Fill cooling system and check for leaks. Start the engine and allow to come to normal operating temperature. Recheck for leaks. Top off the coolant, as necessary, to obtain the proper level.

2.8L and 3.1L Engines

▶ See Figure 24

1. Disconnect the negative battery cable.
2. Drain the engine coolant into a clean container for reuse.
3. Remove the serpentine drive belt.
4. For 1988–92 vehicles, disconnect the radiator and heater hoses.
5. Unfasten the water pump pulley bolts, then remove the pulley.
6. Remove the water pump-to-engine bolts, then remove the water pump from the vehicle. Remove and discard the gasket, then thoroughly clean the gasket mating surfaces.

To install:

7. Install a new gasket, then position the water pump over the gasket. Coat the water pump retaining bolts threads with 1052080 or equivalent sealant.
8. Install the water pump attaching bolts and tighten to 89 inch lbs. (10 Nm).
9. Install the water pump pulley and attaching bolts. Tighten the retaining bolts to 15 ft. lbs. (21 Nm).
10. If removed, connect the radiator and heater hoses.
11. Install the serpentine drive belt.
12. Connect the negative battery cable.
13. Fill cooling system and check for leaks. Start the engine and allow to come to normal operating temperature. Recheck for leaks. Top off the coolant, as necessary to obtain the correct level.

Cylinder Head

REMOVAL & INSTALLATION

✳ CAUTION

When draining the coolant, keep in mind that cats and dogs are attracted by ethylene glycol antifreeze, and are quite likely to drink

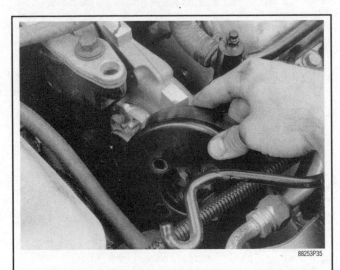

After removing the water pump pulley retaining bolts, remove the pulley

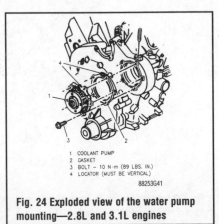

Unfasten the bolts securing the water pump to the engine . . .

. . . then remove the water pump from the engine

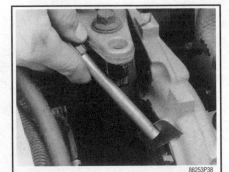

If using a scraper to clean the water pump mating surfaces, be extremely careful not to gouge the surface

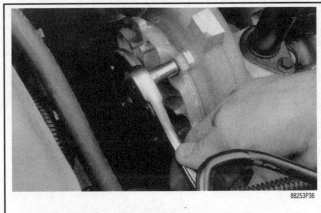

1 COOLANT PUMP
2 GASKET
3 BOLT – 10 N·m (89 LBS. IN.)
4 LOCATOR (MUST BE VERTICAL)

Fig. 24 Exploded view of the water pump mounting—2.8L and 3.1L engines

any that is left in an uncovered container or in puddles on the ground. This will prove fatal in sufficient quantity. Always drain the coolant into a sealable container. Coolant should be reused unless it is contaminated or several years old.

2.0L and 2.2L Engine

➡The engine should be overnight cold before removing the cylinder head.

1988–90 VEHICLES

♦ See Figure 25

1. Properly relieve the fuel system pressure, as outlined in Section 5 of this manual. If not already done, disconnect the negative battery cable.
2. Place a suitable container under the radiator, then drain the cooling system.
3. Remove the TBI cover.
4. Raise and safely support the vehicle.
5. Remove the exhaust shield. Disconnect the exhaust pipe.
6. Remove the heater hose from the intake manifold.
7. Disconnect the accelerator and TV cable bracket.
8. Carefully lower the vehicle.
9. Tag and disconnect the vacuum lines at the intake manifold and thermostat.
10. Disconnect the accelerator linkage at the TBI unit and remove the linkage bracket.
11. Tag and disconnect all necessary wires. Disconnect the upper radiator hose from the thermostat.
12. Remove the serpentine belt.
13. Unbolt the power steering pump and lay aside. Do NOT disconnect the fluid lines.
14. Make sure the fuel system pressure is released, then disconnect and plug the fuel lines.
15. Remove the alternator. Remove the alternator brace from the head and remove the upper mounting bracket.

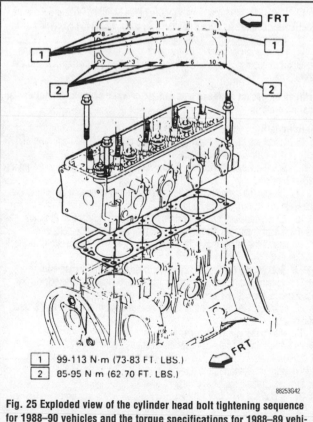

| 1 | 99-113 N·m (73-83 FT. LBS.) |
| 2 | 85-95 N·m (62-70 FT. LBS.) |

88253G42

Fig. 25 Exploded view of the cylinder head bolt tightening sequence for 1988–90 vehicles and the torque specifications for 1988–89 vehicles

16. Remove the cylinder head cover. Remove the rocker arms and pushrods keeping all parts in order for correct installation.
17. Remove the cylinder head bolts. Remove the cylinder head with the TBI unit, intake and exhaust manifolds still attached. Remove and discard the cylinder head gasket.

To install:

18. The gasket surfaces on both the head and the block must be clean of any foreign matter and free of any nicks or heavy scratches. Bolt threads in the block and the bolts must be clean.
19. Place a new cylinder head gasket in position over the dowel pins on the block. Carefully guide the cylinder head into position.
20. Coat the cylinder head bolts with sealing compound and install them finger-tight.
21. Using a torque wrench, tighten the bolts for 1988–89 vehicles, as follows: tighten the long bolts to 73–83 ft lbs. (11 Nm), in the sequence shown in the illustration and tighten the short bolts to 62–70 ft lbs. (84–95 Nm) in the sequence shown in the illustration.
22. For 1990 vehicles, tighten with a torque wrench in 4 steps as follows:
    a. Tighten all bolts in sequence to 41 ft. lbs. (55 Nm).
    b. Tighten all bolts an additional 45° in sequence.
    c. Tighten all bolts an additional 45° in sequence.
    d. Tighten the long bolts—8, 4, 1, 1, 5 and 9 an additional 20° and tighten the short bolts—7, 3, 2, 6 and 10 an additional 10°.

➡The short bolts, exhaust side, should end up with a total rotation of 100° and the long bolts, intake side, should end up with a total rotation of 110°.

23. Reinstall the alternator. Install the power steering pump and brackets.
24. Reconnect the fuel lines and the hoses. Connect the exhaust pipe to the manifold.
25. Install the valve cover and connect the linkage at the TBI unit. Install the air cleaner and fill all the fluids.
26. Connect the negative battery cable, then start the engine and check for leaks. Check the fluid levels, and add if necessary.

1991–96 VEHICLES

♦ See Figure 26

1. Properly relieve the fuel system pressure, as outlined in Section 5 of this manual. If not already done, disconnect the negative battery cable.
2. Place a suitable container under the radiator, then drain the cooling system.
3. Disconnect the air inlet duct.
4. Tag and disconnect the necessary vacuum lines.
5. Detach and unroute the electrical connections from the following:
   a. Engine Coolant Temperature (ECT) sensor
   b. Oxygen sensor
   c. Idle Air Control (IAC) valve
   d. Throttle Position (TP) sensor
   e. Manifold Absolute Pressure (MAP) sensor
   f. EVAP canister purge solenoid
   g. Fuel injector harness
6. Disconnect the accelerator, cruise control and TV cables.
7. Remove the coolant recovery reservoir.
8. Install engine support fixture, tool J 28467-A equivalent to the engine, then remove the right engine mount.
9. Remove the serpentine belt.
10. Remove the alternator rear brace, then remove the alternator.
11. Disconnect the power steering pump lines, then remove the power steering pump.
12. Remove the serpentine drive belt tensioners.
13. Remove the right engine mount bracket.
14. Tag and disconnect the wires from the spark plugs.
15. Detach the EVAP canister purge line from beneath the manifold.
16. Remove the throttle body cable bracket.
17. Disconnect the upper radiator hose from the coolant outlet.
18. Remove the intake manifold brace (on the power steering bracket).
19. Disconnect the coolant inlet hose from the cylinder head.
20. Using a back-up wrench, disconnect the fuel lines.

➡When valve train components are removed for service, they should be kept in order. They must be installed in the same location, with the mating surface from which they were removed.

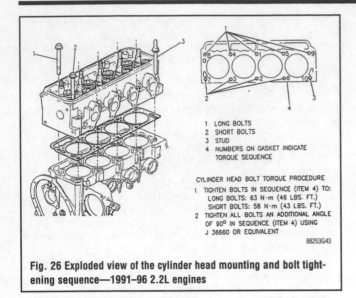

```
1 LONG BOLTS
2 SHORT BOLTS
3 STUD
4 NUMBERS ON GASKET INDICATE
  TORQUE SEQUENCE
```

```
CYLINDER HEAD BOLT TORQUE PROCEDURE
1 TIGHTEN BOLTS IN SEQUENCE (ITEM 4) TO:
  LONG BOLTS: 63 N·m (46 LBS. FT.)
  SHORT BOLTS: 58 N·m (43 LBS. FT.)
2 TIGHTEN ALL BOLTS AN ADDITIONAL ANGLE
  OF 90° IN SEQUENCE (ITEM 4) USING
  J 36660 OR EQUIVALENT
                                    88253G43
```

Fig. 26 Exploded view of the cylinder head mounting and bolt tightening sequence—1991–96 2.2L engines

21. Remove the rocker arm (valve) cover, then remove the rocker arms and pushrods, keeping them in order for installation.
22. Remove the spark plug wire bracket.
23. Remove the engine lift bracket.
24. Raise and safely support the vehicle.
25. Disconnect the exhaust pipe from the lower manifold.
26. Carefully lower the vehicle.
27. Remove the cylinder head retaining bolts.
28. If equipped with an automatic transaxle, remove the transaxle fluid level indicator bracket.
29. Remove the cylinder head from the vehicle. Remove and discard the cylinder head gasket.
30. The gasket surfaces on both the head and the block must be clean of any foreign matter and free of any nicks or heavy scratches. Bolt threads in the block and the bolts must be clean.

To install:
31. Place a new cylinder head gasket in position over the dowel pins on the block. Carefully guide the cylinder head into position.
32. Coat the cylinder head bolts with sealing compound and install them finger tight.
33. Using a torque wrench, tighten the bolts as follows:
    a. Tighten the long bolts in sequence to 46 ft. lbs. (62 Nm).
    b. Tighten the short bolts in sequence to 43 ft. lbs. (58 Nm).
    c. Tighten all bolts in sequence an additional 90° using J 36660, or equivalent torque angle meter.
34. Install the engine lift bracket.
35. Install the spark plug wire bracket.
36. Install the rocker arms and pushrods in the same locations as they were removed from.
37. Install the rocker arm (valve) cover.
38. Install the accelerator, cruise control and TV bracket.
39. Connect the fuel lines and tighten using a back-up wrench.
40. Attach the vacuum lines and electrical connections at the throttle body, as tagged during removal.
41. Connect the coolant inlet hose to the cylinder head.
42. If equipped, install the transaxle fluid level indicator bracket bolt.
43. Install the intake manifold bracket-to-power steering bracket.
44. Connect the upper radiator hose to the outlet housing.
45. Attach the spark plug wires to the plugs, as tagged during removal.
46. Install the right engine bracket.
47. Install the serpentine drive belt tensioner.
48. Install the power steering pump, then connect the fluid lines.
49. Install the alternator and alternator rear brace.
50. Install the serpentine drive belt.
51. Remove the engine support tool.
52. Install the coolant recovery reservoir.
53. Install the air cleaner duct.
54. Connect the accelerator, cruise control and T.V. cables to the throttle body.

55. Route and attach the following electrical connectors:
    a. Engine Coolant Temperature (ECT) sensor
    b. Oxygen sensor
    c. Idle Air Control (IAC) valve
    d. Throttle Position (TP) sensor
    e. Manifold Absolute Pressure (MAP) sensor
    f. EVAP canister purge solenoid
    g. Fuel injector harness
56. Connect the vacuum lines, as tagged during removal.
57. Raise and safely support the vehicle, then attach the exhaust pipe.
58. Carefully lower the vehicle. Fill all fluids and/or lubricants to the proper levels.
59. Connect the negative battery cable, then start the engine and check for leaks. Check the fluid levels, and add if necessary.

2.3L Engine

◆ See Figures 27, 28 amd 29

1. Properly relieve the fuel system pressure, as outlined in Section 5 of this manual.
2. If not already done, disconnect the negative battery cable. Drain the engine coolant into a clean container for reuse.
3. Disconnect the heater inlet and throttle body heater hoses from water outlet. Disconnect upper radiator hose from water outlet.
4. Remove the exhaust manifold.
5. Remove the intake and exhaust camshaft housings.
6. Unfasten the retaining bolt/screw, then remove the engine oil cap and dipstick. Pull the oil fill tube upward to unseat it from the block.
7. Tag and detach the injector harness electrical connector.
8. Disconnect the throttle body-to-air cleaner duct. Remove the throttle cable and bracket and position it aside.
9. Remove the throttle body from the intake manifold with the electrical harness, hoses and cable attached, then position the assembly aside.
10. Tag and disconnect the Manifold Absolute Pressure (MAP) sensor vacuum hose from intake manifold.
11. Remove the intake manifold bracket-to-block bolt, then remove the intake manifold brace.
12. Detach the electrical connectors from the Manifold Absolute Pressure (MAP) sensor, Intake Air Temperature (IAT) sensor and purge solenoid.
13. Tag and detach the 2 coolant sensor connections.
14. Remove the cylinder head-to-block bolts, in the reverse order of the tightening sequence. Remove the cylinder head, then remove and discard the gasket.

➡ **Clean all gasket surfaces with plastic or wood scraper. Do not use any sealing material.**

To install:
15. Install the cylinder head gasket on the cylinder block, then carefully position the cylinder head in place.
16. Sparingly coat the head bolt threads with clean engine oil, allowing any excess oil to drain off before installing.
17. Tighten the cylinder head bolts to the proper torque, in the sequences shown in the accompanying figures.
18. Attach the electrical connectors to the Manifold Absolute Pressure (MAP) sensor, Intake Air Temperature (IAT) sensor and purge solenoid.
19. Install the intake manifold brace and secure with the manifold-to-block bracket bolt.
20. Connect the MAP sensor vacuum hose to the intake manifold.
21. Install the throttle body on the intake manifold with the electrical harness, hoses and cable attached.
22. Connect the throttle body-to-air cleaner duct. Install the throttle cable and bracket.
23. Attach the injector harness electrical connector.
24. Attach the 2 coolant sensor connections.
25. Install the oil cap and dipstick. Install the oil fill tube into the block and secure with the retaining bolt/screw.
26. Install the exhaust and intake camshaft housings.
27. Install the exhaust manifold.
28. Connect the heater inlet and throttle body heater hoses to the water outlet. Connect the upper radiator hose to the water outlet.
29. Fill the cooling system and connect the negative battery cable.

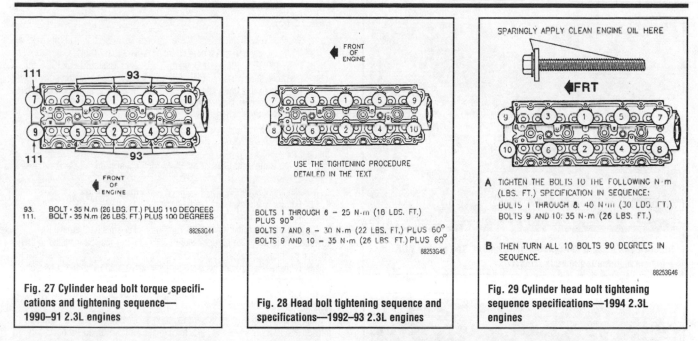

Fig. 27 Cylinder head bolt torque specifications and tightening sequence—1990–91 2.3L engines

93.   BOLT - 35 N.m (26 LBS. FT.) PLUS 110 DEGREES
111. BOLT - 35 N.m (26 LBS. FT.) PLUS 100 DEGREES
88253G44

Fig. 28 Head bolt tightening sequence and specifications—1992–93 2.3L engines

USE THE TIGHTENING PROCEDURE DETAILED IN THE TEXT

BOLTS 1 THROUGH 6 — 25 N·m (18 LBS. FT.) PLUS 90°
BOLTS 7 AND 8 — 30 N·m (22 LBS. FT.) PLUS 60°
BOLTS 9 AND 10 — 35 N·m (26 LBS. FT.) PLUS 60°
88253G45

Fig. 29 Cylinder head bolt tightening sequence specifications—1994 2.3L engines

SPARINGLY APPLY CLEAN ENGINE OIL HERE
◀FRT

A TIGHTEN THE BOLTS TO THE FOLLOWING N·m (LBS. FT.) SPECIFICATION IN SEQUENCE:
BOLTS 1 THROUGH 8, 40 N·m (30 LBS. FT.)
BOLTS 9 AND 10: 35 N·m (26 LBS. FT.)

B THEN TURN ALL 10 BOLTS 90 DEGREES IN SEQUENCE.
88253G46

30. Start the engine, allow it to reach operating temperature then check for leaks. Check the coolant level and add, if necessary.

2.8L and 3.1L Engines

♦ See Figure 30

LEFT SIDE

1. Properly relieve the fuel pressure, as outlined in Section 5 of this manual.
2. If not already done, disconnect the negative battery cable.
3. For 1988–93 vehicles, remove the air cleaner assembly. For 1994–96 vehicles, remove the top half of the air cleaner assembly and throttle body duct.
4. Place a suitable drain pan under the radiator and drain the cooling system.
5. Unfasten the rocker arm (valve) cover attaching bolts, then remove the rocker arm cover(s).
6. Remove the intake manifold and plenum.
7. Remove the engine strut bracket.
8. Remove the exhaust crossover.
9. Remove the left side exhaust manifold.
10. Tag and disconnect the spark plug wires from the left cylinder head.
11. Loosen the rocker arms nuts, turn the rocker arms and remove the pushrods. Keep all of the components in order so they may be installed in their original positions.
12. Disconnect the oil level indicator tube assembly.
13. Unfasten the cylinder head-to-block bolts; starting with the outer bolts and working toward the center. Remove the cylinder head from the vehicle. Remove and discard the cylinder head gasket.

14. Clean the gasket mounting surfaces. Inspect the surfaces of the cylinder head, block and intake manifold damage and/or warpage. Clean the threaded holes in the block and the cylinder head bolt threads.

To install:

15. Align a new cylinder head gasket over the dowels on the block with the note **This Side Up** facing the cylinder head.
16. Position the cylinder head over the gasket on the block.
17. Sparingly coat the cylinder head bolt threads 1052080 or equivalent sealant, then install the bolts hand-tight.
18. Using the proper torque sequence (shown the accompanying figure), tighten the bolts to 33 ft. lbs. (45 Nm). After all bolts are tightened to 33 ft. lbs. (45 Nm), rotate the torque wrench another 90° or ¼ turn. This will apply the correct torque to the bolts.
19. Position a new intake manifold gasket.
20. Install the pushrods in the same order that they were removed. Tighten the rocker arm nuts to 14–20 ft. lbs. (19–27 Nm).
21. Install the intake manifold and plenum.
22. Install the rocker arm (valve) cover and secure with the retaining bolts.
23. Install the oil level indicator tube assembly.
24. Connect the spark plug wires to the plugs, as tagged during removal.
25. Install the left exhaust manifold.
26. Install the crossover pipe.
27. Install the engine strut bracket.
28. For 1988–93 vehicles, install the air cleaner assembly. For 1994–96 vehicles, install the top half of the air cleaner assembly and throttle body duct.
29. Fill the cooling system and connect the negative battery cable.
30. Start the engine, allow it to reach operating temperature then check for leaks. Check the coolant level and add, if necessary.

Unfasten the retainer, then remove the oil level dipstick tube assembly

Starting with the outermost bolts, unfasten the cylinder head-to-block bolts . . .

. . . then remove the cylinder head from the vehicle

Remove and discard the cylinder head gasket. The gasket MUST be replaced anytime the head is removed

The correct tightening sequence and specifications are essential to prevent cylinder head leakage

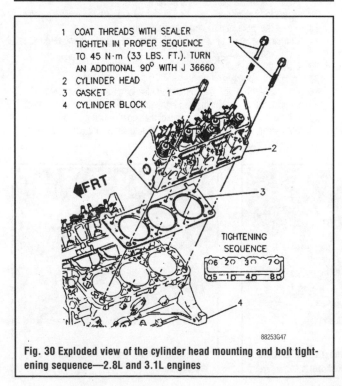

Fig. 30 Exploded view of the cylinder head mounting and bolt tightening sequence—2.8L and 3.1L engines

RIGHT SIDE

1. Properly relieve the fuel pressure, as outlined in Section 5 of this manual.
2. If not already done, disconnect the negative battery cable.
3. For 1988–93 vehicles, remove the air cleaner assembly. For 1994–96 vehicles, remove the top half of the air cleaner assembly and throttle body duct.
4. Place a suitable drain pan under the radiator and drain the cooling system.
5. Raise and safely support the vehicle.
6. Disconnect the exhaust pipe from the crossover.
7. Carefully lower the vehicle.
8. Remove the exhaust crossover heat shield. Remove the crossover from the right manifold.
9. Remove the right exhaust manifold-to-cylinder head bolts and exhaust manifold.
10. Tag and disconnect the spark plug wires from the plugs.
11. Remove the rocker arm (valve) cover.
12. Remove the intake manifold and plenum.
13. Loosen the rocker arms nuts, turn the rocker arms and remove the pushrods. Keep all of the components in order so they may be installed in their original positions.
14. Remove the cylinder head-to-engine bolts, starting with the outer bolts and working towards the center of the head.
15. Lift the cylinder head from the engine. Remove and discard the cylinder head gasket.
16. Throughly clean the gasket mounting surfaces, and cylinder head bolt threads and holes. Inspect the parts for damage and/or warpage; if necessary, have them machined or replace them.

To install:

17. Align a new cylinder head gasket over the dowels on the block with the note **This Side Up** facing the cylinder head.
18. Position the cylinder head over the gasket on the block.
19. Sparingly coat the cylinder head bolt threads 1052080 or equivalent sealant, then install the bolts hand-tight.
20. Using the proper torque sequence (shown the accompanying figure), tighten the bolts to 33 ft. lbs. (45 Nm). After all bolts are tightened to 33 ft. lbs. (45 Nm), rotate the torque wrench another 90° or ¼ turn. This will apply the correct torque to the bolts.
21. Position a new intake manifold gasket.
22. Install the pushrods in the same order as they were removed. Tighten the rocker arm nuts to 14–20 ft. lbs. (19–27 Nm).
23. Install the intake manifold and plenum.
24. Install the rocker arm (valve) cover and secure with the retaining bolts.
25. Connect the spark plug wires to the plugs, as tagged during removal.
26. Install the right exhaust manifold and secure with the manifold-to-cylinder head bolts.
27. Install the crossover heat shield.
28. Raise the vehicle and support it safely.
29. Connect the exhaust pipe to the exhaust manifold and install the exhaust manifold-to-exhaust pipe bolts.
30. Carefully lower the vehicle.
31. For 1988–93 vehicles, install the air cleaner assembly. For 1994–96 vehicles, install the top half of the air cleaner assembly and throttle body duct.
32. Fill the cooling system and connect the negative battery cable.
33. Start the engine, allow it to reach operating temperature then check for leaks. Check the coolant level and add, if necessary.

Oil Pan

REMOVAL & INSTALLATION

✹✹ CAUTION

The EPA warns that prolonged contact with used engine oil may cause a number of skin disorders, including cancer! You should make every effort to minimize your exposure to used engine oil. Protective gloves should be worn when changing the oil. Wash your hands and any other exposed skin areas as soon as possible after exposure to used engine oil. Soap and water, or waterless hand cleaner should be used.

2.0L and 2.2L Engines

♦ See Figure 31

1. Disconnect the negative battery cable.
2. Raise and safely support the vehicle.
3. For 1994–96 vehicles, remove the right front tire and wheel assembly, then remove the right engine splash shield.
4. Position a suitable drain pan under the oil pan, then drain the engine oil. Don't forget to install the drain plug, after the oil is fully drained.
5. If equipped, remove the A/C brace.
6. For 1988–93 vehicles, remove the exhaust heat shield, then disconnect the exhaust pipe from the manifold.
7. Remove the starter bracket from the block, then remove the starter motor and position it out of the way.
8. Remove the transaxle converter cover or flywheel housing cover.
9. For 1988–90 vehicles, remove the four right support bolts. Lower the support slightly to gain clearance for oil pan removal.
10. For 1988–90 vehicles if equipped with automatic transaxle, remove the oil filter and extension.

11. For 1994–96 vehicles, remove the engine mount strut bracket. Remove the oil level sensor.
12. Remove the oil pan nuts and bolts, then lower the oil pan and remove it from the vehicle.

➡ Before installing the oil pan, make sure the sealing surfaces on the pan, cylinder block and front cover are clean and free of oil. If installing the old pan, be sure that all old RTV has been removed.

To install:

13. Apply a ⅒ in. (2mm) wide bead of RTV sealant to the oil pan sealing surface, except for at the rear seal mounting surface. Apply a thin coat of RTV sealer on a new oil pan rear seal, on the ends down to the ears, then install the pan against the case and install bolts. Tighten the bolts to 71–89 inch lbs. (8–10 Nm).
14. Install the remaining components in the reverse of the removal procedure.
15. Fill the crankcase with the proper type and amount of engine oil.
16. Connect the negative battery cable, then start the engine and check for leaks. Recheck the oil level and add if necessary.

2.3L Engine

♦ See Figures 32, 33 and 34

1990–91 VEHICLES

1. Disconnect the negative battery cable.
2. Raise and support the vehicle safely.
3. Remove the flywheel inspection cover.
4. Remove the splash shield-to-suspension support bolt.
5. Remove the exhaust manifold brace.
6. Remove the radiator outlet pipe-to-oil pan bolt.
7. Remove the transaxle-to-oil pan nut and stud using a 7mm socket.
8. Gently pry the spacer out from between oil pan and transaxle.
9. Unfasten the oil pan bolts, then remove the oil pan from the engine.

To install:

10. Position the oil pan to the engine and secure with the retaining bolts. Tighten the chain housing and carrier seal bolts to 106 inch lbs. (12 Nm). Tighten the oil pan-to-block bolts to 17 ft. lbs. (23 Nm).
11. Install the remaining components in the reverse of the removal procedure.
12. Fill the crankcase with the proper type and amount of engine oil.
13. Connect the negative battery cable. Start the engine and check for leaks.
14. Turn the engine off and allow to stand. Check the oil level and add as necessary to obtain the proper level.

1992–94 VEHICLES

1. Disconnect the negative battery cable.
2. Raise and support the vehicle safely.
3. Position a suitable drain pan under the oil pan, then drain the oil pan.

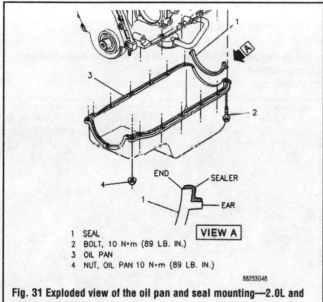

1 SEAL
2 BOLT, 10 N•m (89 LB. IN.)
3 OIL PAN
4 NUT, OIL PAN 10 N•m (89 LB. IN.)

Fig. 31 Exploded view of the oil pan and seal mounting—2.0L and 2.2L engines

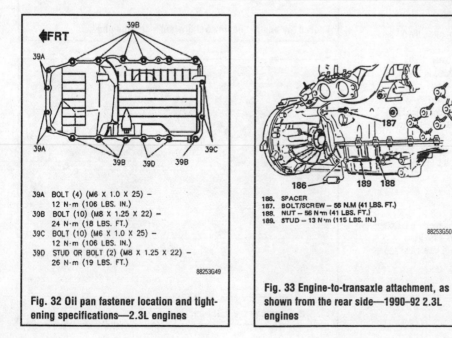

39A BOLT (4) (M6 X 1.0 X 25) –
     12 N•m (106 LBS. IN.)
39B BOLT (10) (M8 X 1.25 X 22) –
     24 N•m (18 LBS. FT.)
39C BOLT (10) (M6 X 1.0 X 25) –
     12 N•m (106 LBS. IN.)
39D STUD OR BOLT (2) (M8 X 1.25 X 22) –
     26 N•m (19 LBS. FT.)

Fig. 32 Oil pan fastener location and tightening specifications—2.3L engines

186. SPACER
187. BOLT/SCREW – 56 N.M (41 LBS. FT.)
188. NUT – 56 N•m (41 LBS. FT.)
189. STUD – 13 N•m (115 LBS. IN.)

Fig. 33 Engine-to-transaxle attachment, as shown from the rear side—1990–92 2.3L engines

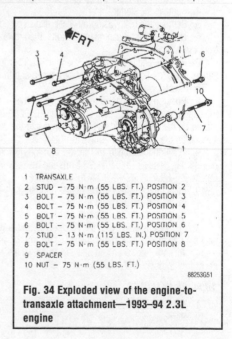

1 TRANSAXLE
2 STUD – 75 N•m (55 LBS. FT.) POSITION 2
3 BOLT – 75 N•m (55 LBS. FT.) POSITION 3
4 BOLT – 75 N•m (55 LBS. FT.) POSITION 4
5 BOLT – 75 N•m (55 LBS. FT.) POSITION 5
6 BOLT – 75 N•m (55 LBS. FT.) POSITION 6
7 STUD – 13 N•m (115 LBS. IN.) POSITION 7
8 BOLT – 75 N•m (55 LBS. FT.) POSITION 8
9 SPACER
10 NUT – 75 N•m (55 LBS. FT.)

Fig. 34 Exploded view of the engine-to-transaxle attachment—1993–94 2.3L engine

4. Place another drain pan under the radiator, then drain the cooling system.

5. Remove the flywheel cover.

6. Remove the right front wheel and tire assembly and the right side splash shield.

7. Relieve the serpentine drive belt tension, then remove the belt.

8. Disconnect the engine mount strut from the engine mount strut bracket.

9. If equipped, remove the A/C compressor from the bracket and suitably support out of the way. Do NOT disconnect the refrigerant lines.

10. Remove the engine mount strut bracket bolts and move the bracket aside.

11. Remove the radiator outlet pipe bolts.

12. Disconnect the air conditioner and radiator outlet pipes from the suspension supports.

13. Remove the exhaust manifold brace.

14. Remove the oil pan-to-flywheel cover bolt and nut.

15. Remove the flywheel cover stud for clearance.

16. Disconnect the radiator outlet pipe from the lower hose and oil pan.

17. Disconnect the oil level sensor wire.

18. Unfasten the oil pan bolts and remove the oil pan. Thoroughly clean the pan mating surfaces, discard the oil pan gasket.

To install:

19. Position a new gasket in the groove of the oil pan, then install the pan and new gasket (no sealer is needed). Loosely install the pan bolts.

20. Place the spacer in its approximate installed location but allow clearance to tighten the pan bolt directly above the spacer.

21. Tighten the chain housing and carrier seal bolts to 106 inch lbs. (12 Nm). Tighten the oil pan-to-block bolts to 17 ft. lbs. (23 Nm).

22. Place the spacer into its proper location and install the stud.

23. Install the oil pan-to-transaxle nut and tighten to 41 ft. lbs. (56 Nm).

24. Attach the oil level sensor wire.

25. Connect the radiator outlet pipe to the lower hose and oil pan.

26. Install the remaining components in the reverse of the removal procedure.

27. Fill the cooling system and the crankcase with the proper type and amount of fluids.

28. Connect the negative battery cable. Start the engine and check for leaks.

29. Turn the engine off and allow to stand. Check the fluid levels and add as necessary to obtain the proper levels.

2.8L and 3.1L Engines

1988–93 VEHICLES

▶ See Figure 35

1. Disconnect the negative battery cable.

2. Raise and safely support the vehicle with jackstands.

3. Position a suitable container under the oil pan, then drain the engine oil. Don't forget to install the drain plug, after the oil has completely drained.

4. Remove the starter.

5. Remove the bellhousing/flywheel inspection cover.

6. Unfasten the oil pan retaining bolts, then lower and remove the oil pan from the vehicle.

7. Remove and discard the oil pan gasket. Thoroughly clean the oil pan flanges, rail, front cover, rear main bearing cap and the threaded bolt holes.

To install:

8. Position a new gasket in the groove on the oil pan. If the rear main bearing cap is being installed, then GM sealant 1052080 or equivalent, must be placed on the oil pan gasket tabs that insert into the gasket groove of the outer surface on the rear main bearing cap.

9. Position the oil pan and secure with the retaining bolts. Tighten the 2 rear oil pan bolts to 18 ft. lbs. (25 Nm), and the remaining oil pan bolts and nuts to 71–89 inch lbs. (8–10 Nm).

10. Install the flywheel inspection/bellhousing.

11. Install the starter motor.

12. Carefully lower the vehicle.

13. Fill the crankcase with the proper type and amount of engine oil. Connect the negative battery cable, then start the engine and check for leaks.

14. Turn the engine off and allow to stand. Check the fluid levels and add as necessary to obtain the proper levels.

1994–96 VEHICLES

1. Disconnect the negative battery cable.

2. Remove the serpentine drive belt.

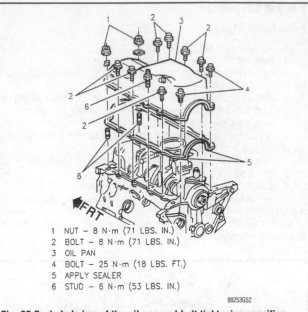

1 NUT – 8 N·m (71 LBS. IN.)
2 BOLT – 8 N·m (71 LBS. IN.)
3 OIL PAN
4 BOLT – 25 N·m (18 LBS. FT.)
5 APPLY SEALER
6 STUD – 6 N·m (53 LBS. IN.)

Fig. 35 Exploded view of the oil pan and bolt tightening specifications—1988–93 2.8L and 3.1L engines

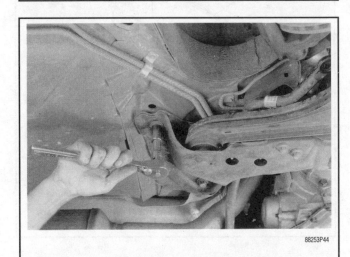

Loosen the engine mount strut bracket side retaining bolt . . .

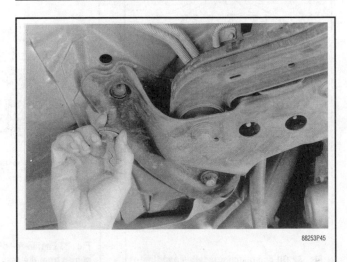

. . . then remove the bolt from the bracket

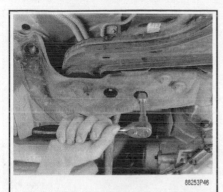

88253P46

Make sure to remove all the bolts from the engine mount strut bracket

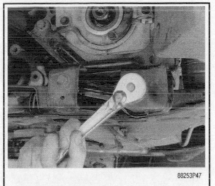

88253P47

Remove the engine mount strut retaining bolt(s) . . .

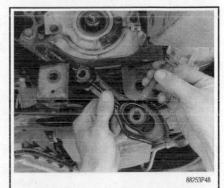

88253P48

. . . then remove the engine mount strut from the vehicle

88253P49

Unfasten the right side suspension support retaining bolts . . .

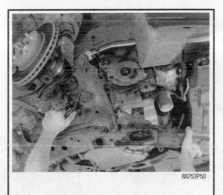

88253P50

. . . then remove the right side suspension support from the vehicle

88253P51

Unfasten the lower A/C compressor mounting bolts . . .

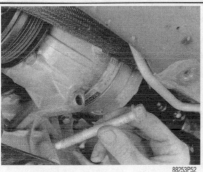

88253P52

. . . then remove the bolts and reposition the compressor, but DO NOT disconnect the lines

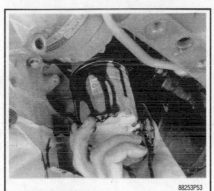

88253P53

Place a drain pan under the oil filter when removing it, because it can get messy

88253P54

If necessary, remove the oil filter adapter retaining bolts . . .

88253P55

. . . then remove the oil filter adapter from the vehicle

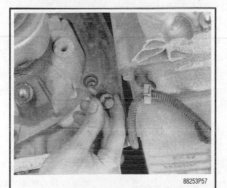

88253P57

Remove the flywheel inspection cover bolts . . .

88253P58

. . . then remove the inspection cover from the vehicle

Unplug the oil level sensor electrical connector

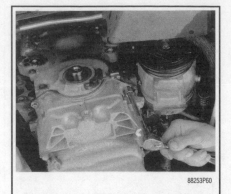

Remove the oil pan side retaining bolts

Unfasten the front oil pan mounting bolts . . .

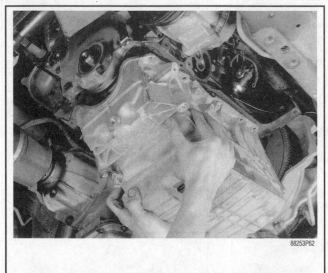

. . . then carefully lower the oil pan and remove it from the vehicle

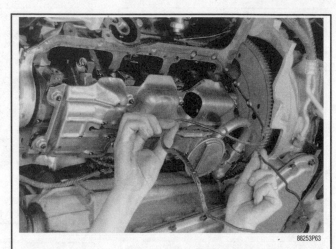

Remove the oil pan gasket and replace it with a new one during installation

3. If equipped, loosen but do not remove the upper A/C compressor.

4. Raise and safely support the vehicle.

5. Position a suitable container under the oil pan, then drain the engine oil. Don't forget to install the drain plug, after the oil has completely drained.

6. Remove the right front wheel and tire assembly, then remove the splash shield.

7. Remove the engine mount strut from the suspension support.

8. Detach the right front ABS wheel speed sensor harness from the right suspension support.

9. Remove the right front ball joint.

10. Remove the right side stabilizer link. Remove the right side suspension support.

11. If equipped, remove the lower A/C compressor bolts, then position the compressor aside and support. Do NOT disconnect the refrigerant lines.

12. Remove the engine mount strut bracket.

13. Remove the engine-to-transaxle brace.

14. Remove the oil filter and the oil filter adapter, if equipped.

15. Remove the starter motor from the vehicle.

16. Remove the flywheel inspection cover.

17. Detach the oil level sensor electrical connector.

18. Unfasten the oil pan retaining bolts, then lower and remove the oil pan from the vehicle.

19. Remove and discard the oil pan gasket. Thoroughly clean the oil pan flanges, rail, front cover, rear main bearing cap and the threaded bolt holes.

To install:

20. Position a new gasket in the groove on the oil pan. If the rear main bearing cap is being installed, then GM sealant 1052080 or equivalent, must be placed on the oil pan gasket tabs that insert into the gasket groove of the outer surface on the rear main bearing cap.

21. Position the oil pan and secure with the retaining bolts. Tighten the retaining bolts to 18 ft. lbs. (25 Nm).

22. Install the oil pan side bolts, then tighten to 37 ft. lbs. (50 Nm).

23. Install the remaining components in the reverse of the removal procedure. Make sure all components are tightened securely.

24. Fill the crankcase with the proper type and amount of engine oil. Connect the negative battery cable, then start the engine and check for leaks.

25. Turn the engine off and allow to stand. Check the fluid levels and add as necessary to obtain the proper levels.

Oil Pump

REMOVAL & INSTALLATION

2.0L and 2.2L Engines

▸ See Figures 36, 37 and 38

1. Remove the engine oil pan, as outlined earlier in this section.

2. Remove the pump-to-rear bearing cap bolt, then remove the pump and extension shaft.

3. Remove the extension shaft and retainer, being careful not to crack the retainer.

To install:

4. Heat the retainer in hot water prior to assembling the extension shaft.

5. Install the extension to the oil pump.

➡Be sure the retainer does not crack upon installation.

6. Install the pump-to-rear bearing cap bolt and tighten to 32 ft. lbs. (43 Nm).

7. Install the oil pan, as outlined earlier in this section.

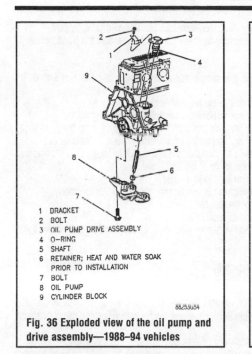

1 BRACKET
2 BOLT
3 OIL PUMP DRIVE ASSEMBLY
4 O-RING
5 SHAFT
6 RETAINER; HEAT AND WATER SOAK
  PRIOR TO INSTALLATION
7 BOLT
8 OIL PUMP
9 CYLINDER BLOCK

88253G54

Fig. 36 Exploded view of the oil pump and drive assembly—1988–94 vehicles

1 BOLT, 43 N·m (32 LBS. FT.)
2 PUMP ASSEMBLY, OIL
3 RETAINER, OIL PUMP SHAFT
  THE RETAINER MUST BE HEATED AND SOAKED
  IN WATER PRIOR TO INSTALLATION. THE
  RETAINER MUST NOT HAVE ANY SPLITS IN IT
  AFTER INSTALLATION.
4 SHAFT, OIL PUMP DRIVE

88253G55

Fig. 37 The oil pump assembly is secured to the bottom of the engine with a bolt—1995–96 2.2L engines

1 BOLT, 25 N·m (18 LBS. FT.)
2 SUPPORT
3 DRIVE ASSEMBLY, OIL PUMP

88253G56

Fig. 38 The oil pump drive is mounted to the top of the engine—1995–96 2.2L engines

2.3L Engine

♦ See Figure 39

1. Disconnect the negative battery cable.
2. Raise and support the vehicle safely.
3. Remove the attaching bolts and the oil pan.
4. Remove the oil pump assembly retainers, bolts and nut.
5. Remove the oil pump assembly and shims if equipped.

➡**Oil pump drive gear backlash must be checked when any of the following components are replaced: oil pump assembly, oil pump drive gear, crankshaft and cylinder block.**

To install:

6. Check and adjust oil pump drive gear backlash as follows:
   a. With oil pump assembly off engine, remove 3 attaching bolts and separate the driven gear cover and screen assembly from the oil pump.
   b. Install the oil pump on the block using the original shims. Tighten the bolts to 33 ft. lbs. (45 Nm) for 1990 vehicles and 40 ft. lbs. (54 Nm) for 1991–94 vehicles.
   c. Install the dial indicator assembly to measure backlash between oil pump to drive gear.

   d. Record oil pump drive to driven gear backlash correct backlash clearance is 0.0091–0.0201 in. (0.23–0.51mm). When taking measurement crankshaft cannot move.
   e. Remove oil pump from block reinstall driven gear cover and screen assembly to pump and tighten to 106 inch lbs. (12 Nm).
   f. Reinstall the pump assembly on block. Tighten oil pump-to-block bolts 33 ft. lbs. (45 Nm).

7. Install the oil pump assembly, including shims if removed.
8. Tighten oil pump to block bolts to 33 ft. lbs. (45 Nm) for 1990 vehicles and 40 ft. lbs. (54 Nm) for 1991–94 vehicles.
9. Install the oil pan and attaching bolts.
10. Carefully lower the vehicle.
11. Fill the crankcase with the proper type and amount of engine oil. Connect the negative battery cable, then start the engine and check for leaks.
12. Turn the engine off and allow to stand. Check oil level, add as necessary.

2.8L and 3.1L Engine

♦ See Figure 40

1. Raise and safely support the vehicle.
2. Remove the oil pan as described earlier in this section.

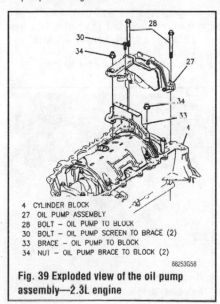

4 CYLINDER BLOCK
27 OIL PUMP ASSEMBLY
28 BOLT – OIL PUMP TO BLOCK
30 BOLT – OIL PUMP SCREEN TO BRACE (2)
33 BRACE – OIL PUMP TO BLOCK
34 NUT – OIL PUMP BRACE TO BLOCK (2)

88253G58

Fig. 39 Exploded view of the oil pump assembly—2.3L engine

88253P64

View of the oil pump, after the pan is removed (see arrow)

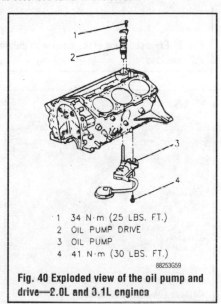

1 34 N·m (25 LBS. FT.)
2 OIL PUMP DRIVE
3 OIL PUMP
4 41 N·m (30 LBS. FT.)

88253G59

Fig. 40 Exploded view of the oil pump and drive—2.0L and 3.1L engines

3. Unfasten and remove the oil pump and driveshaft extension.

To install:

4. Install the oil pump and driveshaft extension.
5. Engage the driveshaft extension into the drive gear.
6. Install the pump-to-rear bearing cap bolt and tighten to 30 ft. lbs. (41 Nm).
7. Install the oil pan, then carefully lower the vehicle.
8. Fill the crankcase with the proper type and amount of engine oil. Connect the negative battery cable, then start the engine and check for leaks.
9. Turn the engine off and allow to stand. Check oil level, add as necessary.

Crankshaft Damper/Balancer

REMOVAL & INSTALLATION

Except 2.3L Engines

♦ See Figure 41

➡The inertia section of the crankshaft balancer is assembly to the hub with a rubber sleeve. Removal and installation MUST be performed with the proper tools and followed exactly to prevent movement of the inertia weight section of the hub causing the torsional damper tuning damage.

1. Remove the air cleaner assembly.
2. Disconnect the negative battery cable.
3. Remove the right side front wheel and tire assembly. Remove the right splash shield.
4. Remove the flywheel cover.
5. Remove the balancer retaining bolt, with an assistant to keep the flywheel from turning.

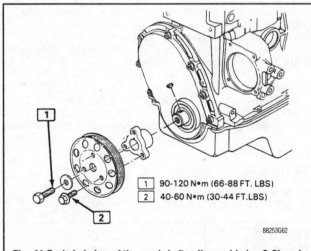

| 1 | 90-120 N•m (66-88 FT. LBS) |
| 2 | 40-60 N•m (30-44 FT.LBS) |

88253G62

Fig. 41 Exploded view of the crankshaft pulley and hub—2.0L and 2.2L engines

6. Install harmonic balancer removal tool J 24420-B or equivalent, installed on the balancer, turn the puller screw, then remove the balancer from the vehicle.

To install:

7. Coat the area of the damper that contacts the front cover seal with clean engine oil.
8. Apply RTV sealant to the key and keyway.
9. Place the balancer in position over the key in the crankshaft.
10. Place balancer installer tool J 29113, or equivalent, onto the crankshaft.
11. Pull the balancer into position, then remove the installation tool.
12. With an assistant to keep the flywheel from turning, install the balancer retaining bolt and tighten to 76 ft. lbs. (103 Nm).
13. Install the transaxle converter cover.
14. Install the right splash shield and the wheel and tire assembly.
15. Carefully lower the vehicle.
16. Install the serpentine drive belt.
17. Connect the negative battery cable, then start the engine and check for leaks.

2.3L Engine

1. Disconnect the negative battery cable.
2. Remove the serpentine drive belt.
3. Raise and safely support the vehicle.
4. Remove the right front wheel and tire assembly. Remove the right splash shield.
5. Remove the balancer retaining bolt, using crankshaft balancer holder tool J 38122 or equivalent, to prevent the crankshaft from rotating when loosening the bolt.
6. Remove the balancer using tool J 24420-B or equivalent puller.

✷✷ WARNING

The automatic transaxle crankshaft balancer must NOT be installed on a vehicle equipped with a manual transaxle.

To install:

7. Lubricate the front seat and the sealing surface of the balancer with chassis grease 1051344 or equivalent.
8. Position the balancer onto the crankshaft, properly indexing the keyway. Tap the balancer into place using a rubber mallet.
9. Install the balancer retaining bolt and washer. Use tool J 38122 or equivalent to hold the crankshaft in place, then tighten as follows:
   a. 1990–92 vehicles: 74 ft. lbs. (100 Nm)
   b. 1993 vehicles: 110 ft. lbs. (150 Nm)
   c. 1994 vehicles: 129 ft. lbs. (175 Nm)

➡Do not use a torque angle meter to final tighten the balancer retaining bolt. The torque capacity of the tool will be exceeded, and the tool will be damaged.

10. To apply the final torque to the retaining bolt, put a mark on the socket next to one of the 4 marks on the balancer holding tool. This mark will represent the zero point. Tighten the bolt by rotating the socket clockwise 90°. At 90°, the socket indexes with the next mark on the tool.
11. Install the splash shield, then install the wheel and tire assembly.

88253P80

Attach a suitable puller to the crankshaft damper (harmonic balancer)

88253P81

Sometimes its necessary to hold the puller in place for leverage while turning the puller screw

88253P82

Remove the crankshaft damper (harmonic balancer) from the vehicle

ENGINE AND ENGINE OVERHAUL **3-37**

12. Carefully lower the vehicle.
13. Install the serpentine drive belt.
14. Connect the negative battery cable, then start the engine and check for leaks.

Timing Chain Cover and Seal

REMOVAL & INSTALLATION

✱✱ CAUTION

When draining the coolant, keep in mind that cats and dogs are attracted by ethylene glycol antifreeze, and are quite likely to drink any that is left in an uncovered container or in puddles on the ground. This will prove fatal in sufficient quantity. Always drain the coolant into a sealable container. Coolant should be reused unless it is contaminated or several years old.

➡The EPA warns that prolonged contact with used engine oil may cause a number of skin disorders, including cancer! You should make every effort to minimize your exposure to used engine oil. Protective gloves should be worn when changing the oil. Wash your hands and any other exposed skin areas as soon as possible after exposure to used engine oil. Soap and water, or waterless hand cleaner should be used.

2.0L and 2.2L Engines

♦ See Figure 42

➡The following procedure requires the use of a special tool.

1. Disconnect the negative battery cable.
2. Remove the serpentine belt and tensioner.
3. For 1993–96 vehicles perform the following:
   a. Install engine support fixture J 28467-A, or equivalent.
   b. Remove the engine mount assembly.
   c. Remove the alternator rear brace, then remove the alternator from the vehicle.
   d. Unbolt the power steering pump, then position it aside, with the fluid lines attached.
4. Raise the vehicle and support it safely.
5. Drain the engine oil into a suitable container.
6. Remove the oil pan-to-front cover bolts, then remove the oil pan from the vehicle.
7. Remove the wheel and tire assembly.
8. Remove the right front inner fender splash.

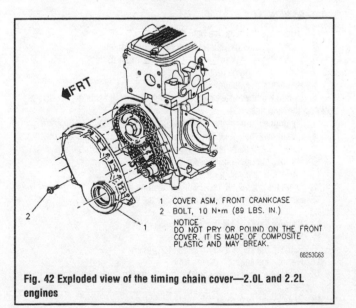

Fig. 42 Exploded view of the timing chain cover—2.0L and 2.2L engines

9. Unscrew the center bolt from the crankshaft pulley and install tool J 24420-B on their pulley, then turn the puller screw and remove the pulley.
10. Remove the front cover-to-block bolts and then remove the front cover. If the front cover is difficult to remove, use a plastic mallet.
   The oil seal can be replaced with the cover either on or off the engine. If the cover is on the engine, remove the crankshaft pulley and hub first. Pry out the seal using a large prytool, being careful not to scratch or distort the seal mating surface. Install the new seal so that the open side or helical side is towards the engine. Press it into place with a seal driver made for the purpose. General Motors recommends a tool, J-35400 Seal Centering Tool. Install the hub if removed.

To install:
11. The surfaces of the block and front cover must be clean and free of oil. Use a new gasket and place the cover over the dowel pins. Tighten the bolts to 89–97 inch lbs. (10–11 Nm).
12. Apply RTV sealant to the keyway in the pulley and place the crankshaft pulley in position over the key on the crankshaft. Pull the crankshaft as follows:
   • Install tool J 29113 into the crankshaft so that at least 6mm of thread is engaged.
   • Pull the pulley into position and remove the tool from the pulley.
13. Tighten the pulley retaining bolt to 66–88 ft. lbs. (89–119 Nm).
14. Install the inner fender splash shield, then install the wheel and tire assembly.
15. Install the oil pan.
16. Carefully lower the vehicle.
17. For 1994–96 vehicles, perform the following:
   a. Position the power steering pump and install the mounting bolts.
   b. Install the alternator and rear brace.
   c. Install the engine mount, then remove the lifting device.
18. Install the serpentine drive belt tensioner and the belt.
19. Fill the crankcase with the proper type and amount of engine oil.
20. Connect the negative battery cable.

2.3L Engine

♦ See Figure 43

1. Disconnect the negative battery cable.
2. Properly drain the cooling system into a suitable container. Remove coolant recovery reservoir.
3. Remove the serpentine drive belt.

➡To avoid personal injury when rotating the serpentine belt tensioner, use a 13mm wrench that is at least 24 in. (610mm) long.

4. For 1992–94 vehicles perform the following:
   a. Remove the alternator and position it aside.
   b. Reinstall the alternator through bolt, then install engine support fixture J 28467-A or equivalent.
5. Remove the upper timing chain cover fasteners.
6. Disconnect the cover vent hose.
7. For 1992–94 vehicles, remove the right engine mount and mount bracket.
8. For 1990–91 vehicles, remove the engine lift bracket.

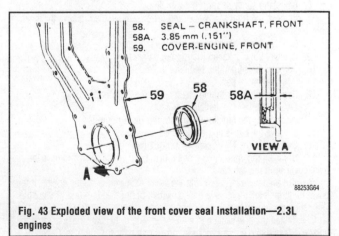

Fig. 43 Exploded view of the front cover seal installation—2.3L engines

9. Raise and safely support the vehicle.

10. Remove right front wheel and tire assembly, then remove right lower splash shield.

11. Remove crankshaft balancer assembly.

12. Remove lower timing chain cover fasteners.

13. Carefully lower the vehicle, then remove the timing chain (front) cover. Inspect the gasket and replace it if it is damaged.

14. If oil seal removal is necessary, support the front cover and drive the oil seal out of the back (timing chain side) of the cover.

To install:

15. If the seal was removed, use front cover crankshaft seal installer, tool J 36010 or equivalent, to install the seal in the cover. The tool will properly position the seal in the cover.

16. Install the gasket and/or seals into the front cover.

17. Place the nuts on the studs to retain the cover, then install the bolts. Tighten the fasteners to 106 inch lbs. (12 Nm).

18. Install the engine lift bracket. Raise and safely support the vehicle. Install the remaining front cover bolts. Tighten the fasteners accessible at this time to 106 inch lbs. (12 Nm).

19. Raise and safely support the vehicle.

20. Install the remaining cover fasteners and tighten to 106 inch lbs. (12 Nm).

21. Lubricate the front oil seal and the sealing surface of the crankshaft balancer with chassis grease 1051344 or equivalent.

22. Install the crankshaft balancer.

23. Install the right splash shield and wheel and tire assembly.

24. Carefully lower the vehicle.

25. For 1990–91 vehicles, install the engine lift bracket.

➡**The right engine mount and bracket bolts must be replaced with new bolts anytime they are removed.**

26. For 1992–94 vehicles perform the following:

a. Install the engine mount bracket and the right engine mount, using NEW bolts.

b. Install the alternator.

c. Remove the engine support fixture.

27. Install the serpentine drive belt.

28. Connect the coolant vent hose.

29. Install the coolant recovery reservoir.

30. Fill the cooling system with the proper type and amount of coolant.

31. Connect the negative battery cable, then start the engine and check for leaks. Check the fluid levels, and add if necessary.

2.8L and 3.1L Engines

♦ **See Figure 44**

1988–94 VEHICLES

1. Disconnect the negative battery cable.

2. Drain the cooling system into a suitable container.

3. Remove the coolant recovery reservoir.

4. Remove the serpentine belt and belt tensioner.

5. Unbolt the power steering pump, then position it aside. Do NOT disconnect the fluid lines.

6. Raise and safely support the vehicle.

7. Remove the right side wheel and tire assembly, then remove the inner splash shield.

8. Remove the flywheel cover from the transaxle.

9. Remove the crankshaft (harmonic) balancer.

10. Remove the serpentine belt idler pulley.

11. Remove the oil pan.

12. Remove the lower timing chain cover retaining bolts.

13. Carefully lower the vehicle.

14. Disconnect the radiator hose from the water pump.

15. Remove the bypass pipe from the front cover.

16. Disconnect the EVAP canister purge hose.

17. Unfasten the upper timing chain (front) cover bolts, then remove the front cover from the vehicle.

The oil seal can be replaced with the cover either on or off the engine. If the cover is on the engine, remove the crankshaft pulley and hub first. Pry out the seal using a large prytool, being careful not to scratch or distort the seal mating surface. Install the new seal so that the open side or helical side is towards the engine. Press it into place with a seal driver made for the purpose. General

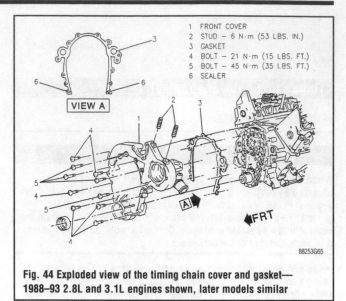

Fig. 44 Exploded view of the timing chain cover and gasket—1988–93 2.8L and 3.1L engines shown, later models similar

Motors recommends a tool, J–35468 Seal Centering Tool. Install the hub if removed.

18. Clean all the gasket mounting surfaces on the front cover and block and place a new gasket to the front cover sealing surface. Apply a sealer (1052080 or equivalent) as shown to the ends of the gasket.

To install:

19. Place the front cover on the engine and install the upper front cover bolts. Tighten the (4) bolts, in the accompanying figure, to 20 ft. lbs. (27 Nm) for 1988–92 vehicles or to 15 ft. lbs. (21 Nm) for 1993–94 vehicles. Tighten the (5) bolts to 38 ft. lbs. (48 Nm) for 1988–92 vehicles or to 35 ft. lbs. (45 Nm) for 1993 vehicles.

20. For 1994 vehicles, tighten the front cover retaining bolts to 15 ft. lbs. (20 Nm).

21. Raise the vehicle and support it safely.

22. Install the oil pan.

23. Install the lower cover bolts. Tighten the (4) bolts, in the accompanying figure, to 20 ft. lbs. (27 Nm) for 1988–92 vehicles or to 15 ft. lbs. (21 Nm) for 1993–94 vehicles. Tighten the (5) bolts to 38 ft. lbs. (48 Nm) for 1988–92 vehicles or to 35 ft. lbs. (45 Nm) for 1993 vehicles.

24. Install the remaining components in the reverse of the removal procedure. Make sure all components are tightened securely.

25. Fill the cooling system with the proper type and amount of coolant.

26. Connect the battery cable, then start the engine and check for leaks.

1995–96 VEHICLES

1. Disconnect the negative battery cable.

2. Drain the cooling system into a suitable container.

3. Install engine support fixture J 28467-A, or equivalent.

4. Remove the engine mount bracket support.

5. Remove the serpentine drive belt.

6. Unbolt the power steering pump, then position it aside but do NOT disconnect the fluid lines.

7. If equipped, loosen the top 2 A/C compressor bolts.

8. Disconnect the coolant bypass pipe from the water pump and manifold.

9. Detach the radiator hose from the coolant outlet housing.

10. Remove the upper front cover bolts.

11. Raise and safely support the vehicle.

12. Drain the engine oil into a suitable container.

13. Remove the right front wheel and tire assembly. Remove the splash shield.

14. Remove the flywheel inspection cover.

15. Remove the crankshaft balancer.

16. Remove the serpentine drive belt tensioner.

17. Remove the engine mount strut.

18. Detach the right wheel speed sensor connector and wire harness from the suspension support.

19. Remove the right side ball joint.

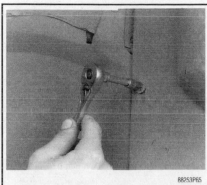

After removing the wheel and tire assembly, unfasten the retainers . . .

. . . then remove the right side inner splash shield

Attach a suitable puller to the crankshaft balancer . . .

. . . then remove the crankshaft balancer from the front cover

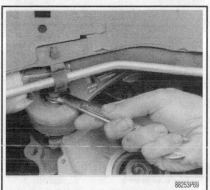

Unfasten the serpentine drive belt tensioner retaining bolt . . .

. . . then remove the drive belt tensioner from the vehicle

Unfasten the Crankshaft Position (CKP) sensor retaining bolts . . .

. . . then remove the CKP sensor from the timing chain (front) cover

Unfasten the lower timing chain cover retaining bolts . . .

20. Detach the stabilizer shaft from the right suspension support and the right control arm.

21. Remove the right suspension support.

22. If equipped, remove the A/C compressor-to-pan bolts.

23. Remove the oil filter and oil filter adapter.

24. Remove the engine mount strut bracket.

25. Remove the engine-to-transaxle brace.

26. Remove the starter motor.

27. Remove the oil pan.

28. Remove the crankshaft sensor.

29. Remove the lower timing chain (front) cover bolts, then remove the front cover from the vehicle..

The oil seal can be replaced with the cover either on or off the engine. If the cover is on the engine, remove the crankshaft pulley and hub first. Pry out the seal using a large prytool, being careful not to scratch or distort the seal mating surface. Install the new seal so that the open side or helical side is towards the engine. Press it into place with a seal driver made for the purpose. General Motors recommends a tool, J 35468 Seal Centering Tool. Install the hub if removed.

30. Clean all the gasket mounting surfaces on the front cover and block and place a new gasket to the front cover sealing surface. Apply a sealer (1052080 or equivalent) as shown to the ends of the gasket.

To install:

31. Place the front cover on the engine. Install the lower front cover bolts. Tighten the small bolts to 15 ft. lbs. (20 Nm) and the large bolts to 35 ft. lbs. (47 Nm).

32. Install the remaining components in the reverse of the removal procedure. Please note the following tightening specifications:

• Upper two front cover bolts: 15 ft. lbs. (20 Nm)

• Engine mount support bracket 8mm bolts: 15 ft. lbs. (20 Nm), plus 45°

• Engine mount support bracket 12mm bolts: to 30 ft. lbs. (40 Nm), plus 45°

33. Install the engine mount assembly, then remove the engine support fixture.

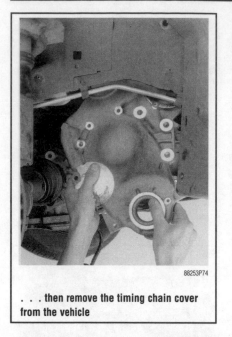

88253P74

. . . then remove the timing chain cover from the vehicle

The front cover oil seal (see arrow) can be removed with the cover on or off the engine

88253P75

Use a scraper to carefully remove any remaining gasket material from the timing chain cover mating surfaces

88253P76

34. Fill the cooling system and crankcase with the proper types and amounts of fluids.

35. Connect the negative battery cable, then start the engine and check for leaks. Check the fluid levels and add if necessary.

Timing Chain and Sprockets

REMOVAL & INSTALLATION

2.0L and 2.2L Engines

▶ See Figures 45, 46 and 47

1. Remove the front cover as previously detailed.
2. Place the No. 1 piston at TDC of the compression stroke so that the marks on the camshaft and crankshaft sprockets are in alignment (see illustration).
3. Either loosen the timing chain tensioner nut as far as possible without actually removing it, or remove the timing chain tensioner retaining bolt.

4. Remove the camshaft sprocket bolt(s), then remove the sprocket and chain assembly. If the sprocket does not slide from the camshaft easily, a light blow with a soft mallet at the lower edge of the sprocket will dislodge it.
5. Remove the Torx bolts, then remove the tensioner assembly.
6. Use gear puller, J–22888 or equivalent to remove the crankshaft sprocket.

To install:

7. Install crankshaft sprocket back onto the crankshaft using tool J 5590 or equivalent installation tool.
8. Compress the tensioner spring, and using a suitable tool (such as a cotter pin or nail), insert the tool into the hole (A) as shown in the accompanying figure.
9. Install the timing chain tensioner and retaining bolts, but do not tighten at this time.
10. Align the crankshaft and camshaft sprocket timing marks with the tab on the tensioner.
11. Install the timing chain over the camshaft sprocket and then around the crankshaft sprocket. Make sure that the marks on the two sprockets are in alignment (see illustration). Lubricate the thrust surface with Molykote® or its equivalent.

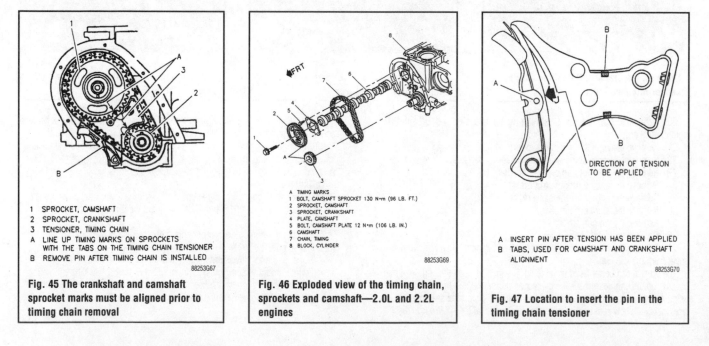

1 SPROCKET, CAMSHAFT
2 SPROCKET, CRANKSHAFT
3 TENSIONER, TIMING CHAIN
A LINE UP TIMING MARKS ON SPROCKETS
   WITH THE TABS ON THE TIMING CHAIN TENSIONER
B REMOVE PIN AFTER TIMING CHAIN IS INSTALLED

88253G67

Fig. 45 The crankshaft and camshaft sprocket marks must be aligned prior to timing chain removal

A TIMING MARKS
1 BOLT, CAMSHAFT SPROCKET 130 N•m (96 LB. FT.)
2 SPROCKET, CAMSHAFT
3 SPROCKET, CRANKSHAFT
4 PLATE, CAMSHAFT
5 BOLT, CAMSHAFT PLATE 12 N•m (106 LB. IN.)
6 CAMSHAFT
7 CHAIN, TIMING
8 BLOCK, CYLINDER

88253G69

Fig. 46 Exploded view of the timing chain, sprockets and camshaft—2.0L and 2.2L engines

DIRECTION OF TENSION
TO BE APPLIED

A INSERT PIN AFTER TENSION HAS BEEN APPLIED
B TABS, USED FOR CAMSHAFT AND CRANKSHAFT
   ALIGNMENT

88253G70

Fig. 47 Location to insert the pin in the timing chain tensioner

12. Align the dowel in the camshaft with the dowel hole in the sprocket and then install the sprocket onto the camshaft. Use the mounting bolt(s) to draw the sprocket onto the camshaft and then tighten to 77 ft. lbs. (105 Nm).

13. Lubricate the timing chain with clean engine oil. Tighten the tensioner retaining bolts to 17 ft. lbs. (23 Nm).

14. Remove the tool used to compress the tensioner spring.

15. Install the timing chain front cover.

16. Fill the cooling system and crankcase with the proper types and amounts of fluids.

17. Connect the negative battery cable, then start the engine and check for leaks. Check the fluid levels and add if necessary.

2.3L Engine

▶ See Figures 48, 49 and 50

➡ Prior to removing the timing chain, review the entire procedure.

1. Disconnect the negative battery cable.

2. Remove the timing chain (front) cover.

3. For 1990–92 vehicles, remove the crankshaft oil slinger.

4. Rotate the crankshaft clockwise, as viewed from front of engine/normal rotation until the camshaft sprockets' timing dowel pin holes line up with the holes in the timing chain housing. The mark on the crankshaft sprocket should line up with the mark on the cylinder block. The crankshaft sprocket keyway should point upwards and line up with the centerline of the cylinder bores. This is the timed position.

5. Remove the 3 timing chain guides.

6. Raise and safely support the vehicle.

7. Gently pry off timing chain tensioner spring retainer sleeve, then remove the spring.

➡ Two styles of tensioner are used. One with a spring post, early production and 1 without a spring post, late production. Both styles are identical in operation and are interchangeable.

8. Remove timing chain tensioner shoe retainer.

9. Make sure all the slack in the timing chain is above the tensioner assembly; remove the chain tensioner shoe. The timing chain must be disengaged from the wear grooves in the tensioner shoe in order to remove the shoe. Slide a prybar under the timing chain while pulling shoe outward.

10. If difficulty is encountered removing chain tensioner shoe, proceed as follows:

   a. Lower the vehicle.

   b. Hold the intake camshaft sprocket with a J 36013 or equivalent holding tool, then remove the sprocket bolt and washer.

   c. Remove the washer from the bolt and re-thread the bolt back into the camshaft by hand, the bolt provides a surface to push against.

   d. Remove intake camshaft sprocket using a 3-jaw puller in the 3 relief holes in the sprocket. Do not attempt to pry the sprocket off the camshaft or damage to the sprocket or chain housing could occur.

11. Remove tensioner assembly attaching bolts and tensioner.

✳✳✳ CAUTION

Be careful, as the tensioner piston is spring loaded and could fly out causing personal injury.

12. For 1990–92 vehicles, remove the chain housing-to-block stud and the timing chain tensioner shoe pivot.

13. Remove the timing chain from the vehicle.

➡ Failure to follow this procedure could result in severe engine damage.

To install:

14. Tighten the intake camshaft sprocket attaching bolt and washer to specification while holding sprocket in place with camshaft sprocket wrench J 36013, or equivalent, if removed.

15. Install camshaft timing alignment pins J 36008 or equivalent through holes in camshaft sprockets into holes in timing chain housing, this positions the camshafts for correct timing.

16. If the camshafts are out of position and must be rotated more than ⅛ turn in order to install the alignment dowel pins, perform the following:

   a. The crankshaft must be rotated 90° clockwise off of TDC in order to give the valves adequate clearance to open.

   b. Once the camshafts are in position and the dowels installed, rotate the crankshaft counterclockwise back to top dead center. Do not rotate the crankshaft clockwise to TDC, valve or piston damage could occur.

17. Install timing chain over exhaust camshaft sprocket, around idler sprocket and around crankshaft sprocket.

18. Remove the alignment dowel pin from the intake camshaft. Using a dowel pin remover tool rotate the intake camshaft sprocket counterclockwise enough to slide the timing chain over the intake camshaft sprocket. Release the camshaft sprocket wrench. The length of chain between the 2 camshaft sprockets will tighten. If properly timed, the intake camshaft alignment dowel pin should slide in easily. If the dowel pin does not fully index, the camshafts are not timed correctly and the procedure must be repeated.

19. Leave the alignment dowel pins installed.

20. With slack removed from chain between intake camshaft sprocket and crankshaft sprocket, the timing marks on the crankshaft and the cylinder block should be aligned. If marks are not aligned, move the chain 1 tooth forward or rearward, remove slack and recheck marks.

21. Tighten chain housing to block stud, timing chain tensioner shoe pivot. Stud is installed under the timing chain. Tighten to 19 ft. lbs. (26 Nm).

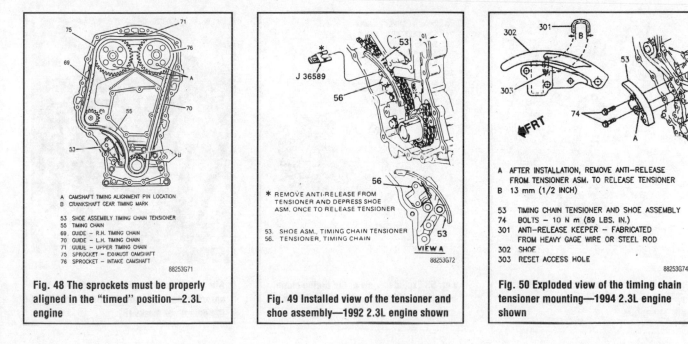

A CAMSHAFT TIMING ALIGNMENT PIN LOCATION
B CRANKSHAFT GEAR TIMING MARK

53 SHOE ASSEMBLY TIMING CHAIN TENSIONER
55 TIMING CHAIN
69 GUIDE – R.H. TIMING CHAIN
70 GUIDE – L.H. TIMING CHAIN
71 GUIDE – UPPER TIMING CHAIN
75 SPROCKET – EXHAUST CAMSHAFT
76 SPROCKET – INTAKE CAMSHAFT

88253G71

Fig. 48 The sprockets must be properly aligned in the "timed" position—2.3L engine

✳ REMOVE ANTI-RELEASE FROM TENSIONER AND DEPRESS SHOE ASM. ONCE TO RELEASE TENSIONER

53. SHOE ASM., TIMING CHAIN TENSIONER
56. TENSIONER, TIMING CHAIN

VIEW A

88253G72

Fig. 49 Installed view of the tensioner and shoe assembly—1992 2.3L engine shown

A AFTER INSTALLATION, REMOVE ANTI-RELEASE FROM TENSIONER ASM. TO RELEASE TENSIONER
B 13 mm (1/2 INCH)

53 TIMING CHAIN TENSIONER AND SHOE ASSEMBLY
74 BOLTS – 10 N·m (89 LBS. IN.)
301 ANTI-RELEASE KEEPER – FABRICATED FROM HEAVY GAGE WIRE OR STEEL ROD
302 SHOE
303 RESET ACCESS HOLE

88253G74

Fig. 50 Exploded view of the timing chain tensioner mounting—1994 2.3L engine shown

22. Reload the timing chain tensioner assembly to its zero position as follows:

a. Assemble the restraint cylinder, spring and nylon plug into the plunger. Index slot in restraint cylinder with peg in plunger. While rotating the restraint cylinder clockwise, push the restraint cylinder into the plunger until it bottoms. Keep rotating the restraint cylinder clockwise but allow the spring to push it out of the plunger. The pin in the plunger will lock the restraint in the loaded position.

b. Install a special plunger installer tool into plunger assembly.

c. Install the plunger assembly into the tensioner body with the long end toward the crankshaft when installed.

23. Install tensioner assembly to chain housing. Recheck plunger assembly installation. It is correctly installed when the long end is toward the crankshaft.

24. Install and tighten timing chain tensioner bolts and tighten to 10 ft. lbs. (14 Nm).

25. Install tensioner shoe and tensioner shoe retainer.

26. Remove the special tool from the plunger and squeeze plunger assembly into tensioner body to unload the plunger assembly.

27. Lower vehicle enough to reach and remove the alignment dowel pins. Rotate crankshaft clockwise 2 full rotations. Align crankshaft timing mark with mark on cylinder block and reinstall alignment dowel pins. Alignment dowel pins will slide in easily if engine is timed correctly.

➡ **If the engine is not correctly timed, severe engine damage could occur.**

28. Install 3 timing chain guides and crankshaft oil slinger (if equipped).
29. Install engine front cover.

30. Connect the negative battery cable. Start engine and check for oil leaks.

2.8L and 3.1L Engines

▶ **See Figures 51, 52 and 53**

1. Disconnect the negative battery cable.
2. Drain the cooling system into a suitable container.
3. Remove the timing chain front cover.
4. Place the No. 1 piston at TDC with the marks on the camshaft and crankshaft sprockets aligned. This is the No. 4 firing position.
5. Remove the bolt(s) that hold the camshaft sprocket to the camshaft. This sprocket is a light press fit on the camshaft and will come off readily. If the sprocket does not come off easily, a light blow on the lower edge of the sprocket with a plastic mallet should dislodge the sprocket. The chain comes off with the camshaft sprocket.
6. Use tool J 5825-A or an equivalent gear puller to remove the crankshaft sprocket.

To install:

7. Without disturbing the position of the engine, mount the crankshaft sprocket on the shaft with tool J 38612 or equivalent sprocket installer.
8. Mount the chain over the camshaft sprocket. Arrange the camshaft sprocket in such a way that the timing marks will line up between the shaft centers and the camshaft locating dowel will enter the dowel hole in the cam sprocket.
9. Place the cam sprocket, with its chain mounted over it, in position on the front of the camshaft and pull up with the bolt(s) that hold it to the camshaft. For 2.8L and 3.1L (VIN T) engines, 18 ft. lbs. (25 Nm). For 3.1L (VIN M) engines, tighten the bolt to 74 ft. lbs. (100 Nm).

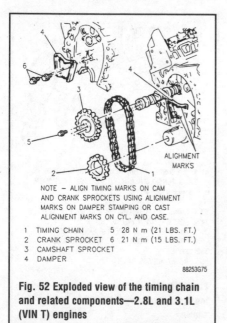

Remove the timing chain (front) cover from the vehicle

The marks on the sprocket, crankshaft shown (A), must align with the cam sprocket and dampener (B)

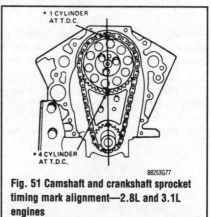

Fig. 51 Camshaft and crankshaft sprocket timing mark alignment—2.8L and 3.1L engines

Fig. 52 Exploded view of the timing chain and related components—2.8L and 3.1L (VIN T) engines

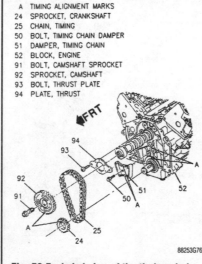

Fig. 53 Exploded view of the timing chain, sprockets and thrust plate—3.1L (VIN M) engines

After rotating the engine 2 times, the sprocket marks (A) should still align with the dampener marks (B)

10. Lubricate the timing chain with clean engine oil.

11. After the sprockets are in place, turn the engine two full revolutions to make certain that the timing marks are in correct alignment between the shaft centers.

12. Install the timing chain front cover.

13. Fill the cooling system and crankcase with the proper types and amounts of fluids.

14. Connect the negative battery cable, then start the engine and check for leaks. Check the fluid levels and add if necessary.

Camshaft, Bearings and Liners

➥To perform the following procedures, the engine must be removed from the vehicle.

REMOVAL & INSTALLATION

> ✳✳ **CAUTION**
>
> When draining the coolant, keep in mind that cats and dogs are attracted by ethylene glycol antifreeze, and are quite likely to drink any that is left in an uncovered container or in puddles on the ground. This will prove fatal in sufficient quantity. Always drain the coolant into a sealable container. Coolant should be reused unless it is contaminated or several years old.

> ✳✳ **CAUTION**
>
> The EPA warns that prolonged contact with used engine oil may cause a number of skin disorders, including cancer! You should make every effort to minimize your exposure to used engine oil. Protective gloves should be worn when changing the oil. Wash your hands and any other exposed skin areas as soon as possible after exposure to used engine oil. Soap and water, or waterless hand cleaner should be used.

2.0L and 2.2L Engines

♦ See Figures 46, 54 and 55

1988–90 VEHICLES

1. Remove the engine from the vehicle and mount on a suitable engine stand.

2. Remove the timing chain and sprockets from the engine.

3. Drain the engine oil into a suitable container, then remove the oil filter.

4. Remove the rocker arm (valve) cover. Loosen the rocker arms, then pivot them 90°. Remove the pushrods and lifters; make sure to note the position of the valve train components for reassembly purposes, as these components MUST be installed in the same positions as they were removed.

5. Remove the oil pump drive.

6. Remove the camshaft thrust plate-to-engine bolts and carefully pull the camshaft from the front of the engine.

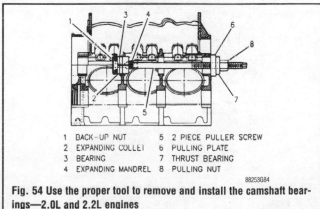

1	BACK-UP NUT	5	2 PIECE PULLER SCREW
2	EXPANDING COLLET	6	PULLING PLATE
3	BEARING	7	THRUST BEARING
4	EXPANDING MANDREL	8	PULLING NUT

88253G84

Fig. 54 Use the proper tool to remove and install the camshaft bearings—2.0L and 2.2L engines

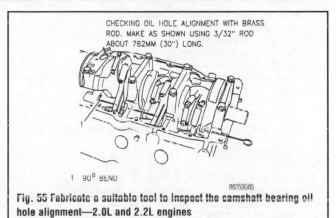

CHECKING OIL HOLE ALIGNMENT WITH BRASS ROD. MAKE AS SHOWN USING 3/32" ROD ABOUT 762MM (30") LONG.

1 90° BEND

88253G85

Fig. 55 Fabricate a suitable tool to inspect the camshaft bearing oil hole alignment—2.0L and 2.2L engines

➥Use care when removing and installing the camshaft; DO NOT damage the camshaft bearings or the bearing surfaces on the camshaft.

7. Using a gasket scraper, thoroughly clean the gasket mounting surfaces.

➥Camshaft bearing removal requires the use of tool J 33049 or equivalent camshaft bearing remover/installer.

8. Remove the camshaft bearings as follows:
a. Select the proper pilot, nut and thrust washer.
b. Assemble camshaft bearing removal/installation tool J 33049. Make sure to puller nut engages with a sufficient number of threads.
c. Pull out the camshaft bearings.

➥Camshaft bearings can NOT be reused once they are removed.

To install:

9. Install the camshaft bearings, as follows:
a. Select front, rear and intermediate camshaft bearings.
b. Select the proper pilot, nut and thrust washer.
c. Assemble camshaft bearing removal/installation tool J 33049.
d. Place the bearing onto the tool, then index the oil holes(s) of the bearing with the oil passage(s) in the cylinder block. Pull the bearing into place.
e. Apply GM sealer 1052914 or equivalent to the camshaft plug, then install the camshaft plug.
f. With a piece of ³⁄₃₂ in. brass rod with a 90° bend at the end, probe the bearing oil holes and make sure they are properly aligned.

10. Lubricate the lobes of the camshaft with GM E.O.S. 1051396 or equivalent and insert the camshaft into the engine.

➥If a new camshaft is being installed, replace all of the valve lifters. Used lifters can only be used on the camshaft that they were originally installed with; provided they are installed in the exact same position they were removed.

11. Align the marks on the camshaft and crankshaft sprockets.

12. Install the timing chain and sprocket.

13. To complete the installation, use new gaskets and reverse the removal procedures.

14. Tighten the rocker arm nuts to 11–18 ft. lbs. (15–24 Nm).

15. Fill the cooling system and crankcase with the proper types and amounts of fluids.

16. Connect the negative battery cable, then start the engine and check for leaks. Check the fluid levels and add if necessary.

1991–96 VEHICLES

1. Remove the engine and transaxle assembly from the vehicle and mount on an engine stand.

2. Remove the serpentine drive belt.

3. Remove the alternator and brackets.

4. Remove the power steering pump.

5. Remove the serpentine drive belt tensioner.

6. Remove the water pump pulley.

7. If not already done, drain the engine oil into a suitable container, then remove the oil filter.

8. Remove the crankshaft pulley and hub.

9. Remove the rocker arm (valve) cover.

10. Remove the rocker arms and pushrods.
11. Remove the valve lifters.
12. Remove the crankshaft front cover.
13. Remove the cam sprocket, timing chain and tensioner.
14. Remove the oil pump drive.
15. Remove the camshaft thrust plate and remove the camshaft carefully without damaging the bearings.
16. Remove the camshaft bearings, if necessary, as follows:
   a. Select the proper pilot, nut and thrust washer.
   b. Assemble tool J 33049 or equivalent, making sure the puller nut engages a sufficient number of threads.
   c. Pull out the bearings.

To install:

17. Install the camshaft bearings, if necessary, as follows:
   a. Select new front rear and intermediate camshaft bearings.
   b. Select the proper pilot, nut and thrust washer.
   c. Assemble tool J 33049 or equivalent, place the bearing onto the tool and index the oil hole(s) of the bearing with the oil passage(s) in the cylinder block.
   d. Pull the bearing into place.
   e. Use a ³⁄₃₂ in. (2.4mm) brass rod with a 90° bend and probe the bearing holes to verify that they are properly aligned.
18. Coat the camshaft lobes with and bearings with GM Engine Oil Supplement (E.O.S.) 1051396 or equivalent and insert the camshaft and thrust plate in the engine.
19. Tighten the thrust plate bolts to 106 inch lbs. (12 Nm).
20. Install the timing chain and sprockets.
21. Install the crankcase front cover.
22. Install the valve lifters in the same bores from which they were removed.

➡ **If a new camshaft is installed, replace all the valve lifters.**

23. Install the oil pump drive.
24. Install the remaining components in the reverse of the removal procedure.
25. Fill the cooling system and crankcase with the proper types and amounts of fluids.
26. Connect the negative battery cable, then start the engine and check for leaks. Check the fluid levels and add if necessary.

2.3L Engine

◆ **See Figures 56 and 57**

INTAKE CAMSHAFT, HOUSING AND LIFTERS—1990–93 VEHICLES

➡ **Any time the camshaft housing to cylinder head bolts are loosened or removed, the camshaft housing to cylinder head gasket must be replaced.**

1. Relieve the fuel system pressure. Disconnect the negative battery cable.
2. Remove ignition coil and module assembly electrical connections mark or tag, if necessary.
3. Remove 4 ignition coil and module assembly to camshaft housing bolts and remove assembly by pulling straight up. Use a special spark plug boot wire remover tool to remove connector assemblies if stuck to the spark plugs.
4. Remove the idle speed power steering pressure switch connector.
5. Loosen 3 power steering pump pivot bolts and remove drive belt.
6. Disconnect the 2 rear power steering pump bracket to transaxle bolts.
7. Remove the front power steering pump bracket to cylinder block bolt.
8. Disconnect the power steering pump assembly and position aside.
9. Using special tools remove power steering pump drive pulley from intake camshaft.
10. Remove oil/air separator bolts and hoses. Leave the hoses attached to the separator, disconnect from the oil fill, chain housing and intake manifold. Remove as an assembly.
11. Remove vacuum line from fuel pressure regulator and fuel injector harness connector.
12. Disconnect fuel line retaining clamp from bracket on top of intake camshaft housing.
13. Remove fuel rail to camshaft housing attaching bolts.
14. Remove fuel rail from cylinder head. Cover injector openings in cylinder head and cover injector nozzles. Leave fuel lines attached and position fuel rail aside.
15. Disconnect timing chain and housing but do not remove from the engine.
16. Remove intake camshaft housing cover-to-camshaft housing attaching bolts.

➡ **The camshaft housing-to-cylinder head bolts MUST be loosened and removed in the reverse order of the tightening sequence.**

17. Remove intake camshaft housing to cylinder head attaching bolts. Use the reverse of the tightening procedure when loosening camshaft housing to cylinder head attaching bolts. Leave 2 bolts loosely in place to hold the camshaft housing while separating camshaft cover from housing.
18. Push the cover off the housing by threading 4 of the housing to head attaching bolts into the tapped holes in the cam housing cover. Tighten the bolts in evenly so the cover does not bind on the dowel pins.
19. Remove the 2 loosely installed camshaft housing to head bolts and remove cover, discard gaskets.
20. Note the position of the chain sprocket dowel pin for reassembly. Remove the camshaft, being careful not to damage the camshaft oil seal from camshaft or journals.

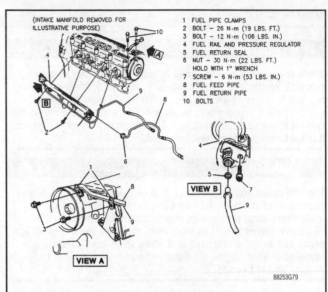

Fig. 56 Exploded view of the fuel rail and lines—2.3L engine

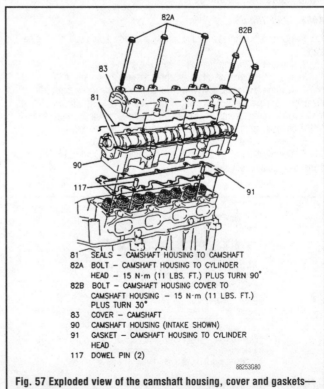

81	SEALS – CAMSHAFT HOUSING TO CAMSHAFT
82A	BOLT – CAMSHAFT HOUSING TO CYLINDER HEAD – 15 N·m (11 LBS. FT.) PLUS TURN 90°
82B	BOLT – CAMSHAFT HOUSING COVER TO CAMSHAFT HOUSING – 15 N·m (11 LBS. FT.) PLUS TURN 30°
83	COVER – CAMSHAFT
90	CAMSHAFT HOUSING (INTAKE SHOWN)
91	GASKET – CAMSHAFT HOUSING TO CYLINDER HEAD
117	DOWEL PIN (2)

Fig. 57 Exploded view of the camshaft housing, cover and gaskets—2.3L engine

21. Remove intake camshaft oil seal from camshaft and discard seal. This seal must be replaced any time the housing and cover are separated.

To install:

➡️**If the camshaft is being replaced, the lifters must also be replaced. Lubricate the camshaft lobes, journals and lifters with camshaft and lifter prelube. The camshaft lobes and journals must be adequately lubricated or engine damage could occur upon start up.**

22. Install camshaft in same position as when removed. The timing chain sprocket dowel pin should be straight up and line up with the centerline of the lifter bores.

23. Install new camshaft housing-to-camshaft housing cover seals into cover. Do not use sealer.

➡️**Cam housing to cover seals are all different.**

24. Apply locking type sealer to camshaft housing and cover attaching bolt threads.

➡️**The camshaft housing bolts MUST be tightened in sequence.**

25. Install bolts and tighten to 11 ft. lbs. (15 Nm). Rotate the bolts an additional 75°, for 1990–93 vehicles or 90° for 1994 vehicles, in sequence.

➡️**Tighten the 2 rear bolts that hold fuel pipe to camshaft housing to 11 ft. lbs. (15 Nm), then rotate the bolts an additional 25° for 1990–93 vehicles or 30° for 1994 vehicles.**

26. Install timing chain housing and timing chain.
27. Uncover fuel injectors and install new fuel injector ring seals lubed with engine oil.
28. Install fuel rail to cylinder head.
29. Install fuel rail to camshaft housing attaching bolts.
30. Connect fuel line retaining clamp to bracket on top of intake camshaft housing.
31. Install vacuum line to fuel pressure regulator and fuel injector harness connector.
32. Install oil/air separator bolts and hoses.
33. Install power steering pump drive pulley to intake camshaft.
34. Install the power steering pump assembly.
35. Install the front power steering pump bracket to cylinder block bolt.
36. Connect the 2 rear power steering pump bracket to transaxle bolts.
37. Tighten the 3 power steering pump pivot bolts and install serpentine belt.
38. Connect the idle speed power steering pressure switch connector.
39. Install ignition module assembly and the 4 ignition coil and module assembly to camshaft housing bolts.

➡️**Clean any loose lubricant that is present on the ignition coil and module assembly to camshaft housing bolts. Apply Loctite® 592 or equivalent onto the ignition coil and module assembly to camshaft housing bolts. Install the bolts and tighten to 13 ft. lbs. (18 Nm).**

40. Connect ignition coil and module assembly electrical connectors.
41. Connect the negative battery cable.

EXHAUST CAMSHAFT, HOUSING AND LIFTERS

➡️**Any time the camshaft housing-to-cylinder head bolts are loosened or removed, the camshaft housing-to-cylinder head gasket must be replaced.**

1. Relieve the fuel system pressure. Disconnect the negative battery cable.
2. Remove electrical connection from ignition coil and module assembly.
3. Remove 4 ignition coil and module assembly to camshaft housing bolts and remove assembly by pulling straight up. Use a special tool to remove connector assembly if stuck to the spark plugs.
4. Detach the electrical connection from oil pressure switch.
5. Remove transaxle fluid level indicator tube assembly from exhaust camshaft cover and position aside.
6. Remove the exhaust camshaft cover and gasket.
7. Disconnect timing chain and housing but do not remove from the engine.

➡️**The camshaft housing-to-cylinder head bolts MUST be loosened and removed in the reverse order of the tightening sequence.**

8. Remove exhaust camshaft housing to cylinder head bolts. Use the reverse of the tightening procedure when loosening camshaft housing while separating camshaft cover from housing.

9. Push the cover off the housing by threading 4 of the housing to head attaching bolts into the tapped holes in the camshaft cover. Tighten the bolts in evenly so the cover does not bind on the dowel pins.
10. Remove the 2 loosely installed camshaft housing to cylinder head bolts and remove cover, discard gaskets.
11. Loosely reinstall 1 camshaft housing to cylinder head bolt to hold the camshaft housing in place during camshaft and lifter removal.
12. Note the position of the chain sprocket dowel pin for reassembly. Remove camshaft being careful not to damage the camshaft or journals.
13. If removing the camshaft housing, remove the valve lifters. Keep the lifters in order so they can be reinstalled in the same location.
14. Remove the camshaft housing and gasket.

To install:

15. Install the camshaft housing and gasket.
16. Loosely install one camshaft housing-to-cylinder head bolt to hold the housing in place.

➡️**Used lifters must be returned to their original position in the camshaft. If the camshaft is being replaced, the lifters must also be replaced. Lubricate camshaft lobe, journals and lifters with camshaft and lifter prelube. The camshaft lobes and journals must be adequately lubricated or engine damage could occur upon start up.**

17. Install the lifters into the lifter bores.
18. Install camshaft in same position as when removed. The timing chain sprocket dowel pin should be straight up and line up with the centerline of the lifter bores.
19. Install new camshaft housing-to-camshaft housing cover seals into cover, no sealer is needed.

➡️**Cam housing to cover seals are all different.**

20. Remove the bolt holding the housing in place. Apply locking type sealer to camshaft housing and cover attaching bolt threads.

To install:

21. Install the camshaft housing cover to the camshaft housing.
22. Install the retaining bolts and tighten, in the sequence shown in the accompanying figure, to 11 ft. lbs. (15 Nm), then rotate, in sequence, an additional 75° for 1990–93 vehicles or 90° for 1994 vehicles.
23. Install the timing chain housing and timing chain.
24. Install the exhaust camshaft housing cover, using a new gasket, then tighten to 10 ft. lbs. (14 Nm).
25. Attach the oil pressure switch electrical connector.
26. Reinstall any spark plug boot connector that was stuck to a spark plug back onto the ignition coil assembly.
27. Locate the ignition coil and module assembly over the spark plugs and push straight down to properly seat the assembly.

➡️**Clean any loose lubricant that is present on the ignition coil and module assembly to camshaft housing bolts.**

28. Apply Loctite® 592 or equivalent to the ignition coil and module assembly to camshaft housing bolts. Install and hand start the ignition coil and module assembly bolts. Tighten to 15 ft. lbs. (20 Nm).
29. Attach the ignition coil and module assembly electrical connectors.
30. Connect the negative battery cable.

2.8L and 3.1L Engine

♦ See Figures 58, 59 and 60

1. Relieve the fuel system pressure. If not already done, disconnect the negative battery cable.
2. Drain the cooling system and the engine oil into suitable containers.
3. Remove the engine from the vehicle and mount on a suitable engine stand.

➡️**Be sure to the valve train components in order for reassembly purposes.**

4. Remove the valve lifters.
5. Remove the timing chain (front) cover, then remove the timing chain and sprockets.
6. If equipped, remove the camshaft thrust plate bolts, then remove the thrust plate.

➡️**The camshaft journals are all the same size. Use extreme care when removing or installing the camshaft not to damage the camshaft bearings or the bearing journals of the camshaft.**

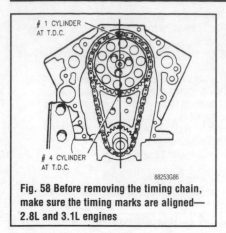

Fig. 58 Before removing the timing chain, make sure the timing marks are aligned— 2.8L and 3.1L engines

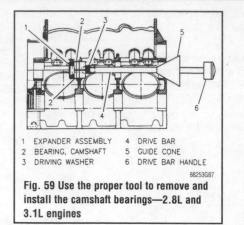

1	EXPANDER ASSEMBLY	4	DRIVE BAR
2	BEARING, CAMSHAFT	5	GUIDE CONE
3	DRIVING WASHER	6	DRIVE BAR HANDLE

Fig. 59 Use the proper tool to remove and install the camshaft bearings—2.8L and 3.1L engines

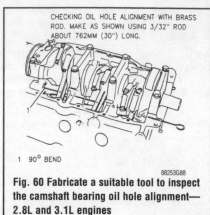

Fig. 60 Fabricate a suitable tool to inspect the camshaft bearing oil hole alignment— 2.8L and 3.1L engines

7. Install a camshaft bolt in the camshaft bolt hole, then carefully rotate and pull the camshaft from the bearings out of the front of the engine.

8. Using a gasket scraper, clean gasket mounting surfaces.

➡**Camshaft bearing removal requires the use of tool J 33049 or equivalent camshaft bearing remover/installer.**

9. If necessary, remove the camshaft bearings as follows:
   a. Select the proper expander assembly.
   b. Assemble camshaft bearing removal/installation tool J 33049.
   c. Carefully tap out the camshaft bearings.

➡**Camshaft bearings can NOT be reused once they are removed.**

To install:

10. Install the camshaft bearings, as follows:
   a. Select front, rear and intermediate camshaft bearings.
   b. Select the proper expander assembly.
   c. Assemble camshaft bearing removal/installation tool J 33049.
   d. Place the bearing onto the tool, then index the oil holes(s) of the bearing with the oil passage(s) in the cylinder block. Tap the bearing into place.
   e. Looking from the front of the engine block, index the front bearing oil holes at 4 and 7 o'clock.
   f. Index all other bearing oil holes at 4 o'clock.
   g. With a piece of ³⁄₃₂ in. brass rod with a 90° bend at the end, probe the bearing oil holes and make sure they are properly aligned.

11. If installing a new camshaft, lubricate the camshaft lobes with GM E.O.S. 1051396 or equivalent and insert the camshaft in the engine.

➡**If a new camshaft is being used replace all of the lifters. Used lifters can only be used on the camshaft that they were originally installed with; provided they are installed in the exact same position they were removed.**

12. Align the camshaft and crankshaft sprocket marks. Install the timing chain and sprocket.

13. Install the front cover and valve train components: Tighten the rocker arm nuts to 14–20 ft. lbs. (19–27 Nm).

14. To complete the installation, reverse the removal procedures. Start the engine, allow it to reach normal operating temperatures and check for leaks.

Rear Main Oil Seal

REMOVAL & INSTALLATION

2.0L and 2.2L Engines

▶ See Figures 61 and 62

1. Raise and safely support the vehicle.
2. Remove the transaxle as outlined in Section 7.
3. Remove the flywheel.

➡**Now is the time to confirm that the rear seal is leaking.**

✼✼ WARNING

Be careful not to damage the crankshaft seal surface with a prytool.

4. Insert a suitable prytool in through the dust lip and pry out the seal by moving the tool around the seal until it is removed.

To install:

5. Before installing, lubricate the seal bore to seal surface with clean engine oil.

6. Install the new seal using tool J–34686 or equivalent rear main bearing oil seal installer.

7. Slide the new seal over the mandrel until the dust lip bottoms squarely against the tool collar.

8. Align the dowel pin of the tool with the dowel pin hole in the crankshaft and attach the tool to the crankshaft. Tighten the attaching screws to 27–62 inch lbs. (3–7 Nm).

9. Tighten the T-handle of the tool to push the seal into the bore. Continue until the tool collar is flush against the block.

10. Loosen the T-handle completely. Remove the attaching screws and the tool.

➡**Check to see that the seal is squarely seated in the bore.**

11. Install the flywheel and transaxle.
12. Carefully lower the vehicle.
13. Start the engine and check for leaks.

2.3L Engine

▶ See Figure 63

1. Remove the transaxle assembly.
2. Remove the clutch and pressure plate and clutch cover. Matchmark the relationship of the pressure plate and clutch cover assembly to the flywheel for reassembly in the same position for proper balance.
3. Remove the bolts attaching the flywheel to the crankshaft flange and flywheel.
4. Remove the oil pan-to-crankshaft seal housing bolts.
5. Support the seal housing for seal removal using 2 wood blocks of equal thickness. With the wood blocks on a flat surface, position the seal housing and blocks so the transaxle side of the seal housing is supported across the dowel pin and center bolt holes on both sides of the seal opening.

✼✼ WARNING

The seal housing could be damaged if not supported during seal removal.

6. Drive the crankshaft seal evenly out of the transaxle side of the seal housing using a small chisel in the 4 relief grooves on the crankshaft side of the seal housing.

✼✼ WARNING

Use care to avoid seal housing sealing surface damage or a leak will result.

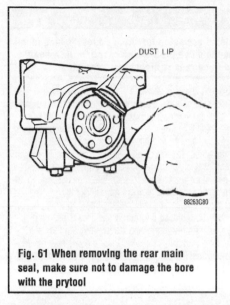

Fig. 61 When removing the rear main seal, make sure not to damage the bore with the prytool

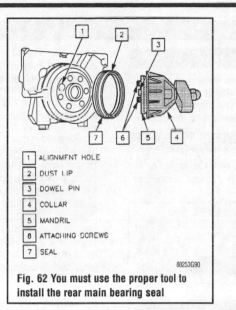

1	ALIGNMENT HOLE
2	DUST LIP
3	DOWEL PIN
4	COLLAR
5	MANDRIL
6	ATTACHING SCREWS
7	SEAL

Fig. 62 You must use the proper tool to install the rear main bearing seal

21	SEAL, REAR CRANKSHAFT
22	BOLT, REAR CRANKSHAFT SEAL HOUSING TO BLOCK (6)
23	HOUSING, REAR CRANKSHAFT SEAL
24	GASKET, REAR CRANKSHAFT SEAL HOUSING TO BLOCK
25	DOWEL PIN, REAR CRANKSHAFT SEAL HOUSING TO BLOCK
38	OIL PAN
39C	BOLT, OIL PAN TO SEAL HOUSING

Fig. 63 Exploded view of the rear main seal and housing—2.3L engines

To install:

7. Press the new seal into the crankshaft using J 36005 seal installer.

8. Position the new seal housing to the block gasket over the alignment dowel pins. The gasket is reversible and no sealant is necessary.

9. Lubricate the lip of the crankshaft seal with engine oil.

10. Install the seal housing assembly to the cylinder block bolts and tighten to 106 inch lbs. (12 Nm).

11. Tighten the oil pan to seal housing bolts to 106 inch lbs. (12 Nm).

12. Install the flywheel with new bolts and thread adhesive.

13. Install the clutch and pressure plate and clutch cover.

14. Install the transaxle assembly.

15. Start the engine and check for leaks.

2.8L and 3.1L Engine

1. Support the engine with J-28467 engine support or equivalent.

2. Remove the transaxle as outlined in Section 7.

3. Remove the flywheel.

➡ **Now is the time to confirm that the rear seal is leaking.**

4. Insert a suitable prytool in through the dust lip and pry out the seal by moving the tool around the seal until it is removed.

※ WARNING

Use care not to damage the crankshaft seal surface with a prytool.

To install:

5. Before installing, lubricate the seal bore to seal surface with clean engine oil.

6. Install the new seal using tool J-34686 or an equivalent rear main seal installation tool.

7. Slide the new seal over the mandrel until the dust lip bottoms squarely against the tool collar.

8. Align the dowel pin of the tool with the dowel pin hole in the crankshaft and attach the tool to the crankshaft. Tighten the attaching screws to 2–5 ft. lbs. (3–7 Nm).

9. Tighten the T-handle of the tool to push the seal into the bore. Continue until the tool collar is flush against the block.

10. Loosen the T-handle completely. Remove the attaching screws and the tool.

➡ **Check to see that the seal is squarely seated in the bore.**

11. Install the flywheel and transmission.

12. Start the engine and check for leaks.

Flywheel

REMOVAL & INSTALLATION

Vehicles Equipped with Manual Transaxles

※ WARNING

The master cylinder pushrod must be disconnected from the clutch pedal or permanent damage to the slave cylinder will occur.

1. Disconnect the negative battery cable.

2. Remove the hush panel from inside the vehicle.

3. Disconnect the master cylinder pushrod from the clutch pedal.

4. Remove the transaxle assembly.

5. Remove the pressure plate and clutch disc assembly.

6. Remove the flywheel attaching bolts, then remove the flywheel from the vehicle.

To install:

7. Install the flywheel and attaching bolts. Tighten the bolts, alternately and evenly as follows:

    a. Except 2.3L engine: 55 ft. lbs. (75 Nm).

    b. 2.3L engine: 22 ft. lbs. (30 Nm) plus an additional 45° rotation.

8. Install the pressure plate and clutch disc assembly.

9. Install the transaxle assembly.

10. Connect the master cylinder pushrod to the clutch pedal.

11. Check cruise control switch adjustment at the clutch pedal bracket.

12. Install the hush panel.

13. Connect the negative battery cable.

Vehicles Equipped with Automatic Transaxles

1. Remove the transaxle assembly.

2. Remove the right splash shield.

3. Remove the flywheel attaching bolts.

4. Remove the retainer.

5. Remove the flywheel.

To install:

6. Remove all thread adhesive from the holes.

7. Apply thread adhesive to all the flywheel bolts.

8. Install the flywheel and retainer and secure with the retaining bolts. Tighten the retaining bolts as follows:

    a. 2.0L and 2.2L engines: 52–55 ft. lbs. (70–75 Nm).

    b. 2.3L engines: 22 ft. lbs. (30 Nm) plus an additional 45° rotation.

    c. 2.8L and 3.1L (VIN T) engines: 52 ft. lbs. (70 Nm).

    d. 3.1L (VIN M) engines: 61 ft. lbs. (83 Nm).

9. Install the transaxle assembly.

EXHAUST SYSTEM

Inspection

➡Safety glasses should be worn at all times when working on or near the exhaust system. Older exhaust systems will almost always be covered with loose rust particles which will shower you when disturbed. These particles are more than a nuisance and could injure your eye.

✳✳ CAUTION

Do NOT perform exhaust repairs or inspection with the engine or exhaust hot. Allow the system to cool completely before attempting

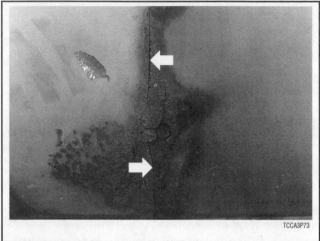

Cracks in the muffler are a guaranteed leak

any work. Exhaust systems are noted for sharp edges, flaking metal and rusted bolts. Gloves and eye protection are required. A healthy supply of penetrating oil and rags is highly recommended.

Your vehicle must be raised and supported safely to inspect the exhaust system properly. Placing 4 safety stands under the vehicle for support should provide enough room for you to slide under the vehicle and inspect the system completely. Start the inspection at the exhaust manifold or turbocharger pipe where the header pipe is attached and work your way to the back of the vehicle. On dual exhaust systems, remember to inspect both sides of the vehicle. Check the complete exhaust system for open seams, holes loose connections, or other deterioration which could permit exhaust fumes to seep into the passenger compartment. Inspect all mounting brackets and hangers for deterioration, some models may have rubber O-rings that can be overstretched and non-supportive. These components will need to be replaced if found. It has always been a practice to use a pointed tool to poke up into the exhaust system where the deterioration spots are to see whether or not they crumble. Some models may have heat shield covering certain parts of the exhaust system , it will be necessary to remove these shields to have the exhaust visible for inspection also.

REPLACEMENT

There are basically two types of exhaust systems. One is the flange type where the component ends are attached with bolts and a gasket in-between. The other exhaust system is the slip joint type. These components slip into one another using clamps to retain them together.

✳✳ CAUTION

Allow the exhaust system to cool sufficiently before spraying a solvent exhaust fasteners. Some solvents are highly flammable and could ignite when sprayed on hot exhaust components.

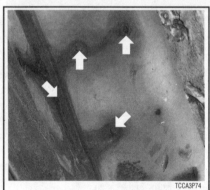

Check the muffler for rotted spot welds and seams

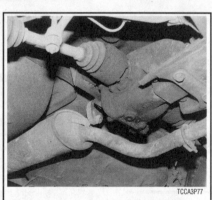

Make sure the exhaust components are not contacting the body or suspension

Check for over-stretched or torn exhaust hangers

Example of a badly deteriorated exhaust pipe

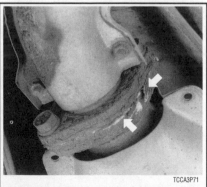

Inspect flanges for gaskets that have deteriorated and need replacement

Some systems, like this one, use large O-rings (donuts) in between the flanges

Before removing any component of the exhaust system, ALWAYS squirt a liquid rust dissolving agent onto the fasteners for ease of removal. A lot of knuckle skin will be saved by following this rule. It may even be wise to spray the fasteners and allow them to sit overnight.

Flange Type

> **⁂ CAUTION**
>
> Do NOT perform exhaust repairs or inspection with the engine or exhaust hot. Allow the system to cool completely before attempting any work. Exhaust systems are noted for sharp edges, flaking metal and rusted bolts. Gloves and eye protection are required. A healthy supply of penetrating oil and rags is highly recommended. Never spray liquid rust dissolving agent onto a hot exhaust component.

Before removing any component on a flange type system, ALWAYS squirt a liquid rust dissolving agent onto the fasteners for ease of removal. Start by unbolting the exhaust piece at both ends (if required). When unbolting the headpipe from the manifold, make sure that the bolts are free before trying to remove them. If you snap a stud in the exhaust manifold, the stud will have to be removed with a bolt extractor, which often means removal of the manifold itself. Next, disconnect the component from the mounting, slight twisting and turning may be required to remove the component completely from the vehicle. You may need to tap on the component with a rubber mallet to loosen the component. If all else fails, use a hacksaw to separate the parts. An oxy-acetylene cutting torch may be faster but the sparks are DANGEROUS near the fuel tank, and at the very least, accidents could happen, resulting in damage to the under-car parts, not to mention yourself.

Slip Joint Type

Before removing any component on the slip joint type exhaust system, ALWAYS squirt a liquid rust dissolving agent onto the fasteners for ease of removal. Start by unbolting the exhaust piece at both ends (if required). When unbolting the headpipe from the manifold, make sure that the bolts are free before trying to remove them. If you snap a stud in the exhaust manifold, the stud will have to be removed with a bolt extractor, which often means removal of the manifold itself. Next, remove the mounting U-bolts from around the exhaust pipe you are extracting from the vehicle. Don't be surprised if the U-bolts break while removing the nuts. Loosen the exhaust pipe from any mounting brackets retaining it to the floor pan and separate the components.

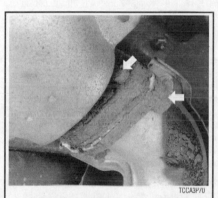

Nuts and bolts will be extremely difficult to remove when deteriorated with rust

Example of a flange type exhaust system joint

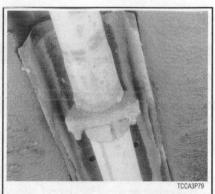

Example of a common slip joint type system

ENGINE RECONDITIONING

Determining Engine Condition

Anything that generates heat and/or friction will eventually burn or wear out (for example, a light bulb generates heat, therefore its life span is limited). With this in mind, a running engine generates tremendous amounts of both; friction is encountered by the moving and rotating parts inside the engine and heat is created by friction and combustion of the fuel. However, the engine has systems designed to help reduce the effects of heat and friction and provide added longevity. The oiling system reduces the amount of friction encountered by the moving parts inside the engine, while the cooling system reduces heat created by friction and combustion. If either system is not maintained, a break-down will be inevitable. Therefore, you can see how regular maintenance can affect the service life of your vehicle. If you do not drain, flush and refill your cooling system at the proper intervals, deposits will begin to accumulate in the radiator, thereby reducing the amount of heat it can extract from the coolant. The same applies to your oil and filter; if it is not changed often enough it becomes laden with contaminates and is unable to properly lubricate the engine. This increases friction and wear.

There are a number of methods for evaluating the condition of your engine. A compression test can reveal the condition of your pistons, piston rings, cylinder bores, head gasket(s), valves and valve seals. An oil pressure test can warn you of possible engine bearing, or oil pump failures. Excessive oil consumption, evidence of oil in the engine air intake area and/or bluish smoke from the tailpipe may indicate worn piston rings, worn valve guides and/or valve seals. As a general rule, an engine that uses no more than one quart of oil every 1000 miles is in good condition. Engines that use one quart of oil or more in less than 1000 miles should first be checked for oil leaks. If any oil leaks are present, have them fixed before determining how much oil is consumed by the engine, especially if blue smoke is not visible at the tailpipe.

COMPRESSION TEST

◆ See Figure 64

A noticeable lack of engine power, excessive oil consumption and/or poor fuel mileage measured over an extended period are all indicators of internal engine wear. Worn piston rings, scored or worn cylinder bores, blown head gaskets, sticking or burnt valves, and worn valve seats are all possible culprits. A check of each cylinder's compression will help locate the problem.

➡ **A screw-in type compression gauge is more accurate than the type you simply hold against the spark plug hole. Although it takes slightly longer to use, it's worth the effort to obtain a more accurate reading.**

1. Make sure that the proper amount and viscosity of engine oil is in the crankcase, then ensure the battery is fully charged.
2. Warm-up the engine to normal operating temperature, then shut the engine **OFF**.
3. Disable the ignition system.
4. Label and disconnect all of the spark plug wires from the plugs.
5. Thoroughly clean the cylinder head area around the spark plug ports, then remove the spark plugs.
6. Set the throttle plate to the fully open (wide-open throttle) position. You can block the accelerator linkage open for this, or you can have an assistant fully depress the accelerator pedal.

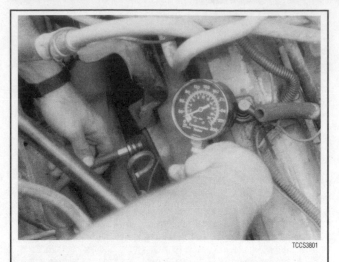

TCCS3801

Fig. 64 A screw-in type compression gauge is more accurate and easier to use without an assistant

7. Install a screw-in type compression gauge into the No. 1 spark plug hole until the fitting is snug.

✳✳ WARNING

Be careful not to crossthread the spark plug hole.

8. According to the tool manufacturer's instructions, connect a remote starting switch to the starting circuit.

9. With the ignition switch in the **OFF** position, use the remote starting switch to crank the engine through at least five compression strokes (approximately 5 seconds of cranking) and record the highest reading on the gauge.

10. Repeat the test on each cylinder, cranking the engine approximately the same number of compression strokes and/or time as the first.

11. Compare the highest readings from each cylinder to that of the others. The indicated compression pressures are considered within specifications if the lowest reading cylinder is within 75 percent of the pressure recorded for the highest reading cylinder. For example, if your highest reading cylinder pressure was 150 psi (1034 kPa), then 75 percent of that would be 113 psi (779 kPa). So the lowest reading cylinder should be no less than 113 psi (779 kPa).

12. If a cylinder exhibits an unusually low compression reading, pour a tablespoon of clean engine oil into the cylinder through the spark plug hole and repeat the compression test. If the compression rises after adding oil, it means that the cylinder's piston rings and/or cylinder bore are damaged or worn. If the pressure remains low, the valves may not be seating properly (a valve job is needed), or the head gasket may be blown near that cylinder. If compression in any two adjacent cylinders is low, and if the addition of oil doesn't help raise compression, there is leakage past the head gasket. Oil and coolant in the combustion chamber, combined with blue or constant white smoke from the tailpipe, are symptoms of this problem. However, don't be alarmed by the normal white smoke emitted from the tailpipe during engine warm-up or from cold weather driving. There may be evidence of water droplets on the engine dipstick and/or oil droplets in the cooling system if a head gasket is blown.

OIL PRESSURE TEST

Check for proper oil pressure at the sending unit passage with an externally mounted mechanical oil pressure gauge (as opposed to relying on a factory installed dash-mounted gauge). A tachometer may also be needed, as some specifications may require running the engine at a specific rpm.

1. With the engine cold, locate and remove the oil pressure sending unit.

2. Following the manufacturer's instructions, connect a mechanical oil pressure gauge and, if necessary, a tachometer to the engine.

3. Start the engine and allow it to idle.

4. Check the oil pressure reading when cold and record the number. You may need to run the engine at a specified rpm, so check the specifications.

5. Run the engine until normal operating temperature is reached (upper radiator hose will feel warm).

6. Check the oil pressure reading again with the engine hot and record the number. Turn the engine **OFF**.

7. Compare your hot oil pressure reading to specification. If the reading is low, check the cold pressure reading against the chart. If the cold pressure is well above the specification, and the hot reading was lower than the specification, you may have the wrong viscosity oil in the engine. Change the oil, making sure to use the proper grade and quantity, then repeat the test.

Low oil pressure readings could be attributed to internal component wear, pump related problems, a low oil level, or oil viscosity that is too low. High oil pressure readings could be caused by an overfilled crankcase, too high of an oil viscosity or a faulty pressure relief valve.

Buy or Rebuild?

Now if you have determined that your engine is worn out, you must make some decisions. The question of whether or not an engine is worth rebuilding is largely a subjective matter and one of personal worth. Is the engine a popular one, or is it an obsolete model? Are parts available? Will it get acceptable gas mileage once it is rebuilt? Is the car it's being put into worth keeping? Would it be less expensive to buy a new engine, have your engine rebuilt by a pro, rebuild it yourself or buy a used engine from a salvage yard? Or would it be simpler and less expensive to buy another car? If you have considered all these matters, and have still decided to rebuild the engine, then it is time to decide how you will rebuild it.

➡ **The editors at Chilton feel that most engine machining should be performed by a professional machine shop. Think of it as an assurance that the job has been done right the first time. There are many expensive and specialized tools required to perform such tasks as boring and honing an engine block or having a valve job done on a cylinder head. Even inspecting the parts requires expensive micrometers and gauges to properly measure wear and clearances. A machine shop can deliver to you clean, and ready to assemble parts, saving you time and aggravation. Your maximum savings will come from performing the removal, disassembly, assembly and installation of the engine and purchasing or renting only the tools required to perform these tasks.**

A complete rebuild or overhaul of an engine involves replacing all of the moving parts (pistons, rods, crankshaft, camshaft, etc.) with new ones and machining the non-moving wearing surfaces of the block and heads. Unfortunately, this may not be cost effective. For instance, your crankshaft may have been damaged or worn, but it can be machined undersize for a minimal fee.

So although you can replace everything inside the engine, it is usually wiser to replace only those parts which are really needed, and, if possible, repair the more expensive ones. Later in this section, we will break the engine down into its two main components: the cylinder head and the engine block. We will discuss each component, and the recommended parts to replace during a rebuild on each.

Engine Overhaul Tips

Most engine overhaul procedures are fairly standard. In addition to specific parts replacement procedures and specifications for your individual engine, this section is also a guide to acceptable rebuilding procedures. Examples of standard rebuilding practice are given and should be used along with specific details concerning your particular engine.

Competent and accurate machine shop services will ensure maximum performance, reliability and engine life. In most instances it is more profitable for the do-it-yourself mechanic to remove, clean and inspect the component, buy the necessary parts and deliver these to a shop for actual machine work.

Much of the assembly work (crankshaft, bearings, piston rods, and other components) is well within the scope of the do-it-yourself mechanic's tools and abilities. You will have to decide for yourself the depth of involvement you desire in an engine repair or rebuild.

TOOLS

The tools required for an engine overhaul or parts replacement will depend on the depth of your involvement. With a few exceptions, they will be the tools found in a mechanic's tool kit (see Section 1 of this manual). More in-depth work will require some or all of the following:

- A dial indicator (reading in thousandths) mounted on a universal base
- Micrometers and telescope gauges
- Jaw and screw-type pullers
- Scraper
- Valve spring compressor
- Ring groove cleaner
- Piston ring expander and compressor
- Ridge reamer
- Cylinder bore or glaze breaker
- Plastigage®
- Engine stand

The use of most of these tools is illustrated in this section. Many can be rented for a one-time use from a local parts jobber or tool supply house specializing in automotive work.

Occasionally, the use of special tools is called for. See the information on Special Tools and the Safety Notice in the front of this book before substituting another tool.

OVERHAUL TIPS

Aluminum has become extremely popular for use in engines, due to its low weight. Observe the following precautions when handling aluminum parts:
- Never hot tank aluminum parts (the caustic hot tank solution will eat the aluminum.)
- Remove all aluminum parts (identification tag, etc.) from engine parts prior to the tanking.
- Always coat threads lightly with engine oil or anti-seize compounds before installation, to prevent seizure.
- Never overtighten bolts or spark plugs especially in aluminum threads.

When assembling the engine, any parts that will be exposed to frictional contact must be prelubed to provide lubrication at initial start-up. Any product specifically formulated for this purpose can be used, but engine oil is not recommended as a prelube in most cases.

When semi-permanent (locked, but removable) installation of bolts or nuts is desired, threads should be cleaned and coated with Loctite® or another similar, commercial non-hardening sealant.

CLEANING

▶ **See Figures 65, 66, 67 and 68**

Before the engine and its components are inspected, they must be thoroughly cleaned. You will need to remove any engine varnish, oil sludge and/or carbon deposits from all of the components to insure an accurate inspection. A crack in the engine block or cylinder head can easily become overlooked if hidden by a layer of sludge or carbon.

Most of the cleaning process can be carried out with common hand tools and readily available solvents or solutions. Carbon deposits can be chipped away using a hammer and a hard wooden chisel. Old gasket material and varnish or sludge can usually be removed using a scraper and/or cleaning solvent. Extremely stubborn deposits may require the use of a power drill with a wire brush. If using a wire brush, use extreme care around any critical machined surfaces (such as the gasket surfaces, bearing saddles, cylinder bores, etc.). USE

OF A WIRE BRUSH IS NOT RECOMMENDED ON ANY ALUMINUM COMPONENTS. Always follow any safety recommendations given by the manufacturer of the tool and/or solvent.

✳✳ CAUTION

Always wear eye protection during any cleaning process involving scraping, chipping or spraying of solvents.

An alternative to the mess and hassle of cleaning the parts yourself is to drop them off at a local garage or machine shop. They should have the necessary equipment to properly clean all of the parts for a nominal fee.

Remove any oil galley plugs, freeze plugs and/or pressed-in bearings and carefully wash and degrease all of the engine components including the fasteners and bolts. Small parts such as the valves, springs, etc., should be placed in a metal basket and allowed to soak. Use pipe cleaner type brushes, and clean all passageways in the components.

Use a ring expander and remove the rings from the pistons. Clean the piston ring grooves with a special tool or a piece of broken ring. Scrape the carbon off of the top of the piston. You should never use a wire brush on the pistons. After preparing all of the piston assemblies in this manner, wash and degrease them again.

✳✳ WARNING

Use extreme care when cleaning around the cylinder head valve seats. A mistake or slip may cost you a new seat.

When cleaning the cylinder head, remove carbon from the combustion chamber with the valves installed. This will avoid damaging the valve seats.

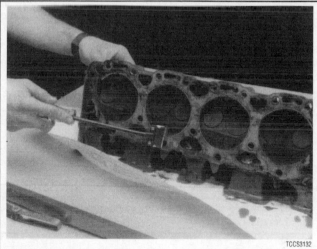

Fig. 65 Use a gasket scraper to remove the old gasket material from the mating surfaces

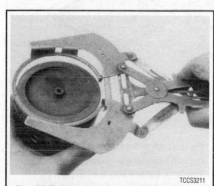

Fig. 66 Before cleaning and inspection, use a ring expander tool to remove the piston rings

Fig. 67 Clean the piston ring grooves using a ring groove cleaner tool, or . . .

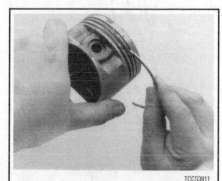

Fig. 68 . . . use a piece of an old ring to clean the grooves. Be careful, the ring can be quite sharp

REPAIRING DAMAGED THREADS

♦ **See Figures 69, 70, 71, 72 and 73**

Several methods of repairing damaged threads are available. Heli-Coil (shown here), Keenserts, and Microdot are among the most widely used. All involve basically the same principle—drilling out stripped threads, tapping the hole and installing a prewound insert—making welding, plugging and oversize fasteners unnecessary.

Two types of thread repair inserts are usually supplied: a standard type for most inch coarse, inch fine, metric course and metric fine thread sizes and a spark lug type to fit most spark plug port sizes. Consult the individual tool manufacturer's catalog to determine exact applications. Typical thread repair kits will contain a selection of prewound threaded inserts, a tap (corresponding to the outside diameter threads of the insert) and an installation tool. Spark plug inserts usually differ because they require a tap equipped with pilot threads and a combined reamer/tap section. Most manufacturers also supply blister-packed thread repair inserts separately in addition to a master kit containing a variety of taps and inserts plus installation tools.

Before attempting to repair a threaded hole, remove any snapped, broken or damaged bolts or studs. Penetrating oil can be used to free frozen threads. The offending item can usually be removed with locking pliers or using a screw/stud extractor. After the hole is clear, the thread can be repaired as shown in the kit manufacturer's instructions.

Engine Preparation

To properly rebuild an engine, you must first remove it from the vehicle, then disassemble and diagnose it. Ideally you should place your engine on an engine stand. This affords you the best access to the engine components. Remove the flywheel or flexplate before installing the engine to the stand.

Now that you have the engine on a stand, and assuming that you have drained the oil and coolant from the engine, it's time to strip it of all but the necessary components. Before you start disassembling the engine, you may want to take a moment to draw some pictures, or fabricate some labels or containers to mark the locations of various components and the bolts and/or studs which fasten them. Modern day engines use a lot of little brackets and clips which hold wiring harnesses and such, and these holders are often mounted on studs and/or bolts that can be easily mixed up. The manufacturer spent a lot of time and money designing your vehicle, and they wouldn't have wasted any of it by haphazardly placing brackets, clips or fasteners on the vehicle. If it's present when you disassemble it, put it back when you assemble, you will regret not remembering that little bracket which holds a wire harness out of the path of a rotating part.

You should begin by unbolting any accessories still attached to the engine, such as the water pump, power steering pump, alternator, etc. Then, unfasten any manifolds (intake or exhaust) which were not removed during the engine removal procedure. Finally, remove any covers remaining on the engine such as the rocker arm, front or timing cover and oil pan. Some front covers may require the vibration damper and/or crank pulley to be removed beforehand. The idea is to reduce the engine to the bare necessities of cylinder head(s), valve train, engine block, crankshaft, pistons and connecting rods, plus any other `in block' components such as oil pumps, balance shafts and auxiliary shafts.

Finally, remove the cylinder head(s) from the engine block and carefully place on a bench. Disassembly instructions for each component follow later in this section.

Cylinder Head

There are two basic types of cylinder heads used on today's automobiles: the Overhead Valve (OHV) and the Overhead Camshaft (OHC). The latter can also be broken down into two subgroups: the Single Overhead Camshaft (SOHC) and

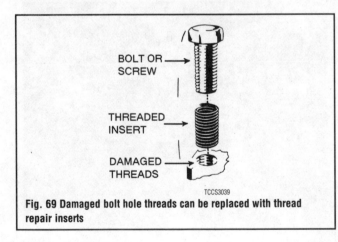

Fig. 69 Damaged bolt hole threads can be replaced with thread repair inserts

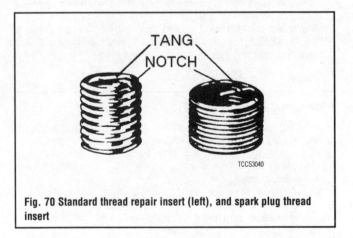

Fig. 70 Standard thread repair insert (left), and spark plug thread insert

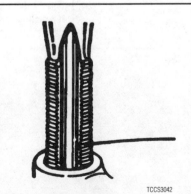

Fig. 71 Drill out the damaged threads with the specified size bit. Be sure to drill completely through the hole or to the bottom of a blind hole

Fig. 72 Using the kit, tap the hole in order to receive the thread insert. Keep the tap well oiled and back it out frequently to avoid clogging the threads

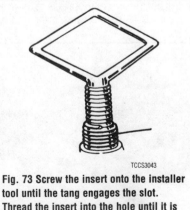

Fig. 73 Screw the insert onto the installer tool until the tang engages the slot. Thread the insert into the hole until it is ¼–½ turn below the top surface, then remove the tool and break off the tang using a punch

the Dual Overhead Camshaft (DOHC). Generally, if there is only a single camshaft on a head, it is just referred to as an OHC head. Also, an engine with an OHV cylinder head is also known as a pushrod engine.

Most cylinder heads these days are made of an aluminum alloy due to its light weight, durability and heat transfer qualities. However, cast iron was the material of choice in the past, and is still used on many vehicles. Whether made from aluminum or iron, all cylinder heads have valves and seats. Some use two valves per cylinder, while the more hi-tech engines will utilize a multi-valve configuration using 3, 4 and even 5 valves per cylinder. When the valve contacts the seat, it does so on precision machined surfaces, which seals the combustion chamber. All cylinder heads have a valve guide for each valve. The guide centers the valve to the seal and allows it to move up and down within it. The clearance between the valve and guide can be critical. Too much clearance and the engine may consume oil, lose vacuum and/or damage the seat. Too little, and the valve can stick in the guide causing the engine to run poorly if at all, and possibly causing severe damage. The last component all automotive cylinder heads have are valve springs. The spring holds the valve against its seat. It also returns the valve to this position when the valve has been opened by the valve train or camshaft. The spring is fastened to the valve by a retainer and valve locks (sometimes called keepers). Aluminum heads will also have a valve spring shim to keep the spring from wearing away the aluminum.

An ideal method of rebuilding the cylinder head would involve replacing all of the valves, guides, seats, springs, etc. with new ones. However, depending on how the engine was maintained, often this is not necessary. A major cause of valve, guide and seat wear is an improperly tuned engine. An engine that is running too rich, will often wash the lubricating oil out of the guide with gasoline, causing it to wear rapidly. Conversely, an engine which is running too lean will place higher combustion temperatures on the valves and seats allowing them to wear or even burn. Springs fall victim to the driving habits of the individual. A driver who often runs the engine rpm to the redline will wear out or break the springs faster then one that stays well below it. Unfortunately, mileage takes it toll on all of the parts. Generally, the valves, guides, springs and seats in a cylinder head can be machined and re-used, saving you money. However, if a valve is burnt, it may be wise to replace all of the valves, since they were all

operating in the same environment. The same goes for any other component on the cylinder head. Think of it as an insurance policy against future problems related to that component.

Unfortunately, the only way to find out which components need replacing, is to disassemble and carefully check each piece. After the cylinder head(s) are disassembled, thoroughly clean all of the components.

DISASSEMBLY

OHV Heads

▶ See Figures 74 thru 79

Before disassembling the cylinder head, you may want to fabricate some containers to hold the various parts, as some of them can be quite small (such as keepers) and easily lost. Also keeping yourself and the components organized will aid in assembly and reduce confusion. Where possible, try to maintain a components original location, this is especially important if there is not going to be any machine work performed on the components.

1. If you haven't already removed the rocker arms and/or shafts, do so now.
2. Position the head so that the springs are easily accessed.
3. Use a valve spring compressor tool, and relieve spring tension from the retainer.

➡ Due to engine varnish, the retainer may stick to the valve locks. A gentle tap with a hammer may help to break it loose.

4. Remove the valve locks from the valve tip and/or retainer. A small magnet may help in removing the locks.
5. Lift the valve spring, tool and all, off of the valve stem.
6. If equipped, remove the valve seal. If the seal is difficult to remove with the valve in place, try removing the valve first, then the seal. Follow the steps below for valve removal.
7. Position the head to allow access for withdrawing the valve.

Fig. 74 When removing an OHV valve spring, use a compressor tool to relieve the tension from the retainer

TCCS3137

Fig. 75 A small magnet will help in removal of the valve locks

TCCS3138

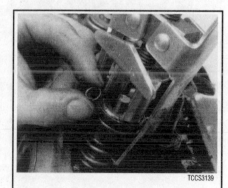

Fig. 76 Be careful not to lose the small valve locks (keepers)

TCCS3139

Fig. 77 Remove the valve seal from the valve stem—O-ring type seal shown

TCCS3140

Fig. 78 Removing an umbrella/positive type seal

TCCS3252

Fig. 79 Invert the cylinder head and withdraw the valve from the valve guide bore

TCCS3141

➡Cylinder heads that have seen a lot of miles and/or abuse may have mushroomed the valve lock grove and/or tip, causing difficulty in removal of the valve. If this has happened, use a metal file to carefully remove the high spots around the lock grooves and/or tip. Only file it enough to allow removal.

8. Remove the valve from the cylinder head.
9. If equipped, remove the valve spring shim. A small magnetic tool or screwdriver will aid in removal.
10. Repeat Steps 3 though 9 until all of the valves have been removed.

OHC Heads

▶ See Figures 80 and 81

Whether it is a single or dual overhead camshaft cylinder head, the disassembly procedure is relatively unchanged. One aspect to pay attention to is careful labeling of the parts on the dual camshaft cylinder head. There will be an intake camshaft and followers as well as an exhaust camshaft and followers and they must be labeled as such. In some cases, the components are identical and could easily be installed incorrectly. DO NOT MIX THEM UP! Determining which is which is very simple; the intake camshaft and components are on the same side of the head as was the intake manifold. Conversely, the exhaust camshaft and components are on the same side of the head as was the exhaust manifold.

CUP TYPE CAMSHAFT FOLLOWERS

▶ See Figures 82, 83 and 84

Most cylinder heads with cup type camshaft followers will have the valve spring, retainer and locks recessed within the follower's bore. You will need a C-clamp style valve spring compressor tool, an OHC spring removal tool (or equivalent) and a small magnet to disassemble the head.

1. If not already removed, remove the camshaft(s) and/or followers. Mark their positions for assembly.
2. Position the cylinder head to allow use of a C-clamp style valve spring compressor tool.

➡It is preferred to position the cylinder head gasket surface facing you with the valve springs facing the opposite direction and the head laying horizontal.

3. With the OHC spring removal adapter tool positioned inside of the follower bore, compress the valve spring using the C-clamp style valve spring compressor.
4. Remove the valve locks. A small magnetic tool or screwdriver will aid in removal.
5. Release the compressor tool and remove the spring assembly.
6. Withdraw the valve from the cylinder head.
7. If equipped, remove the valve seal.

Fig. 80 Exploded view of a valve, seal, spring, retainer and locks from an OHC cylinder head

Fig. 81 Example of a multi-valve cylinder head. Note how it has 2 intake and 2 exhaust valve ports

Fig. 82 Position the OHC spring tool in the follower bore, then compress the spring with a C-clamp type tool

Fig. 83 C-clamp type spring compressor and an OHC spring removal tool (center) for cup type followers

Fig. 84 Most cup type follower cylinder heads retain the camshaft using bolt-on bearing caps

➡Special valve seal removal tools are available. Regular or needlenose type pliers, if used with care, will work just as well. If using ordinary pliers, be sure not to damage the follower bore. The follower and its bore are machined to close tolerances and any damage to the bore will effect this relationship.

8. If equipped, remove the valve spring shim. A small magnetic tool or screwdriver will aid in removal.

9. Repeat Steps 3 through 8 until all of the valves have been removed.

ROCKER ARM TYPE CAMSHAFT FOLLOWERS

♦ See Figures 85 thru 93

Most cylinder heads with rocker arm-type camshaft followers are easily disassembled using a standard valve spring compressor. However, certain models may not have enough open space around the spring for the standard tool and may require you to use a C-clamp style compressor tool instead.

1. If not already removed, remove the rocker arms and/or shafts and the camshaft. If applicable, also remove the hydraulic lash adjusters. Mark their positions for assembly.

2. Position the cylinder head to allow access to the valve spring.

3. Use a valve spring compressor tool to relieve the spring tension from the retainer.

➡Due to engine varnish, the retainer may stick to the valve locks. A gentle tap with a hammer may help to break it loose.

4. Remove the valve locks from the valve tip and/or retainer. A small magnet may help in removing the small locks.

5. Lift the valve spring, tool and all, off of the valve stem.

6. If equipped, remove the valve seal. If the seal is difficult to remove with the valve in place, try removing the valve first, then the seal. Follow the steps below for valve removal.

7. Position the head to allow access for withdrawing the valve.

Fig. 85 Example of the shaft mounted rocker arms on some OHC heads

Fig. 86 Another example of the rocker arm type OHC head. This model uses a follower under the camshaft

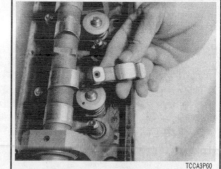

Fig. 87 Before the camshaft can be removed, all of the followers must first be removed . . .

Fig. 88 . . . then the camshaft can be removed by sliding it out (shown), or unbolting a bearing cap (not shown)

Fig. 89 Compress the valve spring . . .

Fig. 90 . . . then remove the valve locks from the valve stem and spring retainer

Fig. 91 Remove the valve spring and retainer from the cylinder head

Fig. 92 Remove the valve seal from the guide. Some gentle prying or pliers may help to remove stubborn ones

Fig. 93 All aluminum and some cast iron heads will have these valve spring shims. Remove all of them as well

➥Cylinder heads that have seen a lot of miles and/or abuse may have mushroomed the valve lock grove and/or tip, causing difficulty in removal of the valve. If this has happened, use a metal file to carefully remove the high spots around the lock grooves and/or tip. Only file it enough to allow removal.

8. Remove the valve from the cylinder head.
9. If equipped, remove the valve spring shim. A small magnetic tool or screwdriver will aid in removal.
10. Repeat Steps 3 though 9 until all of the valves have been removed.

INSPECTION

Now that all of the cylinder head components are clean, it's time to inspect them for wear and/or damage. To accurately inspect them, you will need some specialized tools:
- A 0–1 in. micrometer for the valves
- A dial indicator or inside diameter gauge for the valve guides
- A spring pressure test gauge
If you do not have access to the proper tools, you may want to bring the components to a shop that does.

Valves

▶ See Figures 94 and 95

The first thing to inspect are the valve heads. Look closely at the head, margin and face for any cracks, excessive wear or burning. The margin is the best place to look for burning. It should have a squared edge with an even width all around the diameter. When a valve burns, the margin will look melted and the

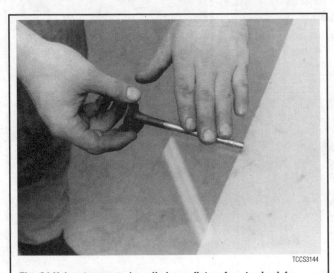

Fig. 94 Valve stems may be rolled on a flat surface to check for bends

edges rounded. Also inspect the valve head for any signs of tulipping. This will show as a lifting of the edges or dishing in the center of the head and will usually not occur to all of the valves. All of the heads should look the same, any that seem dished more than others are probably bad. Next, inspect the valve lock grooves and valve tips. Check for any burrs around the lock grooves, especially if you had to file them to remove the valve. Valve tips should appear flat, although slight rounding with high mileage engines is normal. Slightly worn valve tips will need to be machined flat. Last, measure the valve stem diameter with the micrometer. Measure the area that rides within the guide, especially towards the tip where most of the wear occurs. Take several measurements along its length and compare them to each other. Wear should be even along the length with little to no taper. If no minimum diameter is given in the specifications, then the stem should not read more than 0.001 in. (0.025mm) below the unworn portion of the stem. Any valves that fail these inspections should be replaced.

Springs, Retainers and Valve Locks

▶ See Figures 96 and 97

The first thing to check is the most obvious, broken springs. Next check the free length and squareness of each spring. If applicable, insure to distinguish between intake and exhaust springs. Use a ruler and/or carpenter's square to measure the length. A carpenter's square should be used to check the springs for squareness. If a spring pressure test gauge is available, check each springs rating and compare to the specifications chart. Check the readings against the specifications given. Any springs that fail these inspections should be replaced.

The spring retainers rarely need replacing, however they should still be checked as a precaution. Inspect the spring mating surface and the valve lock retention area for any signs of excessive wear. Also check for any signs of cracking. Replace any retainers that are questionable.

Valve locks should be inspected for excessive wear on the outside contact area as well as on the inner notched surface. Any locks which appear worn or broken and its respective valve should be replaced.

Cylinder Head

There are several things to check on the cylinder head: valve guides, seats, cylinder head surface flatness, cracks and physical damage.

VALVE GUIDES

▶ See Figure 98

Now that you know the valves are good, you can use them to check the guides, although a new valve, if available, is preferred. Before you measure anything, look at the guides carefully and inspect them for any cracks, chips or breakage. Also if the guide is a removable style (as in most aluminum heads), check them for any looseness or evidence of movement. All of the guides should appear to be at the same height from the spring seat. If any seem lower (or higher) from another, the guide has moved. Mount a dial indicator onto the spring side of the cylinder head. Lightly oil the valve stem and insert it into the cylinder head. Position the dial indicator against the valve stem near the tip and zero the gauge. Grasp the valve stem and wiggle towards and away from the dial indicator and observe the readings. Mount the dial indicator 90 degrees from

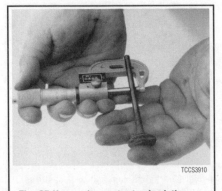

Fig. 95 Use a micrometer to check the valve stem diameter

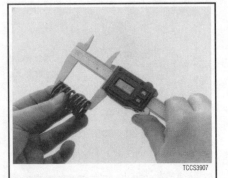

Fig. 96 Use a caliper to check the valve spring free-length

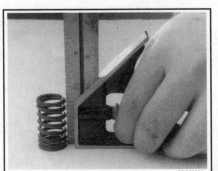

Fig. 97 Check the valve spring for squareness on a flat surface; a carpenter's square can be used

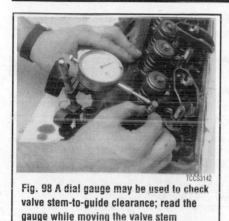

Fig. 98 A dial gauge may be used to check valve stem-to-guide clearance; read the gauge while moving the valve stem

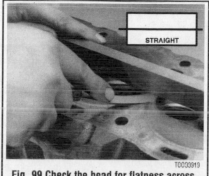

Fig. 99 Check the head for flatness across the center of the head surface using a straightedge and feeler gauge

Fig. 100 Checks should also be made along both diagonals of the head surface

the initial point and zero the gauge and again take a reading. Compare the two readings for an out of round condition. Check the readings against the specifications given. An Inside Diameter (I.D.) gauge designed for valve guides will give you an accurate valve guide bore measurement. If the I.D. gauge is used, compare the readings with the specifications given. Any guides that fail these inspections should be replaced or machined.

VALVE SEATS

A visual inspection of the valve seats should show a slightly worn and pitted surface where the valve face contacts the seat. Inspect the seat carefully for severe pitting or cracks. Also, a seat that is badly worn will be recessed into the cylinder head. A severely worn or recessed seat may need to be replaced. All cracked seats must be replaced. A seat concentricity gauge, if available, should be used to check the seat run-out. If run-out exceeds specifications the seat must be machined (if no specification is available given use 0.002 in. or 0.051mm).

CYLINDER HEAD SURFACE FLATNESS

▶ See Figures 99 and 100

After you have cleaned the gasket surface of the cylinder head of any old gasket material, check the head for flatness.

Place a straightedge across the gasket surface. Using feeler gauges, determine the clearance at the center of the straightedge and across the cylinder head at several points. Check along the centerline and diagonally on the head surface. If the warpage exceeds 0.003 in. (0.076mm) within a 6.0 in. (15.2cm) span, or 0.006 in. (0.152mm) over the total length of the head, the cylinder head must be resurfaced. After resurfacing the heads of a V-type engine, the intake manifold flange surface should be checked, and if necessary, milled proportionally to allow for the change in its mounting position.

CRACKS AND PHYSICAL DAMAGE

Generally, cracks are limited to the combustion chamber, however, it is not uncommon for the head to crack in a spark plug hole, port, outside of the head or in the valve spring/rocker arm area. The first area to inspect is always the hottest: the exhaust seat/port area.

A visual inspection should be performed, but just because you don't see a crack does not mean it is not there. Some more reliable methods for inspecting for cracks include Magnaflux®, a magnetic process or Zyglo®, a dye penetrant. Magnaflux® is used only on ferrous metal (cast iron) heads. Zyglo® uses a spray on fluorescent mixture along with a black light to reveal the cracks. It is strongly recommended to have your cylinder head checked professionally for cracks, especially if the engine was known to have overheated and/or leaked or consumed coolant. Contact a local shop for availability and pricing of these services.

Physical damage is usually very evident. For example, a broken mounting ear from dropping the head or a bent or broken stud and/or bolt. All of these defects should be fixed or, if unrepairable, the head should be replaced.

Camshaft and Followers

Inspect the camshaft(s) and followers as described earlier in this section.

REFINISHING & REPAIRING

Many of the procedures given for refinishing and repairing the cylinder head components must be performed by a machine shop. Certain steps, if the inspected part is not worn, can be performed yourself inexpensively. However, you spent a lot of time and effort so far, why risk trying to save a couple bucks if you might have to do it all over again?

Valves

Any valves that were not replaced should be refaced and the tips ground flat. Unless you have access to a valve grinding machine, this should be done by a machine shop. If the valves are in extremely good condition, as well as the valve seats and guides, they may be lapped in without performing machine work.

It is a recommended practice to lap the valves even after machine work has been performed and/or new valves have been purchased. This insures a positive seal between the valve and seat.

LAPPING THE VALVES

➡**Before lapping the valves to the seats, read the rest of the cylinder head section to insure that any related parts are in acceptable enough condition to continue. Also, remember that before any valve seat machining and/or lapping can be performed, the guides must be within factory recommended specifications.**

1. Invert the cylinder head.
2. Lightly lubricate the valve stems and insert them into the cylinder head in their numbered order.
3. Raise the valve from the seat and apply a small amount of fine lapping compound to the seat.
4. Moisten the suction head of a hand-lapping tool and attach it to the head of the valve.
5. Rotate the tool between the palms of both hands, changing the position of the valve on the valve seat and lifting the tool often to prevent grooving.
6. Lap the valve until a smooth, polished circle is evident on the valve and seat.
7. Remove the tool and the valve. Wipe away all traces of the grinding compound and store the valve to maintain its lapped location.

✳✳ WARNING

Do not get the valves out of order after they have been lapped. They must be put back with the same valve seat with which they were lapped.

Springs, Retainers and Valve Locks

There is no repair or refinishing possible with the springs, retainers and valve locks. If they are found to be worn or defective, they must be replaced with new (or known good) parts.

Cylinder Head

Most refinishing procedures dealing with the cylinder head must be performed by a machine shop. Read the sections below and review your inspection data to determine whether or not machining is necessary.

VALVE GUIDE

➡️If any machining or replacements are made to the valve guides, the seats must be machined.

Unless the valve guides need machining or replacing, the only service to perform is to thoroughly clean them of any dirt or oil residue.

There are only two types of valve guides used on automobile engines: the replaceable-type (all aluminum heads) and the cast-in integral-type (most cast iron heads). There are four recommended methods for repairing worn guides.

- Knurling
- Inserts
- Reaming oversize
- Replacing

Knurling is a process in which metal is displaced and raised, thereby reducing clearance, giving a true center, and providing oil control. It is the least expensive way of repairing the valve guides. However, it is not necessarily the best, and in some cases, a knurled valve guide will not stand up for more than a short time. It requires a special knurlizer and precision reaming tools to obtain proper clearances. It would not be cost effective to purchase these tools, unless you plan on rebuilding several of the same cylinder head.

Installing a guide insert involves machining the guide to accept a bronze insert. One style is the coil-type which is installed into a threaded guide. Another is the thin-walled insert where the guide is reamed oversize to accept a split-sleeve insert. After the insert is installed, a special tool is then run through the guide to expand the insert, locking it to the guide. The insert is then reamed to the standard size for proper valve clearance.

Reaming for oversize valves restores normal clearances and provides a true valve seat. Most cast-in type guides can be reamed to accept an valve with an oversize stem. The cost factor for this can become quite high as you will need to purchase the reamer and new, oversize stem valves for all guides which were reamed. Oversizes are generally 0.003–0.030 in. (0.076–0.762mm), with 0.015 in. (0.381mm) being the most common.

To replace cast-in type valve guides, they must be drilled out, then reamed to accept replacement guides. This must be done on a fixture which will allow centering and leveling off of the original valve seat or guide, otherwise a serious guide-to-seat misalignment may occur making it impossible to properly machine the seat.

Replaceable-type guides are pressed into the cylinder head. A hammer and a stepped drift or punch may be used to install and remove the guides. Before removing the guides, measure the protrusion on the spring side of the head and record it for installation. Use the stepped drift to hammer out the old guide from the combustion chamber side of the head. When installing, determine whether or not the guide also seals a water jacket in the head, and if it does, use the recommended sealing agent. If there is no water jacket, grease the valve guide and its bore. Use the stepped drift, and hammer the new guide into the cylinder head from the spring side of the cylinder head. A stack of washers the same thickness as the measured protrusion may help the installation process.

VALVE SEATS

➡️Before any valve seat machining can be performed, the guides must be within factory recommended specifications. If any machining occurred or if replacements were made to the valve guides, the seats must be machined.

If the seats are in good condition, the valves can be lapped to the seats, and the cylinder head assembled. See the valves section for instructions on lapping.

If the valve seats are worn, cracked or damaged, they must be serviced by a machine shop. The valve seat must be perfectly centered to the valve guide, which requires very accurate machining.

CYLINDER HEAD SURFACE

If the cylinder head is warped, it must be machined flat. If the warpage is extremely severe, the head may need to be replaced. In some instances, it may be possible to straighten a warped head enough to allow machining. In either case, contact a professional machine shop for service.

➡️Any OHC cylinder head that shows excessive warpage should have the camshaft bearing journals align bored after the cylinder head has been resurfaced.

❊❊ **WARNING**

Failure to align bore the camshaft bearing journals could result in severe engine damage including but not limited to: valve and piston damage, connecting rod damage, camshaft and/or crankshaft breakage.

CRACKS AND PHYSICAL DAMAGE

Certain cracks can be repaired in both cast iron and aluminum heads. For cast iron, a tapered threaded insert is installed along the length of the crack. Aluminum can also use the tapered inserts, however welding is the preferred method. Some physical damage can be repaired through brazing or welding. Contact a machine shop to get expert advice for your particular dilemma.

ASSEMBLY

The first step for any assembly job is to have a clean area in which to work. Next, thoroughly clean all of the parts and components that are to be assembled. Finally, place all of the components onto a suitable work space and, if necessary, arrange the parts to their respective positions.

OHV Engines

1. Lightly lubricate the valve stems and insert all of the valves into the cylinder head. If possible, maintain their original locations.
2. If equipped, install any valve spring shims which were removed.
3. If equipped, install the new valve seals, keeping the following in mind:
- If the valve seal presses over the guide, lightly lubricate the outer guide surfaces.
- If the seal is an O-ring type, it is installed just after compressing the spring but before the valve locks.
4. Place the valve spring and retainer over the stem.
5. Position the spring compressor tool and compress the spring.
6. Assemble the valve locks to the stem.
7. Relieve the spring pressure slowly and insure that neither valve lock becomes dislodged by the retainer.
8. Remove the spring compressor tool.
9. Repeat Steps 2 through 8 until all of the springs have been installed.

OHC Engines

◗ See Figure 101

CUP TYPE CAMSHAFT FOLLOWERS

To install the springs, retainers and valve locks on heads which have these components recessed into the camshaft follower's bore, you will need a small screwdriver-type tool, some clean white grease and a lot of patience. You will also need the C-clamp style spring compressor and the OHC tool used to disassemble the head.

TCCA3P64

Fig. 101 Once assembled, check the valve clearance and correct as needed

1. Lightly lubricate the valve stems and insert all of the valves into the cylinder head. If possible, maintain their original locations.

2. If equipped, install any valve spring shims which were removed.

3. If equipped, install the new valve seals, keeping the following in mind:

• If the valve seal presses over the guide, lightly lubricate the outer guide surfaces.

• If the seal is an O-ring type, it is installed just after compressing the spring but before the valve locks.

4. Place the valve spring and retainer over the stem.

5. Position the spring compressor and the OHC tool, then compress the spring.

6. Using a small screwdriver as a spatula, fill the valve stem side of the lock with white grease. Use the excess grease on the screwdriver to fasten the lock to the driver.

7. Carefully install the valve lock, which is stuck to the end of the screwdriver, to the valve stem then press on it with the screwdriver until the grease squeezes out. The valve lock should now be stuck to the stem.

8. Repeat Steps 6 and 7 for the remaining valve lock.

9. Relieve the spring pressure slowly and insure that neither valve lock becomes dislodged by the retainer.

10. Remove the spring compressor tool.

11. Repeat Steps 2 through 10 until all of the springs have been installed.

12. Install the followers, camshaft(s) and any other components that were removed for disassembly.

ROCKER ARM TYPE CAMSHAFT FOLLOWERS

1. Lightly lubricate the valve stems and insert all of the valves into the cylinder head. If possible, maintain their original locations.

2. If equipped, install any valve spring shims which were removed.

3. If equipped, install the new valve seals, keeping the following in mind:

• If the valve seal presses over the guide, lightly lubricate the outer guide surfaces.

• If the seal is an O-ring type, it is installed just after compressing the spring but before the valve locks.

4. Place the valve spring and retainer over the stem.

5. Position the spring compressor tool and compress the spring.

6. Assemble the valve locks to the stem.

7. Relieve the spring pressure slowly and insure that neither valve lock becomes dislodged by the retainer.

8. Remove the spring compressor tool.

9. Repeat Steps 2 through 8 until all of the springs have been installed.

10. Install the camshaft(s), rockers, shafts and any other components that were removed for disassembly.

Engine Block

GENERAL INFORMATION

A thorough overhaul or rebuild of an engine block would include replacing the pistons, rings, bearings, timing belt/chain assembly and oil pump. For OHV engines also include a new camshaft and lifters. The block would then have the cylinders bored and honed oversize (or if using removable cylinder sleeves, new sleeves installed) and the crankshaft would be cut undersize to provide new wearing surfaces and perfect clearances. However, your particular engine may not have everything worn out. What if only the piston rings have worn out and the clearances on everything else are still within factory specifications? Well, you could just replace the rings and put it back together, but this would be a very rare example. Chances are, if one component in your engine is worn, other components are sure to follow, and soon. At the very least, you should always replace the rings, bearings and oil pump. This is what is commonly called a "freshen up".

Cylinder Ridge Removal

Because the top piston ring does not travel to the very top of the cylinder, a ridge is built up between the end of the travel and the top of the cylinder bore.

Pushing the piston and connecting rod assembly past the ridge can be difficult, and damage to the piston ring lands could occur. If the ridge is not removed before installing a new piston or not removed at all, piston ring breakage and piston damage may occur.

➡ It is always recommended that you remove any cylinder ridges before removing the piston and connecting rod assemblies. If you know that new pistons are going to be installed and the engine block will be bored oversize, you may be able to forego this step. However, some ridges may actually prevent the assemblies from being removed, necessitating its removal.

There are several different types of ridge reamers on the market, none of which are inexpensive. Unless a great deal of engine rebuilding is anticipated, borrow or rent a reamer.

1. Turn the crankshaft until the piston is at the bottom of its travel.

2. Cover the head of the piston with a rag.

3. Follow the tool manufacturers instructions and cut away the ridge, exercising extreme care to avoid cutting too deeply.

4. Remove the ridge reamer, the rag and as many of the cuttings as possible. Continue until all of the cylinder ridges have been removed.

DISASSEMBLY

♦ See Figures 102 and 103

The engine disassembly instructions following assume that you have the engine mounted on an engine stand. If not, it is easiest to disassemble the

Fig. 102 Place rubber hose over the connecting rod studs to protect the crankshaft and cylinder bores from damage

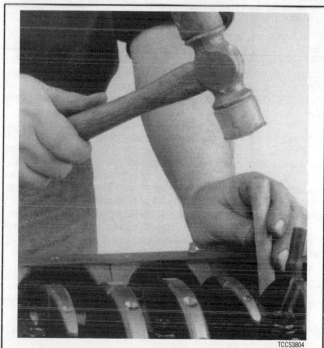

Fig. 103 Carefully tap the piston out of the bore using a wooden dowel

engine on a bench or the floor with it resting on the bell housing or transmission mounting surface. You must be able to access the connecting rod fasteners and turn the crankshaft during disassembly. Also, all engine covers (timing, front, side, oil pan, whatever) should have already been removed. Engines which are seized or locked up may not be able to be completely disassembled, and a core (salvage yard) engine should be purchased.

Pushrod Engines

If not done during the cylinder head removal, remove the pushrods and lifters, keeping them in order for assembly. Remove the timing gears and/or timing chain assembly, then remove the oil pump drive assembly and withdraw the camshaft from the engine block. Remove the oil pick-up and pump assembly. If equipped, remove any balance or auxiliary shafts. If necessary, remove the cylinder ridge from the top of the bore. See the cylinder ridge removal procedure earlier in this section.

OHC Engines

If not done during the cylinder head removal, remove the timing chain/belt and/or gear/sprocket assembly. Remove the oil pick-up and pump assembly and, if necessary, the pump drive. If equipped, remove any balance or auxiliary shafts. If necessary, remove the cylinder ridge from the top of the bore. See the cylinder ridge removal procedure earlier in this section.

All Engines

Rotate the engine over so that the crankshaft is exposed. Use a number punch or scribe and mark each connecting rod with its respective cylinder number. The cylinder closest to the front of the engine is always number 1. However, depending on the engine placement, the front of the engine could either be the flywheel or damper/pulley end. Generally the front of the engine faces the front of the vehicle. Use a number punch or scribe and also mark the main bearing caps from front to rear with the front most cap being number 1 (if there are five caps, mark them 1 through 5, front to rear).

✱✱ WARNING

Take special care when pushing the connecting rod up from the crankshaft because the sharp threads of the rod bolts/studs will score the crankshaft journal. Insure that special plastic caps are installed over them, or cut two pieces of rubber hose to do the same.

Again, rotate the engine, this time to position the number one cylinder bore (head surface) up. Turn the crankshaft until the number one piston is at the bottom of its travel, this should allow the maximum access to its connecting rod. Remove the number one connecting rods fasteners and cap and place two lengths of rubber hose over the rod bolts/studs to protect the crankshaft from damage. Using a sturdy wooden dowel and a hammer, push the connecting rod up about 1 in. (25mm) from the crankshaft and remove the upper bearing insert. Continue pushing or tapping the connecting rod up until the piston rings are out of the cylinder bore. Remove the piston and rod by hand, put the upper half of the bearing insert back into the rod, install the cap with its bearing insert installed, and hand-tighten the cap fasteners. If the parts are kept in order in this manner, they will not get lost and you will be able to tell which bearings came form what cylinder if any problems are discovered and diagnosis is necessary. Remove all the other piston assemblies in the same manner. On V-style engines, remove all of the pistons from one bank, then reposition the engine with the other cylinder bank head surface up, and remove that banks piston assemblies.

The only remaining component in the engine block should now be the crankshaft. Loosen the main bearing caps evenly until the fasteners can be turned by hand, then remove them and the caps. Remove the crankshaft from the engine block. Thoroughly clean all of the components.

INSPECTION

Now that the engine block and all of its components are clean, it's time to inspect them for wear and/or damage. To accurately inspect them, you will need some specialized tools:

• Two or three separate micrometers to measure the pistons and crankshaft journals

• A dial indicator
• Telescoping gauges for the cylinder bores
• A rod alignment fixture to check for bent connecting rods

If you do not have access to the proper tools, you may want to bring the components to a shop that does.

Generally, you shouldn't expect cracks in the engine block or its components unless it was known to leak, consume or mix engine fluids, it was severely overheated, or there was evidence of bad bearings and/or crankshaft damage. A visual inspection should be performed on all of the components, but just because you don't see a crack does not mean it is not there. Some more reliable methods for inspecting for cracks include Magnaflux®, a magnetic process or Zyglo®, a dye penetrant. Magnaflux® is used only on ferrous metal (cast iron). Zyglo® uses a spray on fluorescent mixture along with a black light to reveal the cracks. It is strongly recommended to have your engine block checked professionally for cracks, especially if the engine was known to have overheated and/or leaked or consumed coolant. Contact a local shop for availability and pricing of these services.

Engine Block

ENGINE BLOCK BEARING ALIGNMENT

Remove the main bearing caps and, if still installed, the main bearing inserts. Inspect all of the main bearing saddles and caps for damage, burrs or high spots. If damage is found, and it is caused from a spun main bearing, the block will need to be align-bored or, if severe enough, replacement. Any burrs or high spots should be carefully removed with a metal file.

Place a straightedge on the bearing saddles, in the engine block, along the centerline of the crankshaft. If any clearance exists between the straightedge and the saddles, the block must be align-bored.

Align-boring consists of machining the main bearing saddles and caps by means of a flycutter that runs through the bearing saddles.

DECK FLATNESS

The top of the engine block where the cylinder head mounts is called the deck. Insure that the deck surface is clean of dirt, carbon deposits and old gasket material. Place a straightedge across the surface of the deck along its centerline and, using feeler gauges, check the clearance along several points. Repeat the checking procedure with the straightedge placed along both diagonals of the deck surface. If the reading exceeds 0.003 in. (0.076mm) within a 6.0 in. (15.2cm) span, or 0.006 in. (0.152mm) over the total length of the deck, it must be machined.

CYLINDER BORES

▶ See Figure 104

The cylinder bores house the pistons and are slightly larger than the pistons themselves. A common piston-to-bore clearance is 0.0015–0.0025 in.

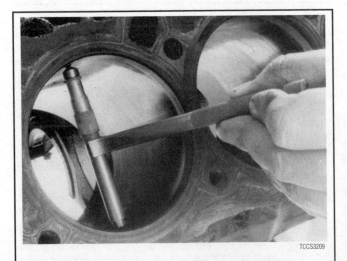

TCCS3209

Fig. 104 Use a telescoping gauge to measure the cylinder bore diameter—take several readings within the same bore

(0.0381mm–0.0635mm). Inspect and measure the cylinder bores. The bore should be checked for out-of-roundness, taper and size. The results of this inspection will determine whether the cylinder can be used in its existing size and condition, or a rebore to the next oversize is required (or in the case of removable sleeves, have replacements installed).

The amount of cylinder wall wear is always greater at the top of the cylinder than at the bottom. This wear is known as taper. Any cylinder that has a taper of 0.0012 in. (0.305mm) or more, must be rebored. Measurements are taken at a number of positions in each cylinder: at the top, middle and bottom and at two points at each position; that is, at a point 90 degrees from the crankshaft centerline, as well as a point parallel to the crankshaft centerline. The measurements are made with either a special dial indicator or a telescopic gauge and micrometer. If the necessary precision tools to check the bore are not available, take the block to a machine shop and have them mike it. Also if you don't have the tools to check the cylinder bores, chances are you will not have the necessary devices to check the pistons, connecting rods and crankshaft. Take these components with you and save yourself an extra trip.

For our procedures, we will use a telescopic gauge and a micrometer. You will need one of each, with a measuring range which covers your cylinder bore size.

1. Position the telescopic gauge in the cylinder bore, loosen the gauges lock and allow it to expand.

➡**Your first two readings will be at the top of the cylinder bore, then proceed to the middle and finally the bottom, making a total of six measurements.**

2. Hold the gauge square in the bore, 90 degrees from the crankshaft centerline, and gently tighten the lock. Tilt the gauge back to remove it from the bore.

3. Measure the gauge with the micrometer and record the reading.

4. Again, hold the gauge square in the bore, this time parallel to the crankshaft centerline, and gently tighten the lock. Again, you will tilt the gauge back to remove it from the bore.

5. Measure the gauge with the micrometer and record this reading. The difference between these two readings is the out-of-round measurement of the cylinder.

6. Repeat steps 1 through 5, each time going to the next lower position, until you reach the bottom of the cylinder. Then go to the next cylinder, and continue until all of the cylinders have been measured.

The difference between these measurements will tell you all about the wear in your cylinders. The measurements which were taken 90 degrees from the crankshaft centerline will always reflect the most wear. That is because at this position is where the engine power presses the piston against the cylinder bore the hardest. This is known as thrust wear. Take your top, 90 degree measurement and compare it to your bottom, 90 degree measurement. The difference between them is the taper. When you measure your pistons, you will compare these readings to your piston sizes and determine piston-to-wall clearance.

Crankshaft

Inspect the crankshaft for visible signs of wear or damage. All of the journals should be perfectly round and smooth. Slight scores are normal for a used crankshaft, but you should hardly feel them with your fingernail. When measuring the crankshaft with a micrometer, you will take readings at the front and rear of each journal, then turn the micrometer 90 degrees and take two more readings, front and rear. The difference between the front-to-rear readings is the journal taper and the first-to-90 degree reading is the out-of-round measurement. Generally, there should be no taper or out-of-roundness found, however, up to 0.0005 in. (0.0127mm) for either can be overlooked. Also, the readings should fall within the factory specifications for journal diameters.

If the crankshaft journals fall within specifications, it is recommended that it be polished before being returned to service. Polishing the crankshaft insures that any minor burrs or high spots are smoothed, thereby reducing the chance of scoring the new bearings.

Pistons and Connecting Rods

PISTONS

♦ See Figure 105

The piston should be visually inspected for any signs of cracking or burning (caused by hot spots or detonation), and scuffing or excessive wear on the skirts. The wrist pin attaches the piston to the connecting rod. The piston

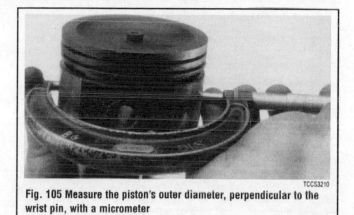

TCCS3210

Fig. 105 Measure the piston's outer diameter, perpendicular to the wrist pin, with a micrometer

should move freely on the wrist pin, both sliding and pivoting. Grasp the connecting rod securely, or mount it in a vise, and try to rock the piston back and forth along the centerline of the wrist pin. There should not be any excessive play evident between the piston and the pin. If there are C-clips retaining the pin in the piston then you have wrist pin bushings in the rods. There should not be any excessive play between the wrist pin and the rod bushing. Normal clearance for the wrist pin is approx. 0.001–0.002 in. (0.025mm–0.051mm).

Use a micrometer and measure the diameter of the piston, perpendicular to the wrist pin, on the skirt. Compare the reading to its original cylinder measurement obtained earlier. The difference between the two readings is the piston-to-wall clearance. If the clearance is within specifications, the piston may be used as is. If the piston is out of specification, but the bore is not, you will need a new piston. If both are out of specification, you will need the cylinder rebored and oversize pistons installed. Generally if two or more pistons/bores are out of specification, it is best to rebore the entire block and purchase a complete set of oversize pistons.

CONNECTING ROD

You should have the connecting rod checked for straightness at a machine shop. If the connecting rod is bent, it will unevenly wear the bearing and piston, as well as place greater stress on these components. Any bent or twisted connecting rods must be replaced. If the rods are straight and the wrist pin clearance is within specifications, then only the bearing end of the rod need be checked. Place the connecting rod into a vice, with the bearing inserts in place, install the cap to the rod and torque the fasteners to specifications. Use a telescoping gauge and carefully measure the inside diameter of the bearings. Compare this reading to the rods original crankshaft journal diameter measurement. The difference is the oil clearance. If the oil clearance is not within specifications, install new bearings in the rod and take another measurement. If the clearance is still out of specifications, and the crankshaft is not, the rod will need to be reconditioned by a machine shop.

➡**You can also use Plastigage® to check the bearing clearances. The assembling section has complete instructions on its use.**

Camshaft

Inspect the camshaft and lifters/followers as described earlier in this section.

Bearings

All of the engine bearings should be visually inspected for wear and/or damage. The bearing should look evenly worn all around with no deep scores or pits. If the bearing is severely worn, scored, pitted or heat blued, then the bearing, and the components that use it, should be brought to a machine shop for inspection. Full-circle bearings (used on most camshafts, auxiliary shafts, balance shafts, etc.) require specialized tools for removal and installation, and should be brought to a machine shop for service.

Oil Pump

➡**The oil pump is responsible for providing constant lubrication to the whole engine and so it is recommended that a new oil pump be installed when rebuilding the engine.**

Completely disassemble the oil pump and thoroughly clean all of the components. Inspect the oil pump gears and housing for wear and/or damage. Insure that the pressure relief valve operates properly and there is no binding or sticking due to varnish or debris. If all of the parts are in proper working condition, lubricate the gears and relief valve, and assemble the pump.

REFINISHING

▶ **See Figure 106**

Almost all engine block refinishing must be performed by a machine shop. If the cylinders are not to be rebored, then the cylinder glaze can be removed with a ball hone. When removing cylinder glaze with a ball hone, use a light or penetrating type oil to lubricate the hone. Do not allow the hone to run dry as this may cause excessive scoring of the cylinder bores and wear on the hone. If new pistons are required, they will need to be installed to the connecting rods. This should be performed by a machine shop as the pistons must be installed in the correct relationship to the rod or engine damage can occur.

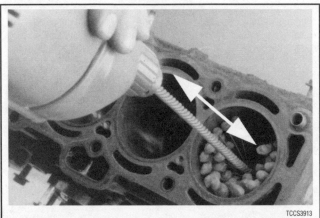

Fig. 106 Use a ball type cylinder hone to remove any glaze and provide a new surface for seating the piston rings

Pistons and Connecting Rods

▶ **See Figure 107**

Only pistons with the wrist pin retained by C-clips are serviceable by the home-mechanic. Press fit pistons require special presses and/or heaters to remove/install the connecting rod and should only be performed by a machine shop.

All pistons will have a mark indicating the direction to the front of the engine and the must be installed into the engine in that manner. Usually it is a notch or arrow on the top of the piston, or it may be the letter F cast or stamped into the piston.

1. Note the location of the forward mark on the piston and mark the connecting rod in relation.
2. Remove the C-clips from the piston and withdraw the wrist pin.

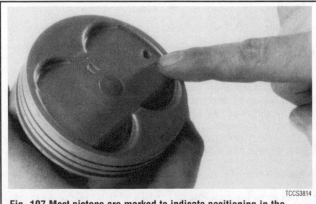

Fig. 107 Most pistons are marked to indicate positioning in the engine (usually a mark means the side facing the front)

➡**Varnish build-up or C-clip groove burrs may increase the difficulty of removing the wrist pin. If necessary, use a punch or drift to carefully tap the wrist pin out.**

3. Insure that the wrist pin bushing in the connecting rod is usable, and lubricate it with assembly lube.
4. Remove the wrist pin from the new piston and lubricate the pin bores on the piston.
5. Align the forward marks on the piston and the connecting rod and install the wrist pin.
6. The new C-clips will have a flat and a rounded side to them. Install both C-clips with the flat side facing out.
7. Repeat all of the steps for each piston being replaced.

ASSEMBLY

Before you begin assembling the engine, first give yourself a clean, dirt free work area. Next, clean every engine component again. The key to a good assembly is cleanliness.

Mount the engine block into the engine stand and wash it one last time using water and detergent (dishwashing detergent works well). While washing it, scrub the cylinder bores with a soft bristle brush and thoroughly clean all of the oil passages. Completely dry the engine and spray the entire assembly down with an anti-rust solution such as WD-40® or similar product. Take a clean lint-free rag and wipe up any excess anti-rust solution from the bores, bearing saddles, etc. Repeat the final cleaning process on the crankshaft. Replace any freeze or oil galley plugs which were removed during disassembly.

Crankshaft

▶ **See Figures 108, 109, 110 and 111**

1. Remove the main bearing inserts from the block and bearing caps.
2. If the crankshaft main bearing journals have been refinished to a definite undersize, install the correct undersize bearing. Be sure that the bearing inserts

Fig. 108 Apply a strip of gauging material to the bearing journal, then install and torque the cap

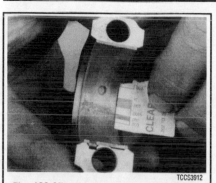

Fig. 109 After the cap is removed again, use the scale supplied with the gauging material to check the clearance

Fig. 110 A dial gauge may be used to check crankshaft end-play

Fig. 111 Carefully pry the crankshaft back and forth while reading the dial gauge for end-play

and bearing bores are clean. Foreign material under inserts will distort bearing and cause failure.

3. Place the upper main bearing inserts in bores with tang in slot.

➡ **The oil holes in the bearing inserts must be aligned with the oil holes in the cylinder block.**

4. Install the lower main bearing inserts in bearing caps.
5. Clean the mating surfaces of block and rear main bearing cap.
6. Carefully lower the crankshaft into place. Be careful not to damage bearing surfaces.
7. Check the clearance of each main bearing by using the following procedure:

   a. Place a piece of Plastigage® or its equivalent, on bearing surface across full width of bearing cap and about ¼ in. off center.

   b. Install cap and tighten bolts to specifications. Do not turn crankshaft while Plastigage® is in place.

   c. Remove the cap. Using the supplied Plastigage® scale, check width of Plastigage® at widest point to get maximum clearance. Difference between readings is taper of journal.

   d. If clearance exceeds specified limits, try a 0.001 in. or 0.002 in. undersize bearing in combination with the standard bearing. Bearing clearance must be within specified limits. If standard and 0.002 in. undersize bearing does not bring clearance within desired limits, refinish crankshaft journal, then install undersize bearings.

8. After the bearings have been fitted, apply a light coat of engine oil to the journals and bearings. Install the rear main bearing cap. Install all bearing caps except the thrust bearing cap. Be sure that main bearing caps are installed in original locations. Tighten the bearing cap bolts to specifications.

9. Install the thrust bearing cap with bolts finger-tight.
10. Pry the crankshaft forward against the thrust surface of upper half of bearing.
11. Hold the crankshaft forward and pry the thrust bearing cap to the rear. This aligns the thrust surfaces of both halves of the bearing.
12. Retain the forward pressure on the crankshaft. Tighten the cap bolts to specifications.
13. Measure the crankshaft end-play as follows:

   a. Mount a dial gauge to the engine block and position the tip of the gauge to read from the crankshaft end.

   b. Carefully pry the crankshaft toward the rear of the engine and hold it there while you zero the gauge.

   c. Carefully pry the crankshaft toward the front of the engine and read the gauge.

   d. Confirm that the reading is within specifications. If not, install a new thrust bearing and repeat the procedure. If the reading is still out of specifications with a new bearing, have a machine shop inspect the thrust surfaces of the crankshaft, and if possible, repair it.

14. Rotate the crankshaft so as to position the first rod journal to the bottom of its stroke.

15. Install the rear main seal.

Pistons and Connecting Rods

◗ **See Figures 112, 113, 114 and 115**

1. Before installing the piston/connecting rod assembly, oil the pistons, piston rings and the cylinder walls with light engine oil. Install connecting rod bolt protectors or rubber hose onto the connecting rod bolts/studs. Also perform the following:

   a. Select the proper ring set for the size cylinder bore.

   b. Position the ring in the bore in which it is going to be used.

   c. Push the ring down into the bore area where normal ring wear is not encountered.

   d. Use the head of the piston to position the ring in the bore so that the ring is square with the cylinder wall. Use caution to avoid damage to the ring or cylinder bore.

   e. Measure the gap between the ends of the ring with a feeler gauge. Ring gap in a worn cylinder is normally greater than specification. If the ring gap is greater than the specified limits, try an oversize ring set.

Fig. 112 Checking the piston ring-to-ring groove side clearance using the ring and a feeler gauge

Fig. 113 The notch on the side of the bearing cap matches the tang on the bearing insert

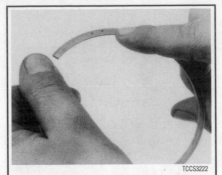

Fig. 114 Most rings are marked to show which side of the ring should face up when installed to the piston

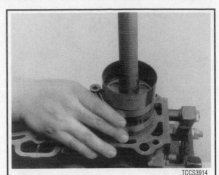

Fig. 115 Install the piston and rod assembly into the block using a ring compressor and the handle of a hammer

f. Check the ring side clearance of the compression rings with a feeler gauge inserted between the ring and its lower land according to specification. The gauge should slide freely around the entire ring circumference without binding. Any wear that occurs will form a step at the inner portion of the lower land. If the lower lands have high steps, the piston should be replaced.

2. Unless new pistons are installed, be sure to install the pistons in the cylinders from which they were removed. The numbers on the connecting rod and bearing cap must be on the same side when installed in the cylinder bore. If a connecting rod is ever transposed from one engine or cylinder to another, new bearings should be fitted and the connecting rod should be numbered to correspond with the new cylinder number. The notch on the piston head goes toward the front of the engine.

3. Install all of the rod bearing inserts into the rods and caps.

4. Install the rings to the pistons. Install the oil control ring first, then the second compression ring and finally the top compression ring. Use a piston ring expander tool to aid in installation and to help reduce the chance of breakage.

5. Make sure the ring gaps are properly spaced around the circumference of the piston. Fit a piston ring compressor around the piston and slide the piston and connecting rod assembly down into the cylinder bore, pushing it in with the wooden hammer handle. Push the piston down until it is only slightly below the top of the cylinder bore. Guide the connecting rod onto the crankshaft bearing journal carefully, to avoid damaging the crankshaft.

6. Check the bearing clearance of all the rod bearings, fitting them to the crankshaft bearing journals. Follow the procedure in the crankshaft installation above.

7. After the bearings have been fitted, apply a light coating of assembly oil to the journals and bearings.

8. Turn the crankshaft until the appropriate bearing journal is at the bottom of its stroke, then push the piston assembly all the way down until the connecting rod bearing seats on the crankshaft journal. Be careful not to allow the bearing cap screws to strike the crankshaft bearing journals and damage them.

9. After the piston and connecting rod assemblies have been installed, check the connecting rod side clearance on each crankshaft journal.

10. Prime and install the oil pump and the oil pump intake tube.

OHV Engines

CAMSHAFT, LIFTERS AND TIMING ASSEMBLY

1. Install the camshaft.
2. Install the lifters/followers into their bores.
3. Install the timing gears/chain assembly.

CYLINDER HEAD(S)

1. Install the cylinder head(s) using new gaskets.
2. Assemble the rest of the valve train (pushrods and rocker arms and/or shafts).

OHC Engines

CYLINDER HEAD(S)

1. Install the cylinder head(s) using new gaskets.
2. Install the timing sprockets/gears and the belt/chain assemblies.

Engine Covers and Components

Install the timing cover(s) and oil pan. Refer to your notes and drawings made prior to disassembly and install all of the components that were removed. Install the engine into the vehicle.

Engine Start-up and Break-in

STARTING THE ENGINE

Now that the engine is installed and every wire and hose is properly connected, go back and double check that all coolant and vacuum hoses are connected. Check that your oil drain plug is installed and properly tightened. If not already done, install a new oil filter onto the engine. Fill the crankcase with the proper amount and grade of engine oil. Fill the cooling system with a 50/50 mixture of coolant/water.

1. Connect the vehicle battery.
2. Start the engine. Keep your eye on your oil pressure indicator; if it does not indicate oil pressure within 10 seconds of starting, turn the vehicle **OFF**.

❊❊ WARNING

Damage to the engine can result if it is allowed to run with no oil pressure. Check the engine oil level to make sure that it is full. Check for any leaks and if found, repair the leaks before continuing. If there is still no indication of oil pressure, you may need to prime the system.

3. Confirm that there are no fluid leaks (oil or other).
4. Allow the engine to reach normal operating temperature (the upper radiator hose will be hot to the touch).
5. At this point any necessary checks or adjustments can be performed, such as ignition timing.
6. Install any remaining components or body panels which were removed.

BREAKING IT IN

Make the first miles on the new engine, easy ones. Vary the speed but do not accelerate hard. Most importantly, do not lug the engine, and avoid sustained high speeds until at least 100 miles. Check the engine oil and coolant levels frequently. Expect the engine to use a little oil until the rings seat. Change the oil and filter at 500 miles, 1500 miles, then every 3000 miles past that.

KEEP IT MAINTAINED

Now that you have just gone through all of that hard work, keep yourself from doing it all over again by thoroughly maintaining it. Not that you may not have maintained it before, heck you could have had one to two hundred thousand miles on it before doing this. However, you may have bought the vehicle used, and the previous owner did not keep up on maintenance. Which is why you just went through all of that hard work. See?

TORQUE SPECIFICATIONS

Component	ft. lbs.	inch lbs.	Nm
Accelerator cable bracket bolts			
2.0L and 2.2L engines	18		25
Camshaft housing			
2.3L engine	11		15
1990-93 vehicles—plus an additional 75°, then 25°			
1994 vehicles—plus an additional 90°, then 30°	11		15
Camshaft sprocket			
2.0L and 2.2L engines	77		105
2.8L and 3.1L (VIN T) engines	18		25
3.1L (VIN M) engine	74		100
Camshaft thrust plate			
2.0L and 2.2L engines		106	12
1991-96 vehicles			
Crankshaft Balancer			
Except 2.3L engine	76		103
2.3L engine			
1990-92 vehicles	74		100
1993 vehicles	110		150
1994 vehicles	129		175
Cylinder head			
2.0L and 2.2L Engines			
1988-89 vehicles			
Long bolts	73-83		99-112
Short bolts	62		70
1990 vehicles			
Step 1:	41		55
Step 2: additional 45°			
Step 3: additional 45°			
Step 4: long bolts an additional 20°			
Step 5: short bolts an additional 10°			
1991-96 Vehicles			
Step 1 long bolts	46		62
Step 2 short bolts	43		58
Step 3 all bolts in sequence an additional 90°			
2.8L and 3.1L engines			
Step 1:	33		45
Step 2: additional 90°			
Electric fan bolts		89	10
Exhaust manifold			
2.0L and 2.2L Engines			
nuts			
1988-90 vehicles	3-11		5-15
1991-96 vehicles		115	13
bolts	6-13		8-18
studs		89	10
2.3L engines	27-31		37-42
2.8L and 3.1L (VIN T) engines			
1988 vehicles	22-30		30-40
1989-93 vehicles	18-21		25-28
Crossover bolts	18		25
3.1L (VIN M) engine			
Manifold bolts	12		16
Heat shield nuts		89	10

88253C11

TORQUE SPECIFICATIONS

Component	ft. lbs.	inch lbs.	Nm
Flywheel			
Manual transaxle			
Except 2.3L engine	55		75
2.3L engine (plus an additional 45° rotation)	22		30
Automatic Transaxle			
2.0L and 2.2L engines	52-55		70-75
2.3L engines (plus an additional 45° rotation)	22		30
2.8L and 3.1L (VIN T) engines	52		70
3.1L (VIN M) engines	61		83
Fuel injector retaining bracket			
2.0L and 2.2L engines		22	3.5
Intake manifold retainers			
2.0L and 2.2L engines			
1988-91 vehicles	15-22		20-30
1992-93 vehicles	22		30
1994-96 vehicles			
studs		89	10
nuts	24		33
2.3L engine			
manifold retainers	18		25
manifold brace retainers	18		25
Nut-to-stud bolt	40		55
Bolt-to-intake manifold	40		55
Bolt-to-cylinder block			
2.8L and 3.1L (VIN T) engines			
1st step:	15		20
2nd step:	24		33
3.1L (VIN M) engine			
Lower intake manifold bolts		115	13
Upper intake manifold bolts	16		25
Oil pan			
2.0L and 2.2L engines		71-89	8-10
2.3L engine			
chain housing and carrier seal bolts		106	12
oil pan-to-block bolts	17		23
2.8L and 3.1L engines			
1988-93 vehicles	18		25
2 rear oil pan bolts			
remaining bolts and nuts		71-89	8-10
1994-96 vehicles			
front and rear bolts	13		25
sidebolts	37		50
Oil pump			
2.0L and 2.2L engines	32		43
2.3L engines			
1990 vehicles	33		45
1991-94 vehicles	40		54
2.8L and 3.1L engines	30		41
Radiator mounting bolts		89	10
Rocker arm (valve) cover bolts			
2.0L and 2.2L engines		89	10
2.8L and 3.1L engines			
1988 vehicles	6-9		8-12
1988-96 vehicles		89	10

88253C12

TORQUE SPECIFICATIONS

Component	ft. lbs.	inch lbs.	Nm
Rocker arm nuts/bolts			
2.0L and 2.2L engines			
1988 vehicles	7-11		10-15
1989-92 vehicles	14		20
1993-96 vehicles	22		30
2.8L and 3.1L engines			
1988 vehicles	18		25
1989-96 vehicles			
nuts	18		25
bolts (plus an additional 30° rotation)		89	10
Thermostat housing retainers			
2.0L and 2.2L engines		89	10
2.3L engines			
1990-93 vehicles	19		26
1994 vehicles (refer to specifications in figure)			
2.8L and 3.1L engines	18		25
Timing chain (front) cover			
2.0L and 2.2L engines		89-97	10-11
2.3L engine		106	12
2.8L and 3.1L engines			
1988-94 vehicles			
4 bolts, in illustration			
1988-92 vehicles	20		27
1993-94 vehicles	15		21
5 bolts, in illustration			
1988-92 vehicles	38		48
1993-94 vehicles	35		45
1995-96 Vehicles			
Lower front cover bolts			
Small bolts	15		20
Large bolts	35		47
Upper front cover bolts	15		20
Timing chain tensioner			
2.0L and 2.2L engines	17		23
2.3L engine	10		14
Water pump			
2.0L and 2.2L engines	18-22		25-30
2.3L engine			
Pump-to-timing chain housing nuts	19		26
Pump-to-pump cover assembly		106	12
Pump cover-to-engine (tighten the bottom bolt first)	19		26
Radiator outlet pipe assembly-to-pump cover		125	14
2.8L and 3.1L engines		89	10
Water pump pulley			
2.0L and 2.2L engines	22		30
2.8L and 3.1L engines	15		21

88253C13

4

DRIVEABILITY AND EMISSION CONTROLS

AIR POLLUTION

The earth's atmosphere, at or near sea level, consists approximately of 78 percent nitrogen, 21 percent oxygen and 1 percent other gases. If it were possible to remain in this state, 100 percent clean air would result. However, many varied sources allow other gases and particulates to mix with the clean air, causing our atmosphere to become unclean or polluted.

Some of these pollutants are visible while others are invisible, with each having the capability of causing distress to the eyes, ears, throat, skin and respiratory system. Should these pollutants become concentrated in a specific area and under certain conditions, death could result due to the displacement or chemical change of the oxygen content in the air. These pollutants can also cause great damage to the environment and to the many man made objects that are exposed to the elements.

To better understand the causes of air pollution, the pollutants can be categorized into 3 separate types, natural, industrial and automotive.

Natural Pollutants

Natural pollution has been present on earth since before man appeared and continues to be a factor when discussing air pollution, although it causes only a small percentage of the overall pollution problem. It is the direct result of decaying organic matter, wind born smoke and particulates from such natural events as plain and forest fires (ignited by heat or lightning), volcanic ash, sand and dust which can spread over a large area of the countryside.

Such a phenomenon of natural pollution has been seen in the form of volcanic eruptions, with the resulting plume of smoke, steam and volcanic ash blotting out the sun's rays as it spreads and rises higher into the atmosphere. As it travels into the atmosphere the upper air currents catch and carry the smoke and ash, while condensing the steam back into water vapor. As the water vapor, smoke and ash travel on their journey, the smoke dissipates into the atmosphere while the ash and moisture settle back to earth in a trail hundreds of miles long. In some cases, lives are lost and millions of dollars of property damage result.

Industrial Pollutants

Industrial pollution is caused primarily by industrial processes, the burning of coal, oil and natural gas, which in turn produce smoke and fumes. Because the burning fuels contain large amounts of sulfur, the principal ingredients of smoke and fumes are sulfur dioxide and particulate matter. This type of pollutant occurs most severely during still, damp and cool weather, such as at night. Even in its less severe form, this pollutant is not confined to just cities. Because of air movements, the pollutants move for miles over the surrounding countryside, leaving in its path a barren and unhealthy environment for all living things.

Working with Federal, State and Local mandated regulations and by carefully monitoring emissions, big business has greatly reduced the amount of pollutant introduced from its industrial sources, striving to obtain an acceptable level. Because of the mandated industrial emission clean up, many land areas and streams in and around the cities that were formerly barren of vegetation and life, have now begun to move back in the direction of nature's intended balance.

Automotive Pollutants

The third major source of air pollution is automotive emissions. The emissions from the internal combustion engines were not an appreciable problem years ago because of the small number of registered vehicles and the nation's small highway system. However, during the early 1950's, the trend of the American people was to move from the cities to the surrounding suburbs. This caused an immediate problem in transportation because the majority of suburbs were not afforded mass transit conveniences. This lack of transportation created an attractive market for the automobile manufacturers, which resulted in a dramatic increase in the number of vehicles produced and sold, along with a marked increase in highway construction between cities and the suburbs. Multi-vehicle families emerged with a growing emphasis placed on an individual vehicle per family member. As the increase in vehicle ownership and usage occurred, so did pollutant levels in and around the cities, as suburbanites drove daily to their businesses and employment, returning at the end of the day to their homes in the suburbs.

It was noted that a smoke and fog type haze was being formed and at times, remained in suspension over the cities, taking time to dissipate. At first this "smog," derived from the words "smoke" and "fog," was thought to result from industrial pollution but it was determined that automobile emissions shared the blame. It was discovered that when normal automobile emissions were exposed to sunlight for a period of time, complex chemical reactions would take place.

It is now known that smog is a photo chemical layer which develops when certain oxides of nitrogen (NOx) and unburned hydrocarbons (HC) from automobile emissions are exposed to sunlight. Pollution was more severe when smog would become stagnant over an area in which a warm layer of air settled over the top of the cooler air mass, trapping and holding the cooler mass at ground level. The trapped cooler air would keep the emissions from being dispersed and diluted through normal air flows. This type of air stagnation was given the name "Temperature Inversion."

TEMPERATURE INVERSION

In normal weather situations, surface air is warmed by heat radiating from the earth's surface and the sun's rays. This causes it to rise upward, into the atmosphere. Upon rising it will cool through a convection type heat exchange with the cooler upper air. As warm air rises, the surface pollutants are carried upward and dissipated into the atmosphere.

When a temperature inversion occurs, we find the higher air is no longer cooler, but is warmer than the surface air, causing the cooler surface air to become trapped. This warm air blanket can extend from above ground level to a few hundred or even a few thousand feet into the air. As the surface air is trapped, so are the pollutants, causing a severe smog condition. Should this stagnant air mass extend to a few thousand feet high, enough air movement with the inversion takes place to allow the smog layer to rise above ground level but the pollutants still cannot dissipate. This inversion can remain for days over an area, with the smog level only rising or lowering from ground level to a few hundred feet high. Meanwhile, the pollutant levels increase, causing eye irritation, respiratory problems, reduced visibility, plant damage and in some cases, even disease.

This inversion phenomenon was first noted in the Los Angeles, California area. The city lies in terrain resembling a basin and with certain weather conditions, a cold air mass is held in the basin while a warmer air mass covers it like a lid.

Because this type of condition was first documented as prevalent in the Los Angeles area, this type of trapped pollution was named Los Angeles Smog, although it occurs in other areas where a large concentration of automobiles are used and the air remains stagnant for any length of time.

HEAT TRANSFER

Consider the internal combustion engine as a machine in which raw materials must be placed so a finished product comes out. As in any machine operation, a certain amount of wasted material is formed. When we relate this to the internal combustion engine, we find that through the input of air and fuel, we obtain power during the combustion process to drive the vehicle. The by-product or waste of this power is, in part, heat and exhaust gases with which we must dispose.

The heat from the combustion process can rise to over 4000°F (2204°C). The dissipation of this heat is controlled by a ram air effect, the use of cooling fans to cause air flow and a liquid coolant solution surrounding the combustion area to transfer the heat of combustion through the cylinder walls and into the coolant. The coolant is then directed to a thin-finned, multi-tubed radiator, from which the excess heat is transferred to the atmosphere by 1 of the 3 heat transfer methods, conduction, convection or radiation.

The cooling of the combustion area is an important part in the control of exhaust emissions. To understand the behavior of the combustion and transfer of its heat, consider the air/fuel charge. It is ignited and the flame front burns progressively across the combustion chamber until the burning charge reaches the cylinder walls. Some of the fuel in contact with the walls is not hot enough to burn, thereby snuffing out or quenching the combustion process. This leaves unburned fuel in the combustion chamber. This unburned fuel is then forced out of the cylinder and into the exhaust system, along with the exhaust gases.

Many attempts have been made to minimize the amount of unburned fuel in the combustion chambers due to quenching, by increasing the coolant temperature and lessening the contact area of the coolant around the combustion area. However, design limitations within the combustion chambers prevent the complete burning of the air/fuel charge, so a certain amount of the unburned fuel is still expelled into the exhaust system, regardless of modifications to the engine.

AUTOMOTIVE EMISSIONS

Before emission controls were mandated on internal combustion engines, other sources of engine pollutants were discovered along with the exhaust emissions. It was determined that engine combustion exhaust produced approximately 60 percent of the total emission pollutants, fuel evaporation from the fuel tank and carburetor vents produced 20 percent, with the final 20 percent being produced through the crankcase as a by-product of the combustion process.

Exhaust Gases

The exhaust gases emitted into the atmosphere are a combination of burned and unburned fuel. To understand the exhaust emission and its composition, we must review some basic chemistry.

When the air/fuel mixture is introduced into the engine, we are mixing air, composed of nitrogen (78 percent), oxygen (21 percent) and other gases (1 percent) with the fuel, which is 100 percent hydrocarbons (HC), in a semi-controlled ratio. As the combustion process is accomplished, power is produced to move the vehicle while the heat of combustion is transferred to the cooling system. The exhaust gases are then composed of nitrogen, a diatomic gas (N_2), the same as was introduced in the engine, carbon dioxide (CO_2), the same gas that is used in beverage carbonation, and water vapor (H_2O). The nitrogen (N_2), for the most part, passes through the engine unchanged, while the oxygen (O_2) reacts (burns) with the hydrocarbons (HC) and produces the carbon dioxide (CO_2) and the water vapors (H_2O). If this chemical process would be the only process to take place, the exhaust emissions would be harmless. However, during the combustion process, other compounds are formed which are considered dangerous. These pollutants are hydrocarbons (HC), carbon monoxide (CO), oxides of nitrogen (NOx) oxides of sulfur (SOx) and engine particulates.

HYDROCARBONS

Hydrocarbons (HC) are essentially fuel which was not burned during the combustion process or which has escaped into the atmosphere through fuel evaporation. The main sources of incomplete combustion are rich air/fuel mixtures, low engine temperatures and improper spark timing. The main sources of hydrocarbon emission through fuel evaporation on most vehicles used to be the vehicle's fuel tank and carburetor float bowl.

To reduce combustion hydrocarbon emission, engine modifications were made to minimize dead space and surface area in the combustion chamber. In addition, the air/fuel mixture was made more lean through the improved control which feedback carburetion and fuel injection offers and by the addition of external controls to aid in further combustion of the hydrocarbons outside the engine. Two such methods were the addition of air injection systems, to inject fresh air into the exhaust manifolds and the installation of catalytic converters, units that are able to burn traces of hydrocarbons without affecting the internal combustion process or fuel economy.

To control hydrocarbon emissions through fuel evaporation, modifications were made to the fuel tank to allow storage of the fuel vapors during periods of engine shut-down. Modifications were also made to the air intake system so that at specific times during engine operation, these vapors may be purged and burned by blending them with the air/fuel mixture.

CARBON MONOXIDE

Carbon monoxide is formed when not enough oxygen is present during the combustion process to convert carbon (C) to carbon dioxide (CO_2). An increase in the carbon monoxide (CO) emission is normally accompanied by an increase in the hydrocarbon (HC) emission because of the lack of oxygen to completely burn all of the fuel mixture.

Carbon monoxide (CO) also increases the rate at which the photo chemical smog is formed by speeding up the conversion of nitric oxide (NO) to nitrogen dioxide (NO_2). To accomplish this, carbon monoxide (CO) combines with oxygen (O_2) and nitric oxide (NO) to produce carbon dioxide (CO_2) and nitrogen dioxide (NO_2). ($CO + O_2 + NO = CO_2 + NO_2$).

The dangers of carbon monoxide, which is an odorless and colorless toxic gas are many. When carbon monoxide is inhaled into the lungs and passed into the blood stream, oxygen is replaced by the carbon monoxide in the red blood cells, causing a reduction in the amount of oxygen supplied to the many parts of the body. This lack of oxygen causes headaches, lack of coordination, reduced mental alertness and, should the carbon monoxide concentration be high enough, death could result.

NITROGEN

Normally, nitrogen is an inert gas. When heated to approximately 2500°F (1371°C) through the combustion process, this gas becomes active and causes an increase in the nitric oxide (NO) emission.

Oxides of nitrogen (NOx) are composed of approximately 97–98 percent nitric oxide (NO). Nitric oxide is a colorless gas but when it is passed into the atmosphere, it combines with oxygen and forms nitrogen dioxide (NO_2). The nitrogen dioxide then combines with chemically active hydrocarbons (HC) and when in the presence of sunlight, causes the formation of photo-chemical smog.

Ozone

To further complicate matters, some of the nitrogen dioxide (NO_2) is broken apart by the sunlight to form nitric oxide and oxygen. (NO_2 + sunlight = NO + O). This single atom of oxygen then combines with diatomic (meaning 2 atoms) oxygen (O_2) to form ozone (O_3). Ozone is one of the smells associated with smog. It has a pungent and offensive odor, irritates the eyes and lung tissues, affects the growth of plant life and causes rapid deterioration of rubber products. Ozone can be formed by sunlight as well as electrical discharge into the air.

The most common discharge area on the automobile engine is the secondary ignition electrical system, especially when inferior quality spark plug cables are used. As the surge of high voltage is routed through the secondary cable, the circuit builds up an electrical field around the wire, which acts upon the oxygen in the surrounding air to form the ozone. The faint glow along the cable with the engine running that may be visible on a dark night, is called the "corona discharge." It is the result of the electrical field passing from a high along the cable, to a low in the surrounding air, which forms the ozone gas. The combination of corona and ozone has been a major cause of cable deterioration. Recently, different and better quality insulating materials have lengthened the life of the electrical cables.

Although ozone at ground level can be harmful, ozone is beneficial to the earth's inhabitants. By having a concentrated ozone layer called the "ozonosphere," between 10 and 20 miles (16–32 km) up in the atmosphere, much of the ultra violet radiation from the sun's rays are absorbed and screened. If this ozone layer were not present, much of the earth's surface would be burned, dried and unfit for human life.

OXIDES OF SULFUR

Oxides of sulfur (SOx) were initially ignored in the exhaust system emissions, since the sulfur content of gasoline as a fuel is less than $\frac{1}{10}$ of 1 percent. Because of this small amount, it was felt that it contributed very little to the overall pollution problem. However, because of the difficulty in solving the sulfur emissions in industrial pollution and the introduction of catalytic converter to the automobile exhaust systems, a change was mandated. The automobile exhaust system, when equipped with a catalytic converter, changes the sulfur dioxide (SO_2) into sulfur trioxide (SO_3).

When this combines with water vapors (H_2O), a sulfuric acid mist (H_2SO_4) is formed and is a very difficult pollutant to handle since it is extremely corrosive. This sulfuric acid mist that is formed, is the same mist that rises from the vents of an automobile battery when an active chemical reaction takes place within the battery cells.

When a large concentration of vehicles equipped with catalytic converters are operating in an area, this acid mist may rise and be distributed over a large ground area causing land, plant, crop, paint and building damage.

PARTICULATE MATTER

A certain amount of particulate matter is present in the burning of any fuel, with carbon constituting the largest percentage of the particulates. In gasoline, the remaining particulates are the burned remains of the various other compounds used in its manufacture. When a gasoline engine is in good internal condition, the particulate emissions are low but as the engine wears internally, the particulate emissions increase. By visually inspecting the tail pipe emissions, a determination can be made as to where an engine defect may exist. An engine with light gray or blue smoke emitting from the tail pipe normally indicates an increase in the oil consumption through burning due to internal engine wear. Black smoke would indicate a defective fuel delivery system, causing the engine to operate in a rich mode. Regardless of the color of the smoke, the internal part of the engine or the fuel delivery system should be repaired to prevent excess particulate emissions.

Diesel and turbine engines emit a darkened plume of smoke from the exhaust system because of the type of fuel used. Emission control regulations are mandated for this type of emission and more stringent measures are being used to prevent excess emission of the particulate matter. Electronic components are being introduced to control the injection of the fuel at precisely the proper time of piston travel, to achieve the optimum in fuel ignition and fuel usage. Other particulate after-burning components are being tested to achieve a cleaner emission.

Good grades of engine lubricating oils should be used, which meet the manufacturers specification. Cut-rate oils can contribute to the particulate emission problem because of their low flash or ignition temperature point. Such oils burn prematurely during the combustion process causing emission of particulate matter.

The cooling system is an important factor in the reduction of particulate matter. The optimum combustion will occur, with the cooling system operating at a temperature specified by the manufacturer. The cooling system must be maintained in the same manner as the engine oiling system, as each system is required to perform properly in order for the engine to operate efficiently for a long time.

Crankcase Emissions

Crankcase emissions are made up of water, acids, unburned fuel, oil fumes and particulates. These emissions are classified as hydrocarbons (HC) and are formed by the small amount of unburned, compressed air/fuel mixture entering the crankcase from the combustion area (between the cylinder walls and piston rings) during the compression and power strokes. The head of the compression and combustion help to form the remaining crankcase emissions.

Since the first engines, crankcase emissions were allowed into the atmosphere through a road draft tube, mounted on the lower side of the engine block. Fresh air came in through an open oil filler cap or breather. The air passed through the crankcase mixing with blow-by gases. The motion of the vehicle and the air blowing past the open end of the road draft tube caused a low pressure area (vacuum) at the end of the tube. Crankcase emissions were simply drawn out of the road draft tube into the air.

To control the crankcase emission, the road draft tube was deleted. A hose and/or tubing was routed from the crankcase to the intake manifold so the blow-by emission could be burned with the air/fuel mixture. However, it was found

that intake manifold vacuum, used to draw the crankcase emissions into the manifold, would vary in strength at the wrong time and not allow the proper emission flow. A regulating valve was needed to control the flow of air through the crankcase.

Testing, showed the removal of the blow-by gases from the crankcase as quickly as possible, was most important to the longevity of the engine. Should large accumulations of blow-by gases remain and condense, dilution of the engine oil would occur to form water, soots, resins, acids and lead salts, resulting in the formation of sludge and varnishes. This condensation of the blow-by gases occurs more frequently on vehicles used in numerous starting and stopping conditions, excessive idling and when the engine is not allowed to attain normal operating temperature through short runs.

Evaporative Emissions

Gasoline fuel is a major source of pollution, before and after it is burned in the automobile engine. From the time the fuel is refined, stored, pumped and transported, again stored until it is pumped into the fuel tank of the vehicle, the gasoline gives off unburned hydrocarbons (HC) into the atmosphere. Through the redesign of storage areas and venting systems, the pollution factor was diminished, but not eliminated, from the refinery standpoint. However, the automobile still remained the primary source of vaporized, unburned hydrocarbon (HC) emissions.

Fuel pumped from an underground storage tank is cool but when exposed to a warmer ambient temperature, will expand. Before controls were mandated, an owner might fill the fuel tank with fuel from an underground storage tank and park the vehicle for some time in warm area, such as a parking lot. As the fuel would warm, it would expand and should no provisions or area be provided for the expansion, the fuel would spill out of the filler neck and onto the ground, causing hydrocarbon (HC) pollution and creating a severe fire hazard. To correct this condition, the vehicle manufacturers added overflow plumbing and/or gasoline tanks with built in expansion areas or domes.

However, this did not control the fuel vapor emission from the fuel tank. It was determined that most of the fuel evaporation occurred when the vehicle was stationary and the engine not operating. Most vehicles carry 5–25 gallons (19–95 liters) of gasoline. Should a large concentration of vehicles be parked in one area, such as a large parking lot, excessive fuel vapor emissions would take place, increasing as the temperature increases.

To prevent the vapor emission from escaping into the atmosphere, the fuel systems were designed to trap the vapors while the vehicle is stationary, by sealing the system from the atmosphere. A storage system is used to collect and hold the fuel vapors from the carburetor (if equipped) and the fuel tank when the engine is not operating. When the engine is started, the storage system is then purged of the fuel vapors, which are drawn into the engine and burned with the air/fuel mixture.

EMISSION CONTROLS

There are three sources of automotive pollutants: crankcase fumes, exhaust gases, and gasoline evaporation. The pollutants formed from these substances fall into three categories: unburnt hydrocarbons (HC), carbon monoxide (CO), and oxides of nitrogen (NOx). The equipment that is used to limit these pollutants is commonly called emission control equipment.

Positive Crankcase Ventilation (PCV) System

♦ **See Figures 1, 2 and 3**

All Corsica/Beretta cars are equipped with a Positive Crankcase Ventilation (PCV) or Crankcase Ventilation (CV) system to control crankcase blow-by vapors. The system functions as follows:

The Positive Crankcase Ventilation (PCV) or Crankcase Ventilation (CV) system is used on all vehicles to evacuate the crankcase vapors. Fresh air from the air cleaner or intake duct is supplied to the crankcase, mixed with blow-by gases and then passed through a Positive Crankcase Ventilation (PCV) valve or Crankcase Ventilation (CV) orifice into the intake manifold or the air plenum.

When manifold vacuum is high, such as at idle, the orifice or valve restricts the flow of blow-by gases allowed into the manifold. If abnormal operating conditions occur, the system will allow excessive blow-by gases to back flow through the hose into the air cleaner. These blow-by gases will then be mixed

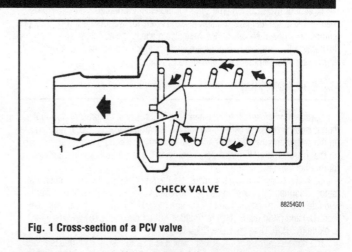

1 CHECK VALVE

88254G01

Fig. 1 Cross-section of a PCV valve

with the intake air in the air cleaner instead of in the manifold. The air cleaner has a small filter attached to the inside wall that connects to the breather hose to trap impurities flowing in either direction.

A plugged PCV valve, orifice or hose may cause rough idle, stalling or slow

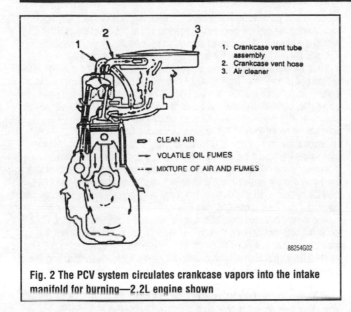

1. Crankcase vent tube assembly
2. Crankcase vent hose
3. Air cleaner

☐ CLEAN AIR
── VOLATILE OIL FUMES
┄┄ MIXTURE OF AIR AND FUMES

88254G02

Fig. 2 The PCV system circulates crankcase vapors into the intake manifold for burning—2.2L engine shown

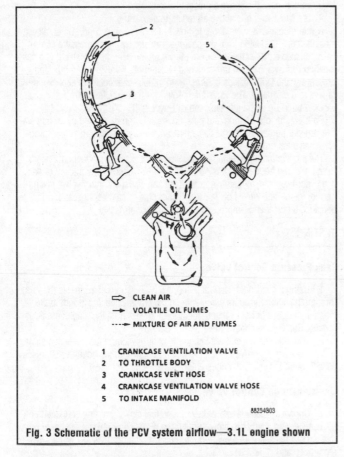

⇨ CLEAN AIR
→ VOLATILE OIL FUMES
┄→ MIXTURE OF AIR AND FUMES

1   CRANKCASE VENTILATION VALVE
2   TO THROTTLE BODY
3   CRANKCASE VENT HOSE
4   CRANKCASE VENTILATION VALVE HOSE
5   TO INTAKE MANIFOLD

88254G03

Fig. 3 Schematic of the PCV system airflow—3.1L engine shown

idle speed, oil leaks, oil in the air cleaner or sludge in the engine. A leak could cause rough idle, stalling or high idle speed. The condition of the grommets in the valve cover will also affect system and engine performance.

Other than checking and replacing the valve/orifice and associated hoses, there is no service required. Engine operating conditions that would direct suspicion to the ventilation system are rough idle, oil present in the air cleaner, oil leaks and excessive oil sludging or dilution. If any of the above conditions exist, remove the PCV valve and shake it. A clicking sound indicates that the valve is free. If no clicking sound is heard, replace the valve. If equipped with a CV orifice, make sure it is not plugged. Inspect the PCV breather in the air cleaner. Replace the breather if it is so dirty that it will not allow gases to pass through.

Check all the PCV hoses for condition and tight connections. Replace any hoses that have deteriorated.

COMPONENT TESTING

▶ See Figure 4

PCV Valve/CV Orifice

1. Start the engine.
2. With the engine at normal operating temperature, run at idle.
3. Remove the PCV valve or CV orifice from the grommet in the valve cover and place thumb over the end to check if vacuum is present. If vacuum is not present, check for plugged hoses or manifold port. Repair or replace as necessary.
4. Stop the engine and remove the valve. Shake the valve and listen for the rattle of the check valve needle. If there is no rattle heard when the valve is shaken, replace the valve.

Crankcase Ventilation System

1. Check to make sure the engine has the correct PCV valve or bleed orifice.
2. Start the engine and bring to normal operating temperature.
3. Block off the PCV system fresh air intake passage.
4. Remove the engine oil dipstick and install a vacuum gauge on the dipstick tube.
5. Run the engine at 1500 rpm for 30 seconds then read the vacuum gauge with the engine at 1500 rpm.
   • If vacuum is present, the PCV system is functioning properly.
   • If there is no vacuum, the engine may not be sealed and/or is drawing in outside air. Check the grommets and valve cover or oil pan gasket for leaks.
   • If the vacuum gauge registers a pressure or the vacuum gauge is pushed out of the dipstick tube, check for the correct PCV valve or bleed orifice, a plugged hose or excessive engine blow-by.

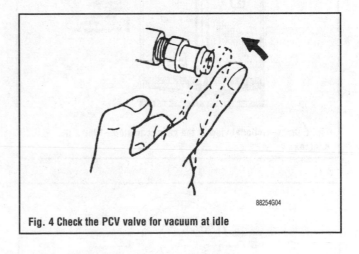

88254G04

Fig. 4 Check the PCV valve for vacuum at idle

REMOVAL & INSTALLATION

Removal and installation procedures of the PCV or CV valve is located in

Evaporative Emission Controls

OPERATION

▶ See Figures 5, 6 and 7

The Evaporative Emission Control System (EECS) is designed to prevent fuel tank vapors from being emitted into the atmosphere. When the engine is not running, gasoline vapors from the tank are stored in a charcoal canister, mounted inside the left rear wheel well. The charcoal canister absorbs the gasoline vapors and stores them until certain engine conditions are met and the

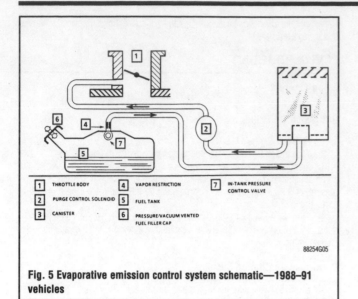

Fig. 5 Evaporative emission control system schematic—1988–91 vehicles

1	THROTTLE BODY	4	VAPOR RESTRICTION
2	PURGE CONTROL SOLENOID	5	FUEL TANK
3	CANISTER	6	PRESSURE/VACUUM VENTED FUEL FILLER CAP
		7	IN-TANK PRESSURE CONTROL VALVE

88254G05

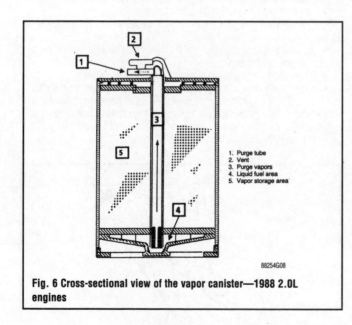

1. Purge tube
2. Vent
3. Purge vapors
4. Liquid fuel area
5. Vapor storage area

88254G08

Fig. 6 Cross-sectional view of the vapor canister—1988 2.0L engines

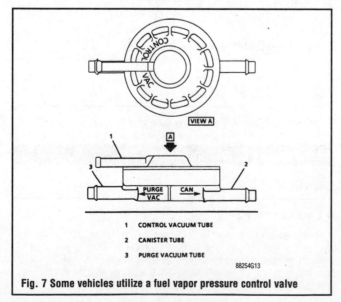

1	CONTROL VACUUM TUBE
2	CANISTER TUBE
3	PURGE VACUUM TUBE

88254G13

Fig. 7 Some vehicles utilize a fuel vapor pressure control valve

vapors can be purged and burned by the engine. In some vehicles, any liquid fuel entering the canister goes into a reservoir in the bottom of the canister to protect the integrity of the carbon element in the canister above. Three different methods are used to control the purge cycle of the charcoal canister.

First, the charcoal canister purge cycle is controlled by throttle position without the use of a valve on the canister. A vacuum line connects the canister to a ported vacuum source on the throttle body. When the throttle is at any position above idle, fresh air is drawn into the bottom of the canister and the fuel vapors are carried into the throttle body at that port. The air/vapor flow volume is only what can be drawn through the vacuum port and is fairly constant.

Second, the flow volume is modulated with throttle position through a vacuum valve. The ported vacuum from the throttle body is used to open a diaphragm valve on top of the canister. When the valve is open, air and vapors are drawn into the intake manifold, usually through the same manifold port as the PCV system. With this method, the purge valve cycle is slaved to the throttle opening; more throttle opening, more purge air flow.

And third, the charcoal canister purge valve cycle is controlled by the ECM through a solenoid valve on the canister. When the solenoid is activated, full manifold vacuum is applied to the top of the purge valve diaphragm to open the valve all the way. A high volume of fresh air is drawn into the canister and the gasoline vapors are purged quickly. The ECM activates the solenoid valve when the following conditions are met:

- The engine is at normal operating temperature.
- After the engine has been running a specified period of time.
- Vehicle speed is above a predetermined speed.
- Throttle opening is above a predetermined value.

A vent pipe allows fuel vapors to flow to the charcoal canister. On some vehicles, the tank is isolated from the charcoal canister by a tank pressure control valve, located either in the tank or in the vapor line near the canister. It is a combination roll-over, integral pressure and vacuum relief valve. When the vapor pressure in the tank exceeds 0.72 psi (5 kPa), the valve opens to allow vapors to vent to the canister. The valve also provides vacuum relief to protect against vacuum build-up in the fuel tank and roll-over spill protection.

Poor engine idle, stalling and poor driveability can be caused by an inoperative canister purge solenoid, a damaged canister or split, damaged or improperly connected hoses.

The most common symptom of problems in this system is fuel odors coming from under the hood. If there is no liquid fuel leak, check for a cracked or damaged vapor canister, inoperative or always open canister control valve, disconnected, misrouted, kinked or damaged vapor pipe or canister hoses; or a damaged air cleaner or improperly seated air cleaner gasket.

TESTING

Tank Pressure Control Valve

1. Using a hand-held vacuum pump, apply a vacuum of 15 in. Hg (51 kPa) through the control vacuum signal tube to the purge valve diaphragm. If the diaphragm does not hold vacuum for at least 20 seconds, the diaphragm is leaking. Replace the control valve.

2. With the vacuum still applied to the control vacuum tube, attach a short piece of hose to the valve's tank tube side and blow into the hose. Air should pass through the valve. If it does not, replace the control valve.

Canister Purge Control Valve

1. Connect a clean length of hose to the fuel tank vapor line connection on the canister and attempt to blow through the purge control valve. It should be difficult or impossible to blow through the valve. If air passes easily, the valve is stuck open and should be replaced.

2. Connect a hand-held vacuum pump to the top vacuum line fitting of the purge control valve. Apply a vacuum of 15 in. Hg (51kPa) to the purge valve diaphragm. If the diaphragm does not hold vacuum for at least 20 seconds the diaphragm is leaking. Replace the control valve. If it is impossible to blow through the valve, it is stuck closed and must be replaced.

3. On vehicles with a solenoid activated purge control valve, unplug the connector and use jumper wires to supply 12 volts to the solenoid connections on the valve. With the vacuum still applied to the control vacuum tube, the purge control valve should open and it should be easy to blow through. If not, replace the valve.

REMOVAL & INSTALLATION

Evaporative Canister

♦ **See Figures 8 and 9**

1. Disconnect the negative battery cable.
2. If necessary for access, remove the coolant recovery reservoir.
3. For 1996 3.1L engines, perform the following:
   a. Raise and safely support the vehicle, then remove the left (driver) side rear wheel and tire assembly.
   b. Remove the left (driver) side rear wheel well liner.
4. Tag and disconnect the vacuum hoses from the canister.
5. Unfasten the retainers, then remove the canister from the vehicle.
6. Installation is the reverse of the removal procedure. Make sure to fasten the canister securely and attach the vacuum lines as tagged during removal.
7. Connect the negative battery cable.

Tank Pressure Control Valve

♦ **See Figure 10**

1. Disconnect the negative battery cable.
2. Tag and disconnect the hoses from the control valve.
3. Remove the mounting hardware.
4. Remove the control valve from the vehicle.
5. Installation is the reverse of the removal procedure.

Canister Purge Solenoid Valve

♦ **See Figure 11**

1. Disconnect the negative battery cable.
2. If necessary for access, raise and safely support the vehicle.
3. Tag and detach the electrical connector and vacuum hose(s) from the valve.
4. Either unfasten the mounting nut or release the locktab on the solenoid bracket.
5. Remove the canister purge solenoid valve from the vehicle.

To install:

6. Position the purge solenoid valve to the bracket. Either snap the valve over the locktabs of the bracket or fasten the retaining nut to secure the valve.
7. Attach the vacuum hose(s) and electrical connector to the valve, as tagged during removal.
8. If necessary, carefully lower the vehicle, then connect the negative battery cable.

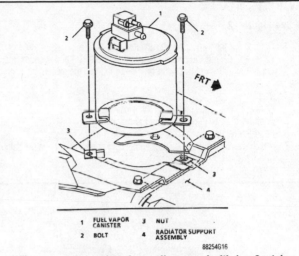

| 1 | FUEL VAPOR CANISTER | 3 | NUT |
| 2 | BOLT | 4 | RADIATOR SUPPORT ASSEMBLY |

88254G16

Fig. 9 The evaporative canister is usually secured with 1 or 2 retaining bolts

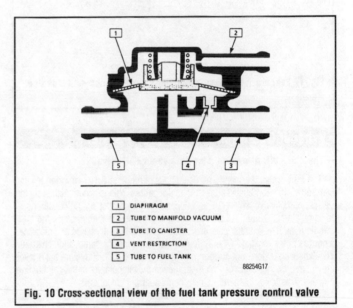

1	DIAPHRAGM
2	TUBE TO MANIFOLD VACUUM
3	TUBE TO CANISTER
4	VENT RESTRICTION
5	TUBE TO FUEL TANK

88254G17

Fig. 10 Cross-sectional view of the fuel tank pressure control valve

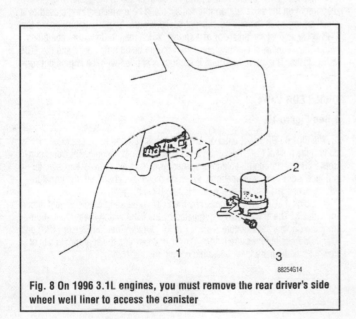

88254G14

Fig. 8 On 1996 3.1L engines, you must remove the rear driver's side wheel well liner to access the canister

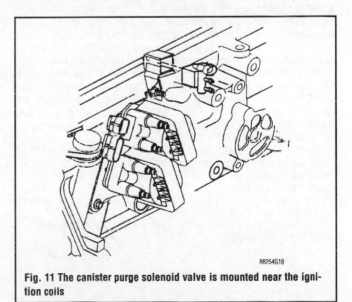

88254G18

Fig. 11 The canister purge solenoid valve is mounted near the ignition coils

EVAP Vacuum Switch

▶ **See Figure 12**

1. Disconnect the negative battery cable.
2. Label and detach the switch electrical connector(s) and vacuum hoses.
3. Bend the retaining tab on the bracket to remove the switch, then remove the switch from the vehicle.
   To install:
4. Connect the vacuum hoses to the switch.
5. Position the vacuum switch on the bracket.
6. Bend the retaining tab to secure the switch to the bracket.
7. Attach the switch electrical connector and connect the negative battery cable.

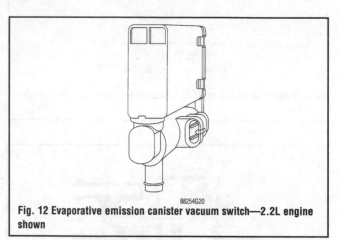

88254G20

Fig. 12 Evaporative emission canister vacuum switch—2.2L engine shown

Exhaust Gas Recirculation (EGR) System

➡ **The 2.3L (VIN A) engine does not use an EGR valve.**

The EGR system is used to reduce oxides of nitrogen (NOx) emission levels caused by high combustion chamber temperatures. This is accomplished by the use of an EGR valve which opens, under specific engine operating conditions, to admit a small amount of exhaust gas into the intake manifold, below the throttle plate. The exhaust gas mixes with the incoming air charge and displaces a portion of the oxygen in the air/fuel mixture entering the combustion chamber. The exhaust gas does not support combustion of the air/fuel mixture but it takes up volume, the net effect of which is to lower the temperature of the combustion process. This lower temperature also helps control detonation.

The EGR valve is a mounted on the intake manifold and has an opening into the exhaust manifold. Except for the digital and linear versions, the EGR valve is opened by manifold vacuum to permit exhaust gas to flow into the intake manifold. With the digital and linear versions, the EGR valve is purely electrical and uses solenoid valves to open the flow passage. If too much exhaust gas enters, combustion will not occur. Because of this, very little exhaust gas is allowed to pass through the valve. The EGR system will be activated once the engine reaches normal operating temperature and the EGR valve will open when engine operating conditions are above idle speed and below Wide Open Throttle (WOT). On California vehicles equipped with a Vehicle Speed Sensor (VSS), the EGR valve opens when the VSS signal is greater than 2 mph (3.2 kph). The EGR system is deactivated on vehicles equipped with a Transmission Converter Clutch (TCC) when the TCC is engaged.

Too much EGR flow at idle, cruise, or during cold operation may result in the engine stalling after cold start, the engine stalling at idle after deceleration, vehicle surge during cruise and rough idle. If the EGR valve is always open, the vehicle may not idle. Too little or no EGR flow allows combustion temperatures to get too high which could result in spark knock (detonation), engine overheating and/or emission test failure.

There are four basic types of systems as described below, differing in the way EGR flow is modulated.

Integrated Electronic EGR Valve

▶ **See Figure 13**

The integrated electronic EGR valve, used on 1988–89 2.8L engines, functions like a port valve with a remote vacuum regulator, except the regulator and a pintle position sensor are sealed in the black plastic cover. The regulator and position sensor are not serviceable items; there is a serviceable filter that provides fresh air to the regulator, along side the vacuum tube.

This valve has a vacuum regulator, to which the ECM provides variable current. This current produces the desired EGR flow using inputs from the manifold air temperature sensor, coolant temperature sensor and engine rpm.

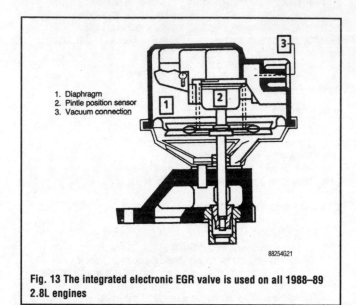

1. Diaphragm
2. Pintle position sensor
3. Vacuum connection

88254G21

Fig. 13 The integrated electronic EGR valve is used on all 1988–89 2.8L engines

Negative Backpressure EGR Valve

▶ **See Figure 14**

The negative backpressure EGR valve, used on the 2.0L and 1990–95 2.2L engines, varies the amount of exhaust gas flow into the intake manifold depending on manifold vacuum and variations in exhaust backpressure. An air bleed valve, located inside the EGR valve assembly acts as a vacuum regulator. The bleed valve controls the amount of vacuum in the vacuum chamber by bleeding vacuum to outside air during the open phase of the cycle. The diaphragm on the valve has an internal air bleed hole which is held closed by a small spring when there is no exhaust backpressure. Engine vacuum opens the EGR valve against the pressure of a spring. When manifold vacuum combines with negative exhaust backpressure, the vacuum bleed hole opens and the EGR valve closes. This valve will open if vacuum is applied with the engine not running.

Digital EGR Valve

▶ **See Figure 15**

The digital EGR valve, used on all 1990–95 3.1L engines, is designed to control the flow of EGR independent of intake manifold vacuum. The valve controls EGR flow through 3 solenoid-opened orifices, which increase in size, to produce 7 possible combinations. When a solenoid is energized, the armature with attached shaft and swivel pintle, is lifted, opening the orifice.

The digital EGR valve is opened by the ECM, grounding each solenoid circuit individually. The flow of EGR is regulated by the ECM which uses information from the Coolant Temperature Sensor (CTS), Throttle Position Sensor (TPS) and Manifold Absolute Pressure (MAP) sensor to determine the appropriate rate of flow for a particular engine operating condition.

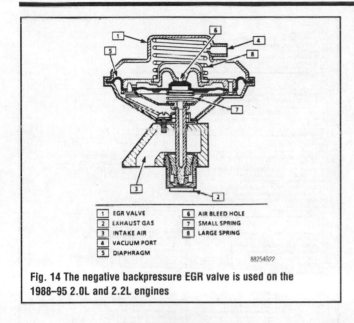

Fig. 14 The negative backpressure EGR valve is used on the 1988–95 2.0L and 2.2L engines

1	EGR VALVE	6	AIR BLEED HOLE
2	EXHAUST GAS	7	SMALL SPRING
3	INTAKE AIR	8	LARGE SPRING
4	VACUUM PORT		
5	DIAPHRAGM		

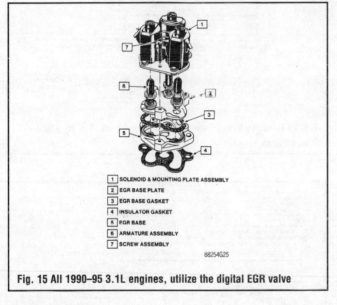

1	SOLENOID & MOUNTING PLATE ASSEMBLY
2	EGR BASE PLATE
3	EGR BASE GASKET
4	INSULATOR GASKET
5	EGR BASE
6	ARMATURE ASSEMBLY
7	SCREW ASSEMBLY

Fig. 15 All 1990–95 3.1L engines, utilize the digital EGR valve

Linear EGR Valve

The linear EGR valve, used on the 1996 2.2L and 3.1L engines, is designed to accurately apply EGR to an engine, independent of intake manifold vacuum. The valve controls EGR flow from the exhaust to the intake manifold through an orifice with a PCM controlled pintle. During operation, the PCM controls pintle position by monitoring the pintle position feedback signal. The PCM uses information from the Engine Coolant Temperature (ECT) sensor, Throttle Position (TP) sensor and the Mass Air Flow (MAF) sensor to determine the appropriate rate of flow for a particular engine operating condition.

COMPONENT TESTING

♦ See Figures 16 thru 23

For EGR testing, please refer to the accompanying charts. Note that some testing procedures require the use of a Tech 1® or equivalent scan tool. Also, when perform the digital EGR system test, the steps must be performed quickly, as the ECM will adjust the idle air control valve to compensate for idle speed.

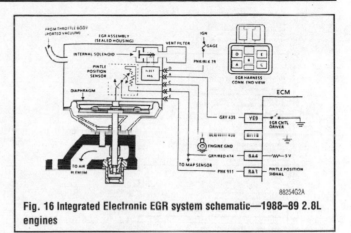

Fig. 16 Integrated Electronic EGR system schematic—1988–89 2.8L engines

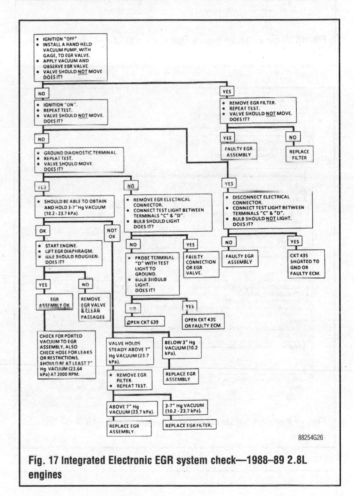

Fig. 17 Integrated Electronic EGR system check—1988–89 2.8L engines

REMOVAL & INSTALLATION

EGR Valve

2.0L AND 1990–95 2.2L ENGINES

♦ See Figure 24

1. Disconnect the negative battery cable.
2. If necessary for access, remove the air cleaner assembly.
3. Disconnect the EGR vacuum hose from the valve.

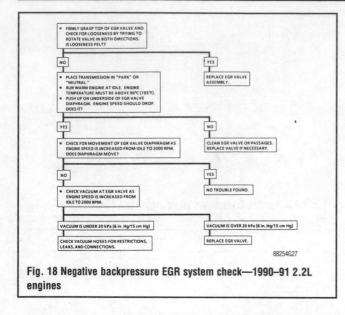

Fig. 18 Negative backpressure EGR system check—1990–91 2.2L engines

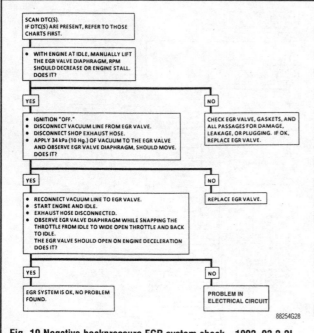

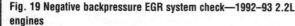

Fig. 19 Negative backpressure EGR system check—1992–93 2.2L engines

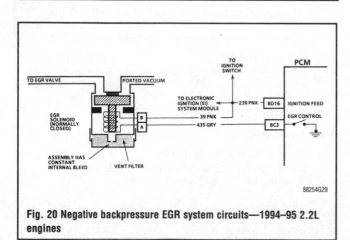

Fig. 20 Negative backpressure EGR system circuits—1994–95 2.2L engines

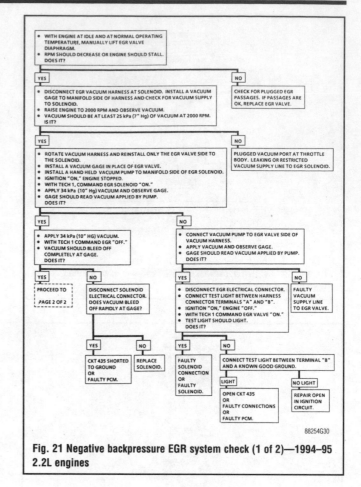

Fig. 21 Negative backpressure EGR system check (1 of 2)—1994–95 2.2L engines

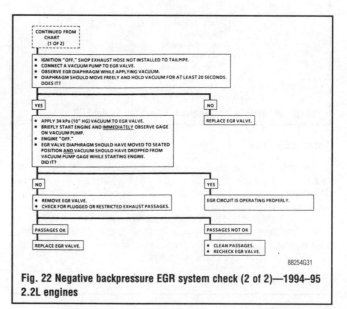

Fig. 22 Negative backpressure EGR system check (2 of 2)—1994–95 2.2L engines

4. Unfasten the EGR retaining bolts, then remove the EGR valve from the manifold.

5. Remove and discard the EGR valve gasket.

6. Inspect the EGR manifold passage and clean any excessive build-up of deposits. Make sure all loose particles are completely removed.

7. With a wire brush or wheel, carefully buff the exhaust deposits from the mounting surface and around the valve. Look for exhaust deposits in the valve outlet and remove with a suitable tool.

8. Clean the mounting surfaces of the intake manifold and valve assembly.

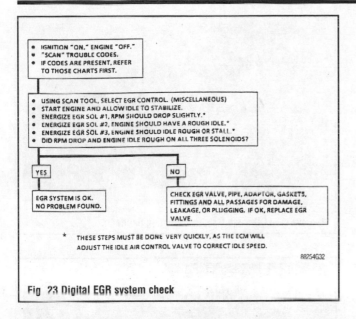

- IGNITION "ON," ENGINE "OFF."
- "SCAN" TROUBLE CODES.
- IF CODES ARE PRESENT, REFER TO THOSE CHARTS FIRST.

- USING SCAN TOOL, SELECT EGR CONTROL. (MISCELLANEOUS)
- START ENGINE AND ALLOW IDLE TO STABILIZE.
- ENERGIZE EGR SOL #1, RPM SHOULD DROP SLIGHTLY.*
- ENERGIZE EGR SOL #2, ENGINE SHOULD HAVE A ROUGH IDLE.*
- ENERGIZE EGR SOL #3, ENGINE SHOULD IDLE ROUGH OR STALL.*
- DID RPM DROP AND ENGINE IDLE ROUGH ON ALL THREE SOLENOIDS?

YES

EGR SYSTEM IS OK. NO PROBLEM FOUND.

NO

CHECK EGR VALVE, PIPE, ADAPTOR, GASKETS, FITTINGS AND ALL PASSAGES FOR DAMAGE, LEAKAGE, OR PLUGGING. IF OK, REPLACE EGR VALVE.

* THESE STEPS MUST BE DONE VERY QUICKLY, AS THE ECM WILL ADJUST THE IDLE AIR CONTROL VALVE TO CORRECT IDLE SPEED.

88254G32

Fig. 23 Digital EGR system check

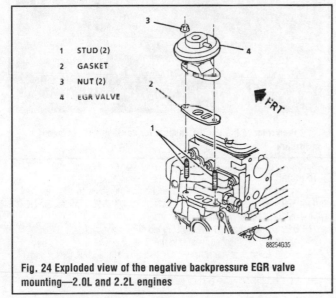

1 STUD (2)
2 GASKET
3 NUT (2)
4 EGR VALVE

FRT

88254G35

Fig. 24 Exploded view of the negative backpressure EGR valve mounting—2.0L and 2.2L engines

9. Installation is the reverse of the removal procedure. Use a new gasket and tighten the retaining bolts and tighten to 11–18 ft. lbs. (15–25 Nm).

2.8L ENGINE

▶ See Figure 25

1. Disconnect the negative battery cable.
2. Detach the EGR vacuum hose from the valve.
3. Unplug the electrical connector.
4. Disconnect the EGR tube from the exhaust manifold.
5. Remove the three EGR mounting nuts from the plenum studs.
6. Remove the EGR tube from the valve by removing the two bolts.
7. Inspect the EGR manifold passage and clean any excessive build-up of deposits. Make sure all loose particles are completely removed.
8. With a wire brush or wheel, clean the exhaust deposits from the mounting surface and around the valve. Look for exhaust deposits in the valve outlet and remove with a suitable tool.
9. Clean the mounting surfaces of the intake manifold and valve assembly.

To install:

10. Install the EGR tube to the EGR valve using a new gasket and tighten to 19 ft. lbs. (26 Nm).
11. Install the EGR valve and tube assembly to the plenum using a new gasket.

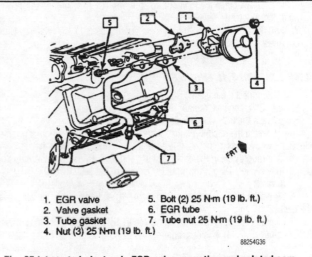

1. EGR valve
2. Valve gasket
3. Tube gasket
4. Nut (3) 25 N·m (19 lb. ft.)
5. Bolt (2) 25 N·m (19 lb. ft.)
6. EGR tube
7. Tube nut 25 N·m (19 lb. ft.)

88254G36

Fig. 25 Integrated electronic EGR valve mounting and related components—2.8l engines

12. Tighten the bolts to 19 ft. lbs. (26 Nm).
13. Install the EGR tube to the exhaust manifold and tighten to 19 ft. lbs. (26 Nm)
14. Attach the electrical connector and vacuum hose to the valve.
15. Connect the negative battery cable.

1990–95 3.1L ENGINE

▶ See Figure 26

1. Disconnect the negative battery cable.
2. Detach the electrical connector from the solenoid.
3. Remove the 2 base-to-flange bolts, then remove the digital EGR valve from the vehicle. Remove the gasket, inspect for damage, and replaced as necessary.

To install:

4. Position the EGR gasket on the pad, aligning it with the holes.
5. Place the EGR valve on the gasket, then install the 2 base to flange bolts finger-tight, aligning the holes through the valve and pad of the upper intake manifold and into the pipe assembly.
6. For 1990–93 vehicles, tighten the bolts in two steps in the following sequence:
   a. Step 1: tighten the long bolt to 11 ft. lbs. (15 Nm) and the short bolt to 11 ft. lbs. (15 Nm).

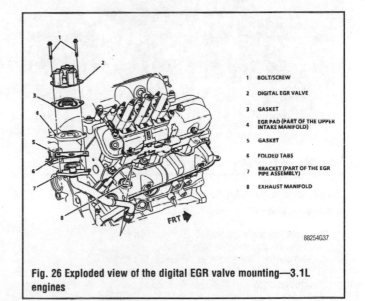

1 BOLT/SCREW
2 DIGITAL EGR VALVE
3 GASKET
4 EGR PAD (PART OF THE UPPER INTAKE MANIFOLD)
5 GASKET
6 FOLDED TABS
7 BRACKET (PART OF THE EGR PIPE ASSEMBLY)
8 EXHAUST MANIFOLD

FRT

88254G37

Fig. 26 Exploded view of the digital EGR valve mounting—3.1L engines

b. Step 2: tighten the long bolt to 30 ft. lbs. (22 Nm) and the short bolt to 30 ft. lbs. (22 Nm).

7. For 1994–95 vehicles, tighten the mounting bolts to 18 ft. lbs. (25 Nm).

8. Attach the electrical connector to the solenoid.

9. Connect the negative battery cable.

1996 2.2L AND 3.1L ENGINES

1. Disconnect the negative battery cable.

2. For 2.2L engines, remove the air cleaner outlet resonator.

3. Detach the EGR valve electrical connector.

4. Unfasten the retaining bolts, then remove the EGR valve from the vehicle. Remove the gasket, inspect for damage and replace, if necessary.

5. Thoroughly clean the gasket mating surfaces, as even a small amount of debris may cause a Diagnostic Trouble Code (DTC) to set.

To install:

6. Position the EGR gasket on the mounting pad, then place the valve over the gasket.

7. Install the retaining bolts and tighten to 16–22 ft. lbs. (22–30 Nm) for 2.2L engines. For 3.1L engines, tighten the retaining bolts to 22 ft. lbs. (30 Nm).

8. Attach the EGR valve electrical connector.

9. If removed, install the air cleaner outlet resonator.

10. Connect the negative battery cable.

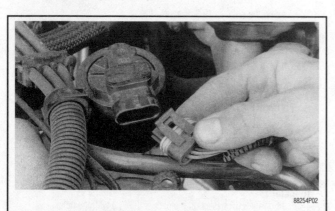

Unplug the EGR valve electrical connector

Remove the EGR valve mounting bolts

EGR Control Valve Relay Solenoid and Injector Valve

♦ See Figure 27

This procedure applies to some 2.2L engines only.

1. Disconnect the negative battery cable.

2. Remove the MAP sensor, as outlined in this section.

3. Detach the electrical connector from the solenoid.

4. Tag and disconnect the vacuum hoses.

5. Unfasten the retaining screw, then remove the EGR solenoid.

Remove the EGR valve from its mounting flange . . .

. . . then remove the gasket, inspect for damage and replace if necessary

To install:

6. Install the solenoid and bracket and tighten the screw to 17 ft. lbs. (24 Nm) for 1992 vehicles or to 22 ft. lbs. (30 Nm) for 1993–95 vehicles. Do NOT overtighten the retainers.

7. Connect the vacuum hoses, as tagged during removal.

8. Attach the electrical connector to the solenoid.

9. Install the seal on the MAP sensor, then install the MAP sensor and tighten the screws to 27 inch lbs. (3 Nm).

10. Connect the negative battery cable.

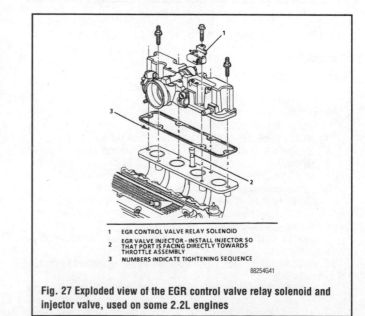

1 EGR CONTROL VALVE RELAY SOLENOID
2 EGR VALVE INJECTOR - INSTALL INJECTOR SO THAT PORT IS FACING DIRECTLY TOWARDS THROTTLE ASSEMBLY
3 NUMBERS INDICATE TIGHTENING SEQUENCE

88254G41

Fig. 27 Exploded view of the EGR control valve relay solenoid and injector valve, used on some 2.2L engines

ELECTRONIC ENGINE CONTROLS

Electronic Control Module (ECM)

OPERATION

→ When the term Electronic Control Module (ECM) is used in this manual it will refer to the engine control computer regardless that it may be a Powertrain Control Module (PCM) or Electronic Control Module (ECM).

The heart of the electronic control system, which is found on the vehicles covered by this manual, is a computer control module. The module gathers information from various sensors, then controls fuel supply and engine emission systems. Most early model vehicles are equipped with an Engine Control Module (ECM) which, as its name implies, controls the engine and related emissions systems. Some ECMs may also control the Torque Converter Clutch (TCC) on automatic transaxle vehicles or the manual upshift light on manual transmission vehicles. Later model vehicles may be equipped with a Powertrain Control Module (PCM). This is similar to the original ECMs, but is designed to control additional systems as well. The PCM may control the manual transmission shift lamp or the shift functions of the electronically controlled automatic transmission.

Regardless of the name, all computer control modules are serviced in a similar manner. Care must be taken when handling these expensive components in order to protect them from damage. Carefully follow all instructions included with the replacement part. Avoid touching pins or connectors to prevent damage from static electricity.

All of these computer control modules contain a Programmable Read Only Memory (PROM) chip, MEM-CAL or EEPROM that contains calibration information which is particular to the vehicle application. For all applications except those equipped with an EEPROM, this chip is not supplied with a replacement module, and must be transferred to the new module before installation. If equipped with an Electronically Erasable Programmable Read Only Memory (EEPROM), it must be reprogrammed after installation. Some later model vehicles have a Knock Sensor (KS) module, mounted in the PCM. The KS module contains the circuitry that allows the PCM to utilize the Knock Sensor signal to diagnose the circuitry.

✷✷ WARNING

To prevent the possibility of permanent control module damage, the ignition switch MUST always be OFF when disconnecting power from or reconnecting power to the module. This includes unplugging the module connector, disconnecting the negative battery cable, removing the module fuse or even attempting to jump your dead battery using jumper cables.

In the event of an ECM failure, the system will default to a pre-programmed set of values. These are compromise values which allow the engine to operate, although at a reduced efficiency. This is variously known as the default, limp-in or back-up mode. Driveability is almost always affected when the ECM enters this mode.

REMOVAL & INSTALLATION

♦ See Figures 28, 29 and 30

For most applications, the computer control module is mounted inside the passenger compartment, attached to a bracket located in the right side upper instrument panel.

1. Make sure the ignition switch is turned **OFF**, then disconnect the negative battery cable.

✷✷ CAUTION

To prevent the possibility of permanent control module damage, the ignition switch MUST always be OFF when disconnecting power from or reconnecting power to the module. This includes unplugging the module connector, disconnecting the negative battery cable, removing the module fuse or even attempting to jump your dead battery using jumper cables.

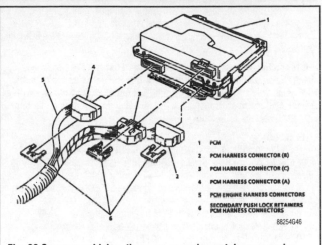

1 PCM
2 PCM HARNESS CONNECTOR (B)
3 PCM HARNESS CONNECTOR (C)
4 PCM HARNESS CONNECTOR (A)
5 PCM ENGINE HARNESS CONNECTORS
6 SECONDARY PUSH LOCK RETAINERS PCM HARNESS CONNECTORS

88254G46

Fig. 28 On some vehicles, there are secondary retainers securing the electrical connectors to the PCM

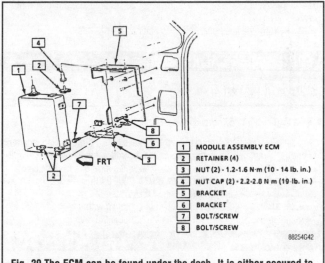

1 MODULE ASSEMBLY ECM
2 RETAINER (4)
3 NUT (2) - 1.2-1.6 N·m (10 - 14 lb. in.)
4 NUT CAP (2) - 2.2-2.8 N·m (19 lb. in.)
5 BRACKET
6 BRACKET
7 BOLT/SCREW
8 BOLT/SCREW

88254G42

Fig. 29 The ECM can be found under the dash. It is either secured to the kick panel . . .

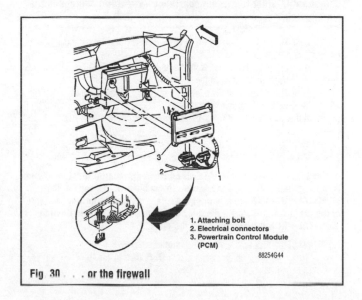

1. Attaching bolt
2. Electrical connectors
3. Powertrain Control Module (PCM)

88254G44

Fig. 30 . . . or the firewall

2. Locate the computer control module. It should be mounted inside the passenger compartment, under the right side of the dash.

3. Remove the interior access panel/right side hush panel.

4. Carefully detach the harness connectors from the ECM.

5. Remove the ECM-to-bracket retaining screws and remove the ECM, then remove the ECM from the engine compartment.

➥If replacing the ECM, when removing the ECM from the package, check the service number to make sure it is the same as the defective ECM. Also when replacing the original computer control module with a service replacement, transfer the broadcast code and production number to the service ECM label.

To install:

6. If the module is being replaced, CAREFULLY replace the EPROM chip, MEM-CAL or Knock Sensor (KS) module, as outlined later in this section.

7. Position the ECM in the vehicle and install the ECM-to-bracket retaining screws.

8. Attach the ECM harness connectors.

9. Install the hush panel/interior access panel.

10. Check that the ignition switch is **OFF**, then connect the negative battery cable.

11. If equipped with a computer control module that contains an EEP-ROM, it must be reprogrammed using a Tech 1® or equivalent scan tool and the latest available software. In all likelihood, the vehicle must be towed to a dealer or repair shop containing the suitable equipment for this service.

12. Perform the functional check, as outlined later in this section.

EPROM/MEM-CAL/KS Module

REMOVAL & INSTALLATION

▶ **See Figures 31, 32 and 33**

As stated earlier, all computer control modules contain information regarding the correct parameters for engine and system operation based on vehicle applications. In most modules, this information takes the form of a EPROM chip or MEM-CAL. Some later model vehicles, also include a Knock Sensor (KS) module which is replaced like the PROM and MEM-CAL.

Replacement computers are normally not equipped with this PROM/MEM-CAL/KS module; you must transfer the chip from the old component.

✳️ WARNING

The PROM/MEM-CAL chip, KS module and computer control module are EXTREMELY sensitive to electrical or mechanical damage. NEVER touch the connector pins or soldered components on the circuit board in order to prevent possible electrostatic damage to the components.

1. Make sure the ignition switch is **OFF**, then remove the computer control module from the vehicle.

2. Remove the access panel. Note the position of the MEM-CAL/PROM/KS module for proper installation in the new ECM.

3. Using 2 fingers, carefully push both retaining clips back away from the MEM-CAL/PROM/KS module. At the same time, grasp it at both ends and lift it up out of the socket. Do not remove the cover of the MEM-CAL/PROM/KS module.

To install:

4. Fit the replacement MEM-CAL/PROM/KS module into the socket.

➥The small notches in the MEM-CAL/PROM/KS module must be aligned with the small notches in the socket. Press only on the ends of the MEM-CAL/PROM/KS module until the retaining clips snap into the ends of the MEM-CAL/PROM/KS module. Do not press on the middle of the MEM-CAL/PROM/KS module, only the ends.

5. Install the access cover and retaining screws.

6. Make sure the ignition switch is still **OFF**, then install the ECM, as outlined earlier in this section.

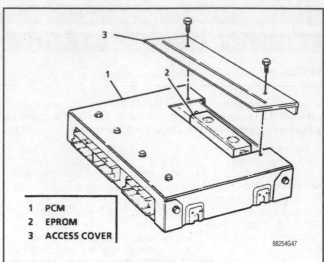

1	PCM
2	EPROM
3	ACCESS COVER

88254G47

Fig. 31 To remove the PROM, MEM-CAL or KS module, you must remove the access cover on the control module

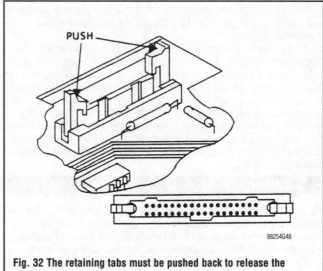

88254G48

Fig. 32 The retaining tabs must be pushed back to release the unit—MEM-CAL shown, others similar

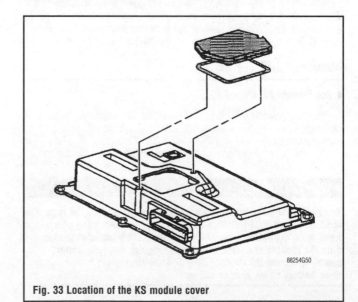

88254G50

Fig. 33 Location of the KS module cover

FUNCTIONAL CHECK

1988–94 Vehicles, Except 1994 3.1L Engine

1. Turn the ignition switch **ON**.
2. Enter diagnostics, as outlined later in this section.
   a. Allow Code 12 to flash 4 times to verify no other codes are present. This indicates the PROM/MEM-CAL is installed properly and the ECM is functioning.
   b. If trouble Codes 42, 43 or 51 occur, or if the Service Engine Soon light is ON constantly with no codes, the MEM-CAL is not fully seated or is defective.
   c. If it is not fully seated, press firmly on the ends of the PROM/MEM-CAL.
3. If installed backwards, replace the PROM/MEM-CAL.

➡**Any time the PROM is installed backwards and the ignition switch is turned ON, the PROM is destroyed.**

4. If the pins are bent, remove the PROM/MEM-CAL, straighten the pins and reinstall the PROM/MEM-CAL. If the bent pins break or crack during straightening, discard the PROM/MEM-CAL and replace with a new PROM/MEM-CAL.

➡**To prevent possible electrostatic discharge damage to the PROM or MEM-CAL, do not touch the component leads and do not remove the integrated circuit from the carrier.**

1994 3.1L Engine and All 1995–96 Vehicles

1. Using a Tech 1® or equivalent scan tool, perform the on-board diagnostic system check.
2. Start the engine and run for one minute.
3. Scan for DTC's using the Tech 1® or equivalent scan tool, as outlined later in this section.
4. If trouble code P0325 occurs, or if the MIL (Service Engine Soon) is ON constantly with no diagnostic trouble codes, the PROM or KS module is not fully seated or is defective. If it is not fully seated, press firmly on the ends of the PROM/KS module.
5. If trouble code P0601 occurs, the EEPROM programming has malfunctioned and must be reprogrammed using a Tech 1® or equivalent scan tool.

Oxygen Sensor

OPERATION

♦ **See Figures 34 and 35**

There are two types of oxygen sensors used in these vehicles. They are the single wire oxygen sensors (O2S) and the heated oxygen sensor (HO2S). The oxygen sensor is a spark plug shaped device that is threaded into the exhaust manifold and protrudes into the exhaust stream which monitors the oxygen content of the exhaust gases. The difference between the oxygen content of the exhaust gases and that of the outside air generates a voltage signal that is sent to the computer control module. The control module monitors this voltage and, depending upon the value of the signal received, issues a command to adjust for a rich or a lean condition.

➡**Some vehicles are equipped with more than one heated oxygen sensor.**

The proper operation of the oxygen sensor depends upon three basic conditions:

1. Good electrical connections. Since the sensor generates low currents, good clean electrical connections at the sensor are a must.
2. Outside air supply. Air must circulate to the internal portion of the sensor. When servicing the sensor, do not restrict the air passages.
3. Proper operating temperatures. The computer control module will not recognize the sensor's signals until the sensor reaches about 600°F (316°C).

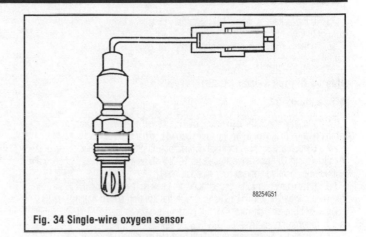

Fig. 34 Single-wire oxygen sensor

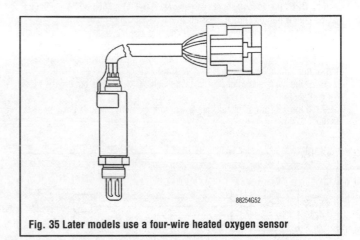

Fig. 35 Later models use a four-wire heated oxygen sensor

TESTING

Single Wire Oxygen Sensor (O2S)

♦ **See Figure 36**

1. Perform a visual inspection of the connector, making sure it is engaged properly and all of the terminals are straight, tight and free of corrosion.
2. Start the engine and run until the engine reaches normal operating temperatures (closed loop, or coolant temperature at 167–203°F.
3. Detach the oxygen sensor connector, then connect a voltmeter to the terminal and a known engine ground.
4. Check the voltage with the engine running above 1200 rpm:
   a. If the voltage is fluctuating between 0.1–1.0 volts (100-999 mV), the system is operating normally.
   b. If the voltage does not fluctuate as specified, replace the sensor.
   c. If the voltage is below 0.35 volts (350 mV), a lean condition exists.
   d. If the voltage is above 0.75 volts (750 mV), a rich condition exists.

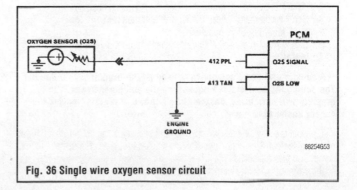

Fig. 36 Single wire oxygen sensor circuit

5. If the voltage is within specifications, check the circuits back to the PCM for continuity.

6. If the sensor and circuits are functioning properly, the PCM may be faulty.

Heated Oxygen Sensor (HO2S)

♦ See Figure 37

1. Visually check the connector, making sure it is engaged properly and all of the terminals are straight, tight and free of corrosion.

2. Detach the sensor electrical connector and check resistance between terminals C and D. Resistance should be 10–15 ohms at 70°F. If resistance is not within specifications, the sensor heater is faulty.

3. If resistance is within specification, check for battery positive (B+) between connector terminals C and D with the ignition **ON**. If battery positive (B+) is not present, check the circuit continuity back to the PCM. If the circuits are functioning properly, the PCM may be faulty.

4. Check the HO2S sensor voltage between terminals A and B with the engine **OFF**. The voltage should be between 350–500 millivolts. If the voltage doesn't fall within that range, the sensor is faulty.

5. If the voltage is within specifications, recheck the voltage after heating the engine to normal operating temperature. With the engine running at 1200 rpm, then voltage should vary between 100–900 millivolts. If the voltage is not varying or not within the range, the sensor is faulty.

6. If the voltage is within specifications, check the circuits back to the PCM for continuity.

7. If the sensor and circuits are functioning properly, the PCM may be faulty.

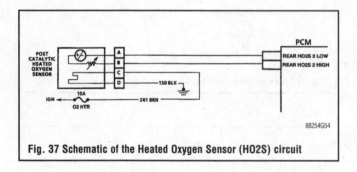

Fig. 37 Schematic of the Heated Oxygen Sensor (HO2S) circuit

REMOVAL & INSTALLATION

♦ See Figure 38

➡The oxygen sensor may be difficult to remove when the engine temperature is below 120°F (49°C). Excessive removal force may damage the threads in the exhaust manifold or pipe; follow the removal procedure carefully.

1. Locate the oxygen sensor. It may protrudes from the center of the exhaust manifold at the front of the engine compartment (it looks somewhat like a spark plug) or be located along the exhaust pipe.

2. If necessary for access to the sensor, remove the exhaust manifold head shield or raise and safely support the vehicle, as necessary.

3. Detach the electrical connector from the oxygen sensor.

4. Spray a commercial heat riser solvent onto the sensor threads and allow it to soak in for at least five minutes.

5. Carefully unscrew and remove the sensor from the vehicle.

To install:

➡A special anti-seize compound is used on the oxygen sensor threads. The compound consists of a liquid graphite and glass beads. The graphite will burn away, but the glass beads will remain, making the sensor easier to remove.

6. Coat the new sensor's threads with GM anti-seize compound No. 5613695 or the equivalent. This is not a conventional anti-seize paste. The use of a regular compound may electrically insulate the sensor, rendering it inoperative. You must coat the threads with an electrically conductive anti-seize compound.

Some vehicles may have an oxygen sensor (see arrow) mounted along the exhaust pipe

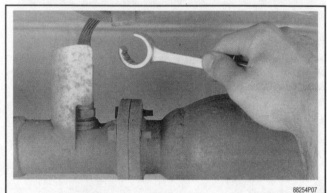

Using an open-ended wrench may make removal of the oxygen sensor easier

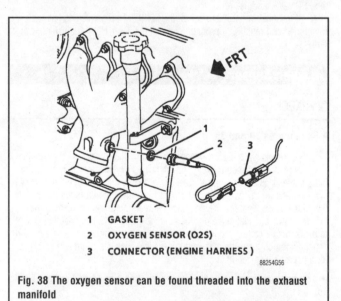

1	GASKET
2	OXYGEN SENSOR (O2S)
3	CONNECTOR (ENGINE HARNESS)

Fig. 38 The oxygen sensor can be found threaded into the exhaust manifold

➡New or service sensors will already have the compound applied to the threads. If a sensor is removed from the engine, and for any reason it is to be reinstalled, the threads must have anti-seize compound applied before reinstallation.

7. Install the sensor and tighten to 28–33 ft. lbs. (42 Nm.). Do not overtighten.

8. Attach the electrical connector. Be careful not to damage the electrical pigtail. Check the sensor boot for proper fit and installation.

9. If removed, install the exhaust manifold heat shield, then connect the negative battery cable.

Idle Air Control (IAC) Valve

OPERATION

▶ See Figure 39

Engine idle speeds are controlled by the PCM through the IAC valve mounted on the throttle body. The PCM sends voltage pulses to the IAC motor windings causing the IAC motor shaft and pintle to move in or out a given distance (number of steps) for each pulse (called counts). The movement of the pintle controls the airflow around the throttle plate, which in turn, controls engine idle speed. IAC valve pintle position counts can be observed using a scan tool. Zero counts correspond to a fully closed passage, while 140 counts or more corresponds to full flow.

Idle speed can be categorized in 2 ways: actual (controlled) idle speed and minimum idle speed. Controlled idle speed is obtained by the PCM positioning the IAC valve pintle. Resulting idle speed is determined by total air flow (IAC/passage + PCV + throttle valve + calibrated vacuum leaks). Controlled idle speed is specified at normal operating conditions, which consists of engine coolant at normal operating temperature, air conditioning compressor **OFF**, manual transmission in neutral or automatic transmission in **D**.

Minimum idle air speed is set at the factory with a stop screw. This setting allows a certain amount of air to bypass the throttle valves regardless of IAC valve pintle positioning. A combination of this air flow and IAC pintle positioning allows the PCM to control engine idle speed. During normal engine idle operation, the IAC valve pintle is positioned a calibrated number of steps (counts) from the seat. No adjustment is required during routine maintenance. Tampering with the minimum idle speed adjustment may result in premature failure of the IAC valve or improperly controlled engine idle operation.

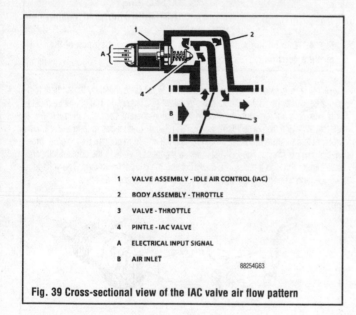

1. VALVE ASSEMBLY - IDLE AIR CONTROL (IAC)
2. BODY ASSEMBLY - THROTTLE
3. VALVE - THROTTLE
4. PINTLE - IAC VALVE
A. ELECTRICAL INPUT SIGNAL
B. AIR INLET

88254G63

Fig. 39 Cross-sectional view of the IAC valve air flow pattern

TESTING

Except 1996 2.2L Engines and 1994–96 3.1L Engines

▶ See Figure 40

1. Visually check the connector, making sure it is connected properly and all of the terminals are straight, tight and free of corrosion.
2. Detach the IAC valve connector, then measure the resistance between the terminals A and B, and between terminals C and D:

a. If the resistance between terminals A and B and terminals C and D measure 40–80 ohms, go to the next step.

b. If the resistance between the terminals A and B or between the terminals C and D does not meet specifications, replace the IAC valve.

3. Check for continuity between the terminals A and D and terminals B and C:

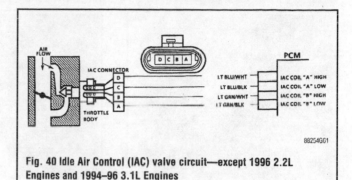

Fig. 40 Idle Air Control (IAC) valve circuit—except 1996 2.2L Engines and 1994–96 3.1L Engines

a. If there is no continuity between terminals A and D and terminals B and C, the valve is OK.

b. If the resistance between the terminals A and D or between terminals B and C does not meet specifications, replace the IAC valve.

1996 2.2L Engines and 1994–96 3.1L Engines

▶ See Figure 41

1. Visually check the connector, making sure it is connected properly and all of the terminals are straight, tight and free of corrosion.
2. Unplug the IAC connector and check resistance between the IAC terminals. Resistance between terminals A to B and terminals C to D should be 40–80 ohms. If resistance is not within specification, the IAC valve must be replaced.
3. Check resistance between the IAC terminals A to C, A to D, B to C and B to D. Resistance should be infinite. If not, the IAC valve is faulty.
4. If the resistance is within specification, check the IAC circuits back to the PCM for continuity.
5. If the valve and circuits are functional, the computer control module may be faulty.

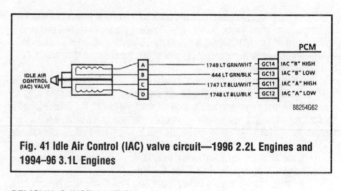

Fig. 41 Idle Air Control (IAC) valve circuit—1996 2.2L Engines and 1994–96 3.1L Engines

REMOVAL & INSTALLATION

▶ See Figure 42

➡On some models it may be necessary to remove the air inlet assembly.

1. Disconnect the negative battery cable.
2. Detach the IAC valve electrical connector.
3. Remove the IAC valve by performing the following:

a. On thread-mounted units, use a 1¼ in. (32mm) wrench.

b. On flange-mounted units, remove the mounting screw assemblies.

4. Remove the IAC valve, then remove the and discard the IAC valve gasket or O-ring.

To install:

5. Clean the mounting surfaces by performing the following:

✳✳ WARNING

NEVER soak the IAC valve in any liquid cleaner or solvent!

Unplug the Idle Air Control (IAC) valve electrical connector

Unfasten the IAC valve-to-throttle body retaining screws

Carefully pull the IAC valve assembly away from the throttle body . . .

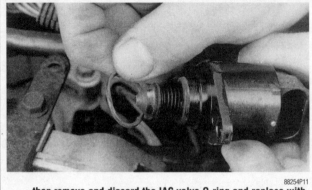

. . . then remove and discard the IAC valve O-ring and replace with a new one during installation

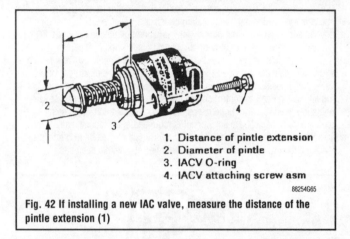

1. Distance of pintle extension
2. Diameter of pintle
3. IACV O-ring
4. IACV attaching screw asm

Fig. 42 If installing a new IAC valve, measure the distance of the pintle extension (1)

a. If servicing a thread-mounted valve, remove the old gasket material from the surface of the throttle body to ensure proper sealing of the new gasket.

b. If servicing a flange-mounted valve, clean the IAC valve surfaces on the throttle body to assure proper seal of the new O-ring and contact of the IAC valve flange.

6. If installing a new IAC valve, measure the distance between the tip of the IAC valve pintle and the mounting flange. If the distance is greater than 1.102 in. (28mm), use finger pressure to slowly retract the pintle. The force required to retract the pintle of a new valve will not cause damage to the valve. If reinstalling the original IAC valve, do not attempt to adjust the pintle in this manner.

7. Install the IAC valve into the throttle body by performing the following:

a. With thread-mounted valves, install with a new gasket. Using a 1¼ in. (32mm) wrench, tighten to 13 ft. lbs. (18 Nm).

b. With flange-mounted valves, lubricate a new O-ring with transmission fluid and install on the IAC valve. Install the IAC valve to the throttle body. Install the mounting screws using a suitable thread locking compound. Tighten to 28 inch lbs. (3.2 Nm).

8. Attach the IAC valve electrical connector.

9. Connect the negative battery cable.

10. No physical adjustment of the IAC valve assembly is required after installation. Reset the IAC valve pintle position by performing the following:

a. Depress the accelerator pedal slightly.

b. Start the engine and run for 5 seconds.

c. Turn the ignition switch to the **OFF** position for 10 seconds.

d. Restart the engine and check for proper idle operation.

Engine Coolant Temperature (ECT) Sensor

OPERATION

▶ See Figure 43

Most engine functions are affected by the coolant temperature. Determining whether the engine is hot or cold is largely dependent on the temperature of the

coolant. An accurate temperature signal to the PCM is supplied by the coolant temperature sensor or Engine Coolant Temperature (ECT) sensor. The coolant temperature sensor is a thermistor mounted in the engine coolant stream. A thermistor is an electrical device that varies its resistance in relation to changes in temperature. Low coolant temperature produces a high resistance and high coolant temperature produces low resistance. The PCM supplies a signal of 5 volts to the coolant temperature sensor through a resistor in the PCM and measures the voltage. The voltage will be high when the engine is cold and low when the engine is hot.

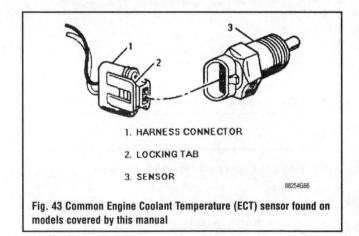

1. HARNESS CONNECTOR

2. LOCKING TAB

3. SENSOR

Fig. 43 Common Engine Coolant Temperature (ECT) sensor found on models covered by this manual

TESTING

▶ See Figures 44, 45 and 46

➡Some vehicles are equipped with a 3-terminal ECT sensor. On these vehicles, terminals A and B are the signal terminals and terminal C supplies voltage to the coolant temperature gauge in the dash.

1. Visually check the connector, making sure it is connected properly and all of the terminals are straight, tight and free of corrosion.
2. Detach the ECT sensor connector.
3. Carefully remove the cap from the cooling system and place a thermometer in the engine coolant.
4. Measure ECT sensor resistance between terminals A and B with the engine cold and at operating temperature.
5. Compare the meter readings with the resistance chart. If the readings aren't within specifications, replace the sensor.

REMOVAL & INSTALLATION

1. Disconnect the negative battery cable.
2. Relieve the cooling system pressure.
3. If necessary, raise and safely support the vehicle, then drain the cooling system into a suitable container, to a level below the ECT sensor.
4. If raised, lower the vehicle.

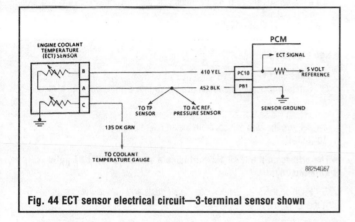

Fig. 44 ECT sensor electrical circuit—3-terminal sensor shown

°C	°F	OHMS
	Temperature vs Resistance Values (Approximate)	
100	212	177
90	194	241
80	176	332
70	158	467
60	140	667
50	122	973
45	113	1188
40	104	1459
35	95	1802
30	86	2238
25	77	2796
20	68	3520
15	59	4450
10	50	5670
5	41	7280
0	32	9420
-5	23	12300
-10	14	16180
-15	5	21450
-20	-4	28680
-30	-22	52700
-40	-40	100700

Fig. 46 Engine Coolant Temperature (ECT) sensor and Intake Air Temperature (IAT) sensor temperature vs. resistance values

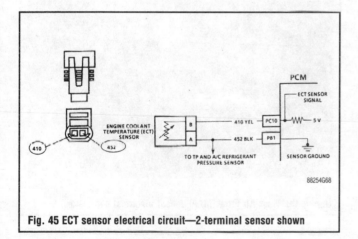

Fig. 45 ECT sensor electrical circuit—2-terminal sensor shown

5. Detach the electrical connector from the Engine Coolant Temperature (ECT) sensor.
6. Carefully back out the ECT sensor.
To Install:
7. Coat the threads of the sensor with a suitable sealer.
8. Install the coolant temperature sensor and tighten as follows:
   a. 2.0L and 2.2L engines: 18.5 ft. lbs. (25 Nm)
   b. 2.3L engine: 9.5 ft. lbs. (13 Nm)
   c. 2.8L and 3.1L engines: 22 ft. lbs. (30 Nm).
9. Attach the sensor electrical connector.
10. Fill the cooling system as required.
11. Connect the negative battery cable, then start the engine and check for leaks.

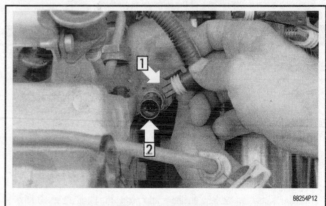

Unplug the electrical connector (1) from the ECT sensor (2)

Intake Air Temperature (IAT) Sensor

OPERATION

♦ See Figure 47

The IAT sensor is a thermistor which supplies intake air temperature information to the PCM. The sensor produces high resistance at low temperatures and low resistance at high temperatures. The PCM supplies a 5 volt signal to the sensor and measures the output voltage. The voltage signal will be low when the air is cold and high when the air is hot. The IAT is located in or near the air intake duct.

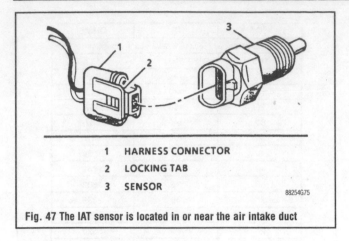

1 HARNESS CONNECTOR
2 LOCKING TAB
3 SENSOR

88254G75

Fig. 47 The IAT sensor is located in or near the air intake duct

TESTING

1. Remove the Intake Air Temperature (IAT) sensor from the vehicle.
2. Connect a digital ohmmeter to the two terminals of the sensor.
3. Using a calibrated thermometer, compare the resistance of the sensor to the temperature of the ambient air. Refer to the temperature vs. resistance chart.
4. Repeat the test at two other temperature points, heating or cooling the air as necessary with a hair dryer or other suitable tool.
5. If the sensor does not meet specifications, it must be replaced.

REMOVAL & INSTALLATION

1. Disconnect the negative battery cable.
2. Detach the sensor electrical connector locking tab and/or unplug detach the connector.
3. If equipped, unfasten the retaining clamp.
4. Carefully remove the sensor.
5. Installation is the reverse of the removal procedure.

Mass Air Flow (MAF) Sensor

OPERATION

The Mass Air Flow (MAF) sensor, found on the 1996 3.1L engine, measures the amount of air passing through it. The PCM uses this information to determine the operating condition of the engine, to control fuel delivery. A large quantity of air indicates acceleration, while a small quantity indicates deceleration or idle.

The MAF sensor used on these vehicles is of the hot-wire type. Current is supplied to the sensing wire to maintain a calibrated temperature, and as air flow increases or decreases the current will vary. This varying current is directly proportional to air mass.

The MAF sensor on the 3.8L engine is attached to the throttle body. On the 5.7L engine, the MAF sensor is mounted between the air ducts.

TESTING

▶ **See Figure 48**

1. Visually check the connector, making sure it is connected properly and all of the terminals are straight, tight and free of corrosion.
2. With the engine running, lightly tap on the MAF sensor and wiggle the wires at the connector and watch for the idle to change. A common problem is MAF sensor wire damage.
3. Backprobe using a DVOM set to the Hertz scale between terminals A and B. Simulate operating conditions by blowing air across the sensor. There should be a frequency swing from the air crossing the wire in the sensor. A normal flow signal will be close to 1200 hertz. If the frequency is not shown, or not proportionate to the air blown across the sensor, the sensor is faulty.
4. Check for battery positive (B+) on terminal C and ground on terminal B. If voltage or ground are not present. check the circuits back to the PCM for continuity.

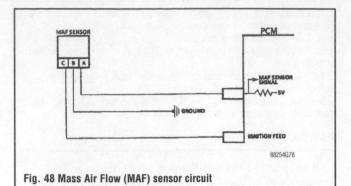

88254G78

Fig. 48 Mass Air Flow (MAF) sensor circuit

5. If you receive the proper amount of voltage at the electrical connector and still have a driveability problem, replace the MAF sensor.
6. If the sensor and circuits are functional, the PCM may be faulty.

REMOVAL & INSTALLATION

▶ **See Figure 49**

1. Disconnect the negative battery cable.
2. Carefully the clamps and remove the air intake ducts from the MAF sensor.
3. Detach the sensor electrical connection.
4. Remove the MAF sensor from the air filter housing.

To install:

➡**The arrows on the MAF sensor indicate air flow and MUST point toward the engine.**

5. Position the MAF sensor into the air ducts and tighten the clamps to 36 inch lbs. (4 Nm).

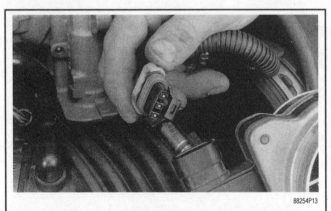

88254P13

Unplug the Mass Air Flow (MAF) sensor electrical connector . . .

88254P14

. . . then remove the MAF sensor from the vehicle

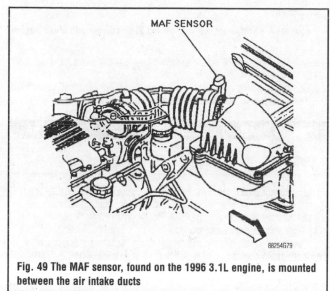

Fig. 49 The MAF sensor, found on the 1996 3.1L engine, is mounted between the air intake ducts

6. Attach the sensor electrical connector.
7. Connect the negative battery cable.

Manifold Absolute Pressure (MAP) Sensor

OPERATION

The MAP sensor measures the changes in intake manifold pressure, which result from engine load/speed changes and converts this information to a voltage output. The MAP sensor reading is the opposite of a vacuum gauge reading: when manifold pressure is high, MAP sensor value is high and vacuum is low. A MAP sensor will produce a low output on engine coast-down with a closed throttle while a wide open throttle will produce a high output. The high output is produced because the pressure inside the manifold is the same as outside the manifold, so 100 percent of the outside air pressure is measured.

The MAP sensor is also used to measure barometric pressure under certain conditions, which allows the PCM to automatically adjust for different altitudes.

The MAP sensor changes the 5 volt signal supplied by the PCM, which reads the change and uses the information to control fuel delivery and ignition timing.

TESTING

Except 1996 2.2L Engines and 1994–96 3.1L Engines

▶ See Figures 50 and 51

1. Visually check the connector, making sure it is connected properly and all of the terminals are straight, tight and free of corrosion.
2. Check the vacuum hose connected to the MAP sensor. Replace the hose if it is in bad condition, plugged or leaking.

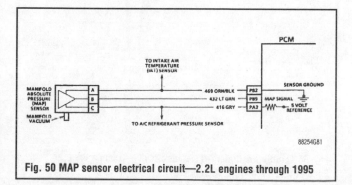

Fig. 50 MAP sensor electrical circuit—2.2L engines through 1995

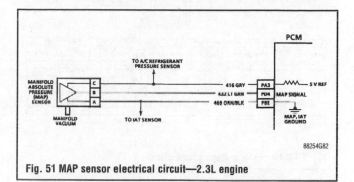

Fig. 51 MAP sensor electrical circuit—2.3L engine

3. Detach the electrical connector from the MAP sensor.
4. Turn the ignition switch to the **ON** position with the engine **OFF**.
5. Connect a voltmeter to a known good ground and terminal C of the harness:
   a. If there is 4.5–5.5 volts, proceed to the next step.
   b. If the voltage is below 4.5 volts or above 5.5 volts, check the MAP sensor reference circuit.
6. With he voltmeter connected to terminal C, connect the other voltmeter lead to terminal A.
   a. If there is 4.5–5.5 volts, proceed to the next step.
   b. If the voltage is below 4.5 volts or above 5.5 volts, check the MAP sensor ground circuit.
7. Turn the ignition switch to the **OFF** position.
8. Attach the electrical connector to the MAP sensor.
9. Remove the vacuum hose from the MAP sensor and connect a hand operated vacuum pump to the MAP sensor.
10. Use a voltmeter to backprobe the connector terminals A and B.
11. Turn the ignition switch to the **ON** position and check the voltage at terminals A and B:
   a. If the voltage is 4.0–4.8 volts, proceed to the next step.
   b. If the voltage is below 4.0 volts or above 4.8 volts, replace the MAP sensor.
12. Observe the voltage measurement while slowly applying 10 inches of vacuum as indicated on the pump gauge. The value should change smoothly and drop 1.5–2.1 volts:
   a. If the MAP sensor voltage drops 1.5–2.1 volts, the sensor is operating properly. Check the vacuum source.
   b. If the MAP sensor voltage drops less than 1.5 volts or more than 2.1 volts, replace the MAP sensor.

1996 2.2L Engines and 1994–96 3.1L Engines

▶ See Figures 52 and 53

1. Visually check the connector, making sure it is connected properly and all of the terminals are straight, tight and free of corrosion.
2. With the ignition **ON**, check the voltage between terminals A and B. It should be above 4 volts. Apply 15 in. Hg of vacuum at the MAP vacuum port and check the voltage again. The voltage should be 2 volts now.

➡**When pumping up and releasing the vacuum, check to make sure the voltage readings are smooth. When applying vacuum to the sensor, the change in voltage should happen instantly. A slow change in voltage could point to a faulty sensor.**

3. If the sensor voltage is not within specification, check for a 5 volt reference at terminal C. If the reference signal is found, the sensor is faulty.

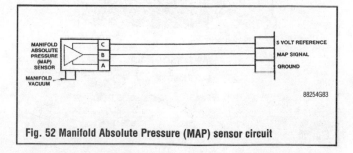

Fig. 52 Manifold Absolute Pressure (MAP) sensor circuit

Altitude—Meters	Altitude—Feet	Pressure—kPa	Voltage Range
Below 305	Below 1000	100–98	3.8–5.5V
305–610	1000–2000	98–95	3.6–5.3V
610–914	2000–3000	95–92	3.5–5.1V
914–1219	3000–4000	92–89	3.3–5.0V
1219–1524	4000–5000	89–86	3.2–4.8V
1524–1829	5000–6000	86–83	3.0–4.6V
1829–2133	6000–7000	83–80	2.9–4.5V
2133–2438	7000–8000	80–77	2.8–4.3V
2438–2743	8000–9000	77–74	2.6–4.2V
2743–3948	9000–10,000	74–71	2.5–4.0V

88254G84

Fig. 53 MAP sensor voltage specifications

4. If the sensor and circuits are functional, the PCM may be faulty.

REMOVAL & INSTALLATION

▶ **See Figures 54 and 55**

1. Disconnect the negative battery cable.
2. Detach the MAP sensor electrical connector. Unplug the vacuum hose.
3. Unfasten the retaining screws/bolts, then remove the MAP sensor from the vehicle.

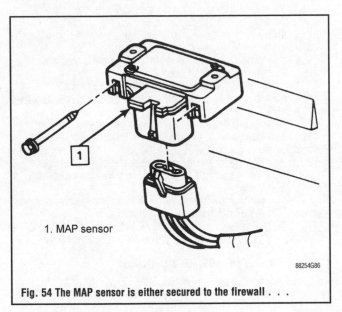

1. MAP sensor

88254G86

Fig. 54 The MAP sensor is either secured to the firewall . . .

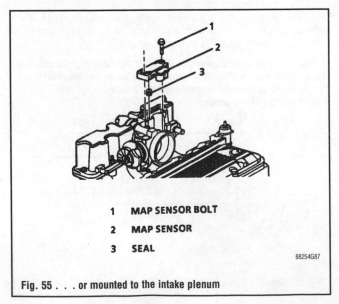

1   MAP SENSOR BOLT

2   MAP SENSOR

3   SEAL

88254G87

Fig. 55 . . . or mounted to the intake plenum

To install:

➡ **If equipped, lightly coat the seal on the MAP sensor with clean engine oil.**

    a. Position the MAP sensor to the intake plenum and attach the vacuum line.
    b. Install the retaining bolts, then attach the sensor electrical connector.
4. Connect the negative battery cable.

Throttle Position Sensor (TPS)

OPERATION

The TP sensor is mounted to the throttle body, opposite the throttle lever and is connected to the throttle shaft. Its function is to sense the current throttle valve position and relay that information to the PCM. Throttle position information allows the PCM to generate the required injector control signals. The TP sensor consists of a potentiometer which alters the flow of voltage according to the position of a wiper on the variable resistor windings, in proportion to the movement of the throttle shaft.

TESTING

Except 1996 2.2L Engines and 1994–96 3.1L Engines

▶ **See Figure 56**

1. Visually check the connector, making sure it is connected properly and all of the terminals are straight, tight and free of corrosion.
2. Connect a voltmeter to a known good engine ground and TPS terminal A (reference signal). Turn the ignition switch to the **ON** position to check the reference voltage:
    a. If 4.5–5.5 volts are present at terminal A, proceed to the next step.
    b. If the voltage is outside of specifications, check the reference circuit.
3. Connect a voltmeter to the TPS connector terminal C (TPS signal voltage) and to terminal B (sensor ground).
4. Turn the ignition switch to the **ON** position, with the engine **OFF**.
5. Check the TPS voltage with the throttle in the fully closed position, then operate the throttle to the full open position, while watching the voltmeter.
6. For 2.0L, 2.2L, 2.8L and 3.1L engines, note the following:
    a. If the voltage at closed throttle is 0.2–0.9 volts and has a smooth increase to 4.5–4.7 volts when the throttle is fully open, the TPS is operating normally.
    b. If the voltage at closed throttle is below 0.2 volts, replace the TPS.
    c. If the voltage at wide open throttle increases above 4.7 volts, replace the TPS.
7. For 2.3L engines, note the following:
    a. If the voltage at closed throttle is 0.29–0.98 volts and has a smooth increase to 4.5–4.7 volts when the throttle is fully open, the TPS is operating normally.
    b. If the voltage at closed throttle is below 0.29 volts, replace the TPS.
    c. If the voltage at wide open throttle increases above 4.8 volts, replace the TPS.

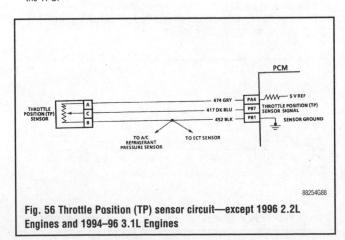

88254G88

Fig. 56 Throttle Position (TP) sensor circuit—except 1996 2.2L Engines and 1994–96 3.1L Engines

1996 2.2L Engines and 1994–96 3.1L Engines

♦ See Figure 57

1. Visually check the connector, making sure it is connected properly and all of the terminals are straight, tight and free of corrosion.
2. With the ignition in the **ON** position, check the voltage at terminal C. The voltage should read less that 0.5 volts.
3. Operate the throttle, while watching the voltage. The voltage should increase smoothly to 5 volts as the throttle is opened.
4. If the voltage is not within specification, check the 5 volt reference signal circuit at terminal A and ground the circuit at terminal B for the proper signal. If the correct signal is found, the sensor is faulty. If the proper signal is not found, check the circuits back to the computer control module for continuity.
5. If the circuits are functional, the PCM may be faulty.

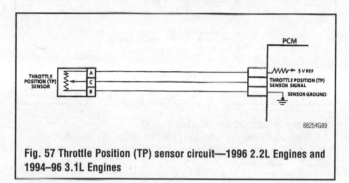

Fig. 57 Throttle Position (TP) sensor circuit—1996 2.2L Engines and 1994–96 3.1L Engines

REMOVAL & INSTALLATION

♦ See Figure 58

1. Disconnect the negative battery cable.
2. Detach the TPS electrical connector.
3. Remove the mounting screws.
4. Remove the TPS and, if equipped, sensor seal from the throttle body.

To install:

5. Place the TP sensor in position. Align the TP sensor lever with the sensor drive lever on the throttle body.
6. Install the TP sensor mounting screws and tighten to 18 inch lbs. (2 Nm).
7. Attach the electrical connector, then connect the negative battery cable.

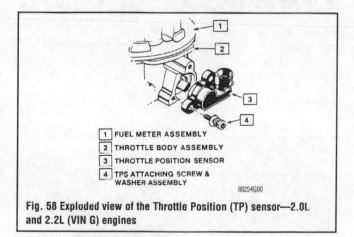

Fig. 58 Exploded view of the Throttle Position (TP) sensor—2.0L and 2.2L (VIN G) engines

Camshaft Position (CMP) Sensor

OPERATION

The PCM uses the CMP sensor to determine the position of the No. 1 piston during its power stroke. This signal is used by the PCM to calculate fuel injection mode of operation.

If the cam signal is lost while the engine is running, the fuel injection system will shift to a calculated fuel injected mode based on the last fuel injection pulse, and the engine will continue to run.

TESTING

➡ The best method to test this sensor is with the use of an oscilloscope.

2.2L (VIN 4) Engine

♦ See Figure 59

➡ This procedure applies to 1996 models only.

The Camshaft Position (CMP) sensor used in these engines is a three wire, Hall effect type sensor. The sensor requires power and ground to function. When performing this test, backprobe all connectors.

1. Visually check the connector, making sure it is connected properly and all of the terminals are straight, tight and free of corrosion.
2. With the ignition in the **ON** position, check the sensor voltage using an oscilloscope. When the starter is briefly operated, a square wave pattern, alternating from 0–12 volts should be seen at terminal C. If the voltage is within specification, the sensor is functional
3. If the sensor voltage is not within specifications, use a DVOM to check terminal A for battery positive (B+). If battery positive (B+) is not present, check the circuit continuity and repair as necessary.
4. If battery positive (B+) is present at terminal C, check terminal B for proper ground. If ground is not present check the circuit for continuity and repair as necessary.
5. If the sensor and circuits are functional, the PCM may be faulty.

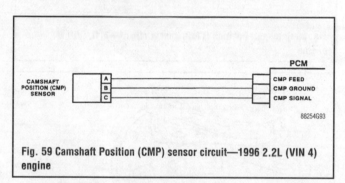

Fig. 59 Camshaft Position (CMP) sensor circuit—1996 2.2L (VIN 4) engine

3.1L (VIN M) Engine

♦ See Figure 60

1. Visually check the connector, making sure it is connected properly and all of the terminals are straight, tight and free of corrosion.
2. With the ignition in the **ON** position, check the sensor voltage using an oscilloscope. When the starter is briefly operated, a square wave pattern, alternating from 0–12 volts should be seen at terminal B. If the voltage is within specification, the sensor is functional
3. If the sensor voltage is not within specifications, use a DVOM to check terminal A for battery positive (B+). If battery positive (B+) is not present, check the circuit continuity and repair as necessary.
4. If battery positive (B+) is present at terminal A, check terminal C for proper ground. If ground is not present check the circuit for continuity and repair as necessary.
5. If the sensor and circuits are functional, the PCM may be faulty.

REMOVAL & INSTALLATION

1996 2.2L (VIN 4) Engine

♦ See Figure 61

1. Disconnect the negative battery cable.
2. Detach the CMP sensor harness connector.
3. Unfasten the CMP sensor bolt, then remove the sensor from the vehicle.

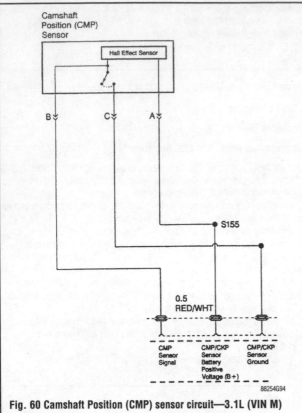

Fig. 60 Camshaft Position (CMP) sensor circuit—3.1L (VIN M) engine

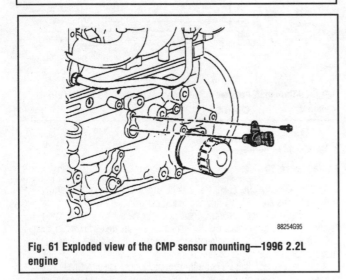

Fig. 61 Exploded view of the CMP sensor mounting—1996 2.2L engine

4. Inspect the sensor O-ring for wear, cracks or deterioration and replaced if necessary.

To install:

5. Lubricate a new sensor O-ring with clean engine oil, then install on the sensor.

6. Install the CMP sensor and secure with the retaining bolt. Tighten the bolt to 6–9 ft. lbs. (9–12 Nm).

7. Attach the sensor harness connector.

8. Connect the negative battery cable.

3.1L Engine

♦ **See Figure 62**

1. Disconnect the negative battery cable.
2. Use a block of wood and a floor jack to properly support the engine oil pan.
3. Remove the right engine mount. It is secured with 5 bolts and 1 nut.

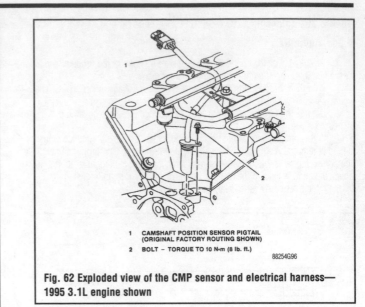

1 CAMSHAFT POSITION SENSOR PIGTAIL (ORIGINAL FACTORY ROUTING SHOWN)
2 BOLT – TORQUE TO 10 N•m (8 lb. ft.)

Fig. 62 Exploded view of the CMP sensor and electrical harness—1995 3.1L engine shown

4. Remove the serpentine drive belt.
5. Remove the retaining nuts and bolt, then remove the alternator braces.
6. Unbolt the power steering pump, then position the pump aside. Do NOT disconnect the fluid lines.
7. Detach the CMP sensor electrical connector.

➡**Use special tool J 38125-A. This tool requires the removal of the plastic connector from the wires for clearance. Do NOT cut the electrical connector.**

8. Remove the retaining bolt, then remove the CMP sensor from the vehicle.

To install:

9. Install the CMP sensor. Reroute the electrical pigtail under the power steering pump and alternator pencil brace.
10. Install the alternator braces.
11. Install the serpentine drive belt.
12. Install the right engine mount, then connect the negative battery cable.

3X/7X Signal Crankshaft Position (CKP) Sensor

OPERATION

The 3x Crankshaft Position (CKP) sensor is used on 1994–95 3.1L (VIN M) engines. The 1996 3.1L engines used the 7x sensor. This sensor provides a signal to the PCM through the ignition control module. The PCM uses this signal to determine RPM and crankshaft position.

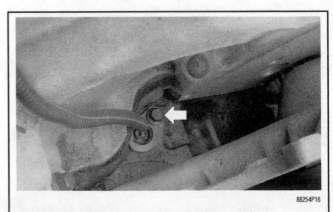

Location of the CMP sensor retaining bolt (see arrow)

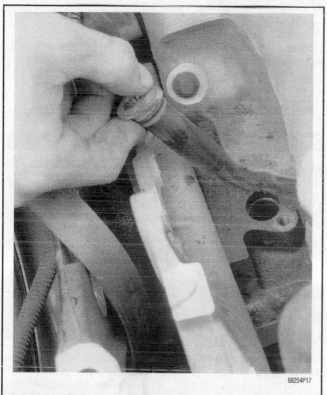

Remove the CMP sensor from the vehicle

88254P17

TESTING

▶ See Figure 63

➡ **The best method to test this sensor is with the use of an oscilloscope.**

1. Visually check the connector, making sure it is connected properly and all of the terminals are straight, tight and free of corrosion.

2. With the ignition in the **ON** position, check the sensor voltage using an oscilloscope. When the starter is briefly operated, a sine wave pattern, alternat-

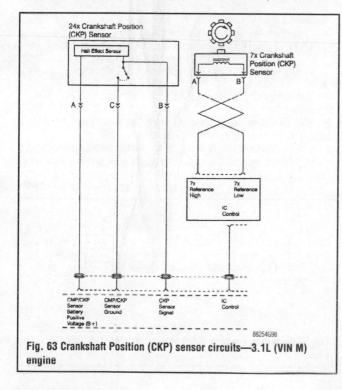

88254G98

Fig. 63 Crankshaft Position (CKP) sensor circuits—3.1L (VIN M) engine

ing from high voltage to low voltage should be seen. If the voltage is less than 0.1 volt the sensor is faulty.

3. If the voltage is within specification, check the resistance at the CKP terminals. If the resistance is not between 900–1200 ohms, the sensor is faulty.

4. If the signal and resistance of the CKP sensor are within specifications, use a DVOM to check for continuity (short, open or high resistance greater than 0.50 ohms) in the CKP circuit wires and repair as necessary.

5. If the sensor and circuits are functional, the computer control module may be faulty.

REMOVAL & INSTALLATION

▶ See Figure 64

1. Turn the steering wheel all the way to the left.
2. Be sure the ignition is in the **OFF** or **LOCK** position, then disconnect the negative battery cable.
3. Raise and safely support the vehicle.
4. Disengage the wiring harness connector from the sensor.
5. Remove the sensor retaining bolt, then carefully remove the sensor from the lower right side of the engine block.

To install:

6. Inspect the sensor O-ring and replace, if necessary.
7. Lubricate the O-ring with clean engine oil, then install the sensor into the hole in the side of the engine block.
8. Install the sensor retaining bolt and tighten to 71 inch lbs. (8 Nm).
9. Engage the sensor wiring harness at the module.
10. Carefully lower the vehicle, then connect the negative battery cable.
11. Turn the steering wheel back to its original position.

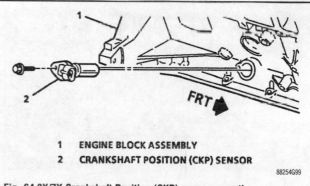

1	**ENGINE BLOCK ASSEMBLY**
2	**CRANKSHAFT POSITION (CKP) SENSOR**

88254G99

Fig. 64 3X/7X Crankshaft Position (CKP) sensor mounting

24X Signal Crankshaft Position (CKP) Sensor

OPERATION

The 24X CKP sensor, found on 1994–96 3.1L engines, is used to improve the idle spark control at engine speeds up to approximately 2000 RPM.

TESTING

➡ **The best method to test this sensor is with the use of an oscilloscope.**

1. Visually check the connector, making sure it is connected properly and all of the terminals are straight, tight and free of corrosion.

2. With the ignition in the **ON** position, check the sensor voltage using an oscilloscope. When the starter is briefly operated, a square wave pattern, alternating between 0–12 volts should be seen at terminal B. If the voltage is within specification, the sensor is functional.

3. If the voltage falls out of range, use a DVOM to check terminal A for battery positive (B+). If battery positive (B+) is not present, check the circuit continuity and repair as necessary.

4. If battery positive (B+) is found at terminal A, check the terminal C for proper ground. If ground is not present, check the circuit for continuity and repair as necessary.

5. If the sensor and circuits are functional, the PCM may be faulty.

REMOVAL & INSTALLATION

3.1L (VIN M) Engine

♦ See Figure 65

1. Be sure the ignition is in the **OFF** or **LOCK** position, then disconnect the negative battery cable.
2. Remove the serpentine belt from the crankshaft pulley.
3. Raise and support the vehicle safely.
4. Remove the crankshaft harmonic balancer assembly from the front of the engine, as follows:
   a. Remove the bolt and washer from the crankshaft harmonic balancer.
   b. Remove the retaining bolts from the crankshaft pulley, then remove the pulley from the balancer.
   c. Using J–24420–B or an equivalent torsional damper remover, pull the balancer from the crankshaft.

➡Note the routing of the CKP sensor harness before removal.

5. Remove the harness retaining clip with the bolt. Detach the sensor harness connector.
6. Remove the sensor retaining bolts, then remove the sensor from the engine.

To install:

7. Install the sensor to the engine and tighten the retaining bolts to 8 ft. lbs. (10 Nm).

The 24X CKP sensor, found on 3.1L (VIN M) engines, is mounted to the timing chain (front) cover

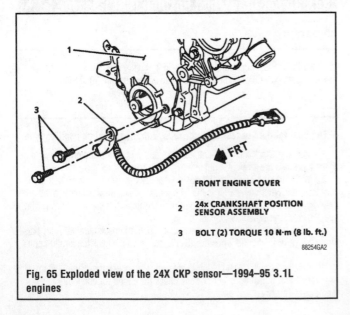

1   FRONT ENGINE COVER

2   24x CRANKSHAFT POSITION
    SENSOR ASSEMBLY

3   BOLT (2) TORQUE 10 N·m (8 lb. ft.)

88254GA2

Fig. 65 Exploded view of the 24X CKP sensor—1994–95 3.1L engines

8. Route the harness as noted during removal, then install the harness retaining clip and secure with the bolt. Tighten the bolt to 8 ft. lbs. (10 Nm).
9. Attach the sensor electrical connector.
10. Use J–29113, or an equivalent installer, to pull the balancer onto the crankshaft. Install the crankshaft balancer bolt and tighten it to 110 ft. lbs. (150 Nm).
11. Install and tighten the crankshaft pulley bolts.
12. Install the serpentine drive belt.
13. Carefully lower the vehicle.
14. Connect the negative battery cable.

Crankshaft Position (CKP) Sensor

OPERATION

The CKP sensor provides a signal through the ignition module which the PCM uses as a reference to calculate RPM and crankshaft position.

TESTING

➡The best method to test this sensor is with the use of an oscilloscope.

2.0L and 2.2L Engines

1988–95 VEHICLES

♦ See Figure 66

1. Visually check the connector, making sure it is connected properly and all of the terminals are straight, tight and free of corrosion.
2. Connect a suitable scan tool to the Data Link Connector (DLC), set the scan tool to check for a rpm signal or the CKP sensor reference pulse. Crank the engine briefly while observing the readings on the scan tool:
   a. If the scan tool registers a rpm reading or has a steady reference pulse from the CKP sensor, the sensor is operating normally.
   b. If the rpm reading or reference pulse is erratic, proceed to the next step.
   c. If there is no rpm reading or reference pulse, proceed to the next step.
3. Turn the ignition switch to the OFF position, then detach the connector from the CKP sensor.
4. Connect a test light between a known good engine ground and terminal C, at the CKP sensor connector:
   a. If the test light illuminates, proceed to the next step.
   b. If the test light does not illuminate, check the CKP sensor feed circuit.
5. Turn the ignition switch to the OFF position.
6. Connect the test light to the positive battery terminal.
7. Connect the test light to terminal B of the CKP sensor connector:
   a. If the test light illuminates, proceed to the next step.
   b. If the test light does not illuminate, check the CKP sensor ground circuit.
8. With the scan tool connected to the DLC, turn the ignition switch to the ON position.
9. With the test light, touch terminal B at the CKP sensor connector, while observing the scan tool for a reference pulse change.
   a. If the reference pulse changes (or increments), replace the CKP sensor.
   b. If the reference pulse does not change, check the reference signal circuit.

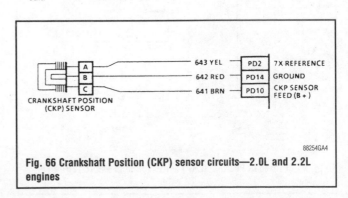

CRANKSHAFT POSITION
(CKP) SENSOR

A	643 YEL	PD2	7X REFERENCE
B	642 RED	PD14	GROUND
C	641 BRN	PD10	CKP SENSOR FEED (B +)

88254GA4

Fig. 66 Crankshaft Position (CKP) sensor circuits—2.0L and 2.2L engines

1996 VEHICLES

The CKP sensor used on these vehicles is a three-wire, Hall effect type sensor. The sensor requires power and ground to function. When performing this test, backprobe all connectors.

1. Visually check the connector, making sure it is connected properly and all of the terminals are straight, tight and free of corrosion.
2. With the ignition in the **ON** position, check the sensor voltage using an oscilloscope. When the starter is briefly operated a square wave pattern, varying between 0–12 volts should be seen at terminal A.
3. If the voltage falls out of range, use a DVOM to check terminal C for battery positive (B+). If battery positive (B+) is not present, check the circuit continuity and repair as necessary.
4. If battery positive (B+) is found at terminal C, check the terminal B for proper ground. If ground is not present, check the circuit for continuity and repair as necessary.
5. If the sensor and circuits are functional, the PCM may be faulty.

2.3L Engine

♦ See Figure 67

1. Visually check the connector, making sure it is connected properly and all of the terminals are straight, tight and free of corrosion.
2. Connect a suitable scan tool to the Data Link Connector (DLC), set the

scan tool to check for a rpm signal or the CKP sensor reference pulse. Crank the engine briefly while observing the readings on the scan tool:
   a. If the scan tool registers a rpm reading or has a steady reference pulse from the CKP sensor, the sensor is operating normally.
   b. If the rpm reading or reference pulse is erratic, proceed to the next step.
   c. If there is no rpm reading or reference pulse, proceed to the next step.
3. Turn the ignition switch to the **OFF** position, then detach the connector from the CKP sensor.
4. Connect a test light between the CKP sensor terminals A and B, then briefly operate the starter motor while watching the voltmeter:
   a. If the voltage is greater than 0.2 volts, proceed to the next step.
   b. If the voltage is 0.2 volts AC or less, replace the CKP sensor.
5. Remove the CKP sensor from the engine.
6. Check the resistance between terminals A and B:
   a. If the resistance is between 500–900 ohms, proceed to the next step.
   b. If the resistance is below 500 ohms or above 900 ohms, replace the CKP sensor.
7. Verify that the CKP sensor is still magnetic:
   a. If the sensor is magnetic, the sensor is good.
   b. If the CKP sensor is not magnetic, replace the sensor.

2.8L and 3.1L (VIN T) Engines

♦ See Figure 68

1. Visually check the connector, making sure it is connected properly and all of the terminals are straight, tight and free of corrosion.
2. Connect a suitable scan tool to the Data Link Connector (DLC), set the scan tool to check for a rpm signal or the CKP sensor reference pulse. Crank the engine briefly while observing the readings on the scan tool:
   a. If the scan tool registers a rpm reading or has a steady reference pulse from the CKP sensor, the sensor is operating normally.
   b. If the rpm reading or reference pulse is erratic, proceed to the next step.
   c. If there is no rpm reading or reference pulse, proceed to the next step.
3. Turn the ignition switch to the **OFF** position, then detach the 2-wire connector from the ignition module.
4. Turn the ignition to the **ON** position.
5. Connect a test light between a known good engine ground and terminal A of the 2-wire ignition module connector:
   a. If the test light illuminates, proceed to the next step.
   b. If the test light does not illuminate, check the power supply circuit.
6. Turn the ignition switch to the **OFF** position.
7. Connect the test light to the positive battery terminal.
8. Connect the test light to terminal B of the 2-wire ignition module connector:
   a. If the test light illuminates, proceed to the next step.
   b. If the test light does not illuminate, check the ignition module ground circuit.

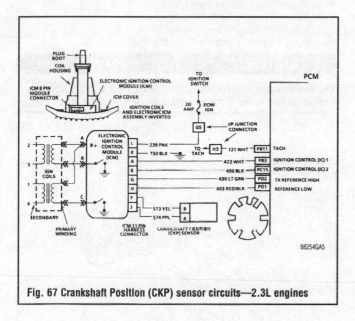

Fig. 67 Crankshaft Position (CKP) sensor circuits—2.3L engines

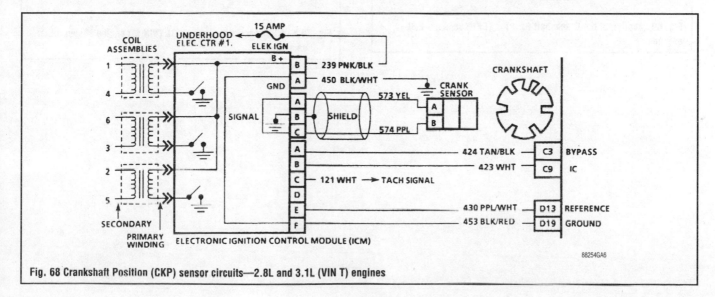

Fig. 68 Crankshaft Position (CKP) sensor circuits—2.8L and 3.1L (VIN T) engines

9. Disconnect the connector from the CKP sensor.
10. Check the resistance between terminals A and B of the CKP sensor:
    a. If the resistance is between 900–1200 ohms, proceed to the next step.
    b. If the resistance is below 900 ohms or above 1200 ohms, replace the CKP sensor.
11. Connect a voltmeter between the CKP sensor terminals A and B, then briefly operate the starter motor while watching the voltmeter:
    a. If the voltage is greater than 0.1 volt AC, the CKP sensor is operating properly.
    b. If the voltage is 0.1 volt AC or less, replace the CKP sensor.

REMOVAL & INSTALLATION

♦ **See Figure 69**

1. Disconnect the negative battery cable.
2. Disconnect the harness connector at the crankshaft sensor.
3. Remove the sensor attaching bolt.
4. Remove the crankshaft sensor from the engine.
5. Inspect the sensor O-ring for wear, cracks or signs of leakage. Replace it if necessary.
   To install:
6. Lubricate the O-ring with engine oil and install it on the sensor.
7. Position the sensor to the engine block and install the attaching bolt. Tighten the attaching bolt to 71–88 inch lbs. (8–10 Nm).
8. Connect the sensor harness connector.
9. Connect the negative battery cable.
10. Start the engine and test engine performance.

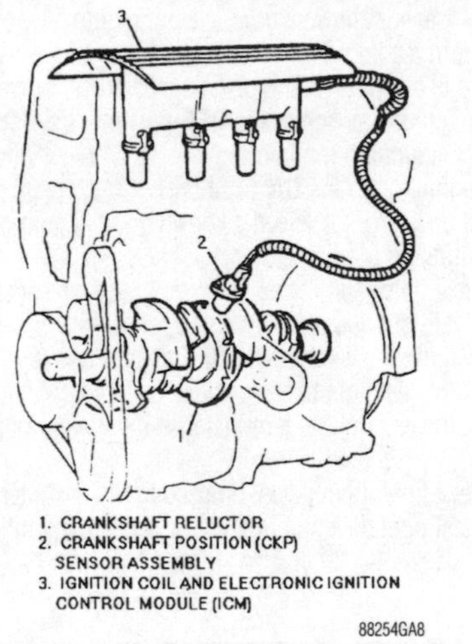

1. CRANKSHAFT RELUCTOR
2. CRANKSHAFT POSITION (CKP) SENSOR ASSEMBLY
3. IGNITION COIL AND ELECTRONIC IGNITION CONTROL MODULE (ICM)

88254GA8

Fig. 69 Location of the Crankshaft Position (CKP) sensor—2.3L engine

Knock Sensor (KS)

OPERATION

The knock sensor is usually mounted to the right lower side of the engine block. When spark knock or pinging is present, the sensor produces a voltage signal which is sent to the PCM. The PCM will then retard the ignition timing based on these signals.

TESTING

1. Connect a timing light to the vehicle, then start the engine.
2. Check that the timing is correct before testing the knock sensor operation.
3. If the timing is correct, tap on the front of the engine block with a metal object while observing the timing to see if the timing retards.
4. If the timing does not retard, the knock sensor may be defective.

REMOVAL & INSTALLATION

♦ **See Figure 70**

1. Disconnect the negative battery cable.
2. Raise and properly support the vehicle.
3. Disconnect the knock sensor wiring harness.
4. Remove the knock sensor from the engine block.

✳✳ CAUTION

The knock sensor is mounted in the engine block cooling passage. Engine coolant in the block will drain when the sensor is removed.

5. Installation is the reverse of removal. Tighten the sensor to 14 ft. lbs. (19 Nm).

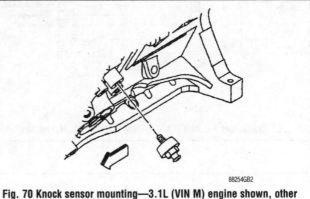

88254GB2

Fig. 70 Knock sensor mounting—3.1L (VIN M) engine shown, other engines similar

COMPONENT LOCATIONS

EMISSION COMPONENT LOCATIONS

1. Engine Coolant Temperature (ECT) sensor (located on lower rear of engine)
2. Camshaft Position (CMP) sensor (located on lower rear of engine)
3. Manifold Absolute Pressure (MAP) sensor
4. Exhaust Gas Recirculation (EGR) valve
5. Throttle Position (TP) sensor
6. Idle Air Control (IAC) valve
7. Mass Air Flow (MAF) sensor
8. Intake Air Temperature (IAT) sensor
9. Positive Crankcase Ventilation (PCV) valve
10. A/C refrigerant pressure sensor

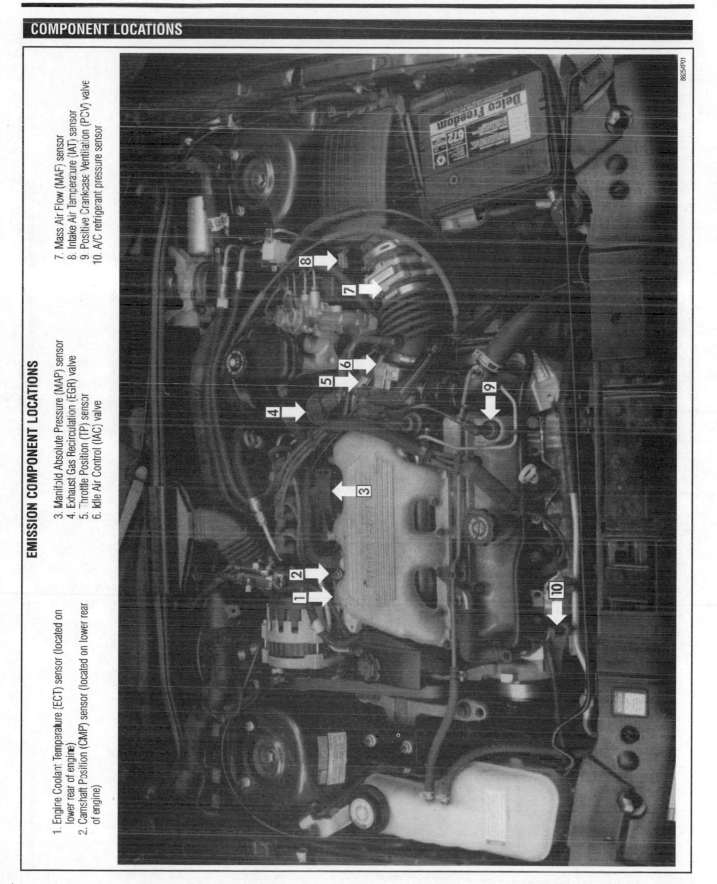

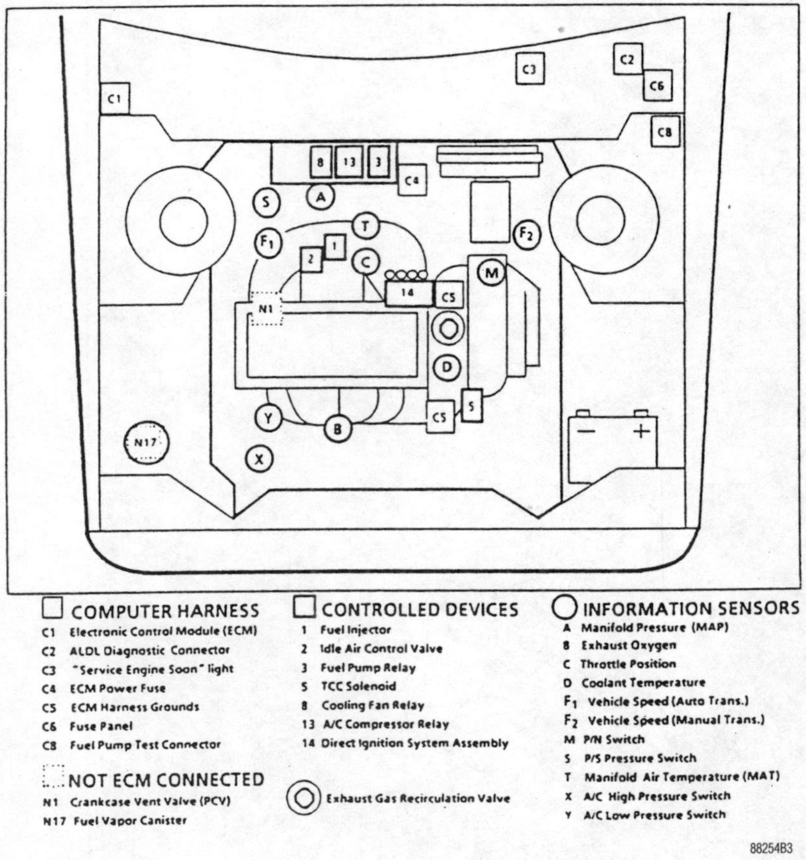
C1
C2
C3
C6
C8
8
13
3
C4
S
A
T
F1
F2
1
2
C
M
N1
14
C5
D
C5
5
Y
B
N17
X
COMPUTER HARNESS
C1 Electronic Control Module (ECM)
C2 ALDL Diagnostic Connector
C3 "Service Engine Soon" light
C4 ECM Power Fuse
C5 ECM Harness Grounds
C6 Fuse Panel
C8 Fuel Pump Test Connector
NOT ECM CONNECTED
N1 Crankcase Vent Valve (PCV)
N17 Fuel Vapor Canister
CONTROLLED DEVICES
1 Fuel Injector
2 Idle Air Control Valve
3 Fuel Pump Relay
5 TCC Solenoid
8 Cooling Fan Relay
13 A/C Compressor Relay
14 Direct Ignition System Assembly
Exhaust Gas Recirculation Valve
INFORMATION SENSORS
A Manifold Pressure (MAP)
B Exhaust Oxygen
C Throttle Position
D Coolant Temperature
F1 Vehicle Speed (Auto Trans.)
F2 Vehicle Speed (Manual Trans.)
M P/N Switch
S P/S Pressure Switch
T Manifold Air Temperature (MAT)
X A/C High Pressure Switch
Y A/C Low Pressure Switch
88254B3

Fig. 71 Component locations—2.0L engine

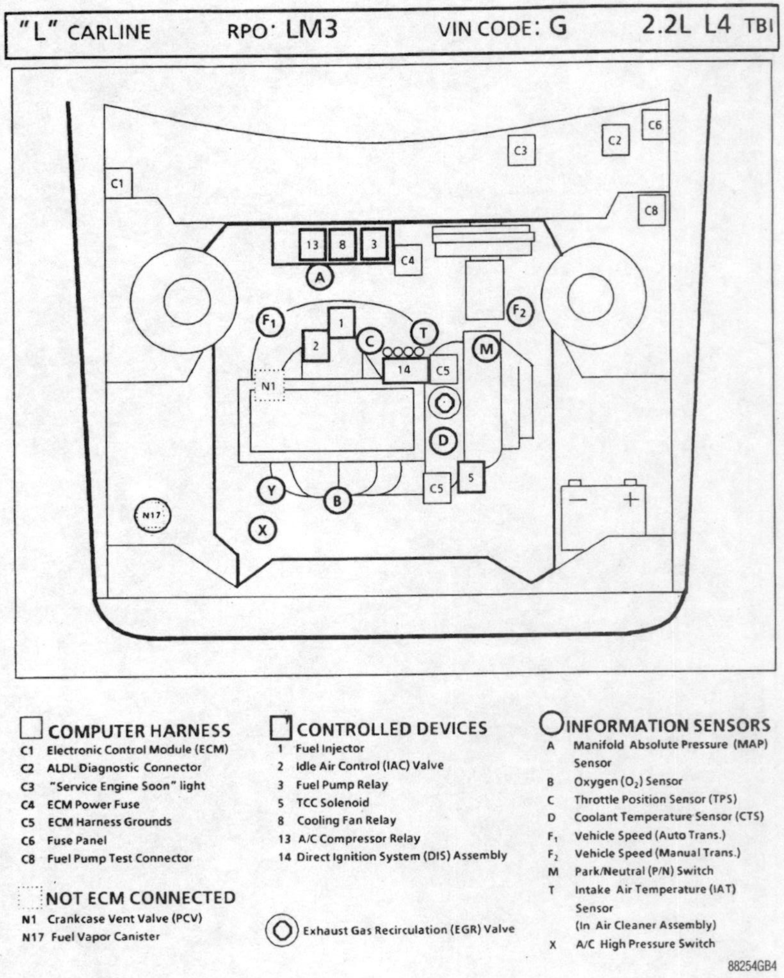
"L" CARLINE RPO: LM3 VIN CODE: G 2.2L L4 TBI
C1
C3
C2
C6
C8
13
8
3
C4
A
F1
1
2
C
T
F2
M
N1
14
C5
D
C5
5
Y
B
N17
X
COMPUTER HARNESS
C1 Electronic Control Module (ECM)
C2 ALDL Diagnostic Connector
C3 "Service Engine Soon" light
C4 ECM Power Fuse
C5 ECM Harness Grounds
C6 Fuse Panel
C8 Fuel Pump Test Connector
NOT ECM CONNECTED
N1 Crankcase Vent Valve (PCV)
N17 Fuel Vapor Canister
CONTROLLED DEVICES
1 Fuel Injector
2 Idle Air Control (IAC) Valve
3 Fuel Pump Relay
5 TCC Solenoid
8 Cooling Fan Relay
13 A/C Compressor Relay
14 Direct Ignition System (DIS) Assembly
Exhaust Gas Recirculation (EGR) Valve
INFORMATION SENSORS
A Manifold Absolute Pressure (MAP) Sensor
B Oxygen (O_2) Sensor
C Throttle Position Sensor (TPS)
D Coolant Temperature Sensor (CTS)
F1 Vehicle Speed (Auto Trans.)
F2 Vehicle Speed (Manual Trans.)
M Park/Neutral (P/N) Switch
T Intake Air Temperature (IAT) Sensor (In Air Cleaner Assembly)
X A/C High Pressure Switch
88254GB4

Fig. 72 Component locations—2.2L (VIN G) engine

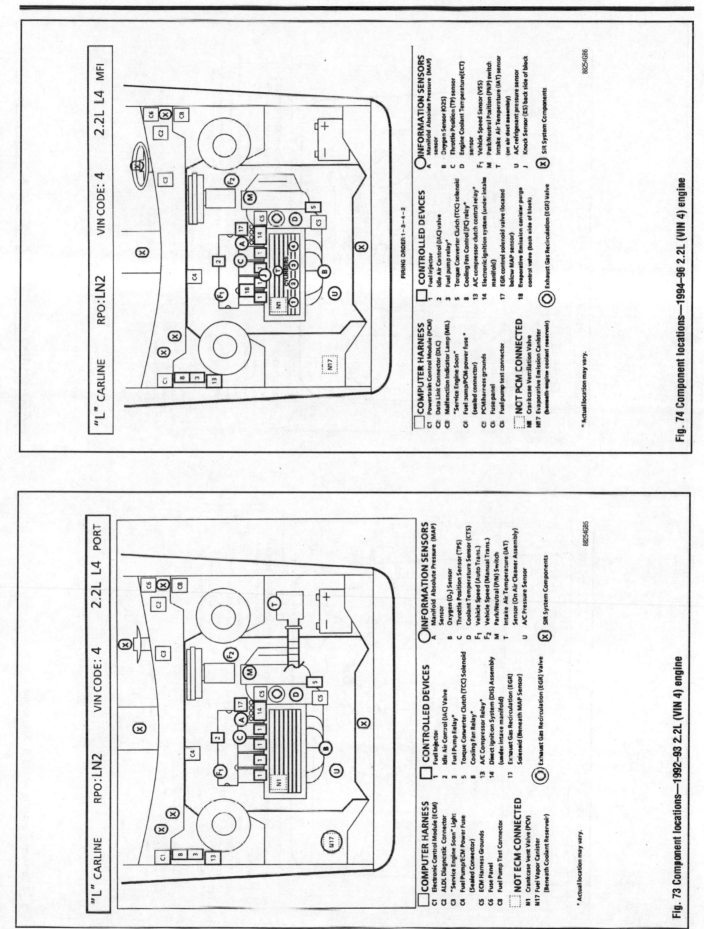

"L" CARLINE   RPO: LN2   VIN CODE: 4   2.2L L4 MFI

FIRING ORDER 1-3-4-2

□ COMPUTER HARNESS
- C1 Powertrain Control Module (PCM)
- C2 Data Link Connector (DLC)
- C3 Malfunction Indicator Lamp (MIL)
- C4 Fuel jump/PCM power fuse *
- "Service Engine Soon" (sealed connector)
- C5 PCM/harness grounds
- C6 Fuse panel
- C8 Fuel pump test connector

NOT PCM CONNECTED
- M1 Crankcase Ventilation Valve
- N17 Evaporative Emission Canister (beneath engine coolant reservoir)

□ CONTROLLED DEVICES
- 1 Fuel injector
- 2 Idle Air Control (IAC) valve
- 3 Fuel pump relay
- 5 Torque Converter Clutch (TCC) solenoid
- 8 Cooling Fan Control (FC) relay *
- 13 A/C compressor clutch control relay *
- 14 Electronic Ignition system (under intake manifold)
- 17 EGR control solenoid valve (located below MAP sensor)
- 18 Evaporative Emission canister purge control valve (back side of block)
- ◎ Exhaust Gas Recirculation (EGR) valve

○ INFORMATION SENSORS
- A Manifold Absolute Pressure (MAP) sensor
- B Oxygen Sensor (O2S)
- C Throttle Position (TP) sensor
- D Engine Coolant Temperature (ECT) sensor
- F1 Vehicle Speed Sensor (VSS)
- M Park/Neutral Position (PNP) switch
- T Intake Air Temperature (IAT) sensor (on air duct assembly)
- U A/C refrigerant pressure sensor
- J Knock Sensor (KS) back side of block
- ⊗ SIR System Components

8825-GB6

* Actual location may vary.

Fig. 74 Component locations—1994-96 2.2L (VIN 4) engine

"L" CARLINE   RPO: LN2   VIN CODE: 4   2.2L L4 PORT

□ COMPUTER HARNESS
- C1 Electronic Control Module (ECM)
- C2 ALDL Diagnostic Connector
- C3 "Service Engine Soon" Light
- C4 Fuel Pump/ECM Power Fuse (Sealed Connector)
- C5 ECM Harness Grounds
- C6 Fuse Panel
- C8 Fuel Pump Test Connector

NOT ECM CONNECTED
- M1 Crankcase Vent Valve (PCV)
- N17 Fuel Vapor Canister (Beneath Coolant Reservoir)

□ CONTROLLED DEVICES
- 1 Fuel Injector
- 2 Idle Air Control (IAC) Valve
- 3 Fuel Pump Relay *
- 5 Torque Converter Clutch (TCC) Solenoid
- 8 Cooling Fan Relay *
- 13 A/C Compressor Relay *
- 14 Direct Ignition System (DIS) Assembly (under intake manifold)
- 17 Exhaust Gas Recirculation (EGR) Solenoid (Beneath MAP Sensor)
- ◎ Exhaust Gas Recirculation (EGR) Valve

○ INFORMATION SENSORS
- A Manifold Absolute Pressure (MAP) Sensor
- B Oxygen (O2) Sensor
- C Throttle Position Sensor (TPS)
- D Coolant Temperature Sensor (CTS)
- F1 Vehicle Speed (Auto Trans.)
- F2 Vehicle Speed (Manual Trans.)
- M Park/Neutral (P/N) Switch
- T Intake Air Temperature (IAT) Sensor (On Air Cleaner Assembly)
- U A/C Pressure Sensor
- ⊗ SIR System Components

8825-GB5

* Actual location may vary.

Fig. 73 Component locations—1992-93 2.2L (VIN 4) engine

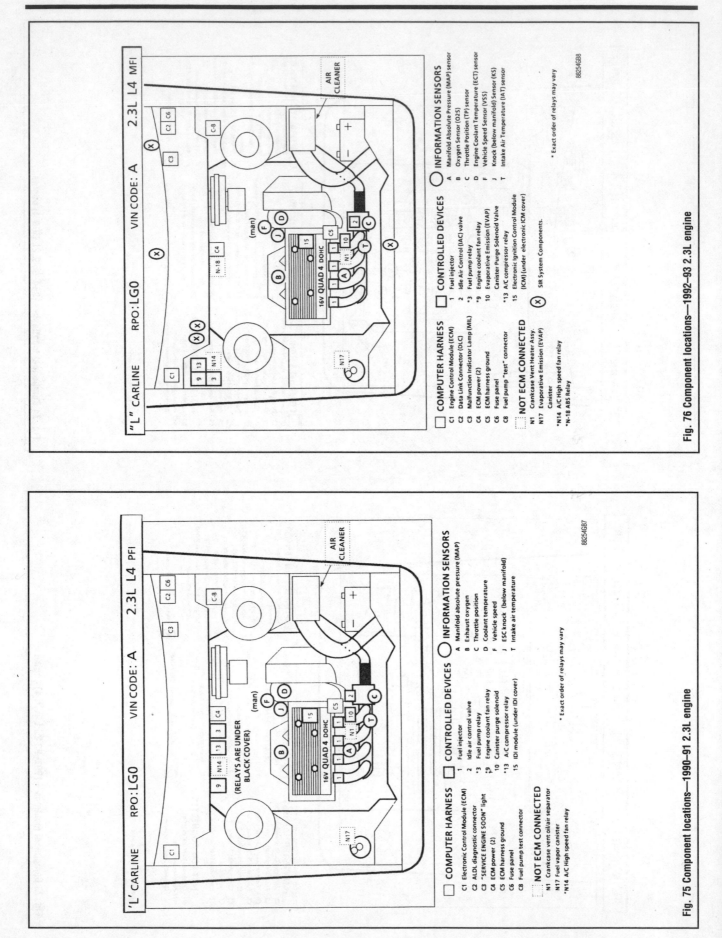

Fig. 76 Component locations—1992-93 2.3L engine

'L' CARLINE RPO:LG0 VIN CODE: A 2.3L L4 MFI

■ COMPUTER HARNESS

C1 Engine Control Module (ECM)
C2 Data Link Connector (DLC)
C3 Malfunction Indicator Lamp (MIL)
C4 ECM power (2)
C5 ECM harness ground
C6 Fuse panel
C8 Fuel pump "test" connector

NOT ECM CONNECTED

N1 Crankcase Vent Heater Assy.
N17 Evaporative Emission (EVAP) Canister
*N14 A/C High speed fan relay
*N-18 ABS Relay

■ CONTROLLED DEVICES

1 Fuel injector
2 Idle Air Control (IAC) valve
*3 Fuel pump relay
*9 Engine coolant fan relay
10 Evaporative Emission (EVAP)
Canister Purge Solenoid Valve
*13 A/C compressor relay
15 Electronic Ignition Control Module (ICM) (under electronic ICM cover)

Ⓧ SIR System Components.

* Exact order of relays may vary

○ INFORMATION SENSORS

A Manifold Absolute Pressure (MAP) sensor
B Oxygen Sensor (O2S)
C Throttle Position (TP) sensor
D Engine Coolant Temperature (ECT) sensor
F Vehicle Speed Sensor (VSS)
J Knock (below manifold) Sensor (KS)
T Intake Air Temperature (IAT) sensor

Fig. 75 Component locations—1990-91 2.3L engine

'L' CARLINE RPO:LG0 VIN CODE: A 2.3L L4 PFI

■ COMPUTER HARNESS

C1 Electronic Control Module (ECM)
C2 ALDI diagnostic connector
C3 "SERVICE ENGINE SOON" light
C4 ECM power (2)
C5 ECM harness ground
C6 Fuse panel
C8 Fuel pump test connector

NOT ECM CONNECTED

N1 Crankcase vent oil/air separator
N17 Fuel vapor canister
*N14 A/C High speed fan relay

■ CONTROLLED DEVICES

1 Fuel injector
2 Idle air control valve
*3 Fuel pump relay
*9 Engine coolant fan relay
10 Canister purge solenoid
*13 A/C compressor relay
15 IDI module (under IDI cover)

* Exact order of relays may vary

○ INFORMATION SENSORS

A Manifold absolute pressure (MAP)
B Exhaust oxygen
C Throttle position
D Coolant temperature
F Vehicle speed
J ESC knock (below manifold)
T Intake air temperature

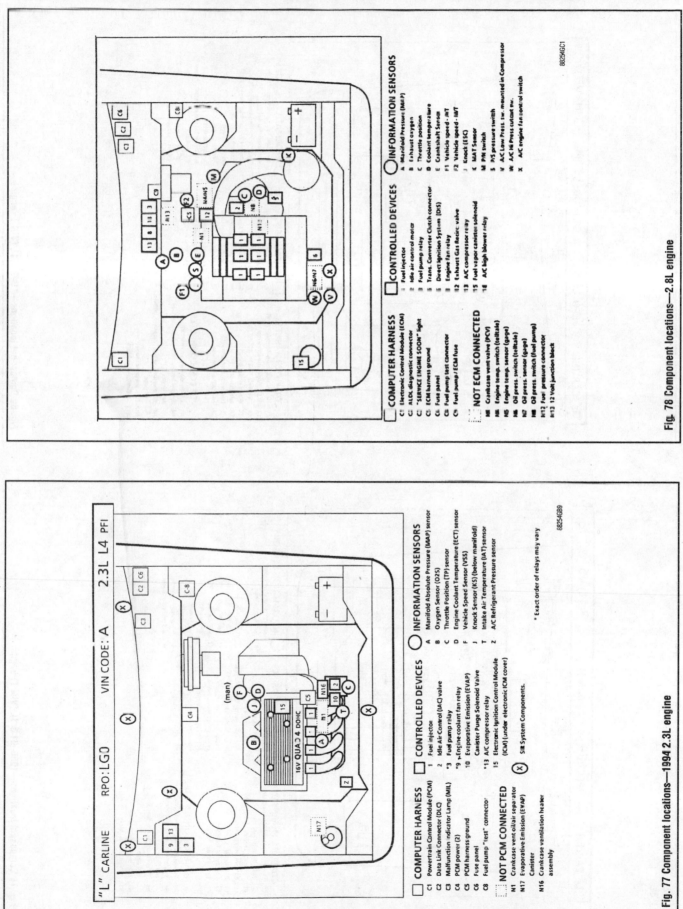

88256GC1

INFORMATION SENSORS
- A Manifold Pressure (MAP)
- B Exhaust oxygen
- C Throttle position
- D Coolant temperature
- E Crankshaft Sensor
- F1 Vehicle speed - MT
- F2 Vehicle speed - MT
- J Knock (ESK)
- M MAT Sensor
- M P/N switch
- N P/S pressure switch
- V A/C Low Press. sw. mounted in Compressor
- W A/C Hi Press cutout sw.
- X A/C engine fan contol switch

CONTROLLED DEVICES
- 1 Fuel injector
- 2 Idle air control motor
- 3 Fuel pump relay
- 4 Trans. Converter Clutch connector
- 6 Direct Ignition System (DIS)
- 9 Engine fan relay
- 12 Exhaust Gas Recirc valve
- 13 A/C compressor relay
- 15 Fuel vapor canister solenoid
- 16 A/C high blower relay

COMPUTER HARNESS
- C1 Electronic Control Module (ECM)
- C2 ALDL diagnostic connector
- C3 "SERVICE ENGINE SOON" light
- C4 ECM harness ground
- C5 Fuse panel
- C6 Fuel pump test connector
- C9 Fuel pump / ECM fuse

NOT ECM CONNECTED
- N6 Crankcase vent valve (PCV)
- N8 Engine temp. switch (telltale)
- N5 Engine temp. sensor (gage)
- N6 Oil press. switch (telltale)
- N7 Oil press. sensor (gage)
- N8 Oil press. switch (fuel pump)
- N12 Fuel pressure connector
- N13 12 Volt junction block

Fig. 78 Component locations—2.8L engine

"L" CARLINE   RPO: LG0   VIN CODE: A   2.3L L4 PFI

88254G89

INFORMATION SENSORS
- A Manifold Absolute Pressure (MAP) sensor
- B Oxygen Sensor (O2S)
- C Throttle Position (TP) sensor
- D Engine Coolant Temperature (ECT) sensor
- F Vehicle Speed Sensor (VSS)
- J Knock Sensor (KS) (below manifold)
- T Intake Air Temperature (IAT) sensor
- Z A/C Refrigerant Pressure sensor

CONTROLLED DEVICES
- 1 Fuel injector
- 2 Idle Air Control (IAC) valve
- 3 Fuel pump relay
- *9 Engine coolant fan relay
- 10 Evaporative Emission (EVAP) Canister Purge Solenoid Valve
- *13 A/C compressor relay
- 15 Electronic Ignition Control Module (ICM) (under electronic ICM cover)
- (X) SIR System Components.

* Exact order of relays may vary

COMPUTER HARNESS
- C1 Powertrain Control Module (PCM)
- C2 Data Link Connector (DLC)
- C3 Malfunction Indicator Lamp (MIL)
- C4 PCM power (2)
- C5 PCM harness ground
- C6 Fuse panel
- C8 Fuel pump "test" connector

NOT PCM CONNECTED
- N1 Crankcase vent oil/air separator
- N17 Evaporative Emission (EVAP) Canister
- N16 Crankcase ventilation heater assembly

Fig. 77 Component locations—1994 2.3L engine

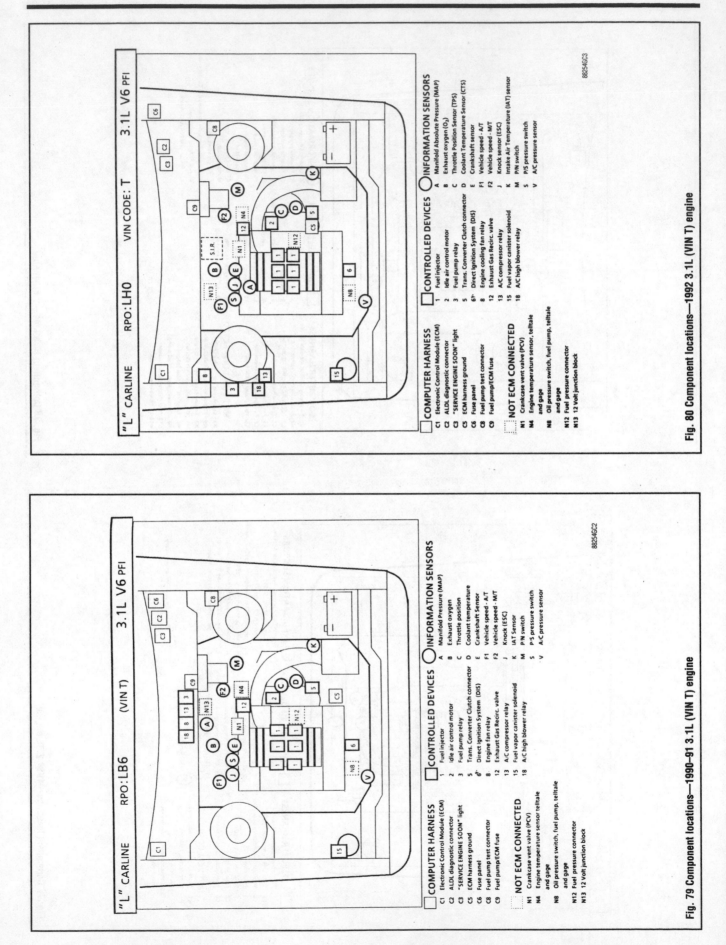

Fig. 80 Component locations—1992 3.1L (VIN T) engine

Fig. 79 Component locations—1990-91 3.1L (VIN T) engine

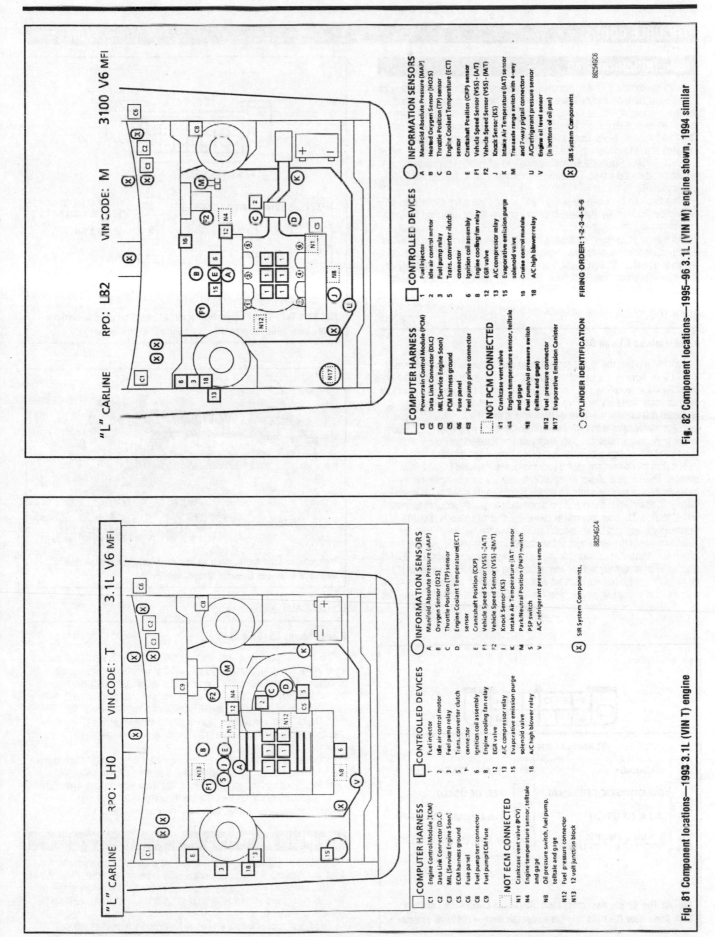

"L" CARLINE   RPO: LB2   VIN CODE: M   3100 V6 MFI

88254GC6

COMPUTER HARNESS

- C1 Powertrain Control Module (PCM)
- C2 Data Link Connector (DLC)
- C3 MIL (Service Engine Soon)
- C6 PCM harness ground
- C8 Fuse panel
- C9 Fuel pump prime connector

NOT PCM CONNECTED

- N1 Crankcase vent valve
- N4 Engine temperature sensor, telltale and gage
- N8 Fuel pump/oil pressure switch (telltale and gage)
- N12 Fuel pressure connector
- N17 Evaporative Emission Canister

CONTROLLED DEVICES

- 1 Fuel injector
- 2 Idle air control motor
- 3 Fuel pump relay
- 5 Trans. converter clutch connector
- 6 Ignition coil assembly
- 8 Engine cooling fan relay
- 12 EGR valve
- 13 A/C compressor relay
- 15 Evaporative emission purge solenoid valve
- 16 Cruise control module
- 18 A/C high blower relay

INFORMATION SENSORS

- A Manifold Absolute Pressure (MAP)
- B Heated Oxygen Sensor (HO2S)
- C Throttle Position (TP) sensor
- D Engine Coolant Temperature (ECT) sensor
- E Crankshaft Position (CKP) sensor
- F1 Vehicle Speed Sensor (VSS) - (A/T)
- F2 Vehicle Speed Sensor (VSS) - (M/T)
- J Knock Sensor (KS)
- K Intake Air Temperature (IAT) sensor
- M Transaxle range switch with 4-way and 7-way pigtail connectors
- U A/C refrigerant pressure sensor
- V Engine oil level sensor (in bottom of oil pan)
- X SIR System Components

CYLINDER IDENTIFICATION

FIRING ORDER: 1-2-3-4-5-6

Fig. 82 Component locations—1995–96 3.1L (VIN M) engine shown, 1994 similar

---

"L" CARLINE   RPO: LH0   VIN CODE: T   3.1L V6 MFI

88254GC4

COMPUTER HARNESS

- C1 Engine Control Module (ECM)
- C2 Data Link Connector (D.C)
- C3 MIL (Service Engine Soon)
- C6 ECM harness ground
- C8 Fuse panel
- C9 Fuel pump test connector
- C9 Fuel pump ECM fuse

NOT ECM CONNECTED

- N1 Crankcase vent valve (PCV)
- N4 Engine temperature sensor, telltale and gage
- N8 Oil pressure switch, fuel pump, telltale and gage
- N12 Fuel pressure connector
- N13 12 volt junction block

CONTROLLED DEVICES

- 1 Fuel injector
- 2 Idle air control motor
- 3 Fuel pump relay
- 5 Trans. converter clutch connector
- 6 Ignition coil assembly
- 8 Engine cooling fan relay
- 12 EGR valve
- 13 A/C compressor relay
- 15 Evaporative emission purge solenoid valve
- 18 A/C high blower relay

INFORMATION SENSORS

- A Manifold Absolute Pressure (MAP)
- B Oxygen Sensor (O2S)
- C Throttle Position (TP) sensor
- D Engine Coolant Temperature (ECT) sensor
- E Crankshaft Position (CKP)
- F1 Vehicle Speed Sensor (VSS) - (A/T)
- F2 Vehicle Speed Sensor (VSS) - (M/T)
- K Knock Sensor (KS)
- M Intake Air Temperature (IAT) sensor
- S Park/Neutral Position (PNP) switch
- S PSP switch
- V A/C refrigerant pressure sensor
- X SIR System Components

Fig. 81 Component locations—1993 3.1L (VIN T) engine

TROUBLE CODES

General Information

Since the computer control module is programmed to recognize the presence and value of electrical inputs, it will also note the lack of a signal or a radical change in values. It will, for example, react to the loss of signal from the vehicle speed sensor or note that engine coolant temperature has risen beyond acceptable (programmed) limits. Once a fault is recognized, a numeric code is assigned and held in memory. The dashboard warning lamp: CHECK ENGINE or SERVICE ENGINE SOON (SES), will illuminate to advise the operator that the system has detected a fault. This lamp is also known as the Malfunction Indicator Lamp (MIL).

More than one code may be stored. Keep in mind not every engine uses every code. Additionally, the same code may carry different meanings relative to each engine or engine family.

In the event of an computer control module failure, the system will default to a pre-programmed set of values. These are compromise values which allow the engine to operate, although possibly at reduced efficiency. This is variously known as the default, limp-in or back-up mode. Driveability is almost always affected when the ECM enters this mode.

SCAN TOOLS

♦ See Figures 83 and 84

On most models, the stored codes may be read with only the use of a small jumper wire, however the use of a hand-held scan tool such as GM's TECH-1® or equivalent is recommended. On 1996 models, an OBD-II compliant scan tool must be used. There are many manufacturers of these tools; a purchaser must be certain that the tool is proper for the intended use. If you own a scan type tool, it probably came with comprehensive instructions on proper use. Be sure to follow the instructions that came with your unit if they differ from what is given here; this is a general guide with useful information included.

The scan tool allows any stored codes to be read from the ECM or PCM memory. The tool also allows the operator to view the data being sent to the computer control module while the engine is running. This ability has obvious diagnostic advantages; the use of the scan tool is frequently required for component testing. The scan tool makes collecting information easier; the data must be correctly interpreted by an operator familiar with the system.

An example of the usefulness of the scan tool may be seen in the case of a temperature sensor which has changed its electrical characteristics. The ECM is reacting to an apparently warmer engine (causing a driveability problem), but the sensor's voltage has not changed enough to set a fault code. Connecting the scan tool, the voltage signal being sent to the ECM may be viewed; comparison to normal values or a known good vehicle reveals the problem quickly.

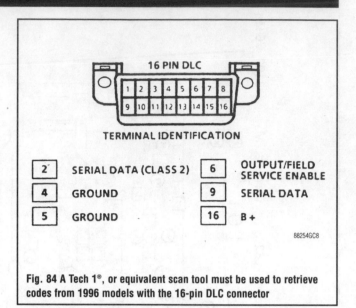

Fig. 84 A Tech 1®, or equivalent scan tool must be used to retrieve codes from 1996 models with the 16-pin DLC connector

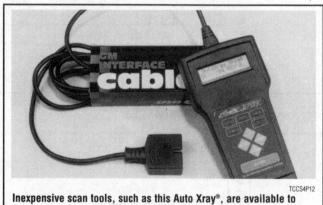

Inexpensive scan tools, such as this Auto Xray®, are available to interface with your General Motors vehicle

ELECTRICAL TOOLS

♦ See Figures 85, 86 and 87

The most commonly required electrical diagnostic tool is the digital multimeter, allowing voltage, ohmage (resistance) and amperage to be read by one instrument. The multimeter must be a high-impedance unit, with 10 megohms of impedance in the voltmeter. This type of meter will not place an additional load on the circuit it is testing; this is extremely important in low voltage circuits. The multimeter must be of high quality in all respects. It should be handled carefully and protected from impact or damage. Replace batteries frequently in the unit.

Other necessary tools include an unpowered test light, a quality tachometer with an inductive (clip-on) pick up, and the proper tools for releasing GM's Metri-Pack, Weather Pack and Micro-Pack terminals as necessary. The Micro-Pack connectors are used at the ECM electrical connector. A vacuum pump/gauge may also be required for checking sensors, solenoids and valves.

Diagnosis and Testing

Diagnosis of a driveability and/or emissions problems requires attention to detail and following the diagnostic procedures in the correct order. Resist the temptation to perform any repairs before performing the preliminary diagnostic steps. In many cases this will shorten diagnostic time and often cure the problem without electronic testing.

The proper troubleshooting procedure for these vehicles is as follows:

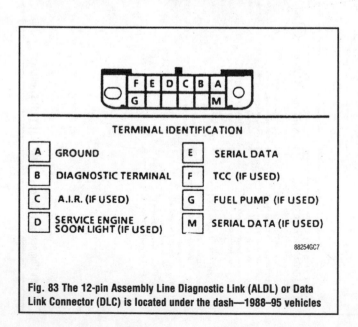

Fig. 83 The 12-pin Assembly Line Diagnostic Link (ALDL) or Data Link Connector (DLC) is located under the dash—1988–95 vehicles

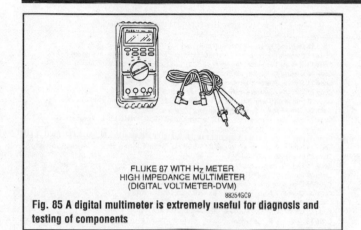

FLUKE 87 WITH H$_z$ METER
HIGH IMPEDANCE MULTIMETER
(DIGITAL VOLTMETER-DVM)

Fig. 85 A digital multimeter is extremely useful for diagnosis and testing of components

Fig. 86 A GM Metri-Pack adapter kit can come in handy for releasing electrical connectors

Fig. 87 You can use a vacuum pump with a gauge to check some types of sensors

VISUAL/PHYSICAL INSPECTION

This is possibly the most critical step of diagnosis and should be performed immediately after retrieving any codes. A detailed examination of connectors, wiring and vacuum hoses can often lead to a repair without further diagnosis. Performance of this step relies on the skill of the technician performing it; a careful inspector will check the undersides of hoses as well as the integrity of hard-to-reach hoses blocked by the air cleaner or other component. Wiring should be checked carefully for any sign of strain, burning, crimping, or terminal pull-out from a connector. Checking connectors at components or in harnesses is required; usually, pushing them together will reveal a loose fit.

INTERMITTENTS

If a fault occurs intermittently, such as a loose connector pin breaking contact as the vehicle hits a bump, the ECM will note the fault as it occurs and energize the dash warning lamp. If the problem self-corrects, as with the terminal pin again making contact, the dash lamp will extinguish after 10 seconds but a code will remain stored in the computer control module's memory.

When an unexpected code appears during diagnostics, it may have been set during an intermittent failure that self-corrected; the codes are still useful in diagnosis and should not be discounted.

CIRCUIT/COMPONENT REPAIR

The fault codes and the scan tool data will lead to diagnosis and checking of a particular circuit. It is important to note that the fault code indicates a fault or loss of signal in an ECM-controlled system, not necessarily in the specific component.

Refer to the appropriate Diagnostic Code chart to determine the codes meaning. The component may then be tested following the appropriate component test procedures found in this section. If the component is OK, check the wiring for shorts or opens. Further diagnoses should be left to an experienced driveability technician.

If a code indicates the ECM to be faulty and the ECM is replaced, but does not correct the problem, one of the following may be the reason:

• There is a problem with the ECM terminal connections: The terminals may have to be removed from the connector in order to check them properly.

• The ECM or PROM is not correct for the application: The incorrect ECM or PROM may cause a malfunction and may or may not set a code.

• The problem is intermittent: This means that the problem is not present at the time the system is being checked. In this case, make a careful physical inspection of all portions of the system involved.

• Shorted solenoid, relay coil or harness: Solenoids and relays are turned on and off by the ECM using internal electronic switches called drivers. Each driver is part of a group of four called Quad-Drivers. A shorted solenoid, relay coil or harness may cause an ECM to fail, and a replacement ECM to fail when it is installed. Use a short tester, J34696, BT 8405, or equivalent, as a fast, accurate means of checking for a short circuit.

• The Programmable Read Only Memory (PROM) or MEM-CAL may be faulty: Although the PROM rarely fails, it operates as part of the ECM. Therefore, it could be the cause of the problem. Substitute a known good PROM/MEM-CAL.

• The replacement ECM may be faulty: After the ECM is replaced, the system should be rechecked for proper operation. If the diagnostic code again indicates the ECM is the problem, substitute a known good ECM. Although this is a very rare condition, it could happen.

Reading Codes

1988–95 VEHICLES

▶ **See Figures 88, 89, 90, 91 and 92**

Listings of the trouble for the various engine control system covered in this manual are located in this section. Remember that a code only points to the faulty circuit NOT necessarily to a faulty component. Loose, damaged or corroded connections may contribute to a fault code on a circuit when the sensor or component is operating properly. Be sure that the components are faulty before replacing them, especially the expensive ones.

The Assembly Line Diagnostic Link (ALDL) connector or Data Link Connector (DLC) may be located under the dash and sometimes covered with a plastic cover labeled DIAGNOSTIC CONNECTOR.

1. The diagnostic trouble codes can be read by grounding test terminal **B**. The terminal is most easily grounded by connecting it to terminal **A** (internal ECM ground). This is the terminal to the right of terminal **B** on the top row of the ALDL connector.

2. Once the terminals have been connected, the ignition switch must be moved to the **ON** position with the engine not running.

3. The Service Engine Soon or Check Engine light should be flashing. If it isn't, turn the ignition **OFF** and remove the jumper wire. Turn the ignition **ON** and confirm that light is now on. If it is not, replace the bulb and try again. If the bulb still will not light, or if it does not flash with the test terminal grounded, the system should be diagnosed by an experienced driveability technician. If the light is OK, proceed as follows.

4. The code(s) stored in memory may be read through counting the flashes of the dashboard warning lamp. The dash warning lamp should begin to flash

CODE	DESCRIPTION	ILLUMINATE "SES"
13	Oxygen (O₂) Sensor Circuit - open circuit	YES
14	Coolant Temperature Sensor (CTS) Circuit - high temperature indicated	YES
15	Coolant Temperature Sensor (CTS) Circuit - low temperature indicated	YES
21	Throttle Position Sensor (TPS) Circuit - signal voltage high	YES
22	Throttle Position Sensor (TPS) Circuit - signal voltage low	YES
23	Intake Air Temperature (IAT) Sensor Circuit - low temperature indicated	YES
24	Vehicle Speed Sensor (VSS) Circuit	YES
25	Intake Air Temperature (IAT) Sensor Circuit - high temperature indicated	YES
32	Exhaust Gas Recirculation (EGR) Circuit Electrical Diagnosis	YES
33	Manifold Absolute Pressure (MAP) Sensor Circuit Signal Voltage high-low vacuum	YES
34	Manifold Absolute Pressure (MAP) Sensor Circuit Signal Voltage low-high vacuum	YES
35	Idle Air Control (IAC) Circuit System Check - Tech 1	YES
41	Cylinder Select Error - faulty or incorrect MEM-CAL	YES
42	Electronic Spark Timing (EST) Circuit	YES
43	Electronic Spark Control (ESC) Circuit	YES
44	Oxygen (O₂) Sensor Circuit - lean exhaust indicated	YES
45	Oxygen (O₂) Sensor Circuit - rich exhaust indicated	YES
54	Fuel Pump Circuit - low voltage	YES
51	MEM-CAL Error - faulty or incorrect MEM-CAL	YES
53	System Over Voltage	YES
61	Degraded Oxygen Sensor	YES
62	Transaxle Gear Switch Signal Circuit	YES
66	A/C Pressure Sensor Circuit	NO

If a code not listed above appears on Tech 1, ground ALDL diagnostic terminal "B" and observe flashed codes. If code does not reappear, Tech 1 data may be faulty. If code does reappear, check for incorrect or faulty MEM-CAL.

88254GD3

Fig. 88 Engine diagnostic trouble codes—1988–93 2.0L and 2.2L, 1988–93 2.8L and 3.1L engines

DTC	DESCRIPTION	ILLUMINATE MIL (SERVICE ENGINE SOON)
13	Oxygen Sensor (O2S) Circuit - open circuit	YES
14	Engine Coolant Temperature (ECT) Sensor Circuit - high temperature	YES
15	Engine Coolant Temperature (ECT) Sensor Circuit - low temperature	YES
19	Intermittent 7X Reference Signal	YES
21	Throttle Position (TP) Sensor Circuit - signal voltage high	YES
22	Throttle Position (TP) Sensor Circuit - signal voltage low	YES
23	Intake Air Temperature (IAT) Sensor Circuit - low temperature	YES
24	Vehicle Speed Sensor (VSS) Circuit	YES
25	Intake Air Temperature (IAT) Sensor Circuit - high temperature	YES
26	Quad-Driver Module (QDSM)	NO
27	Quad-Driver Module (QDM1)	YES
28	Quad-Driver Module (QDM2)	NO
32	Exhaust Gas Recirculation (EGR) Valve	YES
33	Manifold Absolute Pressure (MAP) Sensor Circuit - signal voltage high - low vacuum	YES
34	Manifold Absolute Pressure (MAP) Sensor Circuit - signal voltage low - high vacuum	YES
35	Improper Idle Speed (IAC)	YES
43	Electronic Spark Control (ESC) - knock sensor	YES
44	Oxygen Sensor (O2S) Circuit - lean exhaust indicated	YES
45	Oxygen Sensor (O2S) Circuit - rich exhaust indicated	YES
51	EPROM or PCM Failure	YES
53	Improper Ignition Voltage	YES
55	Lean in Power Enrichment	NO
66	A/C Refrigerant Pressure Sensor Circuit	NO

88254GD5

Fig. 89 Engine diagnostic trouble codes—1994–95 2.2L (VIN 4) engines and 1993–94 2.3L (VIN A) engines

Code 13 Oxygen (O₂) Sensor Circuit (Open Circuit)
Code 14 Coolant Temperature Sensor (CTS) Circuit (High Temperature Indicated)
Code 15 Coolant Temperature Sensor (CTS) Circuit (Low Temperature Indicated)
Code 16 Missing 2X Reference Circuit
Code 21 Throttle Position Sensor (TPS) Circuit (Signal Voltage High)
Code 22 Throttle Position Sensor (TPS) Circuit (Signal Voltage Low)
Code 23 Intake Air Temperature (IAT) Sensor Circuit (Low Temperature Indicated)
Code 24 Vehicle Speed Sensor (VSS) Circuit
Code 25 Intake Air Temperature (IAT) Sensor Circuit (High Temperature Indicated)
Code 26 Quad-Driver (QDM) Circuit
Code 33 Manifold Absolute Pressure (MAP) Sensor Circuit (Signal Voltage High-Low Vacuum)
Code 34 Manifold Absolute Pressure (MAP) Sensor Circuit (Signal Voltage Low-High Vacuum)
Code 35 Idle Speed Error
Code 41 1X Reference Circuit
Code 42 Electronic Spark Timing (EST) Circuit
Code 43 Electronic Spark Control (ESC) Circuit
Code 44 Oxygen (O₂) Sensor Circuit (Lean Exhaust Indicated)
Code 45 Oxygen (O₂) Sensor Circuit (Rich Exhaust Indicated)
Code 51 MEM-CAL Error (Faulty or Incorrect MEM-CAL)
Code 53 Battery Voltage Error
Code 65 Fuel Injector Circuit (Low Current) (1 of 2)
Code 66 A/C Pressure Sensor Circuit

88254GD7

Fig. 90 Engine diagnostic trouble codes—1990–92 2.3L (VIN A) engines

DTC	DESCRIPTION	ILLUMINATE MIL
13	Heated Oxygen Sensor (HO2S) - open circuit	YES
14	Engine Coolant Temperature (ECT) Sensor Circuit (high temperature indicated)	YES
15	Engine Coolant Temperature (ECT) Sensor Circuit (low temperature indicated)	YES
16	System Low Voltage (low battery voltage)	YES
17	Camshaft Position Sensor Circuit Error	NO
21	Throttle Position (TP) Sensor Circuit (signal voltage high)	YES
22	Throttle Position (TP) Sensor Circuit (signal voltage low)	YES
23	Intake Air Temperature (IAT) Sensor Circuit (low temperature indicated)	YES
24	Vehicle Speed Sensor (VSS) Circuit (no signal voltage)	YES
25	Intake Air Temperature (IAT) Sensor Circuit (high temperature indicated)	YES
28	Transmission Range Switch Error	NO
33	Manifold Absolute Pressure (MAP) Sensor Circuit (signal voltage high - high MAP)	YES
34	Manifold Absolute Pressure (MAP) Sensor Circuit (signal voltage low - low MAP)	YES
35	Idle Speed Error	YES
36	Ignition Control 24X Signal Circuit Error	NO
37	TCC Brake Switch Error	NO
41	Ignition Control (EST) Error	NO
42	Ignition Control (EST) Bypass Error	YES
43	Knock Sensor (KS) Circuit Error	YES
44	Heated Oxygen Sensor (HO2S) Circuit (lean exhaust indicated)	YES
45	Heated Oxygen Sensor (HO2S) Circuit (rich exhaust indicated)	YES
46*	PASS KeyII® Circuit (out of frequency range)	NO
51	PROM Error (faulty or incorrect calibration)	YES
53	System Voltage High	YES
54	Fuel Pump Circuit (low voltage)	YES
58	Trans Fluid Temperature (TFT) Sensor Circuit Low (high temperature)	NO
59	Trans Fluid Temperature (TFT) Sensor Circuit High (low temperature)	NO

* If Applicable

88254GE1

Fig. 91 Engine diagnostic trouble codes (1 of 2)—1994–95 3.1L (VIN M) engines

Code 12. The code will display as one flash, a pause and two flashes. Code 12 is not a fault code. It is used as a system acknowledgment or handshake code; its presence indicates that the ECM can communicate as requested. Code 12 is used to begin every diagnostic sequence. Some vehicles also use Code 12 after all diagnostic codes have been sent.

5. After Code 12 has been transmitted 3 times, the fault codes, if any, will each be transmitted 3 times. The codes are stored and transmitted in numeric order from lowest to highest.

➡ **The order of codes in the memory does not indicate the order of occurrence.**

6. If there are no codes stored, but a driveability or emissions problem is evident, the system should be diagnosed by an experienced driveability technician.

7. If one or more codes are stored, record them. Refer to the applicable Diagnostic Code chart in this section.

8. Switch the ignition **OFF** when finished with code retrieval or scan tool readings.

➡ **After making repairs, clear the trouble codes and operate the vehicle to see if it will reset, indicating further problems.**

DTC	DESCRIPTION	ILLUMINATE MIL
66	A/C Refrigerant Pressure Sensor Circuit (low pressure)	NO
70	A/C Refrigerant Pressure Sensor Circuit (high pressure)	NO
72	Vehicle Speed Sensor (VSS) Circuit Signal Error	NO
75	Digital EGR #1 Solenoid (error)	YES
76	Digital EGR #2 Solenoid (error)	YES
77	Digital EGR #3 Solenoid (error)	YES
79	Transmission Fluid Overtemp	NO
80	Transmission Component Error	NO
82	Ignition Control 3X Signal Error	NO
85	PROM Error (faulty or incorrect calibration)	YES
86	Analog/Digital PCM Error	YES
87	Electrically Erasable Programmable Read Only Memory (EEPROM) Error	NO
90	TCC Error	NO
96	Trans System Voltage Low	NO
98	Invalid PCM Program	NO
99	Invalid PCM Program	NO

88254GE2

Fig. 92 Engine diagnostic trouble codes (2 of 2)—1994–95 3.1L (VIN M) engines

1996 VEHICLES

♦ See Figures 93, 94, 95 and 96

On 1996 models, an OBD-II compliant scan tool, such as GM's TECH-1® or equivalent, must be used to retrieve the trouble codes. Follow the scan tool manufacturer's instructions on how to connect the scan tool to the vehicle and how to retrieve the codes.

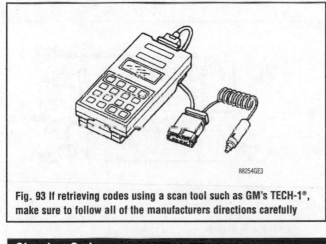

88254GE3

Fig. 93 If retrieving codes using a scan tool such as GM's TECH-1®, make sure to follow all of the manufacturers directions carefully

Clearing Codes

Stored fault codes may be erased from memory at any time by removing power from the ECM for at least 30 seconds. It may be necessary to clear stored codes during diagnosis to check for any recurrence during a test drive, but the stored codes must be written down when retrieved. The codes may still be required for subsequent troubleshooting. Whenever a repair is complete, the stored codes must be erased and the vehicle test driven to confirm correct operation and repair.

✱✱ WARNING

The ignition switch must be OFF any time power is disconnected or restored to the ECM. Severe damage may result if this precaution is not observed.

Depending on the electrical distribution of the particular vehicle, power to the ECM may be disconnected by removing the ECM fuse in the fusebox, disconnecting the in-line fuse holder near the positive battery terminal or disconnecting the ECM power lead at the battery terminal. Disconnecting the negative battery cable to clear codes is not recommended as this will also clear other memory data in the vehicle such as radio presets.

Description	Illuminate MIL
DTC P0101 Mass Air Flow System Performance	Yes
DTC P0102 MAF Sensor Circuit Low Frequency	Yes
DTC P0103 MAF Sensor Circuit High Frequency	Yes
DTC P0106 MAP System Performance	Yes
DTC P0107 MAP Sensor Circuit Low Voltage	Yes
DTC P0108 MAP Sensor Circuit High Voltage	Yes
DTC P0112 IAT Sensor Circuit Low Voltage	Yes
DTC P0113 IAT Sensor Circuit High Voltage	Yes
DTC P0117 ECT Sensor Circuit Low Voltage	Yes
DTC P0118 ECT Sensor Circuit High Voltage	Yes
DTC P0121 TP Sensor Performance	Yes
DTC P0122 TP Sensor Circuit Low Voltage	Yes
DTC P0123 TP Sensor Circuit High Voltage	Yes
DTC P0125 ECT Excessive Time to Closed Loop	Yes
DTC P0131 HO2S Circuit Low Voltage Sensor1	Yes
DTC P0132 HO2S Circuit High Voltage Sensor1	Yes
DTC P0133 HO2S Circuit Slow Response Sensor1	Yes
DTC P0134 HO2S CKT Insufficient Activity Sensor1	Yes
DTC P0135 HO2S Heater Circuit Sensor1	Yes
DTC P0137 HO2S Circuit Low Voltage Sensor2	Yes
DTC P0138 HO2S Circuit High Voltage Sensor2	Yes
DTC P0140 HO2S CKT Insufficient Activity Sensor2	Yes
DTC P0141 HO2S Heater Circuit Sensor2	Yes
DTC P0171 Fuel Trim System Lean	Yes
DTC P0172 Fuel Trim System Rich	Yes
DTC P0300 Engine Misfire Detected	Yes
DTC P0325 Knock Sensor Module Circuit	No
DTC P0326 Knock Sensor Noise Channel High Voltage	No
DTC P0327 Knock Sensor Noise Channel Low Voltage	No
DTC P0336 18X Reference Signal Circuit	Yes
DTC P0341 CMP Sensor Circuit Performance	Yes
DTC P0401 EGR System Flow Insufficient	Yes
DTC P0420 TWC System Low Efficiency	Yes
DTC P0441 EVAP System No Flow During Purge	Yes
P0502 Vehicle Speed Sensor Circuit - Low Input	Yes
P0503 Vehicle Speed Sensor Circuit - Intermittent Input	Yes
DTC P0506 Idle Control System Low RPM	Yes
DTC P0507 Idle Control System High RPM	Yes

88254GE5

Fig. 94 Engine diagnostic trouble codes (1 of 3)—1996 vehicles

Description	Illuminate MIL
DTC P0530 A/C Refrigerant Pressure Sensor Circuit	No
DTC P0560 System Voltage	No
DTC P0601 PCM Memory	Yes
DTC P0602 PCM Not Programmed	No
DTC P0705 Trans Range Switch Circuit	No
DTC P0706 Transaxle Range Switch Performance	No
P0712 Transaxle Fluid Temperature (TFT) Sensor Circuit - Low Signal Voltage	Yes
P0713 Transaxle Fluid Temperature (TFT) Sensor Circuit - High Signal Voltage	Yes
P0719 Brake Switch Circuit Low	No
P0724 Brake Switch Circuit High	No
P0742 Torque Converter Clutch Circuit Stuck On	Yes
P0751 Shift Solenoid 1 - Performance/Stuck Off	Yes
P0753 Shift Solenoid 1 - Electrical	Yes
P0756 Shift Solenoid 2 - Performance/Stuck Off	Yes
P0758 Shift Solenoid 2 - Electrical	Yes
DTC P1106 MAP Sensor CKT Intermittent High Voltage	No
DTC P1107 MAP Sensor CKT Intermittent Low Voltage	No
DTC P1111 IAT Sensor CKT Intermittent High Voltage	No
DTC P1112 IAT Sensor CKT Intermittent Low Voltage	No
DTC P1114 ECT Sensor CKT Intermittent Low Voltage	No
DTC P1115 ECT Sensor CKT Intermittent High Voltage	No
DTC P1121 TP Sensor CKT Intermittent High Voltage	No
DTC P1122 TP Sensor CKT Intermittent Low Voltage	No
DTC P1133 HO2S Insufficient Switching Sensor1	Yes
DTC P1134 HO2S Transition Time Ratio Sensor1	Yes
DTC P1200 Injector Control Circuit	Yes
DTC P1350 Bypass Line Monitor	Yes
DTC P1361 IC Circuit Not Toggling	Yes
DTC P1374 3X Reference Circuit	Yes
DTC P1381 Misfire Detected No EBCM/PCM Serial Data	No
DTC P1406 EGR Valve Pintle Position Circuit	Yes
DTC P1441 EVAP System Flow During Non-Purge	Yes
DTC P1442 EVAP Vacuum Switch Circuit	Yes
DTC P1554 Cruise Control Status Circuit	No
DTC P1626 Theft Deterrent System Fuel Enable CKT	No

88254GE4

Fig. 95 Engine diagnostic trouble codes (2 of 3)—1996 vehicles

Description	Illuminate MIL
DTC P1629 Theft Deterrent Crank Signal Malfunction	No
DTC P1635 5 Volt Reference (A) Circuit	Yes
DTC P1639 5 Volt Reference (B) Circuit	No
DTC P1641 MIL Control Circuit	No
DTC P1651 Fan 1 Relay Control Circuit	Yes
DTC P1652 Fan 2 Relay Control Circuit	Yes
DTC P1654 A/C Relay Control Circuit	No
DTC P1655 EVAP Purge Solenoid Control Circuit	Yes
DTC P1662 Cruise Control Inhibit Control Circuit	No
DTC P1672 Low Engine Oil Level Lamp Control CKT	No
P1812 Transaxle Over Temperature Condition	Yes
P1860 Torque Converter Clutch PWM Solenoid Circuit	Yes
P1864 Torque Converter Clutch Enable Solenoid Circuit	Yes
P1870 Transaxle Component Slipping	Yes

88254GE6

Fig. 96 Engine diagnostic trouble codes (3 of 3)—1996 vehicles

VACUUM DIAGRAMS

Following are vacuum diagrams for most of the engine and emissions package combinations covered by this manual. Because vacuum circuits will vary based on various engine and vehicle options, always refer first to the vehicle emission control information label, if present. Should the label be missing, or should vehicle be equipped with a different engine from the vehicle's original equipment, refer to the diagrams below for the same or similar configuration.

If you wish to obtain a replacement emissions label, most manufacturers make the labels available for purchase. The labels can usually be ordered from a local dealer.

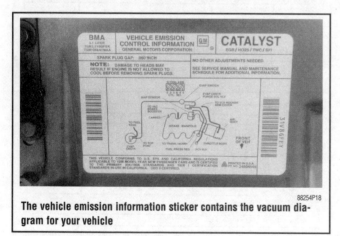

88254P18

The vehicle emission information sticker contains the vacuum diagram for your vehicle

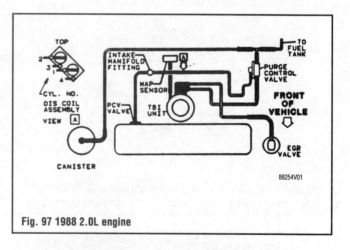

88254V01

Fig. 97 1988 2.0L engine

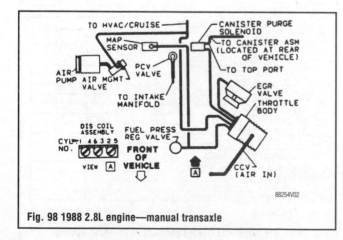

88254V02

Fig. 98 1988 2.8L engine—manual transaxle

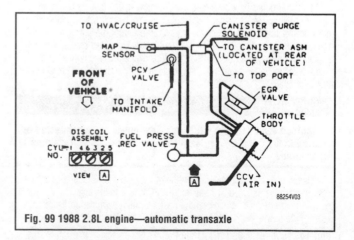

88254V03

Fig. 99 1988 2.8L engine—automatic transaxle

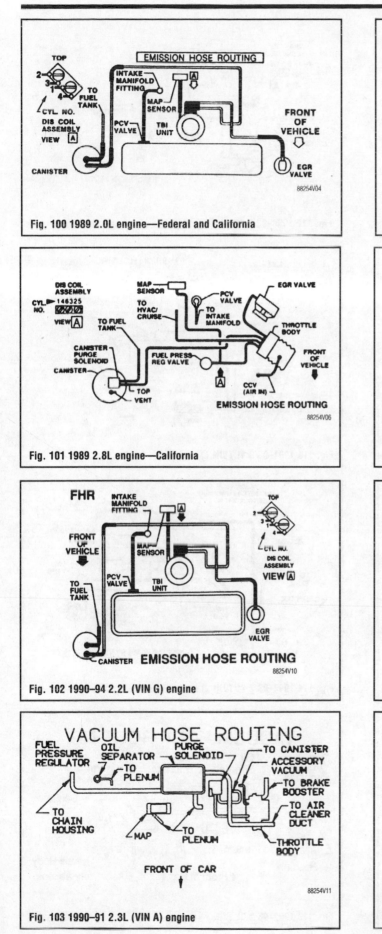

Fig. 100 1989 2.0L engine—Federal and California

Fig. 101 1989 2.8L engine—California

Fig. 102 1990-94 2.2L (VIN G) engine

Fig. 103 1990-91 2.3L (VIN A) engine

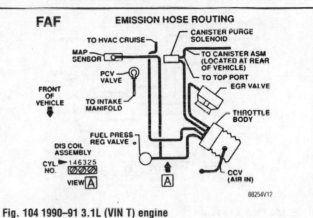

Fig. 104 1990-91 3.1L (VIN T) engine

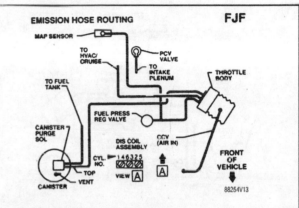

Fig. 105 1990-91 3.1L (VIN T) engine

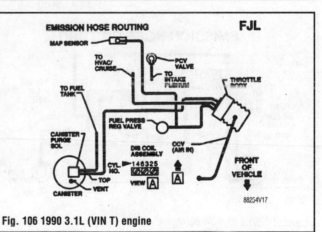

Fig. 106 1990 3.1L (VIN T) engine

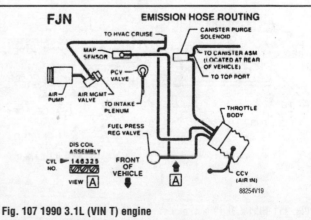

Fig. 107 1990 3.1L (VIN T) engine

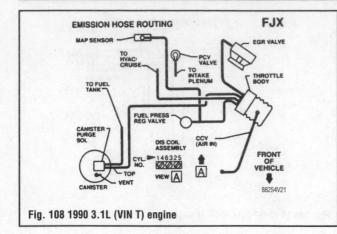

Fig. 108 1990 3.1L (VIN T) engine

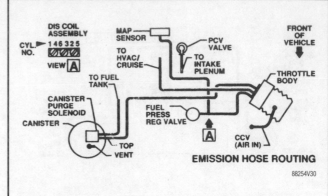

Fig. 112 1990–93 3.1L (VIN T) engine—Federal and California

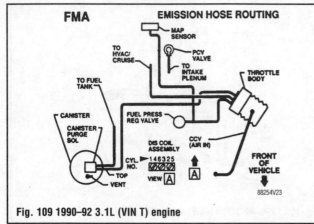

Fig. 109 1990–92 3.1L (VIN T) engine

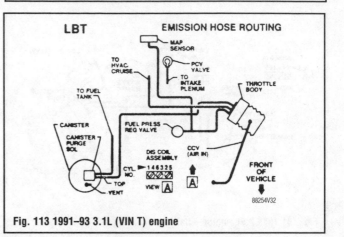

Fig. 113 1991–93 3.1L (VIN T) engine

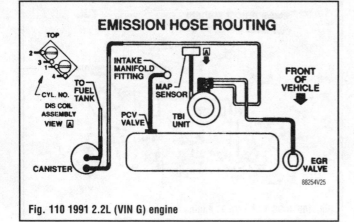

Fig. 110 1991 2.2L (VIN G) engine

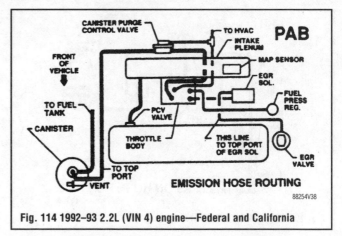

Fig. 114 1992–93 2.2L (VIN 4) engine—Federal and California

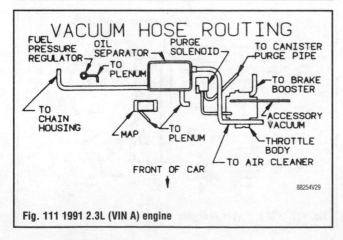

Fig. 111 1991 2.3L (VIN A) engine

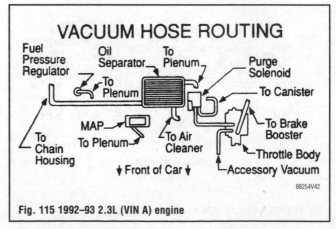

Fig. 115 1992–93 2.3L (VIN A) engine

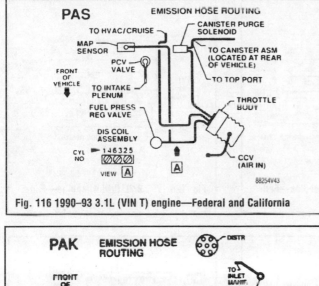

Fig. 116 1990–93 3.1L (VIN T) engine—Federal and California

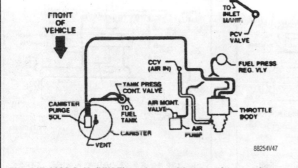

Fig. 117 1992 3.1L (VIN T) engine—with manual transaxle

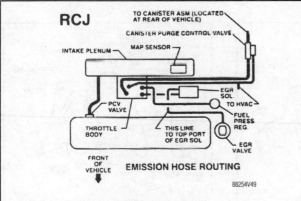

Fig. 118 1993 2.2L (VIN 4) engine—Federal and California

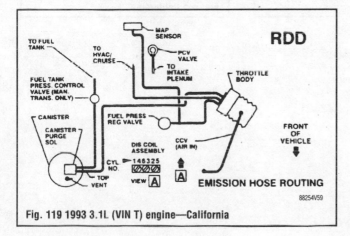

Fig. 119 1993 3.1L (VIN T) engine—California

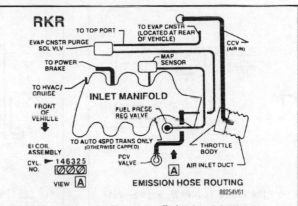

Fig. 120 1993–94 3.1L (VIN T) engine—Federal and California

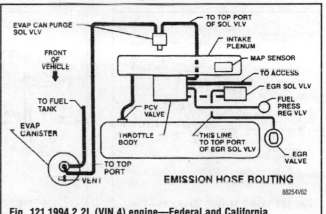

Fig. 121 1994 2.2L (VIN 4) engine—Federal and California

VACUUM HOSE ROUTING

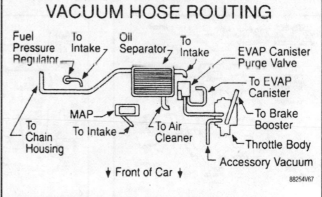

Fig. 122 1994 2.3L (VIN A) engine—California

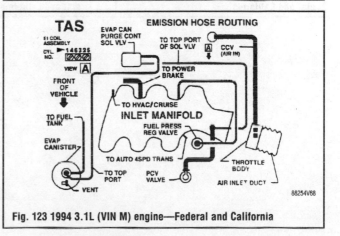

Fig. 123 1994 3.1L (VIN M) engine—Federal and California

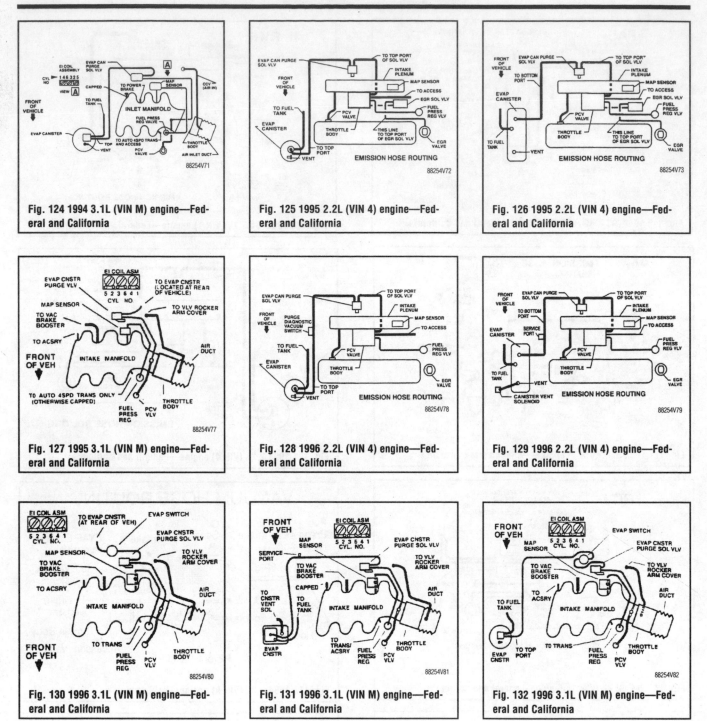

Fig. 124 1994 3.1L (VIN M) engine—Federal and California

Fig. 125 1995 2.2L (VIN 4) engine—Federal and California

Fig. 126 1995 2.2L (VIN 4) engine—Federal and California

Fig. 127 1995 3.1L (VIN M) engine—Federal and California

Fig. 128 1996 2.2L (VIN 4) engine—Federal and California

Fig. 129 1996 2.2L (VIN 4) engine—Federal and California

Fig. 130 1996 3.1L (VIN M) engine—Federal and California

Fig. 131 1996 3.1L (VIN M) engine—Federal and California

Fig. 132 1996 3.1L (VIN M) engine—Federal and California

5

FUEL
SYSTEM

BASIC FUEL SYSTEM DIAGNOSIS

3When there is a problem starting or driving a vehicle, two of the most important checks involve the ignition and the fuel systems. The questions most mechanics attempt to answer first, "is there spark?" and "is there fuel?" will often lead to solving most basic problems. For ignition system diagnosis and testing, please refer to the information on engine electrical components and ignition systems found earlier in this manual. If the ignition system checks out (there is spark), then you must determine if the fuel system is operating properly (is there fuel?).

FUEL LINE FITTINGS

Quick-Connect Fittings

REMOVAL & INSTALLATION

♦ **See Figure 1**

➡**This procedure requires Tool Set J37088–A fuel line quick-connect separator.**

1. Grasp both sides of the fitting. Twist the female connector ¼ turn in each direction to loosen any dirt within the fittings. Using compressed air, blow out the dirt from the quick-connect fittings at the end of the fittings.

✷ CAUTION

Safety glasses MUST be worn when using compressed air to avoid eye injury due to flying dirt particles!

2. For plastic (hand releasable) fittings, squeeze the plastic retainer release tabs, then pull the connection apart.
3. For metal fittings, choose the correct tool from kit J37088–A for the size of the fitting to be disconnected. Insert the proper tool into the female connector, then push inward to release the locking tabs. Pull the connection apart.
4. If it is necessary to remove rust or burrs from the male tube end of a quick-connect fitting, use emery cloth in a radial motion with the tube end to prevent damage to the O-ring sealing surfaces. Using a clean shop towel, wipe off the male tube ends. Inspect all connectors for dirt and burrs. Clean and/or replace if required.

To install:
5. Apply a few drops of clean engine oil to the male tube end of the fitting.
6. Push the connectors together to cause the retaining tabs/fingers to snap into place.
7. Once installed, pull on both ends of each connection to make sure they are secure.

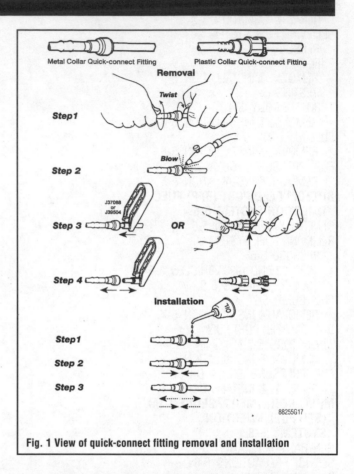

Fig. 1 View of quick-connect fitting removal and installation

THROTTLE BODY INJECTION (TBI) SYSTEM

General Information

➡**The Model 700 throttle body system is used on 1988–91 2.0L and 2.2L engines.**

The Throttle Body Injection (TBI) system is an electronic fuel metering system in which the amount of fuel delivered by the injector is determined by the Electronic Control Module (ECM). This small, on-board microcomputer monitors various engine and vehicle conditions to calculate the fuel delivery time (pulse width) of the injector. The fuel pulse may be modified by the ECM to account for special operating conditions, such as cranking, cold starting, altitude, acceleration and deceleration.

The TBI system provides a mean of fuel distribution for controlling exhaust emissions within legislation's limits. The TBI system, by precisely controlling the air/fuel mixture under all operating conditions, provides as near possible complete combustion.

In order to regulate the fuel delivery in such an efficient manner, then ECM receives electrical inputs from various sensors about engine operating conditions. An oxygen sensor in the main exhaust stream functions to provide feedback information to the ECM regarding oxygen content in the exhaust. The ECM uses this information from the oxygen sensor, and other sensors, in modifying fuel delivery to achieve, as near as possible, an ideal air/fuel ratio of 14.7:1. This air/fuel ratio allows the 3-way catalytic converter to be more efficient in the conversion process of reducing exhaust emissions while, at the same time, providing acceptable levels of driveability and fuel economy.

The TBI unit is made up on 2 major casting assemblies: (1) a throttle body with a valve to control airflow and (2) a fuel body assembly with an integral pressure regulator and fuel injector to supply the required fuel. A device to provide idle speed (IAC) and a device to provide information about throttle valve position (TPS) and included as part of the TBI unit.

Relieving Fuel System Pressure

1. Disconnect the negative battery cable to avoid possible fuel discharge if someone accidentally tries to start the engine.
2. Loosen the fuel filler cap to relieve the tank vapor pressure. Do not tighten the cap until the service procedure is finished.

✷✷ CAUTION

To reduce the chance of personal injury, cover the fuel line with cloth to collect the fuel and then place the cloth in an approved container.

3. The TBI Model 700 used on these engines contains a constant bleed feature to relieve pressure. Therefore, no special procedures are required for reliev-

ing fuel pressure. However, a small amount of fuel may be released after the fuel line is disconnected.

Fuel Pump

The electric fuel pump is attached to the fuel sending unit. The pump used on the 2.0L and 2.2L engines with throttle body injection is a low pressure pump that ranges from 4–13 psi.

REMOVAL & INSTALLATION

♦ **See Figures 2, 3, 4, 5 and 6**

1. Properly relieve the fuel system pressure.
2. If not already done, disconnect the negative battery cable.
3. Raise and safely support the vehicle.
4. Remove the fuel tank, as outlined later in this section.
5. Remove the fuel lever sending unit and pump assembly by using the proper tool to turn the cam lock ring counterclockwise. Lift the assembly from the fuel tank and remove the fuel pump from the fuel level sending unit.
6. Pull the fuel pump up into the attaching hose or pulsator while pulling outward away from the bottom support. After the pump is clear of the bottom support, pull the pump assembly out of the rubber connector or pulsator for removal.

To install:

7. Push the pump into the attaching hose.
8. Install the fuel level sending unit and pump assembly into the tank assembly. Use new O-ring during reassembly.

❉❉ WARNING

Be careful not to fold over or twist the strainer when installing the sending unit as it will restrict fuel flow. Also, be careful the strainer does not block full travel of the float arm.

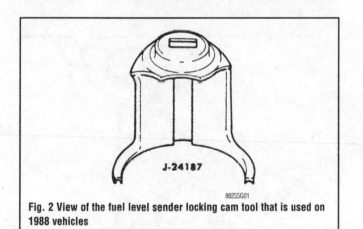

Fig. 2 View of the fuel level sender locking cam tool that is used on 1988 vehicles

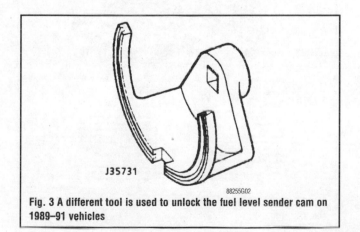

Fig. 3 A different tool is used to unlock the fuel level sender cam on 1989–91 vehicles

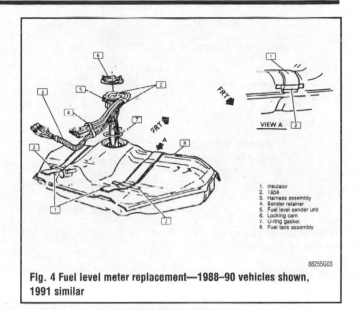

1. Insulator
2. Tape
3. Harness assembly
4. Sender retainer
5. Fuel level sender unit
6. Locking cam
7. O-ring gasket
8. Fuel tank assembly

88255G03

Fig. 4 Fuel level meter replacement—1988–90 vehicles shown, 1991 similar

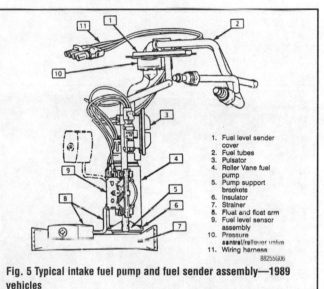

1. Fuel level sender cover
2. Fuel tubes
3. Pulsator
4. Roller Vane fuel pump
5. Pump support brackets
6. Insulator
7. Strainer
8. Float and float arm
9. Fuel level sensor assembly
10. Pressure control/rollover valve
11. Wiring harness

88255G06

Fig. 5 Typical intake fuel pump and fuel sender assembly—1989 vehicles

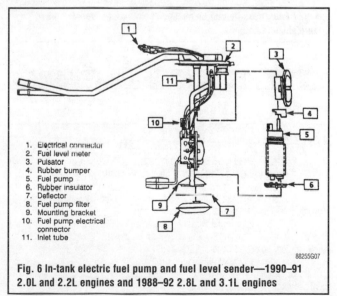

1. Electrical connector
2. Fuel level meter
3. Pulsator
4. Rubber bumper
5. Fuel pump
6. Rubber insulator
7. Deflector
8. Fuel pump filter
9. Mounting bracket
10. Fuel pump electrical connector
11. Inlet tube

88255G07

Fig. 6 In-tank electric fuel pump and fuel level sender—1990–91 2.0L and 2.2L engines and 1988–92 2.8L and 3.1L engines

9. Install the cam lock over the assembly and lock by turning clockwise.
10. Install the fuel tank, as outlined later in this section.
11. Carefully lower the vehicle, then connect the negative battery cable.

TESTING

▶ **See Figure 7**

2.0L Engines

1. Properly relieve the fuel system pressure.
2. With the engine **OFF** off, remove the TBI cover and gasket.
3. Uncouple the fuel supply flexible hose in the engine compartment and attach a gauge between the steel line and the flexible hose. Tighten the gauge inline to ensure no leaks occur during testing.
4. Start the engine and note the reading on the gauge. The pressure should be 9–13 psi.
5. Remove the gauge and reconnect the fuel line. Start the engine and check for leaks.

2.2L Engines

1. Turn the ignition to the **OFF** position.
2. Make sure the fuel tank quantity is sufficient.
3. Install pressure gauge J 29658–B or BT–8205 or equivalent to the fuel line as illustrated.
4. Apply battery voltage to the fuel pump test connector using a 10 amp fused jumper wire.
5. Note the fuel pressure which should be 9–13 psi.

TCCS4P04

Fig. 7 Fuel pressure can be checked using an inexpensive pressure/vacuum gauge

Throttle Body

REMOVAL & INSTALLATION

▶ **See Figures 8 and 9**

1. Properly relieve the fuel system pressure.
2. If not already done, disconnect the negative battery cable.
3. Remove the TBI cover and gasket.
4. Detach the electrical connectors from the Idle Air Control (IAC) valve, Throttle Position (TP) sensor and the fuel injector.
5. Remove the grommet with the wires from the TBI unit.
6. Disconnect the throttle linkage, return spring(s), transmission control cable and cruise control where applicable.
7. Tag and disconnect all vacuum hoses.
8. Unfasten the inlet and outlet fuel line nuts, using a back-up wrench to avoid twisting or warping the lines.

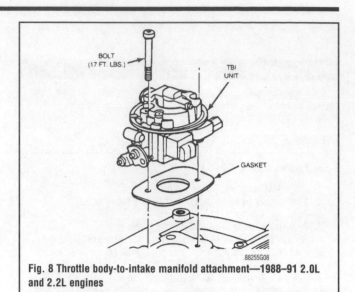

88255G08

Fig. 8 Throttle body-to-intake manifold attachment—1988–91 2.0L and 2.2L engines

9. Remove the fuel line O-rings from the nuts and discard.
10. Remove all TBI mounting hardware and remove the TBI unit and gasket.

✳✳ WARNING

To prevent damage, place the TBI unit in a holding fixture, before performing service.

11. Stuff a clean rag in the manifold opening to prevent dirt from entering.
To install:
12. Clean old gasket material from the surface of the intake manifold.
13. Place a new gasket along with the TBI unit on the manifold and tighten the mounting hardware to 17 ft. lbs. (23 Nm) for 1988 vehicles, or to 18 ft. lbs. (24 Nm) for 1989–91 vehicles.

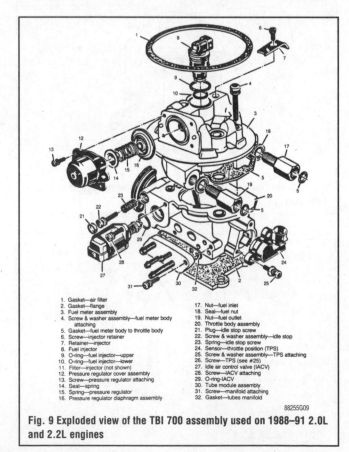

1. Gasket—air filter
2. Gasket—flange
3. Fuel meter assembly
4. Screw & washer assembly—fuel meter body attaching
5. Gasket—fuel meter body to throttle body
6. Screw—injector retainer
7. Retainer—injector
8. Fuel injector
9. O-ring—fuel injector—upper
10. O-ring—fuel injector—lower
11. Filter—injector (not shown)
12. Pressure regulator cover assembly
13. Screw—pressure regulator attaching
14. Seat—spring
15. Spring—pressure regulator
16. Pressure regulator diaphragm assembly
17. Nut—fuel inlet
18. Seal—fuel nut
19. Nut—fuel outlet
20. Throttle body assembly
21. Plug—idle stop screw
22. Screw & washer assembly—idle stop
23. Spring—idle stop screw
24. Sensor—throttle position (TPS)
25. Screw & washer assembly—TPS attaching
26. Screw—TPS (see #25)
27. Idle air control valve (IACV)
28. Screw—IACV attaching
29. O-ring—IACV
30. Tube module assembly
31. Screw—manifold attaching
32. Gasket—tubes manifold

88255G09

Fig. 9 Exploded view of the TBI 700 assembly used on 1988–91 2.0L and 2.2L engines

14. Use new O-rings on the fuel line nuts and install hand-tight.
15. Use a back-up wrench on the TBI unit and tighten the inlet and outlet nuts to 20 ft. lbs. (27 Nm).
16. Attach the vacuum hoses, as tagged during removal.
17. Connect the throttle linkage, return spring(s), transmission control cable and cruise control where applicable.
18. Install the grommet with the wires to the TBI unit.
19. Attach the electrical connectors to the IAC valve, TP sensor and the fuel injector. Make sure they are all fully seated and latched.
20. With the engine OFF, depress the accelerator pedal to the floor to make sure it is free.
21. Install the TBI cover and new gasket if necessary.
22. Connect the negative battery cable, then start the engine and check for leaks.

Fuel Injector

REMOVAL & INSTALLATION

▶ See Figures 10 and 11

❊❊ WARNING

When removing the injectors, be careful not to damage the electrical connector pins (on top of the injector), the injector fuel filter and the nozzle. The fuel injector is serviced as a complete assembly ONLY. The injector is an electrical component and should not be immersed in any kind of cleaner.

1. Properly relieve the fuel system pressure.
2. If not done already, disconnect the negative battery cable.
3. Remove the TBI cover and gasket.
4. Detach the electrical connector from the fuel injector.
5. Remove the injector retainer screw and retainer.
6. Using a fulcrum, place a suitable tool under the ridge opposite the connector end and carefully pry the injector out, as shown in the accompanying figure.
7. Remove and discard the injector upper and lower O-rings, and the O-rings in the fuel injector cavity.

To install:

❊❊ WARNING

Be sure to replace the injector with an identical part. Injectors from other models can fit in the Model 700, but are calibrated for different flow rates. There is a part number located on the top of the injector

8. Inspect the filter for evidence of contamination.
9. Lubricate the new upper and lower O-rings with automatic transmission fluid and place them on the injector. Make sure the upper O-ring is in the groove and the lower one is flush up against the filter.
10. Install the injector assembly by pushing it straight into the fuel injector cavity.

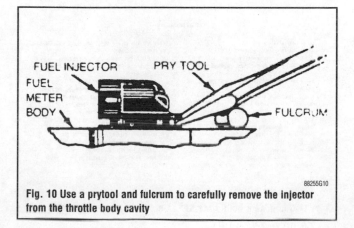

Fig. 10 Use a prytool and fulcrum to carefully remove the injector from the throttle body cavity

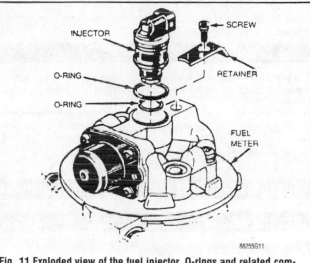

Fig. 11 Exploded view of the fuel injector, O-rings and related components

➡ Make sure the electrical connector end on the injector is facing in the general direction to the cut-out in the fuel meter body for the wire grommet.

11. Install the injector retainer, using appropriate thread locking compound on the retainer attaching screw. Tighten to 27 inch lbs. (3.0 Nm).
12. Attach the fuel injector electrical connector.
13. Connect the negative battery cable. With the engine OFF and the ignition in the ON position, check for fuel leaks.
14. Install the TBI cover and gasket.

Fuel Pressure Regulator

REMOVAL & INSTALLATION

▶ See Figure 12

❊❊ WARNING

To prevent leaks, the pressure regulator diaphragm assembly must be replaced whenever the cover is removed.

1. Properly relieve the fuel system pressure.
2. If not done already, disconnect the negative battery cable.

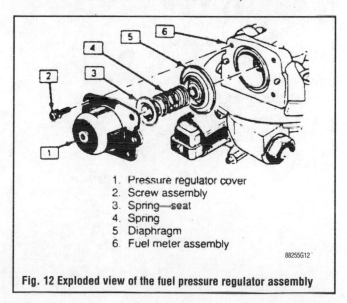

1. Pressure regulator cover
2. Screw assembly
3. Spring—seat
4. Spring
5. Diaphragm
6. Fuel meter assembly

Fig. 12 Exploded view of the fuel pressure regulator assembly

3. Remove the TBI cover and gasket.
4. Remove the 4 pressure regulator attaching screws, while keeping the pressure regulator compressed.

✳✳ CAUTION

The pressure regulator contains a large spring under heavy compression. Use care when removing the screws to prevent personal injury.

5. Remove the pressure regulator cover assembly, then remove the spring seat.
6. Remove the pressure regulator diaphragm assembly.

BOTTOM FEED PORT (BFP) FUEL INJECTION SYSTEM

General Information

◆ See Figures 13 and 14

➤The Bottom Feed Port (BFP) injection system is used on the 1992–96 2.2L. In later years, this system may also be referred to as Multi-port Fuel Injection (MFI) or Sequential Fuel Injection (SFI).

The function of the fuel metering system is to deliver the correct amount of fuel to the engine under all operating conditions. In this system, fuel is delivered to the engine by individual bottom feed-type multi-port fuel injectors mounted in the lower intake manifold near each cylinder.

The computer control module, pulses the fuel injectors in pairs. Alternate parts are pulsed every 180° of crankshaft revolution. This is called Alternating Synchronous Double Fire (ASDF) injection. The ECM uses two injector driver circuits, each controlling a pair of injectors. The current in each circuit is allowed to climb to a peak of 4 amps and then is reduced to 1 amp to hold the injector open. This happens very quickly.

The main control sensor of this system is the Oxygen (O$_2$) sensor, located in the exhaust manifold. This sensor indicates to the computer control module how much oxygen is in the exhaust gas and the ECM changes the air/fuel ratio to the engine by controlling the fuel injectors. The best mixture keep exhaust emissions to a minimum is 14.7:1 which allows the catalytic converter to operate most efficiently. Because of the constant measuring and adjusting of the air/fuel ratio, then fuel injection system is called a "Closed Loop" system.

Relieving Fuel System Pressure

1992–93 AND 1996 VEHICLES

1. Loosen the fuel filler cap to relieve the tank vapor pressure. Leave the cap loose for now.
2. Raise and support the vehicle safely.
3. Detach the fuel pump electrical connector.
4. Lower the vehicle.
5. Start the engine and run until the fuel supply remaining in the fuel pipes is consumed. Engage the starter for 3 seconds to assure relief of any remaining pressure.
6. Raise and support the vehicle safely.
7. Attach the fuel pump electrical connector.
8. Lower the vehicle.
9. Tighten the fuel filler cap.
10. Disconnect the negative battery cable terminal to avoid possible fuel discharge someone accidentally tries to start the engine. The fuel system is now safe for servicing.

1994–95 VEHICLES

1. Loosen the fuel filler cap to relieve the tank vapor pressure. Leave the cap loose for now.
2. Remove the fuel pump fuse from the fuse block.
3. Start the engine and run until the fuel supply remaining in the pipes is used. Engage the starter for 3 seconds for 3 seconds to make sure the pressure is completely relieved.
4. Install the fuel pump fuse in the block.
5. Disconnect the negative battery cable terminal to avoid possible fuel discharge someone accidentally tries to start the engine. The fuel system is now safe for servicing.

To install:
7. Install the pressure regulator diaphragm assembly, making sure it is seated in the groove in the fuel meter body.
8. Install the regulator spring seat and spring into the cover assembly.
9. Install the cover assembly over the diaphragm, while aligning the mounting holes.
10. While maintaining pressure on the regulator spring, install the 4 screw assemblies that have been coated with appropriate thread locking compound. Tighten the screws to 22 inch lbs. (2.4 Nm).
11. Connect the negative battery cable. With the engine **OFF** and the ignition in the **ON** position, check for fuel leaks.
12. Install the TBI cover, using a new gasket.

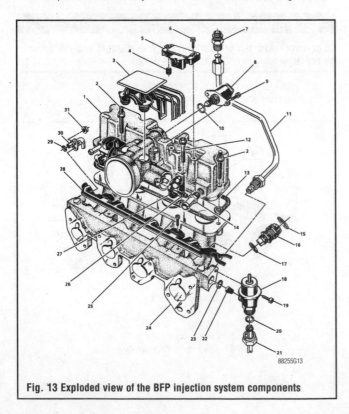

Fig. 13 Exploded view of the BFP injection system components

Part Names		
1 MANIFOLD ASM - UPPER	16	INJECTOR ASM - (BOTTOM FEED) MFI FUEL
2 STUD - UPPER INLET MANIFOLD	17	O-RING - LOWER
3 HARNESS ASM - EGR VALVE AND FUEL PRESSURE REGULATOR VACUUM	18	REGULATOR ASM - FUEL PRESSURE
4 SEAL - MAP SENSOR	19	SCREW - FUEL PRESSURE REGULATOR ATTACHING
5 SENSOR - MANIFOLD ABSOLUTE PRESSURE (MAP)	20	O-RING - FUEL RETURN LINE
6 BOLT - MAP SENSOR ATTACHING	21	PIPE ASM - FUEL INJECTOR FUEL RETURN
7 FITTING AND WASHER ASM	22	SCREEN - FILTER (IF SO EQUIPPED)
8 VALVE ASM - IDLE AIR CONTROL (IAC)	23	O-RING - FUEL INLET FITTING
9 SCREW - IAC VALVE ATTACHING	24	MANIFOLD ASM - LOWER
10 O-RING - IAC VALVE	25	SCREW - INJECTOR RETAINER ATTACHING
11 TUBE ASM - EGR TRANSPORT	26	SCREW - TP SENSOR ATTACHING
12 BOLT - UPPER INLET MANIFOLD	27	SENSOR - THROTTLE POSITION (TP)
13 GASKET - UPPER INLET MANIFOLD	28	RETAINER - INJECTOR
14 FITTING - POWER BRAKE	29	O-RING - FUEL FEED LINE
15 O-RING - FUEL INJECTOR	30	PIPE ASM - FUEL INJECTION FUEL FEED
	31	NUT - FUEL FEED

88255G14

Fig. 14 Component list for the BFP injection system components

Fuel Pump

REMOVAL & INSTALLATION

For fuel pump replacement details, please refer to the Multi-port Fuel Injection (MFI) procedure, located later in this section.

Bottom Feed Port Fuel Injectors

REMOVAL & INSTALLATION

▶ See Figure 15

✳✳ WARNING

Any time the injectors are removed for service, always remove the fuel pressure regulator to drain excess fuel, and prevent fuel from entering the engine cylinders. Flooded cylinders could result in engine damage.

1. Properly relieve the fuel system pressure as outlined earlier.
2. If not already done, disconnect the negative battery cable.
3. Remove the upper manifold assembly, as outlined in Section 3 of this manual.

✳✳ CAUTION

To reduce the chance of personal injury, cover the fuel line connections with a shop towel, when disconnecting.

4. Disconnect the fuel return line retaining bracket nut and move the return line away from the regulator.
5. Remove the fuel pressure regulator assembly.

✳✳ WARNING

Do not try to remove the injectors by lifting up on the injector retaining bracket while the injectors are still installed in the in the bracket slots or damage to the bracket and/or injectors could result.

➡Do not attempt to remove the bracket without first removing the pressure regulator.

6. Remove the injector retainer bracket attaching screws and carefully slide the bracket off to clear the injector slots and regulator.

7. Detach the fuel injector electrical connectors.
8. Remove the fuel injector(s), then remove and discard the O-ring seals.

✳✳ CAUTION

To reduce the risk fire and personal injury, make sure that the lower (small) O-ring of each injector does not remain in the lower manifold. If the O-ring is not removed with the injector, the replacement injector, with new O-rings, will not seat properly in the injector socket and could cause a fuel leak.

9. Cover the injector sockets to prevent dirt from entering the opening.

➡Each fuel injector is calibrated with a different flow rate, so make sure to replace with the identical part numbers.

To install:
10. Lubricate the new injector O-ring seals with clean engine oil and install on the injector assembly.
11. Install the injector assembly into the lower manifold injector socket, with the electrical connectors facing inward.
12. Carefully position the injector retainer bracket so that the injector retaining slots and regulator are aligned with the bracket slots.
13. Attach the injector electrical connectors.
14. Install the pressure regulator assembly.
15. Coat the injector retainer bracket retaining screws with suitable thread locking material, then install them and tighten to 31 inch lbs. (3.5 Nm).
16. Install the accelerator cable bracket with the attaching bolts/nuts finger-tight at this time.

✳✳ WARNING

The accelerator bracket must be aligned with the accelerator cam to prevent cable wear, which could result in cable breakage.

17. Align the accelerator bracket as follows:
   a. Place a steel rule across the bore of the throttle body, with one end in contact with the accelerator bracket.
   b. Adjust the accelerator bracket to obtain a $^{25}/_{64}$ in. (9–11mm) gap between the bracket and the throttle body.
   c. Tighten the top bolt first and tighten all bolts/nuts to 18 ft. lbs. (25 Nm)
18. Tighten the fuel filler cap.
19. Connect the negative battery cable and turn the ignition **ON** for 2 seconds, **OFF** for 10 seconds, then **ON** and check for fuel leaks.
20. Install the air intake duct.

Fuel Pressure Regulator

REMOVAL & INSTALLATION

▶ See Figure 16

1. Properly relieve the fuel system pressure as outlined earlier in this section.

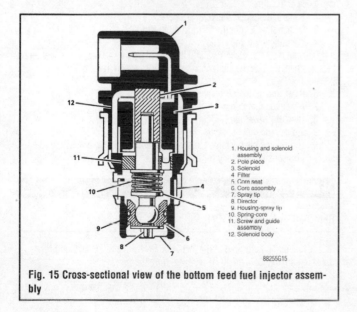

1. Housing and solenoid assembly
2. Pole piece
3. Solenoid
4. Filter
5. Core seat
6. Core assembly
7. Spray tip
8. Director
9. Housing-spray tip
10. Spring-core
11. Screw and guide assembly
12. Solenoid body

88255G15

Fig. 15 Cross-sectional view of the bottom feed fuel injector assembly

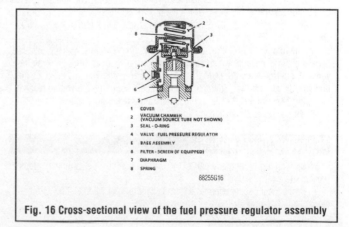

1. COVER
2. VACUUM CHAMBER (VACUUM SOURCE TUBE NOT SHOWN)
3. SEAL - O-RING
4. VALVE - FUEL PRESSURE REGULATOR
5. BASE ASSEMBLY
6. FILTER - SCREEN (IF EQUIPPED)
7. DIAPHRAGM
8. SPRING

88255G16

Fig. 16 Cross-sectional view of the fuel pressure regulator assembly

2. If not already done, disconnect the negative battery cable.

3. Disconnect the vacuum hose from the regulator.

4. Place a rag under the connection, then remove the fuel return pipe clamp.

5. Remove the fuel return pipe and O-ring from the regulator. Discard the O-ring.

6. Unfasten the pressure regulator bracket attaching screw.

7. Remove the pressure regulator assembly and O-ring. Discard the O-ring.

To install:

8. Lubricate a new pressure regulator O-ring with clean engine oil, then install on the pressure regulator.

9. Position the pressure regulator assembly onto the manifold.

10. Coat the pressure regulator bracket attaching screw with the appropriate thread locking material, then install and tighten to 31 inch lbs. (3.5 Nm).

11. Attach the vacuum hose to the regulator.

12. Lubricate a new fuel return pipe O-ring with clean engine oil, then install on the end of the pipe.

13. Connect the fuel return pipe to the pressure regulator and tighten the attaching nut to 22 inch lbs. (30 Nm).

14. Install the fuel return pipe clamp attaching nut to the lower manifold assembly.

15. Tighten the fuel filler cap.

16. Connect the negative battery cable and turn the ignition **ON** for 2 seconds, **OFF** for 10 seconds, then **ON** and check for fuel leaks.

MULTI-PORT (MFI) & SEQUENTIAL (SFI) FUEL INJECTION SYSTEMS

General Information

On 1988–94 2.8L and 3.1L engines, the Multi-port Fuel Injection (MFI) system is available. The MFI system is controlled by a computer control module (ECM/PCM), which monitors engine operation and generates output signals to provide the correct air/fuel mixture, ignition timing and engine idle speed control. Input to the control unit is provided by an oxygen sensor, coolant temperature sensor, detonation sensor, hot film air mass sensor and throttle position sensor. The ECM/PCM also receives information concerning engine rpm, road speed, transmission gear position, power steering and air conditioning.

The 2.3L engines also use a Multi-port Fuel Injection (MFI) system, however, this system incorporates an Alternating Synchronous Double Fire (ASDF) method of injection. Fuel is delivered to the engine by individual fuel injectors mounted in the intake ports of the cylinder head as in an all multi-port type injection system. The difference is that the Electric Control module (ECM) pulses the fuel injectors in pairs. Alternate pairs are pulsed every 180° of crankcase revolution. This system provides better fuel vaporization and improved emission control.

On 1995–96 3.1L engines, a Sequential port Fuel Injection (SFI) system is used for more precise fuel control. With SFI, metered fuel is timed and injected sequentially through injectors into individual cylinder ports. Each cylinder receives one injection per working cycle (every two revolutions), just prior to the opening of the intake valve. The main difference between the two types of fuel injection systems is the manner in which fuel is injected. In the multi-port system, all injectors work simultaneously, injecting half the fuel charge each engine revolution. The control units are different for SFI and MFI systems, but most other components are similar.

1. Both systems use Bosch injectors, on at each intake port, rather than the single injector found on the earlier throttle body system. The injectors are mounted on a fuel rail and are activated by a signal from the electronic control module. The injector is a solenoid-operated valve which remains open depending on the width of the electronic pulses (length of the signal) from the computer control module (ECM/PCM); the longer the open time, then more fuel is injected. In this manner, the air fuel mixture can be precisely controlled for maximum performance with minimum emissions.

Fuel is pumped from the tank by a high pressure fuel pump, located inside the fuel tank. It is a positive displacement roller vane pump. The impeller serves as a vapor separator and pre-charges the high pressure assembly. A pressure regulator maintains 40.5–47 psi (271–315 kPa) in the fuel line to the injectors and the excess fuel is fed back to the tank.

Engine idle is controlled by an Idle Air Control (IAC) valve, which provides a bypass channel through which air can flow. It consists of an orifice and pintle which is controlled by the ECM through a stepper motor. The IAC provides air flow for idle and allows additional air during cold start until the engine reaches operating temperature. As the engine temperature rises, the opening through which air passes is slowly closed.

Service Precautions

When working around any part of the fuel system, take precautionary steps to prevent fire and/or explosion:

• Disconnect negative terminal from battery (except when testing with battery voltage is required).

• When ever possible, use a flashlight instead of a drop light.

• Keep all open flame and smoking material out of the area.

• Use a shop cloth or similar to catch fuel when opening a fuel system.

• Relieve fuel system pressure before servicing.

• Use eye protection.

• Always keep a dry chemical (class B) fire extinguisher near the area.

Relieving Fuel System Pressure

✴✴ CAUTION

To reduce the risk of fire or personal injury, it is necessary to relieve the fuel system pressure before servicing the fuel system.

EXCEPT 1991–94 2.3L & 1995–96 3.1L ENGINES

1. Disconnect the negative battery cable, to prevent fuel spray if someone accidentally tries to start the engine.

2. Loosen the fuel filler cap to relieve tank vapor pressure.

3. Connect a J–34730–1 fuel gauge or equivalent, to the fuel pressure valve. Wrap a shop towel around the fitting while connecting the gauge to avoid spillage.

4. Install a bleed hose into an approved container and open the valve to bleed the system pressure. The fuel system is now safe for servicing.

5. Drain any remaining fuel in the gauge into an approved container.

1991–94 2.3L & 1995–96 3.1L ENGINES

1. Loosen the full filler cap to relieve the tank vapor pressure. Leave the cap loose at this time.

2. Raise and support the vehicle safely.

3. Detach the fuel pump electrical connector.

4. Carefully lower the vehicle.

5. Start the engine and run until the fuel supply remaining in the fuel pipes is consumed. Engage the starter for 3 seconds to assure relief of any remaining pressure.

6. Raise and support the vehicle safely.

7. Attach the fuel pump electrical connector.

8. Carefully lower the vehicle.

9. Tighten the fuel filler cap.

10. Disconnect the negative battery cable terminal to avoid possible fuel spray if someone accidentally tries to start the engine.

Fuel Pump

REMOVAL & INSTALLATION

The fuel pump is located in the fuel tank. Removal and installation procedures require the fuel tank to be removed from the vehicle.

The fuel system pressure must be relieved before attempting any service procedures. Use caution to avoid the risk of fire by disposing of any fuel and fuel soaked rags properly.

1988–92 Vehicles

▶ See Figures 6, 17 and 18

1. Properly relieve the fuel system pressure.
2. If not done already, disconnect the negative battery cable.
3. Using a siphon hose and pump, drain the fuel from the fuel tank into an approved container.
4. Raise and safely support the vehicle.
5. Support the fuel tank securely, then disconnect the retaining straps.
6. Lower the tank enough to disconnect the sending unit wire, the hoses and the ground strap. Remove the fuel tank from the vehicle.
7. Using a locking cam tool, remove the sending unit retaining cam from the fuel tank.
8. Remove the fuel pump and sending unit assembly from the tank. Remove and discard the O-ring gasket.

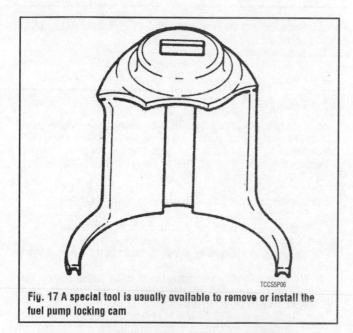

Fig. 17 A special tool is usually available to remove or install the fuel pump locking cam

TCCS5P06

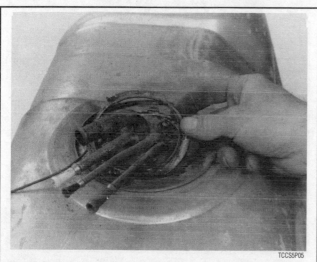

Fig. 18 Once the locking cam is released it can be removed to free the fuel pump

TCCS5P05

To Install:

9. Install a new O-ring and gasket. Carefully install the fuel pump and sending unit assembly into the fuel tank.
10. Install the retaining cam and lock and secure the sending unit in place to the fuel tank.
11. Raise the tank in position to connect the sending unit wire, the hoses and the ground strap. Install the tank retaining straps and secure the tank in place.
12. Carefully lower the vehicle, then refill the tank with fuel.
13. Connect the negative battery cable. Turn the ignition switch to the **ON** position, to restore system pressure.
14. Start the engine and check for fuel leaks.

1993–96 Vehicles

▶ See Figures 19, 20 and 21

1. Properly relieve the fuel system pressure.
2. If not done already, disconnect the negative battery cable.
3. Using a siphon hose and pump, drain the fuel from the fuel tank into an approved container.
4. Raise and safely support the vehicle.
5. Remove the fuel tank from the vehicle, as outlined later in this section.

When removing the modular sender, be careful as the sender may spring up from its position. Also, during removal, the reservoir bucket is full of fuel and must be tipped slightly during removal to avoid damage to the float.

6. While holding the modular fuel sender assembly down, remove the snapring from the designated slots located on the retainer. Remove and discard the fuel sender O-ring and replace with a new one during installation.
7. Remove the external fuel strainer.
8. Remove Connector Position Assurance (CPA) #8 from the electrical connector, then detach the fuel pump electrical connector.
9. Gently release the tabs on the sides of the fuel sender to the cover assembly. Begin by squeezing the sides of the reservoir and releasing the tab opposite the fuel level sensor. Move clockwise to release the second and third tab using the same procedure.
10. Lift the cover out far enough to detach the fuel pump electrical connector.
11. Rotate the fuel pump baffle #18 counterclockwise and remove the baffle and pump from retainer #7. Refer to the accompanying illustration for details.
12. Slide the fuel pump outlet out of the slot.
13. Remove the fuel pump outlet seal.

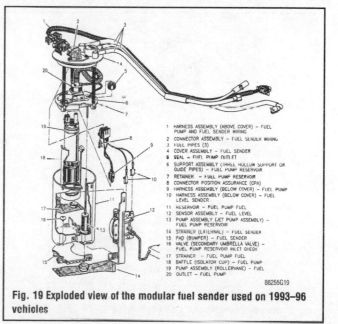

1 HARNESS ASSEMBLY (ABOVE COVER) – FUEL PUMP AND FUEL SENDER WIRING
2 CONNECTOR ASSEMBLY – FUEL SENDER WIRING
3 FUEL PIPES (3)
4 COVER ASSEMBLY – FUEL SENDER
5 SEAL – FUEL PUMP OUTLET
6 SUPPORT ASSEMBLY (THREE HOLLOW SUPPORT OR GUIDE PIPES) – FUEL PUMP RESERVOIR
7 RETAINER – FUEL PUMP RESERVOIR
8 CONNECTOR POSITION ASSURANCE (CPA)
9 HARNESS ASSEMBLY (BELOW COVER) – FUEL PUMP
10 HARNESS ASSEMBLY (BELOW COVER) – FUEL LEVEL SENDER
11 RESERVOIR – FUEL PUMP FUEL
12 SENSOR ASSEMBLY – FUEL LEVEL
13 PUMP ASSEMBLY (JET PUMP ASSEMBLY) – FUEL PUMP RESERVOIR
14 STRAINER (EXTERNAL) – FUEL SENDER
15 PAD (BUMPER) – FUEL SENDER
16 VALVE (SECONDARY UMBRELLA VALVE) – FUEL PUMP RESERVOIR INLET CHECK
17 STRAINER – FUEL PUMP FUEL
18 BAFFLE (ISOLATOR CUP) – FUEL PUMP
19 PUMP ASSEMBLY (ROLLERVANE) – FUEL
20 OUTLET – FUEL PUMP

88255G19

Fig. 19 Exploded view of the modular fuel sender used on 1993–96 vehicles

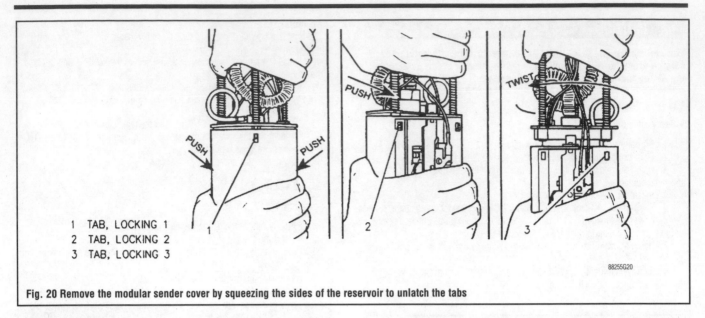

1 TAB, LOCKING 1
2 TAB, LOCKING 2
3 TAB, LOCKING 3

88255G20

Fig. 20 Remove the modular sender cover by squeezing the sides of the reservoir to unlatch the tabs

To install:

14. Install the fuel pump outlet seal.

15. Slide the fuel pump outlet in the slots of reservoir cover.

16. Install the fuel pump and baffle assembly onto the reservoir retainer #7 and rotate clockwise until seated.

17. Lower retainer assembly #7 partially into the reservoir. Line up all three sleeve tabs. Press the retainer onto the reservoir making sure all three tabs are firmly seated. Gently pull on the fuel pump reservoir retainer to be sure a secure fastening was achieved. If not secure, replace the entire fuel sender.

18. Attach the fuel pump connector.

19. Install CPA #8 to the fuel sender cover #7.

20. Install a new external fuel strainer #14.

21. Install new O-ring on the modular fuel sender to the tank.

22. Align the tab on the front of the sender with the slot on the front of the retainer snapring.

23. Slowly apply pressure to the top of the spring loaded sender, until the sender aligns flush with the retainer on the tank.

24. Insert the snapring into the designated slots. Make sure the snapring is fully seated within the tab slots.

25. Install the fuel tank, as outlined later in this section.

26. Carefully lower the vehicle, then refill the tank with fuel.

27. Connect the negative battery cable. Turn the ignition switch to the **ON** position, to restore system pressure.

28. Start the engine and check for fuel leaks.

TESTING

▶ **See Figure 22**

When the ignition switch is turned **ON**, the Electronic Control Module (ECM) will turn **ON** the in-tank fuel pump. It will remain **ON** as long as the engine is cranking or running, and the ECM is receiving references pulses. If there are no reference pulses, the ECM will shut **OFF** the fuel pump within 2 seconds after ignition **ON** or engine stops.

The pump will deliver fuel to the fuel rail and injectors, then to the pressure regulator, where the system pressure is controlled to about 34–47 psi. Excess fuel is then returned to the fuel tank.

1. Wrap a towel around the fuel pressure connector to absorb any small amount of fuel leakage that may occur while installing the gauge.

2. The ignition should be off for at least 10 seconds and the air conditioning **OFF**.

3. With the ignition **ON** the fuel pump should run for about 2 seconds. The ignition **ON** fuel pump pressure should be 40.5–47 psi. This pressure is controlled by the spring pressure within the regulator assembly.

1 RESERVOIR ASSEMBLY
2 TUBE, OUTLET
3 PUMP, FUEL ASSEMBLY
4 MEMBER, FLEX
5 RESERVOIR, RETAINER—FUEL PUMP

88255G21

Fig. 21 Rotate the baffle and pump to remove

TCCS4P04

Fig. 22 Fuel pressure can be checked using an inexpensive pressure/vacuum gauge

4. When the engine is idling, the manifold pressure is low (high vacuum) and is applied to the fuel regulator diaphragm. This will offset the spring and lower the fuel pressure. This idle pressure will vary somewhat depending on the barometric pressure, however the pressure idling should be less indicating pressure regulator control.

5. Pressure that continues to fall is caused by 1 of the following:
- In-tank fuel pump check valve not holding
- Pump coupling hose or pulsator leaking
- Fuel pressure regulator valve leaking
- Injector(s) sticking open

➡A Injector sticking open can best be determined by checking for a fouled or saturated spark plug(s).

Throttle Body

REMOVAL & INSTALLATION

▶ **See Figures 23 thru 29**

1. Properly relieve the fuel system pressure.
2. If not already done, disconnect the negative battery cable.
3. Partially drain the radiator enough to allow the coolant hoses at the throttle body to be removed.
4. Disconnect the air cleaner duct from the throttle body.
5. Detach the electrical connectors from the IAC valve and TP sensor.
6. Tag and disconnect the vacuum hoses from the throttle body.
7. Detach the throttle, cruise and transmission control cables from the throttle body.
8. Remove the accelerator cable bracket attaching nut and bolt, then remove the bracket.
9. Disconnect the power brake vacuum hose from the throttle body.

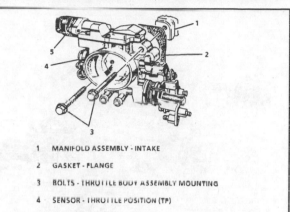

1	MANIFOLD ASSEMBLY - INTAKE
2	GASKET - FLANGE
3	BOLTS - THROTTLE BODY ASSEMBLY MOUNTING
4	SENSOR - THROTTLE POSITION (TP)
5	VALVE - IDLE AIR CONTROL (IAC)

88255G26

Fig. 25 The throttle body is secured with 2 bolts on 1988–93 2.8L and 3.1L engines

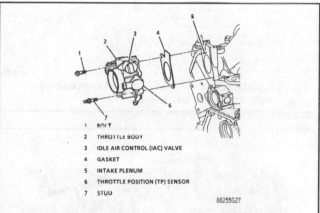

1	BOLT
2	THROTTLE BODY
3	IDLE AIR CONTROL (IAC) VALVE
4	GASKET
5	INTAKE PLENUM
6	THROTTLE POSITION (TP) SENSOR
7	STUD

88255G27

Fig. 26 Exploded view of the throttle body and gasket—1994–96 3.1L engines

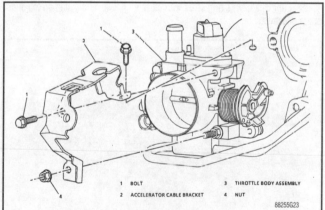

| 1 | BOLT | 3 | THROTTLE BODY ASSEMBLY |
| 2 | ACCELERATOR CABLE BRACKET | 4 | NUT |

88255G23

Fig. 23 Unfasten the retaining nut and bolt, then remove the accelerator cable bracket—2.3L engine

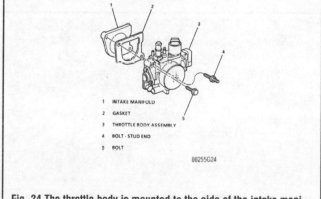

1	INTAKE MANIFOLD
2	GASKET
3	THROTTLE BODY ASSEMBLY
4	BOLT - STUD END
5	BOLT

88255G24

Fig. 24 The throttle body is mounted to the side of the intake manifold on 2.3L engines

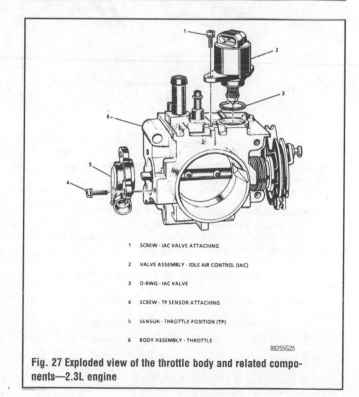

1	SCREW - IAC VALVE ATTACHING
2	VALVE ASSEMBLY - IDLE AIR CONTROL (IAC)
3	O-RING - IAC VALVE
4	SCREW - TP SENSOR ATTACHING
5	SENSOR - THROTTLE POSITION (TP)
6	BODY ASSEMBLY - THROTTLE

88255G25

Fig. 27 Exploded view of the throttle body and related components—2.3L engine

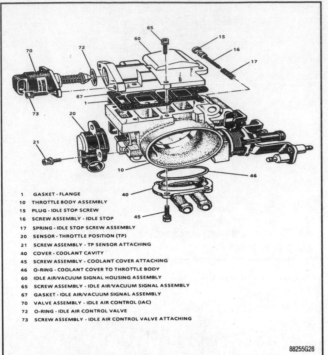

1	GASKET - FLANGE
10	THROTTLE BODY ASSEMBLY
15	PLUG - IDLE STOP SCREW
16	SCREW ASSEMBLY - IDLE STOP
17	SPRING - IDLE STOP SCREW ASSEMBLY
20	SENSOR - THROTTLE POSITION (TP)
21	SCREW ASSEMBLY - TP SENSOR ATTACHING
40	COVER - COOLANT CAVITY
45	SCREW ASSEMBLY - COOLANT COVER ATTACHING
46	O-RING - COOLANT COVER TO THROTTLE BODY
60	IDLE AIR/VACUUM SIGNAL HOUSING ASSEMBLY
65	SCREW ASSEMBLY - IDLE AIR/VACUUM SIGNAL ASSEMBLY
67	GASKET - IDLE AIR/VACUUM SIGNAL ASSEMBLY
70	VALVE ASSEMBLY - IDLE AIR CONTROL (IAC)
72	O-RING - IDLE AIR CONTROL VALVE
73	SCREW ASSEMBLY - IDLE AIR CONTROL VALVE ATTACHING

88255G28

Fig. 28 Exploded view of the throttle body and related components—1988–93 2.8L and 3.1L engines

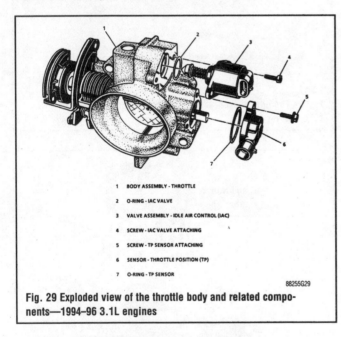

1	BODY ASSEMBLY - THROTTLE
2	O-RING - IAC VALVE
3	VALVE ASSEMBLY - IDLE AIR CONTROL (IAC)
4	SCREW - IAC VALVE ATTACHING
5	SCREW - TP SENSOR ATTACHING
6	SENSOR - THROTTLE POSITION (TP)
7	O-RING - TP SENSOR

88255G29

Fig. 29 Exploded view of the throttle body and related components—1994–96 3.1L engines

10. Remove the throttle body attaching bolt and stud.
11. Loosen the throttle body from the manifold.
12. Disconnect the coolant lines and remove the throttle body and gasket from the manifold. Remove and discard the gasket.
To install:
13. Reposition the throttle body next to the manifold and reconnect the coolant hoses.
14. Install a new mounting gasket and tighten the bolt and stud and tighten the bolts to 19 ft. lbs. (26 Nm).
15. Connect the power brake vacuum hose at the throttle body.
16. Attach the throttle, cruise and transmission control cables to the throttle body.
17. Install the accelerator cable bracket attaching nut and bolt and tighten the nut to 18 ft. lbs. (25 Nm) and the bolt to 106 inch lbs. (12 Nm).

18. Connect the vacuum hoses to the throttle body, as tagged during removal.
19. Attach the electrical connectors to the IAC valve and TPS.
20. Connect the air cleaner duct to the throttle body.
21. Refill the radiator.
22. Connect the negative battery cable.
23. With the engine off, check to see that the accelerator pedal is free.
24. Reset the IAC pintle position as follows:
  a. Turn the ignition switch to the **ON** position (engine **OFF**).
  b. Ground the diagnostic test terminal for 5 seconds.
  c. Remove the ground.
  d. Turn the ignition switch to the **OFF** position for 10 seconds.
  e. Start the engine and check for proper idle information.

Fuel Injectors

REMOVAL & INSTALLATION

1. Properly relieve the fuel system pressure.
2. If not already done, disconnect the negative battery cable.

➡**It is not necessary to separate the rail from the fuel pipes.**

3. Remove the fuel rail from the vehicle.
4. Detach the fuel injector electrical connector.
5. Remove the injector retaining clip by spreading the open end of the clip slightly and removing from the rail.
6. Remove the injector(s). Discard the injector retaining clip.
7. Remove and discard the O-rings from both ends of the injectors.
To install:

➡**Each fuel injector is calibrated with a different flow rate. Make sure the replacement injector has the identical part number.**

8. Lubricate new O-ring seals with clean engine oil and install on the ends of the injectors.

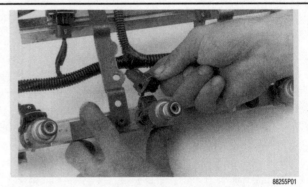

88255P01

Remove the fuel rail from the manifold, then detach the fuel injector electrical connector

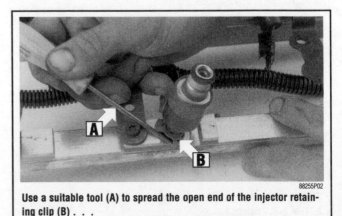

88255P02

Use a suitable tool (A) to spread the open end of the injector retaining clip (B) . . .

. . . then remove the injector from the fuel rail

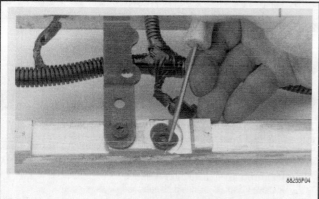

Carefully remove and discard the fuel rail injector O-ring . . .

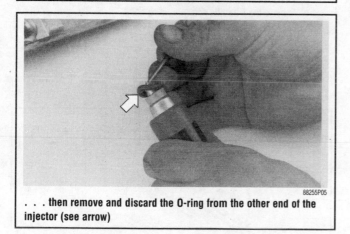

. . . then remove and discard the O-ring from the other end of the injector (see arrow)

9. Place new injector retaining clips on the injector assembly. Position the clip on the right side of the injector electrical connector.

10. Install the injector assembly(ies) into the fuel rail socket(s) with the electrical connector facing outward. Push in far enough to engage the retainer clip over the rail extrusion flange.

11. Install the fuel rail assembly.

12. Connect the negative battery cable

Fuel Rail Assembly

REMOVAL & INSTALLATION

2.3L Engines

▶ See Figures 30, 31 and 32

1. Properly relieve the fuel system pressure.
2. If not done already, disconnect the negative battery cable.

3. Disconnect the hoses from the front and side of the crankcase ventilation oil/air separator. Leave the vacuum hose attached to the canister purge solenoid.

4. Remove the bolts attaching the crankcase ventilation oil/air separator and canister purge solenoid.

5. Disconnect the hose from the bottom of the separator, then remove the separator. Position the canister purge solenoid out of the way.

6. Remove the fuel pipe clamp bolt.

7. Disconnect the vacuum hose at the pressure regulator.

8. Remove the fuel rail attaching bolts, then remove the fuel rail from the cylinder head.

9. Remove the injector electrical connectors by pushing in the wire connector clip, while pulling the connector away from the injector.

10. Disconnect the fuel inlet pipe at the fuel rail. Use a back-up wrench on the fuel rail inlet fitting to prevent it from turning.

11. Loosen the fuel return pipe retaining bracket attaching screw and rotate the retaining bracket to allow the fuel pipe to be removed.

12. Disconnect the fuel return pipe from the pressure regulator.

13. Remove the fuel rail assembly.

14. If necessary, unfasten the quick connect fittings at fuel pipes from the fuel feed and return lines as follows:

   a. Grasp both ends of the fuel line connection and twist the quick con-

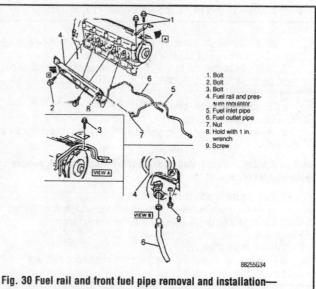

1. Bolt
2. Bolt
3. Bolt
4. Fuel rail and pressure regulator
5. Fuel inlet pipe
6. Fuel outlet pipe
7. Nut
8. Hold with 1 in. wrench
9. Screw

Fig. 30 Fuel rail and front fuel pipe removal and installation—1991–94 2.3L engines shown, 1990 similar

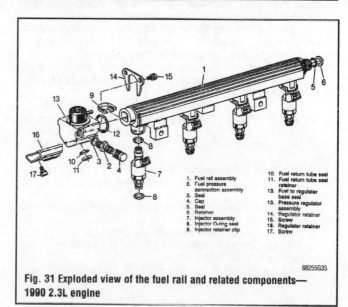

1. Fuel rail assembly
2. Fuel pressure connection assembly
3. Seal
4. Cap
5. Seal
6. Retainer
7. Injector assembly
8. Injector O-ring seal
9. Injector retainer clip
10. Fuel return tube seal
11. Fuel return tube seal retainer
12. Fuel to regulator base seal
13. Pressure regulator assembly
14. Regulator retainer
15. Screw
16. Regulator retainer
17. Screw

Fig. 31 Exploded view of the fuel rail and related components—1990 2.3L engine

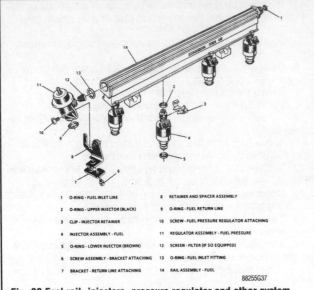

1 O-RING - FUEL INLET LINE	8 RETAINER AND SPACER ASSEMBLY
2 O-RING - UPPER INJECTOR (BLACK)	9 O-RING - FUEL RETURN LINE
3 CLIP - INJECTOR RETAINER	10 SCREW - FUEL PRESSURE REGULATOR ATTACHING
4 INJECTOR ASSEMBLY - FUEL	11 REGULATOR ASSEMBLY - FUEL PRESSURE
5 O-RING - LOWER INJECTOR (BROWN)	12 SCREEN - FILTER (IF SO EQUIPPED)
6 SCREW ASSEMBLY - BRACKET ATTACHING	13 O-RING - FUEL INLET FITTING
7 BRACKET - RETURN LINE ATTACHING	14 RAIL ASSEMBLY - FUEL

88255G37

Fig. 32 Fuel rail, injectors, pressure regulator and other system components—1992–94 2.3L engines shown, 1991 similar

nect fitting ¼ turn in each direction to loosen any dirt within the fitting. Repeat for the other nylon fuel connecting line fitting.

b. Select the correct tool from J 37088 tool set or its equivalent, and insert the tool into the female connector, then push inward to release the male connector.

c. Repeat for the other fitting.

15. Disassemble as follows:

a. Remove the injector O-ring seal from the spray tip of each injector and discard.

➡ **If an injector was separated from the rail during removal, remove both injector O-rings.**

b. Remove the injector clips, if necessary.

c. If the fuel pipes were disconnect from the fuel rail, remove the fuel inlet and return tube O-ring seals and tube seals and discard.

To install

16. Assemble as follows:

a. Lubricate new injector O-ring seals with clean engine oil, and install on the injectors.

b. Install new injector retaining clips, if necessary.

c. If separated from the fuel rail, install the injector(s) into the fuel rail injector sockets, with the electrical connector facing outward. Push in far enough to engage the retainer clip over the fuel rail extrusion flange.

d. If the fuel pipes were disconnected from the fuel rail, install new inlet and return tube O-ring seals and retainers. Press the retainer in to contact the O-ring. Lubricate the seals with clean engine oil.

17. If the fuel rail was disconnected from the fuel pipes, apply a few drops of clean engine oil to the male end of the fuel pipes and reconnect the fuel pipes to the rail at this time.

18. Attach the return pipe to the regulator, aligning the bracket. Apply Loctite® 262, or equivalent, to the threads of the fuel return pipe bracket screw and tighten to 53 inch lbs. (6 Nm).

19. Using a back-up wrench, install the fuel inlet nut to 22 ft. lbs. (30 Nm).

20. Position the fuel rail over the cylinder head, and connect the injector electrical connectors. Rotate the injector(s) as required to avoid stretching the wire harness.

21. Install the fuel rail assembly to the cylinder head and tighten the attaching bolts to 19 ft. lbs. (26 Nm).

22. Install the vacuum hose to the pressure regulator.

23. If the fuel pipes were disconnected at the fuel feed and return line quick-connect fittings, reconnect them as follows:

a. Apply a few drops of clean engine oil to the male tube ends of the engine fuel feed and return pipes.

✷✷ CAUTION

During normal operation, O-rings, located in the female connector will swell and may prevent proper reconnection if not lubricated. This will prevent a possible fuel leak.

b. Push the connectors together to cause the retaining the retaining tabs/fingers to snap into place. Pull on both ends of each connection to make sure they are secure. Repeat for the other fitting.

24. Install the fuel pipe clamp bolt and tighten to 106 inch lbs. (12 Nm).

25. Connect the hose to the bottom of the crankcase ventilation oil/air separator.

26. Position the separator and canister purge solenoid over the attaching bosses.

27. Install the separator and solenoid attaching bolts and tighten to 71 inch lbs. (8 Nm).

28. Connect the hoses to the front and the sides of the separator.

29. Tighten the fuel filler cap and connect the negative battery cable.

2.8L and 3.1L Engines

1988–95 VEHICLES

▶ **See Figures 33, 34, 35 and 36**

✷✷ CAUTION

To reduce the risk of fire or personal injury, it is necessary to relieve the fuel system pressure before servicing the fuel system.

1. Properly relieve the fuel system pressure.
2. Disconnect the negative battery cable.
3. Remove the intake manifold plenum, as follows:

a. Tag and disconnect the vacuum lines.

b. Remove the EGR-to-plenum nuts.

c. Remove the 2 throttle body mounting bolts.

d. Unfasten the throttle cable-to-bracket bolts.

e. Remove the ignition wire plastic shield bolts.

f. Unfasten the plenum bolts, then remove the plenum and gasket.

4. Remove the fuel line bracket bolt.
5. Use a back-up wrench to disconnect the fuel lines from the rail.

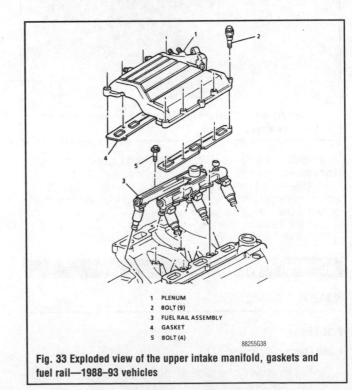

1	PLENUM
2	BOLT (9)
3	FUEL RAIL ASSEMBLY
4	GASKET
5	BOLT (4)

88255G38

Fig. 33 Exploded view of the upper intake manifold, gaskets and fuel rail—1988–93 vehicles

FUELSYSTEM

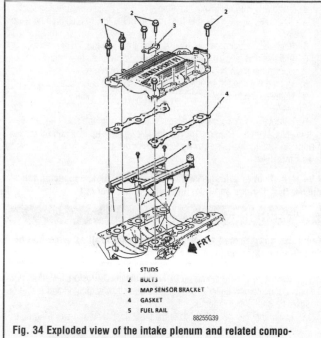

1 STUDS
2 BOLTS
3 MAP SENSOR BRACKET
4 GASKET
5 FUEL RAIL

88255G39

Fig. 34 Exploded view of the intake plenum and related components—1994–95 vehicles

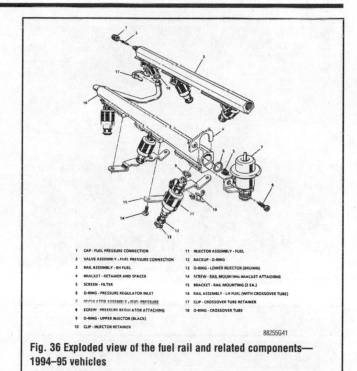

1	CAP - FUEL PRESSURE CONNECTION	11	INJECTOR ASSEMBLY - FUEL
2	VALVE ASSEMBLY - FUEL PRESSURE CONNECTION	12	BACKUP - O-RING
3	RAIL ASSEMBLY - RH FUEL	13	O-RING - LOWER INJECTOR (BROWN)
4	BRACKET - RETAINER AND SPACER	14	SCREW - RAIL MOUNTING BRACKET ATTACHING
5	SCREEN - FILTER	15	BRACKET - RAIL MOUNTING (2 EA.)
6	O-RING - PRESSURE REGULATOR INLET	16	RAIL ASSEMBLY - LH FUEL (WITH CROSSOVER TUBE)
7	REGULATOR ASSEMBLY - FUEL PRESSURE	17	CLIP - CROSSOVER TUBE RETAINER
8	SCREW - PRESSURE REGULATOR ATTACHING	18	O-RING - CROSSOVER TUBE
9	O-RING - UPPER INJECTOR (BLACK)		
10	CLIP - INJECTOR RETAINER		

88255G41

Fig. 36 Exploded view of the fuel rail and related components—1994–95 vehicles

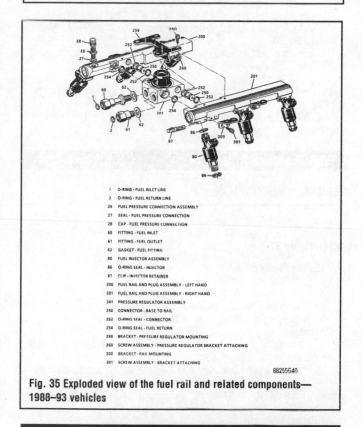

1   O-RING - FUEL INLET LINE
2   O-RING - FUEL RETURN LINE
26   FUEL PRESSURE CONNECTION ASSEMBLY
27   SEAL - FUEL PRESSURE CONNECTION
28   CAP - FUEL PRESSURE CONNECTION
60   FITTING - FUEL INLET
61   FITTING - FUEL OUTLET
62   GASKET - FUEL FITTING
80   FUEL INJECTOR ASSEMBLY
86   O-RING SEAL - INJECTOR
87   CLIP - INJECTOR RETAINER
200 FUEL RAIL AND PLUG ASSEMBLY - LEFT HAND
201 FUEL RAIL AND PLUG ASSEMBLY - RIGHT HAND
241 PRESSURE REGULATOR ASSEMBLY
250 CONNECTOR - BASE TO RAIL
252 O-RING SEAL - CONNECTOR
254 O-RING SEAL - FUEL RETURN
259 BRACKET - PRESSURE REGULATOR MOUNTING
260 SCREW ASSEMBLY - PRESSURE REGULATOR BRACKET ATTACHING
300 BRACKET - RAIL MOUNTING
301 SCREW ASSEMBLY - BRACKET ATTACHING

88255G40

Fig. 35 Exploded view of the fuel rail and related components—1988–93 vehicles

✳✳ CAUTION

Wrap a cloth around the fuel lines to collect spilled fuel, then place the fuel in an approved container.

6. Remove and discard the fuel inlet and return line O-rings.
7. Disconnect the vacuum line from the pressure regulator.
8. Remove the rail retaining bolts.
9. Detach the injector electrical connectors.
10. Remove the fuel rail assembly from the vehicle.

11. If necessary, disassemble by removing the O-ring seal from each of the spray tip end of the injector.

To install:

12. Lubricate new O-ring seals with clean engine oil, then install on each of the spray tip ends of the injector.

13. Install the fuel rail assembly to the intake manifold. Tilt the fuel rail assembly to install the injectors.

14. Install the fuel rail attaching bolts and tighten to 19 ft. lbs. (25 Nm) for 1988 vehicles, and to 88 inch lbs. (10 Nm) for 1989–95 vehicles.

15. Attach the injector electrical connectors.

16. Connect the vacuum line to the pressure regulator.

17. Install new O-rings on the inlet and return fuel lines, then connect the fuel inlet and outlet fittings, using a back-up wrench to tighten the lines. Tighten the fuel pipe nuts to 22 ft. lbs. (30 Nm).

18. Connect the negative battery cable. Tighten the fuel filler cap.

19. Turn the ignition switch to the **ON** position for 2 seconds, then turn to the **OFF** position for 10 seconds. Turn the ignition switch to the **ON** position again and check for leaks.

20. Install the intake manifold plenum.

1996 VEHICLES

1. Properly relieve the fuel system pressure.
2. Disconnect the negative battery cable.

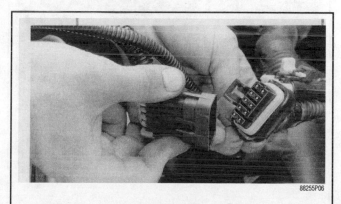

88255P06

Unplug the main injector harness electrical connector

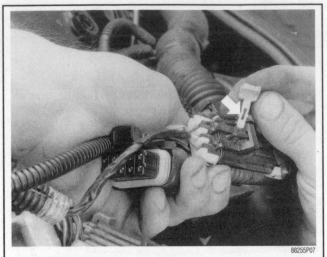

Some connectors have a Connector Position Assurance (CPA) retaining clip (see arrow)

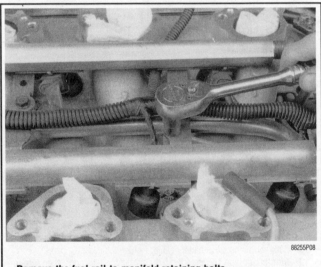

Remove the fuel rail-to-manifold retaining bolts . . .

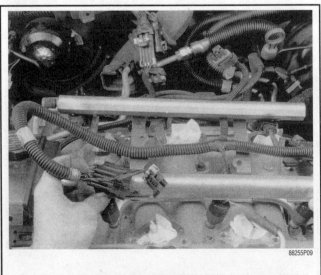

. . . then remove the fuel rail assembly from the intake manifold

3. Remove the upper intake manifold.
4. Disconnect the engine fuel feed pipe from the fuel rail, using a back-up wrench.
5. Remove the fuel pressure regulator from the fuel rail.
6. Remove and discard the fuel inlet pipe and pressure regulator O-rings.
7. Detach the main injector harness electrical connector.
8. Unplug the coolant temperature sensor electrical connector.
9. Unfasten the fuel rail retaining bolts, then remove the fuel rail assembly from the vehicle.
10. Remove and discard the injector O-ring seal from the spray tip end of each injector. With the O-ring removed, the O-ring back-up may slip off the injector. Be sure to retain the O-ring back-up for reuse.

To install:

➡Be careful not to damage the fuel injector electrical connector, the injector tips, O-rings and inlet and outlet of the fuel rail.

❊❊ WARNING

Never use compressed air or immerse the fuel rail as a method of cleaning the rail assembly.

11. Make sure the O-ring back-ups are on the injector before installing new O-rings. Lubricate new injector O-ring seals with clean engine oil and install on the spray tip end of each injector.
12. Install the fuel rail in the intake manifold. Install the rail attaching bolts and tighten to 7 ft. lbs. (10 Nm).
13. Attach the coolant temperature sensor electrical connector.
14. Connect the main injector wiring harness.
15. Install new O-rings on the fuel rail inlet line and fuel pressure regulator.
16. Install the fuel feed and tighten the pipe nut to 13 ft. lbs. (17 Nm), using a back-up wrench.
17. Install the fuel pressure regulator.
18. Install the upper intake manifold.
19. Install the fuel filler cap.
20. Turn the ignition switch to the **ON** position for 2 seconds, then turn to the **OFF**
position for 10 seconds. Turn the ignition switch to the **ON** position again and check for leaks.

Fuel Pressure Regulator

REMOVAL & INSTALLATION

2.3L Engines

▶ **See Figure 37**

1. Properly relieve the fuel system pressure.
2. Disconnect the negative battery cable.
3. Remove the fuel rail assembly from the cylinder head.
4. Remove the pressure regulator attaching screws.
5. Twist back and forth and remove the regulator from the fuel rail.

To install:

6. Lubricate the new rail to the regulator inlet fitting O-ring seal with clean engine oil and install in the regulator.
7. Install the pressure regulator by aligning the retainer and spacer assembly mounting holes and tightening the retaining screws, with thread locking material, to 49 inch lbs. (5.5 Nm) for 1990 vehicles and 102 inch lbs. (11.5 Nm) for 1991–94 vehicles.
8. Install the fuel rail assembly.
9. Connect the negative battery cable. Tighten the fuel filler cap.
10. Turn the ignition switch to the **ON** position for 2 seconds, then turn to the **OFF** position for 10 seconds. Turn the ignition switch to the **ON** position again and check for leaks.

2.8L and 3.1L Engines

1988–93 VEHICLES

1. Properly relieve the fuel system pressure.
2. If not already done, disconnect the negative battery cable.

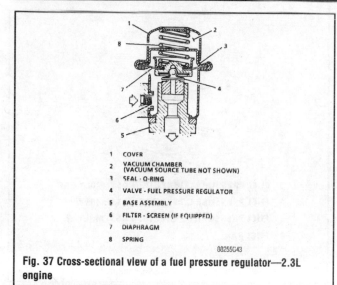

1 COVER
2 VACUUM CHAMBER
  (VACUUM SOURCE TUBE NOT SHOWN)
3 SEAL - O-RING
4 VALVE - FUEL PRESSURE REGULATOR
5 BASE ASSEMBLY
6 FILTER - SCREEN (IF EQUIPPED)
7 DIAPHRAGM
8 SPRING

88255G43

Fig. 37 Cross-sectional view of a fuel pressure regulator—2.3L engine

3. Remove the fuel rail and place on a suitable workbench.
4. Remove the fuel inlet and outlet fittings and gaskets.
5. Remove the pressure regulator bracket attaching screws and mounting bracket.
6. Remove the right and left hand fuel rail assemblies from the pressure regulator assembly.
7. Remove the base-to-rail connectors from the regulator or rails.
8. Disassemble the connector O-rings from the base to rail connectors.
9. Remove the fuel return O-ring from the fuel rails.

To install:
10. Lubricate new fuel return O-rings with clean engine oil and install on the fuel rails.
11. Lubricate new connector O-rings with clean engine oil and install to the base-to-rail connectors.
12. Install the base to rail connectors in the regulator assembly.
13. Install the right and left hand fuel rail assemblies to the pressure regulator assembly.
14. Install the pressure regulator mounting bracket with the attaching screws. Tighten the screws to 28 inch lbs. (3.2 Nm).
15. Install new fuel inlet and outlet fitting gaskets and tighten the fittings to 20 ft lbs. (27 Nm) for 1988 vehicles or, for 1989–96 vehicles, tighten the fuel inlet fitting to 35 ft. lbs. (48 Nm) and the fuel outlet fitting to 30 ft. lbs. (40 Nm).
16. Install the fuel rail assembly.
17. Connect the negative battery cable. Tighten the fuel filler cap.
18. Turn the ignition switch to the **ON** position for 2 seconds, then turn to the **OFF** position for 10 seconds. Turn the ignition switch to the **ON** position again and check for leaks.

1994–96 VEHICLES

♦ See Figure 38

1. Properly relieve the fuel system pressure.
2. If not already done, disconnect the negative battery cable.
3. Remove the upper intake manifold.
4. Disconnect the fuel pressure regulator vacuum line.
5. Unfasten the pressure regulator retaining screw.
6. Position a shop towel under the regulator, to catch any spilled fuel, then lift and twist the regulator to remove it from the fuel rail.
7. Remove and discard the retainer and spacer bracket from the fuel rail.
8. Remove the fuel pressure regulator from the engine fuel return pipe.
9. Remove and discard the pressure regulator inlet O-ring.
10. Check the filter screen for contamination. If contamination is found, discard the filter screen.

To install:
11. Lubricate a new pressure regulator inlet O-ring with clean engine oil, then install on the regulator inlet.
12. Install a new retainer and spacer bracket into the slot on the fuel rail.

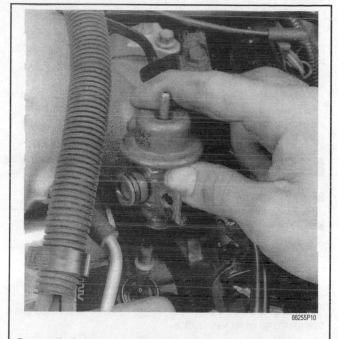

88255P10

Remove the fuel pressure regulator from the fuel rail assembly

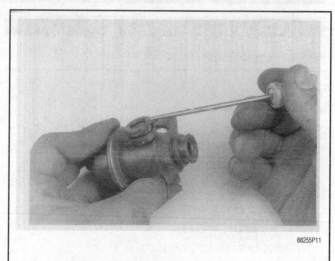

88255P11

Remove and discard the pressure regulator O-ring

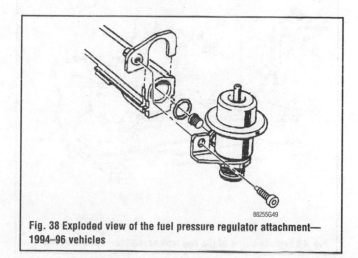

88255G49

Fig. 38 Exploded view of the fuel pressure regulator attachment—1994–96 vehicles

13. Position the pressure regulator to the fuel rail. Install the engine fuel return pipe nut to 13 ft. lbs. (17 Nm).

14. Install the pressure regulator attaching screw. Connect the vacuum line to the regulator. Tighten the regulator attaching screw to 6 ft. lbs. (8.5 Nm).

15. Make sure the retainer and spacer bracket is engaged in the slots in the fuel rail. Pull on the regulator to be sure it is properly seated.

16. Connect the negative battery cable. Tighten the fuel filler cap.

17. Turn the ignition switch to the **ON** position for 2 seconds, then turn to the **OFF** position for 10 seconds. Turn the ignition switch to the **ON** position again and check for leaks.

Fuel Pressure Connection

REMOVAL & INSTALLATION

◊ **See Figure 39**

1. Properly relieve the fuel system pressure.
2. If not done already, disconnect the negative battery cable.
3. Remove the fuel pressure connection and seal. Discard the seal.

To install:

4. Place a new seal on the fuel pressure connection.
5. Place the fuel pressure connection in the fuel rail. Tighten the fuel pressure connection 88 inch lbs. (10 Nm).

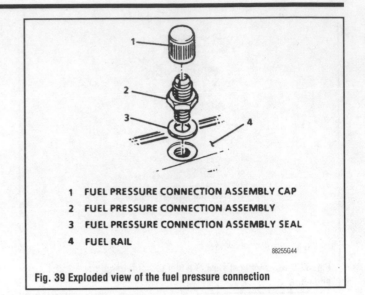

1 **FUEL PRESSURE CONNECTION ASSEMBLY CAP**
2 **FUEL PRESSURE CONNECTION ASSEMBLY**
3 **FUEL PRESSURE CONNECTION ASSEMBLY SEAL**
4 **FUEL RAIL**

88255G44

Fig. 39 Exploded view of the fuel pressure connection

6. Tighten the fuel filler cap.
7. Connect the negative battery cable and turn the ignition **ON** for 2 seconds, **OFF** for 10 seconds, then **ON** and check for fuel leaks.

FUEL TANK

Tank Assembly

REMOVAL & INSTALLATION

1988–89 Vehicles

◊ **See Figure 40**

1. Relieve the fuel system pressure as outlined earlier in this section.
2. If not already done, disconnect the negative cable from the battery.
3. Raise and safely support the vehicle.
4. Drain the fuel tank into an approved container. There is no drain plug; remaining fuel in the tank must be siphoned through the fuel feed line (the line to the fuel pump), because of the restrictor in the filler neck.
5. Disconnect the hose and the vapor return hose from the level sending unit fittings.
6. Remove the ground wire screw.
7. Unplug the level sending unit electrical connector.

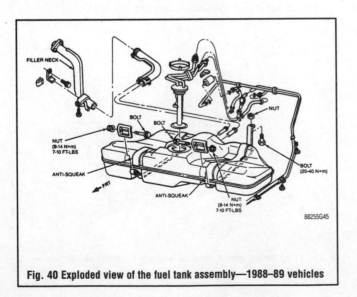

Fig. 40 Exploded view of the fuel tank assembly—1988–89 vehicles

8. Disconnect the vent hose.
9. Unbolt the support straps, and lower and remove the tank.
10. Installation is the reverse of the removal procedure. Tighten the front retaining strap bolts to 26 ft. lbs. (35 Nm) and the rear strap bolts to 8 ft. lbs. (11 Nm).

1990–92 Vehicles

◊ **See Figure 41**

1. Relieve the fuel system pressure as outlined earlier in this section.
2. If not already done, disconnect the negative cable from the battery.
3. Raise and safely support the vehicle.
4. Drain the tank. There is no drain plug; remaining fuel in the tank must be siphoned through the fuel filler tube.
5. Remove the exhaust pipe rubber hangers.
6. Remove the muffler hanger attaching bolts.
7. Remove the heat shield attaching screws and remove the heat shield.
8. Remove the filler tube and clamp at the fuel tank.
9. Disconnect the fuel tank vent tube and clamp at the fuel tank vent hose.
10. Detach the electrical connector.
11. Disconnect the vapor connecting hose from the fuel level meter.
12. If the nylon feed or return connecting lines become kinked, and cannot be straightened, they must be replaced as follows:

   a. Grasp the fuel level meter fuel feed tube and nylon fuel feed connecting line quick connect fitting and twist the quick connect fitting ¼ turn in each direction to loosen any dirt within the fitting. Repeat for the return nylon fuel connecting line fitting.

   b. For the fuel return quick connect fittings, squeeze the plastic tabs of the male end connector and pull the connection apart.

   c. For the fuel feed quick connect fitting, select the correct tool from J 37088 tool set or its equivalent, and insert the tool into the female connector, then push inward to release the male connector.

13. With the aid of an assistant, support the fuel tank and remove the rear fuel tank retaining strap attaching bolts, fuel tank and both fuel tank retaining straps.

To install:

14. With the aid of an assistant, position and support the fuel tank and install the retaining strap attaching bolts. Tighten to 22 ft. lbs. (30 Nm).

15. Connect the nylon fuel feed and return connecting line quick connect fittings to the fuel level meter as follow:

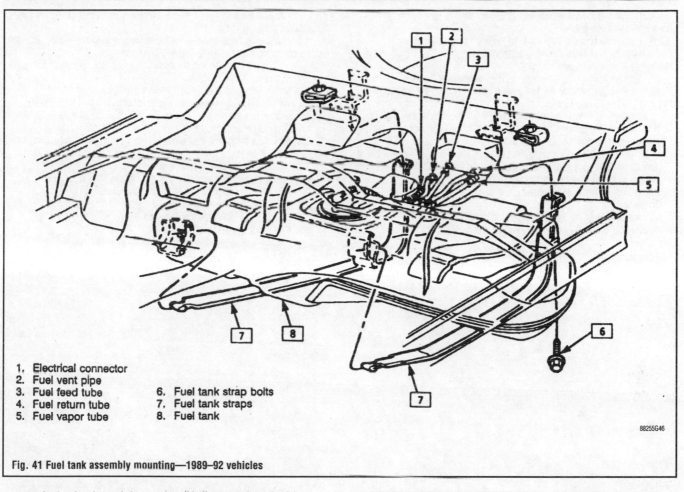

1. Electrical connector
2. Fuel vent pipe
3. Fuel feed tube
4. Fuel return tube
5. Fuel vapor tube
6. Fuel tank strap bolts
7. Fuel tank straps
8. Fuel tank

88255G46

Fig. 41 Fuel tank assembly mounting—1989–92 vehicles

a. Apply a few drops of clean engine oil to the male tube ends of the engine fuel feed and return pipes.

✳✳ CAUTION

During normal operation, O-rings, located in the female connector will swell and may prevent proper reconnection if not lubricated. This will prevent a possible fuel leak.

b. Push the connectors together to cause the retaining the retaining tabs/fingers to snap into place. Pull on both ends of each connection to make sure they are secure. Repeat for the other fitting.
16. Install the vapor connecting hose.
17. Attach the electrical connector.
18. Install the fuel tank vent hose and clamp.
19. Install the heat shield and retain with the attaching screws.
20. Install the muffler hanger, then secure with the attaching bolts and tighten to 11 ft. lbs. (15 Nm).
21. Install the exhaust pipe rubber hangers.
22. Add fuel and install the fuel filler cap.
23. Connect the negative battery cable.

1993–96 Vehicles

♦ **See Figure 42**

1. Relieve the fuel system pressure as outlined earlier in this section.
2. If not already done, disconnect the negative cable from the battery.
3. Drain the fuel tank into an approved container.
4. Raise and safely support the vehicle.
5. Detach the fuel sender electrical connector.
6. Remove the muffler hanger bolts.
7. Remove the exhaust rubber hangers and allow the exhaust system to rest on the rear axle.

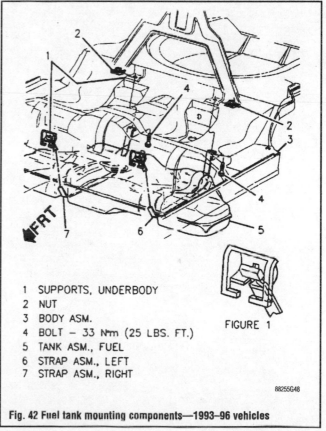

1. SUPPORTS, UNDERBODY
2. NUT
3. BODY ASM.
4. BOLT – 33 N·m (25 LBS. FT.)
5. TANK ASM., FUEL
6. STRAP ASM., LEFT
7. STRAP ASM., RIGHT

FIGURE 1

88255G48

Fig. 42 Fuel tank mounting components—1993–96 vehicles

8. Disconnect the quick-connect hoses from the fuel tank sender, as outlined earlier in this section.

9. Detach the hoses at the tank from the filer vent and vapor pipes.

10. With the help of an assistant, support the fuel tank, then disconnect the two fuel tank retaining straps.

11. Remove the tank from the vehicle, then remove the sound insulators.

12. If necessary, remove the fuel sender assembly from the tank, as follows:

    a. Hold the modular fuel sender assembly down, then remove the snapring from the designated slots located on the retainer. Be careful, as the modular fuel sender may spring up from its position.

    b. When removing the sender, be careful as the reservoir bucket is full of fuel. It must be tipped slightly during removal to avoid float damage. Discard the fuel sender O-ring and replace with a new one.

    c. Carefully discard the reservoir fuel into an approved container.

To install:

13. Install the fuel sender assembly, as follows:

    a. Install a new O-ring on the modular fuel sender to the tank.

    b. Align the tab on the front of the sender with the slot on the front of the retainer snapring.

    c. Slowly apply pressure to the top of the spring loaded sender until the sender aligns flush with the retainer on the tank.

    d. Insert the snapring into the designated slots. Be sure the snap ring is fully seated within the tab slots.

14. Install the sound insulators.

15. With the help of an assistant, position the fuel tank to the body and secure with the retaining straps. Tighten the strap bolts to 24 ft. lbs. (33 Nm).

16. Connect the hoses to the filler, vent and vapor pipes.

17. Attach the nylon fuel feed and return connecting line quick-connect fittings to the fuel sender.

18. Install the exhaust rubber hangers.

19. Install the muffler hanger bolts and tighten to 11 ft. lbs. (15 Nm).

20. Attach the fuel tank sender electrical connector.

21. Carefully lower the vehicle.

22. Add fuel and install the fuel filler cap.

23. Connect the negative battery cable.

6

CHASSIS ELECTRICAL

UNDERSTANDING AND TROUBLESHOOTING ELECTRICAL SYSTEMS

Basic Electrical Theory

▶ See Figure 1

For any 12 volt, negative ground, electrical system to operate, the electricity must travel in a complete circuit. This simply means that current (power) from the positive (+) terminal of the battery must eventually return to the negative (-) terminal of the battery. Along the way, this current will travel through wires, fuses, switches and components. If, for any reason, the flow of current through the circuit is interrupted, the component fed by that circuit will cease to function properly.

Perhaps the easiest way to visualize a circuit is to think of connecting a light bulb (with two wires attached to it) to the battery—one wire attached to the negative (-) terminal of the battery and the other wire to the positive (+) terminal. With the two wires touching the battery terminals, the circuit would be complete and the light bulb would illuminate. Electricity would follow a path from the battery to the bulb and back to the battery. It's easy to see that with longer wires on our light bulb, it could be mounted anywhere. Further, one wire could be fitted with a switch so that the light could be turned on and off.

The normal automotive circuit differs from this simple example in two ways. First, instead of having a return wire from the bulb to the battery, the current travels through the frame of the vehicle. Since the negative (-) battery cable is attached to the frame (made of electrically conductive metal), the frame of the vehicle can serve as a ground wire to complete the circuit. Secondly, most automotive circuits contain multiple components which receive power from a single circuit. This lessens the amount of wire needed to power components on the vehicle.

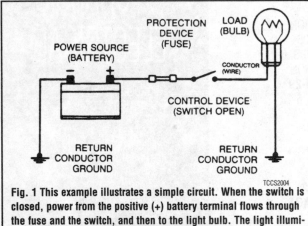

TCCS2004

Fig. 1 This example illustrates a simple circuit. When the switch is closed, power from the positive (+) battery terminal flows through the fuse and the switch, and then to the light bulb. The light illuminates and the circuit is completed through the ground wire back to the negative (-) battery terminal. In reality, the two ground points shown in the illustration are attached to the metal frame of the vehicle, which completes the circuit back to the battery

HOW DOES ELECTRICITY WORK: THE WATER ANALOGY

Electricity is the flow of electrons—the subatomic particles that constitute the outer shell of an atom. Electrons spin in an orbit around the center core of an atom. The center core is comprised of protons (positive charge) and neutrons (neutral charge). Electrons have a negative charge and balance out the positive charge of the protons. When an outside force causes the number of electrons to unbalance the charge of the protons, the electrons will split off the atom and look for another atom to balance out. If this imbalance is kept up, electrons will continue to move and an electrical flow will exist.

Many people have been taught electrical theory using an analogy with water. In a comparison with water flowing through a pipe, the electrons would be the water and the wire is the pipe.

The flow of electricity can be measured much like the flow of water through a pipe. The unit of measurement used is amperes, frequently abbreviated as amps (a). You can compare amperage to the volume of water flowing through a pipe. When connected to a circuit, an ammeter will measure the actual amount of current flowing through the circuit. When relatively few electrons flow

through a circuit, the amperage is low. When many electrons flow, the amperage is high.

Water pressure is measured in units such as pounds per square inch (psi); The electrical pressure is measured in units called volts (v). When a voltmeter is connected to a circuit, it is measuring the electrical pressure.

The actual flow of electricity depends not only on voltage and amperage, but also on the resistance of the circuit. The higher the resistance, the higher the force necessary to push the current through the circuit. The standard unit for measuring resistance is an ohm. Resistance in a circuit varies depending on the amount and type of components used in the circuit. The main factors which determine resistance are:

- Material—some materials have more resistance than others. Those with high resistance are said to be insulators. Rubber materials (or rubber-like plastics) are some of the most common insulators used in vehicles as they have a very high resistance to electricity. Very low resistance materials are said to be conductors. Copper wire is among the best conductors. Silver is actually a superior conductor to copper and is used in some relay contacts, but its high cost prohibits its use as common wiring. Most automotive wiring is made of copper.
- Size—the larger the wire size being used, the less resistance the wire will have. This is why components which use large amounts of electricity usually have large wires supplying current to them.
- Length—for a given thickness of wire, the longer the wire, the greater the resistance. The shorter the wire, the less the resistance. When determining the proper wire for a circuit, both size and length must be considered to design a circuit that can handle the current needs of the component.
- Temperature—with many materials, the higher the temperature, the greater the resistance (positive temperature coefficient). Some materials exhibit the opposite trait of lower resistance with higher temperatures (negative temperature coefficient). These principles are used in many of the sensors on the engine.

OHM'S LAW

There is a direct relationship between current, voltage and resistance. The relationship between current, voltage and resistance can be summed up by a statement known as Ohm's law.

Voltage (E) is equal to amperage (I) times resistance (R): $E = I \times R$

Other forms of the formula are $R = E/I$ and $I = E/R$

In each of these formulas, E is the voltage in volts, I is the current in amps and R is the resistance in ohms. The basic point to remember is that as the resistance of a circuit goes up, the amount of current that flows in the circuit will go down, if voltage remains the same.

The amount of work that the electricity can perform is expressed as power. The unit of power is the watt (w). The relationship between power, voltage and current is expressed as:

Power (w) is equal to amperage (I) times voltage (E): $W = I \times E$

This is only true for direct current (DC) circuits; The alternating current formula is a tad different, but since the electrical circuits in most vehicles are DC type, we need not get into AC circuit theory.

Electrical Components

POWER SOURCE

Power is supplied to the vehicle by two devices: The battery and the alternator. The battery supplies electrical power during starting or during periods when the current demand of the vehicle's electrical system exceeds the output capacity of the alternator. The alternator supplies electrical current when the engine is running. Just not does the alternator supply the current needs of the vehicle, but it recharges the battery.

The Battery

In most modern vehicles, the battery is a lead/acid electrochemical device consisting of six 2 volt subsections (cells) connected in series, so that the unit is capable of producing approximately 12 volts of electrical pressure. Each subsection consists of a series of positive and negative plates held a short distance apart in a solution of sulfuric acid and water.

The two types of plates are of dissimilar metals. This sets up a chemical reaction, and it is this reaction which produces current flow from the battery when its positive and negative terminals are connected to an electrical load . The power removed from the battery is replaced by the alternator, restoring the battery to its original chemical state.

The Alternator

On some vehicles there isn't an alternator, but a generator. The difference is that an alternator supplies alternating current which is then changed to direct current for use on the vehicle, while a generator produces direct current. Alternators tend to be more efficient and that is why they are used.

Alternators and generators are devices that consist of coils of wires wound together making big electromagnets. One group of coils spins within another set and the interaction of the magnetic fields causes a current to flow. This current is then drawn off the coils and fed into the vehicles electrical system.

GROUND

Two types of grounds are used in automotive electric circuits. Direct ground components are grounded to the frame through their mounting points. All other components use some sort of ground wire which is attached to the frame or chassis of the vehicle. The electrical current runs through the chassis of the vehicle and returns to the battery through the ground (-) cable; if you look, you'll see that the battery ground cable connects between the battery and the frame or chassis of the vehicle.

➡**It should be noted that a good percentage of electrical problems can be traced to bad grounds.**

PROTECTIVE DEVICES

▶ **See Figure 2**

It is possible for large surges of current to pass through the electrical system of your vehicle. If this surge of current were to reach the load in the circuit, the surge could burn it out or severely damage it. It can also overload the wiring,

Fig. 2 Most vehicles use one or more fuse panels. This one is located on the driver's side kick panel

TCCA6P01

causing the harness to get hot and melt the insulation. To prevent this, fuses, circuit breakers and/or fusible links are connected into the supply wires of the electrical system. These items are nothing more than a built-in weak spot in the system. When an abnormal amount of current flows through the system, these protective devices work as follows to protect the circuit:

• Fuse—when an excessive electrical current passes through a fuse, the fuse "blows" (the conductor melts) and opens the circuit, preventing the passage of current.

• Circuit Breaker—a circuit breaker is basically a self-repairing fuse. It will open the circuit in the same fashion as a fuse, but when the surge subsides, the circuit breaker can be reset and does not need replacement.

• Fusible Link—a fusible link (fuse link or main link) is a short length of special, high temperature insulated wire that acts as a fuse. When an excessive electrical current passes through a fusible link, the thin gauge wire inside the link melts, creating an intentional open to protect the circuit. To repair the circuit, the link must be replaced. Some newer type fusible links are housed in plug-in modules, which are simply replaced like a fuse, while older type fusible links must be cut and spliced if they melt. Since this link is very early in the electrical path, it's the first place to look if nothing on the vehicle works, yet the battery seems to be charged and is properly connected.

✳✳ CAUTION

Always replace fuses, circuit breakers and fusible links with identically rated components. Under no circumstances should a component of higher or lower amperage rating be substituted.

SWITCHES & RELAYS

▶ **See Figures 3 and 4**

Switches are used in electrical circuits to control the passage of current. The most common use is to open and close circuits between the battery and the various electric devices in the system. Switches are rated according to the amount of amperage they can handle. If a sufficient amperage rated switch is not used in a circuit, the switch could overload and cause damage.

Some electrical components which require a large amount of current to operate use a special switch called a relay. Since these circuits carry a large amount of current, the thickness of the wire in the circuit is also greater. If this large wire were connected from the load to the control switch, the switch would have to carry the high amperage load and the fairing or dash would be twice as large to accommodate the increased size of the wiring harness. To prevent these problems, a relay is used.

Relays are composed of a coil and a set of contacts. When the coil has a current passed though it, a magnetic field is formed and this field causes the contacts to move together, completing the circuit. Most relays are normally open,

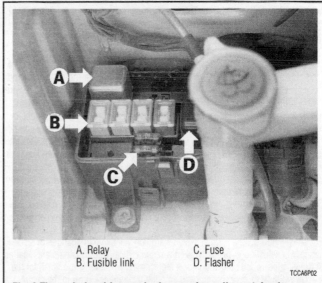

A. Relay   C. Fuse
B. Fusible link   D. Flasher

TCCA6P02

Fig. 3 The underhood fuse and relay panel usually contains fuses, relays, flashers and fusible links

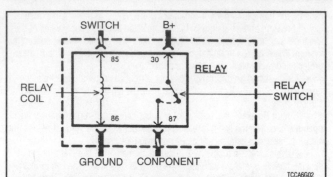

Fig. 4 Relays are composed of a coil and a switch. These two components are linked together so that when one operates, the other operates at the same time. The large wires in the circuit are connected from the battery to one side of the relay switch (B+) and from the opposite side of the relay switch to the load (component). Smaller wires are connected from the relay coil to the control switch for the circuit and from the opposite side of the relay coil to ground

preventing current from passing through the circuit, but they can take any electrical form depending on the job they are intended to do. Relays can be considered "remote control switches." They allow a smaller current to operate devices that require higher amperages. When a small current operates the coil, a larger current is allowed to pass by the contacts. Some common circuits which may use relays are the horn, headlights, starter, electric fuel pump and other high draw circuits.

LOAD

Every electrical circuit must include a "load" (something to use the electricity coming from the source). Without this load, the battery would attempt to deliver its entire power supply from one pole to another. This is called a "short circuit." All this electricity would take a short cut to ground and cause a great amount of damage to other components in the circuit by developing a tremendous amount of heat. This condition could develop sufficient heat to melt the insulation on all the surrounding wires and reduce a multiple wire cable to a lump of plastic and copper.

WIRING & HARNESSES

The average vehicle contains meters and meters of wiring, with hundreds of individual connections. To protect the many wires from damage and to keep them from becoming a confusing tangle, they are organized into bundles, enclosed in plastic or taped together and called wiring harnesses. Different harnesses serve different parts of the vehicle. Individual wires are color coded to help trace them through a harness where sections are hidden from view.

Automotive wiring or circuit conductors can be either single strand wire, multi-strand wire or printed circuitry. Single strand wire has a solid metal core and is usually used inside such components as alternators, motors, relays and other devices. Multi-strand wire has a core made of many small strands of wire twisted together into a single conductor. Most of the wiring in an automotive electrical system is made up of multi-strand wire, either as a single conductor or grouped together in a harness. All wiring is color coded on the insulator, either as a solid color or as a colored wire with an identification stripe. A printed circuit is a thin film of copper or other conductor that is printed on an insulator backing. Occasionally, a printed circuit is sandwiched between two sheets of plastic for more protection and flexibility. A complete printed circuit, consisting of conductors, insulating material and connectors for lamps or other components is called a printed circuit board. Printed circuitry is used in place of individual wires or harnesses in places where space is limited, such as behind instrument panels.

Since automotive electrical systems are very sensitive to changes in resistance, the selection of properly sized wires is critical when systems are repaired. A loose or corroded connection or a replacement wire that is too small for the circuit will add extra resistance and an additional voltage drop to the circuit.

The wire gauge number is an expression of the cross-section area of the conductor. Vehicles from countries that use the metric system will typically

describe the wire size as its cross-sectional area in square millimeters. In this method, the larger the wire, the greater the number. Another common system for expressing wire size is the American Wire Gauge (AWG) system. As gauge number increases, area decreases and the wire becomes smaller. An 18 gauge wire is smaller than a 4 gauge wire. A wire with a higher gauge number will carry less current than a wire with a lower gauge number. Gauge wire size refers to the size of the strands of the conductor, not the size of the complete wire with insulator. It is possible, therefore, to have two wires of the same gauge with different diameters because one may have thicker insulation than the other.

It is essential to understand how a circuit works before trying to figure out why it doesn't. An electrical schematic shows the electrical current paths when a circuit is operating properly. Schematics break the entire electrical system down into individual circuits. In a schematic, usually no attempt is made to represent wiring and components as they physically appear on the vehicle; switches and other components are shown as simply as possible. Face views of harness connectors show the cavity or terminal locations in all multi-pin connectors to help locate test points.

CONNECTORS

▶ See Figures 5 and 6

Three types of connectors are commonly used in automotive applications—weatherproof, molded and hard shell.

• Weatherproof—these connectors are most commonly used where the connector is exposed to the elements. Terminals are protected against moisture and dirt by sealing rings which provide a weathertight seal. All repairs require the use of a special terminal and the tool required to service it. Unlike standard blade type terminals, these weatherproof terminals cannot be straightened once they are bent. Make certain that the connectors are properly seated and all of the sealing rings are in place when connecting leads.

Fig. 5 Hard shell (left) and weatherproof (right) connectors have replaceable terminals

Fig. 6 Weatherproof connectors are most commonly used in the engine compartment or where the connector is exposed to the elements

• Molded—these connectors require complete replacement of the connector if found to be defective. This means splicing a new connector assembly into the harness. All splices should be soldered to insure proper contact. Use care when probing the connections or replacing terminals in them, as it is possible to create a short circuit between opposite terminals. If this happens to the wrong terminal pair, it is possible to damage certain components. Always use jumper wires between connectors for circuit checking and NEVER probe through weatherproof seals.

• Hard Shell—unlike molded connectors, the terminal contacts in hard-shell connectors can be replaced. Replacement usually involves the use of a special terminal removal tool that depresses the locking tangs (barbs) on the connector terminal and allows the connector to be removed from the rear of the shell. The connector shell should be replaced if it shows any evidence of burning, melting, cracks, or breaks. Replace individual terminals that are burnt, corroded, distorted or loose.

Test Equipment

Pinpointing the exact cause of trouble in an electrical circuit is most times accomplished by the use of special test equipment. The following describes different types of commonly used test equipment and briefly explains how to use them in diagnosis. In addition to the information covered below, the tool manufacturer's instructions booklet (provided with the tester) should be read and clearly understood before attempting any test procedures.

JUMPER WIRES

✳✳ CAUTION

Never use jumper wires made from a thinner gauge wire than the circuit being tested. If the jumper wire is of too small a gauge, it may overheat and possibly melt. Never use jumpers to bypass high resistance loads in a circuit. Bypassing resistances, in effect, creates a short circuit. This may, in turn, cause damage and fire. Jumper wires should only be used to bypass lengths of wire or to simulate switches.

Jumper wires are simple, yet extremely valuable, pieces of test equipment. They are basically test wires which are used to bypass sections of a circuit. Although jumper wires can be purchased, they are usually fabricated from lengths of standard automotive wire and whatever type of connector (alligator clip, spade connector or pin connector) that is required for the particular application being tested. In cramped, hard-to-reach areas, it is advisable to have insulated boots over the jumper wire terminals in order to prevent accidental grounding. It is also advisable to include a standard automotive fuse in any jumper wire. This is commonly referred to as a "fused jumper". By inserting an in-line fuse holder between a set of test leads, a fused jumper wire can be used for bypassing open circuits. Use a 5 amp fuse to provide protection against voltage spikes.

Jumper wires are used primarily to locate open electrical circuits, on either the ground (-) side of the circuit or on the power (+) side. If an electrical component fails to operate, connect the jumper wire between the component and a good ground. If the component operates only with the jumper installed, the ground circuit is open. If the ground circuit is good, but the component does not operate, the circuit between the power feed and component may be open. By moving the jumper wire successively back from the component toward the power source, you can isolate the area of the circuit where the open is located. When the component stops functioning, or the power is cut off, the open is in the segment of wire between the jumper and the point previously tested.

You can sometimes connect the jumper wire directly from the battery to the "hot" terminal of the component, but first make sure the component uses 12 volts in operation. Some electrical components, such as fuel injectors or sensors, are designed to operate on about 4 to 5 volts, and running 12 volts directly to these components will cause damage.

TEST LIGHTS

◆ See Figure 7

The test light is used to check circuits and components while electrical current is flowing through them. It is used for voltage and ground tests. To use a 12 volt test light, connect the ground clip to a good ground and probe wherever necessary with the pick. The test light will illuminate when voltage is detected. This does not necessarily mean that 12 volts (or any particular amount of voltage) is present; it only means that some voltage is present. It is advisable before using the test light to touch its ground clip and probe across the battery posts or terminals to make sure the light is operating properly.

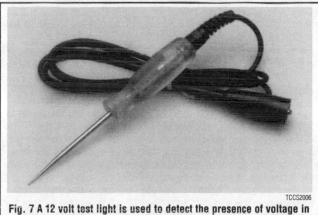

TCCS2006

Fig. 7 A 12 volt test light is used to detect the presence of voltage in a circuit

✳✳ WARNING

Do not use a test light to probe electronic ignition, spark plug or coil wires. Never use a pick-type test light to probe wiring on computer controlled systems unless specifically instructed to do so. Any wire insulation that is pierced by the test light probe should be taped and sealed with silicone after testing.

Like the jumper wire, the 12 volt test light is used to isolate opens in circuits. But, whereas the jumper wire is used to bypass the open to operate the load, the 12 volt test light is used to locate the presence of voltage in a circuit. If the test light illuminates, there is power up to that point in the circuit; if the test light does not illuminate, there is an open circuit (no power). Move the test light in successive steps back toward the power source until the light in the handle illuminates. The open is between the probe and a point which was previously probed.

The self-powered test light is similar in design to the 12 volt test light, but contains a 1.5 volt penlight battery in the handle. It is most often used in place of a multimeter to check for open or short circuits when power is isolated from the circuit (continuity test).

The battery in a self-powered test light does not provide much current. A weak battery may not provide enough power to illuminate the test light even when a complete circuit is made (especially if there is high resistance in the circuit). Always make sure that the test battery is strong. To check the battery, briefly touch the ground clip to the probe; if the light glows brightly, the battery is strong enough for testing.

➡A self-powered test light should not be used on any computer controlled system or component. The small amount of electricity transmitted by the test light is enough to damage many electronic automotive components.

MULTIMETERS

Multimeters are an extremely useful tool for troubleshooting electrical problems. They can be purchased in either analog or digital form and have a price range to suit any budget. A multimeter is a voltmeter, ammeter and ohmmeter (along with other features) combined into one instrument. It is often used when testing solid state circuits because of its high input impedance (usually 10 megaohms or more). A brief description of the multimeter main test functions follows:

• Voltmeter—the voltmeter is used to measure voltage at any point in a circuit, or to measure the voltage drop across any part of a circuit. Voltmeters usually have various scales and a selector switch to allow the reading of different voltage ranges. The voltmeter has a positive and a negative lead. To avoid damage to the meter, always connect the negative lead to the negative (-) side of the circuit (to ground or nearest the ground side of the circuit) and connect the positive lead to the positive (+) side of the circuit (to the power source or the nearest power source). Note that the negative voltmeter lead will always be black and that the positive voltmeter will always be some color other than black (usually red).

• Ohmmeter—the ohmmeter is designed to read resistance (measured in ohms) in a circuit or component. Most ohmmeters will have a selector switch which permits the measurement of different ranges of resistance (usually the selector switch allows the multiplication of the meter reading by 10, 100, 1,000 and 10,000). Some ohmmeters are "auto-ranging" which means the meter itself will determine which scale to use. Since the meters are powered by an internal battery, the ohmmeter can be used like a self-powered test light. When the ohmmeter is connected, current from the ohmmeter flows through the circuit or component being tested. Since the ohmmeter's internal resistance and voltage are known values, the amount of current flow through the meter depends on the resistance of the circuit or component being tested. The ohmmeter can also be used to perform a continuity test for suspected open circuits. In using the meter for making continuity checks, do not be concerned with the actual resistance readings. Zero resistance, or any ohm reading, indicates continuity in the circuit. Infinite resistance indicates an opening in the circuit. A high resistance reading where there should be none indicates a problem in the circuit. Checks for short circuits are made in the same manner as checks for open circuits, except that the circuit must be isolated from both power and normal ground. Infinite resistance indicates no continuity, while zero resistance indicates a dead short.

⁂ WARNING

Never use an ohmmeter to check the resistance of a component or wire while there is voltage applied to the circuit.

• Ammeter—an ammeter measures the amount of current flowing through a circuit in units called amperes or amps. At normal operating voltage, most circuits have a characteristic amount of amperes, called "current draw" which can be measured using an ammeter. By referring to a specified current draw rating, then measuring the amperes and comparing the two values, one can determine what is happening within the circuit to aid in diagnosis. An open circuit, for example, will not allow any current to flow, so the ammeter reading will be zero. A damaged component or circuit will have an increased current draw, so the reading will be high. The ammeter is always connected in series with the circuit being tested. All of the current that normally flows through the circuit must also flow through the ammeter; if there is any other path for the current to follow, the ammeter reading will not be accurate. The ammeter itself has very little resistance to current flow and, therefore, will not affect the circuit, but it will measure current draw only when the circuit is closed and electricity is flowing. Excessive current draw can blow fuses and drain the battery, while a reduced current draw can cause motors to run slowly, lights to dim and other components to not operate properly.

Troubleshooting Electrical Systems

When diagnosing a specific problem, organized troubleshooting is a must. The complexity of a modern automotive vehicle demands that you approach any problem in a logical, organized manner. There are certain troubleshooting techniques, however, which are standard:

• Establish when the problem occurs. Does the problem appear only under certain conditions? Were there any noises, odors or other unusual symptoms?

Isolate the problem area. To do this, make some simple tests and observations, then eliminate the systems that are working properly. Check for obvious problems, such as broken wires and loose or dirty connections. Always check the obvious before assuming something complicated is the cause.

• Test for problems systematically to determine the cause once the problem area is isolated. Are all the components functioning properly? Is there power going to electrical switches and motors? Performing careful, systematic checks will often turn up most causes on the first inspection, without wasting time checking components that have little or no relationship to the problem.

• Test all repairs after the work is done to make sure that the problem is fixed. Some causes can be traced to more than one component, so a careful verification of repair work is important in order to pick up additional malfunctions that may cause a problem to reappear or a different problem to arise. A blown fuse, for example, is a simple problem that may require more than another fuse to repair. If you don't look for a problem that caused a fuse to blow, a shorted wire (for example) may go undetected.

Experience has shown that most problems tend to be the result of a fairly simple and obvious cause, such as loose or corroded connectors, bad grounds or damaged wire insulation which causes a short. This makes careful visual inspection of components during testing essential to quick and accurate troubleshooting.

Testing

OPEN CIRCUITS

▶ **See Figure 8**

This test already assumes the existence of an open in the circuit and it is used to help locate the open portion.
1. Isolate the circuit from power and ground.
2. Connect the self-powered test light or ohmmeter ground clip to the ground side of the circuit and probe sections of the circuit sequentially.
3. If the light is out or there is infinite resistance, the open is between the probe and the circuit ground.
4. If the light is on or the meter shows continuity, the open is between the probe and the end of the circuit toward the power source.

SHORT CIRCUITS

➡**Never use a self-powered test light to perform checks for opens or shorts when power is applied to the circuit under test. The test light can be damaged by outside power.**

1. Isolate the circuit from power and ground.
2. Connect the self-powered test light or ohmmeter ground clip to a good ground and probe any easy-to-reach point in the circuit.
3. If the light comes on or there is continuity, there is a short somewhere in the circuit.

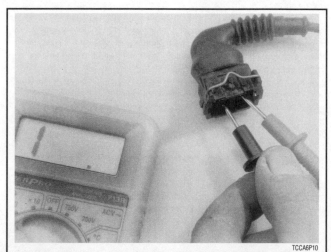

TCCA6P10

Fig. 8 The infinite reading on this multimeter indicates that the circuit is open

4. To isolate the short, probe a test point at either end of the isolated circuit (the light should be on or the meter should indicate continuity).

5. Leave the test light probe engaged and sequentially open connectors or switches, remove parts, etc. until the light goes out or continuity is broken.

6. When the light goes out, the short is between the last two circuit components which were opened.

VOLTAGE

This test determines voltage available from the battery and should be the first step in any electrical troubleshooting procedure after visual inspection. Many electrical problems, especially on computer controlled systems, can be caused by a low state of charge in the battery. Excessive corrosion at the battery cable terminals can cause poor contact that will prevent proper charging and full battery current flow.

1. Set the voltmeter selector switch to the 20V position.

2. Connect the multimeter negative lead to the battery's negative (–) post or terminal and the positive lead to the battery's positive (+) post or terminal.

3. Turn the ignition switch **ON** to provide a load.

4. A well charged battery should register over 12 volts. If the meter reads below 11.5 volts, the battery power may be insufficient to operate the electrical system properly.

VOLTAGE DROP

♦ See Figure 9

When current flows through a load, the voltage beyond the load drops. This voltage drop is due to the resistance created by the load and also by small resistances created by corrosion at the connectors and damaged insulation on the wires. The maximum allowable voltage drop under load is critical, especially if there is more than one load in the circuit, since all voltage drops are cumulative.

1. Set the voltmeter selector switch to the 20 volt position.

2. Connect the multimeter negative lead to a good ground.

3. Operate the circuit and check the voltage prior to the first component (load).

4. There should be little or no voltage drop in the circuit prior to the first component. If a voltage drop exists, the wire or connectors in the circuit are suspect.

5. While operating the first component in the circuit, probe the ground side of the component with the positive meter lead and observe the voltage readings. A small voltage drop should be noticed. This voltage drop is caused by the resistance of the component.

6. Repeat the test for each component (load) down the circuit.

7. If a large voltage drop is noticed, the preceding component, wire or connector is suspect.

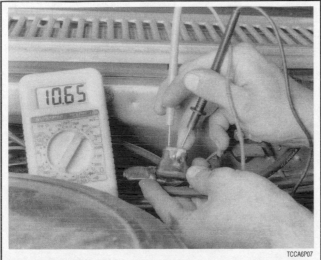

Fig. 9 This voltage drop test revealed high resistance (low voltage) in the circuit

RESISTANCE

♦ See Figures 10 and 11

✱✱ WARNING

Never use an ohmmeter with power applied to the circuit. The ohmmeter is designed to operate on its own power supply. The normal 12 volt electrical system voltage could damage the meter!

1. Isolate the circuit from the vehicle's power source.

2. Ensure that the ignition key is **OFF** when disconnecting any components or the battery.

3. Where necessary, also isolate at least one side of the circuit to be checked, in order to avoid reading parallel resistances. Parallel circuit resistances will always give a lower reading than the actual resistance of either of the branches.

4. Connect the meter leads to both sides of the circuit (wire or component) and read the actual measured ohms on the meter scale. Make sure the selector switch is set to the proper ohm scale for the circuit being tested, to avoid misreading the ohmmeter test value.

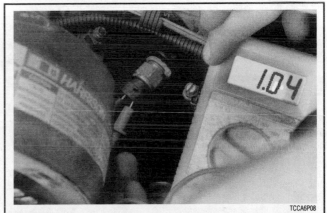

Fig. 10 Checking the resistance of a coolant temperature sensor with an ohmmeter. Reading is 1.04 kilohms

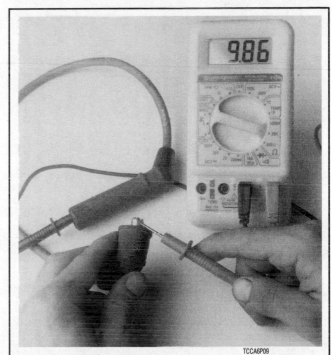

Fig. 11 Spark plug wires can be checked for excessive resistance using an ohmmeter

Wire and Connector Repair

Almost anyone can replace damaged wires, as long as the proper tools and parts are available. Wire and terminals are available to fit almost any need. Even the specialized weatherproof, molded and hard shell connectors are now available from aftermarket suppliers.

Be sure the ends of all the wires are fitted with the proper terminal hardware and connectors. Wrapping a wire around a stud is never a permanent solution and will only cause trouble later. Replace wires one at a time to avoid confusion. Always route wires exactly the same as the factory.

➡**If connector repair is necessary, only attempt it if you have the proper tools. Weatherproof and hard shell connectors require special tools to release the pins inside the connector. Attempting to repair these connectors with conventional hand tools will damage them.**

BATTERY CABLES

Disconnecting the Cables

When working on any electrical component on the vehicle, it is always a good idea to disconnect the negative (-) battery cable. This will prevent potential damage to many sensitive electrical components such as the Engine Control Module (ECM), radio, alternator, etc.

➡**Any time you disengage the battery cables, it is recommended that you disconnect the negative (-) battery cable first. This will prevent your accidentally grounding the positive (+) terminal to the body of the vehicle when disconnecting it, thereby preventing damage to the above mentioned components.**

Before you disconnect the cable(s), first turn the ignition to the **OFF** position. This will prevent a draw on the battery which could cause arcing (electricity trying to ground itself to the body of a vehicle, just like a spark plug jumping the gap) and, of course, damaging some components such as the alternator diodes.

When the battery cable(s) are reconnected (negative cable last), be sure to check that your lights, windshield wipers and other electrically operated safety components are all working correctly. If your vehicle contains an Electronically Tuned Radio (ETR), don't forget to also reset your radio stations. Ditto for the clock.

SUPPLEMENTAL INFLATABLE RESTRAINT (SIR) SYSTEM

General Information

Beginning in 1991, driver's side air bags became standard equipment for the Beretta and Corsica vehicles. The Supplemental Inflatable Restraint (SIR) system offers protection in addition to that provided by the seat belt by deploying an air bag from the center of the steering wheel or dash panel. The air bag deploys when the vehicle is involved in a frontal crash of sufficient force up to 30° off the centerline of the vehicle. To further absorb the crash energy, there is also a knee bolster located beneath the instrument panel in the driver's area and the steering wheel is collapsible.

The system has an energy reserve, which can store a large enough electrical charge to deploy the air bag(s) for up to ten minutes after the battery has been disconnected or damaged. The system **MUST** be disabled before any service is performed on or around SIR components or SIR wiring.

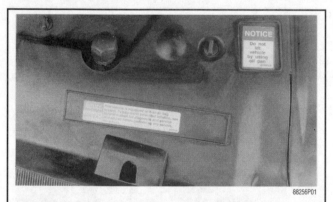

Your vehicle should have an SIR system sticker located in the engine compartment

SYSTEM OPERATION

The SIR system consists of a Diagnostic Energy Reserve Module (DERM), the driver inflator module, the SIR coil assembly, and the AIR BAG warning lamp in the instrument cluster. The DERM, SIR coil assembly, inflator module and connector wires make up the deployment loops. The function of the deployment loops is to supply current through the inflator modules, which will cause deployment of the air bag in the event of a frontal crash of sufficient force, up to 30 degrees off the centerline of the vehicle. The inflator modules are only supplied enough current to deploy when the DERM detects vehicle velocity changes severe enough the warrant deployment. The SDM supplies the necessary power, even if the battery has been damaged.

The deployment loop is made up of the arming sensors, coil assembly, inflator module and the discriminating sensors. The inflator module is only supplied sufficient current when the arming sensor and at least one of the two discriminating sensors close simultaneously. The function of the SDM is to supply the deployment loop a 36 Volt Loop Reserve (36VLR) to assure sufficient voltage to deploy the air bag if ignition voltage is lost in a frontal crash.

The DERM, in conjunction with the sensor resistors, makes it possible to detect circuit and component malfunctions within the deployment loop. If the voltages monitored by the DERM fall outside expected limits, the DERM will indicate a malfunction by storing a diagnostic trouble code and illuminating the AIR BAG lamp.

SYSTEM COMPONENTS

▶ **See Figures 12 and 13**

Diagnostic Energy Reserve Module (DERM)

The DERM is designed to perform five main functions: energy reserve, malfunction detection, malfunction recording, driver notification and frontal crash recording.

The DERM maintains a reserve voltage supply to provide deployment energy for a few seconds when the vehicle voltage is low or lost in a frontal crash. The DERM performs diagnostic monitoring of the SIR system and records malfunctions in the form of diagnostic trouble codes, which can be obtained from a

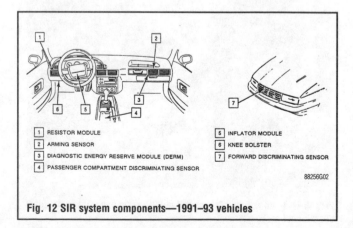

1 RESISTOR MODULE	5 INFLATOR MODULE
2 ARMING SENSOR	6 KNEE BOLSTER
3 DIAGNOSTIC ENERGY RESERVE MODULE (DERM)	7 FORWARD DISCRIMINATING SENSOR
4 PASSENGER COMPARTMENT DISCRIMINATING SENSOR	

Fig. 12 SIR system components—1991–93 vehicles

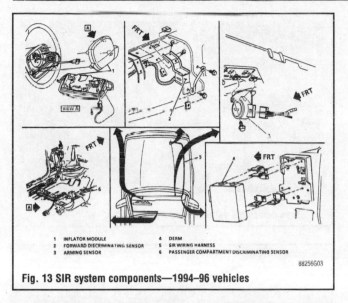

Fig. 13 SIR system components—1994–96 vehicles

1	INFLATOR MODULE	4	DERM
2	FORWARD DISCRIMINATING SENSOR	5	SIR WIRING HARNESS
3	ARMING SENSOR	6	PASSENGER COMPARTMENT DISCRIMINATING SENSOR

88256G03

hand scan tool and/or on-board diagnostics. The DERM warns the driver of SIR system malfunctions by controlling the AIR BAG warning lamp and records SIR system status during a frontal crash.

Air Bag Warning Lamp

The AIR BAG warning/indicator lamp is used to verify lamp and DERM operation by flashing 7 times when the ignition is first turned **ON**. It is also used to warn the driver of an SIR system malfunction.

SIR Coil Assembly

♦ See Figure 14

The SIR coil assembly consists of two current carrying coils. They are attached to the steering column and allow rotation of the steering wheel while maintaining continuous deployment loop contact through the inflator module.

There is a shorting bar on the lower steering column connector that connects the SIR coil to the SIR wiring harness. The shorting bar shorts the circuit when the connector is disengaged. The circuit to the inflator module is shorted in this way to prevent unwanted air bag deployment when servicing the steering column or other SIR components.

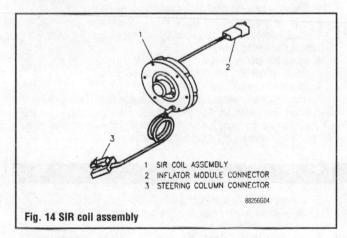

1	SIR COIL ASSEMBLY
2	INFLATOR MODULE CONNECTOR
3	STEERING COLUMN CONNECTOR

88256G04

Fig. 14 SIR coil assembly

Inflator Module

♦ See Figure 15

The inflator module consists of an inflatable bag and an inflator (a canister of gas-generating material and an initiating device). When the vehicle is in a frontal crash of sufficient force to close the arming sensor and at least one discriminating sensor simultaneously, current flows through the deployment loop. Current passing through the initiator ignites the material in the inflator

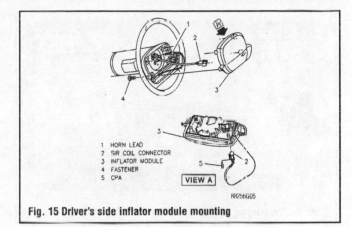

1	HORN LEAD
2	SIR COIL CONNECTOR
3	INFLATOR MODULE
4	FASTENER
5	CPA

VIEW A

88256G05

Fig. 15 Driver's side inflator module mounting

module, causing a reaction which produces a gas that rapidly inflates the air bag.

All vehicles are equipped with a driver's side inflator module located in the steering wheel.

SERVICE PRECAUTIONS

♦ See Figure 16

• When performing service around the SIR system components or wiring, the SIR system **MUST** be disabled. Failure to do so could result in possible air bag deployment, personal injury or unneeded SIR system repairs.

• When carrying a live inflator module, make sure that the bag and trim cover are pointed away from you. Never carry the inflator module by the wires or connector on the underside of the module. In case of accidental deployment, the bag will then deploy with minimal chance of injury.

• When placing a live inflator module on a bench or other surface, always face the bag and trim cover up, away from the surface.

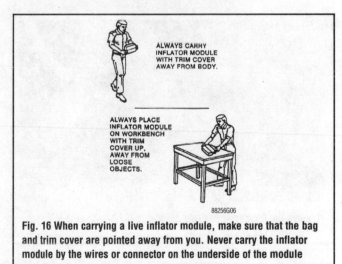

ALWAYS CARRY INFLATOR MODULE WITH TRIM COVER AWAY FROM BODY.

ALWAYS PLACE INFLATOR MODULE ON WORKBENCH WITH TRIM COVER UP, AWAY FROM LOOSE OBJECTS.

88256G06

Fig. 16 When carrying a live inflator module, make sure that the bag and trim cover are pointed away from you. Never carry the inflator module by the wires or connector on the underside of the module

DISABLING THE SYSTEM

♦ See Figure 17

→With the AIR BAG fuse removed and the ignition switch ON, the AIR BAG warning lamp will be on. The is normal and does not indicate any system malfunction.

1. Turn the steering wheel so that the vehicle's wheels are pointing straight ahead.

2. Turn the ignition switch to **LOCK**, remove the key, then disconnect the negative battery cable.

3. Remove the AIR BAG fuse (fuse 3) from the fuse block.

4. Remove the steering column filler panel/left-hand sound insulator.

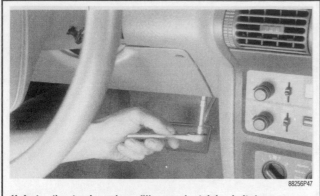
Unfasten the steering column filler panel retaining bolts/screws . . .

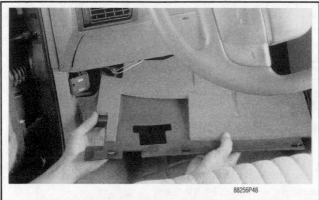
. . . then remove the filler panel from under the steering column

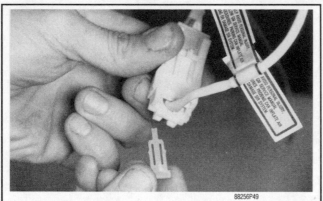
Remove the Connector Position Assurance (CPA) retaining clip (see arrow) from the SIR connector . . .

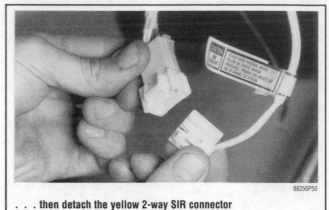
. . . then detach the yellow 2-way SIR connector

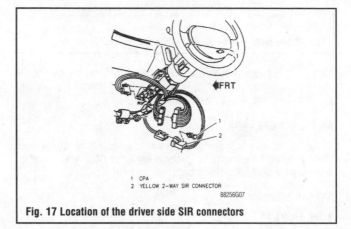

1 CPA
2 YELLOW 2-WAY SIR CONNECTOR

88256G07

Fig. 17 Location of the driver side SIR connectors

5. Disengage the Connector Position Assurance (CPA) and the yellow 2-way connector, located near the base of the steering column.
6. Connect the negative battery cable.

ENABLING THE SYSTEM

▶ **See Figure 17**

1. Disconnect the negative battery cable.
2. Turn the ignition switch to **LOCK**, then remove the key.
3. Engage the yellow SIR connector and corresponding CPA located near the base of the steering column.
4. Install the steering column filler panel/lower trim panel.
5. Install the AIR BAG fuse (fuse 3) to the fuse block.
6. Connect the negative battery cable.
7. Turn the ignition switch to **RUN** and make sure that the AIR BAG warning lamp flashes seven times and then shuts off. If the warning lamp does not shut off, make sure that the wiring is properly connected. If the light remains on, take the vehicle to a reputable repair facility for service.

HEATER & AIR CONDITIONING

Blower Motor

REMOVAL & INSTALLATION

▶ **See Figures 18 and 19**

1988–89 Vehicles

1. Disconnect the negative battery cable.
2. Disconnect the electrical connections at the blower motor and blower resistor.

3. Remove the plastic water shield from the right side of the cowl.
4. On vehicles equipped with V6 engine and air conditioning, it may be necessary to remove the alternator.
5. Remove the blower motor retaining screws and then pull the blower motor and cage out.
6. Hold the blower motor cage and remove the cage retaining nut from the blower motor shaft.
7. Remove the blower motor and cage.
8. Installation is the reverse of removal.

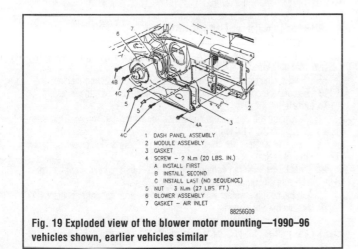

1. Blower motor
2. Blower fan
3. Nut
4. Blower module
5. Blower motor resistor
6. Motor cooling tube

88256G00

Fig. 18 Exploded view of a typical blower motor and fan assembly

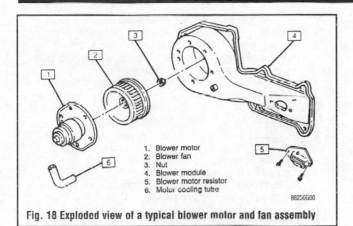

1. DASH PANEL ASSEMBLY
2. MODULE ASSEMBLY
3. GASKET
4. SCREW — 2 N.m (20 LBS. IN.)
   A INSTALL FIRST
   B INSTALL SECOND
   C INSTALL LAST (NO SEQUENCE)
5. NUT 3 N.m (27 LBS FT.)
6. BLOWER ASSEMBLY
7. GASKET – AIR INLET

88256G09

Fig. 19 Exploded view of the blower motor mounting—1990–96 vehicles shown, earlier vehicles similar

1990-96 Vehicles

1. Disconnect the negative battery cable.
2. For 3.1L engines, perform the following:
   a. Remove the serpentine drive belt.
   b. Remove the alternator from the vehicle.
3. Detach the electrical connection(s) from the blower motor.
4. Disconnect the motor cooling tube.
5. Remove the motor retaining bolts/screws, then remove the motor and fan assembly.

➡On 1991–96 models, the blower motor and fan is serviced as an assembly.

6. If necessary, remove the nut from the blower motor shaft, then separate remove the fan from the motor.

To install:

7. Position the fan onto the blower motor shaft, then install the retaining nut.
8. Install the blower motor assembly, then secure with the retaining screws.
9. Connect the motor cooling tube.
10. Attach the electrical connection(s) to the blower motor.
11. On vehicles equipped with the 3.1L, perform the following:
    a. Install the alternator.
    b. Install the serpentine drive belt.
12. Connect the negative battery cable, then check for proper blower motor operation.

Heater Core

REMOVAL & INSTALLATION

♦ See Figures 20 and 21

✳✳ CAUTION

When draining the coolant, keep in mind that cats and dogs are attracted by cthylone glycol antifreeze, and are quite likely to drink any that is left in an uncovered container or in puddles on the ground. This will prove fatal in sufficient quantity. Always drain the coolant into a sealable container. Coolant should be reused unless it is contaminated or several years old.

Vehicles Without A/C

1988–90 VEHICLES

1. Disconnect the negative battery cable.
2. Drain the cooling system into a suitable container.
3. Disconnect the heater inlet and outlet hoses from the heater core.
4. Remove the heater outlet deflector.
5. Unfasten the retaining screws, then remove the heater core cover.
6. Remove the heater core retaining straps, then remove the heater core from the vehicle.
7. Installation is the reverse of removal.

1991 VEHICLES

1. Disconnect the negative battery cable.
2. Drain the cooling system into a suitable container.
3. Properly disable the SIR system, as outlined earlier in this section.
4. Remove the instrument panel as outlined in this section.
5. Remove the screws and floor outlet, turning clockwise and to the right to release from the rear floor air outlet.
6. Raise the vehicle and support it safely.
7. Detach the heater hoses from the heater core.
8. Disconnect the drain tube elbow from the heater core cover.
9. Carefully lower the vehicle.
10. Unfasten the retaining screws, then remove the heater core cover.

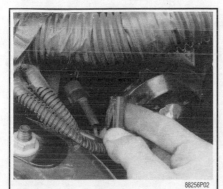

88256P02

Unplug the blower motor electrical connection(s)

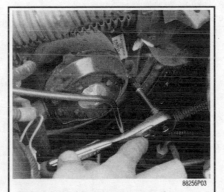

88256P03

Unfasten the blower motor mounting bolts/screws . . .

88256P04

. . . then remove the blower motor and fan assembly from the vehicle

11. Remove the core screws, clamps and heater core from the vehicle.
12. Installation is the reverse of the removal procedure.
13. Fill the cooling system with the proper type and amount of coolant.
14. Enable the SIR system, as outlined earlier in this section.
15. Connect the negative battery cable, then start the engine and check for coolant leaks. Check the coolant level, and add if necessary.

1992–93 VEHICLES

1. Disable the SIR system, as outlined earlier in this section.
2. Disconnect the negative battery cable.
3. Drain the cooling system into a suitable container.
4. Remove the radio as outlined in this section.
5. Reach through the radio opening and release the heater core cover from the retention clips.
6. Remove the screws and floor outlet, turning clockwise and to the right to release from the rear floor air outlet.
7. Raise the vehicle and support it safely.
8. Disconnect the heater hoses from the heater core.
9. Detach the drain tube elbow from the heater core cover.
10. Carefully lower the vehicle.
11. Unfasten the retaining screws and remove the heater core cover.
12. Remove the core screws, clamps and heater core from the vehicle.

To install:
13. Reposition the heater core and install the straps and screws. Tighten the retaining screws to 12 inch lbs. (1.4 Nm).
14. Install the heater core cover and attaching screws. Tighten the cover attaching screws to 12 inch lbs. (1.4 Nm).
15. Reach through the radio opening, position the cover under the retention clips.
16. Install the remaining components in the reverse of the removal procedure.
17. Fill the cooling system with the proper type and amount of coolant.
18. Enable the SIR system.
19. Connect the negative battery cable, then start the engine and check for coolant leaks. Check the coolant level, and add if necessary.

1994–96 VEHICLES

For heater core removal on these vehicles, please refer to the procedure for vehicles with A/C.

Vehicles With A/C

1988–90 VEHICLES

1. Disconnect the negative battery cable.
2. Drain the cooling system into a suitable container.
3. Raise and safely support the front of the vehicle.
4. Disconnect the drain tube from the heater case.
5. Detach the heater hoses from the heater core.
6. Carefully lower the car.
7. Remove the right and left hush panels, the steering column trim cover, the heater outlet duct and the glove box.
8. Remove the heater core cover. Be sure to pull the cover straight to the rear so as not to damage the drain tube.
9. Remove the heater core clamps, then remove the core from the vehicle.
10. Installation is the reverse of the removal procedure.
11. Fill the cooling system with the proper type and amount of coolant.
12. Connect the negative battery cable, then start the engine and check for coolant leaks. Check the coolant level, and add if necessary.

1991 VEHICLES

1. Disable the SIR system, as outlined earlier in this section.
2. Disconnect the negative battery cable.
3. Drain the cooling system into a suitable container.
4. Remove the instrument panel as outlined in this section.
5. Remove the screws and floor outlet, turning clockwise and to the right to release from the rear floor air outlet.
6. Raise the vehicle and support it safely.
7. Disconnect the heater hoses from the heater core.
8. Detach the drain tube elbow from the heater core cover.
9. Carefully lower the vehicle.

10. Remove the screws and remove the heater core cover.
11. Remove the core screws, clamps and heater core from the vehicle.
12. Reposition the heater core and install the straps and screws.
13. Install the remaining components in the reverse of the removal procedure. Make sure all components are tightened securely.
14. Fill the cooling system with the proper type and amount of coolant.
15. Enable the SIR system.
16. Connect the negative battery cable, then start the engine and check for coolant leaks. Check the coolant level, and add if necessary.

1992–93 VEHICLES

1. Disable the SIR system.
2. Disconnect the negative battery cable.
3. Drain the cooling system into a suitable container.
4. Raise the vehicle and support it safely.
5. Disconnect the drain tube from the heater case.
6. Detach the heater hoses from the heater core.
7. Carefully lower the vehicle.
8. Remove the console, if equipped.
9. Remove the right and left sound insulators.
10. Remove the steering column opening filler.
11. Remove the screws and floor outlet, turning clockwise and to the right to release from the rear floor air outlet.
12. Unfasten the retaining screws, then remove the heater core cover.
13. Remove the core screws, clamps and heater core from the vehicle.

To install:
14. Reposition the heater core and install the straps and screws. Tighten the screws to 12 inch lbs. (1.4 Nm).
15. Install the heater core cover and attaching screws. Tighten the screws to 12 inch lbs. (1.4 Nm).
16. Install the remaining components in the reverse of the removal procedure. Make sure all components are tightened securely.
17. Fill the cooling system with the proper type and amount of coolant.
18. Enable the SIR system.
19. Connect the negative battery cable, then start the engine and check for coolant leaks. Check the coolant level, and add if necessary.

1994–96 VEHICLES

1. Properly disable the SIR system, as outlined earlier in this section.
2. Disconnect the negative battery cable.
3. Drain the cooling system into a suitable container.
4. Raise and safely support the vehicle.
5. Disconnect the drain tube from the heater case.
6. Detach the heater hoses from the heater core.
7. Carefully lower the vehicle.
8. Remove the right and left sound insulators.
9. Remove the steering column opening filler.
10. Remove the floor air outlet duct.
11. Remove the heater core cover.
12. Unfasten the heater core mounting clamps, then remove the heater core from the vehicle.
13. Position the heater core in the vehicle and secure with the mounting straps.

The heater core is located in the passenger's side footwell, below the glove compartment

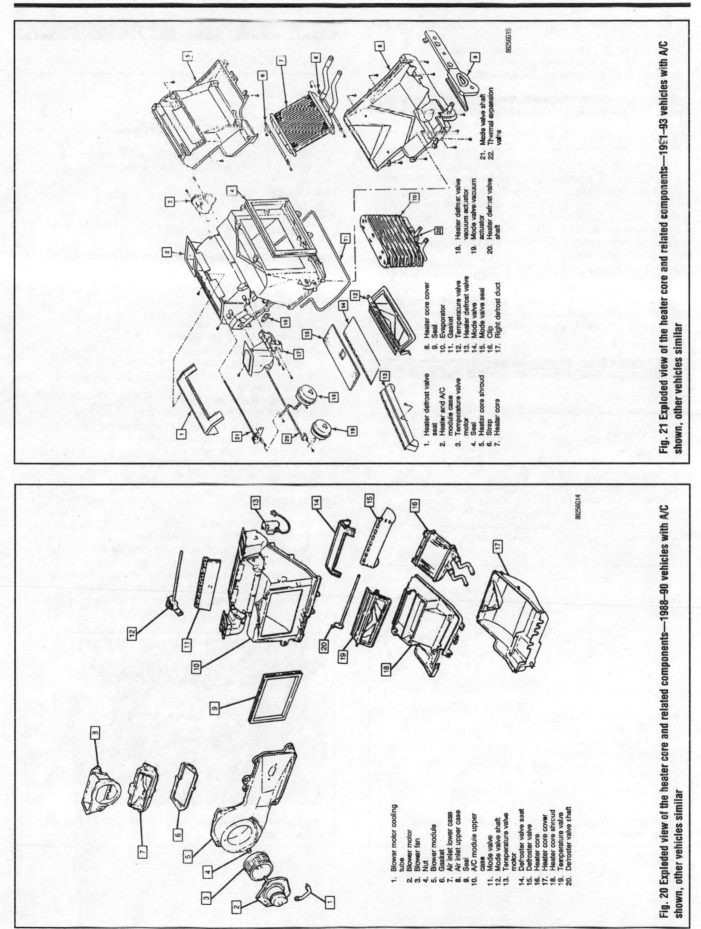

1. Heater defrost valve seat
2. Heater and A/C module case
3. Temperature valve motor
4. Seal
5. Heater core shroud
6. Strap
7. Heater core

8. Heater core cover
9. Seal
10. Evaporator
11. Gasket
12. Temperature valve
13. Heater defrost valve
14. Mode valve
15. Mode valve seal
16. Clip
17. Right defrost duct

18. Heater defrost valve vacuum actuator
19. Mode valve vacuum actuator
20. Heater defrost valve shaft
21. Mode valve shaft
22. Thermal expansion valve

Fig. 21 Exploded view of the heater core and related components—1991–93 vehicles with A/C shown, other vehicles similar

1. Blower motor cooling tube
2. Blower motor
3. Blower fan
4. Nut
5. Blower module
6. Gasket
7. Air inlet lower case
8. Air inlet upper case
9. Seal
10. A/C module upper case
11. Mode valve
12. Mode valve shaft
13. Temperature valve motor
14. Defroster valve seat
15. Defroster valve
16. Heater core
17. Heater core cover
18. Heater core shroud
19. Temperature valve
20. Defroster valve shaft

Fig. 20 Exploded view of the heater core and related components—1988–90 vehicles with A/C shown, other vehicles similar

14. Install the remaining components in the reverse of the removal procedure.
15. Enable the SIR system, as outlined earlier in this section.
16. Connect the negative battery cable, then start the engine and check for coolant leaks. Check the coolant level, and add if necessary.

Air Conditioning Components

REMOVAL & INSTALLATION

Repair or service of air conditioning components is not covered by this manual, because of the risk of personal injury or death, and because of the legal ramifications of servicing these components without the proper EPA certification and experience. Cost, personal injury or death, environmental damage, and legal considerations (such as the fact that it is a federal crime to vent refrigerant into the atmosphere), dictate that the A/C components on your vehicle should be serviced only by a Motor Vehicle Air Conditioning (MVAC) trained, and EPA certified automotive technician.

➡️If your vehicle's A/C system uses R-12 refrigerant and is in need of recharging, the A/C system can be converted over to R-134a refrigerant (less environmentally harmful and expensive). Refer to Section 1 for additional information on R-12 to R-134a conversions, and for additional considerations dealing with your vehicle's A/C system.

Control Cables

REMOVAL & INSTALLATION

1988–90 Vehicles

▶ See Figure 22

1. Disconnect the negative battery cable..
2. Remove the glove box and the right side sound insulator.
3. Disconnect the cables from the heater module.
4. Remove the heater control assembly trim plate.
5. Disconnect the cables from the heater control assembly.
6. Installation is the reverse of the removal procedure.

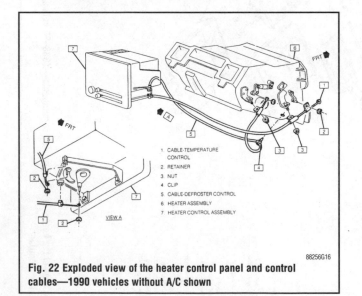

1. CABLE-TEMPERATURE CONTROL
2. RETAINER
3. NUT
4. CLIP
5. CABLE-DEFROSTER CONTROL
6. HEATER ASSEMBLY
7. HEATER CONTROL ASSEMBLY

VIEW A

88256G16

Fig. 22 Exploded view of the heater control panel and control cables—1990 vehicles without A/C shown

Control Panel

REMOVAL & INSTALLATION

1988–89 Vehicles

1. Disconnect the negative battery cable.
2. Remove the glove box and the right sound insulator.
3. Disconnect the cables from the module.
4. Remove the control panel trim plate, then remove the control assembly.
5. Installation is the reverse of the removal procedure.

1990 Vehicles

MODELS WITHOUT A/C

1. Disconnect the negative battery cable.
2. Disconnect the control cables.
3. Remove the control cable retaining screws, then remove the control assembly from the vehicle.
4. Installation is the reverse of the removal procedure.

MODELS WITH A/C

1. Disconnect the negative battery cable.
2. For Corsicas, perform the following:
   a. Unsnap the radio trim ring.
   b. Remove the 4 radio retaining screws.
   c. Detach the electrical and vacuum harness from the rear of the radio/control assembly.
3. For Berettas, perform the following:
   a. Remove the 2 screws securing the control trim panel and trim panel.
   b. Disconnect the vacuum and electrical harness from the rear of the heater and A/C control assembly.
4. Remove the four screws securing the heater and A/C control assembly to the radio face plate, then remove the control assembly from the vehicle.
5. Installation is the reverse of the removal procedure.

1991–96 Vehicles

1. Disconnect the negative battery cable.
2. Remove the bezel from the instrument panel.
3. Remove the heater control assembly retaining screws.
4. Detach the electrical connector from the heater control assembly.
5. Disconnect the vacuum harness from the heater control assembly.
6. Remove the heater and A/C control assembly from the vehicle.
7. Install the remaining components in the reverse of the removal procedure. Make sure all components are tightened securely.

88256P05

On the Corsica, remove the bezel by carefully prying it from the instrument panel

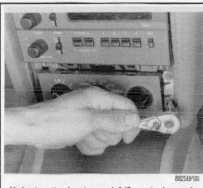

Unfasten the heater and A/C control panel retaining screws

Pull the control assembly partially away from the instrument panel . . .

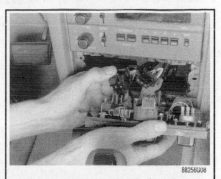

. . . then detach the electrical and vacuum connections and remove the control assembly from the vehicle

CRUISE CONTROL

General Information

▶ See Figures 23, 24, 25 and 26

Cruise control is a speed control system that maintains a desired vehicle speed under normal driving conditions. However, steep grades up or down may cause variations in the selected speeds. The electronic cruise control system has the capability to cruise, coast, resume speed, accelerate, "tap-up" and "tap-down".

The main parts of the cruise control system are the functional control switches, cruise control module assembly, vehicle speed sensor and the release switches.

The cruise control system uses the module assembly to obtain the desired operation. Two components in the module help to do this. One is the electronic controller and the second is the electric stepper motor. The controller monitors the vehicle speed and operates the stepper motor. The motor moves a ribbon and throttle linkage in response to the controller. The cruise control module assembly contains a low speed limit which will prevent system engagement below 25 mph (40 km/h). The module is controlled by the functional switches in the turn signal/headlamp switch and windshield wiper lever.

The release switches are mounted on the brake/clutch/accelerator pedal bracket. When the brake or clutch pedal is depressed, the cruise control system is electrically disengaged and the throttle is returned to the idle position.

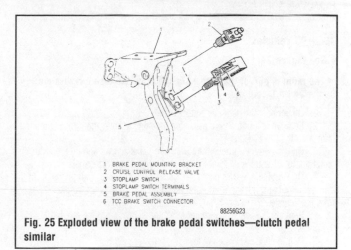

1 BRAKE PEDAL MOUNTING BRACKET
2 CRUISE CONTROL RELEASE VALVE
3 STOPLAMP SWITCH
4 STOPLAMP SWITCH TERMINALS
5 BRAKE PEDAL ASSEMBLY
6 TCC BRAKE SWITCH CONNECTOR

88256G23

Fig. 25 Exploded view of the brake pedal switches—clutch pedal similar

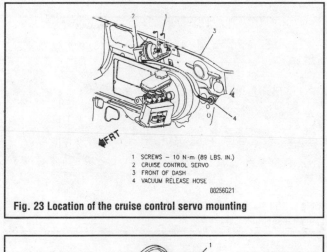

1 SCREWS – 10 N·m (89 LBS. IN.)
2 CRUISE CONTROL SERVO
3 FRONT OF DASH
4 VACUUM RELEASE HOSE

88256G21

Fig. 23 Location of the cruise control servo mounting

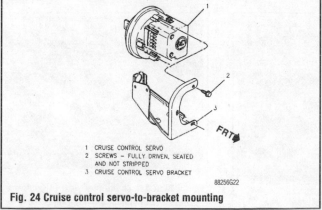

1 CRUISE CONTROL SERVO
2 SCREWS – FULLY DRIVEN, SEATED AND NOT STRIPPED
3 CRUISE CONTROL SERVO BRACKET

88256G22

Fig. 24 Cruise control servo-to-bracket mounting

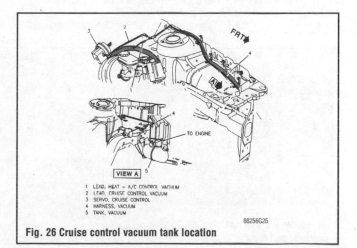

1 LEAD, HEAT – A/C CONTROL VACUUM
2 LEAD, CRUISE CONTROL VACUUM
3 SERVO, CRUISE CONTROL
4 HARNESS, VACUUM
5 TANK, VACUUM

88256G25

Fig. 26 Cruise control vacuum tank location

CRUISE CONTROL TROUBLESHOOTING

Problem	Possible Cause
Will not hold proper speed	Incorrect cable adjustment
	Binding throttle linkage
	Leaking vacuum servo diaphragm
	Leaking vacuum tank
	Faulty vacuum or vent valve
	Faulty stepper motor
	Faulty transducer
	Faulty speed sensor
	Faulty cruise control module
Cruise intermittently cuts out	Clutch or brake switch adjustment too tight
	Short or open in the cruise control circuit
	Faulty transducer
	Faulty cruise control module
Vehicle surges	Kinked speedometer cable or casing
	Binding throttle linkage
	Faulty speed sensor
	Faulty cruise control module
Cruise control inoperative	Blown fuse
	Short or open in the cruise control circuit
	Faulty brake or clutch switch
	Leaking vacuum circuit
	Faulty cruise control switch
	Faulty stepper motor
	Faulty transducer
	Faulty speed sensor
	Faulty cruise control module

Note: Use this chart as a guide. Not all systems will use the components listed.

TCCA6C01

ENTERTAINMENT SYSTEMS

Radio

REMOVAL & INSTALLATION

1988–90 Vehicles

▶ See Figure 27

➡The radio is part of the accessory center, which also includes the heater and A/C controls.

1. Disconnect the negative battery cable.
2. Remove left side sound insulator attaching screws and remove the insulator from the lower dash.
3. On the Beretta, remove the lower trim panel screws and pull the trim panel out to release the clips at the top and remove the trim panel.
4. On Corsica, the trim panel has no attaching screws. Carefully pull the trim panel out and release it from the retaining clips, then remove the trim panel from the vehicle.
5. Remove the accessory center attaching screws from the top and from the bottom.
6. Pull the accessory center away from the carrier.
7. On vehicles with A/C, remove the electrical and vacuum harness from the back of the heater and A/C control assembly.
8. On vehicles without A/C, remove the cables from the control module.

9. Detach the antenna connection and tag and unplug the attaching electrical connections.
10. Pull the accessory center assembly from the dash.
11. Place the assembly on a clean working area.
12. Remove all controls knobs by pulling them straight off.
13. Remove the screws attaching the trim plate to the radio. Separate the radio from the trim plate.

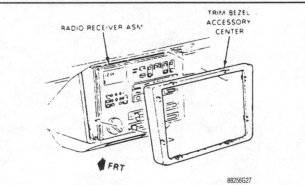

Fig. 27 On the 1988–90 Corsica, the accessory trim plate bezel does not have retaining screws

To remove the trim panel on the Corsica, carefully pull it away from the instrument panel

Carefully pull the radio assembly away from its mounting position . . .

. . . then detach the electrical (A) and antenna (B) connections from the back of the radio

To install:

14. Assemble the radio to the trim plate and accessory center. Install the attaching screws.

15. Install the knobs by pushing them in place.

16. Position the accessory center assembly to the dash and attach the electrical harness connections.

17. On vehicles with A/C, connect the electrical and vacuum harnesses at the rear of the heater and A/C control assembly.

18. On vehicles without A/C, connect the control cables to the control module.

19. Connect the antenna lead to the radio.

20. Slide the accessory center into place in the dash. Install the attaching screws at the top and bottom.

21. Install the trim panel in place.

22. Install the left side sound insulator to lower dash and cowl and install the attaching screws.

23. Connect the negative battery cable.

1991–92 Vehicles

1. Disconnect the negative battery cable.

2. Remove the accessory center trim bezel by inserting a suitable flat-bladed tool to carefully separate the bezel from the panel and disengage the clips. Remove the bezel.

➡ **If equipped with air conditioning, the outlets need not be removed prior to removing the bezel.**

3. Remove the bracket-to-panel screws.

4. Partially lift out the radio in order to access the wiring.

5. Disconnect the antenna cable.

6. Remove the bracket, clip-retained bolts and clip-retained rear guide.

7. Remove the radio receiver from the vehicle.

To install:

8. Install the clip-retained bolts, rear guide and bracket to the radio receiver.

9. Position the receiver and connect the antenna lead.

10. Press the guide receiver into the opening.

➡ **Ensure the rear guide is engaged into the slot in the instrument panel.**

11. Install the attaching screws.

12. Place the trim bezel into position, align the clips to the holes in the panel and press in to secure.

13. Connect the negative battery cable.

1993–96 Vehicles

1. Disconnect the negative battery cable.

2. Pull out from the slot in the bottom edge of the instrument panel trim bezel and disengage the clips.

3. Press the sides of the A/C outlets to disengage the clips.

4. Remove the clips from the instrument panel trim bezel.

5. Unfasten the bracket retaining screws.

6. Pull the radio partially out of the mounting bracket to detach the antenna and electrical connectors.

7. Remove the radio from the vehicle.

To install:

8. Connect the antenna and electrical connectors to the rear of the radio assembly.

9. Install the radio in the mounting bracket, then install the retaining screws. Tighten the screws to 18 inch lbs. (2 Nm)

10. Fasten the clips to the instrument panel trim bezel.

11. Install the air conditioner outlets, press to engage the clips.

12. Position the bezel, align the clips to the holes in the panel, then press to secure.

13. Connect the negative battery cable.

Front Speakers

REMOVAL & INSTALLATION

1988–90 Vehicles

1. Disconnect the negative battery cable.

2. Using a suitable flat bladed tool, carefully pry off the grille.

3. Remove the screws retaining the speaker to the instrument panel.

4. Detach the speaker electrical connection, then remove the speaker from the vehicle.

5. Installation is the reverse of the removal procedure.

1991–96 Vehicles

➡ See Figure 28

➡ **The shroud side trim panels incorporate the front speakers.**

1. Disable the SIR system, as outlined earlier in this section.

2. If not already done, disconnect the negative battery cable.

3. Remove the shroud side trim panel as follows:

   a. Remove the sound insulator.

   b. Remove the carpet retainer.

   c. Remove the upper screw from the hood release bracket.

   d. Loosen the instrument panel sound insulator.

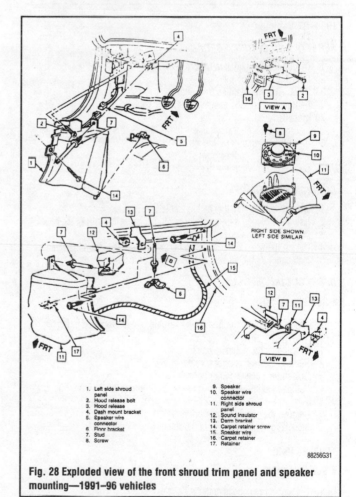

1. Left side shroud panel
2. Hood release bolt
3. Hood release
4. Dash mount bracket
5. Speaker wire connector
6. Floor bracket
7. Stud
8. Screw
9. Speaker
10. Speaker wire connector
11. Right side shroud panel
12. Sound insulator
13. Dash bracket
14. Carpet retainer screw
15. Speaker wire
16. Carpet retainer
17. Retainer

88256G31

Fig. 28 Exploded view of the front shroud trim panel and speaker mounting—1991–96 vehicles

e. Remove the stud to bracket on the dash panel.

f. Slide the panel toward the rear of the vehicle to disengage the retainer from the floor bracket (left side), or stud (right side).

g. Disconnect the speaker wire.

4. Remove the speaker-to-trim panel bolts, then remove the speaker from the vehicle.

To install:

5. Position the speaker to the trim panel, then tighten the bolts to 16 inch lbs. (1.8 Nm).

6. Connect the speaker wire.

7. Install the shroud side trim panel as follows:

a. Insert the retainer on the panel into the floor support bracket (left side), or stud (right side).

b. Position the panel to hinge pillar over the hood release bracket and align the bolt hole. Align the upper hole in the panel with the dash mat support bracket (left side). On the right side, align the upper hole with the bracket and dash mat support bracket.

c. Apply sufficient pressure to allow the installation of the stud and tighten the stud to 17 inch lbs. (1.9 Nm).

d. Install the carpet retainer and sound insulator.

8. Enable the SIR system, then connect the negative battery cable.

Rear Speakers

REMOVAL & INSTALLATION

1988–92 Vehicles

BERETTA AND CORSICA SEDAN

1. Disconnect the negative battery cable.
2. Detach the wire connectors.
3. Disengage the retainers from the tab.
4. Remove the speaker assembly from the vehicle.

To install:

5. Insert the tabs on the speaker into the slots in the rear window panel.
6. Place the retainers into the tab.
7. Attach the wire connectors.
8. Connect the negative battery cable.

CORSICA HATCHBACK

1. Disconnect the negative battery cable.
2. Use a flat-bladed tool, carefully pry the speaker cover from the housing.
3. Remove the speaker-to-housing fasteners.
4. Detach the wire connector, then remove the speaker from the vehicle.
5. Installation is the reverse of the removal procedure.

BERETTA CONVERTIBLE

▶ See Figure 29

The rear speakers on the Beretta convertible are incorporated in the rear quarter trim panel.

1. Disconnect the negative battery cable.
2. Remove the rear quarter trim panel.
3. Detach the speaker wire connector.
4. Remove the speaker push-on nuts, then remove the speaker from the vehicle.
5. Remove the speaker cover grille.
6. Installation is the reverse of the removal procedure.

1993–96 Vehicles

▶ See Figure 30

1. Disconnect the negative battery cable.
2. Remove the rear seat-to-back window trim panel, as follows:

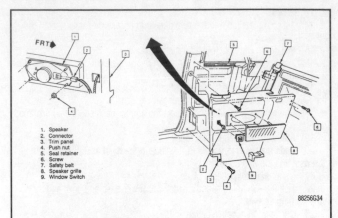

1. Speaker
2. Connector
3. Trim panel
4. Push nut
5. Seal retainer
6. Screw
7. Safety belt
8. Speaker grille
9. Window Switch

88256G34

Fig. 29 On the convertible Beretta, the rear speakers are mounted in the rear quarter trim panel

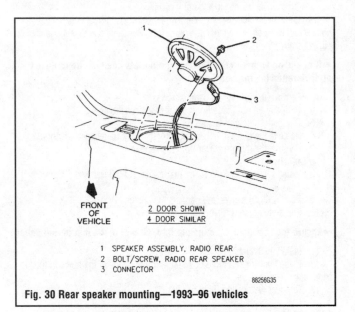

FRONT OF VEHICLE

2 DOOR SHOWN
4 DOOR SIMILAR

1 SPEAKER ASSEMBLY, RADIO REAR
2 BOLT/SCREW, RADIO REAR SPEAKER
3 CONNECTOR

88256G35

Fig. 30 Rear speaker mounting—1993–96 vehicles

a. Remove the rear seat cushion.

b. Remove the rear seat back.

c. Remove the center high-mounted stop light and the stop light bracket.

d. Remove the fasteners, then remove the trim panel.

3. Remove the rear radio speaker retaining screws.

4. Remove the rear radio speaker from the shelf panel, then detach the connector and remove the speaker from the vehicle.

To install:

5. Feed the connector through the speaker opening in the shelf panel and secure to the speaker.

6. Position the speaker into the opening with the connector terminals pointing toward the center of the vehicle.

7. Install the speaker retaining screws and tighten them securely.

8. Install the rear seat-to-back window trim panel, as follows:

a. Position the trim panel, aligning the slots in the trim panels to the holes in the body panel.

b. Install the retaining fasteners.

c. Install the center high-mounted stop light bracket and light.

d. Install the rear seatback and rear seat cushion.

9. Connect the negative battery cable.

WINDSHIELD WIPERS AND WASHERS

Windshield Wiper Blade and Arm

REMOVAL & INSTALLATION

1988–89 Vehicles

♦ **See Figure 31**

1. Turn the ignition to the **ON** position.
2. With the wipers ON, turn the ignition **OFF** when the wiper arm is at the mid-wipe position.
3. Lift the wiper arm from the windshield and pull the retaining latch.
4. Remove the wiper arm and blade assembly from the transmission shaft.

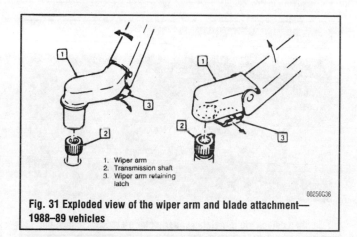

1. Wiper arm
2. Transmission shaft
3. Wiper arm retaining latch

00256G36

Fig. 31 Exploded view of the wiper arm and blade attachment— 1988–89 vehicles

To install:

5. Install the arm on the transmission shaft.
6. Push the retaining latch in and return the arm to the windshield.
7. Turn the ignition to the **ON** position, then put the wipers in the park position.

1990–96 Vehicles

♦ **See Figures 32 and 33**

1. Turn the ignition **ON**, place the wiper system in the park position, then turn the ignition **OFF**
2. Detach the washer fluid hose from the connector of the washer hose assembly.
3. Remove the protective plastic cap from the wiper arm shaft.
4. Lift the wiper arm, then insert a suitable pin completely through the 2 holes located next the pivot of the arm.
5. Remove the nut securing the wiper arm.
6. Remove the arm by lifting off the shaft, using an up and down rocking motion. It may be necessary to use a tool such as a battery terminal puller to remove the arm from the shaft.
7. If necessary, replace the wiper blade at this time, as outlined in Section 1 of this manual.
To install:
8. Clean the metal shavings from the knurls of the shaft before installation.
9. Place the wiper arm and blade assembly on the transmission drive shaft so the wiper arm assembly is 1 in. (25mm) below the stop surface of the park ramp. See accompanying figure for details.
10. Remove the pivot prevention pin from the wiper arm.

➡**You MUST use a torque wrench to tighten the wiper arm nut to the proper specifications.**

88256P11

Disconnect the windshield washer fluid hose from the hose connector

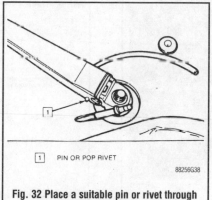

1 PIN OR POP RIVET

88256G38

Fig. 32 Place a suitable pin or rivet through the 2 holes next to the pivot of the arm

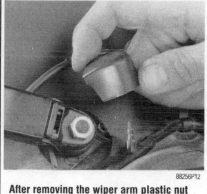

88256P12

After removing the wiper arm plastic nut cover . . .

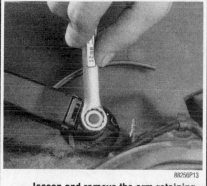

88256P13

. . . loosen and remove the arm retaining nut

88256P14

When installing the wiper arm, make sure it is in the correct position

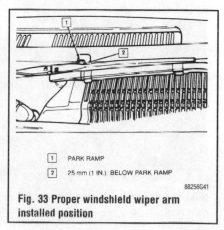

1 PARK RAMP
2 25 mm (1 IN.) BELOW PARK RAMP

88256G41

Fig. 33 Proper windshield wiper arm installed position

11. Install a new nut and tighten, using a torque wrench, to 14.7–17.7 ft. lbs. (20–27 Nm) for 1990–92 vehicles or to 22.5 ft. lbs. (30.5 Nm) for 1993–96 vehicles.

12. Attach the wiper arm hose to the connector of the washer hose assembly, then install the protective cap.

13. Run the wiper system and check for a correct wiper pattern. The left side blade tip should wipe to a limit of 1.5 in. (38mm) from the outside edge of the glass. The right side blade should overlap slightly into the left side wipe pattern,

14. Turn the windshield wipers off, then check for proper park position.

Windshield Wiper Motor

REMOVAL & INSTALLATION

▶ **See Figures 34, 35 and 36**

1. Disconnect the negative battery cable.
2. Remove the left and right side wiper blade and arm assemblies.
3. Remove the air inlet screen/cowl panel.
4. For 1988–92 vehicles, loosen the 2 drive link adjusting screws, then remove the drive link from the motor crank arm.
5. Detach the wiper motor electrical connectors and/or washer hoses.
6. For 1993–96 vehicles, separate the transmission drive link socket from the crank arm ball of the wiper motor assembly using tool J 39232, or equivalent transmission separator.
7. Remove the wiper motor mounting bolts/screws, then remove the wiper motor by guiding the crank arm through the hole.
8. If necessary, remove the crank arm from the motor.
9. Remove the gasket or seal from the wiper motor.

To install:

10. Install the crank arm on the new wiper motor shaft and install the attaching nut.
11. Position the gasket on the wiper motor.
12. Install the wiper motor while guiding the crank arm through the hole.

Use a proper tool to remove the cowl panel retaining "buttons"

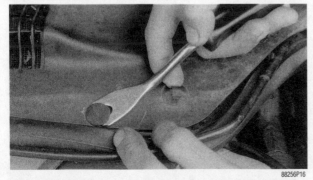

Make sure to remove all of the retainers, then remove the left and right cowl panels

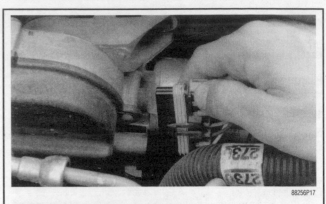

Unplug the connector from the wiper motor cover . . .

. . . then detach the remaining wiper motor electrical connection

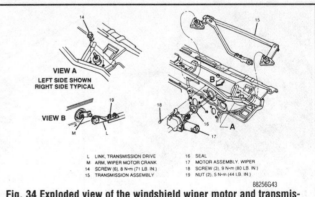

VIEW A
LEFT SIDE SHOWN
RIGHT SIDE TYPICAL

VIEW B

L	LINK, TRANSMISSION DRIVE	16	SEAL
M	ARM, WIPER MOTOR CRANK	17	MOTOR ASSEMBLY, WIPER
14	SCREW (6), 8 N·m (71 LB. IN.)	18	SCREW (3), 9 N·m (80 LB. IN.)
15	TRANSMISSION ASSEMBLY	19	NUT (2), 5 N·m (44 LB. IN.)

Fig. 34 Exploded view of the windshield wiper motor and transmission assemblies

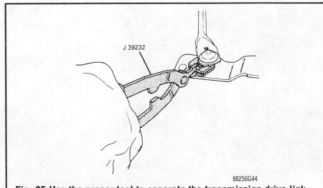

Fig. 35 Use the proper tool to separate the transmission drive link socket from the crank arm ball

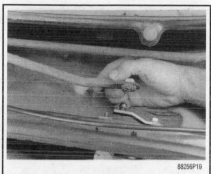

After using the proper tool, the drive link socket will be separated from the crank arm ball

Unfasten the windshield wiper motor retaining bolts . . .

. . . then remove the wiper motor from the vehicles, guiding the crank arm through the hole

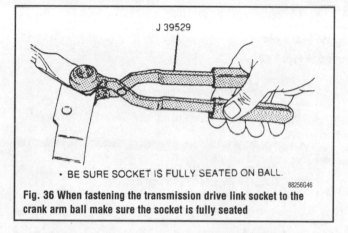

- BE SURE SOCKET IS FULLY SEATED ON BALL.

Fig. 36 When fastening the transmission drive link socket to the crank arm ball make sure the socket is fully seated

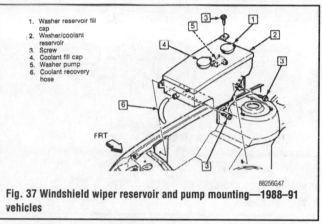

1. Washer reservoir fill cap
2. Washer/coolant reservoir
3. Screw
4. Coolant fill cap
5. Washer pump
6. Coolant recovery hose

FRT

Fig. 37 Windshield wiper reservoir and pump mounting—1988–91 vehicles

13. Install the wiper motor to the chassis and install the attaching bolts/screws. Tighten the bolts/screws to 80 inch lbs. (9 Nm).

14. Attach the wiper motor electrical connectors and/or connect the washer hoses.

15. For 1988–92 vehicles, connect the wiper arm drive link to the crank arm. Tighten the drive link adjusting screws to 44 inch lbs. (5 Nm).

16. For 1993–96 vehicles, fasten the transmission drive link socket to the crank arm ball of the wiper motor assembly using tool J 39232 or equivalent. Make sure the socket is fully seated on the ball.

17. Install the top vent screen/cowl panel.

18. Install the left and right wiper arm and blade assemblies.

19. Connect the negative battery cable.

Windshield Washer Motor and/or Reservoir

REMOVAL & INSTALLATION

1988–91 Vehicles

▶ See Figure 37

1. Disconnect the negative battery cable.
2. Remove the washer solvent from the reservoir.
3. Remove the reservoir screws.
4. Detach the electrical connectors and hose.
5. Remove the washer pump from the reservoir.
6. Installation is the reverse of the removal procedure.

➡Make sure the new washer pump is pushed all the way into the reservoir gasket.

1992–96 Vehicles

1. Disconnect the negative battery cable.
2. Remove the washer solvent from the reservoir.
3. Unfasten the screws to allow the inner fender panel (A) to be pulled to get access to the solvent container and pump.
4. Detach the electrical connectors and washer hose.
5. For 1993–96 vehicles, perform the following:
   a. Remove the screw from the mounting tab at the neck of the washer fluid reservoir.
   b. Remove the 2 screws from the container mounting brackets.
   c. Remove the container from the inner fender.
6. Remove the washer pump from the reservoir.

To install:

➡Make sure the new washer pump is pushed all the way into the reservoir gasket.

7. Position the pump in the windshield washer container.
8. For 1993–96 vehicles, perform the following:
   a. Insert the neck of the container into the engine compartment, then attach the container with the three retaining screws. Tighten the screws to 44 inch lbs. (5 Nm).
9. Attach the electrical connectors and washer hose.
10. Install the inner fender panel (A) and retaining screws.
11. Fill the reservoir with the proper type and amount of washer fluid.
12. Connect the negative battery cable.

INSTRUMENTS AND SWITCHES

Instrument Cluster Bezel

REMOVAL & INSTALLATION

1988–89 Vehicles

▶ **See Figures 38 and 39**

1. Disconnect the negative battery cable.
2. Remove the left side sound insulator attaching screws and remove the insulator from the lower dash and cowl.
3. Unfasten the 2 screws from the top of the trim cover, then remove the trim cover.

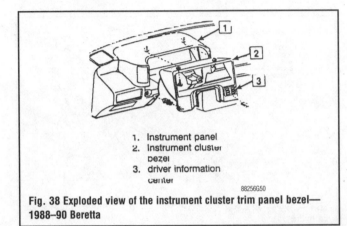

1. Instrument panel
2. Instrument cluster bezel
3. driver information center

88256G50

Fig. 38 Exploded view of the instrument cluster trim panel bezel—1988–90 Beretta

4. Remove the 2 bolts from the upper part of the column and bolt(s) from the lower part of the column. Lower and support the column to prevent tension on the flex joint.
5. Remove the instrument cluster trim panel attaching hardware. Pull the trim panel rearward.
6. Tag and detach the necessary electrical connectors.
7. Remove the trim panel from the vehicle.

To install:

8. Position the instrument cluster trim panel close to the wiring harness, in order to attach the electrical connectors.
9. Install the cluster trim panel and attaching hardware.
10. Raise the steering wheel into position and install the bolt(s) at the bottom part of the column and 2 bolts at the top of the column.
11. Install the trim cover and 2 attaching screws.
12. The remainder of installation is the reverse of the removal procedure.
13. Connect the negative battery cable.

1991–96 Vehicles

▶ **See Figure 40**

1. Disconnect the negative battery cable.
2. Remove the bezel-to-instrument panel screws.
3. Carefully pull the bezel rearward to disengage the retaining clips.
4. Unplug the headlight and windshield wiper switch electrical connectors.
5. If removing the switches, remove the screws attaching the switches to the bezel.
6. Remove the clips, as required.
7. Installation is the reverse of the removal procedure.
8. Connect the negative battery cable.

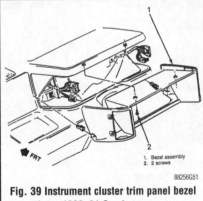

1. Bezel assembly
2. 2 screws

88256G51

Fig. 39 Instrument cluster trim panel bezel mounting—1988–91 Corsica

88256P22

Unfasten the bezel-to-instrument panel screws located under the wiper switch

88256G23

You will also find bezel-to-panel retaining screws under the headlight switch

88256P24

Pull the cluster bezel away from the cluster and panel, carefully as not to damage the retaining clips

88256P25

When pulling the cluster bezel away, detach the headlight and wiper switch electrical connectors

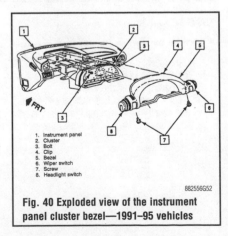

1. Instrument panel
2. Cluster
3. Bolt
4. Clip
5. Bezel
6. Wiper switch
7. Screw
8. Headlight switch

882556G52

Fig. 40 Exploded view of the instrument panel cluster bezel—1991–95 vehicles

Instrument Cluster

REMOVAL & INSTALLATION

❊❊❊ WARNING

Whenever working on any electronic equipment, make sure to have a clean, static free environment in which to work. Always cover the work surface with a mat that is grounded and static free. Static electricity from walking across the floor or sliding across a car seat is enough to damage any equipment.

1988–90 Vehicles

1. Disconnect the negative battery cable.
2. Remove the instrument cluster bezel/trim panel.
3. Remove the 4 screws attaching instrument cluster. There are 2 screws at the top and 2 at the bottom of the cluster.
4. Pull the cluster forward, then detach the electrical connectors.
5. Remove the instrument cluster from the vehicle.
To install:
6. Position the instrument cluster close to the wiring harness, in order to attach the harness. Ensure the cluster connectors plug in securely to the connectors in the cluster carrier.
7. Slide the instrument cluster into position and install the mounting screws.
8. Install the instrument cluster bezel/trim panel.
9. Connect the negative battery cable.

1991–96 Vehicles

1. Disconnect the negative battery cable.
2. Remove the instrument panel trim/cluster bezel.

3. Unfasten the instrument cluster-to-instrument panel attaching bolts/screws.
4. Rock the instrument cluster rearward and remove it from the vehicle. The electrical connector will release as the cluster is removed.
To install:
5. Carefully, align the instrument cluster and press into proper position. The electrical connector will align and engage as the cluster is pushed into position.
6. Install the cluster retaining screws and tighten to 12 inch lbs. (1.4 Nm).
7. Install the instrument cluster bezel.
8. Connect the negative battery cable.

Gauges

The speedometer and gauge cluster are replaced as an assembly. If any part(s) require servicing, with the exception of bulbs and sockets, the cluster will have to be exchanged or repaired by an authorized service center.

Windshield Wiper Switch

REMOVAL & INSTALLATION

1988–90 Vehicles

▶ See Figure 41

1. Disconnect the negative battery cable.
2. Remove the switch by using a suitable flat-bladed tool to gently pry behind the switch.
3. Pull the switch away from the instrument panel, then detach the wiring.
4. Remove the switch from the vehicle.
5. Installation is the reverse of the removal procedure.
6. Connect the negative battery cable, then check for proper wiper operation.

88256P26

Once the instrument cluster bezel is removed, you can access the cluster retainers (see arrows)

88256G27

Remove the cluster-to-instrument panel retaining bolts . . .

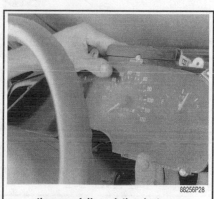

88256P28

. . . then carefully rock the cluster rearward and remove it from the vehicle

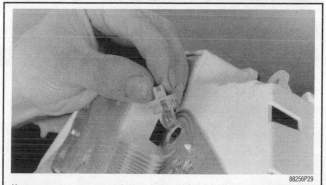

88256P29

If necessary, you can replace any burned out bulbs in the instrument cluster at this time

88256P30

Align the cluster so when pressing it into position the electrical connector will engage properly

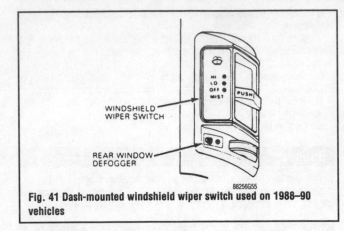

Fig. 41 Dash-mounted windshield wiper switch used on 1988–90 vehicles

1991–96 Vehicles

▶ **See Figure 42**

1. Disconnect the negative battery cable.
2. Remove the instrument cluster bezel/trim panel.
3. Squeeze the small knob at the side, then pull straight out.
4. Insert a small flat-bladed tool into the slots adjacent to the center of the inner knob to disengage the knob from the switch.
5. Unfasten the screws attaching the wiper switch to the bezel.
6. Remove the wiper switch from the vehicle.

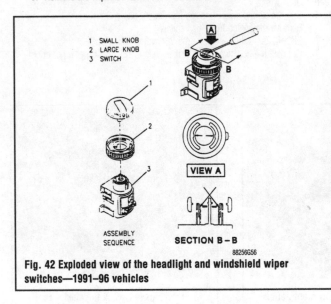

Fig. 42 Exploded view of the headlight and windshield wiper switches—1991–96 vehicles

To install:
7. Position the switch to the bezel, then secure with the attaching screws.
8. Place the inner knob on the switch. Ensure the tabs are lined up with the slots and press to secure the knob.
9. Position the outer knob on the switch and align the D-shaped hole in the knob to the shaft on the switch and press to secure the knob.
10. Install the instrument cluster bezel/trim plate.
11. Connect the negative battery cable.

Headlight Switch

REMOVAL & INSTALLATION

1988–90 Vehicles

▶ **See Figure 43**

1. Disconnect the negative battery cable.
2. Remove the switch by gently prying behind the switch.
3. Pull the switch away from the instrument panel, then detach the wiring.
4. Remove the switch from the vehicle.
5. Installation is the reverse of the removal procedure.
6. Connect the negative battery cable, then test for proper switch operation.

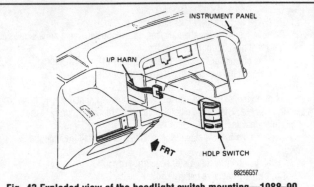

Fig. 43 Exploded view of the headlight switch mounting—1988–90 vehicles

1991–96 Vehicles

▶ **See Figure 42**

1. Disconnect the negative battery cable.
2. Remove the instrument cluster bezel/trim panel.
3. Squeeze the small knob at the side and pull it straight out.
4. Insert a small flat-bladed tool into the slots adjacent to the center of the inner knob to disengage the knob from the switch.
5. Unfasten the screws attaching the headlight switch to the bezel.
6. Remove the switch from the vehicle.
To install:
7. Install the switch to the bezel. Install the attaching screws.
8. Position the inner knob on the switch. Ensure the tabs are lined up with the slots and press to secure the knob.
9. Position the outer knob on the switch and align the D-shaped hole in the knob to the shaft on the switch and press to secure the knob.
10. Install the instrument cluster bezel.
11. Connect the negative battery cable.

Back-Up Light Switch

The Back-Up/Neutral Start switch procedure is located in Section 7 of this manual.

Ignition Switch

The ignition switch is mounted in the steering column and is covered in Section 8 of this manual.

LIGHTING

Headlights

REMOVAL & INSTALLATION

On the vehicles covered by this manual, composite style headlamps, which contain replacement bulbs, are used (instead of the sealed beam type headlights). The bulb located inside the headlamp assembly, can be removed from under the hood.

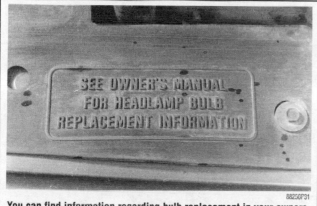

You can find information regarding bulb replacement in your owners manual

✳✳ CAUTION

Halogen bulbs contain gas under pressure. Handling the bulbs incorrectly could cause it to shatter into flying glass fragments. Do NOT leave the light switch ON. Always allow the bulb to cool before removal. Handle the bulb only by the base; avoid touching the glass itself. Whenever handling a halogen bulb, ALWAYS follow these precautions:

- Turn the headlight switch OFF and allow the bulb to cool before changing it. Leave the switch OFF until the change is complete.
- ALWAYS wear eye protection when changing a halogen bulb.
- Handle the bulb only by its base. Avoid touching the glass.
- DO NOT drop or scratch the bulb.
- Keep dirt and moisture off of the bulb.
- Carefully place the old bulb in the new bulb's carton and dispose of properly.
- Keep halogen bulbs out of reach of children.

Beretta

1. Open the hood, then disconnect the negative battery cable.
2. Remove the two retainers holding the filler panel over the headlight assembly.
3. If you are replacing just the bulb, perform the following:
   a. Remove the bulb socket.
   b. Detach the electrical connector by carefully opening the tabs.
   c. Remove the bulb assembly.
4. If removing the headlight assembly, perform the following:
   a. Remove the retainer located near the radiator by carefully prying it off.
   b. Remove the bolt from the front of the filler panel
   c. Remove the two bolts from the top of the headlight assembly.
   d. Remove the headlight assembly by lifting it up and out, then pulling forward. Lift the filler panel slightly for clearance to remove the light assembly.
5. Remove the sockets from the headlight.

To install:

6. For installation of the headlight assembly, perform the following:
   a. Fasten the sockets securely in the headlight assembly.
   b. Position the headlight assembly, making sure the inner side is behind the grille.
   c. Install the retaining bolt located at the rear of the assembly.
   d. Install the two top headlight assembly retaining bolts.
   e. Fold the filler panel over to its original position.
   f. Install the bolt to the front of the filler panel.
   g. Fasten the retainer near the radiator by pressing it into place.
7. If installing a new bulb only, perform the following:
   a. Install a new bulb in the socket.
   b. Attach the electrical connector.
   c. Install the socket into the headlight assembly.
8. Install the two retainers on the filler panel.
9. Close the hood.
10. Connect the negative battery cable and check the headlight operation. Take the vehicle to a reputable repair shop to have the headlight aim check and adjusted, if necessary.

Corsica

1. Open the hood, then disconnect the negative battery cable.
2. Remove the two retainers holding the filler panel over the headlight assembly.
3. Fold the filler panel back for access to the headlight assembly.
4. Remove the two retainers securing the top of the headlight assembly.
5. Remove the headlight assembly by lifting it up to clear the guide pin at the right, then pulling it forward.
6. Remove the socket(s) from the headlight assembly.
7. Carefully remove the bulb(s) from the socket(s).

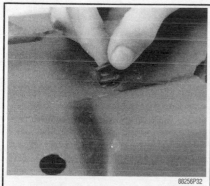

Remove filler panel retainers in order to access the headlight assembly

Loosen the and remove the retainers securing the top of the headlight assembly

If necessary, you can unplug the electrical connector from the headlight bulb socket

Carefully twist, then remove the headlight bulb from the socket

88256P35

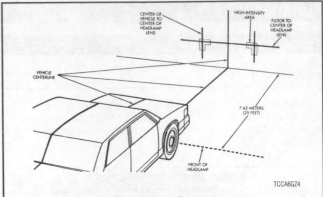

Fig. 45 Low-beam headlight pattern alignment

TCCA6GZ4

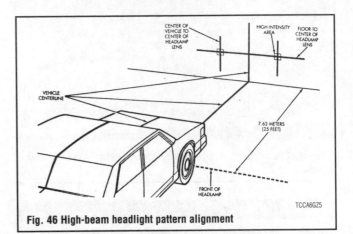

Fig. 46 High-beam headlight pattern alignment

TCCA6GZ5

To install:

8. Install a new bulb into the socket.
9. Install the socket into the headlight assembly.
10. Position the headlight assembly, making sure the guide pins on the back of the assembly are inserted properly in the holes in the headlight housing panel.
11. Fasten the two retainers into the headlight assembly.
12. Install the filler panel and secure with the two retainers.
13. Close the hood.
14. Connect the negative battery cable and check the headlight operation. Take the vehicle to a reputable repair shop to have the headlight aim check and adjusted, if necessary.

HEADLIGHT AIMING

◆ **See Figures 44, 45 and 46**

The headlights must be properly aimed to provide the best, safest road illumination. The lights should be checked for proper aim and adjusted as necessary. Certain state and local authorities have requirements for headlight aiming; these should be checked before adjustment is made.

※※ CAUTION

About once a year, when the headlights are replaced or any time front end work is performed on your vehicle, the headlight should be accurately aimed by a reputable repair shop using the proper equipment. Headlights not properly aimed can make it virtually impossible to see and may blind other drivers on the road, possibly causing an accident. Note that the following procedure is a temporary fix, until you can take your vehicle to a repair shop for a proper adjustment.

Headlight adjustment may be temporarily made using a wall, as described below, or on the rear of another vehicle. When adjusted, the lights should not glare in oncoming car or truck windshields, nor should they illuminate the pas-

senger compartment of vehicles driving in front of you. These adjustments are rough and should always be fine-tuned by a repair shop which is equipped with headlight aiming tools. Improper adjustments may be both dangerous and illegal.

For most of the vehicles covered by this manual, horizontal and vertical aiming of each sealed beam unit is provided by two adjusting screws which move the retaining ring and adjusting plate against the tension of a coil spring. There is no adjustment for focus; this is done during headlight manufacturing.

➡ **Because the composite headlight assembly is bolted into position, no adjustment should be necessary or possible. Some applications, however, may be bolted to an adjuster plate or may be retained by adjusting screws. If so, follow this procedure when adjusting the lights, BUT always have the adjustment checked by a reputable shop.**

Before removing the headlight bulb or disturbing the headlamp in any way, note the current settings in order to ease headlight adjustment upon reassembly. If the high or low beam setting of the old lamp still works, this can be done using the wall of a garage or a building:

1. Park the vehicle on a level surface, with the fuel tank about ½ full and with the vehicle empty of all extra cargo (unless normally carried). The vehicle should be facing a wall which is no less than 6 feet (1.8m) high and 12 feet (3.7m) wide. The front of the vehicle should be about 25 feet from the wall.
2. If aiming is to be performed outdoors, it is advisable to wait until dusk in order to properly see the headlight beams on the wall. If done in a garage, darken the area around the wall as much as possible by closing shades or hanging cloth over the windows.
3. Turn the headlights **ON** and mark the wall at the center of each light's low beam, then switch on the brights and mark the center of each light's high beam. A short length of masking tape which is visible from the front of the vehicle may be used. Although marking all four positions is advisable, marking one position from each light should be sufficient.
4. If neither beam on one side is working, and if another like-sized vehicle is available, park the second one in the exact spot where the vehicle was and mark the beams using the same-side light. Then switch the vehicles so the one

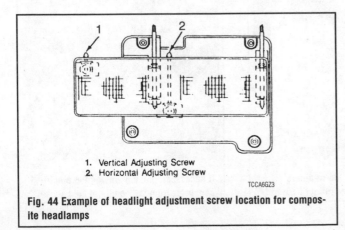

1. Vertical Adjusting Screw
2. Horizontal Adjusting Screw

TCCA6GZ3

Fig. 44 Example of headlight adjustment screw location for composite headlamps

to be aimed is back in the original spot. It must be parked no closer to or farther away from the wall than the second vehicle.

5. Perform any necessary repairs, but make sure the vehicle is not moved, or is returned to the exact spot from which the lights were marked. Turn the headlights **ON** and adjust the beams to match the marks on the wall.

6. Have the headlight adjustment checked as soon as possible by a reputable repair shop.

Signal and Marker Lamps

REMOVAL & INSTALLATION

Front Parking/Turn Signal Lamps

BERETTA

♦ **See Figure 47**

1. Raise the hood, then disconnect the negative battery cable.
2. Remove the headlight assembly as outlined earlier.
3. Remove the radiator-to-grille covers.

➡ **The 2 center bolts can be loosened rather than be removed.**

4. Unfasten the 12 bolts holding the headlight mounting panel.
5. Detach the wiring harness clips from the headlamp panel.
6. Remove the headlight mounting panel with the grille attached.
7. If necessary for access, remove the front energy absorber and rear shim as outlined in Section 10 of this manual.
8. Remove the socket by reaching from under the vehicle, pressing the tab (inner bulb) and twisting. If necessary, remove the bulb from the socket.
9. Remove the 2 screws from the bottom of the assembly.
10. Remove the retaining screw from the upper rear, then remove the lamp assembly.

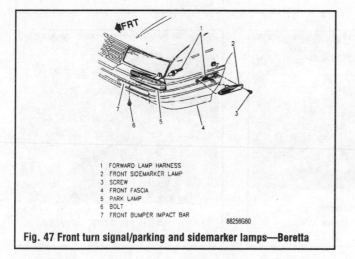

```
1  FORWARD LAMP HARNESS
2  FRONT SIDEMARKER LAMP
3  SCREW
4  FRONT FASCIA
5  PARK LAMP
6  BOLT
7  FRONT BUMPER IMPACT BAR
                              88256G60
```

Fig. 47 Front turn signal/parking and sidemarker lamps—Beretta

To install:

11. Position the lamp assembly, then secure with the 3 retaining screws.
12. Install a new bulb into the socket, then install the socket into the lamp assembly.
13. If removed, install the front energy absorber and rear shim as outlined in Section 10 of this manual.
14. Reposition the headlight mounting panel with the grille attached.
15. Attach the wiring harness clips to the headlamp panel.
16. Install the 12 bolts holding the headlight mounting panel.
17. Connect the radiator to grille cover.
18. Install the headlight assembly.
19. Connect the negative battery cable, close the hood, then check for proper light operation.

CORSICA

♦ **See Figure 48**

1. Disconnect the negative battery cable.
2. Remove the bulb socket by reaching from under the vehicle, pressing the tab (Inner bulb) and twisting. If necessary, remove the bulb from the socket.
3. Using a socket wrench with a long extension, reach through the hole in the front fascia and remove the bolt from the bottom of the light assembly.
4. Working through the light opening in the front fascia, remove the 2 bolts from the front of the assembly.
5. Carefully remove the lamp assembly through the front fascia opening.

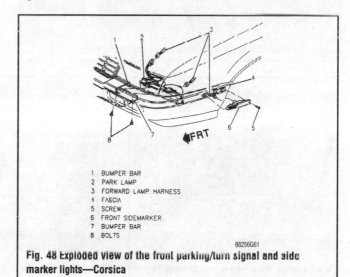

```
1  BUMPER BAR
2  PARK LAMP
3  FORWARD LAMP HARNESS
4  FASCIA
5  SCREW
6  FRONT SIDEMARKER
7  BUMPER BAR
8  BOLTS
                              88256G61
```

Fig. 48 Exploded view of the front parking/turn signal and side marker lights—Corsica

To install:

6. Install the lamp assembly, making sure the bolt holes on the top are above the bolt holes in the fascia.
7. Install the 2 bolts at the front of the assembly, but do not fully tighten until the bottom bolt is installed.
8. Install the bolt at the bottom of the assembly. Tighten all of the bolts securely.
9. If necessary install a new bulb in the socket, then install the socket in the lamp assembly.
10. Connect the negative battery cable, close the hood, then check for proper light operation.

Front Side Marker Light

1. Disconnect the negative battery cable.
2. Remove the Torx® screw from the front side marker light assembly, then remove the marker light assembly.
3. Remove the socket from the assembly.
4. Remove the bulb, if replacing.
5. Installation is the reverse of the removal procedure.

Rear Turn Signal, Brake and Parking Lights

♦ **See Figure 49**

❊❊❊ WARNING

Make sure to prevent water leaks if the sealing surfaces are disturbed. Damaged gaskets must be replaced and sealer used as necessary.

1. Disconnect the negative battery cable.
2. Open the trunk and remove the rear compartment inner trim, if equipped.

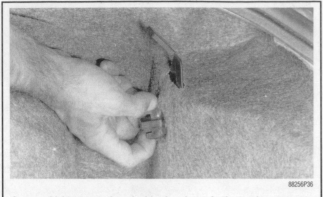

Some vehicles are equipped with trim pieces in the trunk

3. Remove the 3 (Beretta) or 4 (Corsica) wing nuts, holding the taillamp assembly.
4. Remove the taillamp assembly by pulling straight back.
5. Remove the socket from the taillamp assembly.
6. Remove the bulb(s) from the socket(s), if replacing.

To install:
7. Place a new bulb in the socket, if necessary.
8. Install the socket into the tail lamp assembly.

➡ Check for proper gasket sealing before tightening the wing nuts.

9. Position the taillamp assembly, then install the retaining wing nuts, 3 or 4 as applicable, securing the taillamp assembly.
10. If equipped, install the rear compartment inner trim. Close the trunk.
11. Connect the negative battery cable, then check for proper lamp operation.

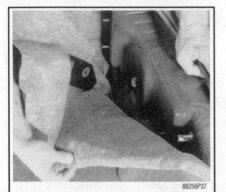

Remove the inner trim from the trunk in order to access the lamp retainers

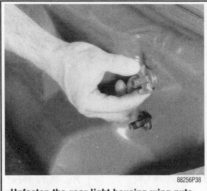

Unfasten the rear light housing wing nuts from inside the trunk

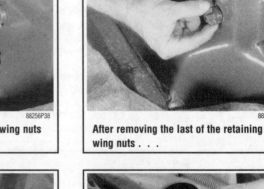

After removing the last of the retaining wing nuts . . .

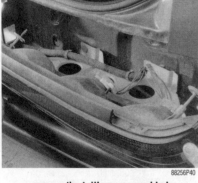

. . . remove the taillamp assembly by pulling it straight back

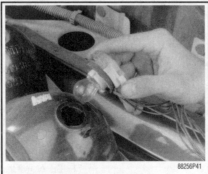

Twist the brake bulb socket to unlock it, then pull the socket from the taillamp housing

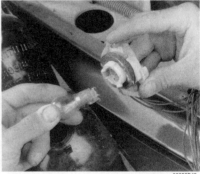

If replacement is necessary, simply pull the bulb straight out from the socket

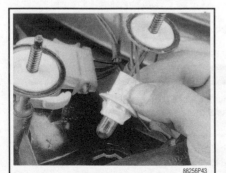

If the turn signal bulb is burned out, twist and remove the socket from the housing . . .

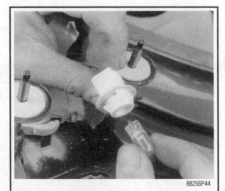

. . . then pull the bulb from the socket and replace with a new one

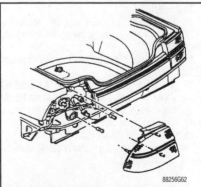

Fig. 49 Rear turn signal, brake and parking light assembly mounting—Beretta

Rear Side Marker Light

CORSICA

The rear side marker lights are and integral part of the rear turn signal, brake and parking light assembly. For removal and installation please refer to that procedure, located earlier in this section.

BERETTA

Beretta has 2 side marker lights, one is part of the rear tail/stop/turn signal light assembly and one on the side of the vehicle. For information on the taillight assembly, refer to the procedure above.

1. Disconnect the negative battery cable.
2. Remove the Torx® from the front of the rear side marker light assembly and remove the side marker light.
3. Remove the socket from the assembly.
4. If necessary, remove the bulb from the socket and replace if with a new one.
5. Installation is the reverse of the removal procedure.

Center High-Mounted Brake Light

EXCEPT LUGGAGE CARRIER, HATCHBACK OR CONVERTIBLE

1. Disconnect the negative battery cable.
2. Remove the two retaining screws, one from each side of the light base.
3. Slide the assembly rearward.
4. Detach the electrical connector, by carefully opening the tab.
5. Remove the light assembly from the vehicle.
6. Installation is the reverse of the removal procedure.

LUGGAGE CARRIER MOUNTED

1. Disconnect the negative battery cable.
2. Open the trunk and remove the nuts holding the luggage carrier outer supports.
3. Remove the luggage carrier outer supports and crossbar.
4. Remove the gasket on the bottom of the light assembly.
5. Unfasten the 2 nuts from the light assembly, then remove the light assembly from the carrier.
6. Detach the light electrical connector
7. Installation is the reverse of the removal procedure.
8. Close the trunk, then connect the negative battery cable and check for proper lamp operation.

HATCHBACK

1. Remove the interior finish panel.
2. Remove the 2 nuts from the light assembly.
3. Slide out the assembly.
4. Disconnect the electrical connector, by carefully opening the tab.
5. Remove the light assembly and replace the bulb, as necessary.
6. Installation is the reverse of removal.

CONVERTIBLE

1. Disconnect the negative battery cable.
2. Unfasten the stoplamp-to-spoiler retaining screws.
3. Pull the stoplamp up and away from the spoiler, then detach the wiring from the light.
4. Remove the brake light assembly.
5. Installation is the reverse of removal.

Dome Light

EXCEPT CONVERTIBLE

1. Disconnect the negative battery cable.
2. Remove the courtesy lamp's fuse.
3. Remove the lens by it straight pulling down.
4. Unfasten the 2 clips by loosening them slightly with a suitable prytool, then carefully pull with pliers.
5. Remove the assembly by lowering the rear of the light and pulling backward to release the clip at the front.

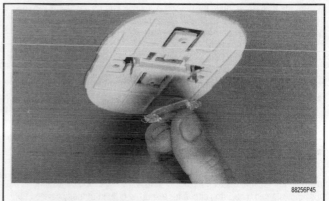

Removing the dome light bulb

To install:

6. Position the dome light assembly, making sure the clip on the front goes over the bracket.
7. Fasten the 2 clips by pushing them into place.
8. Install the lens and the fuse.
9. Connect the negative battery cable.

CONVERTIBLE

1. Disconnect the negative battery cable.
2. Remove the screw and the lens from the lamp at the center of the stationary bow in the passenger compartment.
3. Remove the 2 bulbs from the clips in the lamp housing.
4. Unfasten the screw attaching the lamp housing from the stationary bow.
5. Disconnect the dome lamp housing from the wiring.
6. Installation is the reverse of the removal procedure.

License Plate Light

CORSICA

The license plate light is an integral part of the rear turn signal, brake and parking light assembly. Refer to the located earlier in this section.

BERETTA

1. Disconnect the negative battery cable.
2. Remove the 2 screws from the light assembly.
3. Unfasten the assembly by pulling out through the opening.
4. Remove the socket from the light assembly.
5. Remove the bulb, if replacing.
6. Installation is the reverse of the removal procedure.

CIRCUIT PROTECTION

Fuses Block and Fuses

▶ See Figure 50

Fuses protect all the major electrical systems in the car. In case of an electrical overload, the fuse melts, breaking the circuit and stopping the flow of electricity.

If a fuse blows, the cause should be investigated and corrected before the installation of a new fuse. This, however, is easier to say than to do. Because each fuse protects a limited number of components, your job is narrowed down somewhat. Begin your investigation by looking for obvious fraying, loose connections, breaks in insulation, etc. Use the techniques outlined at the beginning of this section. Electrical problems are almost always a real headache to solve, but if you are patient and persistent, and approach the problem logically (that is, don't start replacing electrical components randomly), you will eventually find the solution.

Each fuse block uses miniature fuses (normally plug-in blade terminal-type for these vehicles) which are designed for increased circuit protection and greater reliability. The compact plug-in or blade terminal design allows for fingertip removal and replacement.

Although most fuses are interchangeable in size, the amperage values are not. Should you install a fuse with too high a value, damaging current could be allowed to destroy the component you were attempting to protect by using a fuse in the first place. The plug-in type fuses have a volt number molded on them and are color coded for easy identification. Be sure to only replace a fuse with the proper amperage rated substitute.

A blown fuse can easily be checked by visual inspection or by continuity checking.

The fuse block is located on the lower left side of the instrument panel. To access the fuse panel, open the driver's side door. Pull off the fuse panel cover to get to the fuses. Spare fuses and a fuse puller should always be kept here. Various convenience connectors, which snap-lock into the fuse block, add to the serviceability of this unit.

REPLACEMENT

▶ **See Figures 51 and 52**

1. Locate the fuse for the circuit in question.

➡ **When replacing the fuse, always use a replacement fuse of the same amperage value. NEVER use one with a higher amperage rating.**

2. Check the fuse by pulling it from the fuse block and observing the element. If it is broken, install a replacement fuse the same amperage rating. If the fuse blows again, check the circuit for a short to ground or faulty device in the circuit protected by the fuse.
3. Continuity can also be checked with the fuse installed in the fuse block with the use of a test light connected across the 2 test points on the end of the fuse. If the test light lights, replace the fuse. Check the circuit for a short to ground or faulty device in the circuit protected by the fuse.

Fusible Links

In addition to circuit breakers and fuses, the wiring harness incorporates fusible links to protect the wiring. Links are used rather than a fuse, in wiring circuits that are not normally fused, such as the ignition circuit. The fusible links are color coded red in the charging and load circuits to match the color coding of the circuits they protect. Each link is four gauges smaller than the cable it protects, and is marked on the insulation with the gauge size because the insulation makes it appear heavier than it really is. The engine compartment wiring harness has several fusible links. The same size wire with a special Hypalon insulation must be used when replacing a fusible link.

➡ **For more details, see the information on fusible links at the beginning of this section.**

The links are located in the following areas:
1. A molded splice at the starter solenoid **Bat** terminal, a 14 gauge red wire.
2. A 16 gauge red fusible link at the junction block to protect the unfused wiring of 12 gauge or larger wire. This link stops at the bulkhead connector.
3. The alternator warning light and field circuitry is protected by a 20 gauge red wire fusible link used in the battery feed–to–voltage regulator number 3 terminal. The link is installed as a molded splice in the circuit at the junction block.
4. The ammeter circuit is protected by two 20 gauge fusible links installed as molded splices in the circuit at the junction block and battery to starter circuit.

Circuit Breakers

REPLACEMENT

Circuit breakers differ from fuses in that they are reusable. Circuit breakers open when the flow of current exceeds specified value and will close after a few

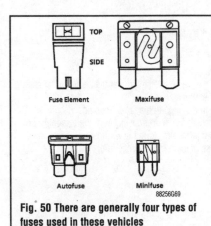

Fig. 50 There are generally four types of fuses used in these vehicles

On some vehicles, you may have to remove a cover for access to the main fuse block

The fuse panel cover has a label with the fuse designations on it

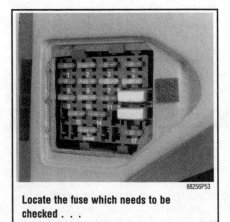

Locate the fuse which needs to be checked . . .

. . . then pull it out of the fuse block

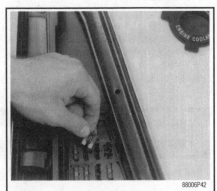

A fuse block is also located in the engine compartment

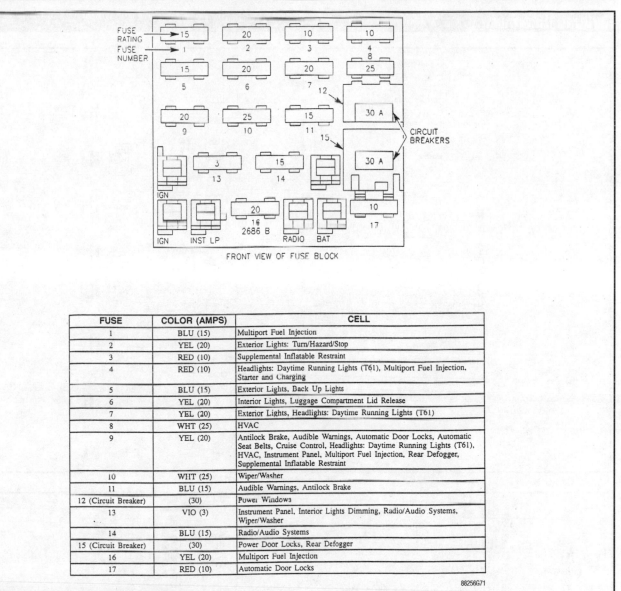

FRONT VIEW OF FUSE BLOCK

FUSE	COLOR (AMPS)	CELL
1	BLU (15)	Multiport Fuel Injection
2	YEL (20)	Exterior Lights: Turn/Hazard/Stop
3	RED (10)	Supplemental Inflatable Restraint
4	RED (10)	Headlights: Daytime Running Lights (T61), Multiport Fuel Injection, Starter and Charging
5	BLU (15)	Exterior Lights, Back Up Lights
6	YEL (20)	Interior Lights, Luggage Compartment Lid Release
7	YEL (20)	Exterior Lights, Headlights: Daytime Running Lights (T61)
8	WHT (25)	HVAC
9	YEL (20)	Antilock Brake, Audible Warnings, Automatic Door Locks, Automatic Seat Belts, Cruise Control, Headlights: Daytime Running Lights (T61), HVAC, Instrument Panel, Multiport Fuel Injection, Rear Defogger, Supplemental Inflatable Restraint
10	WHT (25)	Wiper/Washer
11	BLU (15)	Audible Warnings, Antilock Brake
12 (Circuit Breaker)	(30)	Power Windows
13	VIO (3)	Instrument Panel, Interior Lights Dimming, Radio/Audio Systems, Wiper/Washer
14	BLU (15)	Radio/Audio Systems
15 (Circuit Breaker)	(30)	Power Door Locks, Rear Defogger
16	YEL (20)	Multiport Fuel Injection
17	RED (10)	Automatic Door Locks

88256G71

Fig. 51 Fuse locations and component identification

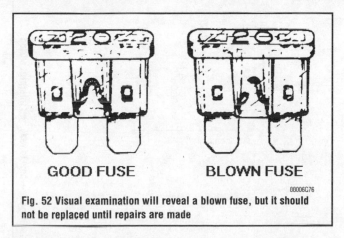

GOOD FUSE   BLOWN FUSE

88006C76

Fig. 52 Visual examination will reveal a blown fuse, but it should not be replaced until repairs are made

seconds when current flow returns to normal. Some of the circuits protected by circuit breakers include electric windows and power accessories. Circuits breakers are used in these applications due to the fact that they must operated at times under prolonged high current flow due to demand even though there is not malfunction in the circuit.

There are 2 types of circuit breakers. The first type opens when high current flow is detected. A few seconds after the excessive current flow has been removed, the circuit breaker will close. If the high current flow is experienced again, the circuit will open again.

The second type is referred to as the Positive Temperature Coefficient (PTC) circuit breaker. When excessive current flow passes through the PTC circuit breaker, the circuit is not opened but its resistance increases. As the device heats ups with the increase in current flow, the resistance increases to the point where the circuit is effectively open. Unlike other circuit breakers, the PTC circuit breaker will not reset until the circuit is opened, removing voltage from the terminals. Once the voltage is removed, the circuit breaker will re-close within a few seconds.

Replace the circuit breaker by unplugging the old one and plugging in the new one. Confirm proper circuit operation.

Flashers

The turn signal flasher is mounted in a clip on the right side of the steering column support bracket. The hazard flasher is located in the component center, under the instrument panel, on the right side. Replace the flasher by unplugging the old one and plugging in the new one.

WIRING DIAGRAMS

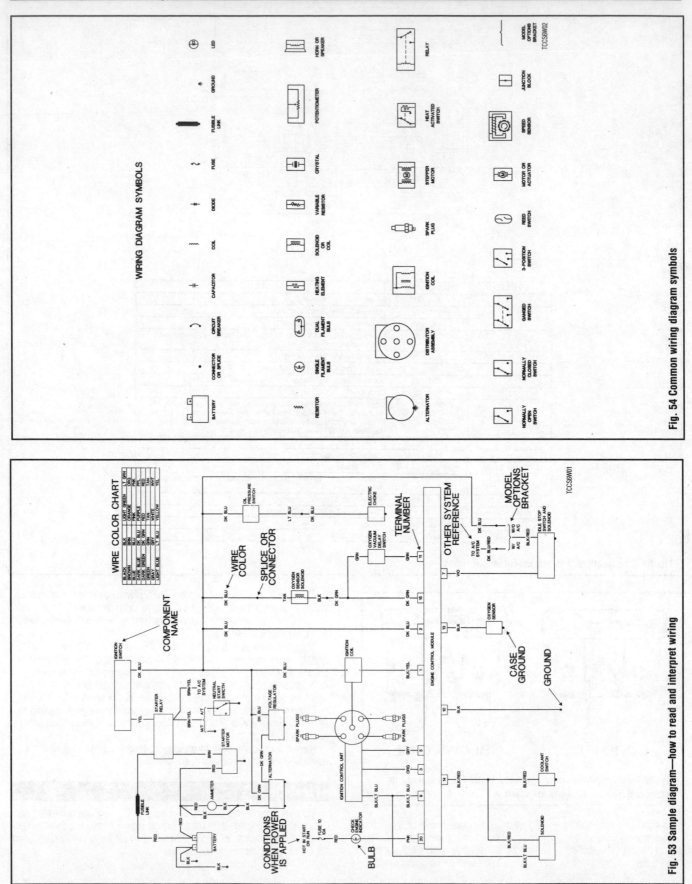

Fig. 54 Common wiring diagram symbols

Fig. 53 Sample diagram—how to read and interpret wiring

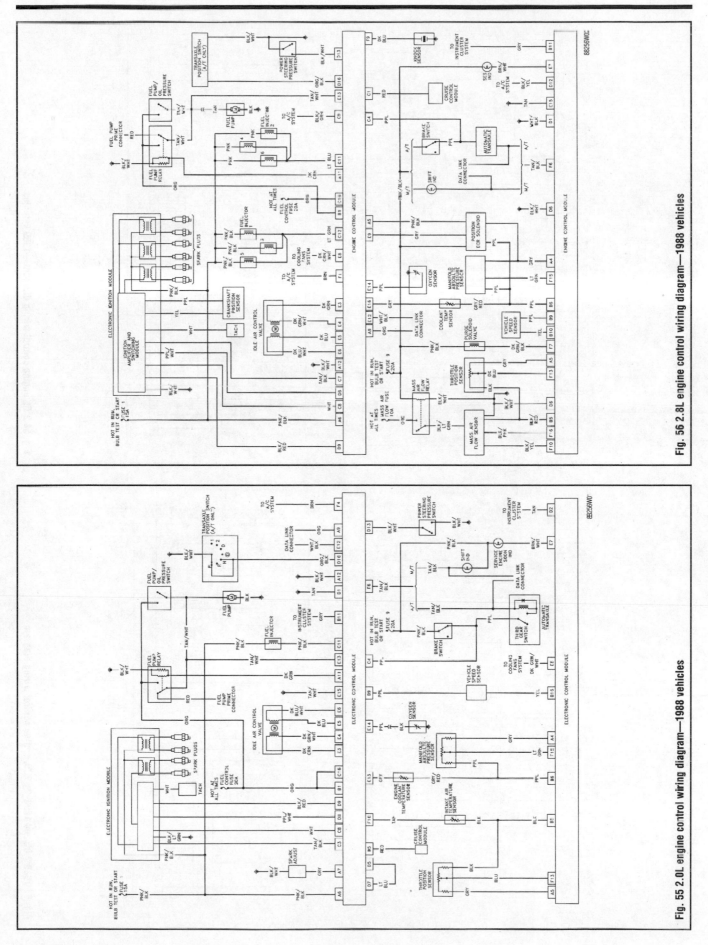

Fig. 56 2.8L engine control wiring diagram—1988 vehicles

Fig. 55 2.0L engine control wiring diagram—1988 vehicles

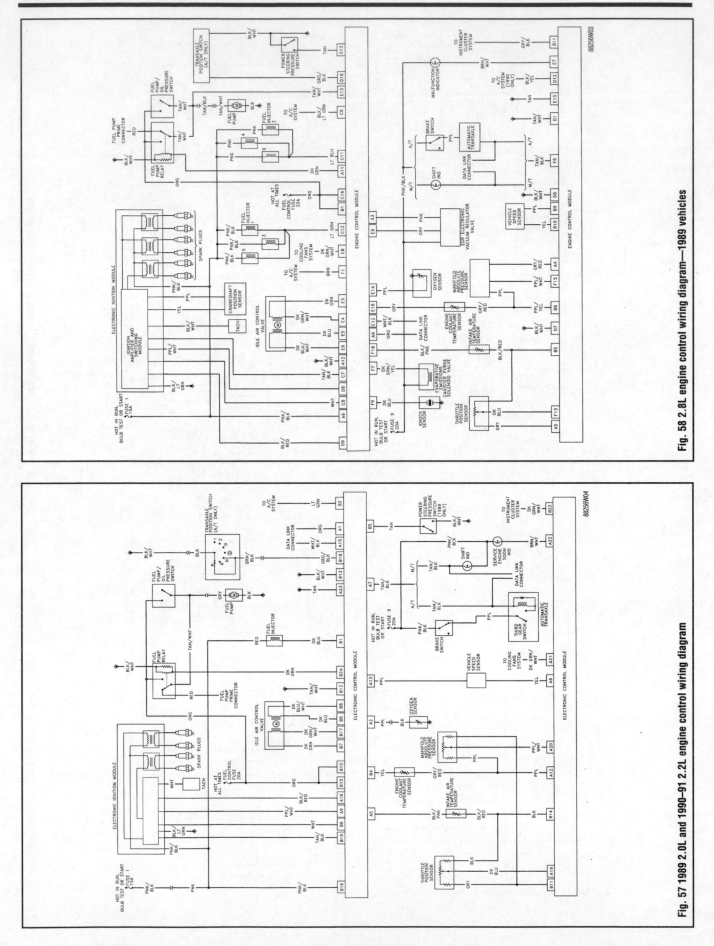

Fig. 58 2.8L engine control wiring diagram—1989 vehicles

Fig. 57 1989 2.0L and 1990-91 2.2L engine control wiring diagram

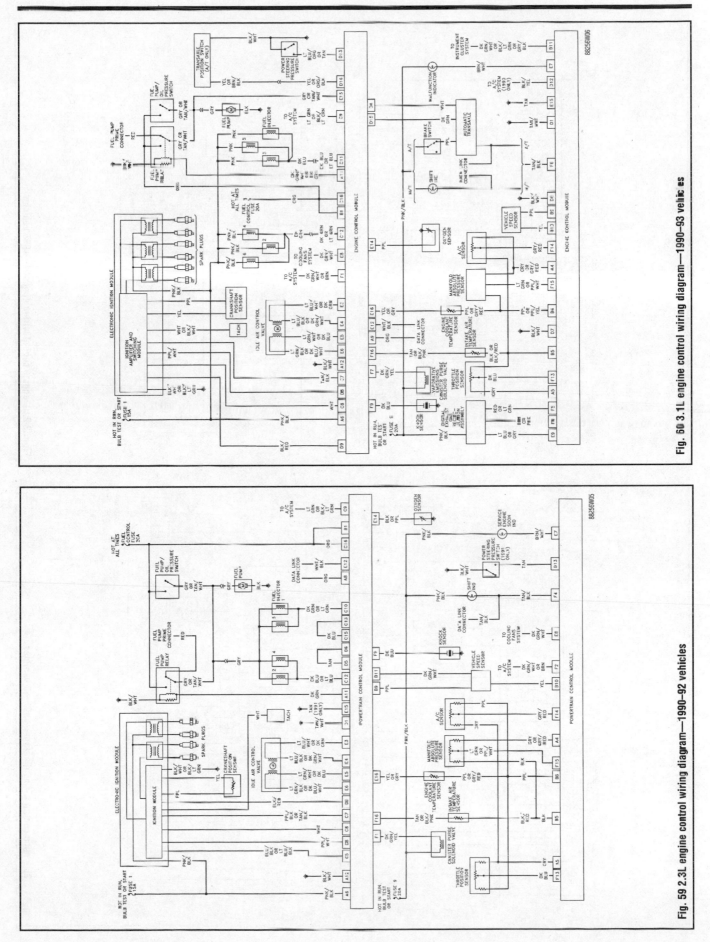

Fig. 60 3.1L engine control wiring diagram—1990-93 vehicles

Fig. 59 2.3L engine control wiring diagram—1990-92 vehicles

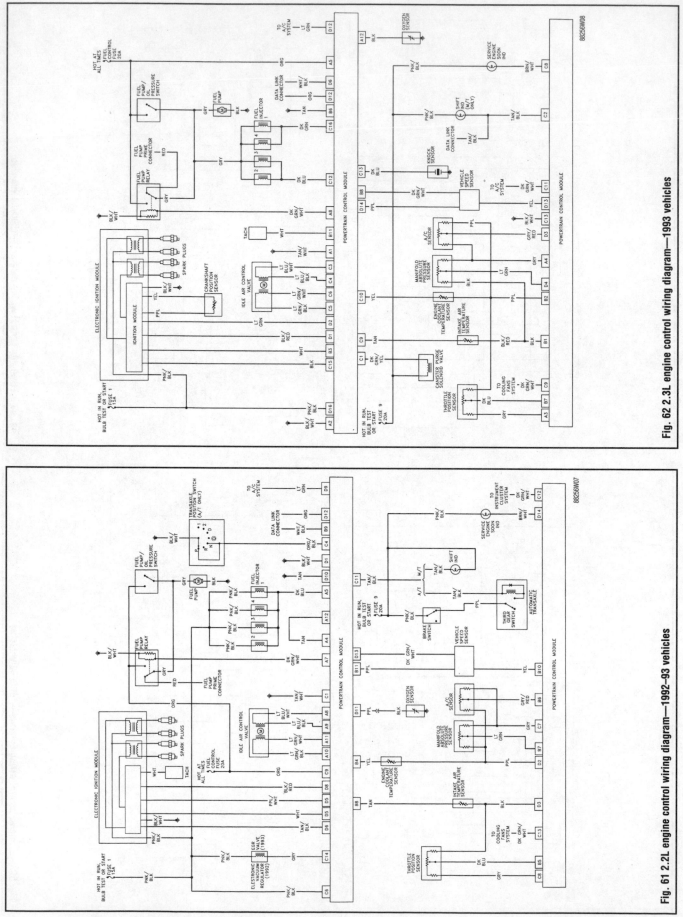

Fig. 62 2.3L engine control wiring diagram—1993 vehicles

Fig. 61 2.2L engine control wiring diagram—1992-93 vehicles

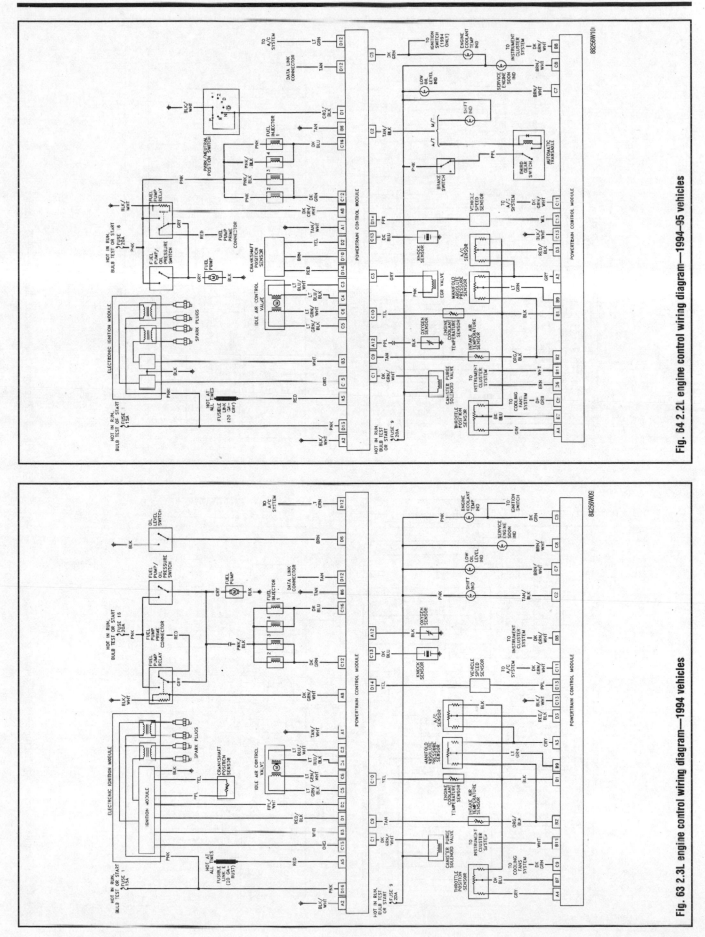

Fig. 64 2.2L engine control wiring diagram—1994–95 vehicles

Fig. 63 2.3L engine control wiring diagram—1994 vehicles

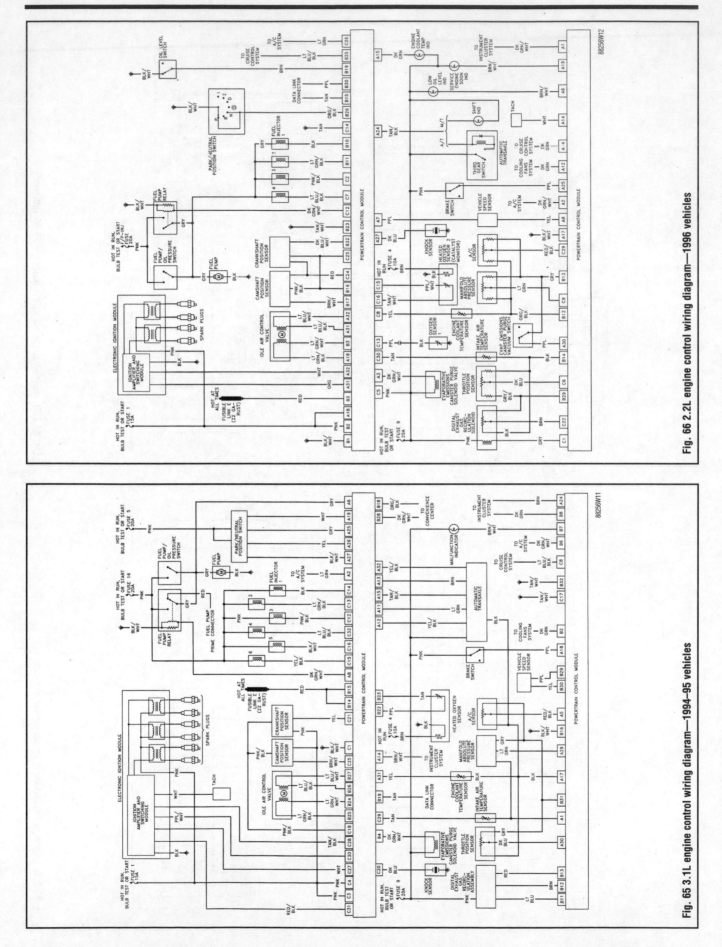

Fig. 66 2.2L engine control wiring diagram—1996 vehicles

Fig. 65 3.1L engine control wiring diagram—1994-95 vehicles

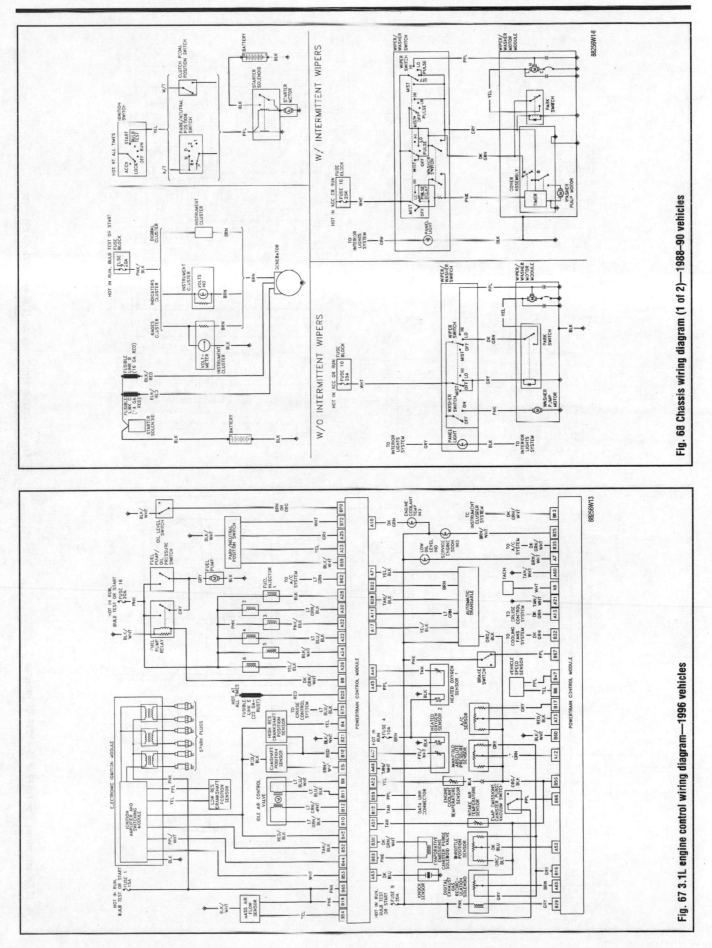

Fig. 68 Chassis wiring diagram (1 of 2)—1988-90 vehicles

Fig. 67 3.1L engine control wiring diagram—1996 vehicles

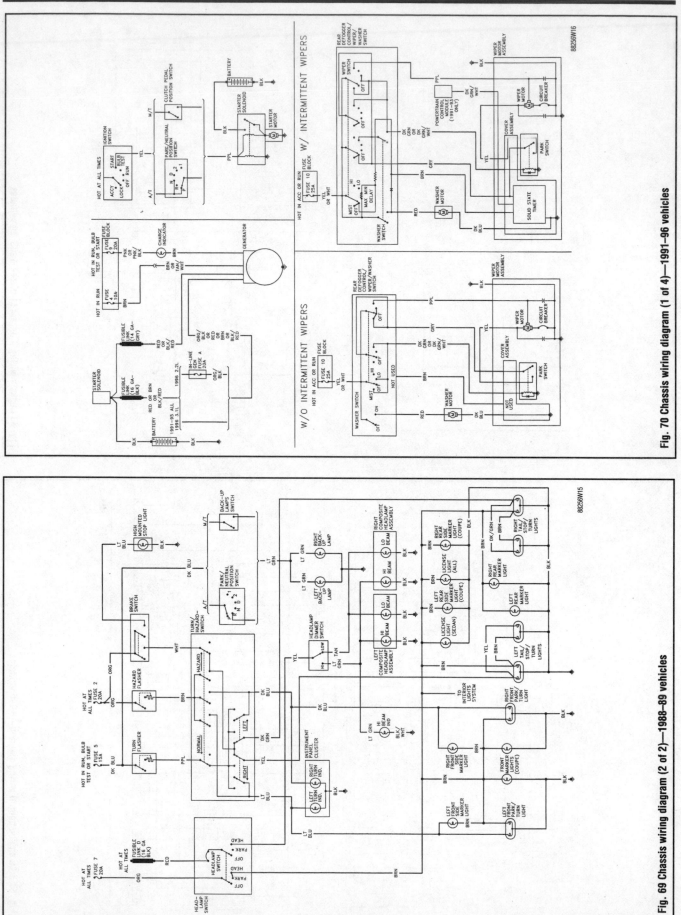

Fig. 70 Chassis wiring diagram (1 of 4)—1991–96 vehicles

Fig. 69 Chassis wiring diagram (2 of 2)—1988–89 vehicles

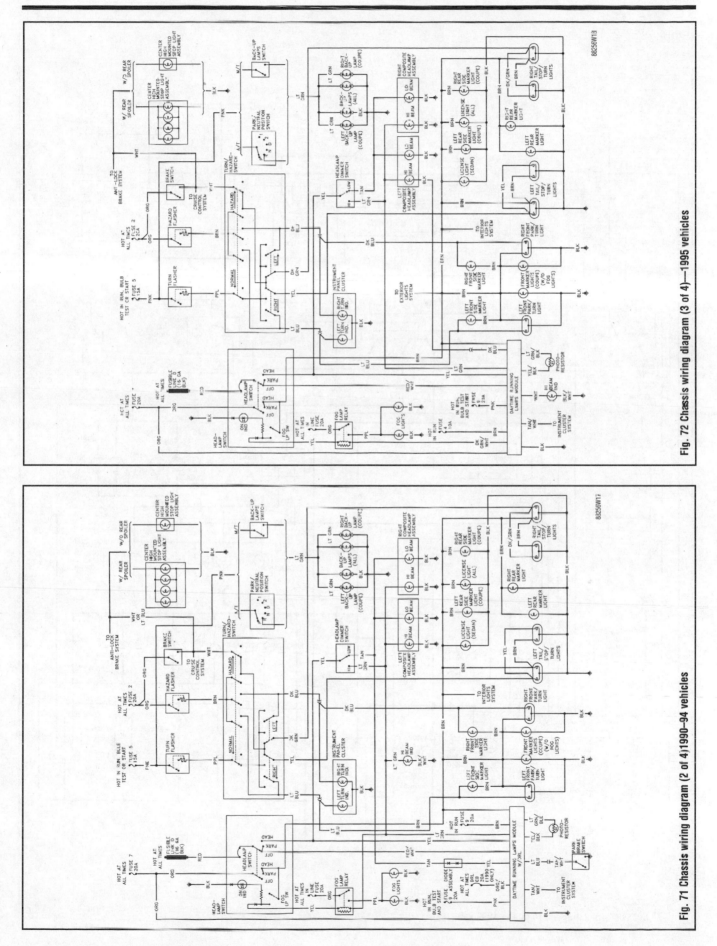

Fig. 72 Chassis wiring diagram (3 of 4)—1995 vehicles

Fig. 71 Chassis wiring diagram (2 of 4)1990-94 vehicles

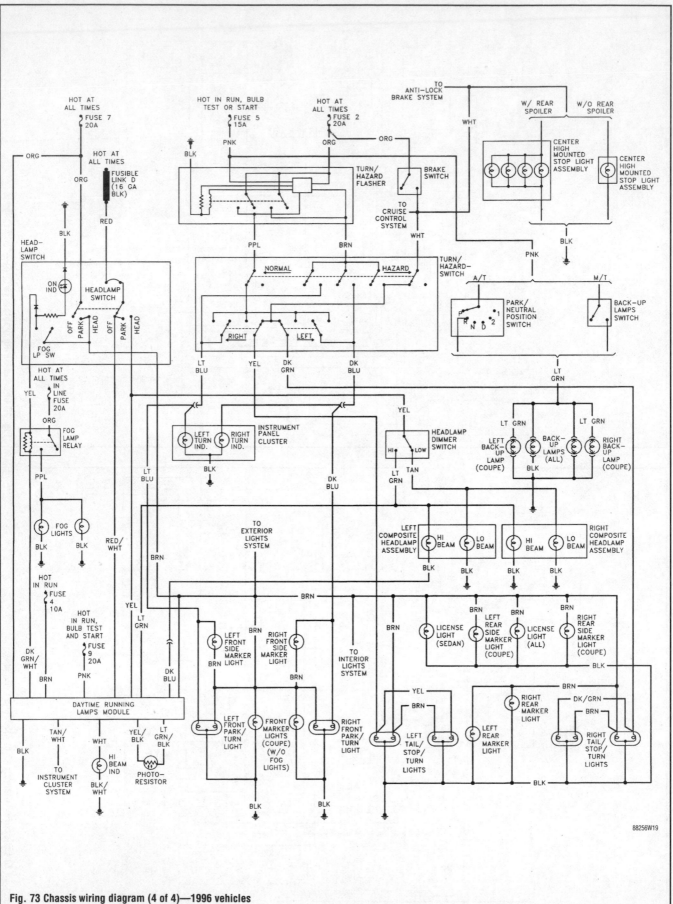

Fig. 73 Chassis wiring diagram (4 of 4)—1996 vehicles

7

DRIVE TRAIN

MANUAL TRANSAXLE

Back-Up Light Switch

REMOVAL & INSTALLATION

▶ **See Figures 1 and 2**

The switch is located in the top of the transaxle case and accessible from the engine compartment.

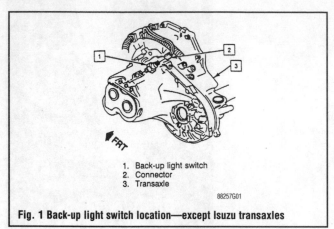

1. Back-up light switch
2. Connector
3. Transaxle

88257G01

Fig. 1 Back-up light switch location—except Isuzu transaxles

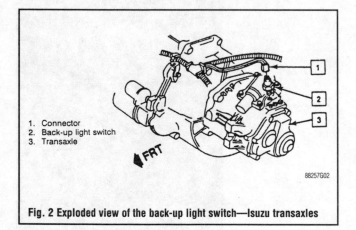

1. Connector
2. Back-up light switch
3. Transaxle

88257G02

Fig. 2 Exploded view of the back-up light switch—Isuzu transaxles

1. Disconnect the negative battery cable.
2. Unplug the back-up light switch wiring harness.
3. Unscrew the switch, then remove it from the transaxle case.

To install:

4. Apply a suitable pipe sealant on the threads, then install the switch. Tighten the switch to 84 inch lbs. (9 Nm) for 1988–90 vehicles and to 24 ft. lbs. (33 Nm) for 1991–96 vehicles.
5. Attach the back-up light switch electrical connector.
6. Connect the negative battery cable.

Manual Transaxle Assembly

REMOVAL & INSTALLATION

▶ **See Figures 3 thru 15**

➡**Before performing any maintenance that requires the removal of the slave cylinder, transaxle or clutch housing, the clutch master cylinder push rod must first be disconnected from the clutch pedal. Failure to disconnect the push rod will result in permanent damage to the slave cylinder if the clutch pedal is depressed with the slave cylinder disconnected.**

Except Isuzu Transaxle

1. Disconnect the negative terminal from the battery.
2. Using the Engine Support Fixture tool No. J–28467 or equivalent and Adapter tool No. J–35953 or equivalent, install them on the engine and raise the engine enough to take the engine weight off of the engine mounts.
3. Remove the left side sound insulator.
4. Disconnect the clutch master cylinder push rod from the clutch pedal.
5. Remove the air cleaner and duct assembly.
6. Disconnect the clutch slave cylinder-to-transaxle support bolts and position the cylinder aside.
7. Remove the transaxle-to-mount through bolt.
8. Raise and support the front of the vehicle.
9. Remove the 2 exhaust crossover bolts at the right side manifold.
10. Lower the vehicle. Remove the left side exhaust manifold.
11. Disconnect the transaxle mounting bracket.
12. Disconnect the shifter cables.
13. Remove the upper transaxle-to-engine bolts.
14. Raise and support the front of the vehicle.
15. Remove the left front tire assembly and the left side inner splash shield.
16. Remove the transaxle strut and bracket.

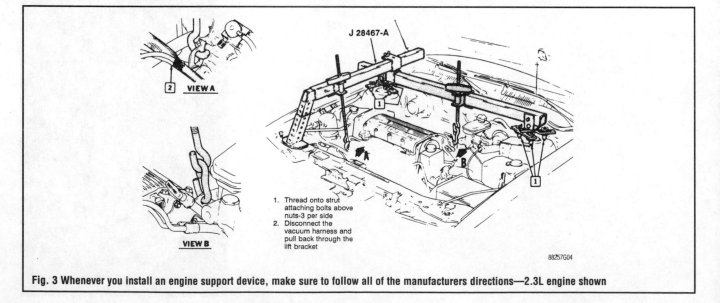

1. Thread onto strut attaching bolts above nuts-3 per side
2. Disconnect the vacuum harness and pull back through the lift bracket

88257G04

Fig. 3 Whenever you install an engine support device, make sure to follow all of the manufacturers directions—2.3L engine shown

17. Place a drain pan under the transaxle, remove the drain plug and drain the fluid from the transaxle.

18. Remove the clutch housing cover bolts.

19. Disconnect the speedometer wire.

20. From the left suspension support and control arm, disconnect the stabilizer shaft.

21. Remove the left suspension support mounting bolts and move the support aside.

22. Disconnect both halfshafts from the transaxle and remove the left halfshaft from the vehicle.

23. Using a transmission jack, attach it to and support the transaxle.

24. Remove the remaining transaxle-to-engine bolts.

25. Slide the transaxle away from the engine, lower it and remove the right side halfshaft.

To install:

26. When installing, guide the right side halfshaft into the transaxle while it is being installed in the vehicle.

27. Torque the transaxle-to-engine bolts to 60 ft. lbs. (81 Nm), the transaxle mount-to-body bolt to 80 ft. lbs. (108 Nm).

28. Install the left halfshaft into its bore at the transaxle then seat both halfshafts at the transaxle.

29. Install the left suspension support mounting bolts.

30. Connect the stabilizer shaft to the left suspension support and control arm.

31. Connect the speedometer wire.

32. Connect the clutch housing cover bolts.

33. Install the transaxle strut and bracket.

34. Install the left front tire assembly and the left side inner splash shield.

35. Lower the car.

36. Install the upper transaxle to engine bolts and torque to 55 ft. lbs. (75 Nm).

37. Install the remaining components in the reverse of the removal procedure.

38. Install the negative battery cable.

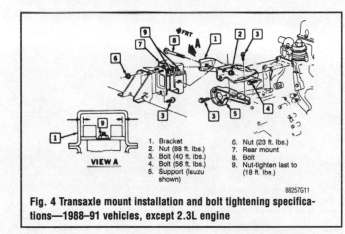

1. Bracket
2. Nut (88 ft. lbs.)
3. Bolt (40 ft. lbs.)
4. Bolt (56 ft. lbs.)
5. Support (Isuzu shown)
6. Nut (23 ft. lbs.)
7. Rear mount
8. Bolt
9. Nut-tighten last to (18 ft. lbs.)

88257G11

Fig. 4 Transaxle mount installation and bolt tightening specifications—1988–91 vehicles, except 2.3L engine

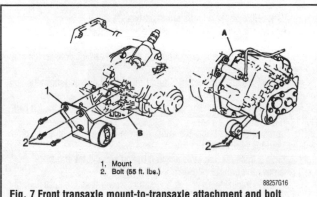

1. Mount
2. Bolt (55 ft. lbs.)

88257G16

Fig. 7 Front transaxle mount-to-transaxle attachment and bolt torques

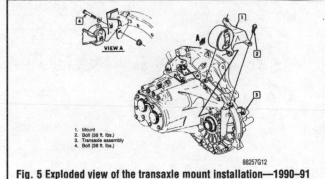

1. Mount
2. Bolt (38 ft. lbs.)
3. Transaxle assembly
4. Bolt (38 ft. lbs.)

88257G12

Fig. 5 Exploded view of the transaxle mount installation—1990–91 2.3L engines shown, 1992–96 vehicles similar, except the bolts are tightened to 55 ft. lbs.

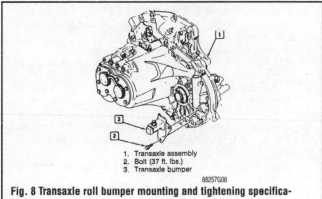

1. Transaxle assembly
2. Bolt (37 ft. lbs.)
3. Transaxle bumper

88257G08

Fig. 8 Transaxle roll bumper mounting and tightening specifications—1990–91 3.1L engines

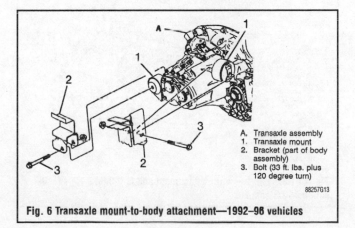

A. Transaxle assembly
1. Transaxle mount
2. Bracket (part of body assembly)
3. Bolt (33 ft. lbs. plus 120 degree turn)

88257G13

Fig. 6 Transaxle mount-to-body attachment—1992–96 vehicles

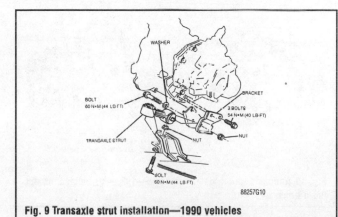

88257G10

Fig. 9 Transaxle strut installation—1990 vehicles

Isuzu Transaxle

1. Disconnect the negative terminal from the battery.
2. Using the Engine Support Fixture tool No. J–28467 or equivalent and Adapter tool No. J–35953 or equivalent, install them on the engine and raise the engine enough to take the engine weight off of the engine mounts.
3. Remove the left side sound insulator.
4. Disconnect the clutch master cylinder push rod from the clutch pedal.
5. Disconnect the clutch slave cylinder-to-transaxle support bolts and position the cylinder aside.
6. Remove the wiring harness from the transaxle mount bracket and the shift wire electrical connector.
7. Remove the transaxle-to-mount bolts and the transaxle mount bracket-to-chassis nuts/bolts.
8. Disconnect the shift cables and remove the retaining clamp from the transaxle. Remove the ground cables from the transaxle mounting studs.
9. Raise and support the front of the vehicle.
10. Remove the left front tire assembly and the left side inner splash shield.
11. Remove the transaxle front strut and bracket.
12. Remove the clutch housing cover bolts. Disconnect the speedometer wire connector.
13. From the left suspension support and control arm, disconnect the stabilizer shaft.
14. Remove the left suspension support mounting bolts and move the support aside.
15. Disconnect both halfshafts from the transaxle and remove the left halfshaft from the vehicle.
16. Place a drain pan under the transaxle, remove the drain plug and drain the fluid from the transaxle.
17. Using a transmission jack, attach it to and support the transaxle.
18. Remove the transaxle-to-engine bolts.
19. Slide the transaxle away from the engine, lower it and remove the right side halfshaft.

To install:

20. When installing, guide the right side halfshaft into the transaxle while it is being installed in the vehicle.
21. Install and torque the transaxle-to-engine bolts to 55 ft. lbs. (75 Nm)
22. Install the left halfshaft into its bore at the transaxle then seat both halfshafts at the transaxle.
23. Install the left suspension support mounting bolts.
24. Connect the stabilizer shaft to the left suspension support and control arm.
25. Connect the speedometer wire.
26. Connect the clutch housing cover bolts and tighten to 89 inch lbs. (10 Nm).
27. Install the transaxle strut and bracket. Torque the transaxle strut to body bolt to 40 ft. lbs. (54 Nm) and the transaxle strut to transaxle to 50 ft. lbs. (68 Nm). See applicable illustration.
28. Install the left front tire assembly and the left side inner splash shield.
29. Lower the car.

30. Install the ground cables at the transaxle mounting studs.
31. Install the wires for the shift light.
32. Install the slave cylinder to the transaxle bracket aligning the push rod into the pocket of the clutch release lever and installing the retaining nuts and tighten evenly.
33. Install the transaxle mount bracket. Tighten the rear mount bracket to transaxle to 40 ft. lbs. (54 Nm). See applicable illustration.
34. Install the transaxle mount to side frame and tighten to 23 ft. lbs. (30 Nm). See applicable illustration.
35. Install the wire harness at the mount bracket.
36. Install the bolt attaching the mount to the transaxle bracket and tighten to 88 ft. lbs. (120 Nm). See applicable illustration.
37. Remove the engine support.
38. Install the shift cables.
39. Connect the negative cable.

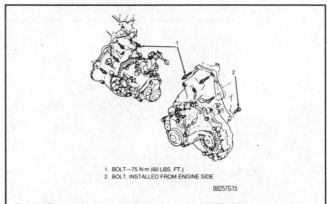

1. BOLT—75 N·m (60 LBS. FT.)
2. BOLT, INSTALLED FROM ENGINE SIDE

88257G15

Fig. 11 Transaxle-to-engine attachments—1988–89 Isuzu transaxles

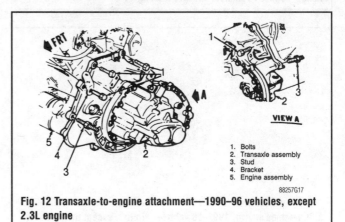

1. Bolts
2. Transaxle assembly
3. Stud
4. Bracket
5. Engine assembly

88257G17

Fig. 12 Transaxle-to-engine attachment—1990–96 vehicles, except 2.3L engine

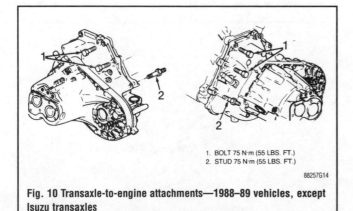

1. BOLT 75 N·m (55 LBS. FT.)
2. STUD 75 N·m (55 LBS. FT.)

88257G14

Fig. 10 Transaxle-to-engine attachments—1988–89 vehicles, except Isuzu transaxles

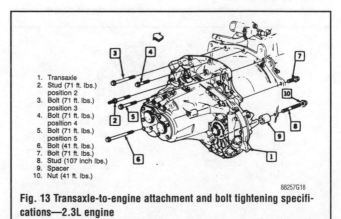

1. Transaxle
2. Stud (71 ft. lbs.) position 2
3. Bolt (71 ft. lbs.) position 3
4. Bolt (71 ft. lbs.) position 4
5. Bolt (71 ft. lbs.) position 5
6. Bolt (41 ft. lbs.)
7. Bolt (71 ft. lbs.)
8. Stud (107 inch lbs.)
9. Spacer
10. Nut (41 ft. lbs.)

88257G18

Fig. 13 Transaxle-to-engine attachment and bolt tightening specifications—2.3L engine

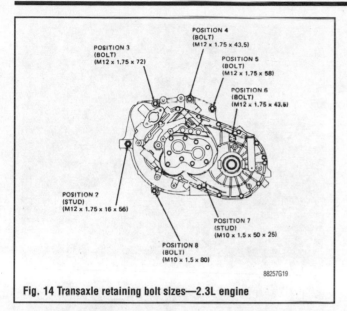

Fig. 14 Transaxle retaining bolt sizes—2.3L engine

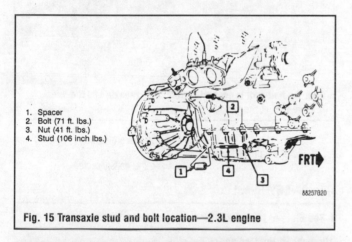

1. Spacer
2. Bolt (71 ft. lbs.)
3. Nut (41 ft. lbs.)
4. Stud (106 inch lbs.)

Fig. 15 Transaxle stud and bolt location—2.3L engine

Halfshafts

REMOVAL & INSTALLATION

1988–89 Vehicles

▶ See Figures 16 and 17

The inner joint on the right side halfshaft uses a male spline that locks into the transaxle gears. The left side halfshaft uses a female spline that is installed over the stub shaft on the transaxle.

1. With the vehicle on the ground, loosen the hub nut.
2. Raise and support the vehicle. Remove the wheel and tire assembly.
3. Remove the hub nut.
4. Install boot protectors on the boots.
5. Remove the brake caliper with the line attached and support it (on a wire) out of the way; DO NOT allow the caliper to hang from the line.
6. Remove the brake rotor and caliper mounting bracket.
7. Remove the strut to steering knuckle bolts. Pull the steering knuckle out of the strut bracket.
8. Using the Halfshaft Removal tool No. J–33008 or equivalent and the Extension tool No. J–29794 or equivalent, remove the halfshafts from the transaxle and support them safely.
9. Using a Spindle Remover tool No. J–28733 or equivalent, remove the halfshaft from the hub and bearing.
10. Remove the halfshaft assembly from the vehicle.
To install:
11. Loosely place the halfshaft on the transaxle and in the hub and bearing.

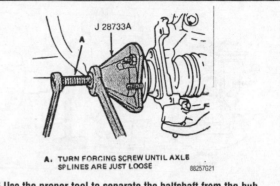

A. TURN FORCING SCREW UNTIL AXLE SPLINES ARE JUST LOOSE

Fig. 16 Use the proper tool to separate the halfshaft from the hub and bearing assembly

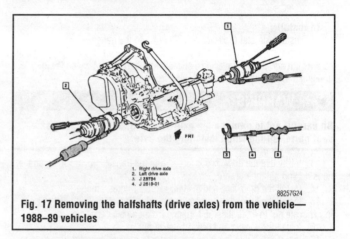

1. Right drive axle
2. Left drive axle
3. J 28794
4. J 2619-01

Fig. 17 Removing the halfshafts (drive axles) from the vehicle— 1988–89 vehicles

12. Properly position the steering knuckle to the strut bracket and install the bolt. Torque the bolts to 133 ft. lbs. (180 Nm).
13. Install the brake rotor, caliper bracket and caliper. Place a holding device in the rotor to prevent it from turning.
14. Install the hub nut and washer. Torque the nut to 71 ft. lbs. (96 Nm).
15. Seat the halfshafts into the transaxle using a prybar on the groove on the inner retainer.
16. Verify that the shafts are seated by grasping the CV-joint and pulling outwards; DO NOT grasp the shaft. If the snapring is seated, the halfshaft will remain in place.
17. To complete the installation, reverse the removal procedures. When the vehicle is lowered with the weight on the wheels, final torque the hub nut to 191 ft. lbs. (259 Nm)

1990–96 Vehicles

▶ See Figure 18

1. Raise the car and suitably support.
2. Remove the wheel and tire assembly.
3. Install drive seal protector J34754 or equivalent, on the outer joint.
4. Insert a drift into the into the caliper and rotor to prevent the rotor from turning.
5. Remove the shaft nut and washer.
6. Remove the lower ball joint cotter pin and nut and loosen the joint using tool J 38892 or equivalent. If removing the right axle, turn the wheel to the left, if removing the left axle, turn the wheel to the right.
7. Separate the joint, with a pry bar between the suspension support.
8. Disengage the axle from the hub and bearing using J 28733–A or equivalent.
9. Separate the hub and bearing assembly from the drive axle and move the strut and knuckle assembly rearward.
10. Disconnect the inner joint from the transaxle using tool J–28468 or J–33008 attached to J–29794 and J–2619–01 or from the intermediate shaft (V6 and 2.3L engines), if equipped.

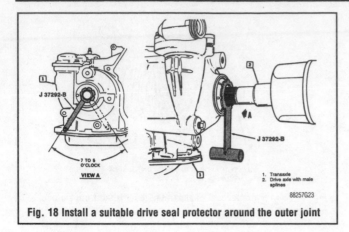

Fig. 18 Install a suitable drive seal protector around the outer joint

To install:

11. Install axle seal protector J–37292–A into the transaxle.

12. Insert the drive axle into the transaxle or intermediate shaft (V6 and 2.3L engines), if equipped, by placing a suitable tool into the groove on the joint housing and tapping until seated.

⁂ WARNING

Be careful not to damage the axle seal or dislodge the transaxle seal garter spring when installing the axle.

13. Verify that the drive axle is seated into the transaxle by grasping on the housing and pulling outward.

14. Install the drive axle into the hub and bearing assembly.

15. Install the lower ball joint to the knuckle. Tighten the ball joint to steering knuckle nut to 41 ft. lbs. (55 Nm) and install a new cotter pin.

16. Install the washer and new driveshaft nut.

17. Insert a drift into the caliper and rotor to prevent the rotor from turning and tighten the driveshaft nut to 185 ft. lbs. (260 Nm).

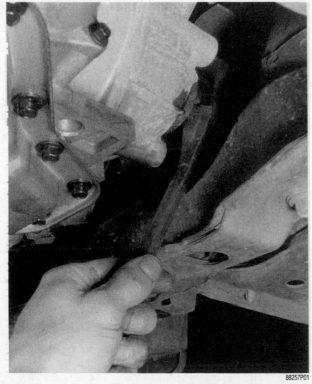

You can try to separate the halfshaft from the transaxle by using a large prytool

After the halfshaft is separated from the transaxle and the hub, remove it from the vehicle

18. Remove both J–37292–B and J–34754 seal protectors.

19. Install the tire and wheel assembly.

20. Lower the vehicle and connect the negative battery cable.

CV- JOINT OVERHAUL

▶ **See Figures 19 and 20**

1988–90 Tri-Pot Design

All driveshafts except the left side inboard joint of the automatic transaxles incorporates a male spline and interlocks with the transaxle gears through the use of a barrel type snap rings. The left side inboard shaft attachment on the automatic transaxle, utilizes a female spline which installs over a stub shaft protruding from the transaxle.

For all overhaul procedures for the 1988–90 Tri-Pot type drive axles, please refer to the illustrated procedures.

1988–96 Cross Groove and 1991–96 Tri-Pot Design

The inner joint on cars with the HM-282, 5TM40 and NVT-550 5-speed transaxles, is a Cross-Groove type. All other applications use the Tri-Pot inner joint.

The following overhaul procedures incorporate both designs, unless otherwise noted.

Outer Deflector Ring

▶ **See Figures 21 and 22**

1. Remove the halfshaft/drive axle from the vehicle.

2. Clamp the halfshaft in a soft jawed vise.

3. Using a brass drift and a hammer, remove the deflecting ring from the CV outer race.

To install:

4. Position and square up the deflecting ring at press diameter of CV outer race.

5. Using a 3 in. (76mm) pipe coupling, M24 1.5 nut a fabricated sheet metal sleeve, tighten the nut until the deflector bottoms against the shoulder of the outer CV-joint.

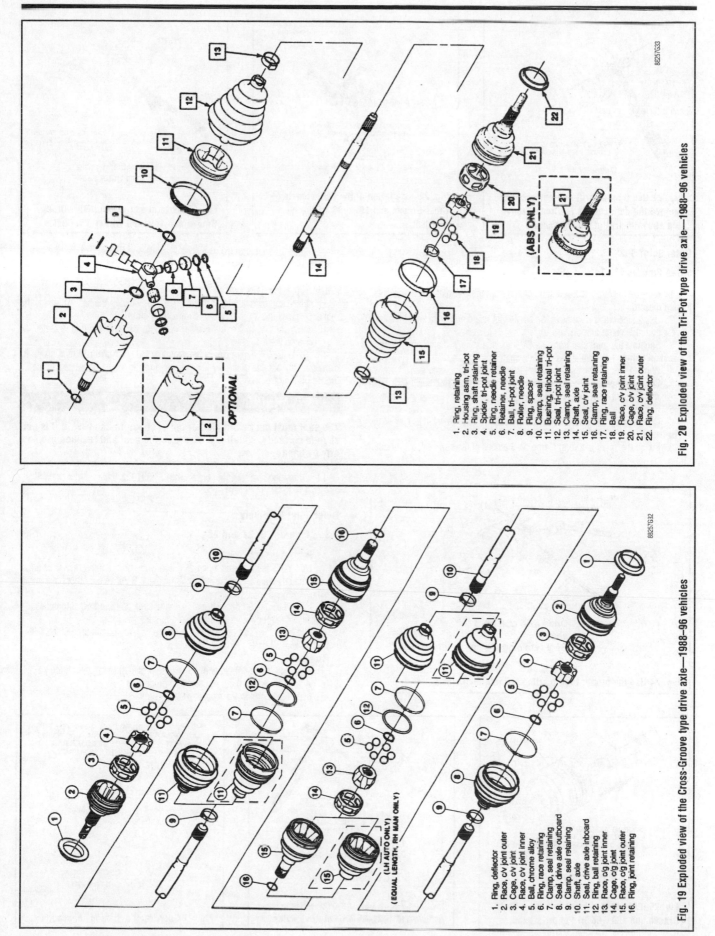

Fig. 20 Exploded view of the Tri-Pot type drive axle—1988-96 vehicles

1. Ring, retaining
2. Housing asm, tri-pot
3. Ring, shaft retaining
4. Spider, tri-pot joint
5. Ring, needle retainer
6. Retainer, needle
7. Ball, tri-pot joint
8. Roller, needle
9. Ring, spacer
10. Clamp, seal retaining
11. Bushing, trilobal tri-pot
12. Seal, tri-pot joint
13. Clamp, seal retaining
14. Shaft, axle
15. Seal, c/v joint
16. Clamp, seal retaining
17. Ring, race retaining
18. Ball
19. Race, c/v joint inner
20. Cage, c/v joint
21. Race, c/v joint outer
22. Ring, deflector

Fig. 19 Exploded view of the Cross-Groove type drive axle—1988-96 vehicles

1. Ring, deflector
2. Race, c/v joint outer
3. Cage, c/v joint
4. Race, c/v joint inner
5. Ball, chrome alloy
6. Ring, race retaining
7. Clamp, seal retaining
8. Seal, drive axle outboard
9. Clamp, seal retaining
10. Shaft, axle
11. Seal, drive axle inboard
12. Ring, ball retaining
13. Race, c/g joint inner
14. Cage, c/g joint
15. Race, c/g joint outer
16. Ring, joint retaining

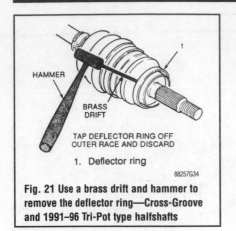

Fig. 21 Use a brass drift and hammer to remove the deflector ring—Cross-Groove and 1991–96 Tri-Pot type halfshafts

SHEET STEEL (3mm MIN THICKNESS) WITH 26mm DRILLED HOLE

3" PIPE COUPLING

M24X1.5 NUT

SQUARE UP DEFLECTOR RING AND TIGHTEN NUT UNTIL RING BOTTOMS AGAINST SHOULDER OF OUTER RACE

1. Deflector ring
2. CV joint outer race

88257G35

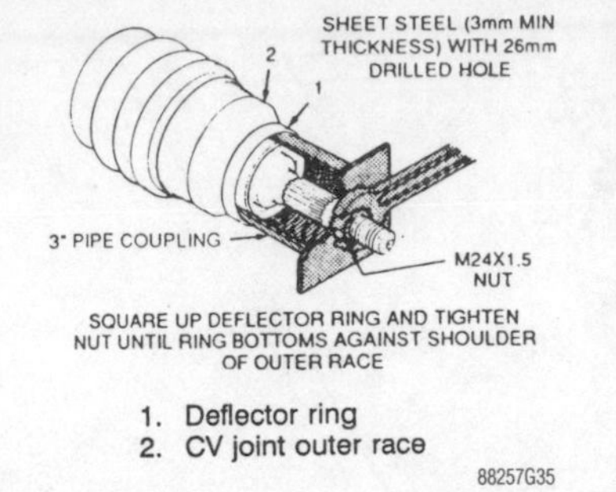

Fig. 22 Installation of the deflector ring—Cross-Groove and 1991–96 Tri-Pot type halfshafts

J 8059

SPREAD RETAINING RING EARS AND SLIDE C/V JOINT OFF AXLE SHAFT

1. Race retaining ring
2. CV joint outer race

88257G36

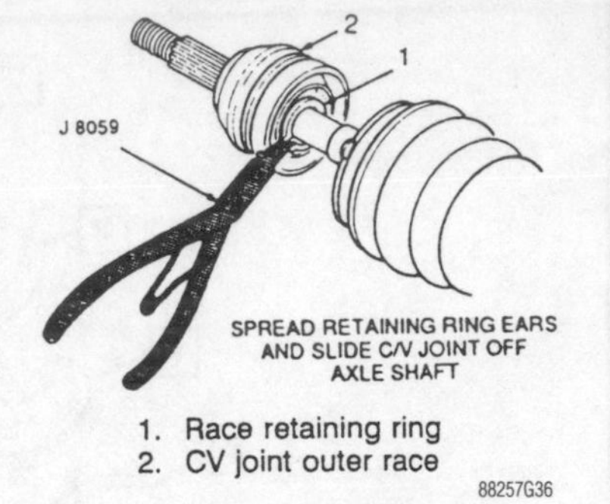

Fig. 23 CV-joint axle separation—Cross-Groove and 1991–96 Tri-Pot drive axles

Outer Joint Seal

◆ See Figures 23, 24 and 25

1. Remove the large seal retaining clamp from the CV joint with a side cutter and discard.
2. Use a side cutter to remove the small seal retaining clamp from the axle shaft with a side cutter and discard.
3. Separate the joint seal from the CV join race at large diameter and slide the seal away from the joint along the axle shaft.
4. Wipe the excess grease from the face of the CV joint inner race.
5. Spread the ears on the race retaining ring with snap ring pliers and remove the CV joint from the axle shaft.
6. Remove the seal from the axle shaft.
7. Disassemble the joint and flush the grease prior to installing a new seal.
To install:
8. Install the small retaining clamp on the neck of the new seal, but do not crimp.

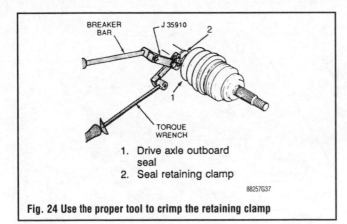

Fig. 24 Use the proper tool to crimp the retaining clamp

1. Drive axle outboard seal
2. Seal retaining clamp

88257G37

9. Slide the seal onto the axle shaft and position the neck of the seal in the seal groove on the axle shaft.
10. Crimp the seal retaining clamp with J 35910 seal clamp tool or equivalent, to 100 ft. lbs. (136 Nm).
11. Place approximately half of the grease provided in the seal kit, inside the seal and repack the CV joint with the remaining grease.
12. Push the CV joint onto the axle shaft until the retaining ring is seated in the groove on the axle shaft.
13. Slide the large diameter of the seal with the large seal retaining clamp in place over the outside of the CV joint race and locate the lip of the seal in the groove on the race.

✳✳ WARNING

The seal must not be dimpled or out of shape in any way. If it is not shaped correctly, equalize pressure in the seal and reshape properly by hand.

14. Crimp the seal retaining clamp with J 35910 seal clamp tool or equivalent, to 130 ft. lbs. (176 Nm).

Outer Joint Assembly

◆ See Figures 26, 27 and 28

1. Remove the outer joint seal as outlined earlier.
2. Using a brass drift and a hammer, lightly tap on the inner race cage until it has tilted sufficiently to remove one of the balls. Remove the other balls in the same manner.
3. Pivot the cage 90 degrees and, with the cage ball windows aligned with the outer joint windows, lift out the cage and the inner race.
4. The inner race can be removed from the cage by pivoting it 90° and lifting out. Clean all parts thoroughly and inspect for wear.
To install:
5. To install, put a light coat of the grease provided in the rebuilding kit onto the ball grooves of the inner race and outer joint.
6. Install the parts in the reverse order of removal.

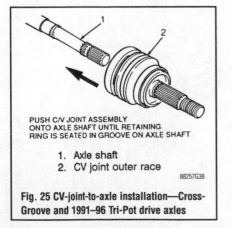

PUSH C/V JOINT ASSEMBLY ONTO AXLE SHAFT UNTIL RETAINING RING IS SEATED IN GROOVE ON AXLE SHAFT

1. Axle shaft
2. CV joint outer race

88257G38

Fig. 25 CV-joint-to-axle installation—Cross-Groove and 1991–96 Tri-Pot drive axles

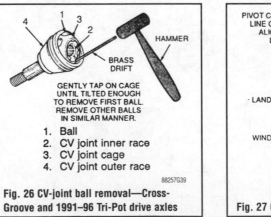

BRASS DRIFT

HAMMER

GENTLY TAP ON CAGE UNTIL TILTED ENOUGH TO REMOVE FIRST BALL. REMOVE OTHER BALLS IN SIMILAR MANNER.

1. Ball
2. CV joint inner race
3. CV joint cage
4. CV joint outer race

88257G39

Fig. 26 CV-joint ball removal—Cross-Groove and 1991–96 Tri-Pot drive axles

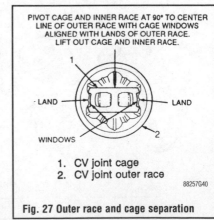

PIVOT CAGE AND INNER RACE AT 90° TO CENTER LINE OF OUTER RACE WITH CAGE WINDOWS ALIGNED WITH LANDS OF OUTER RACE. LIFT OUT CAGE AND INNER RACE.

LAND

LAND

WINDOWS

1. CV joint cage
2. CV joint outer race

88257G40

Fig. 27 Outer race and cage separation

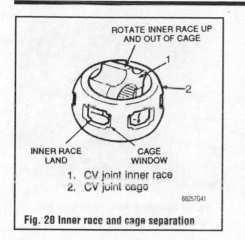

ROTATE INNER RACE UP AND OUT OF CAGE

INNER RACE LAND   CAGE WINDOW

1. CV joint inner race
2. CV joint cage

88257G41

Fig. 28 Inner race and cage separation

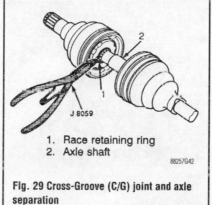

1. Race retaining ring
2. Axle shaft

88257G42

Fig. 29 Cross-Groove (C/G) joint and axle separation

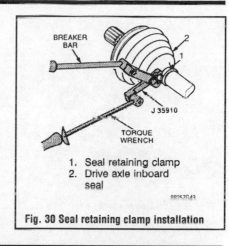

BREAKER BAR

J 35910

TORQUE WRENCH

1. Seal retaining clamp
2. Drive axle inboard seal

88257G43

Fig. 30 Seal retaining clamp installation

→Make sure that the retaining ring side of the inner race faces the axle shaft.

7. Install the outer seal as outlined earlier

Cross Groove Joint Seal

♦ See Figures 29, 30, 31 and 32

1. Cut the seal retaining clamps with a side cutter.
2. Separate the seal from the C/G joint race at the large diameter and slide the seal away from the joint along the axle shaft.
3. Wipe the excess grease from the C/G joint inner race.
4. Spread the ears on the retaining ring with snap ring pliers and remove the C/G joint from the axle shaft.
5. Remove the seal from the axle shaft.
6. Remove the seal from the shaft.

→The cross-groove joint design uses precision grinding and selected dimensional component fits for proper assembly and operation. Due to its complexity, disassembly is not recommended.

7. Flush the grease from the joint prior to installing a new seal.

To install:
8. Install the small retaining clamp on the neck of the new seal, but do not crimp yet.
9. Slide the seal onto the axle shaft and position the neck of the seal in the seal groove on the axle shaft.
10. Crimp the seal retaining clamp with J 35910 seal clamp tool or equivalent, to 100 ft. lbs. (136 Nm).
11. Place approximately half of the grease provided in the seal kit, inside the seal and repack the C/G joint with the remaining grease.
12. Push the C/G joint onto the axle shaft until the retaining ring is seated in the groove on the axle shaft.
13. Slide the large diameter of the seal over the outside of the C/G joint and locate the lip of the seal in the groove on ball retainer.

✳✳ WARNING

The seal must not be dimpled or out of shape in any way. If it is not shaped correctly, equalize pressure in the seal and reshape properly by hand.

14. Crimp the seal retaining clamp with J 35910 seal clamp tool or equivalent, to 130 ft. lbs. (176 Nm).

Inner Tri-Pot Seal

♦ See Figures 33 thru 44

1. Remove the larger seal retaining clamp from the tri-pot joint with a side cutter and discard.

✳✳ WARNING

Do not cut through the seal and damage the sealing surface of the tri-pot outer housing and trilobal bushing.

2. Remove the small seal retaining clamp from the axle shaft with a side cutter and discard.
3. Separate the seal from the trilobal tri-pot bushing at the large diameter and slide the seal away from the joint along the axle shaft.
4. Remove the tri-pot housing from the spider and shaft.
5. Spread the spacer ring with snap ring pliers and slide the spacer ring and tri-pot spider back on the axle shaft.
6. Remove the shaft retaining ring from the groove on the axle shaft and slide the spider assembly off of the shaft.
7. Check the tri-pot balls and needle rollers for damage or wear.

→Use care when handling the spider assembly as the tri-pot balls and rollers may separate from the spider trunnions.

8. Remove the trilobal tri-pot bushing from the tri-pot housing.
9. Remove the spacer ring and seal from the axle shaft.

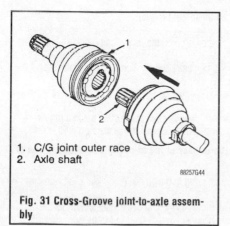

1. C/G joint outer race
2. Axle shaft

88257G44

Fig. 31 Cross-Groove joint-to-axle assembly

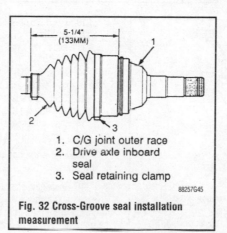

5-1/4" (133MM)

1. C/G joint outer race
2. Drive axle inboard seal
3. Seal retaining clamp

88257G45

Fig. 32 Cross-Groove seal installation measurement

TCCS7031

Fig. 33 Removing the outer band from the CV-boot

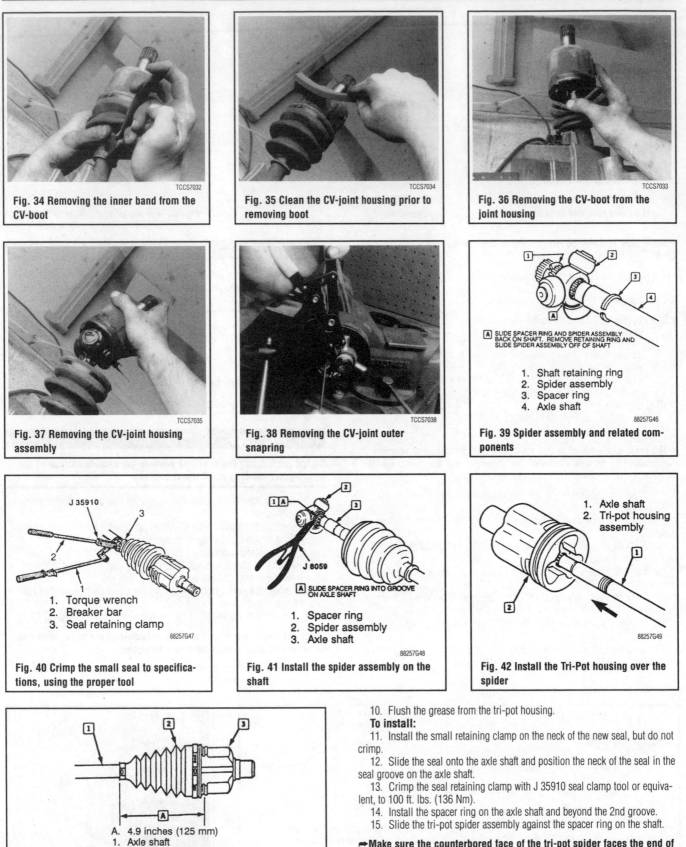

Fig. 34 Removing the inner band from the CV-boot

Fig. 35 Clean the CV-joint housing prior to removing boot

Fig. 36 Removing the CV-boot from the joint housing

Fig. 37 Removing the CV-joint housing assembly

Fig. 38 Removing the CV-joint outer snapring

1. Shaft retaining ring
2. Spider assembly
3. Spacer ring
4. Axle shaft

A SLIDE SPACER RING AND SPIDER ASSEMBLY BACK ON SHAFT. REMOVE RETAINING RING AND SLIDE SPIDER ASSEMBLY OFF OF SHAFT.

Fig. 39 Spider assembly and related components

1. Torque wrench
2. Breaker bar
3. Seal retaining clamp

Fig. 40 Crimp the small seal to specifications, using the proper tool

1. Spacer ring
2. Spider assembly
3. Axle shaft

A SLIDE SPACER RING INTO GROOVE ON AXLE SHAFT

Fig. 41 Install the spider assembly on the shaft

1. Axle shaft
2. Tri-pot housing assembly

Fig. 42 Install the Tri-Pot housing over the spider

A. 4.9 inches (125 mm)
1. Axle shaft
2. Tri-pot joint seal
3. Tri-pot housing assembly

Fig. 43 Tri-pot seal installation dimensions

10. Flush the grease from the tri-pot housing.

To install:

11. Install the small retaining clamp on the neck of the new seal, but do not crimp.

12. Slide the seal onto the axle shaft and position the neck of the seal in the seal groove on the axle shaft.

13. Crimp the seal retaining clamp with J 35910 seal clamp tool or equivalent, to 100 ft. lbs. (136 Nm).

14. Install the spacer ring on the axle shaft and beyond the 2nd groove.

15. Slide the tri-pot spider assembly against the spacer ring on the shaft.

➡**Make sure the counterbored face of the tri-pot spider faces the end of the shaft.**

16. Install the shaft retaining ring in the groove of the axle shaft with the snap ring pliers.

17. Slide the tri-pot spider towards the end of the shaft and reseat the spacer ring in the groove on the shaft.

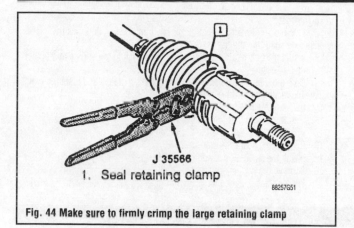

J 35566
1. Seal retaining clamp

88257G51

Fig. 44 Make sure to firmly crimp the large retaining clamp

18. Place approximately half of the grease provided in the seal kit, inside the seal and repack the tri-pot housing with the remaining grease.
19. Install the trilobal tri-pot bushing to the tri-pot housing.
20. Position the larger clamp on the seal.
21. Slide the tri-pot housing over the tri-pot spider.
22. Slide the large diameter of the seal, with the larger clamp in place, over the outside of the trilobal bushing and locate the lip of the seal in the bushing groove.
23. Position the tri-pot assembly at the proper vehicle dimension as shown.

❄ WARNING

The seal must not be dimpled or out of shape in any way. If it is not shaped correctly, equalize pressure by carefully inserting a thin flat blunt tool (no sharp edges) between the large seal opening and the bushing and reshape properly by hand.

24. Crimp the seal retaining clamp with J 35566 seal clamp tool or equivalent.

Intermediate Shaft

REMOVAL & INSTALLATION

1988–89 Vehicles

♦ See Figure 45

1. Raise the car and suitably support.
2. Remove the wheel and tire assembly.
3. Drain the transaxle into a suitable container.
4. Install the modified outer seal protector J–34754.
5. Remove the stabilizer shaft from the right control arm.
6. Remove the right ball joint from the knuckle.
7. Disconnect the drive axle from the intermediate axle shaft.
8. Remove the 2 housing to bracket bolts.
9. Remove the bottom bracket to engine bolt and loosen the top bolt, rotate the bracket out of the way.
10. Remove the 3 bolts holding the housing to the transaxle.
To install:
11. Place the intermediate shaft into position and lock the intermediate axle shaft into the transaxle.
12. Install the 3 bolts holding the housing to the transaxle and tighten to 18 ft. lbs. (25 Nm).
13. Rotate the bracket into position and install the bottom bolt, tighten both bolts to 37 ft. lbs. (50 Nm).
14. Install the 2 housing to bracket bolts and tighten to 37 ft. lbs. (50 Nm).
15. Coat the splines with chassis grease.
16. Attach the drive axle to the intermediate axle shaft.
17. Connect the right ball joint to the knuckle.
18. Install the stabilizer shaft to the right control arm.
19. Remove the modified outer seal protector J–34754.
20. Install the wheel and tire assembly.

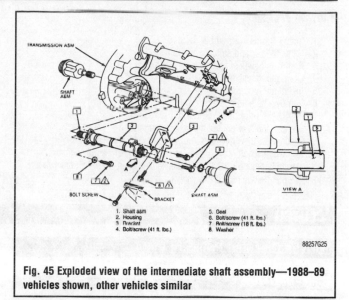

1. Shaft asm
2. Housing
3. Bracket
4. Bolt/screw (41 ft. lbs.)
5. Seal
6. Bolt/screw (41 ft. lbs.)
7. Bolt/screw (18 ft. lbs.)
8. Washer

88257G25

Fig. 45 Exploded view of the intermediate shaft assembly—1988–89 vehicles shown, other vehicles similar

21. Lower the car and fill the transaxle with the proper type and amount of fluid.

1990 Vehicles

♦ See Figure 46

1. Install engine support bar J–28467.
2. Raise the car and suitably support.
3. Remove the wheel assembly.
4. Drain the transaxle.
5. Install the modified outer seal protector J–34754.
6. Remove the stabilizer shaft from the right control arm.
7. Remove the right ball joint from the knuckle.
8. For 2.3L engines, remove the rear engine mount through bolt.
9. For 3.1L engines, disconnect the rear engine mount.
10. Disconnect the drive axle from the intermediate axle shaft.
11. Remove the bolt retaining the intermediate shaft to the engine.
12. Carefully disengage the intermediate axle shaft from the transaxle and remove the intermediate shaft assembly.
To install:
13. Place the intermediate shaft assembly into position and lock the intermediate axle shaft into the transaxle.
14. Install the bolt retaining the intermediate shaft to the engine and tighten to 38 ft. lbs. (52 Nm).
15. Coat the intermediate axle shaft with chassis grease and install the intermediate axle shaft to the drive axle.
16. Install the remaining components in the reverse of the removal procedure.
17. Fill the transaxle with the proper fluid.

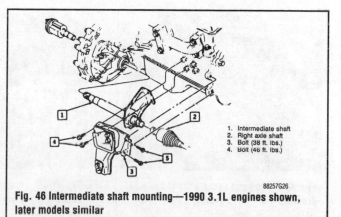

1. Intermediate shaft
2. Right axle shaft
3. Bolt (38 ft. lbs.)
4. Bolt (46 ft. lbs.)

88257G26

Fig. 46 Intermediate shaft mounting—1990 3.1L engines shown, later models similar

1991–96 Vehicles

1. Install engine support bar J–28467.
2. Raise the car and suitably support.
3. Remove the wheel assembly.
4. Drain the transaxle.
5. Install the modified outer seal protector J–34754.
6. Remove the stabilizer shaft from the right control arm.
7. Remove the right ball joint from the knuckle.
8. Remove the rear engine mount through bolt.
9. Disconnect the drive axle from the intermediate axle shaft.
10. Remove the bolt retaining the intermediate shaft to the engine.
11. Carefully disengage the intermediate axle shaft from the transaxle and remove the intermediate shaft assembly.

To install:

12. Place the intermediate shaft assembly into position and lock the intermediate axle shaft into the transaxle.
13. Install the bolt retaining the intermediate shaft to the engine and tighten to 35 ft. lbs. (47 Nm).
14. Coat the intermediate axle shaft with chassis grease and install the intermediate axle shaft to the drive axle.
15. Install the rear engine mount through bolt.
16. Install the right ball joint to the knuckle.
17. Install the stabilizer shaft to the right control arm.
18. Remove the seal protector tool.
19. Install the wheel and lower the vehicle.
20. Remove the engine support bar holding fixture.
21. Fill the transaxle with the proper fluid.

CLUTCH

Driven Disc and Pressure Plate

✳✳ CAUTION

The clutch driven disc contains asbestos, which has been determined to be a cancer causing agent. Never clean clutch surfaces with compressed air! Avoid inhaling any dust from any clutch surface! When cleaning clutch surfaces, use a commercially available brake cleaning fluid.

REMOVAL & INSTALLATION

◆ **See Figures 47 thru 57**

1. Disconnect the negative battery cable.
2. From inside the vehicle, remove the hush panel.

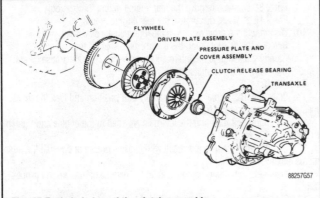

Fig. 47 Exploded view of the clutch assembly

FLYWHEEL
DRIVEN PLATE ASSEMBLY
PRESSURE PLATE AND COVER ASSEMBLY
CLUTCH RELEASE BEARING
TRANSAXLE

88257G57

3. Disconnect the clutch master cylinder push rod from the clutch pedal.
4. Refer to the "Transaxle, Removal and Installation" procedures in this section and remove the transaxle.
5. With the transaxle removed, matchmark the pressure plate and flywheel assembly to insure proper balance during reassembly.
6. Loosen the pressure plate-to-flywheel bolts (one turn at a time) until the spring pressure is removed.
7. Support the pressure plate and remove the bolts.
8. Remove the pressure plate and disc assembly; be sure to note the flywheel side of the clutch disc.
9. Clean and inspect the clutch assembly, flywheel, release bearing, clutch fork and pivot shaft for signs of wear. Replace any necessary parts.

To install:

10. Position the clutch disc and pressure plate in the appropriate position, align the "Heavy Side" of the flywheel assembly stamped with an **X** with the clutch cover "Light Side" marked with paint. Support the assembly with Alignment tool No. J–290742 or equivalent.

➡**The clutch disc is installed with the damper springs offset towards the transaxle. Stamped letters on the clutch disc identify "Flywheel Side". Make sure the clutch disc is facing the same direction it was when removed. If the same pressure plate is being reused, align the marks made during the removal.**

11. Install the pressure plate-to-flywheel retaining bolts.
12. For 1988–90 vehicles, tighten the flywheel-to-pressure plate bolts to 15 ft. lbs. (20 Nm)
13. For 1991–96 vehicles, tighten the flywheel-to-pressure plate bolts as follows:
    a. Install and lightly seat bolts 1, 2, 3 then 4, 5, 6.
    b. Tighten bolts 1, 2, 3 to 12 ft. lbs. (16 Nm).
    c. Tighten bolts 4, 5, 6 to 12 ft. lbs. (16 Nm).
    d. Tighten bolts 1, 2, 3 then 4, 5, 6 to 15 ft. lbs. (20 Mm) plus 30 degree rotation.
14. Remove the alignment tool.

Fig. 48 Loosen and remove the clutch and pressure plate bolts evenly, a little at a time . . .

TCCS7116

PRESSURE PLATE
CLUTCH DISC

Fig. 49 . . . then carefully removing the clutch and pressure plate assembly from the flywheel

TCCS7118

Fig. 50 Check across the flywheel surface, it should be flat

TCCS7125

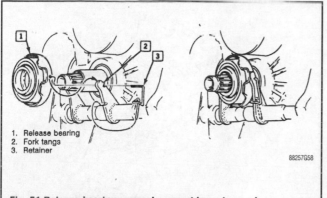

1. Release bearing
2. Fork tangs
3. Retainer

88257G58

Fig. 51 Release bearing removal—except Isuzu transaxle

Fig. 52 Be sure that the flywheel surface is clean, before installing the clutch

TCCS7127

Fig. 53 Install a clutch alignment arbor, to align the clutch assembly during installation

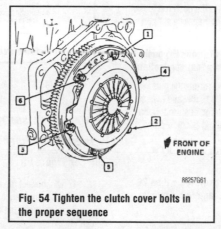

FRONT OF ENGINE

88257G61

Fig. 54 Tighten the clutch cover bolts in the proper sequence

TCCS7131

Fig. 55 You may want to use a thread locking compound on the clutch assembly bolts

TCCS7133

Fig. 56 Be sure to use a torque wrench to tighten all bolts

15. Lightly lubricate the clutch fork ends. Fill the recess ends of the release bearing with grease. Lubricate the input shaft with a light coat of grease.

16. To complete the installation, reverse the removal procedures.

➡The clutch lever must not be moved towards the flywheel until the transaxle is bolted to the engine. Damage to the transaxle, release bearing and clutch fork could occur if this is not followed.

17. Bleed the clutch system and check the clutch operation when finished.

Master and Slave Cylinder Assembly

A hydraulic clutch mechanism is used on all clutch equipped vehicles. This mechanism uses a clutch master cylinder with a remote reservoir and a slave cylinder connected to the master cylinder.

Except on 1990–91 2.3L and 3.1L engines, the clutch master and slave cylinders are removed from the vehicle as an assembly. After assembly the clutch hydraulic system must be bled.

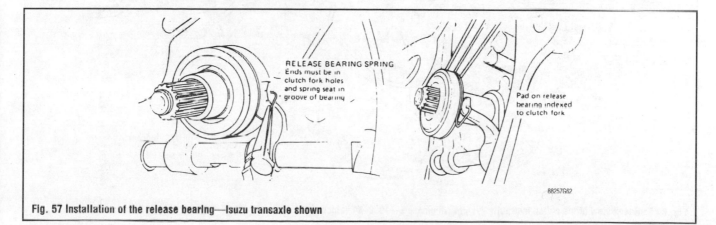

RELEASE BEARING SPRING
Ends must be in clutch fork holes and spring seat in groove of bearing

Pad on release bearing indexed to clutch fork

88257G62

Fig. 57 Installation of the release bearing—Isuzu transaxle shown

REMOVAL & INSTALLATION

All 1988–89 Vehicles; 1990–96 Vehicles With 2.2L Engines

▶ **See Figures 58 and 59**

1. Disconnect the negative battery cable.
2. From inside the vehicle, remove the hush panel.

➡ **If equipped with a 2.8L engine, remove the air cleaner assembly.**

3. Disconnect the clutch master cylinder push rod from the clutch master cylinder.
4. From the front of the dash, remove the trim cover.
5. Remove the clutch master cylinder-to-clutch pedal bracket nuts and the remote reservoir-to-chassis screws.
6. Remove the slave cylinder-to-transaxle nuts and the slave cylinder.
7. Remove the hydraulic system (as a unit) from the vehicle.
   To install:
8. Install the slave cylinder-to-transaxle support, align the push rod to the clutch fork outer lever pocket. Tighten the slave cylinder-to-transaxle support nuts to 16 ft. lbs. (22 Nm).

➡ **If installing a new clutch hydraulic system, DO NOT break the push rod plastic retainer; the straps will break on the first pedal application.**

9. Install the master cylinder-to-clutch pedal bracket. Torque the nuts evenly (to prevent damaging the master cylinder) to 15–20 ft. lbs. and reverse the removal procedures. Remove the pedal restrictor from the push rod. Lubricate the push rod bushing on the clutch pedal; if the bushing is cracked or worn, replace it.
10. If equipped with cruise control, check the switch adjustment at the clutch pedal bracket.

➡ **When adjusting the cruise control switch, do not exert more than 20 lbs. of upward force on the clutch pedal pad for damage to the master cylinder push rod retaining rod can result.**

11. Depress the clutch pedal several times to break the plastic retaining straps; DO NOT remove the plastic button from the end of the push rod.

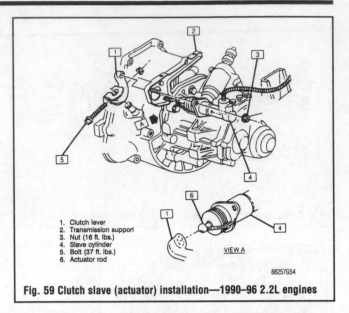

1. Clutch lever
2. Transmission support
3. Nut (16 ft. lbs.)
4. Slave cylinder
5. Bolt (37 ft. lbs.)
6. Actuator rod

Fig. 59 Clutch slave (actuator) installation—1990–96 2.2L engines

12. To complete the installation, reverse the removal procedures.
13. Bleed the clutch hydraulic system.

1990–91 2.3L and 3.1L Engines

MASTER CYLINDER

▶ **See Figure 60**

1. Disconnect the negative battery cable.
2. From inside the vehicle, remove the hush panel.
3. Disconnect the clutch master cylinder push rod from the clutch master cylinder.
4. From the front of the dash, remove the trim cover.

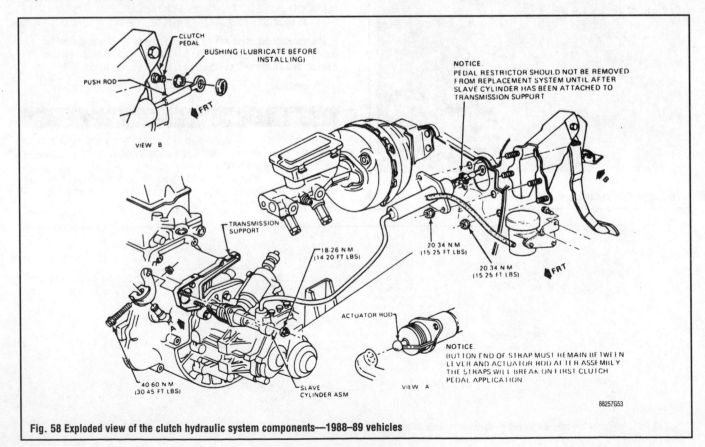

Fig. 58 Exploded view of the clutch hydraulic system components—1988–89 vehicles

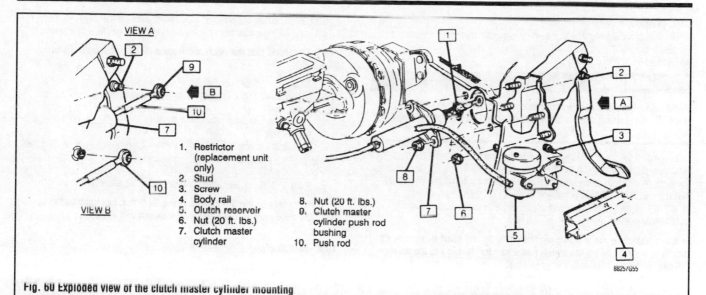

1. Restrictor (replacement unit only)
2. Stud
3. Screw
4. Body rail
5. Clutch reservoir
6. Nut (20 ft. lbs.)
7. Clutch master cylinder
8. Nut (20 ft. lbs.)
9. Clutch master cylinder push rod bushing
10. Push rod

Fig. 60 Exploded view of the clutch master cylinder mounting

5. Remove the air cleaner assembly.
6. Remove the clutch master cylinder-to-clutch pedal bracket nuts and the remote reservoir-to-chassis screws.
7. Disconnect the quick-connect fitting on the hydraulic line and remove the master cylinder from the vehicle.

To install:

8. Connect the quick connect fitting on the hydraulic line and install the master cylinder to the vehicle.
9. With the master cylinder installed to the front of the dash tighten the retaining nuts to 20 ft. lbs. (27 Nm). Install the reservoir mounting screws.
10. Remove the pedal restrictor from the push rod on the new replacement. Lubricate the push rod bushing on the clutch pedal; if the bushing is cracked or worn, replace it.
11. If equipped with cruise control, check the switch adjustment at the clutch pedal bracket.

➡When adjusting the cruise control switch, do not exert more than 20 lbs. of upward force on the clutch pedal pad for damage to the master cylinder push rod retaining rod can result.

12. Install the hush panel.
13. Connect the negative battery cable.

SLAVE CYLINDER

♦ See Figure 61

1. Disconnect the negative battery cable.
2. Remove the air cleaner assembly.
3. Disconnect the slave cylinder nuts at the transaxle.
4. Disconnect the quick connect fitting on the hydraulic line and remove the slave cylinder from the vehicle.

To install:

5. Attach the quick-connect fitting on the hydraulic line and install the master cylinder to the vehicle.
6. Install the slave cylinder to the transmission support bracket, aligning the pushrod into the pocket on the clutch fork lever. Tighten the retaining nuts evenly to 19 ft. lbs. (25 Nm).
7. Depress the clutch pedal several times to break the plastic retaining straps; DO NOT remove the plastic button from the end of the push rod.
8. Install the air cleaner assembly.
9. Connect the negative battery cable.

1992-96 2.3L and 3.1L Engines

1. Disconnect the negative battery cable.
2. From inside the vehicle, remove the hush panel.
3. Remove the air cleaner duct assembly.
4. Disconnect the left fender brace.
5. Remove the battery.

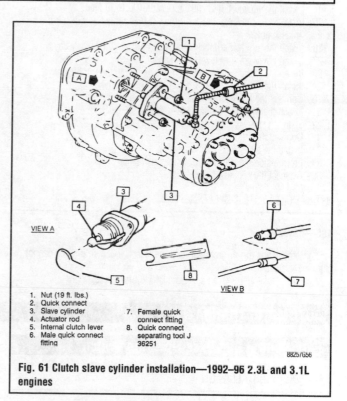

1. Nut (19 ft. lbs.)
2. Quick connect
3. Slave cylinder
4. Actuator rod
5. Internal clutch lever
6. Male quick connect fitting
7. Female quick connect fitting
8. Quick connect separating tool J 36251

Fig. 61 Clutch slave cylinder installation—1992-96 2.3L and 3.1L engines

6. Disconnect the MAT/IAT sensor lead at the air cleaner.
7. Disconnect the Mass Air Flow (MAF) sensor lead.
8. Remove the PCV pipe retaining clamp at the air intake duct.
9. Remove the clamp retaining the air intake duct to the throttle body.
10. Remove the MAF sensor.
11. Remove the air cleaner bracket mounting bolts at the battery tray.
12. Remove the air cleaner, Mass Air Flow sensor and the air intake duct as an assembly.
13. Disconnect the electrical lead at the washer bottle, remove the attaching bolts and remove the bottle.
14. Disconnect the cruise control mounting bracket retaining nuts from the strut tower, if equipped.
15. Disconnect the clutch master cylinder push rod from the clutch pedal.
16. From the front of the dash, remove the trim cover, if so equipped.
17. Remove the clutch master cylinder retaining nuts at the dash.
18. Remove the actuator cylinder-to-transaxle nuts.
19. Remove the hydraulic system (as a unit) from the vehicle.

To install:

20. Install the actuator cylinder-to-transaxle support, align the push rod to the clutch fork outer lever pocket. Tighten the slave cylinder-to-transaxle support nuts to 16 ft. lbs. (22 Nm).

✳✳ WARNING

If installing a new clutch hydraulic system, DO NOT break the push rod plastic retainer; the straps will break on the first pedal application.

21. Install the master cylinder to the front of the dash. Tighten the nuts evenly (to prevent damaging the master cylinder) to 16 ft. lbs. (22 Nm). Remove the pedal restrictor from the push rod. Lubricate the push rod bushing on the clutch pedal; if the bushing is cracked or worn, replace it.

22. If equipped with cruise control, check the switch adjustment at the clutch pedal bracket.

➡When adjusting the cruise control switch, do not exert more than 20 lbs. of upward force on the clutch pedal pad for damage to the master cylinder push rod retaining rod can result.

23. Depress the clutch pedal several times to break the plastic retaining straps; DO NOT remove the plastic button from the end of the push rod.
24. Install the washer bottle and connect the electrical lead.
25. Install the air cleaner, Mass Air Flow (MAF) sensor and the air intake duct as an assembly.
26. Install the air cleaner bracket mounting bolts at the battery tray.
27. Install the Mass Air Flow (MAF) sensor.
28. Install the clamp retaining the air intake duct to the throttle body.
29. Install the PCV pipe retaining clamp at the air intake duct.
30. Connect the MAF sensor lead.
31. Attach the MAT/IAT sensor lead at the air cleaner.
32. Install the battery.
33. Connect the left fender brace.
34. Install the air cleaner duct assembly.
35. From inside the vehicle, install the hush panel.
36. Connect the negative battery cable.

HYDRAULIC SYSTEM BLEEDING

1988–89 Vehicles

1. Remove any dirt or grease around the reservoir cap so that dirt cannot enter the system.
2. Fill the reservoir with an approved DOT 3 brake fluid.

3. Loosen, but do not remove, the bleeder screw on the slave cylinder.
4. Fluid will now flow from the master cylinder to the slave cylinder.

➡It is important that the reservoir remain filled throughout the procedure.

5. Air bubbles should now appear at the bleeder screw.
6. Continue this procedure until a steady stream of fluid without any air bubbles is present.
7. Tighten the bleeder screw. Check the fluid level in the reservoir and refill to the proper mark.
8. The system is now fully bled. Check the clutch operation by starting the engine, pushing the clutch pedal to the floor and placing the transmission in reverse.
9. If any grinding of the gears is noted, repeat the entire procedure.

➡Never under any circumstances reuse fluid that has been in the system. The fluid may be contaminated with dirt and moisture.

1990–96 Vehicles

1. Disconnect the slave cylinder from the transaxle.
2. Loosen the master cylinder mounting attaching nuts. Do not remove the master cylinder.
3. Remove any dirt or grease around the reservoir cap so dirt cannot enter the system. Fill the reservoir with an approved DOT 3 brake fluid.
4. Depress the hydraulic actuator cylinder pushrod approximately 0.787 in. (20mm) into the slave cylinder bore and hold.
5. install the diaphragm and cap on the reservoir while holding the slave cylinder pushrod.
6. Release the slave cylinder pushrod.
7. Hold the slave cylinder vertically with the pushrod end facing the ground.

➡The slave cylinder should be lower than the master cylinder.

8. Press the pushrod into the slave cylinder bore with short 0.390 in. (10mm) strokes.
9. Observe the reservoir for air bubbles. Continue until air bubbles no longer enter the reservoir.
10. Connect the slave cylinder to the transaxle.
11. Tighten the master cylinder attaching nuts.
12. Top-up the clutch master cylinder reservoir.
13. To test the system, start the engine and push the clutch pedal to the floor. Wait 10 seconds and select reverse gear. There should be no gear clash. If clash is present, air may still be present in the system. Repeat bleeding procedure.

AUTOMATIC TRANSAXLE

Park/Neutral And Back-Up Lamp Switch

REMOVAL & INSTALLATION

♦ See Figure 62

1. Disconnect the negative battery cable.
2. Disconnect the shift linkage.
3. Detach the switch electrical connector.
4. Unfasten the mounting bolts and remove the switch from the vehicle.
To install
5. If reinstalling the OLD SWITCH, proceed as follows:
   a. Place the shift shaft in **NEUTRAL**.
   b. Align the flats of the shift shaft with the switch.
   c. Assemble the mounting bolts to the case loosely.
   d. Insert a 3/32 in. (2.4mm) drill bit in the service adjustment hole and rotate the switch until the pin drops to a depth of 9/64 in. (3.6mm).
   e. Tighten the bolts to 22 ft. lbs. (30 Nm).
   f. Remove the gauge pin.

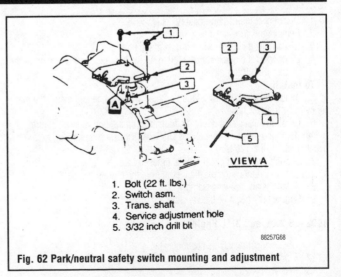

1. Bolt (22 ft. lbs.)
2. Switch asm.
3. Trans. shaft
4. Service adjustment hole
5. 3/32 inch drill bit

Fig. 62 Park/neutral safety switch mounting and adjustment

✳✳ CAUTION

After switch adjustment, verify that the engine will only start in PARK or NEUTRAL. If engine will start in any other position readjust switch.

6. If installing a NEW SWITCH, proceed as follows:
   a. Place the shift shaft in **NEUTRAL**.
   b. Align the flats of the shift shaft with the switch.
   c. Tighten the mounting bolts to 22 ft. lbs. (30 Nm).

➥If the bolt holes do not align with the mounting boss on the transaxle, verify the shift shaft is in NEUTRAL position, do not rotate the switch. The switch is pinned in the NEUTRAL position

7. If the switch has been rotated and the pin broken, the switch an be adjusted by using the Old Switch replacement procedure.

✳✳ CAUTION

After switch installation, verify that the engine will only start in PARK or NEUTRAL. If engine will start in any other position readjust the switch using the replacement of the Old Switch procedure.

ADJUSTMENT

▸ See Figure 62

1. Place the transaxle control shifter assembly in the **NEUTRAL** notch in the detent plate.
2. Loosen the switch attaching screws.
3. Rotate the switch on the shifter assembly to align the service adjustment hole with the carrier tang hole.
4. Insert a 3/32 in. (2.4mm) drill bit in the service adjustment hole and rotate the switch until the pin drops to a depth of 9/64 in. (3.6mm).
5. Tighten the attaching screws to 22 ft. lbs. (30 Nm).
6. Remove the gauge pin.

Transaxle

REMOVAL & INSTALLATION

2.0L and 2.2L Engines

▸ See Figures 63, 64, 65 and 66

1. Disconnect the negative battery cable. Remove the air cleaner and air intake assembly.

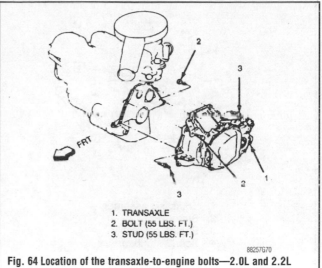

1. TRANSAXLE
2. BOLT (55 LBS. FT.)
3. STUD (55 LBS. FT.)

88257G70

Fig. 64 Location of the transaxle-to-engine bolts—2.0L and 2.2L engines, except 1990 2.2L engine

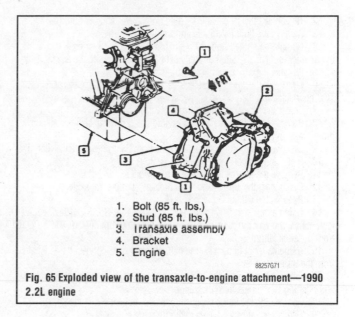

1. Bolt (85 ft. lbs.)
2. Stud (85 ft. lbs.)
3. Transaxle assembly
4. Bracket
5. Engine

88257G71

Fig. 65 Exploded view of the transaxle-to-engine attachment—1990 2.2L engine

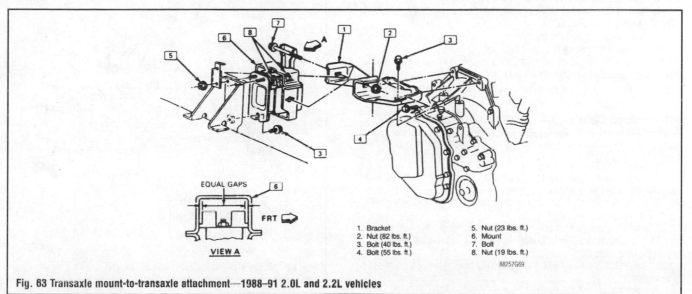

EQUAL GAPS

VIEW A

FRT ➡

1. Bracket	5. Nut (23 lbs. ft.)
2. Nut (82 lbs. ft.)	6. Mount
3. Bolt (40 lbs. ft.)	7. Bolt
4. Bolt (55 lbs. ft.)	8. Nut (19 lbs. ft.)

88257G69

Fig. 63 Transaxle mount-to-transaxle attachment—1988–91 2.0L and 2.2L vehicles

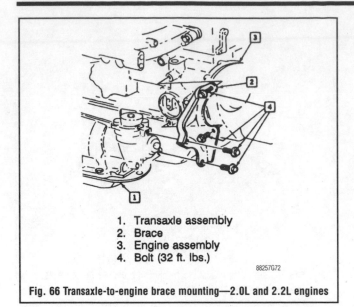

1. Transaxle assembly
2. Brace
3. Engine assembly
4. Bolt (32 ft. lbs.)

88257G72

Fig. 66 Transaxle-to-engine brace mounting—2.0L and 2.2L engines

2. Disconnect the TV cable from the throttle lever and the transaxle.

3. Remove the fluid level indicator and the filler tube.

4. Using the Engine Support Fixture tool No. J–28467 or equivalent and the Adapter tool No. J–35953 or equivalent, install them onto the engine.

5. Remove the wiring harness-to-transaxle nut.

6. Label and disconnect the electrical connectors for the speed sensor, TCC connector and the neutral safety/backup light switch.

7. Disconnect the shift linkage from the transaxle.

8. Remove the top 2 transaxle-to-engine bolts, the transaxle mount and bracket assembly.

9. Disconnect the rubber hose that runs from the transaxle to the vent pipe.

10. Raise and support the front of the vehicle.

11. Remove the front wheels and tire assemblies.

12. Disconnect the shift linkage and bracket from the transaxle.

13. Remove the left side splash shield.

14. Using a modified Drive Axle Seal Protector tool No. J–34754 or equivalent, install one on each drive axle to protect the seal from damage and the joint from possible failure.

15. Using care not to damage the halfshaft boots, disconnect the halfshafts from the transaxle.

16. Remove the transaxle strut. Remove the left side stabilizer link pin bolt and bushing clamp nuts from the support.

17. Remove the left frame support bolts and move it out of the way.

18. Disconnect the speedometer wire from the transaxle.

19. Remove the transaxle converter cover and matchmark the torque converter-to-flywheel for reassembly.

20. Disconnect and plug the transaxle cooler pipes.

21. Remove the transaxle-to-engine support.

22. Using a transmission jack, position and secure the jack to the transaxle. Remove the remaining transaxle-to-engine bolts.

23. Making sure the torque converter does not fall out, remove the transaxle from the vehicle.

➡The transaxle cooler and lines should be flushed any time the transaxle is removed for overhaul or replacing the pump, case or converter.

To install:

24. Put a small amount of grease on the pilot hub of the converter and make sure that the converter is properly engaged with the pump.

25. Raise the transaxle to the engine while guiding the right side halfshaft into the transaxle.

26. Install the lower transaxle mounting bolts and remove the jack.

27. Align the converter with the marks made previously on the flywheel and install the bolts hand tight.

28. Torque the converter bolts to 46 ft. lbs. (62 Nm); retorque the first bolt after the others.

29. Install the remaining components in the reverse of the removal procedure. Make sure all components are tightened securely and all connectors are properly attached.

30. Fill with fluid and check for leaks.

2.3L Engine

♦ See Figures 67, 68 and 69

1. Disconnect the negative battery cable.
2. Drain the cooling system into a suitable container.
3. Detach the heater hoses from the heater core.
4. Disconnect the intake air duct.
5. Remove the cable control cover.
6. Disconnect the throttle and TV cables.
7. Disconnect the shift cable and bracket.
8. Disconnect the throttle cable from the throttle body.
9. Tag and disconnect all vacuum lines and electrical connections.
10. Remove the power steering pump and set aside.
11. Remove the fluid fill tube.
12. Install engine support fixture J 28467–A or equivalent.
13. Remove the 4 top engine to transaxle bolts.
14. Raise and support the vehicle safely.
15. Remove both front tire and wheel assemblies.
16. Disconnect the left inner splash shield from the control arm assembly.
17. Disconnect both lower ball joints.
18. Disconnect the stabilizer shaft links.
19. Remove the front air deflector.
20. Disconnect the left suspension support.
21. Install drive axle seal protectors and remove both drive axles.
22. Disconnect the engine to transaxle brace.
23. Remove the flywheel cover.
24. Remove the flywheel-to-torque converter bolts.
25. Disconnect the transaxle cooler pipes.
26. Disconnect the ground wires from the engine-to-transaxle bolt.
27. Disconnect the cooler pipe brace.
28. Disconnect the exhaust brace.
29. Remove the bolts from the engine and transaxle mount.
30. Remove the transaxle mount to body bolts.
31. Support the transaxle with a jack.
32. Remove the remaining engine-to-transaxle bolts and remove the transaxle.

To install:

33. Put a small amount of grease on the pilot hub of the converter and make sure that the converter is properly engaged with the pump.

34. Raise the transaxle to the engine while guiding the right side halfshaft into the transaxle.

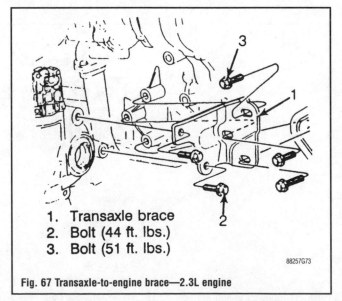

1. Transaxle brace
2. Bolt (44 ft. lbs.)
3. Bolt (51 ft. lbs.)

88257G73

Fig. 67 Transaxle-to-engine brace—2.3L engine

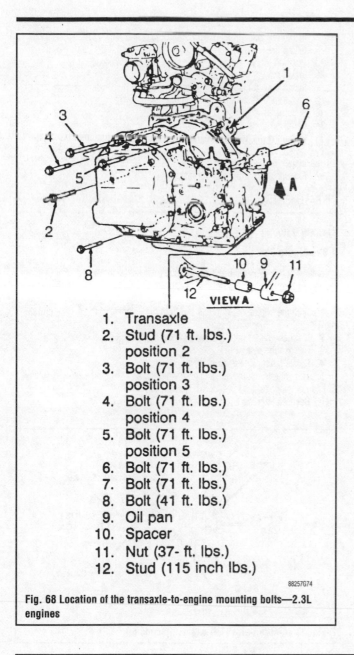

1. Transaxle
2. Stud (71 ft. lbs.)
   position 2
3. Bolt (71 ft. lbs.)
   position 3
4. Bolt (71 ft. lbs.)
   position 4
5. Bolt (71 ft. lbs.)
   position 5
6. Bolt (71 ft. lbs.)
7. Bolt (71 ft. lbs.)
8. Bolt (41 ft. lbs.)
9. Oil pan
10. Spacer
11. Nut (37- ft. lbs.)
12. Stud (115 inch lbs.)

88257G74

Fig. 68 Location of the transaxle-to-engine mounting bolts—2.3L engines

35. Install the lower engine to transaxle bolts.
36. Install the transaxle mount to body bolts.
37. Install the bolts to the engine and transaxle mount.
38. Install the remaining components in the reverse of the removal procedure. Make sure all components are tightened securely and all connectors are properly attached.
39. Fill the cooling system.
40. Connect the negative battery cable.
41. Fill the transaxle.
42. Adjust the TV cable and shift linkage as necessary.

2.8L and 3.1L Engines

♦ See Figures 70, 71 and 72

1. Disconnect the negative battery cable. Remove the air cleaner, bracket, mass air flow (MAF) sensor and air tube as an assembly.
2. Disconnect the exhaust crossover from the right side manifold and remove the left side exhaust manifold. Raise and support the manifold/crossover assembly.
3. Disconnect the TV cable from the throttle lever and the transaxle.
4. Remove the vent hose and the shift cable from the transaxle.
5. Remove the fluid level indicator and the filler tube.
6. Using the Engine Support Fixture tool No. J–28467 or equivalent and the Adapter tool No. J–35953 or equivalent, install them on the engine.
7. Remove the wiring harness-to-transaxle nut.
8. Label and disconnect the wires for the speed sensor, TCC connector and the neutral safety/backup light switch.
9. Remove the upper transaxle-to-engine bolts.
10. Remove the transaxle-to-mount through bolt, the transaxle mount bracket and the mount.
11. Raise and support the vehicle.
12. Remove the front wheel and tire assemblies.
13. Disconnect the shift cable bracket from the transaxle.
14. Remove the left side splash shield.
15. Using a modified Drive Axle Seal Protector tool No. J–34754 or equivalent, install one on each drive axle to protect the seal from damage and the joint from possible failure.
16. Using care not to damage the halfshaft boots, disconnect the halfshafts from the transaxle.
17. Remove the torsional and lateral strut from the transaxle. Remove the left side stabilizer link pin bolt.
18. Remove the left frame support bolts and move it out of the way.
19. Disconnect the speedometer wire from the transaxle.
20. Remove the transaxle converter cover and matchmark the converter-to-flywheel for assembly.
21. Disconnect and plug the transaxle cooler pipes.
22. Remove the transaxle-to-engine support.
23. Using a transmission jack, position and secure it to the transaxle. Remove the remaining transaxle-to-engine bolts.

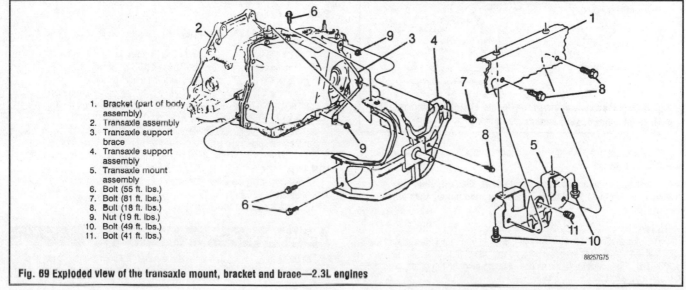

1. Bracket (part of body assembly)
2. Transaxle assembly
3. Transaxle support brace
4. Transaxle support assembly
5. Transaxle mount assembly
6. Bolt (55 ft. lbs.)
7. Bolt (81 ft. lbs.)
8. Bolt (18 ft. lbs.)
9. Nut (19 ft. lbs.)
10. Bolt (49 ft. lbs.)
11. Bolt (41 ft. lbs.)

88257G75

Fig. 69 Exploded view of the transaxle mount, bracket and brace—2.3L engines

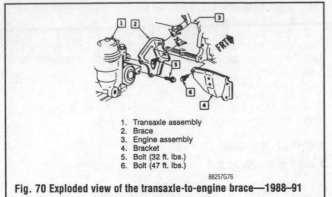

1. Transaxle assembly
2. Brace
3. Engine assembly
4. Bracket
5. Bolt (32 ft. lbs.)
6. Bolt (47 ft. lbs.)

88257G76

Fig. 70 Exploded view of the transaxle-to-engine brace—1988–91 2.8L and 3.1L engines shown, 1992–96 similar

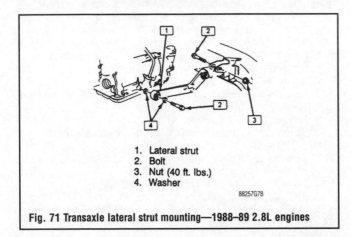

1. Lateral strut
2. Bolt
3. Nut (40 ft. lbs.)
4. Washer

88257G78

Fig. 71 Transaxle lateral strut mounting—1988–89 2.8L engines

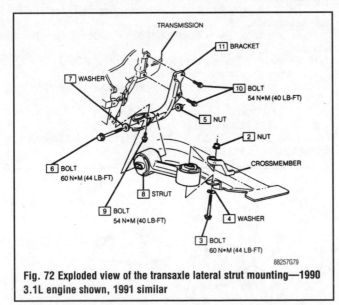

Fig. 72 Exploded view of the transaxle lateral strut mounting—1990 3.1L engine shown, 1991 similar

24. Make sure that the torque converter does not fall out and remove the transaxle from the vehicle.

➡The transaxle cooler and lines should be flushed any time the transaxle is removed for overhaul, to replace the pump, case or converter.

To install:

25. Put a small amount of grease on the pilot hub of the converter and make sure that the converter is properly engaged with the pump.

26. Raise the transaxle to the engine while guiding the right side halfshaft into the transaxle.

27. Install the lower transaxle mounting bolts and remove the jack.
28. Install the cooler lines at the transmission.
29. Position the left side drive axle shaft into the transaxle.
30. Install the left frame support bolts.
31. Install the left stabilizer shaft bushing clamp nuts at the support.
32. Install the left stabilizer bar link pin bolt.
33. Seat the drive axles in the transaxle.
34. Remove the drive axle seal protectors.
35. Install the remaining components in the reverse of the removal procedure.
36. Install the negative battery cable.
37. Fill with fluid and check for leaks.

ADJUSTMENTS

Throttle Valve (TV) Cable

▶ **See Figure 73**

Setting of the TV cable must be done by rotating the throttle lever at the carburetor or throttle body. Do not use the accelerator pedal to rotate the throttle lever.

1. With the engine off, depress and hold the reset tab at the engine end of the TV cable.
2. Move the slider until it stops against the fitting.
3. Release the rest tab.
4. Rotate the throttle lever to its full travel.
5. The slider must move (ratchet) toward the lever when the lever is rotated to its full travel position.
6. Recheck after the engine is hot and road test the vehicle.

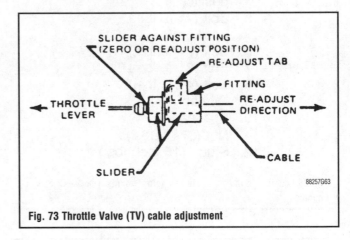

Fig. 73 Throttle Valve (TV) cable adjustment

Park/Lock Cable

▶ **See Figures 74, 75, 76 and 77**

1. Place the floor shift lever in the **PARK** position.
2. Turn the column lock cylinder to the **LOCK** position.
3. Unseat the body housing lock from the body housing.
4. With the body housing still attached to the shift control mounting bracket, adjust the outer cable conduit to obtain proper location for the white plastic housing in the ignition switch.
5. There must be no gap between the metal terminal stop and the protruding end of the white plastic collar.
6. The white plastic collar must either be flush or recessed approximately 0.04 inch (1 mm) within the ignition park lock housing.
7. While holding the outer cable conduit in position, seat the body housing lock in the body housing.
8. Check for proper operation.

Halfshaft

The procedures for automatic transaxle halfshaft removal, installation and overhaul are the same as those outlined earlier for the manual transaxle.

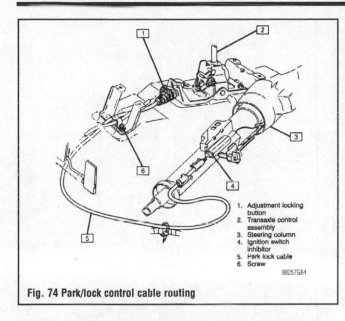

1. Adjustment locking button
2. Transaxle control assembly
3. Steering column
4. Ignition switch inhibitor
5. Park lock cable
6. Screw

88257G64

Fig. 74 Park/lock control cable routing

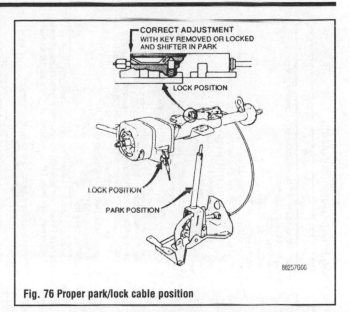

CORRECT ADJUSTMENT
WITH KEY REMOVED OR LOCKED
AND SHIFTER IN PARK

LOCK POSITION

LOCK POSITION

PARK POSITION

88257G66

Fig. 76 Proper park/lock cable position

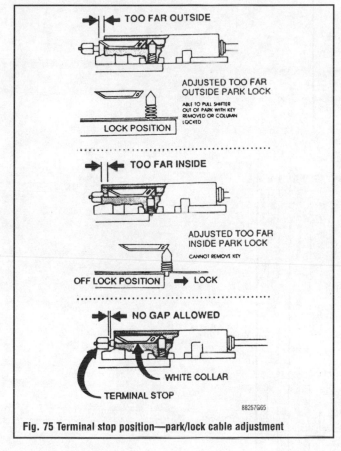

TOO FAR OUTSIDE

ADJUSTED TOO FAR OUTSIDE PARK LOCK
ABLE TO PULL SHIFTER OUT OF PARK WITH KEY REMOVED OR COLUMN LOCKED

LOCK POSITION

TOO FAR INSIDE

ADJUSTED TOO FAR INSIDE PARK LOCK
CANNOT REMOVE KEY

OFF LOCK POSITION → LOCK

NO GAP ALLOWED

WHITE COLLAR

TERMINAL STOP

88257G65

Fig. 75 Terminal stop position—park/lock cable adjustment

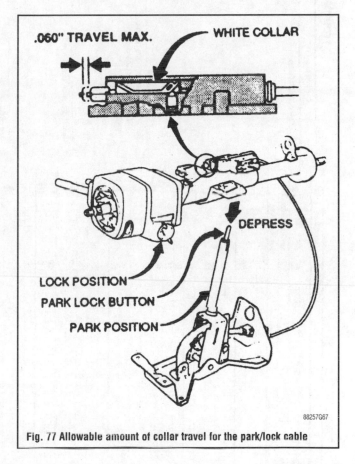

.060" TRAVEL MAX.

WHITE COLLAR

DEPRESS

LOCK POSITION

PARK LOCK BUTTON

PARK POSITION

88257G67

Fig. 77 Allowable amount of collar travel for the park/lock cable

TORQUE SPECIFICATIONS

Component	ft. lbs.	Inch lbs.	Nm
Automatic Transaxle			
Neutral safety/back-up light switch	22		30
Transaxle-to-engine bolts	see illustrations		
Transaxle mounting bolts	see illustrations		
Back-up light switch			
1988-90 vehicles		84	9
1991-96 vehicles	24		33
Clutch			
Clutch start switch		53	6
Master cylinder retaining nuts	20		27
Pressure plate-to-flywheel bolts			
1988-89 vehicles	15		20
1990-96 vehicles	16		22
Step 1	12		16
Step 2 (plus an additional 30° rotation)	15		20
Slave (actuator) cylinder nuts			
1988-89 vehicles	16		22
1990-96 2.2L engines	16		22
1990 2.3L and 3.1L engines	19		25
Halfshaft			
Cross-groove design			
Inner seal clamp	130		176
Outer seal clamp	100		136
Tri-pot design			
Inner seal clamp	130		176
Outer seal clamp	130		176
Intermediate shaft			
Shaft housing-to-engine	18		25
Housing-to-bracket bolts			
1988-89 vehicles	37		50
Shaft-to-engine bolts			
1990 vehicles	38		52
1991 vehicles	37		50
1992-96 vehicles	35		47
Manual transaxle			
Transaxle-to-engine bolts	see illustrations		
Transaxle mounting	see illustrations		

8825TC01

Troubleshooting Basic Clutch Problems

Problem	Cause
Excessive clutch noise	Throwout bearing noises are more audible at the lower end of pedal travel. The usual causes are: • Riding the clutch • Too little pedal free-play • Lack of bearing lubrication A bad clutch shaft pilot bearing will make a high pitched squeal, when the clutch is disengaged and the transmission is in gear or within the first 2" of pedal travel. The bearing must be replaced. Noise from the clutch linkage is a clicking or snapping that can be heard or felt as the pedal is moved completely up or down. This usually requires lubrication. Transmitted engine noises are amplified by the clutch housing and heard in the passenger compartment. They are usually the result of insufficient pedal free-play and can be changed by manipulating the clutch pedal.
Clutch slips (the car does not move as it should when the clutch is engaged)	This is usually most noticeable when pulling away from a standing start. A severe test is to start the engine, apply the brakes, shift into high gear and SLOWLY release the clutch pedal. A healthy clutch will stall the engine. If it slips it may be due to: • A worn pressure plate or clutch plate • Oil soaked clutch plate • Insufficient pedal free-play
Clutch drags or fails to release	The clutch disc and some transmission gears spin briefly after clutch disengagement. Under normal conditions in average temperatures, 3 seconds is maximum spin-time. Failure to release properly can be caused by: • Too light transmission lubricant or low lubricant level • Improperly adjusted clutch linkage
Low clutch life	Low clutch life is usually a result of poor driving habits or heavy duty use. Riding the clutch, pulling heavy loads, holding the car on a grade with the clutch instead of the brakes and rapid clutch engagement all contribute to low clutch life.

9064TC00

8

SUSPENSION AND STEERING

WHEELS

Wheel Assembly

REMOVAL & INSTALLATION

♦ See Figure 1

1. Park the vehicle on a level surface.
2. Remove the jack, tire iron and, if necessary, the spare tire from their storage compartments.
3. Check the owner's manual or refer to Section 1 of this manual for the jacking points on your vehicle. Then, place the jack in the proper position.
4. If equipped with lug nut trim caps, remove them by either unscrewing or pulling them off the lug nuts, as appropriate. Consult the owner's manual, if necessary.
5. If equipped with a wheel cover or hub cap, insert the tapered end of the tire iron in the groove and pry off the cover.
6. Apply the parking brake and block the diagonally opposite wheel with a wheel chock or two.

➡Wheel chocks may be purchased at your local auto parts store, or a block of wood cut into wedges may be used. If possible, keep one or two of the chocks in your tire storage compartment, in case any of the tires has to be removed on the side of the road.

7. If equipped with an automatic transmission/transaxle, place the selector lever in **P** or Park; with a manual transmission/transaxle, place the shifter in Reverse.
8. With the tires still on the ground, use the tire iron/wrench to break the lug nuts loose.

➡If a nut is stuck, never use heat to loosen it or damage to the wheel and bearings may occur. If the nuts are seized, one or two heavy hammer blows directly on the end of the bolt usually loosens the rust. Be careful, as continued pounding will likely damage the brake drum or rotor.

9. Using the jack, raise the vehicle until the tire is clear of the ground. Support the vehicle safely using jackstands.
10. Remove the lug nuts, then remove the tire and wheel assembly.

To install:

11. Make sure the wheel and hub mating surfaces, as well as the wheel lug studs, are clean and free of all foreign material. Always remove rust from the wheel mounting surface and the brake rotor or drum. Failure to do so may cause the lug nuts to loosen in service.
12. Install the tire and wheel assembly and hand-tighten the lug nuts.
13. Using the tire wrench, tighten all the lug nuts, in a crisscross pattern, until they are snug.
14. Raise the vehicle and withdraw the jackstand, then lower the vehicle.
15. Using a torque wrench, tighten the lug nuts in a crisscross pattern to 100 ft. lbs. (140 Nm). Check your owner's manual or refer to Section 1 of this manual for the proper tightening sequence.

✳✳ WARNING

Do not overtighten the lug nuts, as this may cause the wheel studs to stretch or the brake disc (rotor) to warp.

16. If so equipped, install the wheel cover or hub cap. Make sure the valve stem protrudes through the proper opening before tapping the wheel cover into position.
17. If equipped, install the lug nut trim caps by pushing them or screwing them on, as applicable.
18. Remove the jack from under the vehicle, and place the jack and tire iron/wrench in their storage compartments. Remove the wheel chock(s).
19. If you have removed a flat or damaged tire, place it in the storage compartment of the vehicle and take it to your local repair station to have it fixed or replaced as soon as possible.

INSPECTION

Inspect the tires for lacerations, puncture marks, nails and other sharp objects. Repair or replace as necessary. Also check the tires for treadwear and air pressure as outlined in Section 1 of this manual. Check the wheel assemblies for dents, cracks, rust and metal fatigue. Repair or replace as necessary.

Wheel Lug Studs

REPLACEMENT

With Disc Brakes

♦ See Figures 2 and 3

1. Raise and support the appropriate end of the vehicle safely using jackstands, then remove the wheel.
2. Remove the brake pads and caliper. Support the caliper aside using wire or a coat hanger. For details, please refer to Section 9 of this manual.
3. Remove the hub and bearing assembly, then lift off the rotor. For details on wheel bearing removal, installation and adjustment, please refer to the procedure located in this section.
4. Properly support the rotor using press bars, then drive the stud out using an C-clamp tool J 6627–A, or equivalent, and remove the stud from the hub and bearing assembly.

➡If the tool is not available, CAREFULLY drive the old stud out using a blunt drift. MAKE SURE the rotor is properly and evenly supported or it may be damaged.

To install:

5. Clean the stud hole with a wire brush and start the new stud with a hammer and drift pin. Do not use any lubricant or thread sealer.

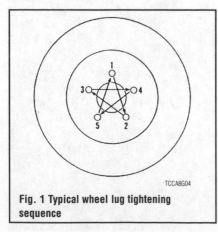

TCCA8G04

Fig. 1 Typical wheel lug tightening sequence

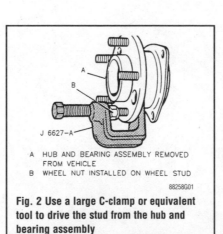

A HUB AND BEARING ASSEMBLY REMOVED FROM VEHICLE
B WHEEL NUT INSTALLED ON WHEEL STUD

J 6627–A

88258G01

Fig. 2 Use a large C-clamp or equivalent tool to drive the stud from the hub and bearing assembly

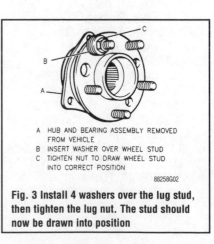

A HUB AND BEARING ASSEMBLY REMOVED FROM VEHICLE
B INSERT WASHER OVER WHEEL STUD
C TIGHTEN NUT TO DRAW WHEEL STUD INTO CORRECT POSITION

88258G02

Fig. 3 Install 4 washers over the lug stud, then tighten the lug nut. The stud should now be drawn into position

➡Start the lug stud through the bore in the hub, then position about 4 flat washers over the stud and thread the lug nut. Hold the hub/rotor while tightening the lug nut, and the stud should be drawn into position. **MAKE SURE THE STUD IS FULLY SEATED, then remove the lug nut and washers.**

6. Install the rotor and adjust the wheel bearings.
7. Install the brake caliper and pads.
8. Install the wheel, then remove the jackstands and carefully lower the vehicle.
9. Tighten the lug nuts to the proper torque.

With Drum Brakes

♦ **See Figures 4 and 5**

1. Raise the vehicle and safely support it with jackstands, then remove the wheel.

2. Remove the brake drum.
3. If necessary to provide clearance, remove the brake shoes, as outlined in Section 9 of this manual.
4. Using a large C-clamp and socket, press the stud from the axle flange.
5. Coat the serrated part of the stud with liquid soap and place it into the hole.

To install:

6. Position about 4 flat washers over the stud and thread the lug nut. Hold the flange while tightening the lug nut, and the stud should be drawn into position. MAKE SURE THE STUD IS FULLY SEATED, then remove the lug nut and washers.
7. If applicable, install the brake shoes.
8. Install the brake drum.
9. Install the wheel, then remove the jackstands and carefully lower the vehicle.
10. Tighten the lug nuts to the proper torque.

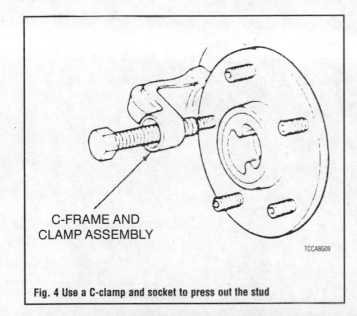

Fig. 4 Use a C-clamp and socket to press out the stud

C-FRAME AND CLAMP ASSEMBLY

TCCA8G09

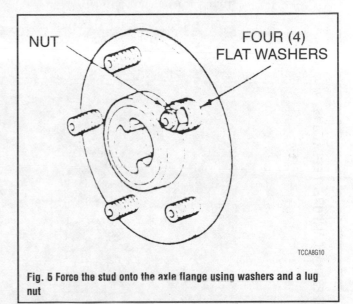

NUT

FOUR (4) FLAT WASHERS

TCCA8G10

Fig. 5 Force the stud onto the axle flange using washers and a lug nut

FRONT SUSPENSION

♦ **See Figures 6 and 7**

The Corsica and Beretta use MacPherson strut front suspension designs. A MacPherson strut combines the functions of a shock absorber and an upper suspension member (upper arm) into 1 unit. The strut is surrounded by a coil spring, which provides normal front suspension functions.

The strut bolts to the body shell at its upper end, and to the steering knuckle at the lower end. The strut pivots with the steering knuckle by means of a sealed mounting assembly at the upper end which contains a preloaded, non-adjustable bearing.

The steering knuckle is connected to the chassis at the lower end by a conventional lower control arm, and pivots in the arm in a preloaded ball joint of standard design. The knuckle is fastened to the ball joint stud by means of a castellated nut and cotter pin.

Advantages of the MacPherson strut design, aside from its relative simplicity, include reduced weight and friction, minimal intrusion into the engine and passenger compartments, and ease of service.

✳✳ **WARNING**

When servicing suspension components always install drive axle boot protector J–33162, in order to prevent damage to the drive axle boot.

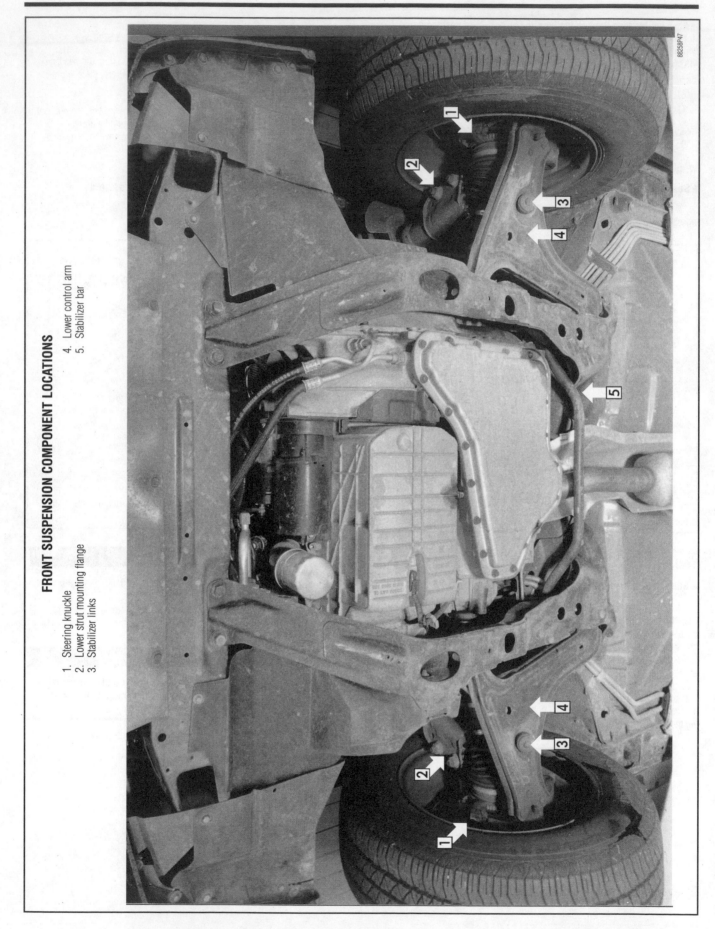

FRONT SUSPENSION COMPONENT LOCATIONS

1. Steering knuckle
2. Lower strut mounting flange
3. Stabilizer links
4. Lower control arm
5. Stabilizer bar

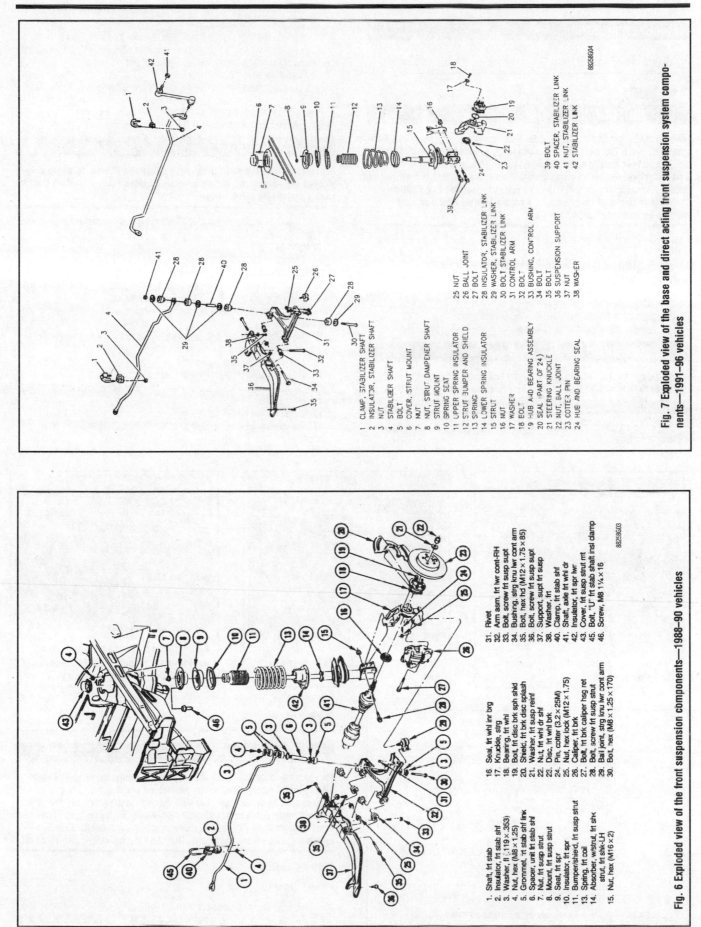

88258G04

1 CLAMP, STABILIZER SHAFT
2 INSULATOR, STABILIZER SHAFT
3 NUT
4 STABILIZER SHAFT
5 BOLT
6 COVER, STRUT MOUNT
7 NUT
8 NUT, STRUT DAMPENER SHAFT
9 STRUT MOUNT
10 SPRING SEAT
11 UPPER SPRING INSULATOR
12 STRUT BUMPER AND SHIELD
13 SPRING
14 LOWER SPRING INSULATOR
15 STRUT
16 NUT
17 WASHER
18 BOLT
19 HUB AND BEARING ASSEMBLY
20 SEAL (PART OF 24)
21 STEERING KNUCKLE
22 NUT, BALL JOINT
23 COTTER PIN
24 HUB AND BEARING SEAL

25 NUT
26 BALL JOINT
27 BOLT
28 INSULATOR, STABILIZER LINK
29 WASHER, STABILIZER LINK
30 BOLT STABILIZER LINK
31 CONTROL ARM
32 BOLT
33 BUSHING, CONTROL ARM
34 BOLT
35 BOLT
36 SUSPENSION SUPPORT
37 NUT
38 WASHER

39 BOLT
40 SPACER, STABILIZER LINK
41 NUT, STABILIZER LINK
42 STABILIZER LINK

Fig. 7 Exploded view of the base and direct acting front suspension system components—1991–96 vehicles

88258G03

1. Shaft, frt stab
2. Insulator, frt stab shf
3. Nut, hex (M8 × 1.25)
4. Washer, fl (.119 x .353)
5. Grommet, frt stab shf link
6. Spacer, unit frt stab shf
7. Nut, frt susp strut
8. Mount, frt susp strut
9. Seal, frt spr
10. Insulator, frt spr
11. Bumper/shield, frt susp strut
12. Spring, frt coil
13. Spring, frt coil
14. Absorber, w/strut, frt shk-LH
    strut, frt shk-LH
15. Nut, hex (M16×2)

16. Seal, frt whl lnr brg
17. Knuckle, strg
18. Bearing, frt whl
19. Bolt, frt disc brk sph shld
20. Shield, frt brk disc splash
21. Washer, frt susp reinf
22. Nut, frt whl dr shf
23. Disc, frt whl brk
24. Pin, cotter (3.2 × 25M)
25. Nut, hex lock (M12 × 1.75)
26. Caliper, frt brk
27. Bolt, frt brk caliper hsg ret
28. Bolt, screw frt susp strut
29. Ball joint, strg knu lwr cont arm
30. Bolt, hex (M8 × 1.25 ×170)

31. Rivet
32. Arm asm, frt lwr cont-RH
33. Bolt, screw frt susp supt
34. Bushing, strg knu lwr cont arm
35. Bolt, hex hd (M12 × 1.75 × 85)
36. Bolt, screw frt susp supt
37. Support, supt frt susp
38. Washer, frt
40. Clamp, frt stab shf
41. Shaft, axle frt whl dr
42. Insulator, frt spr lwr
43. Cover, frt susp strut frt
45. Bolt, "U" frt stab shaft insl clamp
46. Screw, M8 1¼ × 16

Fig. 6 Exploded view of the front suspension components—1988–90 vehicles

MacPherson Struts

REMOVAL & INSTALLATION

▶ **See Figures 8 and 9**

✳ CAUTION

The struts retain the springs under tremendous pressure even when removed from the car. For these reasons, several expensive special tools and substantial specialized knowledge are required to safely and effectively work on these parts. We recommend that if spring or shock absorber repair work is required, you remove the strut or struts involved and take them to a repair facility which is fully equipped and familiar with the car.

1. Open the hood, then unfasten the nuts and bolt securing the top of the strut.
2. Break the lug nuts loose, then raise and safely support the vehicle, allowing the suspension to hang free:
   a. Place jackstands under the front suspension supports.
   b. Carefully lower the vehicle slightly so the weight of the vehicle rest on the suspension supports and NOT on the control arms.
3. Remove the wheel and tire assembly.

✳ WARNING

Care must be taken not to allow the tri-pot joints from being over extended when either end of the shaft is disconnected. Over extension could result in separation of the internal components.

4. Install modified inner drive axle seal protector J 34754, to prevent possible boot damage.

5. Remove the brake line bracket.
6. Remove the cotter pin and nut, then separate the tie rod end from the strut assembly, using tool J 24319-01 or equivalent 2-jawed puller to press the tie rod out of the strut bracket. Discard the cotter pin.
7. Scribe the strut flange as follows:
   a. Using a sharp tool, scribe the knuckle along the lower outboard strut radius.
   b. Scribe the strut flange on the inboard side along the curve of the knuckle.
   c. Make a scribe mark across the strut/knuckle interface.

✳ WARNING

When removing the strut from the vehicle, be careful to avoid chipping or scratching the spring coating. Damage to the coating could cause premature strut failure.

8. Unfasten the strut-to-knuckle retaining bolts, then carefully remove the strut from the vehicle.
To install:
9. Place the strut into position and hand-tighten the nuts attaching the top of the strut to the body.
10. Align the steering knuckle with the strut flange scribe marks and install the bolts and nuts and tighten to 133 ft. lbs. (180 Nm).
11. Position the tie rod end into the strut assembly, then install the nut and new cotter pin.
12. Tighten the nuts and bolt attaching the top of the strut assembly to the body to 18 ft. lbs. (25 Nm).
13. Install the brake line bracket.
14. Remove the modified drive axle seal protector.
15. Slightly raise the vehicle and remove the jackstands from under the suspension supports.
16. Install the tire and wheel assembly, then carefully lower the vehicle.
17. Take the vehicle to a reputable repair shop and have the front end alignment checked.

Remove any retainers blocking access to the upper strut nuts

Unfasten the upper strut-to-body retaining nuts

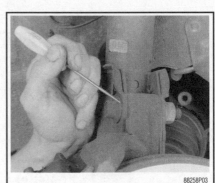

Before removal, scribe the area around the lower strut mounting bolts, to promote proper alignment upon reassembly

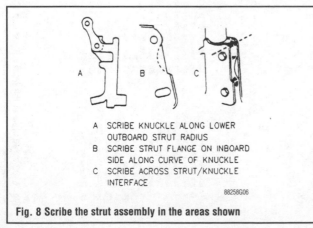

A SCRIBE KNUCKLE ALONG LOWER
  OUTBOARD STRUT RADIUS
B SCRIBE STRUT FLANGE ON INBOARD
  SIDE ALONG CURVE OF KNUCKLE
C SCRIBE ACROSS STRUT/KNUCKLE
  INTERFACE

88258G06

Fig. 8 Scribe the strut assembly in the areas shown

OVERHAUL

✳ CAUTION

This procedure requires the use of a spring compressor and several other special tools. It cannot be performed without them. If you do not have access to these tools, DO NOT attempt to disassemble the strut. The coil springs are retained under extremely high pressure. They can exert enough force to cause serious injury or even death. Exercise extreme caution when disassembling the strut for coil spring removal.

1988–90 Vehicles

▶ **See Figure 10**

1. Remove the strut assembly from the vehicle.
2. Clamp the spring compressor, tool J-26584, in a vise. Position the strut

assembly in the bottom adapter of the compressor and install the special tool J26584–400 (see illustration). Be sure that the adapter captures the strut and that the locating pins are engaged.

3. Place the top adapter, J–26584–430, on the strut cap. Note that the adapter has drilled holes designating each specific vehicle.

4. Using a 1 in. socket, turn the screw on top of the compressor clockwise until the top support flange contacts the adapters. Continue turning the screw until the coil spring is compressed approximately ½ in. (13mm); 4 complete turns. Never bottom the spring or the strut damper rod.

5. Unscrew the nut from the strut damper shaft and place the J–34013–27 alignment rod on the top of the damper shaft. Use this rod to guide the damper shaft straight down through the spring cap while decompressing the spring.

Unfasten the two lower strut assembly mounting bolts

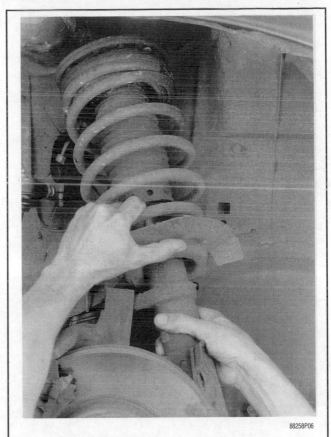

After removing the retainers, maneuver the strut assembly out of the vehicle

Support the strut assembly, then remove the lower mounting bolts

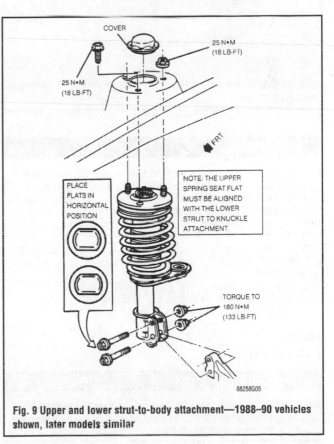

Fig. 9 Upper and lower strut-to-body attachment—1988–90 vehicles shown, later models similar

6. Turn the compressor adjusting screw counterclockwise until the spring tension has been relieved. Remove the adapters and then remove the coil spring.

To assemble:

7. Clamp the strut compressor body J 26584 in a vise.

8. Position the strut assembly in the compressor using bottom adapter J–26584–400. Make sure the adapter captures the strut and the locating pins are engaged.

9. Position the spring on the strut. Make sure the spring is properly seated on the bottom of the spring plate.

10. Install all shields, bumpers and insulators on the spring seat.

11. Install the spring strut seat assembly on top of the spring and make sure they are centered together and aligned properly.

➡ **The ends of the spring coil are to be located within 0 to 10 mm from the end of the groove in the upper insulator and 10 to 15mm from the end of the groove in the lower insulator.**

12. Place the top adapter, J–26584–430, on the strut cap. Lower the compressor to capture the cap. Pull up the damper rod to full extension and clamp in place with J–34013–20.

13. Insert alignment rod, J–34013–27 through the bearing and spring caps and position on top of the damper rod. Compress the spring and guide the damper rod through the bearing cap using the alignment rod during compression.

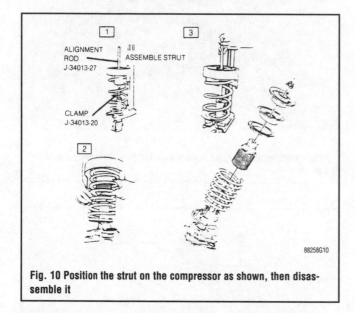

Fig. 10 Position the strut on the compressor as shown, then disassemble it

❈❈ WARNING

During compression of the spring be sure to use the guide rod to guide the shaft through the exact center of the bearing. If the threads of the damper rod catch on the bearing cap and prevent the rod from passing cleanly through the bearing, stop compressing immediately. Decompress the spring and begin again.

14. Compress the spring until approximately 1 in. (25mm) of the damper rod protrudes through the bearing cap. Do not compress the spring any further. Install and tighten the nut to 59 ft. lbs. (80 Nm).

15. Remove the damper rod clamp J–34013–20.

16. Back off the spring compressor and remove the strut assembly.

17. Install the strut in the vehicle.

1991–96 Vehicles

◆ See Figure 11

❈❈ WARNING

When removing or overhauling the strut, be careful to avoid chipping or scratching the spring coating. Damage to the coating could cause premature component failure.

1. Remove the strut assembly from the vehicle.

2. Mount strut compressor J 34013 in holding fixture J 3289–20.

3. Mount the strut into the strut compressor. Note that the strut compressor has strut mounting holes drilled for the specific vehicle.

4. Compress the strut about ½ its height after the initial contact with the top cap.

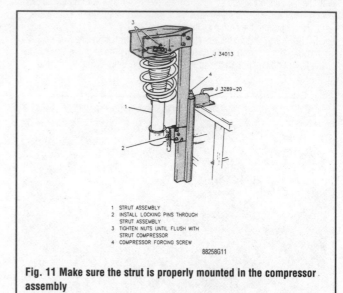

```
1  STRUT ASSEMBLY
2  INSTALL LOCKING PINS THROUGH
   STRUT ASSEMBLY
3  TIGHTEN NUTS UNTIL FLUSH WITH
   STRUT COMPRESSOR
4  COMPRESSOR FORCING SCREW
```

88258G11

Fig. 11 Make sure the strut is properly mounted in the compressor assembly

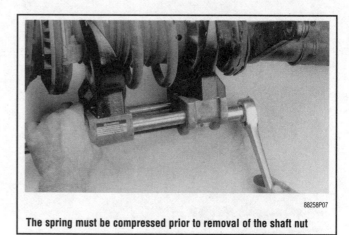

88258P07

The spring must be compressed prior to removal of the shaft nut

❈❈ WARNING

NEVER bottom the spring or dampener rod.

5. Remove the nut from the strut dampener shaft and place guiding rod, J 34013–27, on top of the dampener shaft. Use this rod to guide the dampener shaft straight down through the bearing cap while decompressing the spring.

6. Disassemble the strut and spring components.

To assemble:

7. Install the bearing cap onto the strut compressor, if previously removed.

8. Mount the strut into the strut compressor using the bottom locking pin only. Extend the dampener shaft and install clamp J 34013–20 on the dampener shaft.

9. Install the spring over the dampener and swing the assembly up so that the upper locking pin can be installed. Install the upper insulator, shield bumper and upper spring seat. be sure the flat on the upper spring seat is facing in the proper direction. The spring seat flat should be facing the same direction as the centerline of the strut assembly spindle.

10. Install the guiding rod and turn the forcing screw while the guiding rod centers the assembly. When the threads on the dampener shaft are visible,

It may be necessary to use a back-up wrench to loosen the dampener shaft nut

Remove the strut mount

Remove the strut dust shield

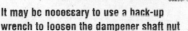

Remove the spring upper insulator . . .

. . . then remove the jounce bumper from the insulator

Remove the spring lower insulator

remove the guiding rod and install the nut. Use a crowfoot line wrench, while holding the dampener shaft with a socket and tighten the nut to 65 ft. lbs. (88 Nm).

11. Remove the clamp.
12. Install the strut assembly in the vehicle.

Lower Ball Joint

INSPECTION

1. Raise and safely support the front of the car, allowing the suspension to hang free.
2. Grasp the wheel at the top and the bottom and shake it in an in-and-out motion. Check for any horizontal movement of the steering knuckle relative to the lower control arm. Replace the ball joint if such movement is noted.
3. If the ball stud is disconnected from the steering knuckle and any looseness is detected, or if the ball stud can be twisted in its socket using finger pressure, replace the ball joint.

REMOVAL & INSTALLATION

Only a lower ball joint is used in each lower arm. The MacPherson strut design does not use an upper ball joint.

1988–90 Vehicles

♦ See Figure 12

1. With the vehicle on the ground, break the lug nuts loose.
2. Raise and safely support the vehicle, then remove the wheel and tire assembly.
3. Use a ⅛ in. (3mm) drill bit to drill a hole through the center of each of the 3 ball joint rivets.

4. Use a ½ in. (13mm) drill bit to drill completely through the rivet.
5. Use a hammer and punch to remove the rivets. Drive them out from the bottom.
6. Use the special tool J–29330 or equivalent ball joint removal tool to separate the ball joint from the steering knuckle (see illustration). Don't forget to remove and discard the cotter pin.

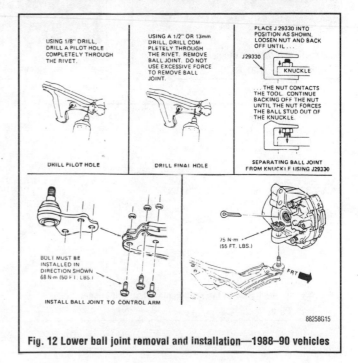

Fig. 12 Lower ball joint removal and installation—1988–90 vehicles

7. Disconnect the stabilizer bar from the lower control arm, then remove the ball joint.

To install:

8. Install the new ball joint into the control arm with the 3 bolts supplied as shown and tighten to 50 ft. lbs. (68 Nm).

9. Installation of the remaining components is in the reverse order of removal.

10. Tighten the castellated nut on the ball joint to 55 ft. lbs. (75 Nm) and use a new cotter pin.

11. Install the wheel and tire assembly, then carefully lower the vehicle.

12. Take the vehicle to a reputable repair shop to have the toe setting checked and adjusted if necessary.

1991–96 Vehicles

▶ See Figure 13

1. With the vehicle on the ground, break the lug nuts loose.
2. Raise and safely support the vehicle.
3. Place jackstands under the suspension supports.
   a. Carefully lower the vehicle slightly, so the weight of the vehicle rest on the suspension supports and NOT on the control arms.
4. Remove the wheel and tire assembly.

✳✳ WARNING

Care must be taken not to allow the tri-pot joints from being over extended when either end of the shaft is disconnected. Over extension could result in separation of the internal components.

5. Install modified inner drive axle seal protector J 34754, to prevent possible boot damage.

✳✳ WARNING

Failure to use the recommended tool could result in ball joint and seal damage.

6. Remove the cotter pin and nut from the ball joint and separate the ball joint from the steering knuckle, using tool J 29330 or equivalent.

7. Use a ⅛ in. (3mm) drill bit to drill a hole through the center of each of the 3 ball joint rivets.

8. Use a ½ in. (13mm) drill bit to drill completely through the rivet.

9. Use a hammer and punch to remove the rivets. Drive them out from the bottom.

10. Unfasten the nut attaching the stabilizer link to the stabilizer shaft.

11. Remove the ball joint from the steering knuckle and control arm.

To install:

12. Position the ball joint to the control arm and install the bolts and nuts as shown in the ball joint kit. Tighten to 50 ft. lbs. (68 Nm).

13. Insert the ball stud through the steering knuckle and install the ball joint nut. Tighten the nut to 26 ft. lbs. (35 Nm) plus an additional 60 degree rotation for 1991 vehicles, and to a minimum of 41 ft lbs. (55 Nm) and a maximum of 50 ft. lbs. (65 Nm) for 1992–96 vehicles.

14. Install a new cotter pin.

15. Install the nut attaching the stabilizer link to the stabilizer shaft and tighten to 13 ft. lbs. (17 Nm) for 1991 vehicles, except GTZ models, and 70 ft. lbs. (95 Nm) for 1991 GTZ models and all 1992–96 models.

16. Remove the modified inner drive belt seal protector.

17. Slightly raise the vehicle and remove the jackstands from under the suspension supports.

18. Install the tire and wheel assembly, then carefully lower the vehicle.

19. Take the vehicle to a reputable repair shop and have the front end alignment checked.

Remove and discard the cotter pin from the lower ball joint nut . . .

88258P14

. . . then remove the lower ball joint nut

88258P15

Separate the lower ball joint from the steering knuckle

88258P16

1 SERVICE BALL JOINT
2 BALL JOINT MOUNTING BOLTS
3 NUT
4 LOWER CONTROL ARM
5 STEERING KNUCKLE
6 NUT – 55 N·m (41 LBS. FT.) MINIMUM TORQUE
   65 N·m (48 LBS. FT.) MAXIMUM TORQUE
   TO INSTALL PIN
7 PIN

88258G17

Fig. 13 Exploded view of the replacement ball joint assembly— 1991–96 vehicles

Stabilizer Bar

REMOVAL & INSTALLATION

1988–90 Vehicles

▶ See Figure 14

1. Open the hood, then install engine support tool J 28467, as instructed by the manufacturer.

2. Raise and safely support the vehicle, allowing the front lower control arms to hang free.

3. Remove the left front wheel and tire.

4. Disconnect the stabilizer shaft from the control arms.

5. Disconnect the stabilizer shaft from the support assemblies.

6. Loosen the front bolts and remove the bolts from the rear and center of the support assemblies.

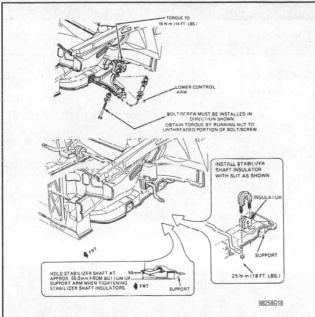

Fig. 14 Exploded view of the stabilizer shaft and bushings—1988–90 vehicles

To install:

7. When installing the stabilizer, loosely assemble all components while insuring that the stabilizer is centered, side to side.

8. Tighten the stabilizer shaft to stabilizer link nut to 14 ft. lbs. (18 Nm) and the stabilizer clamp nuts to 18 ft. lbs. (25 Nm).

9. The remainder of installation is the reverse of the removal procedure.

1991–96 Vehicles

▶ See Figures 15 and 16

1. Raise and safely support the vehicle, allowing the front lower control arms to hang free.

2. Remove the front wheel and tire assemblies.

3. Unfasten the nuts attaching the stabilizer shafts to the stabilizer links.

4. Remove the stabilizer shaft-to-suspension support clamps.

5. Remove the bolts from the rear and center of the support assemblies, then loosen the front bolts.

6. Remove the stabilizer shaft with the insulators from the vehicle.

To install:

➡ **When installing the stabilizer, loosely assemble all components while insuring that the stabilizer is centered, side to side.**

7. Position the stabilizer shaft with the insulators, into the vehicle.

8. Install the clamps securing the stabilizer shaft to the suspension support assemblies and hand-tighten the retainers.

9. Place the suspension support assemblies into position, then install the retaining bolts hand-tight.

10. Install the nuts attaching the stabilizer shaft to the stabilizer links and tighten to 13 ft. lbs. (17 Nm) for 1991 vehicles, except GTZ models and to 70 ft. lbs. (95 Nm) for 1991 GTZ models. For 1992–96 vehicles, tighten to 15–22 ft. lbs. for vehicles with the base suspension and to 70 ft. lbs. (95 Nm) for vehicles with the direct acting suspension.

11. Tighten the suspension support bolts; rear first, center second and front third to 66 ft. lbs. (90 Nm) for 1991–94 vehicles or to 89 ft. lbs. (120 Nm) for 1995–96 vehicles.

12. Tighten the clamp nuts to 17–22 ft. lbs. (23–30 Nm)

13. Install the front wheel and tire assemblies, then carefully lower the vehicle.

14. Take the vehicle to a reputable repair shop and have the front end alignment checked.

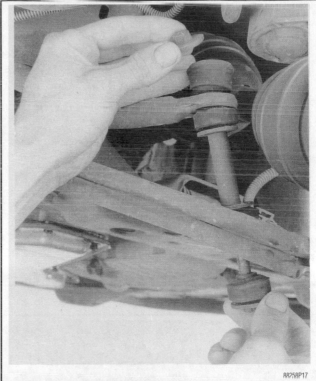

Remove the stabilizer link retaining nut and bolt

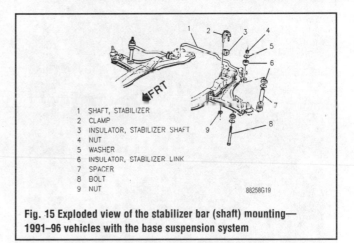

1 SHAFT, STABILIZER
2 CLAMP
3 INSULATOR, STABILIZER SHAFT
4 NUT
5 WASHER
6 INSULATOR, STABILIZER LINK
7 SPACER
8 BOLT
9 NUT

Fig. 15 Exploded view of the stabilizer bar (shaft) mounting—1991–96 vehicles with the base suspension system

Stabilizer Link

REMOVAL & INSTALLATION

1. Raise and safely support the vehicle, allowing the front lower control arms to hang free.

2. Remove the front wheel and tire assemblies.

3. Unfasten the nut attaching the stabilizer link to the stabilizer shaft.

4. On vehicles equipped with the base suspension system, remove the bolt, insulators, spacer and washers.

5. On vehicles equipped with the direct acting stabilizer system, remove the nut attaching the stabilizer link to the strut bracket.

6. Remove the stabilizer link from the vehicle.

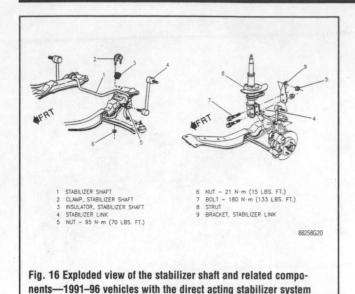

1 STABILIZER SHAFT
2 CLAMP, STABILIZER SHAFT
3 INSULATOR, STABILIZER SHAFT
4 STABILIZER LINK
5 NUT – 95 N·m (70 LBS. FT.)
6 NUT – 21 N·m (15 LBS. FT.)
7 BOLT – 180 N·m (133 LBS. FT.)
8 STRUT
9 BRACKET, STABILIZER LINK

88258G20

Fig. 16 Exploded view of the stabilizer shaft and related components—1991–96 vehicles with the direct acting stabilizer system

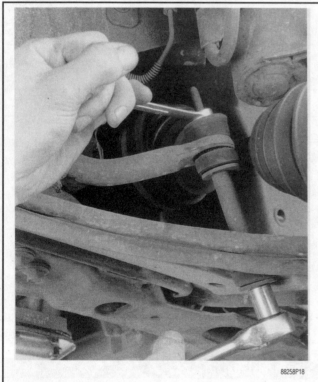

88258P18

Tighten the stabilizer link retainers

To install:

7. For vehicles equipped with the base suspension system, install the bolt, insulators, spacer and washers.

8. Install the nut securing the stabilizer link to the shaft. Tighten the nut to 15–20 ft. lbs. (20–30 Nm) for vehicles with the base suspension system. For vehicles with direct acting suspension, tighten the nut to 70 ft. lbs. (95 Nm).

9. For vehicles with the direct acting stabilizer system, install the nuts attaching the stabilizer link to the strut bracket and tighten to 70 ft. lbs. (95 Nm).

10. Install the front wheel and tire assemblies, then carefully lower the vehicle.

Lower Control Arm

REMOVAL & INSTALLATION

1988–90 Vehicles

▶ **See Figure 17**

1. Raise and safely support the front of the vehicle. Remove the wheel and tire assembly.

2. Disconnect the stabilizer bar from the control arm and/or support, as outliner earlier in this section.

3. Separate the ball joint from the steering knuckle using tool J 29330 or equivalent.

4. Remove the 2 control arm-to-support bolts, then remove the control arm from the vehicle.

5. If control arm support bar removal is necessary, unscrew the 6 mounting bolts and remove the support.

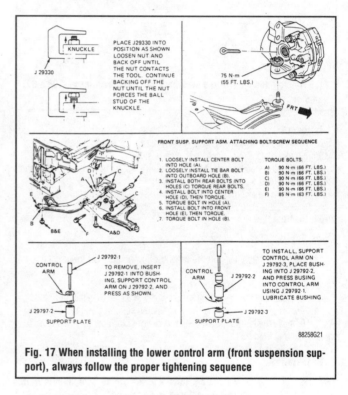

88258G21

Fig. 17 When installing the lower control arm (front suspension support), always follow the proper tightening sequence

To install:

6. Installation is the reverse of the removal procedure.

7. Tighten the control arm support rail bolts in the sequence shown in the accompanying figure.

8. Have a reputable repair shop check the toe and adjust as necessary.

1991–96 Vehicles

▶ **See Figure 18**

1. Break the lug nuts loose, then raise and safely support the vehicle.

   a. Place jackstands under the suspension supports.

   b. Carefully lower the vehicle slightly so the weight of the vehicle rest on the suspension supports and NOT on the control arms.

2. Remove the wheel and tire.

✵✵ WARNING

Care must be taken not to allow the tri-pot joints from being over extended when either end of the shaft is disconnected.

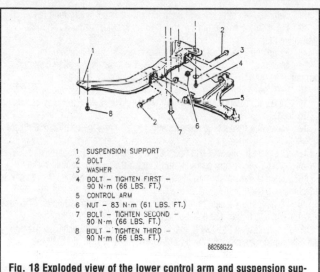

1 SUSPENSION SUPPORT
2 BOLT
3 WASHER
4 BOLT – TIGHTEN FIRST –
  90 N·m (66 LBS. FT.)
5 CONTROL ARM
6 NUT – 83 N·m (61 LBS. FT.)
7 BOLT – TIGHTEN SECOND –
  90 N·m (66 LBS. FT.)
8 BOLT – TIGHTEN THIRD –
  90 N·m (66 LBS. FT.)

88258G22

Fig. 18 Exploded view of the lower control arm and suspension support assembly—1993 shown, other years similar

Over extension could result in separation of the internal components.

3. Install modified inner drive axle seal protector J 34754, to prevent possible boot damage.

4. Remove the cotter pin and nut from the ball joint and separate the ball joint from the steering knuckle, using tool J 29330 or equivalent. Discard the cotter pin.

✳✳ WARNING

Failure to use the recommended tool could result in ball joint and seal damage.

5. On 1991 models equipped with the 2.3L engine only, install overhead engine support, J 28467–A or equivalent and remove the nuts attaching the front engine mount crossmember to the suspension support.

6. Remove the bolts attaching the suspension support to the vehicle.

7. Remove the bolts attaching the control arm to the suspension support.

To install:

8. Position the control arm and loosely install the bolts attaching the control arm to the suspension support.

9. Place the suspension support into position, guiding the ball joint into the steering knuckle and loosely install the bolts.

10. Install the nuts attaching the stabilizer shaft clamp to the suspension support and tighten to 17 ft. lbs. (23 Nm).

11. On 1991 models equipped with the 2.3L engine only, install the nuts attaching the front engine mount crossmember to the suspension support and tighten to 30 ft. lbs. (40 Nm).

12. Install the nut attaching the ball joint to the steering knuckle and tighten to 26 ft. lbs. (35 Nm) plus a 60 degree rotation for 1991 vehicles, and 41–50 ft. lbs. (55–65 Nm) for 1992–96 vehicles.

13. Install the nuts attaching the stabilizer link to the stabilizer shaft and tighten to 13 ft. lbs. (17 Nm) for except GTZ models and 70 ft. lbs. (95 Nm) for GTZ models.

14. Remove the modified drive axle seal protector.

15. Slightly raise the vehicle and remove the jackstands from under the suspension supports.

16. Install the tire and wheel assembly.

17. On 1991 models equipped with the 2.3L engine, remove the overhead engine support, J 28467–A or equivalent.

18. With the vehicle at curb height, tighten the suspension support attaching bolts, as follows:

   a. For 1991 vehicles, tighten the rear first, center second and front third, to 66 ft. lbs. (90 Nm).

   b. For 1992–96 vehicles, tighten the center first to 66 ft. lbs. (90 Nm), front second to 65 ft. lbs. (88 Nm) and rear third to 65 ft. lbs. (88 Nm).

19. With the vehicle at curb height tighten the control arm attaching bolts to 44 ft. lbs. (60 Nm) plus an additional 60 degree rotation.

20. Check the front end alignment.

CONTROL ARM BUSHING REPLACEMENT

♦ See Figure 19

→Lower control arm bushing replacement requires the use of Front Control Arm Horizontal Bushing Service Set (J 29792) and Front Control Arm Rear Vertical Bushing Service Set (J 39971) or equivalent tools.

1. Remove the lower control arm from the vehicle.

2. Coat the threads of tool J 29792 with an extreme pressure lubricant.

3. Install the bushing removal tools, as shown in the accompanying figure.

4. Remove the control arm bushings.

To install:

5. Install the lower control arm bushings. To make installation easier, coat the outer casing of the new bushing with a suitable lubricant.

6. Install the lower control arm in the vehicle, as outlined earlier in this section.

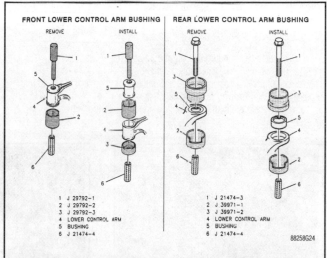

FRONT LOWER CONTROL ARM BUSHING | REAR LOWER CONTROL ARM BUSHING
REMOVE   INSTALL   REMOVE   INSTALL

1 J 29792–1
2 J 29792–2
3 J 29792–3
4 LOWER CONTROL ARM
5 BUSHING
6 J 21474–4

1 J 21474–3
2 J 39971–1
3 J 39971–2
4 LOWER CONTROL ARM
5 BUSHING
6 J 21474–4

88258G24

Fig. 19 Exploded view of front and rear lower control arm bushing removal

Front Engine Mount Crossmember

REMOVAL & INSTALLATION

This procedure applies to 1991 2.3L engines only.

1. Install overhead engine support, J 28467–A or equivalent.

2. Remove the front engine mount upper nut.

3. Carefully raise the engine, making sure to follow the tool manufacturers instructions.

4. Raise the vehicle and support it safely.

5. Remove the front engine mount-to-crossmember nuts.

6. Remove the engine mount crossmember with the front engine mount.

7. Separate the engine mount from the crossmember.

To install:

8. Place the engine mount crossmember into position with the front engine mount.

9. Install the crossmember plates through the suspension supports, then loosely install the nuts.

10. Position the front engine mount to the crossmember and loosely install the nuts.

11. Carefully lower the vehicle, then lower the engine.

12. Remove the engine support tool.

13. Install the front engine mount upper nut to 55 ft. lbs. (75 Nm).

14. Tighten the lower engine mount nuts to 30 ft. lbs. (40 Nm) and the engine mount crossmember plate nuts to 40 ft. lbs. 54 Nm).

Front Hub and Bearing

REMOVAL & INSTALLATION

▶ See Figures 20, 21 and 22

✲✲ WARNING

You will need a special tool to pull the bearing free of the halfshaft (drive axle), GM tool no. J–28733 or the equivalent. You should also use a halfshaft boot protector, GM tool no. J–33162 or the equivalent to protect the parts from damage on cars equipped with the 2.0L engine and boot protector J–34754 on all other engines.

1. With the vehicle weight on the tires, break the hub nut loose.
2. Raise and safely support the vehicle. Remove the wheel and tire assembly.
3. Install a boot cover over the outer CV-joint boot.
4. Remove the brake caliper and support it aside (on a wire); do not allow the caliper to hang on the brake line.
5. Remove the rotor.
6. Remove the hub nut.
7. Unfasten the hub and bearing mounting bolts.
8. Remove the brake rotor splash shield.
9. Install J 28733 or equivalent hub puller tool, then turn the bolt and press the hub and bearing from the halfshaft.
10. Disconnect the stabilizer link from the lower control arm.
11. Remove the cotter pin and the ball joint-to-knuckle attaching nut.
12. Separate the ball joint from the steering knuckle, using J 29330 or equivalent tool.
13. Remove the halfshaft from the knuckle and support it aside.
14. Matchmark the strut in relationship to the knuckle, for alignment purposes and remove the strut-to-knuckle attaching nuts.
15. Remove the knuckle from the strut.
16. Using a brass drift, remove the inner knuckle seal.

To install:

17. Clean and inspect the steering knuckle bore and the bearing mating surfaces.
18. Lubricate a new seal and the bearing with a high temperature wheel bearing grease, then using a driving tool, install the seal in the knuckle.
19. Connect the ball joint to the knuckle and install the ball joint-to-knuckle attaching nut, hand tight.
20. Position the knuckle to the strut and install the attaching bolts. Align the matchmarks and tighten the attaching bolts to 129 ft. lbs. (175 Nm) for 1988–90 vehicles, and to 133 ft. lbs. (180 Nm) for 1991–96 vehicles. Tighten the ball joint-to-knuckle attaching nut to 55 ft. lbs. (75 Nm) for 1988–90 vehicles, and to 26 ft. lbs. (35 Nm) plus 60 degree rotation for 1991–96 vehicles.
21. Install a new O-ring between the bearing and knuckle assembly.
22. Install the splash shield, hub/bearing assembly, to the knuckle and install the attaching bolts. Tighten the attaching bolts to 67 ft. lbs. (90 Nm) for 1988–90 vehicles and 70 ft. lbs. (95 Nm) for 1991–92 vehicles.
23. Remove the boot cover from the outer CV-joint boot and slide the halfshaft into the knuckle assembly.
24. Install the hub washer and attaching nut, (use and new nut) on the halfshaft. Tighten the attaching nut to a partial torque of 71 ft. lbs. (100 Nm), at this time.

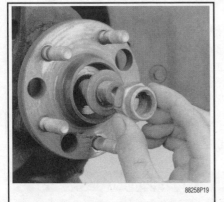

Remove the hub nut

Remove the hub and bearing assembly mounting bolts

Attach a suitable puller to the hub and bearing to separate it from the halfshaft

Remove the hub and bearing assembly from the vehicle

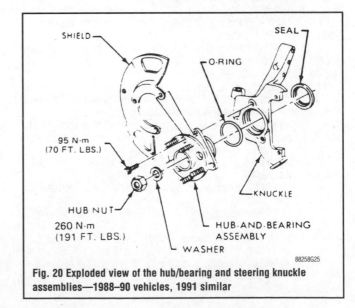

Fig. 20 Exploded view of the hub/bearing and steering knuckle assemblies—1988–90 vehicles, 1991 similar

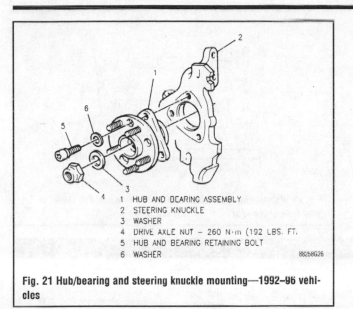

1 HUB AND BEARING ASSEMBLY
2 STEERING KNUCKLE
3 WASHER
4 DRIVE AXLE NUT – 260 N·m (192 LBS. FT.)
5 HUB AND BEARING RETAINING BOLT
6 WASHER

88258G26

Fig. 21 Hub/bearing and steering knuckle mounting—1992–96 vehicles

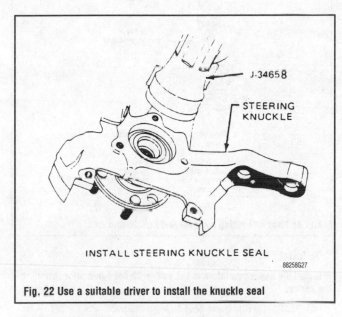

INSTALL STEERING KNUCKLE SEAL

88258G27

Fig. 22 Use a suitable driver to install the knuckle seal

25. Connect the stabilizer link to the lower control arm.
26. Install the brake rotor, caliper and the wheel/tire assembly.
27. Lower the vehicle and final-tighten the hub nut to 191 ft. lbs. (259 Nm).

Wheel Alignment

If the tires are worn unevenly, if the vehicle is not stable on the highway or if the handling seems uneven in spirited driving, the wheel alignment should be checked. If an alignment problem is suspected, first check for improper tire inflation and other possible causes. These can be worn suspension or steering components, accident damage or even unmatched tires. If any worn or damaged components are found, they must be replaced before the wheels can be properly aligned. Wheel alignment requires very expensive equipment and involves minute adjustments which must be accurate; it should only be performed by a trained technician. Take your vehicle to a properly equipped shop.

Following is a description of the alignment angles which are adjustable on most vehicles and how they affect vehicle handling. Although these angles can apply to both the front and rear wheels, usually only the front suspension is adjustable.

CASTER

♦ See Figure 23

Looking at a vehicle from the side, caster angle describes the steering axis rather than a wheel angle. The steering knuckle is attached to a control arm or strut at the top and a control arm at the bottom. The wheel pivots around the line between these points to steer the vehicle. When the upper point is tilted back, this is described as positive caster. Having a positive caster tends to make the wheels self-centering, increasing directional stability. Excessive positive caster makes the wheels hard to steer, while an uneven caster will cause a pull to one side. Overloading the vehicle or sagging rear springs will affect caster, as will raising the rear of the vehicle. If the rear of the vehicle is lower than normal, the caster becomes more positive.

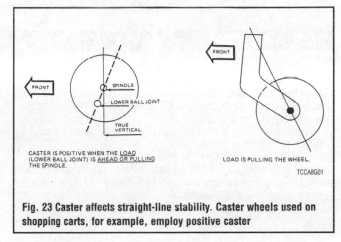

TCCA8G01

Fig. 23 Caster affects straight-line stability. Caster wheels used on shopping carts, for example, employ positive caster

CAMBER

♦ See Figure 24

Looking from the front of the vehicle, camber is the inward or outward tilt of the top of wheels. When the tops of the wheels are tilted in, this is negative camber; if they are tilted out, it is positive. In a turn, a slight amount of negative camber helps maximize contact of the tire with the road. However, too much negative camber compromises straight-line stability, increases bump steer and torque steer.

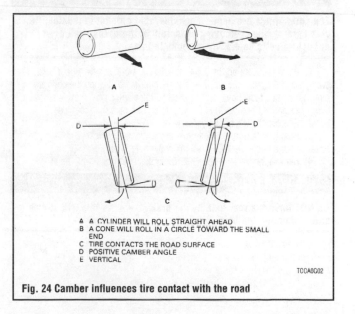

A A CYLINDER WILL ROLL STRAIGHT AHEAD
B A CONE WILL ROLL IN A CIRCLE TOWARD THE SMALL END
C TIRE CONTACTS THE ROAD SURFACE
D POSITIVE CAMBER ANGLE
E VERTICAL

TCCA0G02

Fig. 24 Camber influences tire contact with the road

TOE

♦ **See Figure 25**

Looking down at the wheels from above the vehicle, toe angle is the distance between the front of the wheels, relative to the distance between the back of the wheels. If the wheels are closer at the front, they are said to be toed-in or to have negative toe. A small amount of negative toe enhances directional stability and provides a smoother ride on the highway.

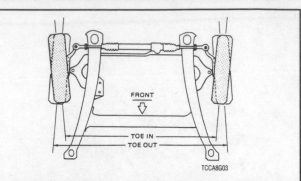

Fig. 25 With toe-in, the distance between the wheels is closer at the front than at the rear

REAR SUSPENSION

The Corsica and Beretta have a semi-independent rear suspension system which consists of an axle with trailing arms and a twisting cross beam, for the Corsica and a tubular trailing arm for the Beretta, 2 coil springs and 2 shock absorbers, 2 upper spring insulators and 2 spring compression bumpers. The axle assembly attaches to the body through a rubber bushing located at the front of each control arm. The brackets are integral with the underbody side rails. A stabilizer bar is available as an option.

Two coil springs are used, each being retained between a seat in the underbody and one on the control arm. A rubber cushion is used to isolate the coil spring upper end from the underbody seat, while the lower end sits on a combination bumper and spring insulator.

The double acting shock absorbers are filled with a calibrated amount of fluid and sealed during production. They are non-adjustable, non-refillable and cannot be disassembled.

A single unit hub and bearing assembly is bolted to both ends of the rear axle assembly; it is a sealed unit and must be replaced if found to be defective.

Coil Springs

REMOVAL & INSTALLATION

♦ **See Figure 26**

※※ CAUTION

The coil springs are under a considerable amount of tension. Be very careful when removing or installing them; they can exert enough force to cause very serious injuries.

1. Raise and support the car on a hoist. Do not use a twin-post hoist. The swing arc of the axle may cause it to slip from the hoist when the bolts are removed. If a suitable hoist is not available, raise and safely support the vehicle using jackstands, then position an adjustable jack under the rear axle.
2. Remove the wheel and tire assembly.
3. Remove the right and left brake hose attaching brackets, allowing the hoses to hang freely. Do NOT disconnect the fluid lines.
4. Remove both shock absorber lower attaching bolts from the axle.

※※ WARNING

Do NOT have the rear axle by the brake hose, as this will stretch and/or damage the brake lines.

5. Carefully lower the rear axle, then remove the coil spring and/or insulator from the vehicle.

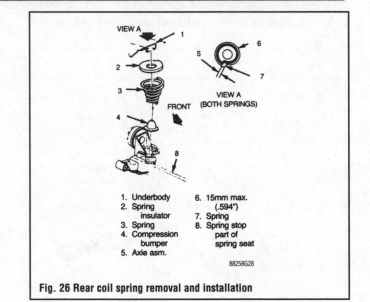

1. Underbody
2. Spring insulator
3. Spring
4. Compression bumper
5. Axle asm.
6. 15mm max. (.594")
7. Spring
8. Spring stop part of spring seat

Fig. 26 Rear coil spring removal and installation

To install:

➡Install the upper insulators to the body with adhesive prior installing the spring.

6. Position the spring and insulator in the seats and raise the axle. The ends of the upper coil of the spring must be must be positioned in the seat of the body and within 7/16 in. (15mm) of the spring stop.

➡**It will be necessary to bring the axle assembly to curb height prior to tightening the bolts on the shocks.**

7. Attach the lower shock absorbers to the rear axle, then tighten the mounting nut and/or bolt, as follows:
    a. For 1988 models, tighten the lower mount nut and bolt to 35 ft. lbs. (47 Nm) for Corsica and to 43 ft. lbs. (58 Nm) for Beretta.
    b. For 1989–90 models, tighten the lower mount nut and bolt to 35 ft. lbs. (47 Nm) for Corsica and 21 ft. lbs. (28 Nm) for Beretta.
    c. For 1991–96 models, tighten the lower mount nut for Beretta to 35 ft. lbs. (47 Nm) and the lower mount bolt for Corsica to 35 ft. lbs. (47 Nm).
8. Attach the brake line brackets to the body.
9. Install the wheel and tire assembly.
10. Remove the jackstands, then carefully lower the vehicle.

REAR SUSPENSION COMPONENT LOCATIONS

1. Shock absorber
2. Spring
3. Spring seat
4. Rear axle

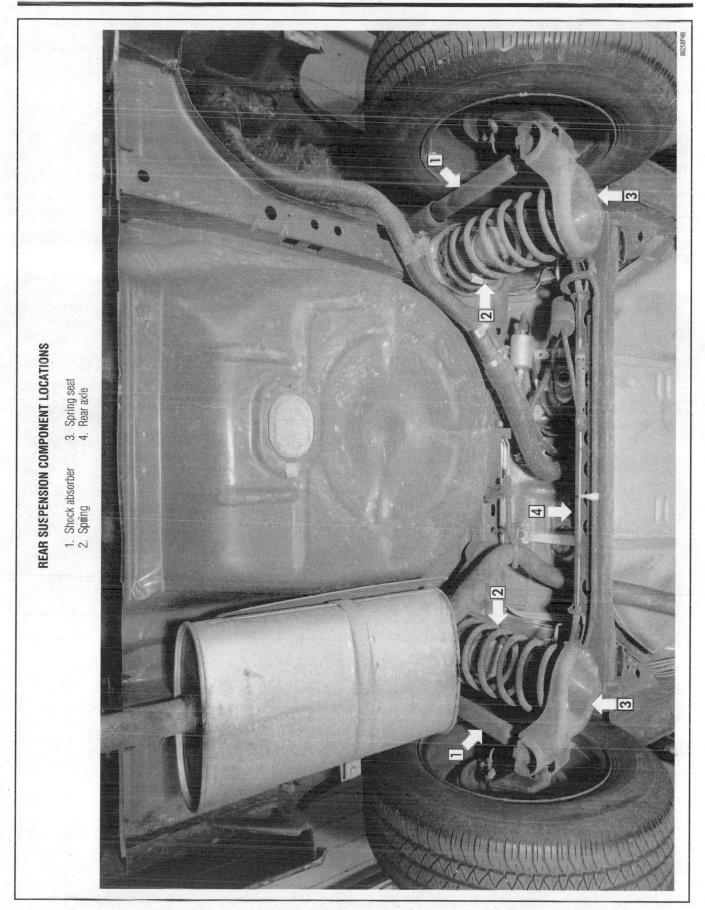

88258P48

Shock Absorbers

REMOVAL & INSTALLATION

▶ **See Figures 27, 28 and 29**

1. Open the trunk lid, remove any necessary trim panels or nut cover, and remove the upper shock absorber nut.

> ✳✳✳ **WARNING**
>
> **When replacing both shock absorbers, remove one at a time. Do not remove both shock absorbers at once, as suspending the rear axle at full length could result in damage to the brake lines and hoses.**

2. Raise the and safely support the vehicle, the support the rear axle assembly with adjustable jackstands to remove the weight from the shock absorbers.

3. Remove the lower attaching bolt or nut, then remove the shock absorber from the vehicle.

To install:

4. Position the shock and install the lower attaching retainer hand-tight.

5. Carefully lower the vehicle enough to guide the upper stud through the body opening and install the upper shock mounting nut loosely.

6. Tighten the lower mounting retainer as follows:

   a. For 1988 models, tighten the lower mount nut and bolt to 35 ft. lbs. (47 Nm) for Corsica and 43 ft. lbs. (58 Nm) for Beretta.

   b. For 1989–90 models, tighten the lower mount nut and bolt to 35 ft. lbs. (47 Nm) for Corsica and 21 ft. lbs. (28 Nm) for Beretta.

   c. For 1991–96 models, tighten the lower mount nut for Beretta to 35 ft. lbs. (47 Nm) and the lower mount bolt for Corsica to 35 ft. lbs. (47 Nm).

7. Remove the axle support, then carefully lower the vehicle the rest of the way.

8. Tighten the upper shock absorber mounting nut, as follows:

   a. For 1988–92 vehicles, tighten the 2 upper outer nuts to 13 ft. lbs. (18 Nm) and the center upper nut to 22 ft. lbs. (30 Nm).

   b. For 1993–96 vehicles, tighten the upper mounting nut to 21 ft. lbs. (29 Nm).

9. Install the upper shock absorber mounting nut cover.

TESTING

The purpose of the shock absorber is simply to limit the motion of the spring during compression and rebound cycles. If the vehicle is not equipped with these motion dampers, the up and down motion would multiply until the vehicle was alternately trying to leap off the ground and to pound itself into the pavement.

Countrary to popular rumor, the shocks do not affect the ride height of the vehicle. This is controlled by other suspension components such as springs and tires. Worn shock absorbers can affect handling; if the front of the vehicle is rising or falling excessively, the "footprint" of the tires changes on the pavement and steering is affected.

The most simple test of the shock absorber is simply push down on one corner of the unladen vehicle and release it. Observe the motion of the body as it is released. In most cases, it will come up beyond it original rest position, dip

Open the trunk, remove the nut cover (A) to access the upper retaining nuts (B)

88258P23

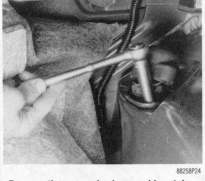

Remove the upper shock assembly retaining nuts

88258P24

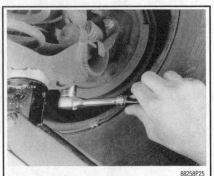

Make sure to properly support the rear axle when removing the retaining bolt from the shock absorber

88258P25

After removing the lower bolt, remove the shock absorber from the vehicle

88258P26

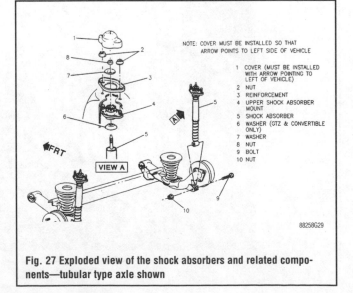

NOTE: COVER MUST BE INSTALLED SO THAT ARROW POINTS TO LEFT SIDE OF VEHICLE

1. COVER (MUST BE INSTALLED WITH ARROW POINTING TO LEFT OF VEHICLE)
2. NUT
3. REINFORCEMENT
4. UPPER SHOCK ABSORBER MOUNT
5. SHOCK ABSORBER
6. WASHER (GTZ & CONVERTIBLE ONLY)
7. WASHER
8. NUT
9. BOLT
10. NUT

FRT

VIEW A

88258G29

Fig. 27 Exploded view of the shock absorbers and related components—tubular type axle shown

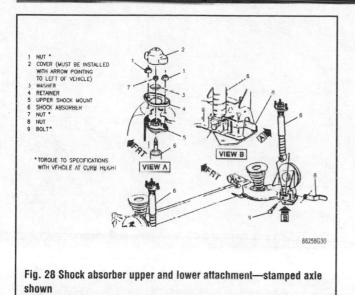

Fig. 28 Shock absorber upper and lower attachment—stamped axle shown

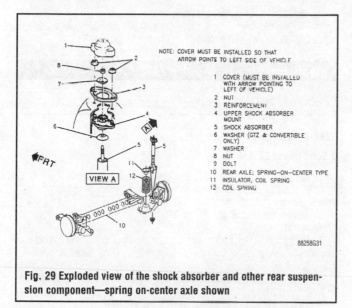

Fig. 29 Exploded view of the shock absorber and other rear suspension component—spring on-center axle shown

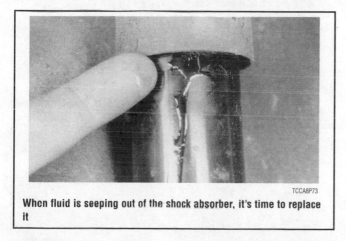

When fluid is seeping out of the shock absorber, it's time to replace it

back below it and settle quickly to rest. This shows that the damper is controlling the spring action. Any tendency to excessive pitch (up-and-down) motion or failure to return to rest within 2-3 cycles is a sign of poor function within the shock absorber. Oil-filled shocks may have a light film of oil around the seal, resulting from normal breathing and air exchange. This should NOT be taken as

a sign of failure, but any sign of thick or running oil definitely indicates failure. Gas filled shocks may also show some film at the shaft; if the gas has leaked out, the shock will have almost no resistance to motion.

While each shock absorber can be replaced individually, it is recommended that they be changed as a pair (both front or both rear) to maintain equal response on both sides of the vehicle. Chances are quite good that if one has failed, its mate is weak also.

Rear Axle/Lower Control Arm Assembly

The control arms and axle are one unit. The axle structure itself maintains the geometrical relationship of the wheels relative to the body. The axle assembly attaches to the underbody through a rubber bushing located at the front of each control arm. Each control arm bolts to underbody brackets.

REMOVAL & INSTALLATION

1988–90 Vehicles

♦ See Figure 30

1. Raise and safely support the vehicle, then place jackstands under the control arms.
2. Remove the stabilizer bar from the axle assembly.
3. Remove the wheel and tire assembly and brake drum.

❋❋ WARNING

Do not hammer on the brake drum as damage to the bearing could result.

4. Remove the shock absorber lower attaching bolts and paddle nuts at the axle and disconnect the shocks from the control arm.
5. Disconnect the parking brake cable from the axle assembly.
6. Disconnect the brake line at the brackets from the axle assembly.
7. Lower the rear axle and remove the coil springs and insulators.
8. Remove the control arm bolts from the underbody bracket, then lower the axle.
9. Remove the hub attaching bolts and remove the hub, bearing and backing plate assembly.
10. Install the hub, bearing and backing plate assembly. Hold the nuts and tighten the attaching bolts to 38 ft. lbs. (51 Nm).
To install:
11. Install the stabilizer bar to the axle assembly.
12. Place the axle assembly on a transmission jack and raise into position. Attach the control arms to the underbody bracket with bolts and nuts. Do not tighten the bolts at this time. It will be necessary to tighten the bolt the bolt of the control arm at standing height.

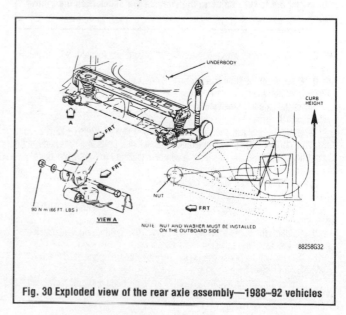

Fig. 30 Exploded view of the rear axle assembly—1988–92 vehicles

13. Install the brake line connections to the axle assembly.

14. Attach the brake cable to the rear axle assembly.

15. Position the coil springs and insulators in seats and raise the rear axle.

16. The end of the upper coil on the springs must be parallel to the axle assembly and seated in the pocket.

17. Install the shock absorber lower attachment bolts and paddle nuts to the rear axle and tighten the bolt to 35 ft. lbs. (47 Nm) for Corsica, and to 43 ft. lbs. (58 Nm) for Beretta.

18. Install the parking brake cable to the guide hook and adjust as necessary.

19. Install the brake drums and wheel and tire assemblies. Tighten the lug nuts to 100 ft. lbs. (140 Nm).

20. Partially lower the vehicle, then bleed the brake system, as outlined in Section 9.

21. Carefully lower the car.

22. Tighten the lower control arm-to-body bracket attaching bolts to 66 ft. lbs. (90 Nm).

1991–96 Vehicles

♦ See Figure 31

1. Raise and safely support the vehicle with jackstands.

2. Support the rear axle assembly with a jackstand.

3. Remove the rear wheel and tire assemblies.

4. Disconnect the brake pipe from the brake pipe brackets on the axle assembly. This will ensure that the axle is not suspended by the brake pipes and hoses.

5. Remove the shock absorber lower attaching bolts and nuts at the axle and disconnect the shocks from the control arm.

6. Lower the rear axle, then remove the springs and insulators.

7. Disconnect the parking brake cable at the equalizer unit and right wheel assembly.

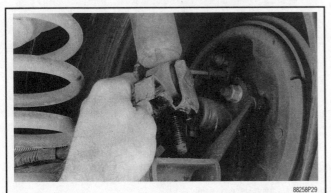

Unfasten the lower retainers, then detach the shock from the control arm

8. Detach the ABS wiring connector and mount clip located near the fuel tank.

9. Disconnect the right and left brake lines.

10. Unfasten the control arm bolts from the underbody bracket, then carefully lower the axle from the vehicle.

To install:

11. Place the axle assembly on a transmission jack and raise into position. Attach the control arms to the underbody bracket with bolts and nuts hand-tight. Do not tighten the bolts at this time. It will be necessary to tighten the bolts of the control arm at standing height.

12. Connect the right and left brake lines.

13. Attach the ABS electrical connectors.

14. Connect the parking brake cable at the equalizer unit and right wheel assembly.

15. Position the upper and lower insulators, using adhesive, and install the springs in the seats and raise the rear axle.

16. The end of the upper coil on the springs must be parallel to the axle assembly and seated in the pocket.

17. Install the shock absorber lower attachment bolts and nuts to the rear axle and tighten the bolt to 35 ft. lbs. (47 Nm).

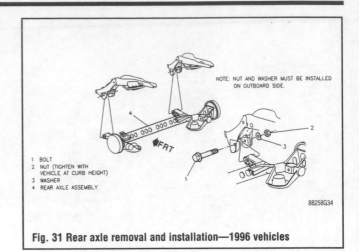

Fig. 31 Rear axle removal and installation—1996 vehicles

18. Install the right and left side brake line bracket mount bolts to the body and tighten to 8 ft. lbs. (11 Nm).

19. Install the wheel and tire assemblies. Tighten the lug nuts to 100 ft. lbs. (140 Nm).

20. Bleed the brake system and lower the car.

21. Tighten the lower control arm-to-body bracket attaching bolts to 52–59 ft. lbs. (70–80 Nm) plus an additional 120 degree rotation.

Stabilizer Bar

REMOVAL & INSTALLATION

1988–90 Vehicles

♦ See Figures 32 and 33

1. Raise and safely support the vehicle with jackstands.

2. Remove the nuts and bolts at both the axle and control arm attachments, then remove the control arm.

3. Remove the bracket, insulator and stabilizer bar.

To install:

4. Install the U-bolts, upper clamp, spacer and insulators in the trailing axle. Position the stabilizer bar in the insulators and loosely install the lower clamp and nuts.

5. Attach the end of the stabilizer bar to the control arms and tighten all nuts to 16 ft. lbs. (22 Nm).

6. Tighten the axle attaching nut to 13 ft. lbs. (18 Nm).

7. Remove the jackstands, then carefully lower the vehicle.

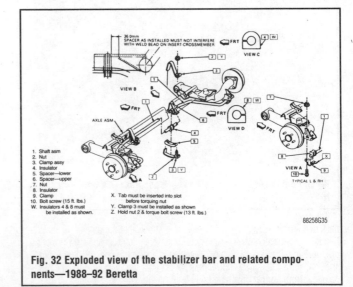

Fig. 32 Exploded view of the stabilizer bar and related components—1988–92 Beretta

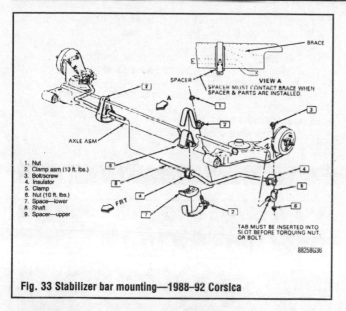

Fig. 33 Stabilizer bar mounting—1988–92 Corsica

1991–96 Vehicles

CORSICA

1. Raise and safely support the vehicle with jackstands.
2. Remove the nuts and bolts at both the axle and control arm attachments and remove the control arm and remove the bracket, insulator and stabilizer bar.

To install:

3. Install the U-bolts, upper clamp, spacer and insulators in the trailing axle. Position the stabilizer bar in the insulators and loosely install the lower clamp and nuts.
4. Attach the end of the stabilizer bar to the control arms and tighten all nuts to 16 ft. lbs. (22 Nm).
5. Tighten the axle attaching nut to 13 ft. lbs. (18 Nm).
6. Lower the vehicle.

BERETTA

♦ **See Figure 34**

1. Raise and safely support the vehicle with jackstands.
2. Remove the nuts and bolts from both ends of the stabilizer shaft.
3. Remove the stabilizer shaft from the vehicle.

To install:

4. Position the stabilizer shaft and install retaining the nuts and bolts.
5. Tighten the nuts to 103 ft. lbs. (139 Nm) for 1991–92 vehicles and to 16 ft. lbs. (22 Nm).
6. Carefully lower the vehicle.

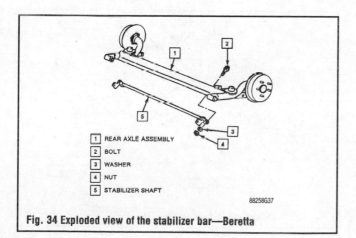

1	REAR AXLE ASSEMBLY
2	BOLT
3	WASHER
4	NUT
5	STABILIZER SHAFT

Fig. 34 Exploded view of the stabilizer bar—Beretta

Rear Hub and Bearing

REMOVAL & INSTALLATION

♦ **See Figure 35**

1. Loosen the wheel lug nuts.
2. Raise and safely support the vehicle, then remove the wheel and tire assembly.

Unfasten the hub and bearing retaining bolts . . .

. . . then remove the hub and bearing from the vehicle

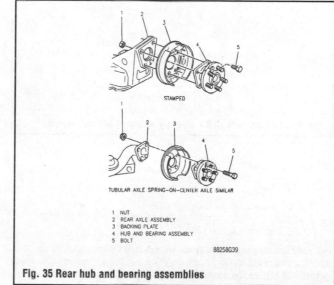

STAMPED

TUBULAR AXLE SPRING-ON-CENTER AXLE SIMILAR

1 NUT
2 REAR AXLE ASSEMBLY
3 BACKING PLATE
4 HUB AND BEARING ASSEMBLY
5 BOLT

Fig. 35 Rear hub and bearing assemblies

Do not hammer on the brake drum to remove; damage to the bearing will result.

3. Remove the brake drum, as outlined in Section 9.
4. If equipped, detach the ABS wheel speed sensor electrical connector.
5. Remove the 4 hub and bearing retaining bolts or nuts, as applicable and remove the assembly from the axle. The top rear attaching bolt will not clear the

brake shoe when removing the hub and bearing assembly. Partially remove the hub and bearing assembly prior to removing this bolt.

To install:
6. Attach the ABS wheel speed sensor electrical connector.
7. Position the top attaching bolt in the hub and bearing assembly prior to the installation in the axle assembly.
8. Install the remaining hub and bearing bolts nuts and tighten them to 38–43 ft. lbs. (52–58 Nm).
9. Install the brake drum.
10. Install the wheel and tire assembly.
11. Carefully lower the vehicle.

STEERING

Steering Wheel

REMOVAL & INSTALLATION

1988–90 Vehicles

▶ **See Figure 36**

1. Disconnect the negative battery cable. Turn the steering wheel so the wheels are in the straight ahead position.
2. From the rear of the steering wheel, remove the horn cover-to-steering wheel screws. Detach the horn electrical connector from the steering wheel.
3. Remove the steering wheel-to-column retainer, nut, washer (if equipped) and damper assembly.
4. Using a marking tool, mark the steering wheel alignment with the steering shaft for realignment purposes.
5. Using the Steering Wheel Puller tool No. J-1859–03 or equivalent, press the steering wheel from the steering column.
6. To install, reverse the removal procedures. Tighten the steering wheel nut to 30 ft. lbs. (41 Nm).

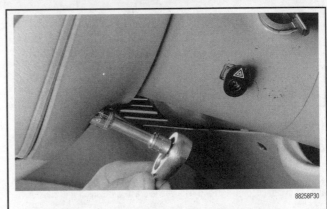

Unfasten the screws from the back of the SIR inflator module

Pull the inflator module partially away from the steering wheel

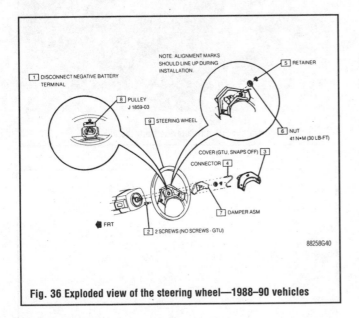

Fig. 36 Exploded view of the steering wheel—1988–90 vehicles

1991–96 Vehicles

▶ **See Figure 37**

1. Disconnect the negative battery cable.
2. If equipped, disable the SIR system as outlined in Section 6, then remove the inflator module as follows:

➡ **Rotate the steering wheel so the access holes on the back of the steering wheel are at the 12 and 6 o'clock positions. This will allow tool access and reduce the possibility of marring the steering column cover.**

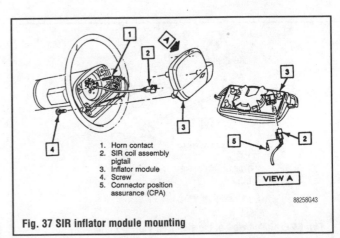

1. Horn contact
2. SIR coil assembly pigtail
3. Inflator module
4. Screw
5. Connector position assurance (CPA)

Fig. 37 SIR inflator module mounting

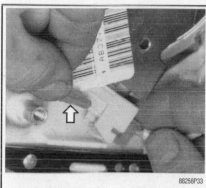

Remove the CPA retaining clip from the inflator module electrical connector . . .

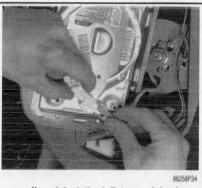

. . . then detach the inflator module electrical connector

Detach the horn contact from the steering wheel

Unfasten the steering wheel retaining nut and washer

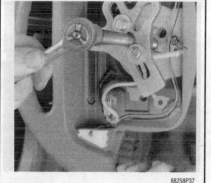

Install a suitable puller on the steering wheel

Once loosened, pull the steering wheel from the shaft

a. Remove the 4 screws from the back of the inflator module.

b. Remove the inflator module from the steering wheel.

c. Remove the Connector Positive Assurance (CPA) from the inflator module electrical connector and detach the connector.

3. For vehicles without air bags, remove the horn cover-to-steering wheel screws.

4. Disconnect the horn electrical connector from the steering wheel and remove the horn contact.

5. Remove the steering wheel-to-column retainer, nut and washer.

6. Mark the steering wheel alignment with the steering shaft for installation purposes.

7. Using a steering wheel puller, press the steering wheel from the steering column.

➡️Under no circumstances should the steering wheel or shaft be hammered on. Sharp blows to the steering column could loosen the plastic injections which maintain column rigidity.

To install:

8. If equipped with SIR, feed the coil assembly connector through the steering wheel.

9. Align the matchmarks made during removal and install the steering wheel.

10. Align the steering wheel with the turn signal cancelling cam assembly.

11. Install the hexagon locking nut. Tighten the steering wheel nut to 31 ft. lbs. (42 Nm).

12. If equipped with SIR, install the inflator module, as follows:

13. If equipped, install the inflator module, as follow:

a. Connect the coil assembly connector. Install the CPA into the connector.

➡️Ensure that no wires at the back of the inflator module are pinched when aligning the inflator module to the steering wheel.

b. Install the inflator module and the 4 attaching bolts.

c. Enable the SIR system.

14. Connect the negative battery cable.

Turn Signal Switch

REMOVAL & INSTALLATION

1988–90 Vehicles

♦ See Figures 38, 39 and 40

➡️Tool No. J–35689–A or equivalent, is required to remove the terminals from the connector on the turn signal switch.

1. Disconnect the negative battery cable.

2. Remove the steering wheel.

3. Pull the turn signal canceling cam assembly from the steering shaft.

4. Remove the hazard warning knob-to-steering column screw and the knob.

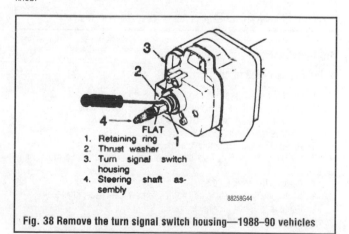

1. Retaining ring
2. Thrust washer
3. Turn signal switch housing
4. Steering shaft assembly

Fig. 38 Remove the turn signal switch housing—1988–90 vehicles

➡Before removing the turn signal assembly, position the turn signal lever so the turn signal assembly-to-steering column screws can all be removed.

5. Remove the column housing cover-to-column housing bowl screw and the cover.

➡If equipped with cruise control, detach the cruise control electrical connector.

6. Remove the turn signal lever-to-pivot assembly screw and the lever; one screw is in the front and one is in the rear.

7. Using the Terminal Remover tool No. J-35689–A or equivalent, disconnect and label the wires "F" and "G" on the connector at the buzzer switch assembly from the turn signal switch electrical harness connector.

8. Remove the turn signal switch-to-steering column screws and the switch.

9. To install, reverse the removal procedures. Tighten the turn signal switch-to-steering column screws to 35 inch lbs. (4 Nm) and the steering wheel nut to 30 ft. lbs. (41 Nm).

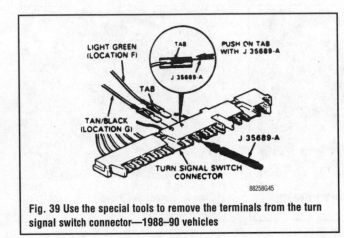

Fig. 39 Use the special tools to remove the terminals from the turn signal switch connector—1988–90 vehicles

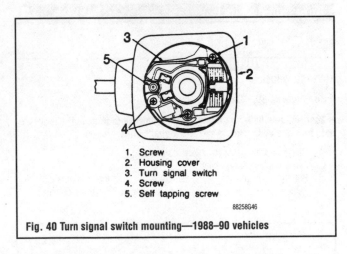

1. Screw
2. Housing cover
3. Turn signal switch
4. Screw
5. Self tapping screw

88258G46

Fig. 40 Turn signal switch mounting—1988–90 vehicles

1991–92 Vehicles

◆ See Figures 41 thru 46

1. Disable the SIR system, as outlined in Section 6 of this manual.
2. If not already done, disconnect the negative battery cable.
3. Place the ignition to the **LOCK** position.
4. Remove the steering wheel.
5. Remove the coil assembly retaining ring.
6. Lift the coil assembly from the end of the steering shaft and allow coil to hang freely.
7. Remove the wave washer.
8. If equipped with a standard column, remove the spacer shaft lock.
9. Remove the shaft lock retaining ring using tool J–23653–C or equivalent, to compress the shaft lock.

10. Pry off the retaining ring.
11. Remove the shaft lock.
12. Remove the turn signal cancelling cam assembly.
13. Remove the upper bearing spring.
14. Position the turn signal lever to the right turn position.
15. Remove the multi-function lever by performing the following:
   a. Ensure the lever is in the center or **OFF** position.
   b. If equipped with cruise control, detach the cruise control connector from the steering column assembly.
   c. Pull the lever straight out of the turn signal switch.
16. Remove the hazard knob assembly.
17. Remove the screw and signal switch arm. If equipped with tilt column and cruise control, allow the switch arm to hang freely.
18. Remove the turn signal switch screws. Allow the switch to hang freely.
19. Disconnect the turn signal/hazard switch assembly terminal from the instrument panel harness.
20. If equipped with tilt column, disconnect the buzzer switch assembly terminals from the turn signal/hazard assembly connector. Remove the tan/black wire lead from cavity E and the light green wire from the cavity F.
21. Remove the upper steering column bolts.
22. Remove the wiring protector.
23. Connect a length of wire to the turn signal/hazard assembly terminal connector to aid in reassembly.
24. Gently pull the wire harness through the steering column housing shroud, steering column housing and lock assembly cover.
25. Detach the wire from the connector.

To install:

26. Attach the wire to the turn signal/hazard switch assembly connector.
27. Gently pull the connector through the steering column housing shroud, steering column housing and lock assembly cover.
28. Remove the wire.
29. Install the wiring protector.
30. If disconnected, connect the buzzer switch terminals to the turn signal/hazard switch assembly connector. Insert the tan/black wire lead into cavity E and the light green wire into cavity F.
31. Attach the turn signal/hazard switch assembly connector to the instrument panel harness.
32. Install the steering column support bracket bolts to the steering column. Tighten to 22 ft. lbs. (30 Nm).
33. Install the steering column upper support bolts. Tighten to 20 ft. lbs. (27 Nm).
34. Install the turn signal switch assembly and attaching screws. Tighten to 20 inch lbs. (2.3 Nm).
35. Install the hazard knob assembly.
36. Install the multi-function lever by performing the following:
   a. Align the tab on the turn signal switch with the notch in the pivot of the turn signal switch.
   b. Push the lever into the turn signal switch.
   c. If equipped with cruise control, connect the connector to the steering column assembly.
37. Install the turn signal cancelling cam assembly. Lubricate with a synthetic grease.

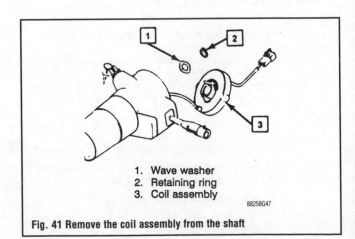

1. Wave washer
2. Retaining ring
3. Coil assembly

88258G47

Fig. 41 Remove the coil assembly from the shaft

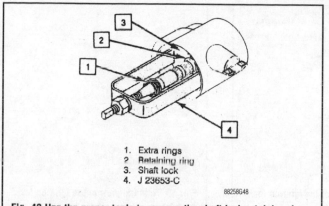

1. Extra rings
2. Retaining ring
3. Shaft lock
4. J 23653-C

88258G48

Fig. 42 Use the proper tools to remove the shaft lock retaining ring

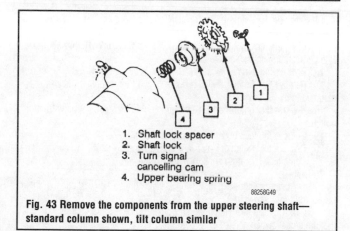

1. Shaft lock spacer
2. Shaft lock
3. Turn signal cancelling cam
4. Upper bearing spring

88258G49

Fig. 43 Remove the components from the upper steering shaft—standard column shown, tilt column similar

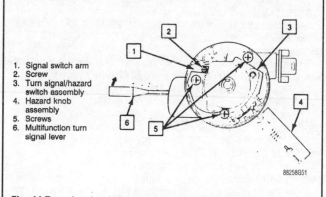

1. Signal switch arm
2. Screw
3. Turn signal/hazard switch assembly
4. Hazard knob assembly
5. Screws
6. Multifunction turn signal lever

88258G51

Fig. 44 Turn signal switch mounting—standard column

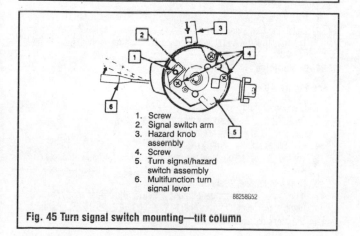

1. Screw
2. Signal switch arm
3. Hazard knob assembly
4. Screw
5. Turn signal/hazard switch assembly
6. Multifunction turn signal lever

88258G52

Fig. 45 Turn signal switch mounting—tilt column

38. Install the shaft lock.
39. Install the shaft lock retaining ring, lining up to block tooth on the shaft. Use tool J–23653–C to compress the shaft lock.
40. If equipped with a standard column, install the spacer shaft lock.
41. Install the wave washer.
42. Ensure the coil assembly is centered.

➡ **The coil assembly will become uncentered if the steering column is separated from the steering gear and is allowed to rotate or the centering spring is pushed down, letting the hub rotate while the coil is removed from the steering column.**

43. Install the coil assembly using the horn tower on the cancelling cam assembly inner ring and projections on the outer ring for alignment.
44. Install the coil assembly retaining ring. The ring must be firmly seated in the groove on the shaft. Gently pull the lower coil assembly wire to remove any wire kinks that may be inside the column.
45. Install the steering wheel.
46. If equipped, enable the SIR system.
47. Connect the negative battery cable.

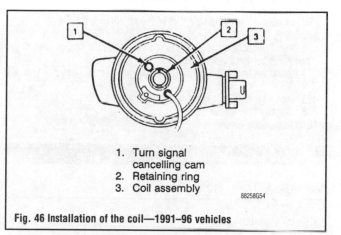

1. Turn signal cancelling cam
2. Retaining ring
3. Coil assembly

88258G54

Fig. 46 Installation of the coil—1991–96 vehicles

Ignition Switch

REMOVAL & INSTALLATION

♦ **See Figure 47**

1. Disconnect the negative battery cable.
2. If equipped, disable the Supplemental Inflatable Restraint (SIR) system.
3. Place the ignition switch in the **OFF-LOCK** position.
4. Remove the left side sound insulator panel.
5. Remove the bolts from the lower steering column support.
6. Remove the flange and coupling pinch bolt.
7. Remove the upper and lower bolts from the upper steering column support.
8. Detach the dimmer and ignition switch electrical connectors.
9. Carefully lower the steering column.
10. Remove the hexagonal nut and bolt/screw attaching the dimmer switch.
11. Disengage the dimmer switch actuator and remove the switches.
To install:
12. Make sure the ignition lock-cylinder is in the **OFF-LOCK** position.
13. Position the switches on the column.
14. Engage the dimmer switch actuator rod in the switch.
15. Install the nut and bolt/screw. Do not tighten.
16. Adjust the dimmer switch by inserting a 1/32 in. (0.8mm) drill bit or a 2.34mm diameter gauge pin into the adjustment hole in the dimmer switch. Push the switch against the actuator rod to remove all the lash.
17. Tighten the nut and screw to 35 inch lbs. (4 Nm).
18. Remove the adjustment tool from the dimmer switch.
19. Support the steering column and install the column into the flange and coupling assembly.

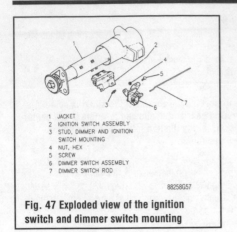

1 JACKET
2 IGNITION SWITCH ASSEMBLY
3 STUD, DIMMER AND IGNITION
  SWITCH MOUNTING
4 NUT, HEX
5 SCREW
6 DIMMER SWITCH ASSEMBLY
7 DIMMER SWITCH ROD

88258G57

Fig. 47 Exploded view of the ignition switch and dimmer switch mounting

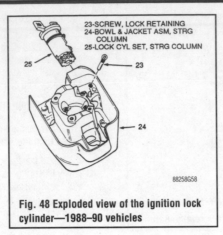

23-SCREW, LOCK RETAINING
24-BOWL & JACKET ASM, STRG
   COLUMN
25-LOCK CYL SET, STRG COLUMN

88258G58

Fig. 48 Exploded view of the ignition lock cylinder—1988–90 vehicles

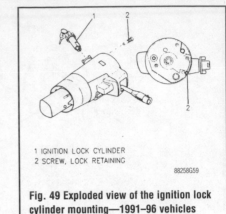

1 IGNITION LOCK CYLINDER
2 SCREW, LOCK RETAINING

88258G59

Fig. 49 Exploded view of the ignition lock cylinder mounting—1991–96 vehicles

20. Attach the dimmer and ignition switch electrical connectors.

21. Raise the column into position and loosely install the lower bolts to the upper steering column support bracket.

22. Install the lower steering column support bracket bolts. Tighten to 22 ft. lbs. (30 Nm).

23. Install the upper bolts to the upper steering column support bracket. Tighten the upper and lower bolts to 21 ft. lbs. (28 Nm).

24. Install the flange and coupling assembly pinch bolt. Tighten to 30 ft. lbs. (41 Nm).

25. Install the right side sound insulator panel.

26. Connect the negative battery cable.

27. If equipped, enable the SIR system.

Ignition Lock Cylinder

REMOVAL & INSTALLATION

1988–90 Vehicles

▶ See Figure 48

1. Disconnect the negative battery cable.

2. Remove the left-side lower trim panel.

3. If equipped with tilt steering, tilt the column up as far as it will go and remove the left-side lower trim panel.

4. Remove the steering column-to-support screws and lower the steering column.

➡Vehicles equipped with floor shift and automatic transaxles use an ignition switch inhibitor and park lock cable. On these models the park lock cable must be disconnected from the ignition switch inhibitor, by releasing the locking tab, before removing the column.

5. Detach the dimmer switch and turn signal switch connectors.

6. Remove the wiring harness-to-firewall nuts and steering column.

7. Remove the steering column-to-steering gear bolt and the steering column from the vehicle.

8. Remove the combination switch, as outlined in this section.

9. For tilt steering wheels, perform the following:

   a. Using a flat-type pry blade, position it in the square opening of the spring retainer, push downward (to the left) to release the spring retainer. Remove the wheel tilt spring.

   b. Remove the spring retainer, the tilt spring and the tilt spring guide.

   c. Remove the shoe pin retaining cap. Using the Pivot Pin Removal tool No. J–21854–01 or equivalent, remove the 2 pivot pins.

10. Place the lock cylinder in the **RUN** position.

11. If equipped with tilt steering, pull the shoe release lever and release the steering column housing. Remove the column housing.

12. Remove the steering shaft assembly and turn signal switch housing as an assembly.

13. Using the Terminal Remover tool No. J–35689–A or equivalent, disconnect and label the wires "F" and "G" on the connector at the buzzer switch assembly from the turn signal switch electrical harness connector.

14. Place the lock cylinder in the **RUN** position and remove the buzzer switch.

15. Place the lock cylinder in the **ACCESSORY** position. Remove the lock cylinder retaining screw and the lock cylinder.

16. Remove the dimmer switch nut/bolt, the dimmer switch and actuator rod.

17. Remove the dimmer switch mounting stud (the mounting nut was mounted to it).

18. Remove the ignition switch-to-steering column screws and the ignition switch.

19. Remove the lock bolt screws and the lock bolt.

20. Remove the switch actuator rack and ignition switch.

21. Remove the steering shaft lock and spring.

To install:

22. Observe the following tightening specifications when installing. Tighten the steering lock screw to 27 inch lbs. (3 Nm), the dimmer switch stud to 35 inch lbs. (4 Nm), the turn signal switch housing screws to 88 inch lbs. (10 Nm), the turn signal switch screws to 35 inch lbs. (4 Nm) and the steering wheel lock nut to 30 ft. lbs. (41 Nm).

23. To install the lock bolt, lubricate it with lithium grease and install the lock bolt, spring and retaining plate.

24. Lubricate the teeth on the switch actuator rack. Install the rack and the ignition switch through the opening in the steering bolt until it rests on the retaining plate.

25. Install the steering column lock cylinder set by holding the barrel of the lock cylinder, insert the key and turn it to the **ACCESSORY** position.

26. Install the lock set in the steering column while holding the rack against the lock plate.

27. Install the lock retaining screw. Insert the key in the lock cylinder and turn the lock cylinder to the START position and the rack will extend.

28. Center the slotted holes on the ignition switch mounting plate and install the ignition switch mounting screw and nut.

29. Install the dimmer switch and actuator rod into the center slot on the switch mounting plate.

30. Install the buzzer switch and turn the lock cylinder to the RUN position. Push the switch in until it is bottomed out with the plastic tab that covers the lock retaining screw.

31. Install the steering shaft and turn signal housing as an assembly.

32. Install the turn signal switch.

33. The remainder of installation is the reverse of the removal procedures.

1991–96 Vehicles

▶ See Figure 49

1. Disconnect the negative battery cable.

2. Disable the SIR system as outlined in Section 6.

3. Remove the steering wheel.

4. Remove the coil assembly retaining ring.

5. Lift the coil assembly from the end of the steering shaft and allow coil to hang freely.

6. Remove the wave washer.

7. If equipped with a standard column, remove the spacer shaft lock.

8. Remove the shaft lock retaining ring using tool J–23653–C or equivalent, to compress the shaft lock.

9. Pry off the retaining ring.
10. Remove the shaft lock.
11. Remove the turn signal cancelling cam assembly.
12. Remove the upper bearing spring.
13. Position the turn signal lever to the right turn position.
14. Remove the multi-function lever by performing the following:
    a. Ensure the lever is in the center or **OFF** position.
    b. If equipped with cruise control, disconnect the cruise control connector from the steering column assembly.
    c. Pull the lever straight out of the turn signal switch.
15. Remove the hazard knob assembly.
16. Remove the screw and signal switch arm. If equipped with tilt column and cruise control, allow the switch arm to hang freely.
17. Remove the turn signal switch screws. Allow the switch to hang freely.
18. Disconnect the turn signal/hazard switch assembly terminal from the instrument panel harness.
19. If equipped with tilt column, disconnect the buzzer switch assembly terminals from the turn signal/hazard assembly connector. Remove the tan/black wire lead from cavity E and the light green wire from the cavity F.
20. Remove the upper steering column bolts.
21. Remove the wiring protector.
22. Connect a length of wire to the turn signal/hazard assembly terminal connector to aid in reassembly.
23. Gently pull the wire harness through the steering column housing shroud, steering column housing and lock assembly cover.
24. Detach the wire from the connector.
25. Ensure the lock cylinder is in the **LOCK** position. Remove the lock cylinder attaching screw.
26. Remove the lock cylinder from the column.

To install:
27. Install the lock cylinder and attaching screw. Tighten to 40 inch lbs. (4.5 Nm).
28. Turn the ignition key to the **RUN** position.
29. Install the buzzer switch.
30. Connect the wire to the turn signal/hazard switch assembly connector.
31. Gently pull the connector through the steering column housing shroud, steering column housing and lock assembly cover.
32. Remove the wire.
33. Install the wiring protector.
34. If disconnected, connect the buzzer switch terminals to the turn signal/hazard switch assembly connector. Insert the tan/black wire lead into cavity E and the light green wire into cavity F.
35. Connect the turn signal/hazard switch assembly connector to the instrument panel harness.
36. Install the steering column support bracket bolts to the steering column. Tighten to 22 ft. lbs. (30 Nm).
37. Install the steering column upper support bolts. Tighten to 20 ft. lbs. (28 Nm).
38. Install the turn signal switch assembly and attaching screws. Tighten to 20 inch lbs. (2 Nm).
39. Install the hazard knob assembly.
40. Install the multi-function lever by performing the following:

a. Align the tab on the turn signal switch with the notch in the pivot of the turn signal switch.
b. Push the lever into the turn signal switch.
c. If equipped with cruise control, connect the connector to the steering column assembly.
41. Install the turn signal cancelling cam assembly. Lubricate with a synthetic grease.
42. Install the shaft lock.
43. Install the shaft lock retaining ring, lining up to block tooth on the shaft. Use tool J–23653–C to compress the shaft lock.
44. If equipped with a standard column, install the spacer shaft lock.
45. Install the wave washer.
46. Ensure the coil assembly is centered.

➡**The coil assembly will become uncentered if the steering column is separated from the steering gear and is allowed to rotate or the centering spring is pushed down, letting the hub rotate while the coil is removed from the steering column.**

47. Install the coil assembly using the horn tower on the cancelling cam assembly inner ring and projections on the outer ring for alignment.
48. Install the coil assembly retaining ring. The ring must be firmly seated in the groove on the shaft. Gently pull the lower coil assembly wire to remove any wire kinks that may be inside the column.
49. Install the steering wheel.
50. Enable the SIR system as outlined earlier in this section.
51. Connect the negative battery cable.

Tie Rod Ends

REMOVAL & INSTALLATION

Outer Tie Rod End

1. Raise and support the front of the vehicle on jackstands. Remove the wheel and tire assembly.
2. Remove and discard the cotter pin and nut from the outer tie rod end.
3. Loosen the outer tie rod pinch bolts.
4. Using the Ball Joint Remover tool No. J-24319–01 or equivalent, separate the tie rod from the steering knuckle.
5. Remove the outer tie rod from the adjuster by counting the exact number of turns required to remove it. This will allow proper installation without having to reset the toe in.

To install:
6. Install the new tie rod end by turning it in the same amount of turns as during the removal.
7. To complete the installation, connect the tie rod to the steering knuckle and reverse the removal procedures. Tighten the ball joint-to-steering knuckle nut to 35–50 ft. lbs. and the tie rod pinch bolts to 35 ft. lbs. (46 Nm) for 1988–90 and to 41 ft. lbs. (55 Nm) for 1991–92 vehicles.

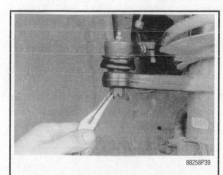
Use needle-nose pliers to remove the cotter pin from the outer tie rod end nut. Discard the cotter pin

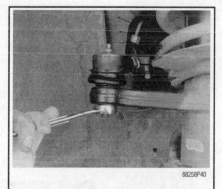
Use a wrench to loosen the tie rod end castellated nut . . .

. . . then remove the nut from the tie rod end

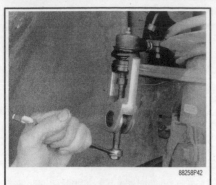

After loosening the pinch bolts, install a puller on the outer tie rod end . . .

. . . then separate the tie rod end from the steering knuckle

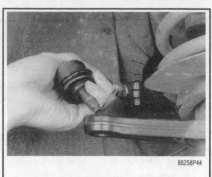

As you are unscrewing the outer tie rod end, count the number of rotations for proper installation . . .

. . . then remove the outer tie rod end from the vehicle

Inner Tie Rod End

♦ See Figure 50

1. Remove the inner tie rod end lock plate bolt. If both inner tie rods are being replaced, discard the used lock plate.

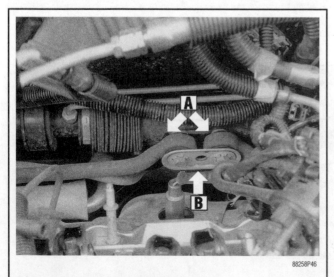

Inner tie rod end (A) and lock plate (B) mounting

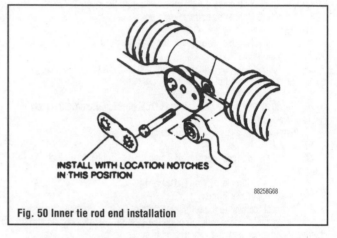

INSTALL WITH LOCATION NOTCHES IN THIS POSITION

Fig. 50 Inner tie rod end installation

2. Slide the inner tie rod out from between the plate and the steering rack.

3. Reinstall the lock plate bolt to insure proper tie rod-to-steering gear realignment.

4. Remove the cotter pin and nut from the outer tie rod end. Discard the cotter pin.

5. Using the Ball Joint Remover tool No. J–24319–01 or equivalent, separate the tie rod from the steering knuckle.

6. Remove the inner and outer tie rod assembly from the vehicle.

7. Note the position of the inner and outer tie rods in relation to each other. Place the assembly in a vise and loosen the adjuster pinch bolts.

8. Remove the outer tie rod from the adjuster by counting the exact number of turns required to remove it. This will allow proper installation without having to reset the toe in.

To install:

9. Place the new inner tie rod in the vise and install the outer tie rod end and adjuster the same amount of turns as when removing it.

10. Check the alignment between the inner and outer tie rods is the same as during removal.

11. To complete the installation, use a new lock plate and reverse the removal procedures. Tighten the inner tie rod-to-lock plate bolts to 65 ft. lbs. (90 Nm).

Rack And Pinion Steering Gear

REMOVAL & INSTALLATION

♦ See Figure 51

✷✷ WARNING

On 1991–96 models, the wheels of the vehicle must be in the straight ahead position and the ignition switch in the LOCK position before

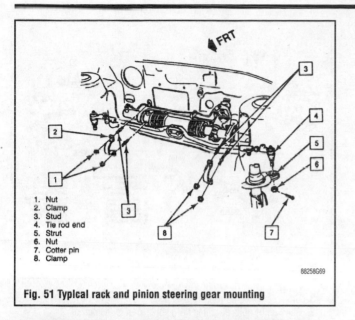

1. Nut
2. Clamp
3. Stud
4. Tie rod end
5. Strut
6. Nut
7. Cotter pin
8. Clamp

88258G69

Fig. 51 Typical rack and pinion steering gear mounting

disconnecting the flange and coupling assembly from the steering column or the rack and pinion steering gear. Failure to do so may cause the Supplemental Inflatable Restraint (SIR) coil assembly to become uncentered, which will damage the SIR coil assembly.

1. From inside the vehicle, remove the left-side lower sound insulator.
2. Remove the upper steering shaft-to-steering rack coupling pinch bolt.
3. Place a drain pan under the steering gear and disconnect the pressure lines from the steering gear.
4. Raise and support the front of the vehicle.
5. Remove both front wheel and tire assemblies.
6. Using the Ball Joint Remover tool No. J–24319–01 or equivalent, disconnect the tie rod ends from the steering knuckles.
7. Lower the vehicle.
8. Remove both steering gear-to-chassis clamps.
9. Slide the steering gear forward and remove the lower steering shaft-to-steering rack coupling pinch bolt.
10. From the firewall, disconnect the coupling and seal from the steering gear.

11. Raise and support the front of the vehicle.
12. Through the left-wheel opening, remove the steering gear with the tie rods.

➡If the studs were removed with the mounting clamps, reinstall the studs into the cowl panel and tighten to the studs are fully seated against the dash panel. The torque should not exceed 15 ft. lbs. (20 Nm). After a second use of the stud a thread locking compound should be used.

To install:

13. Install the rack and pinion through the left wheel opening.
14. Install the dash seal on the rack and pinion assembly.
15. Move the rack and pinion assembly forward and install the coupling lower pinch bolt and tighten to 30 ft. lbs. (41 Nm).
16. Install the gear inlet and outlet pipes to the steering gear and tighten to 19 ft. lbs. (26 Nm).
17. Hand tighten the camp nuts, then tighten the left side clamp nuts first to 22 ft. lbs. (30 Nm), then tighten the right side clamp nuts to 22 ft. lbs. (30 Nm).
18. Raise and safely support the vehicle.
19. Install the tie rod ends to the struts and install the cotter pins after tightening the nuts to 34 ft. lbs. (47 Nm).
20. Install the wheel and tire assemblies.
21. Lower the vehicle and install the steering column upper pinch bolt to 30 ft. lbs. (41 Nm).
22. Refill power steering pump reservoir and bleed the power steering system.

Power Steering Pump

REMOVAL & INSTALLATION

Except 2.3L Engine

◆ **See Figures 52 and 53**

1. Disconnect the negative battery cable.
2. Remove the pressure and return hoses from the pump and drain the system into a suitable container.
3. Cap or plug the fittings at the pump.
4. Using a 12 in. (305mm) adjustable wrench, on the tensioner casting, loosen the belt tensioner. Lift the belt off the pulley.

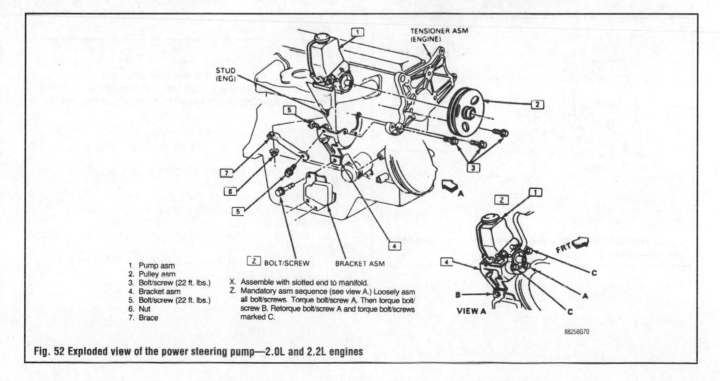

1. Pump asm
2. Pulley asm
3. Bolt/screw (22 ft. lbs.)
4. Bracket asm
5. Bolt/screw (22 ft. lbs.)
6. Nut
7. Brace

Z BOLT/SCREW   BRACKET ASM

X. Assemble with slotted end to manifold.
Z. Mandatory asm sequence (see view A). Loosely asm all bolt/screws. Torque bolt/screw A. Then torque bolt/screw B. Retorque bolt/screw A and torque bolt/screws marked C.

88258G70

Fig. 52 Exploded view of the power steering pump—2.0L and 2.2L engines

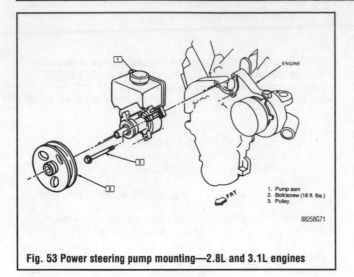

Fig. 53 Power steering pump mounting—2.8L and 3.1L engines

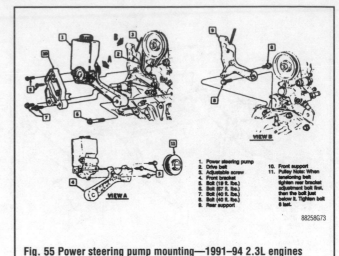

Fig. 55 Power steering pump mounting—1991–94 2.3L engines

5. Locate the 3 pump attaching bolts through the access hole in the pulley and remove the bolts.

6. On the 2.0L and 2.2L engine, remove the bolt from the rear of the pump.

7. Remove the pump assembly.

8. To install, reverse the removal procedure. Tighten the power steering pump bolts to 22 ft. lbs. (30 Nm) for the 2.8L and 3.1L engines and to 18 ft. lbs. (25 Nm) for the 2.0L and 2.2L cylinder engines.

9. Refill power steering pump reservoir and bleed the system as outlined later in this section.

2.3L Engine

♦ **See Figures 54 and 55**

1. Remove the air cleaner assembly.

2. Disconnect the power brake booster line.

3. Remove the poly-groove drive belt.

4. Detach the electrical connector from the idle speed power steering pressure switch.

5. Remove the pump bracket bolts and bracket.

6. Unfasten the hose clamp and return hose.

7. Remove the attaching bolt and remove the pressure pipe to the pump.

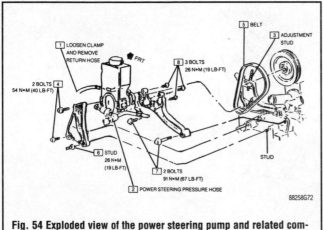

Fig. 54 Exploded view of the power steering pump and related components—1990 2.3L engine

8. Unfasten the pump pivot bracket bolts, then remove the bracket.

9. Remove the bolts attaching the pivot bracket to the pump.

10. Remove the pulley from the pump, as necessary.

To install:

11. Install the pulley to the pump, as necessary.

12. Install the bolts attaching the pivot bracket to the pump and tighten to 23 ft. lbs. (31 Nm).

13. Install the pump pivot bracket with the pump into position and tighten the bolt hand-tight.

14. Install the poly groove drive belt.

15. Tighten the pivot bracket bolts to specifications. Tighten the bolt closest to the pump to 19 ft. lbs. (26 Nm) and tighten the bolt furthest to the pump to 72 ft. lbs. (98 Nm).

16. Install the pump bracket and bolts to 39 ft. lbs. (53 Nm) for the bottom, 39 ft. lbs. (53 Nm) for the stud and 19 ft. lbs. (26 Nm) for the bottom.

17. Install the pressure pipe to the pump and tighten to 18 ft. lbs. (25 Nm).

18. Install the bolt attaching the pressure pipe to the pump and tighten to 23 ft. lbs. (31 Nm).

19. Install the return hose and clamp.

20. Install the air cleaner assembly.

21. Bleed the power steering system, as outlined later in this section.

BLEEDING

♦ **See Figure 56**

➡ **Automatic transmission fluid is NOT compatible with the seals and hoses of the power steering system. Under no circumstances should automatic transmission be used in place of power steering fluid in this system.**

1. With the engine turned OFF, turn the wheels all the way to the left.

2. Fill the reservoir with power steering fluid until the level is at the COLD mark on the reservoir.

3. Start and operate the engine at fast idle for 15 seconds. Turn the engine OFF.

4. Recheck the fluid level and fill it to the COLD mark.

5. Start the engine and bleed the system by turning the wheels in both directions slowly to the stops.

6. Stop the engine and check the fluid. Fluid that still has air in it will be a light tan color.

7. Repeat this procedure until all air is removed from the system.

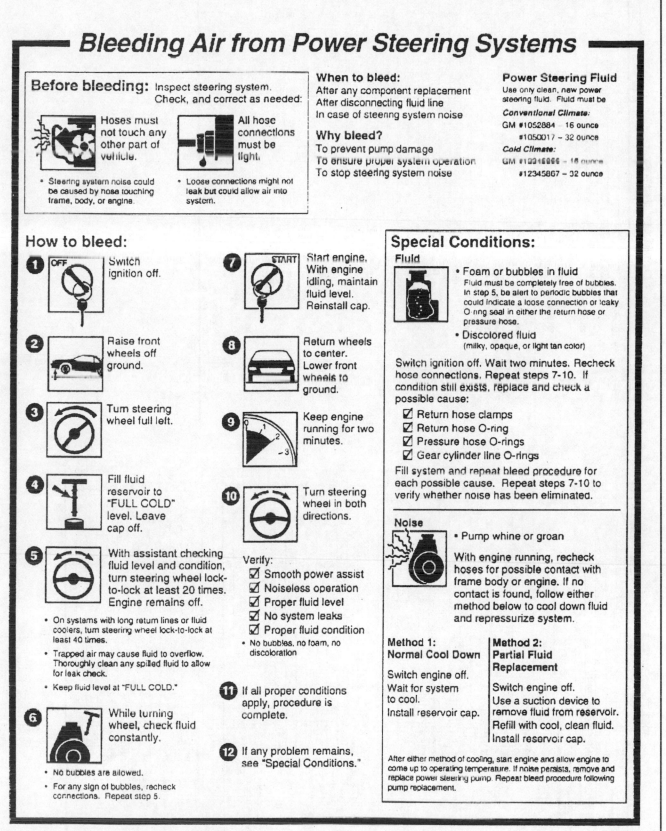

Bleeding Air from Power Steering Systems

Before bleeding: Inspect steering system. Check, and correct as needed:

Hoses must not touch any other part of vehicle.

- Steering system noise could be caused by hose touching frame, body, or engine.

All hose connections must be tight.

- Loose connections might not leak but could allow air into system.

When to bleed:
After any component replacement
After disconnecting fluid line
In case of steering system noise

Why bleed?
To prevent pump damage
To ensure proper system operation
To stop steering system noise

Power Steering Fluid
Use only clean, new power steering fluid. Fluid must be

Conventional Climate:
GM #1052884 – 16 ounce
     #1050017 – 32 ounce

Cold Climate:
GM #12345666 – 16 ounce
     #12345867 – 32 ounce

How to bleed:

1 Switch ignition off.

2 Raise front wheels off ground.

3 Turn steering wheel full left.

4 Fill fluid reservoir to "FULL COLD" level. Leave cap off.

5 With assistant checking fluid level and condition, turn steering wheel lock-to-lock at least 20 times. Engine remains off.

- On systems with long return lines or fluid coolers, turn steering wheel lock-to-lock at least 40 times.
- Trapped air may cause fluid to overflow. Thoroughly clean any spilled fluid to allow for leak check.
- Keep fluid level at "FULL COLD."

6 While turning wheel, check fluid constantly.

- No bubbles are allowed.
- For any sign of bubbles, recheck connections. Repeat step 5.

7 Start engine. With engine idling, maintain fluid level. Reinstall cap.

8 Return wheels to center. Lower front wheels to ground.

9 Keep engine running for two minutes.

10 Turn steering wheel in both directions.

Verify:
- ☑ Smooth power assist
- ☑ Noiseless operation
- ☑ Proper fluid level
- ☑ No system leaks
- ☑ Proper fluid condition
- No bubbles, no foam, no discoloration

11 If all proper conditions apply, procedure is complete.

12 If any problem remains, see "Special Conditions."

Special Conditions:

Fluid

- Foam or bubbles in fluid
  Fluid must be completely free of bubbles. In step 5, be alert to periodic bubbles that could indicate a loose connection or leaky O-ring seal in either the return hose or pressure hose.

- Discolored fluid
  (milky, opaque, or light tan color)

Switch ignition off. Wait two minutes. Recheck hose connections. Repeat steps 7-10. If condition still exists, replace and check a possible cause:

- ☑ Return hose clamps
- ☑ Return hose O-ring
- ☑ Pressure hose O-rings
- ☑ Gear cylinder line O-rings

Fill system and repeat bleed procedure for each possible cause. Repeat steps 7-10 to verify whether noise has been eliminated.

Noise

- Pump whine or groan

With engine running, recheck hoses for possible contact with frame body or engine. If no contact is found, follow either method below to cool down fluid and repressurize system.

**Method 1:
Normal Cool Down**

Switch engine off.
Wait for system to cool.
Install reservoir cap.

**Method 2:
Partial Fluid Replacement**

Switch engine off.
Use a suction device to remove fluid from reservoir.
Refill with cool, clean fluid.
Install reservoir cap.

After either method of cooling, start engine and allow engine to come up to operating temperature. If noise persists, remove and replace power steering pump. Repeat bleed procedure following pump replacement.

88258G74

Fig. 56 Power steering system bleeding procedure

TORQUE SPECIFICATIONS

Component	ft. lbs.	inch lbs.	Nm
Front Suspension			
Ball joint castellated nut			
1988-90 vehicles	55		75
1991 vehicles (plus an additional 60° rotation)	26		35
1992-96 vehicles	41-50		55-65
Ball joint-to-control arm nuts and bolts	50		68
Control arm and suspension support bolts			
1988-90 vehicles		see procedure	
1991 vehicles			
Step 1: rear	66		90
Step 2: center	66		90
Step 3: front	66		90
1992-96 vehicles			
Step 1: center	66		90
Step 2: front	65		88
Step 3: rear	65		88
Front engine mount crossmember			
1991 2.3L engine only			
Front engine mount upper nut	55		75
Lower engine mount nuts	30		40
Crossmember plate nuts	40		54
Hub and bearing assembly			
1988-90 vehicles	67		90
1991-96 vehicles	70		95
MacPherson strut			
Strut-to-knuckle bolts	133		180
Upper strut-to-body nuts	18		25
Outer tie rod end nuts			
1988-90 vehicles	35		50
1991-96 vehicles	55		75
Stabilizer link-to-stabilizer shaft			
1988-90 vehicles	14		18
1991 vehicles			
Except GTZ	13		17
GTZ	70		95
1992-96 vehicles	70		95
Upper spring retaining nuts			
1988-90 vehicles	59		80
1991-96 vehicles	65		88
Rear Suspension			
Rear axle assembly			
Control arm-to-body bracket			
1988-90 vehicles	66		90
1991-96 vehicles (plus a 120° rotation)	52		70
Rear hub and bearing assembly bolts	38		52
Shock absorbers			
2 upper outer nuts	13		18
1 upper center nut	22		30
Lower mount nut and bolt			
1988 Corsica	35		47
1988 Beretta	43		58
1989-90 Corsica	35		47
1989-90 Beretta	21		28
1991-96 vehicles	35		47

88258C01

TORQUE SPECIFICATIONS

Component	ft. lbs.	inch lbs.	Nm
Stabilizer bar			
1988-90 vehicles			
Stabilizer-to-control arm	16		22
Stabilizer-to-axle	13		18
1991-96 Corsica			
Stabilizer-to-control arm	16		22
Stabilizer-to-axle	13		18
1991-96 Beretta			
Stabilizer retaining nuts	103		139
Steering			
Ignition and dimmer switch nut		35	4
Inner tie rod-to-lock plate	65		90
Power steering pump attaching bolts			
2.0L and 2.2L engines	18		25
2.8L and 3.1L engines	22		30
2.3L engine			
Bottom bracket bolts	39		53
Front bracket bolts	19		26
Rear bracket bolts	72		98
Top bracket bolts	19		26
Bracket stud	39		53
Outer tie rod end			
Ball joint-to-knuckle nut	35-55		47-75
Tie rod pinch bolts			
1988-90 vehicles	35		46
1991-96 vehicles	41		55
Steering column			
1988-90 vehicles			
Capsule bolts	20		27
Coupling pinch bolt	29		40
Lower shackle bolt	22		30
1991-96 vehicles			
Column support bracket	22		30
Coupling pinch bolt	29-30		40-41
Upper support bolts	20-21		26-27
Steering wheel retaining nut			
1988-90 vehicles	30		41
1991-96 vehicles	31		42
Turn signal switch			
1988-90 vehicles		35	4
1991-96 vehicles		20	2.3

88258C02

9

BRAKES

BRAKE OPERATING SYSTEM

Basic Operating Principles

Hydraulic systems are used to actuate the brakes of all modern automobiles. The system transports the power required to force the frictional surfaces of the braking system together from the pedal to the individual brake units at each wheel. A hydraulic system is used for two reasons.

First, fluid under pressure can be carried to all parts of an automobile by small pipes and flexible hoses without taking up a significant amount of room or posing routing problems.

Second, a great mechanical advantage can be given to the brake pedal end of the system, and the foot pressure required to actuate the brakes can be reduced by making the surface area of the master cylinder pistons smaller than that of any of the pistons in the wheel cylinders or calipers.

The master cylinder consists of a fluid reservoir along with a double cylinder and piston assembly. Double type master cylinders are designed to separate the front and rear braking systems hydraulically in case of a leak. The master cylinder coverts mechanical motion from the pedal into hydraulic pressure within the lines. This pressure is translated back into mechanical motion at the wheels by either the wheel cylinder (drum brakes) or the caliper (disc brakes).

Steel lines carry the brake fluid to a point on the vehicle's frame near each of the vehicle's wheels. The fluid is then carried to the calipers and wheel cylinders by flexible tubes in order to allow for suspension and steering movements.

In drum brake systems, each wheel cylinder contains two pistons, one at either end, which push outward in opposite directions and force the brake shoe into contact with the drum.

In disc brake systems, the cylinders are part of the calipers. At least one cylinder in each caliper is used to force the brake pads against the disc.

All pistons employ some type of seal, usually made of rubber, to minimize fluid leakage. A rubber dust boot seals the outer end of the cylinder against dust and dirt. The boot fits around the outer end of the piston on disc brake calipers, and around the brake actuating rod on wheel cylinders.

The hydraulic system operates as follows: When at rest, the entire system, from the piston(s) in the master cylinder to those in the wheel cylinders or calipers, is full of brake fluid. Upon application of the brake pedal, fluid trapped in front of the master cylinder piston(s) is forced through the lines to the wheel cylinders. Here, it forces the pistons outward, in the case of drum brakes, and inward toward the disc, in the case of disc brakes. The motion of the pistons is opposed by return springs mounted outside the cylinders in drum brakes, and by spring seals, in disc brakes.

Upon release of the brake pedal, a spring located inside the master cylinder immediately returns the master cylinder pistons to the normal position. The pistons contain check valves and the master cylinder has compensating ports drilled in it. These are uncovered as the pistons reach their normal position. The piston check valves allow fluid to flow toward the wheel cylinders or calipers as the pistons withdraw. Then, as the return springs force the brake pads or shoes into the released position, the excess fluid reservoir through the compensating ports. It is during the time the pedal is in the released position that any fluid that has leaked out of the system will be replaced through the compensating ports.

Dual circuit master cylinders employ two pistons, located one behind the other, in the same cylinder. The primary piston is actuated directly by mechanical linkage from the brake pedal through the power booster. The secondary piston is actuated by fluid trapped between the two pistons. If a leak develops in front of the secondary piston, it moves forward until it bottoms against the front of the master cylinder, and the fluid trapped between the pistons will operate the rear brakes. If the rear brakes develop a leak, the primary piston will move forward until direct contact with the secondary piston takes place, and it will force the secondary piston to actuate the front brakes. In either case, the brake pedal moves farther when the brakes are applied, and less braking power is available.

All dual circuit systems use a switch to warn the driver when only half of the brake system is operational. This switch is usually located in a valve body which is mounted on the firewall or the frame below the master cylinder. A hydraulic piston receives pressure from both circuits, each circuit's pressure being applied to one end of the piston. When the pressures are in balance, the piston remains stationary. When one circuit has a leak, however, the greater pressure in that circuit during application of the brakes will push the piston to one side, closing the switch and activating the brake warning light.

In disc brake systems, this valve body also contains a metering valve and, in some cases, a proportioning valve. The metering valve keeps pressure from traveling to the disc brakes on the front wheels until the brake shoes on the rear wheels have contacted the drums, ensuring that the front brakes will never be used alone. The proportioning valve controls the pressure to the rear brakes to lessen the chance of rear wheel lock-up during very hard braking.

Warning lights may be tested by depressing the brake pedal and holding it while opening one of the wheel cylinder bleeder screws. If this does not cause the light to go on, substitute a new lamp, make continuity checks, and, finally, replace the switch as necessary.

The hydraulic system may be checked for leaks by applying pressure to the pedal gradually and steadily. If the pedal sinks very slowly to the floor, the system has a leak. This is not to be confused with a springy or spongy feel due to the compression of air within the lines. If the system leaks, there will be a gradual change in the position of the pedal with a constant pressure.

Check for leaks along all lines and at wheel cylinders. If no external leaks are apparent, the problem is inside the master cylinder.

DISC BRAKES

Instead of the traditional expanding brakes that press outward against a circular drum, disc brake systems utilize a disc (rotor) with brake pads positioned on either side of it. An easily-seen analogy is the hand brake arrangement on a bicycle. The pads squeeze onto the rim of the bike wheel, slowing its motion. Automobile disc brakes use the identical principle but apply the braking effort to a separate disc instead of the wheel.

The disc (rotor) is a casting, usually equipped with cooling fins between the two braking surfaces. This enables air to circulate between the braking surfaces making them less sensitive to heat buildup and more resistant to fade. Dirt and water do not drastically affect braking action since contaminants are thrown off by the centrifugal action of the rotor or scraped off the by the pads. Also, the equal clamping action of the two brake pads tends to ensure uniform, straight line stops. Disc brakes are inherently self-adjusting. There are three general types of disc brake:

1. A fixed caliper.
2. A floating caliper.
3. A sliding caliper.

The fixed caliper design uses two pistons mounted on either side of the rotor (in each side of the caliper). The caliper is mounted rigidly and does not move.

The sliding and floating designs are quite similar. In fact, these two types are often lumped together. In both designs, the pad on the inside of the rotor is moved into contact with the rotor by hydraulic force. The caliper, which is not held in a fixed position, moves slightly, bringing the outside pad into contact with the rotor. There are various methods of attaching floating calipers. Some pivot at the bottom or top, and some slide on mounting bolts. In any event, the end result is the same.

DRUM BRAKES

Drum brakes employ two brake shoes mounted on a stationary backing plate. These shoes are positioned inside a circular drum which rotates with the wheel assembly. The shoes are held in place by springs. This allows them to slide toward the drums (when they are applied) while keeping the linings and drums in alignment. The shoes are actuated by a wheel cylinder which is mounted at the top of the backing plate. When the brakes are applied, hydraulic pressure forces the wheel cylinder's actuating links outward. Since these links bear directly against the top of the brake shoes, the tops of the shoes are then forced against the inner side of the drum. This action forces the bottoms of the two shoes to contact the brake drum by rotating the entire assembly slightly (known as servo action). When pressure within the wheel cylinder is relaxed, return springs pull the shoes back away from the drum.

Most modern drum brakes are designed to self-adjust themselves during application when the vehicle is moving in reverse. This motion causes both shoes to rotate very slightly with the drum, rocking an adjusting lever, thereby causing rotation of the adjusting screw. Some drum brake systems are designed to self-adjust during application whenever the brakes are applied. This on-board adjustment system reduces the need for maintenance adjustments and keeps both the brake function and pedal feel satisfactory.

POWER BRAKE BOOSTERS

Power brakes operate just as standard brake systems except in the actuation of the master cylinder pistons. A vacuum diaphragm is located on the front of the master cylinder and assists the driver in applying the brakes, reducing both the effort and travel he must put into moving the brake pedal.

The vacuum diaphragm housing is connected to the intake manifold by a vacuum hose. A check valve is placed at the point where the hose enters the diaphragm housing, so that during periods of low manifold vacuum brake assist vacuum will not be lost.

Depressing the brake pedal closes off the vacuum source and allows atmospheric pressure to enter on one side of the diaphragm. This causes the master cylinder pistons to move and apply the brakes. When the brake pedal is released, vacuum is applied to both sides of the diaphragm, and return springs return the diaphragm and master cylinder pistons to the released position. If the vacuum fails, the brake pedal rod will butt against the end of the master cylinder actuating rod, and direct mechanical application will occur as the pedal is depressed.

The hydraulic and mechanical problems that apply to conventional brake systems also apply to power brakes, and should be checked for if the following tests do not reveal the problem.

Test for a system vacuum leak as described below:

1. Operate the engine at idle with the transaxle in Neutral without touching the brake pedal for at least one minute.
2. Turn off the engine, and wait one minute.
3. Test for the presence of assist vacuum by depressing the brake pedal and releasing it several times. Light application will produce less and less pedal travel, if vacuum was present. If there is no vacuum, air is leaking into the system somewhere.
4. Test for system operation as follows:
   a. Pump the brake pedal (with engine off) until the supply vacuum is entirely gone.
   b. Put a light, steady pressure on the pedal.
   c. Start the engine, and operate it at idle with the transaxle in Neutral. If the system is operating, the brake pedal should fall toward the floor if constant pressure is maintained on the pedal.

Power brake systems may be tested for hydraulic leaks just as ordinary systems are tested, except that the engine should be idling with the transaxle in Neutral throughout the test.

Brake Light Switch

REMOVAL & INSTALLATION

♦ See Figure 1

1. Disconnect the negative battery cable.
2. Remove the lower left trim panel. Locate the stoplight switch on the brake pedal support.

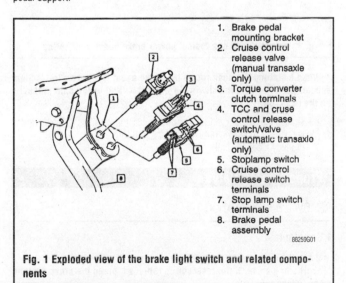

1. Brake pedal mounting bracket
2. Cruise control release valve (manual transaxle only)
3. Torque converter clutch terminals
4. TCC and cruse control release switch/valve (automatic transaxle only)
5. Stoplamp switch
6. Cruise control release switch terminals
7. Stop lamp switch terminals
8. Brake pedal assembly

88259G01

Fig. 1 Exploded view of the brake light switch and related components

3. Detach the electrical connector from the switch, then remove the switch by twisting it out of the tubular retaining clip.
To install:
4. Using a new retaining clip, install the switch and attach the electrical connector.
5. To adjust the switch, pull back on the brake pedal, push the switch through the retaining clip noting the "clicks"; repeat this procedure until no more "clicks" can be heard.
6. Connect the negative battery cable and check the switch operation.

Master Cylinder

REMOVAL & INSTALLATION

✳✳ WARNING

Clean, high quality brake fluid is essential to the safe and proper operation of the brake system. You should always buy the highest quality brake fluid that is available. If the brake fluid becomes contaminated, drain and flush the system, then refill the master cylinder with new fluid. Never reuse any brake fluid. Any brake fluid that is removed from the system should be discarded. Also, do not allow any brake fluid to come in contact with a painted surface; it will damage the paint.

1988–91 Vehicles

1. Disconnect the negative battery cable.
2. Detach the electrical connector from the fluid level sensor.
3. Disconnect and cap or plug the four (4) brake lines on the master cylinder.
4. Remove the master cylinder-to-power booster nuts, then remove the master cylinder with the reservoir attached from the vehicle.
To install:
5. Position the master cylinder and tighten the retaining nuts to 20 ft. lbs. (27 Nm).
6. Uncap the brake lines, then connect them to the master cylinder and tighten to 13–15 ft. lbs. (17–20 Nm).
7. Attach the fluid level electrical sensor wires.
8. Connect the negative battery cable.
9. Refill the reservoir with an approved DOT 3 brake fluid and bleed the brake system.

1992–96 Vehicles

♦ See Figure 2

1. Disconnect the negative battery cable.
2. Unplug the electrical connectors from both solenoids.
3. Detach the electrical connector from the fluid level sensor.
4. Detach the 3-pin and 6 pin motor pack electrical connectors.
5. Disconnect and cap the four (4) brake lines from the master cylinder and modulator.
6. Remove the master cylinder-to-power booster bolts/nuts and remove the master cylinder and modulator assembly.

88259P01

Detach the solenoid electrical connectors

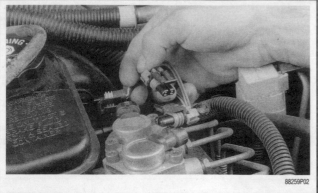

Unplug the fluid level electrical connector

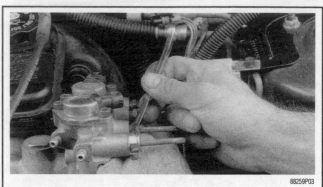

Place a shop rag under the fittings, then disconnect and plug the brake lines from the master cylinder

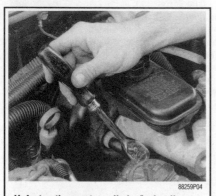

Unfasten the master cylinder/hydraulic modulator-to-power booster retainers . . .

. . . then remove the master cylinder/ hydraulic modulator assembly from its mounting

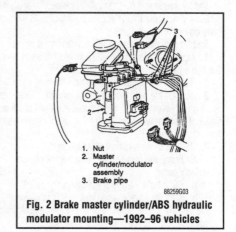

1. Nut
2. Master cylinder/modulator assembly
3. Brake pipe

Fig. 2 Brake master cylinder/ABS hydraulic modulator mounting—1992–96 vehicles

To install:

7. Position the master cylinder and tighten the retaining nuts to 20 ft. lbs. (27 Nm). and the brake lines-to-master cylinder and modulator to 15 ft. lbs. (20 Nm).

8. Connect the fluid level electrical sensor wires.

9. Attach the electrical connectors to both solenoids.

10. Connect the 3-pin and 6 pin motor pack electrical connectors.

11. Connect the negative battery cable.

12. Refill the reservoir with an approved DOT 3 brake fluid and bleed the brake system.

Power Brake Booster

REMOVAL & INSTALLATION

♦ See Figure 3

➡It is not necessary to remove or disconnect the master cylinder from the vehicle in order to remove the vacuum booster. However, if both the vacuum booster and master cylinder are to be removed, remove the master cylinder first as described earlier.

1. Remove the brake master cylinder, as outlined earlier in this section. Move the master cylinder forward just enough to clear the studs on the vacuum booster. This will flex the pipes slightly. Be careful not to bend or distort the brake pipes.

➡Place the master cylinder in an upright position to prevent fluid loss.

2. It may be necessary on some models to remove the left lower trim panel inside the vehicle, then disconnect the brake pedal-to-booster push rod from the brake pedal.

3. Disconnect the vacuum line from the booster.

4. Unfasten the brake booster mounting nuts, then remove the booster from the firewall.

To install:

5. To install, reverse the removal procedures.

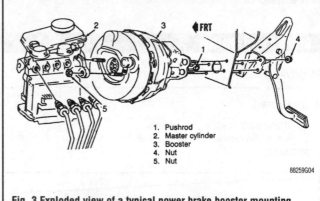

1. Pushrod
2. Master cylinder
3. Booster
4. Nut
5. Nut

Fig. 3 Exploded view of a typical power brake booster mounting

➡When installing the push rod to the brake pedal, tilt the entire vacuum booster push rod onto the clevis pin without putting undue side pressure on the push rod.

6. Tighten the master cylinder-to-power booster to 20 ft. lbs. (28 Nm) and the power booster mounting nuts to 20 ft. lbs. (28 Nm).

7. Properly bleed the brake system.

Proportioning Valve

REMOVAL & INSTALLATION

♦ See Figure 4

➡It may be necessary to remove the reservoir in order to remove the proportioning valve. If the reservoir is removed, bleed the brake system when finished.

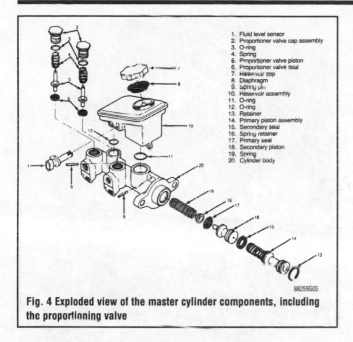

1. Fluid level sensor
2. Proportioner valve cap assembly
3. O-ring
4. Spring
5. Proportioner valve piston
6. Proportioner valve seal
7. Reservoir cap
8. Diaphragm
9. Spring pin
10. Reservoir assembly
11. O-ring
12. O-ring
13. Retainer
14. Primary piston assembly
15. Secondary seal
16. Spring retainer
17. Primary seal
18. Secondary piston
19. Spring
20. Cylinder body

88259G05

Fig. 4 Exploded view of the master cylinder components, including the proportioning valve

1. Disconnect the negative battery cable.
2. Remove the proportioning valve cap on the master cylinder.
3. Remove and discard the O-rings.
4. Remove the springs, the proportioning valve pistons and the seals from the valves.
5. Inspect the valves for corrosion or abnormal wear; to replace, if necessary.
6. Clean all parts in denatured alcohol and dry them with compressed air before reassembling.

To install:

7. To install, use new O-rings (coated with silicone grease) and reverse the removal procedures.
8. Install the new seals on the pistons with the lip facing the cap. Tighten the caps to 20 ft. lbs. (27 Nm).
9. Connect the negative battery cable.
10. Refill the reservoir and bleed the brake system.

Brake Hoses and Pipes

Metal lines and rubber brake hoses should be checked frequently for leaks and external damage. Metal lines are particularly prone to crushing and kinking under the vehicle. Any such deformation can restrict the proper flow of fluid and therefore impair braking at the wheels. Rubber hoses should be checked for cracking or scraping; such damage can create a weak spot in the hose and it could fail under pressure.

✳✳ CAUTION

Brake fluid contains polyglycol ethers and polyglycols. Avoid contact with the ,eyes and wash your hands thoroughly after handling brake fluid. If you do get brake fluid in your eyes, flush your eyes with clean, running water for 15 minutes. If eye irritation persists, or if you have taken brake fluid internally, IMMEDIATELY seek medical assistance.

Any time the lines are removed or disconnected, extreme cleanliness must be observed. Clean all joints and connections before disassembly (use a stiff bristle brush and clean brake fluid); be sure to plug the lines and ports as soon as they are opened. New lines and hoses should be flushed clean with brake fluid before installation to remove any contamination.

REMOVAL & INSTALLATION

▶ See Figures 5, 6, 7 and 8

1. Disconnect the negative battery cable.
2. Raise and safely support the vehicle on jackstands.
3. Remove any wheel and tire assemblies necessary for access to the particular line you are removing.
4. Thoroughly clean the surrounding area at the joints to be disconnected.
5. Place a suitable catch pan under the joint to be disconnected.
6. Using two wrenches (one to hold the joint and one to turn the fitting), disconnect the hose or line to be replaced.
7. Disconnect the other end of the line or hose, moving the drain pan if necessary. Always use a back-up wrench to avoid damaging the fitting.
8. Disconnect any retaining clips or brackets holding the line and remove the line from the vehicle.

➡ **If the brake system is to remain open for more time than it takes to swap lines, tape or plug each remaining clip and port to keep contaminants out and fluid in.**

To install:

9. Install the new line or hose, starting with the end farthest from the master cylinder. Connect the other end, then confirm that both fittings are correctly threaded and turn smoothly using finger pressure. Make sure the new line will not rub against any other part. Brake lines must be at least 1/2 in. (13mm) from the steering column and other moving parts. Any protective shielding or insulators must be reinstalled in the original location.

✳✳ WARNING

Make sure the hose is NOT kinked or touching any part of the frame or suspension after installation. These conditions may cause the hose to fail prematurely.

10. Using two wrenches as before, tighten each fitting.
11. Install any retaining clips or brackets on the lines.

TCCA9P09

Fig. 5 Use a brush to clean the fittings of any debris

TCCA9P10

Fig. 6 Use two wrenches to loosen the fitting. If available, use flare nut type wrenches

TCCA9P11

Fig. 7 Any gaskets/crush washers should be replaced with new ones during installation

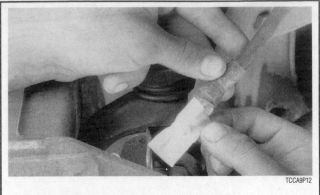

Fig. 8 Tape or plug the line to prevent contamination

12. If removed, install the wheel and tire assemblies, then carefully lower the vehicle to the ground.

13. Refill the brake master cylinder reservoir with clean, fresh brake fluid, meeting DOT 3 specifications. Properly bleed the brake system.

14. Connect the negative battery cable.

Bleeding Brake System

➡**For vehicles equipped with the Anti-Lock Brake System (ABS), please refer to the bleeding procedure in that section.**

The purpose of bleeding the brakes is to expel air trapped in the hydraulic system. The system must be bled whenever the pedal feels spongy, indicating that compressible air has entered the system. It must also be bled whenever the system has been opened or repaired. You will need a helper for this job.

✳✳ CAUTION

Never reuse brake fluid which has been bled from the brake system.

1. The sequence for bleeding is right rear, left front, left rear and right front. If the car has power brakes, remove the vacuum by applying the brakes several times. Do not run the engine while bleeding the brakes.

2. Clean all the bleeder screws. You may want to give each one a shot of penetrating solvent to loosen it up; seizure is a common problem with bleeder screws, which then break off, sometimes requiring replacement of the part to which they are attached.

3. Fill the master cylinder with DOT 3 brake fluid.

✳✳ WARNING

Brake fluid absorbs moisture from the air. Don't leave the master cylinder or the fluid container uncovered any longer than necessary. Be careful handling the fluid; it eats paint.

Bleeding the rear wheel drum brakes

Check the level of the fluid often when bleeding, and refill the reservoirs as necessary. Don't let them run dry, or you will have to repeat the process.

4. Attach a length of clear vinyl tubing to the bleeder screw on the wheel cylinder. Insert the other end of the tube into a clear, clean jar half filled with brake fluid.

5. Have your assistant slowly depress the brake pedal. As this is done, open the bleeder screw ⅓–½ of a turn, and allow the fluid to run through the tube. Then close the bleeder screw before the pedal reaches the end of its travel. Have your assistant slowly release the pedal. Repeat this process until no air bubbles appear in the expelled fluid.

6. Repeat the procedure on the other three brakes, checking the level of fluid in the master cylinder reservoir often.

After you're done, there should be no sponginess in the brake pedal feel. If there is, either there is still air in the line, in which case the process should be repeated, or there is a leak somewhere, which of course must be corrected before the car is moved.

FRONT DISC BRAKES

Older brake pads or shoes may contain asbestos, which has been determined to be a cancer causing agent. Never clean the brake surfaces with compressed air! Avoid inhaling any dust from any brake surface! When cleaning brake surfaces, use a commercially available brake cleaning fluid.

Pads

REMOVAL & INSTALLATION

1988–91 Vehicles

♦ **See Figures 9 thru 15**

1. Using a clean turkey baster or equivalent, siphon ⅔ of the brake fluid from the master cylinder reservoir and place in a suitable container.

2. Loosen the wheel lug nuts and raise the car. Remove the wheel and tire assembly, then reinstall two lug nuts to retain the rotor.

✳✳ WARNING

If you haven't removed some brake fluid from the master cylinder, it will overflow when the piston is retracted.

3. Position a 12 in. (305mm) pair of adjustable pliers over the inboard brake shoe tab and the inboard caliper housing so that the caliper piston bottoms in its bore.

4. Remove the allen head caliper mounting bolts. Inspect the bolts for corrosion, and replace as necessary.

5. Remove the caliper from the steering knuckle and suspend it from the body of the car with a length of wire. Do NOT allow the caliper to hang by its hose.

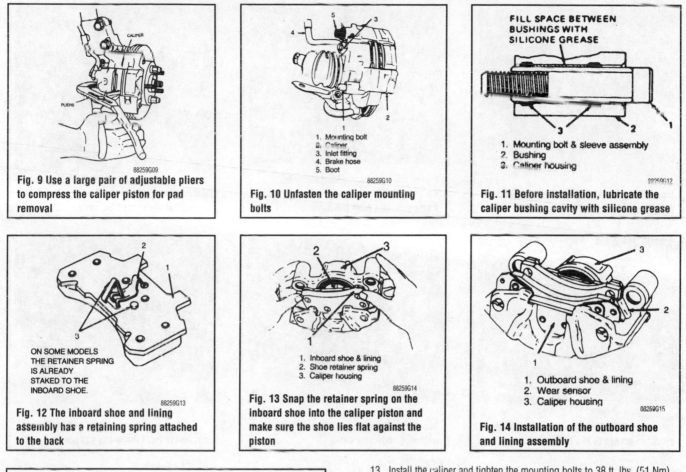

Fig. 9 Use a large pair of adjustable pliers to compress the caliper piston for pad removal

Fig. 10 Unfasten the caliper mounting bolts

1. Mounting bolt
2. Caliper
3. Inlet fitting
4. Brake hose
5. Boot

FILL SPACE BETWEEN BUSHINGS WITH SILICONE GREASE

1. Mounting bolt & sleeve assembly
2. Bushing
3. Caliper housing

Fig. 11 Before installation, lubricate the caliper bushing cavity with silicone grease

ON SOME MODELS THE RETAINER SPRING IS ALREADY STAKED TO THE INBOARD SHOE.

Fig. 12 The inboard shoe and lining assembly has a retaining spring attached to the back

1. Inboard shoe & lining
2. Shoe retainer spring
3. Caliper housing

Fig. 13 Snap the retainer spring on the inboard shoe into the caliper piston and make sure the shoe lies flat against the piston

1. Outboard shoe & lining
2. Wear sensor
3. Caliper housing

Fig. 14 Installation of the outboard shoe and lining assembly

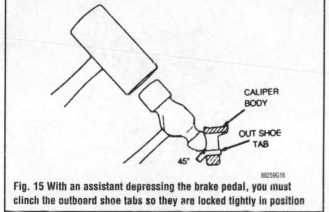

CALIPER BODY

OUT SHOE TAB

45°

Fig. 15 With an assistant depressing the brake pedal, you must clinch the outboard shoe tabs so they are locked tightly in position

6. Use a 12 in. (305mm) pair of adjustable pliers to straighten the bent over shoe tabs, then remove the outboard shoe and lining from the caliper.

7. Remove the inboard shoe and lining from the caliper.

8. Remove the rubber bushings from the mounting bolt holes.

To install:

9. Install new bushings and lubricate with a light coating of silicone grease before installation. These bushings must always be replaced when the pads are replaced. They are usually included in the pad replacement kits.

10. Install the retainer spring on the inboard pad. A new spring should be included in the pad replacement. On some models the spring is already staked to the inboard shoe.

11. Install the inboard shoe by snapping the retainer spring into the piston ID. The shoe must lay flat against the piston.

12. Install the outboard pad into the caliper with the wear sensor at the leading edge of the shoe during forward wheel rotation. The back of the shoe must lay flat against the caliper.

13. Install the caliper and tighten the mounting bolts to 38 ft. lbs. (51 Nm). Install the boots securely.

14. Partially lower the vehicle in order to apply the brake pedal at least three times to seat the linings.

15. Pry on the outboard shoe with a large flat-bladed tool between the outboard shoe flange and the hat section of the rotor. Keep the tool wedged in place for the following step.

16. Have an assistant apply moderate force on the brake pedal and clinch the outboard shoe tabs. The outboard shoe should be locked tightly in position.

17. Install the wheel and tire assembly, then carefully lower the car.

18. Fill the master cylinder to its proper level with fresh brake fluid meeting DOT 3 specifications. Since the brake hose wasn't disconnected, it isn't really necessary to bleed the brakes, although most mechanics do this as a matter of course.

1992–96 Vehicles

See Figures 16 and 17

1. Siphon ⅔ of the brake fluid from the master cylinder reservoir.

2. Loosen the wheel lug nuts, then raise and safely support the vehicle.

3. Remove the wheel and tire assembly, then reinstall two wheel nuts to retain the rotor.

4. You must push the piston into the caliper bore to provide clearance between the linings and rotors as follows:

   a. Install a large C-clamp over the top of the caliper housing and against the back of the outboard shoe.

   b. Slowly tighten the C-clamp until the piston is pushed into the caliper bore enough to slide the caliper assembly off the rotor.

5. Remove the mounting bolts and sleeve assemblies and remove the caliper from the rotor and knuckle. Suspend the caliper from the strut using a wire hook.

6. Use a suitable pry tool to disengage the buttons on the shoe from the holes in the caliper housing.

7. Remove the inboard shoe and lining.

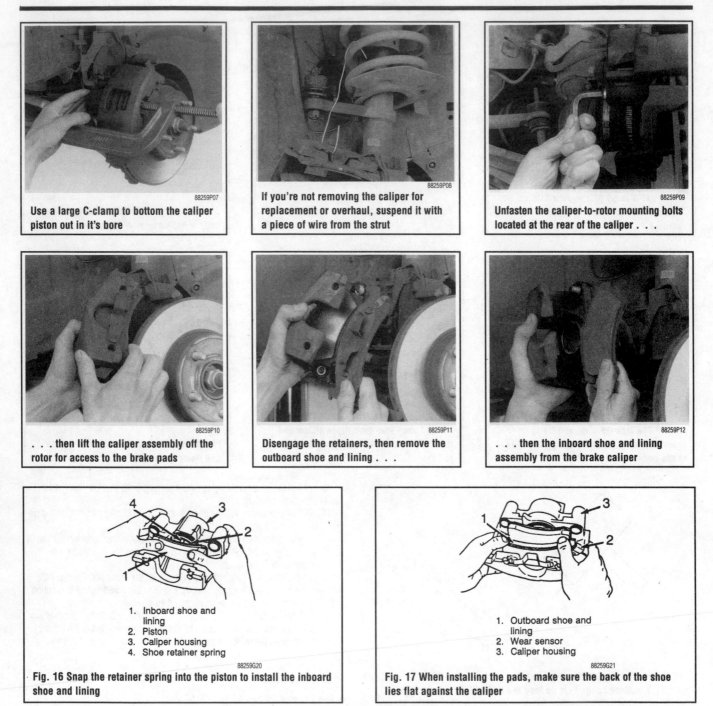

Use a large C-clamp to bottom the caliper piston out in it's bore

If you're not removing the caliper for replacement or overhaul, suspend it with a piece of wire from the strut

Unfasten the caliper-to-rotor mounting bolts located at the rear of the caliper . . .

. . . then lift the caliper assembly off the rotor for access to the brake pads

Disengage the retainers, then remove the outboard shoe and lining . . .

. . . then the inboard shoe and lining assembly from the brake caliper

1. Inboard shoe and lining
2. Piston
3. Caliper housing
4. Shoe retainer spring

Fig. 16 Snap the retainer spring into the piston to install the inboard shoe and lining

1. Outboard shoe and lining
2. Wear sensor
3. Caliper housing

Fig. 17 When installing the pads, make sure the back of the shoe lies flat against the caliper

To install:

8. Place the C-clamp over the caliper housing and into the piston. Carefully tighten the piston into the caliper bore.

9. After bottoming the piston, lift the inner edge of the boot and press out any trapped air. the boot must lay flat.

10. Install the inboard shoe by snapping the retainer spring into the piston.

11. Install the outboard pad into the caliper with the wear sensor at the leading edge of the shoe during forward wheel rotation. The back of the shoe must lay flat against the caliper.

12. Install the caliper and tighten the mounting bolts to 38 ft. lbs. (51 Nm). Install the boots securely.

13. Apply the brake pedal at least three times to seat the linings.

14. Install the wheel and lower the car.

15. Fill the master cylinder to its proper level with fresh brake fluid meeting DOT 3 specifications. Since the brake hose wasn't disconnected, it isn't really necessary to bleed the brakes, although most mechanics do this as a matter of course.

INSPECTION

The pad thickness should be inspected every time that the tires are removed for rotation. The outer pad an be checked by looking in at each end, which is the point at which the highest rate of wear occurs. The inner pad can be checked by looking down through the inspection hole in the top of the caliper. If the thickness of the pad is worn to within 1/32 in. (0.8mm) of the rivet at either end of the pad, all the pads should be replaced. This is the factory recommended measurement; your state's automobile inspection laws may not agree with this.

➡**Always replace all pads on both front wheels at the same time. Failure to do so will result in uneven braking action and premature wear.**

Caliper

REMOVAL & INSTALLATION

1. Remove the caliper from the rotor. Follow the procedure outlined under brake pad removal.
2. Unfasten the bolt securing the brake hose to the caliper. Plug or cap the brake line.
3. Remove the mounting bolts, then remove the caliper from the vehicle.
4. Inspect the caliper mounting bolts for corrosion and replace them if necessary.

To install:

5. With the pads installed as outlined in pad replacement, install the caliper and mounting bolts and torque to 38 ft. lbs. (51 Nm).
6. Connect the brake hose fitting and tighten to 33 ft. lbs. (45 Nm).
7. The remainder of installation is the reverse of the removal procedure.
8. After installation is complete, properly bleed the brake system, as outlined in this section.

OVERHAUL

▶ See Figures 18 thru 27

➡Some vehicles may be equipped dual piston calipers. The procedure to overhaul the caliper is essentially the same with the exception of multiple pistons, O-rings and dust boots.

1. Remove the caliper from the vehicle and place on a clean workbench.

✳✳ CAUTION

NEVER place your fingers in front of the pistons in an attempt to catch or protect the pistons when applying compressed air. This could result in personal injury!

➡Depending upon the vehicle, there are two different ways to remove the piston from the caliper. Refer to the brake pad replacement procedure to make sure you have the correct procedure for your vehicle.

2. The first method is as follows:
   a. Stuff a shop towel or a block of wood into the caliper to catch the piston.
   b. Remove the caliper piston using compressed air applied into the caliper inlet hole. Inspect the piston for scoring, nicks, corrosion and/or worn or damaged chrome plating. The piston must be replaced if any of these conditions are found.
3. For the second method, you must rotate the piston to retract it from the caliper.
4. If equipped, remove the anti-rattle clip.
5. Use a prytool to remove the caliper boot, being careful not to scratch the housing bore.
6. Remove the piston seals from the groove in the caliper bore.
7. Carefully loosen the brake bleeder valve cap and valve from the caliper housing.
8. Inspect the caliper bores, pistons and mounting threads for scoring or excessive wear.
9. Use crocus cloth to polish out light corrosion from the piston and bore.
10. Clean all parts with denatured alcohol and dry with compressed air.

To assemble:

11. Lubricate and install the bleeder valve and cap.
12. Install the new seals into the caliper bore grooves, making sure they are not twisted.
13. Lubricate the piston bore.
14. Install the pistons and boots into the bores of the calipers and push to the bottom of the bores.
15. Use a suitable driving tool to seat the boots in the housing.

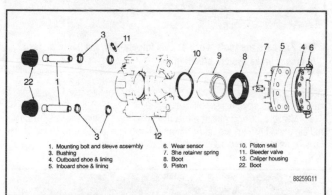
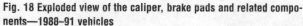

Fig. 18 Exploded view of the caliper, brake pads and related components—1988–91 vehicles

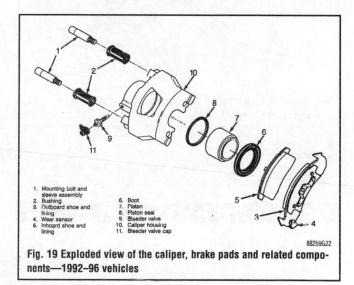

Fig. 19 Exploded view of the caliper, brake pads and related components—1992–96 vehicles

Fig. 20 For some types of calipers, use compressed air to drive the piston out of the caliper, but make sure to keep your fingers clear

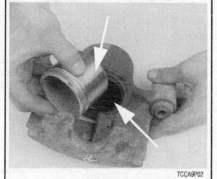

Fig. 21 Withdraw the piston from the caliper bore

Fig. 22 On some vehicles, you must remove the anti-rattle clip

Fig. 23 Use a prytool to carefully pry around the edge of the boot . . .

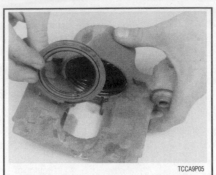

Fig. 24 . . . then remove the boot from the caliper housing, taking care not to score or damage the bore

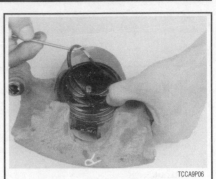

Fig. 25 Use extreme caution when removing the piston seal; DO NOT scratch the caliper bore

Fig. 26 Use the proper size driving tool and a mallet to properly seal the boots in the caliper housing

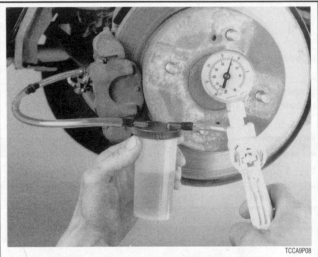

Fig. 27 There are tools, such as this Mighty-Vac, available to assist in proper brake system bleeding

16. Install the caliper in the vehicle.
17. Install the wheel and tire assembly, then carefully lower the vehicle.
18. Properly bleed the brake system.

Brake Disc (Rotor)

REMOVAL & INSTALLATION

1. Siphon ⅔ of the brake fluid from the master cylinder reservoir.
2. Loosen the wheel lug nuts, then raise and safely support the vehicle.
3. Remove the wheel and tire assembly, then reinstall two wheel nuts to retain the rotor.
4. Remove the caliper from the vehicle.
5. Remove the rotor by pulling it straight off the wheel lug studs and hub assembly.
6. To install, reposition the rotor and install the caliper and pads as outlined earlier.

INSPECTION

1. Check the rotor surface for wear or scoring. Deep scoring, grooves or rust pitting can be removed by refacing, a job to be referred to your local machine shop or garage. Minimum thickness is stamped on the rotor (21.08 mm). If the rotor will be thinner than this after refinishing, it must be replaced.
2. Check the rotor parallelism (thickness variation); it must vary less than 0.01mm measured at four or more points around the circumference. Make all measurements at the same distance in from the edge of the rotor. Refinish the rotor if it fails to meet this specification.

3. Measure the disc runout with a dial indicator. If runout exceeds 0.10mm, and the wheel bearings are OK (if runout is being measured with the disc on the car), the rotor must be refaced or replaced as necessary.

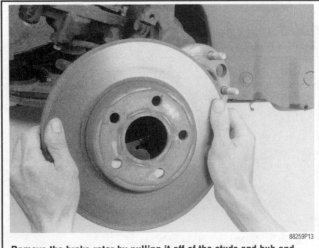

Remove the brake rotor by pulling it off of the studs and hub and bearing assembly

REAR DRUM BRAKES

Brake Drums

REMOVAL & INSTALLATION

1. Loosen the wheel lug nuts, then raise and support the car. Matchmark the relationship of the wheel to the axle and remove the wheel.
2. Mark the relationship of the drum to the axle and remove the drum. If it cannot be slipped off easily, try the following:

REAR DRUM BRAKE COMPONENTS

1. Return springs
2. Actuator link
3. Hold-down springs
4. Hold-down pins
5. Actuator lever
6. Lever return spring
7. Primary shoe and lining
8. Parking brake lever
9. Adjusting screw spring
10. Adjusting screw
11. Secondary shoe and lining
12. Parking brake strut and spring

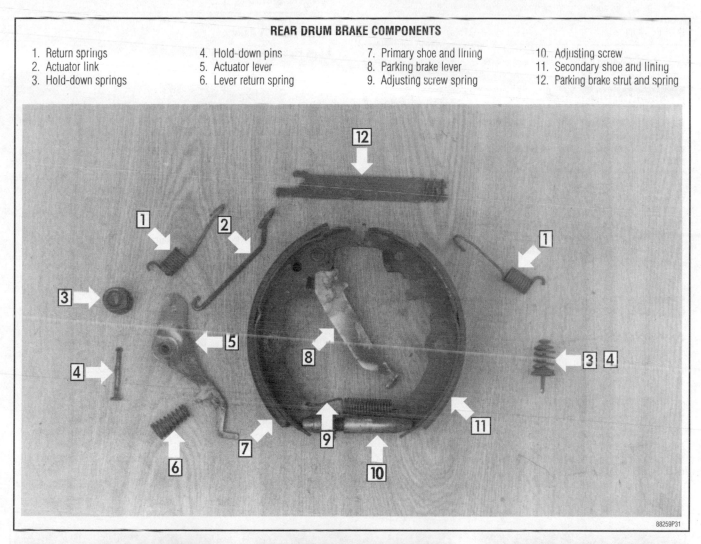

Some vehicles may have a retainer that must be removed before you can take off the drum

Usually, the drum will slip off the hub and bearing with ease

The brake drum has a wear limit specifications stamped on it (see arrows)

a. Check to see that the parking brake is fully released. If so, the brake shoes are probably locked against the drum. See the Adjustment procedure located under brake pad removal for details on how to back off the adjuster.

b. Remove the access hole plug from the backing plate and insert a suitable tool through the hole to push the parking brake lever off its stop. This will allow the shoe linings to retract slightly.

c. Insert a punch tool through the hole at the bottom of the splash shield. Tap gently on the tool to loosen the drum.

d. Use a rubber mallet to tap gently on the outer rim of the drum.

3. To install, reposition the drum making sure to align the matchmarks made during removal.

4. Install the wheel and tire assembly, then carefully lower the vehicle

5. The lug nut tightening specifications is 100 ft. lbs. (136 Nm).

INSPECTION

1. After removing the brake drum, wipe out the accumulated dust with a damp cloth.

✳✳ CAUTION

Do not blow the brake dust out of the drums with compressed air or lung power. Brake linings may contain asbestos, a known cancer causing substance. Dispose of the cloth used to clean the parts after use.

2. Inspect the drums for cracks, deep grooves, roughness, scoring, or out-of-roundness. Replace any drum which is cracked; do not try to weld it up.

3. Smooth any slight scores by polishing the friction surface with fine emery cloth. Heavy or extensive scoring will cause excessive lining wear and should be removed from the drum through resurfacing, a job to be referred to your local machine shop or garage. The maximum finished diameter of the drums is 200.64mm. The drum must be replaced if the diameter is 201.40mm or greater.

Brake Shoes

INSPECTION

After removing the brake drum, inspect the brake shoes. If the lining is worn down to within $\frac{1}{32}$ in. (0.8mm) of a rivet, the shoes must be replaced.

➡**This figure may disagree with your state's automobile inspection laws.**

If the brake lining is soaked with brake fluid or grease, it must be replaced. If this is the case, the brake drum should be sanded with crocus cloth to remove all traces of brake fluid, and the wheel cylinders should be rebuilt. Clean all grit from the friction surface of the drum before replacing it.

If the lining is chipped, cracked, or otherwise damaged, it must be replaced with a new lining.

➡**Always replace the brake linings in sets of two on both ends of the axle. Never replace just one shoe, or both shoes on one side and not the other. When replacing the brakes, it is a good idea to replace one side at a time so that you always have an example to refer to if you get confused during reassembly.**

Check the condition of the shoes, retracting springs, and hold-down springs for signs of overheating. If the shoes or springs have a slight blue color, this indicates overheating and replacement of the shoes and springs is recommended. The wheel cylinders should be rebuilt as a precaution against future problems.

REMOVAL & INSTALLATION

Except 1988–91 Beretta

▶ **See Figure 28**

1. Loosen the lug nuts on the wheel to be serviced, raise and support the car, and remove the wheel and brake drum.

➡**It is not really necessary to remove the hub and wheel bearing assembly from the axle, but it does make the job easier. If you can work with the hub and bearing assembly in place, skip down to Step 3.**

2. Remove the four hub and bearing assembly retaining bolts and remove the assembly from the axle.

3. Remove the return springs from the shoes with a pair of needle nose pliers. There are also special brake spring pliers for this job.

4. Remove the hold-down springs by gripping them with a pair of pliers, then pressing down and turning 90°. There are special tools to grab and turn these parts, but pliers work fairly well.

5. Remove the shoe hold-down pins from behind the brake backing plate. They will simply slide out once the hold-down spring tension is relieved.

6. Lift up the actuator lever for the self-adjusting mechanism and remove the actuating link. Remove the actuator lever, pivot, and the pivot return spring.

7. Spread the shoes apart to clear the wheel cylinder pistons and remove the parking brake strut and spring.

8. If the hub and bearing assembly is still in place, spread the shoes far enough apart to clear it.

9. Disconnect the parking brake cable from the lever. Remove the shoes, still connected by their adjusting screw spring, from the car.

10. With the shoes removed, note the position of the adjusting spring and remove the spring and adjusting screw.

11. Remove the C-clip from the parking brake lever and remove the lever from the secondary shoe.

12. Use a damp cloth to remove all dirt and dust from the backing plate and brake parts. See the warning about brake dust in the drum removal procedure.

13. Check the wheel cylinders by carefully pulling the lower edges of the wheel cylinder boots away from the cylinders. If there is excessive leakage, the inside of the cylinder will be moist with fluid. If leakage exists, a wheel cylinder overhaul is in order. Do not delay, because brake failure could result.

88259P17

Before beginning brake shoe removal, spray the components with a commercially available cleaner

88259P18

Use a suitable tool to unhook the return springs

88259P19

Unhook the right side return spring with a suitable brake spring removal tool . . .

. . . then remove the other return spring from the assembly

Use the brake tool to compress the hold-down spring and twist the plate to free the pin

After removing the actuating link, remove the actuator lever and pivot return spring

Remove the parking brake strut and spring

Spread the brake shoes enough to clear the hub and bearing . . .

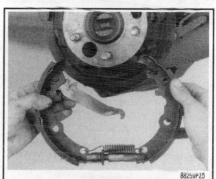

. . . then disconnect the parking brake cable and remove the shoe and spring assembly from the vehicle

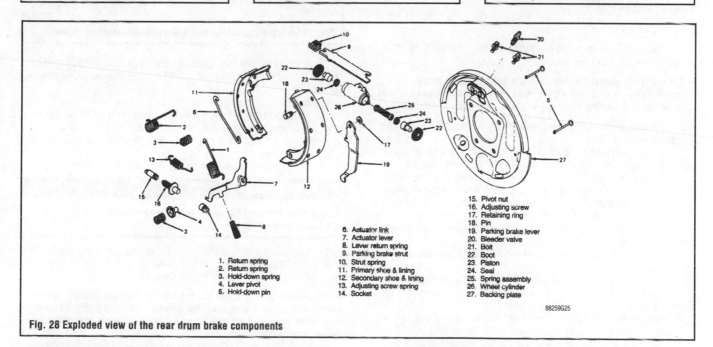

1. Return spring
2. Return spring
3. Hold-down spring
4. Lever pivot
5. Hold-down pin
6. Actuator link
7. Actuator lever
8. Lever return spring
9. Parking brake strut
10. Strut spring
11. Primary shoe & lining
12. Secondary shoe & lining
13. Adjusting screw spring
14. Socket
15. Pivot nut
16. Adjusting screw
17. Retaining ring
18. Pin
19. Parking brake lever
20. Bleeder valve
21. Bolt
22. Boot
23. Piston
24. Seal
25. Spring assembly
26. Wheel cylinder
27. Backing plate

Fig. 28 Exploded view of the rear drum brake components

➡A small amount of fluid will be present to act as a lubricant for the wheel cylinder pistons. Fluid spilling from the boot center hole, after the piston is removed, indicates cup leakage and the necessity for cylinder overhaul.

To install

14. Check the backing plate attaching bolts to make sure that they are tight. Use fine emery cloth to clean all rust and dirt from the shoe contact surfaces on the plate.

15. Lubricate the fulcrum end of the parking brake lever with brake grease specially made for the purpose. Install the lever on the secondary shoe and secure with C-clip.

16. Install the adjusting screw and spring on the shoes, connecting them together. The coils of the spring must not be over the star wheel on the adjuster. The left and right hand springs are not interchangeable. Do not mix them up.

17. Lubricate the shoe contact surfaces on the backing plate with the brake grease. Be certain when you are using this stuff that none of it actually gets on

the linings or drums. Apply the same grease to the point where the parking brake cable contacts the plate. Use the grease sparingly.

18. Spread the shoe assemblies apart and connect the parking brake cable. Install the shoes on the backing plate, engaging the shoes at the top temporarily with the wheel cylinder pistons. Make sure that the star wheel on the adjuster is lined up with the adjusting hole in the backing plate, if the hole is back there.

19. Spread the shoes apart slightly and install the parking brake strut and spring. Make sure that the end of the strut without the spring engages the parking brake lever. The end with the spring engages the primary shoe (the one with the shorter lining).

20. Install the actuator pivot, lever and return spring. Install the actuating link in the shoe retainer. Lift up the actuator lever and hook the link into the lever.

21. Install the hold-down pins through the back of the plate, install the lever pivots and hold-down springs. Install the shoe return springs with a pair of pliers. Be very careful not to stretch or otherwise distort these springs.

22. Take a look at everything. Make sure the linings are in the right place, the self-adjusting mechanism is correctly installed, and the parking brake parts are all hooked up. If in doubt, remove the other wheel and take a look at that one for comparison.

23. Measure the width of the linings, then measure the inside width of the drum. Adjust the linings by means of the adjuster so that the drum will fit onto the linings.

24. Install the hub and bearing assembly onto the axle if removed. Tighten the retaining bolts to 38 ft. lbs. (51 Nm).

25. Install the drum and wheel, tightening the lug nuts to 100 ft. lbs. (136 Nm). Adjust the brakes using the procedure given in this section. Be sure to install a rubber hole cover in the knock-out hole after the adjustment is complete. Adjust the parking brake.

26. Lower the car and check the pedal for any sponginess or lack of a hard feel. Check the braking action and the parking brake. The brakes must not be applied severely immediately after installation. They should be used moderately for the first 200 miles of city driving or 1000 miles of highway driving, to allow the linings to conform to the shape of the drum.

1988–91 Beretta

▶ **See Figure 29**

1. Loosen the lug nuts on the wheel to be serviced, raise and support the car, and remove the wheel and brake drum.

➡**It is not really necessary to remove the hub and wheel bearing assembly from the axle, but it does make the job easier. If you can work with the hub and bearing assembly in place, skip down to Step 3.**

2. Remove the four hub and bearing assembly retaining bolts and remove the assembly from the axle.

3. Remove the actuator and return spring from the shoes with a pair of needle nose pliers. There are also special brake spring pliers for this job.

4. Remove the spring connecting link, adjuster actuator and spring washer.

5. Remove the hold down springs by gripping them with a pair of pliers, then pressing down and turning 90°. There are special tools to grab and turn these parts, but pliers work fairly well.

6. Remove the shoe hold-down pins from behind the brake backing plate. They will simply slide out once the hold-down spring tension is relieved.

7. Disconnect the parking brake cable and remove the shoe and lining assemblies.

8. Remove the adjusting screw assembly and the lower return spring.

9. Remove the retaining ring, pin, spring washer and park brake lever from the shoe and lining.

10. Use a damp cloth to remove all dirt and dust from the backing plate and brake parts. See the warning about brake dust in the drum removal procedure.

11. Check the wheel cylinders by carefully pulling the lower edges of the wheel cylinder boots away from the cylinders. If there is excessive leakage, the inside of the cylinder will be moist with fluid. If leakage exists, a wheel cylinder overhaul is in order. Do not delay, because brake failure could result.

➡**A small amount of fluid will be present to act as a lubricant for the wheel cylinder pistons. Fluid spilling from the boot center hole, after the piston is removed, indicates cup leakage and the necessity for cylinder overhaul.**

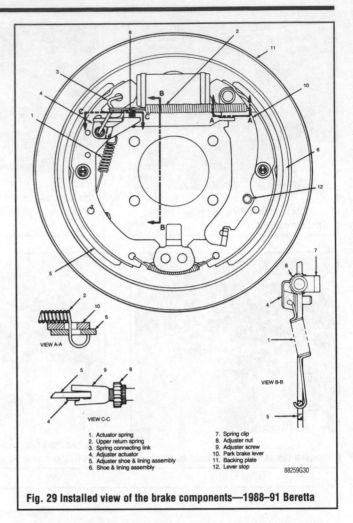

1. Actuator spring
2. Upper return spring
3. Spring connecting link
4. Adjuster actuator
5. Adjuster shoe & lining assembly
6. Shoe & lining assembly
7. Spring clip
8. Adjuster nut
9. Adjuster screw
10. Park brake lever
11. Backing plate
12. Lever stop

88259G30

Fig. 29 Installed view of the brake components—1988–91 Beretta

12. Check the backing plate attaching bolts to make sure that they are tight. Use fine emery cloth to clean all rust and dirt from the shoe contact surfaces on the plate.

To install

13. Lubricate the fulcrum end of the parking brake lever with brake grease specially made for the purpose. Also lubricate the adjusting screw threads, inside diameter of the socket and the socket face. Install the adjuster spring clip in the same position as when removed.

14. Install the lower return spring between the shoe and linings.

✳✳ WARNING

Do not over-stretch the lower return spring more than 3.88 in. (98.5mm) or it will be damaged.

15. Connect the parking brake cable to the adjuster shoe then install both shoe and lining assemblies with the hold down springs and pins. The lower return spring should be positioned under the anchor plate.

➡**The adjuster shoe and lining is the one in which the adjuster pin was installed in the shoe web. Also, the adjuster shoe and lining is to the front of the car on the left side brake assembly or to the rear of the car on the right side brake assembly.**

16. Install the adjuster screw assembly between the two shoe and lining assemblies and position to the backing plate.

➡**Proper installation of the adjusting screw is with the adjuster screw engaging the notch in the adjuster shoe and the spring clip pointing towards the backing plate.**

17. Install the spring washer with the concave side against the web of the adjuster shoe and lining.

18. Install the adjuster actuator so that the top leg engages the notch in the adjuster screw.

19. Install the spring connecting link and hold in place.

20. Install the upper return spring by inserting the angled hook end of the spring through the park brake lever and the shoe and lining. Grasp the long straight section of the spring with suitable pliers and pull the spring straight across and then down to hook into the crook on the spring connecting link.

✳✳ WARNING

Do not over-stretch the upper return spring more than 5.49 in. (139.5mm) or it will be damaged.

21. Install the actuator spring with suitable pliers.

22. Take a look at everything. Make sure the linings are in the right place, the self-adjusting mechanism is correctly installed, and the parking brake parts are all hooked up. If in doubt, remove the other wheel and take a look at that one for comparison.

23. Measure the width of the linings, then measure the inside width of the drum. Adjust the linings by means of the adjuster so that the drum will fit onto the linings.

24. Install the hub and bearing assembly onto the axle if removed. Tighten the retaining bolts to 38 ft. lbs.

25. Install the drum and wheel tightening the lug nuts to 100 ft. lbs. Adjust the brakes using the procedure given earlier in this Section. Make sure the parking brake lever is on its stop.(See drum removal). Be sure to install a rubber hole cover in the knock-out hole after the adjustment is complete. Adjust the parking brake.

26. Lower the car and check the pedal for any sponginess or lack of a hard feel. Check the braking action and the parking brake. The brakes must not be applied severely immediately after installation. They should be used moderately for the first 200 miles of city driving or 1000 miles of highway driving, to allow the linings to conform to the shape of the drum.

ADJUSTMENTS

▶ See Figures 30, 31 and 32

On the Corsica the drum brakes are designed to self-adjust when applied with the car moving in reverse. On the Beretta the drum brakes self-adjust during normal service. Both drum brake systems can also be adjusted manually however, and should be whenever the linings are replaced.

1. Raise and support the vehicle safely.
2. Remove the tire and wheel assembly.
3. Mark the relationship of the wheel to the axle flange, then remove the brake drum.
4. Measure the drum inside diameter using tool J 2177–A, or equivalent.
5. Turn the star wheel, and adjust the shoe and lining diameter to be 0.050 in. (1.27mm) for 1988–90 or 0.030 in. (0.76mm) for 1991–96 vehicles.
6. Install the drums and wheels aligning the previous marks.
7. Carefully lower the vehicle.
8. Tighten the wheel nuts to 100 ft. lbs. (140 Nm).
9. Make several alternate forward and reserve stops applying firm force to the brake pedal until ample pedal reserve is built up.

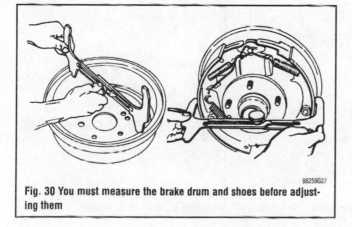

Fig. 30 You must measure the brake drum and shoes before adjusting them

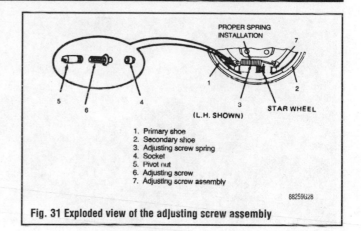

1. Primary shoe
2. Secondary shoe
3. Adjusting screw spring
4. Socket
5. Pivot nut
6. Adjusting screw
7. Adjusting screw assembly

Fig. 31 Exploded view of the adjusting screw assembly

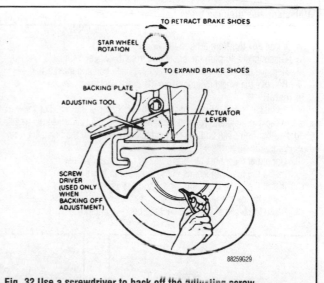

Fig. 32 Use a screwdriver to back off the adjusting screw

Wheel Cylinders

REMOVAL & INSTALLATION

Except 1988–91 Beretta

1. Raise and safely support the rear of the vehicle with jackstands.
2. Remove the tire and wheel assembly, then remove the brake drum.
3. Clean any dirt from around the wheel cylinder.
4. Disconnect and plug the brake line from the wheel cylinder.
5. Remove the wheel cylinder bolts using a #6 Torx® socket.
6. Remove the wheel cylinder from the brake backing plate.

To install:

7. Position the wheel cylinder assembly and hold in place with a wooden block between the cylinder and axle flange.
8. Install the wheel cylinder bolts using a # 6 Torx socket. Tighten the bolts to 15 ft. lbs. (20 Nm).
9. Uncap and attach the fluid line, then tighten the tube nut to 13 ft. lbs. (17 Nm).
10. Install the brake drum and the wheel and tire assembly.
11. Carefully lower the vehicle.
12. Bleed the brake system. Inspect the brake operation.

1988–91 Beretta

1. Raise and support the rear of the vehicle on jackstands.
2. Remove the tire and wheel assembly, then remove the brake drum.
3. Remove the brake shoes and attaching hardware.

Unfasten, then plug the brake line from the wheel cylinder

Unfasten the wheel cylinder-to-brake backing plate bolts . . .

4. Clean any dirt from around the wheel cylinder.
5. Disconnect and plug the brake line from the wheel cylinder.
6. Remove the wheel cylinder-to-backing plate bolt and lockwasher.
7. Remove the wheel cylinder from the brake backing plate.

To install:

8. To install, apply a liquid gasket to the shoulder of the wheel cylinder that faces the backing plate and reverse the removal procedures. Tighten the wheel cylinder-to-backing plate bolt to 106 inch lbs. (12 Nm) and the brake line-to-wheel cylinder to 13 ft. lbs. (17 Nm).
9. Unplug and connect the brake line to the wheel cylinder
10. Install the brake shoes, as outlined earlier in this section.
11. Install the brake drum and wheel and tire assembly.
12. Carefully lower the vehicle.
13. Bleed the brake system. Inspect the brake operation.

OVERHAUL

Wheel cylinder overhaul kits may be available, but often at little or no savings over a reconditioned wheel cylinder. It often makes sense with these components to substitute a new or reconditioned part instead of attempting an overhaul.

If no replacement is available, or you would prefer to overhaul your wheel cylinders, the following procedure may be used. When rebuilding and installing wheel cylinders, avoid getting any contaminants into the system. Always use clean, new, high quality brake fluid. If dirty or improper fluid has been used, it will be necessary to drain the entire system, flush the system with proper brake fluid, replace all rubber components, then refill and bleed the system.

1. Remove the wheel cylinder from the vehicle and place on a clean work-bench.

Remove the outer boots from the wheel cylinder

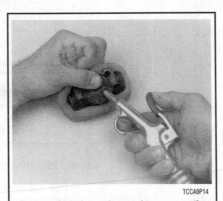

Compressed air can be used to remove the pistons and seals

Remove the pistons, cup seals and spring from the cylinder

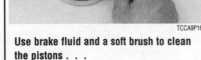

Use brake fluid and a soft brush to clean the pistons . . .

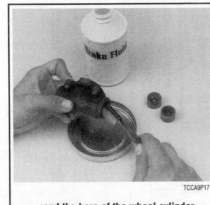

. . . and the bore of the wheel cylinder

Once cleaned and inspected, the wheel cylinder is ready for assembly

Lubricate the cup seals with brake fluid

Install the spring, then the cup seals in the bore

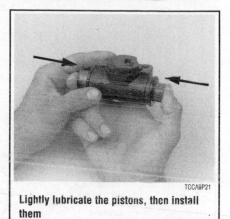

Lightly lubricate the pistons, then install them

The boots can now be installed over the wheel cylinder ends

2. First remove and discard the old rubber boots, then withdraw the pistons. Piston cylinders are equipped with seals and a spring assembly, all located behind the pistons in the cylinder bore.

3. Remove the remaining inner components, seals and spring assembly. Compressed air may be useful in removing these components. If no com-

pressed air is available, be VERY careful not to score the wheel cylinder bore when removing parts from it. Discard all components for which replacements were supplied in the rebuild kit.

4. Wash the cylinder and metal parts in denatured alcohol or clean brake fluid.

✳✳ WARNING

Never use a mineral-based solvent such as gasoline, kerosene or paint thinner for cleaning purposes. These solvents will swell rubber components and quickly deteriorate them.

5. Allow the parts to air dry or use compressed air. Do not use rags for cleaning, since lint will remain in the cylinder bore.

6. Inspect the piston and replace it if it shows scratches.

7. Lubricate the cylinder bore and seals using clean brake fluid.

8. Position the spring assembly.

9. Install the inner seals, then the pistons.

10. Insert the new boots into the counterbores by hand. Do not lubricate the boots.

11. Install the wheel cylinder.

PARKING BRAKE

Cable

REMOVAL & INSTALLATION

♦ **See Figures 33 and 34**

Front Cable

1. Raise and safely support the vehicle on jackstands.
2. Loosen, but do not remove, the equalizer nut to remove the cable.
3. Disconnect the cable from the equalizer and right rear cable.
4. Remove the hand grip from the parking brake lever inside the vehicle.
5. Remove the console.
6. Disconnect the cable from the parking brake lever.
7. Remove the nut holding the cable to the floor.
8. Remove the exhaust hanger bracket mounting nuts.
9. Remove the catalytic converter shield.
10. Remove the cable.
11. To install, lubricate the cable and reverse the removal procedures. Adjust the parking brake.

Rear Cable

1988–89 VEHICLES

1. Raise and support the vehicle on jackstands.
2. Loosen the equalizer nut until the cable tension is released. Must be separated from the threaded rod, if removing the left cable.

3. Disconnect the right side cable button from the connector.
4. Disconnect the conduit end of the cable from the bracket on the axle.
5. Remove the tire and the brake drum.
6. Disconnect the cable from the parking brake lever attached to the brake shoes.
7. Remove the conduit end from the brake shoe backing plate.
8. To install, lubricate the cable and reverse the removal procedures. Adjust the parking brake.

1990–91 VEHICLES

1. Raise and support the vehicle on jackstands.
2. Loosen the equalizer nut until the cable tension is released. Must be separated from the threaded rod, if removing the right cable.
3. Disconnect the left side cable button from the connector.
4. Disconnect the conduit end of the cable from the bracket on the axle.
5. Remove the tire and the brake drum.
6. Disconnect the cable from the parking brake lever attached to the brake shoes.
7. Remove the conduit end from the brake shoe backing plate.
8. To install, lubricate the cable and reverse the removal procedures. Adjust the parking brake.

1992–96 VEHICLES

1. Raise and support the vehicle on jackstands.
2. Loosen the equalizer nut until the cable tension is released. Must be separated from the threaded rod, if removing the left cable.
3. Remove the tire and the brake drum.

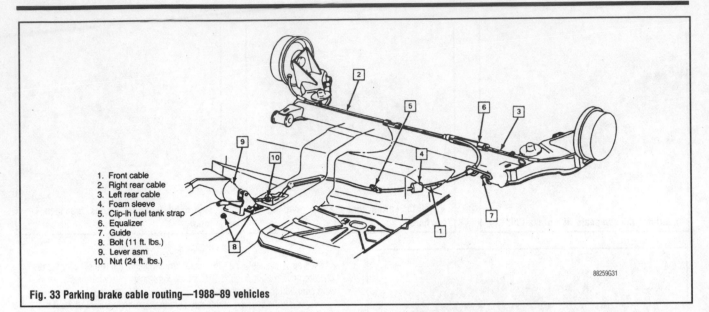

1. Front cable
2. Right rear cable
3. Left rear cable
4. Foam sleeve
5. Clip-lh fuel tank strap
6. Equalizer
7. Guide
8. Bolt (11 ft. lbs.)
9. Lever asm
10. Nut (24 ft. lbs.)

88259G31

Fig. 33 Parking brake cable routing—1988–89 vehicles

4. Insert a screwdriver between the brake shoe and the top part of the brake adjuster bracket.

5. Push the bracket to the front and release the top adjuster bracket rod.

6. Disconnect the hold down the spring, actuator lever and lever return spring.

7. Disconnect the adjuster screw spring.

8. Disconnect the top rear brake shoe return spring.

9. Disconnect the parking brake cable from the parking brake lever.

10. Disconnect the conduit fitting from the backing plate while depressing the conduit fitting retaining tangs.

11. Disconnect the cable end button from the connector, right side only.

12. Disconnect the conduit fitting from the axle bracket while depressing the conduit fitting retaining tangs.

To install:

13. Connect the conduit retaining tangs and conduit fitting into the axle bracket.

14. Connect the cable end button to the connector, right side only.

15. Connect the conduit fitting to the backing plate.

16. Connect the parking brake cable to the parking brake lever.

17. Connect the top rear brake shoe return spring.

18. Connect the adjuster screw spring.

19. Connect the lever return spring, actuator lever, and rear hold down spring.

20. Connect the top adjuster bracket rod.

21. Install the brake drum and tire and wheel assembly.

22. Adjust the parking brake cable and lower the vehicle.

ADJUSTMENT

Except 1988–91 Beretta

1. Adjust the brakes as described earlier in this section.

2. If the vehicle is equipped with a hand parking brake, apply the parking brake lever exactly 5 clicks. If the vehicle has a foot operated parking brake, depress the parking brake pedal 2 ratchet clicks.

3. Raise and safely support the rear of the vehicle on jackstands.

➥**Make sure the equalizer nut groove is liberally lubricated with grease.**

4. Tighten the adjusting nut until the right rear wheel can just be turned rearward using two hands but is locked when forward rotation is attempted.

5. Release the parking brake and check to see if both wheels turn freely in either direction by hand.

6. Carefully lower the vehicle.

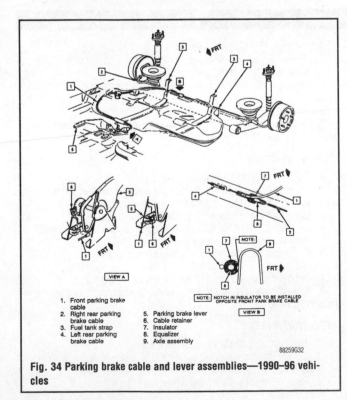

1. Front parking brake cable
2. Right rear parking brake cable
3. Fuel tank strap
4. Left rear parking brake cable
5. Parking brake lever
6. Cable retainer
7. Insulator
8. Equalizer
9. Axle assembly

NOTE: NOTCH IN INSULATOR TO BE INSTALLED OPPOSITE FRONT PARK BRAKE CABLE

VIEW A

VIEW B

88259G32

Fig. 34 Parking brake cable and lever assemblies—1990–96 vehicles

88259P29

The cable is adjusted at the equalizer

1988–91 Beretta

♦ **See Figure 35**

1. Adjust the brakes as described earlier in this section.
2. Apply and release the parking brake 6 times to 10 clicks. Release the parking brake.

➡ **Check to see that both rear wheels turn freely.**

3. Check the parking brake pedal assembly for full release by turning the ignition to **ON** and inspecting the BRAKE warning lamp. The lamp should be off. If the Brake lamp is on and the brake appears to be released, operate the pedal release lever and pull downward on the front parking brake cable to remove the slack from the assembly.
4. Apply the parking brake to 4 clicks.
5. Raise and support the rear of the vehicle on jackstands.
6. Locate the access hole in the backing plate and adjust the parking brake cable until a ⅛ in. (3mm) drill bit can be inserted between the brake shoe webbing and the parking brake lever.
7. Check to make sure that a ¼ in. (6mm) drill bit will NOT fit in the same position.
8. Release the parking brake and check to see if both wheels turn freely by hand.
9. Carefully lower the vehicle.

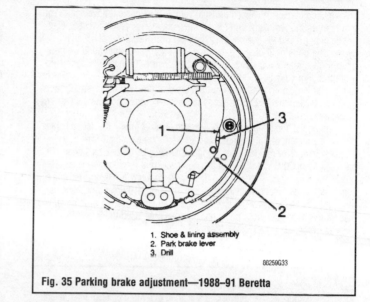

1. Shoe & lining assembly
2. Park brake lever
3. Drill

86259G33

Fig. 35 Parking brake adjustment—1988–91 Beretta

ANTI-LOCK BRAKE SYSTEM

General Information

The Anti-Lock Brake System (ABS), used on 1992–96 vehicles, has been designed to improve the controllability and steerability of a vehicle during braking that would cause one or more wheels to lock. ABS-VI accomplishes this objective by controlling the hydraulic pressure applied to each wheel brake.

BASIC KNOWLEDGE REQUIRED

Before using this section, it is important that you have a basic knowledge of the following items. Without this basic knowledge, it will be difficult to use the diagnostic procedures contained in this section.

Basic Electrical Circuits—You should understand the basic theory of electricity and know the meaning of voltage, current (amps) and resistance (ohms). You should understand what happens in a circuit with an open or shorted wire. You should be able to read and understand a wiring diagram.

Use Of Circuit Testing Tools—You should know how to use a test light and how to use jumper wires to bypass components to test circuits. You should be familiar with the High Impedance Multimeter (DVM) J 34029–A. You should be able to measure voltage, resistance and current and be familiar with the meter controls and how to use them correctly.

PRECAUTIONS

Failure to observe the following precautions may result in system damage.
• Before performing electric arc welding on the vehicle, disconnect the Electronic Brake Control Module (EBCM) and the hydraulic modulator connectors.
• When performing painting work on the vehicle, do not expose the Electronic Brake Control Module (EBCM) to temperatures in excess of 185°F (85°C) for longer than 2 hrs. The system may be exposed to temperatures up to 200°F (95°C) for less than 15 min.
• Never disconnect or connect the Electronic Brake Control Module (EBCM) or hydraulic modulator connectors with the ignition switch ON.
• Never disassemble any component of the Anti-Lock Brake System (ABS) which is designated non-serviceable; the component must be replaced as an assembly.
• When filling the master cylinder, always use Delco Supreme 11 brake fluid or equivalent, which meets DOT-3 specifications; petroleum base fluid will destroy the rubber parts.

Diagnosis and Testing

ONBOARD DIAGNOSTICS

The ABS-VI contains sophisticated onboard diagnostics that, when accessed with a bi-directional "Scan" tool, are designed to identify the source of any system fault as specifically as possible, including whether or not the fault is intermittent. There are 58 diagnostic fault codes to assist the service technician with diagnosis. The last diagnostic fault code to occur is specifically identified, and specific ABS data is stored at the time of this fault, also, the first five codes set. Additionally, using a bi-directional "Scan" tool, each input and output can be monitored, thus enabling fault confirmation and repair verification. Manual control of components and automated functional tests are also available when using a GM approved "Scan" tool. Details of many of these functions are contained in the following sections.

ENHANCED DIAGNOSTICS

Enhanced Diagnostic Information, found in the CODE HISTORY function of the bi-directional "Scan" tool, is designed to provide the service technician with specific fault occurrence information. For each of the first five (5) and the very last diagnostic fault codes stored, data is stored to identify the specific fault code number, the number of failure occurrences, and the number of drive cycles since the failure first and last occurred (a drive cycle occurs when the ignition is turned "ON" and the vehicle is driven faster than 10 mph). However, if a fault is present, the drive cycle counter will increment by turning the ignition "ON" and "OFF". These first five (5) diagnostic fault codes are also stored in the order of occurrence. The order in which the first 5 faults occurred can be useful in determining if a previous fault is linked to the most recent faults, such as an intermittent wheel speed sensor which later becomes completely open.

During difficult diagnosis situations, this information can be used to identify fault occurrence trends. Does the fault occur more frequently now than it did during the last time when it only failed 1 out of 35 drive cycles? Did the fault only occur once over a large number of drive cycles, indication an unusual condition present when the fault occurred? Does the fault occur infrequently over a large number of drive cycles, indication special diagnosis techniques may be required to identify the source of the fault?

If a fault occurred 1 out of 20 drive cycles, the fault is intermittent and has not reoccurred for 19 drive cycles. This fault may be difficult or impossible to duplicate and may have been caused by a severe vehicle impact (large pot hole, speed bump at high speed, etc.) that momentarily opened an electrical connector or caused unusual vehicle suspension movement. Problem resolution is unlikely, and the problem may never reoccur (check diagnostic aids proved for that code). If the fault occurred 3 out of 15 drive cycles, the odds of finding the cause are still not good, but you know how often it occurs and you can determine whether or not the fault is becoming more frequent based on an additional or past occurrences visit if the source of the problem can not or could not be found. If the fault occurred 10 out of 20 drive cycles, the odds of finding the cause are very good, as the fault may be easily reproduced.

By using the additional fault data, you can also determine if a failure is randomly intermittent or if it has not reoccurred for long periods of time due to weather changes or a repair prior to this visit. Say a diagnostic fault code occurred 10 of 20 drive cycles but has not reoccurred for 10 drive cycles. This means the failure occurred 10 of 10 drive cycles but has not reoccurred since. A significant environmental change or a repair occurred 10 drive cycles ago. A repair may not be necessary if a recent repair can be confirmed. If no repair was made, the service can focus on diagnosis techniques used to locate difficult to recreate problems.

INTERMITTENT FAILURES

As with most electronic systems, intermittent failures may be difficult to accurately diagnose. The following is a method to try to isolate an intermittent failure especially wheel speed circuitry failures.

If an ABS fault occurs, the "ABS" warning light indicator will be "ON" during the ignition cycle in which the fault was detected. If it is an intermittent problem which seems to have corrected itself ("ABS" warning light "OFF"), a history trouble code will be stored. Also stored will be the history data of the code at the time the fault occurred. The Tech 1 must be used to read ABS history data.

INTERMITTENTS AND POOR CONNECTIONS

Most intermittents are caused by faulty electrical connections or wiring, although occasionally a sticking relay or solenoid can be a problem. Some items to check are:

1. Poor mating of connector halves, or terminals not fully seated in the connector body (backed out).
2. Dirt or corrosion on the terminals. The terminals must be clean and free of any foreign material which could impede proper terminal contact.
3. Damaged connector body, exposing the terminals to moisture and dirt, as well as not maintaining proper terminal orientation with the component or mating connector.
4. Improperly formed or damaged terminals. All connector terminals in problem circuits should be checked carefully to ensure good contact tension. Use a corresponding mating terminal to check for proper tension. Refer to "Checking Terminal Contact" in this section for the specific procedure.
5. The J 35616–A Connector Test Adapter Kit must be used whenever a diagnostic procedure requests checking or probing a terminal. Using the adapter will ensure that no damage to the terminal will occur, as well as giving an idea of whether contact tension is sufficient. If contact tension seems incorrect, refer to "Checking Terminal Contact" in this section for specifics.
6. Poor terminal-to-wire connection. Checking this requires removing the terminal from the connector body. Some conditions which fall under this description are poor crimps, poor solder joints, crimping over wire insulation rather than the wire itself, corrosion in the wire-to-terminal contact area, etc.
7. Wire insulation which is rubbed through, causing an intermittent short as the bare area touches other wiring or parts of the vehicle.
8. Wiring broken inside the insulation. This condition could cause a continuity check to show a good circuit, but if only 1 or 2 strands of a multi-strand type wire are intact, resistance could be far too high.

Checking Terminal Contact

When diagnosing an electrical system that uses Metri-Pack 150/280/480/630 series terminals (refer to Terminal Repair Kit J 38125–A instruction manual J 38125–4 for terminal identification), it is important to check terminal contact between a connector and component, or between inline connectors, before replacing a suspect component.

Frequently, a diagnostic chart leads to a step that reads "Check for poor connection". Mating terminals must be inspected to ensure good terminal contact. A poor connection between the male and female terminal at a connector may be the result of contamination or deformation.

Contamination is caused by the connector halves being improperly connected, a missing or damaged connector seal, or damage to the connector itself, exposing the terminals to moisture and dirt. Contamination, usually in underhood or underbody connectors, leads to terminal corrosion, causing an open circuit or an intermittently open circuit.

Deformation is caused by probing the mating side of a connector terminal without the proper adapter, improperly joining the connector halves or repeatedly separating and joining the connector halves. Deformation, usually to the female terminal contact tang, can result in poor terminal contact causing an open or intermittently open circuit.

Follow the procedure below to check terminal contact.
1. Separate the connector halves. Refer to Terminal Repair Kit J 38125–A instruction manual J 38125–4, if available.
2. Inspect the connector halves for contamination. Contamination will result in a white or green buildup within the connector body or between terminals, causing high terminal resistance, intermittent contact or an open circuit. An underhood or underbody connector that shows signs of contamination should be replaced in its entirety: terminals, seals, and connector body.
3. Using an equivalent male terminal from the Terminal Repair Kit J 38125–A, check the retention force of the female terminal in question by inserting and removing the male terminal to the female terminal in the connector body. Good terminal contact will require a certain amount of force to separate the terminals.
4. Using an equivalent female terminal from the Terminal Repair Kit J 38125–A, compare the retention force of this terminal to the female terminal in question by joining and separating the male terminal to the female terminal in question. If the retention force is significantly different between the two female terminals, replace the female terminal in question, using a terminal from Terminal Repair Kit J 38125–A.

DISPLAYING CODES

◆ See Figures 36 thru 41

Diagnostic fault codes can only be read through the use of a TECH 1® or equivalent bi-directional scan tool. There are no provisions for flash code diagnostics.

CLEARING CODES

The trouble codes in EBCM memory are erased in one of two ways:
1. TECH 1® "Clear Codes" selection.
2. Ignition cycle default.
These two methods are detailed below. Be sure to verify proper system operation and absence of codes when clearing procedure is completed. The EBCM will not permit code clearing until all of the codes have been displayed. Also, codes cannot be cleared by unplugging the EBCM, disconnecting the battery cables, or turning the ignition "OFF" (except on an ignition cycle default).

TECH 1® "Clear Codes" Method

Select F2 for trouble codes. After codes have been viewed completely, TECH 1® will ask, "CLEAR ABS CODES"; ANSWER "yes." TECH 1® will then read, "DISPLAY CODE HIST. DATA"? "LOST" IF CODES CLEARED. "NO" TO CLEAR CODES. Answer "NO" and codes will be cleared.

Ignition Cycle Default

If no diagnostic fault code occurs for 100 drive cycles (a drive cycle occurs when the ignition is turned "ON" and the vehicle is driven faster than 10 mph), any existing fault codes are cleared from the EBCM memory.

TROUBLE CODE	DESCRIPTION
A011	ABS Warning Light Circuit Open or Shorted to Ground
A013	ABS Warning Light Circuit Shorted to Battery
A014	Enable Relay Contacts Or Fuse Open
A015	Enable Relay Contacts Shorted to Battery
A016	Enable Relay Coil Circuit Open
A017	Enable Relay Coil Circuit Shorted to Ground
A018	Enable Relay Coil Circuit Shorted to Battery
A021	Left Front Wheel Speed = 0 (1 of 2)
A022	Right Front Wheel Speed = 0 (1 of 2)
A023	Left Rear Wheel Speed = 0 (1 of 2)
A024	Right Rear Wheel Speed = 0 (1 of 2)
A025	Left Front Excessive Wheel Speed Variation (1 of 2)
A026	Right Front Excessive Wheel Speed Variation (1 of 2)
A027	Left Rear Excessive Wheel Speed Variation (1 of 2)
A028	Right Rear Excessive Wheel Speed Variation (1 of 2)
A031	Two Wheel Speeds = 0 (1 of 2) (Non-Tubular Rear Axle)
A031	Two Wheel Speeds = C (1 of 2) (Tubular Rear Axle)
A036	Low System Voltage
A037	High System Voltage
A038	Left Front EMB Will Not Hold Motor
A041	Right Front EMB Will Not Hold Motor
A042	Rear Axle ESB Will Not Hold Motor
A044	Left Front Channel Will Not Move
A045	Right Front Channel Will Not Move
A046	Rear Axle Channel Will Not Move
A047	Left Front Motor Free Spins
A048	Right Front Motor Free Spins
A051	Rear Axle Motor Free Spins
A052	Left Front Channel in Release Too Long
A053	Right Front Channel In Release Too Long
A054	Rear Axle Channel in Release Too Long
A055	Motor Driver Fault Detected
A056	Left Front Motor Circuit Open
A057	Left Front Motor Circuit Shorted to Ground
A058	Left Front Motor Circuit Shorted to Battery or Motor Shorted
A061	Right Front Motor Circuit Open
A062	Right Front Motor Circuit Shorted to Ground
A063	Right Front Motor Circuit Shorted to Battery or Motor Shorted

88259634

Fig. 36 ABS Diagnostic Trouble Code list (page 1 of 2)—1992-93 vehicles

TROUBLE CODE	DESCRIPTION
A064	Rear Axle Motor Circuit Open
A065	Rear Axle Motor Circuit Shorted to Ground
A066	Rear Axle Motor Circuit Shorted to Battery or Motor Shorted
A067	Left Front EMB Circuit Open or Shorted to Ground
A068	Left Front EMB Circuit Shorted to Battery or EMB Shorted
A071	Right Front EMB Circuit Open or Shorted to Ground
A072	Right Front EMB Circuit Shorted to Battery or EMB Shorted
A076	Left Front Solenoid Circuit Shorted to Battery or Open
A077	Left Front Solenoid Circuit Shorted to Ground or Driver Open
A078	Right Front Solenoid Circuit Shorted to Battery or Open
A081	Right Front Solenoid Circuit Shorted to Ground or Driver Open
A082	Calibration Memory Failure
A086	Red Brake Warning Light Activated by ABS
A087	Red Brake Warning Light Circuit Open
A088	Red Brake Warning Light Circuit Shorted to Battery
A091	Open Brake Switch Contacts During Deceleration
A092	Open Brake Switch Contacts When ABS Was Required
A093	Code 91 or 92 Set in Current or Previous Ignition Cycle
A094	Brake Switch Contacts Always Closed
A095	Brake Switch Circuit Open
A096	Brake Lights Circuit Open

88259G35

Fig. 37 ABS Diagnostic Trouble Code list (page 2 of 2)—1992-93 vehicles

DIAGNOSTIC TROUBLE CODE	DESCRIPTION
11	ABS Warning Lamp Circuit Malfunction (1 of 2)
14	ABS Enable Relay Contact Circuit Open (1 of 3)
15	ABS Enable Relay Contact Circuit Shorted to Battery or Always Closed
16	ABS Enable Relay Coil Circuit Open
17	ABS Enable Relay Coil Circuit Shorted to Ground
18	ABS Enable Relay Coil Circuit Shorted to Battery or Coil Shorted
21	Left Front Wheel Speed = 0 or Unreasonable (1 of 2)
22	Right Front Wheel Speed = 0 or Unreasonable (1 of 2)
23	Left Rear Wheel Speed = 0 or Unreasonable (1 of 4)
24	Right Rear Wheel Speed = 0 or Unreasonable (1 of 4)
25	Left Front Excessive Wheel Speed Variation (1 of 2)
26	Right Front Excessive Wheel Speed Variation (1 of 2)
27	Left Rear Excessive Wheel Speed Variation (1 of 4)
28	Right Rear Excessive Wheel Speed Variation (1 of 4)
36	Low System Voltage
37	High System Voltage
38	Left Front EMB Will Not Hold Motor
41	Right Front EMB Will Not Hold Motor
42	Rear ESB Will Not Hold Motor
44	Left Front ABS Channel Will Not Move (1 of 2)
45	Right Front ABS Channel Will Not Move (1 of 2)
46	Rear ABS Channel Will Not Move
47	Left Front ABS Motor Free Spins (1 of 2)
48	Right Front ABS Motor Free Spins (1 of 2)
51	Rear ABS Motor Free Spins (1 of 2)
52	Left Front ABS Channel in Release Too Long
53	Right Front ABS Channel in Release Too Long
54	Rear ABS Channel in Release Too Long
55	EBCM Malfunction
56	Left Front ABS Motor Circuit Open
57	Left Front ABS Motor Circuit Shorted to Ground
58	Left Front ABS Motor Circuit Shorted to Battery or Motor Shorted
61	Right Front ABS Motor Circuit Open
62	Right Front ABS Motor Circuit Shorted to Ground
63	Right Front ABS Motor Circuit Shorted to Battery or Motor Shorted
64	Rear ABS Motor Circuit Open
65	Rear ABS Motor Circuit Shorted to Ground
66	Rear ABS Motor Circuit Shorted to Battery or Motor Shorted

Fig. 38 ABS Diagnostic Trouble Code list (page 1 of 2)—1994–95 vehicles

CHART	SYMPTOM
67	Left Front EMB Circuit Open or Shorted to Ground
68	Left Front EMB Circuit Shorted to Battery or Driver Open
71	Right Front EMB Circuit Open or Shorted to Ground
72	Right Front EMB Circuit Shorted to Battery or Driver Open
76	Left Front Solenoid Circuit Open or Shorted to Battery
77	Left Front Solenoid Circuit Shorted to Ground or Driver Open
78	Right Front Solenoid Circuit Open or Shorted to Battery
81	Right Front Solenoid Circuit Shorted to Ground or Driver Open
82	Calibration Malfunction
86	EBCM Turned "ON" the Red "BRAKE" Warning Lamp
87	Red "BRAKE" Warning Lamp Circuit Open
88	Red "BRAKE" Warning Lamp Circuit Shorted to Battery
91	Open Brake Switch Contacts During Deceleration
92	Open Brake Switch Contacts When ABS Was Required
93	DTC 91 or 92 Set in Current or Previous Ignition Cycle
94	Brake Switch Contacts Always Closed
95	Brake Switch Circuit Open
96	Brake Lamp Circuit Open

Fig. 39 ABS Diagnostic Trouble Code list (page 2 of 2)—1994–95 vehicles

BRAKES 9-23

DIAGNOSTIC TROUBLE CODE	DESCRIPTION
11	ABS warning Lamp Circuit Malfunction
14	ABS Relay Contacts Circuit Open
15	ABS Relay Contacts Circuit Shorted to Battery
16	ABS Relay Coil Circuit Open
17	ABS Relay Coil Circuit Shorted to Ground
18	ABS Relay Coil Circuit Shorted to Battery or Coil Shorted
21	Left Front Wheel Speed = 0
22	Right Front Wheel Speed = 0
23	Left Rear Wheel Speed = 0
24	Right Rear Wheel Speed = 0
25	Left Front Excessive Wheel Speed Variation
26	Right Front Excessive Wheel Speed Variation
27	Left Rear Excessive Wheel Speed Variation
28	Right Rear Excessive Wheel Speed Variation
32	Left Front Wheel Speed Sensor Circuit Open or Shorted to Ground /Battery
33	Right Front Wheel Speed Sensor Circuit Open or Shorted to Ground /Battery
34	Left Rear Wheel Speed Sensor Circuit Open or Shorted to Ground /Battery
35	Right Rear Wheel Speed Sensor Circuit Open or Shorted to Ground /Battery
36	Low System Voltage
37	High System Voltage
38	Left Front ESB Will Not Hold Motor
41	Right Front ESB Will Not Hold Motor
42	Rear ESB Will Not Hold Motor
44	Left Front Channel Will Not Move
45	Right Front Channel Will Not Move
46	Rear Channel Will Not Move
47	Left Front Motor Free Spins
48	Right Front Motor Free Spins
51	Rear Motor Free Spins
52	Left Front Channel in Release Too Long
53	Right Front Channel in Release Too Long
54	Rear Channel in Release Too Long
55	EBCM Malfunction
56	Left Front Motor Circuit Open
57	Left Front Motor Circuit Shorted to Ground
58	Left Front Motor Circuit Shorted to Battery or Motor Shorted

Fig. 40 ABS Diagnostic Trouble Code list (page 1 of 2)—1996 vehicles

DIAGNOSTIC TROUBLE CODE	DESCRIPTION
61	Right Front Motor Circuit Open
62	Right Front Motor Circuit Shorted to Ground
63	Right Front Motor Circuit Shorted to Battery or Motor Shorted
64	Rear Motor Circuit Open
65	Rear Motor Circuit Shorted to Ground
66	Rear Motor Circuit Shorted to Battery or Motor Shorted
76	Left Front Solenoid Circuit Open or Shorted to Ground
77	Left Front Solenoid Circuit Shorted to Battery
78	Right Front Solenoid Circuit Open or Shorted to Ground
81	Right Front Solenoid Circuit Shorted to Battery
82	Calibration Malfunction
86	EBCM Turned "ON" the Red "BRAKE" Warning Lamp
87	Red "BRAKE" Warning Lamp Circuit Malfunction
91	Open Brake Switch Contacts During Deceleration
92	Open Brake Switch Contacts When ABS Was Required
93	DTCs 91 or 92 Set in Current or Previous Ignition Cycle
94	Brake Switch Contacts Always Closed
95	Brake Switch Circuit Open

Fig. 41 ABS Diagnostic Trouble Code list (page 2 of 2)—1996 vehicles

DIAGNOSTIC PROCESS

▶ **See Figures 42 thru 54**

When servicing the ABS-VI, the following steps should be followed in order. Failure to follow these steps may result in the loss of important diagnostic data and may lead to difficult and time consuming diagnosis procedures.

1. Using a TECH 1®, or equivalent bi-directional "Scan" tool, read all current and history diagnostic codes. Be certain to note which codes are current diagnostic code failures. DO NOT CLEAR CODES unless directed to do so.

2. Using a bi-directional "Scan" tool, read the CODE HISTORY data. Note the diagnostic fault codes stored and their frequency of failure. Specifically note the last failure that occurred and the conditions present when this failure occurred. This "last failure" should be the starting point for diagnosis and repair.

3. Perform a vehicle preliminary diagnosis inspection. This should include:

a. Inspection of the compact master cylinder for proper brake fluid level.

b. Inspection of the ABS hydraulic modulator for any leaks or wiring damage.

c. Inspection of brake components at all four (4) wheels. Verify no drag exists. Also verify proper brake apply operation.

d. Inspection for worn or damaged wheel bearings that allow a wheel to "wobble."

e. Inspection of the wheel speed sensors and their wiring. Verify correct air gap range, solid sensor attachment, undamaged sensor toothed ring, and undamaged wiring, especially at vehicle attachment points.

f. Verify proper outer CV joint alignment and operation.

g. Verify tires meet legal tread depth requirements.

4. If no codes are present, or mechanical component failure codes are present, perform the automated modulator test using the Tech 1 or T-100 to isolate the cause of the problem. If the failure is intermittent and not reproducible, test drive the vehicle while using the automatic snapshot feature of the bi-directional "Scan" tool.

Perform normal acceleration, stopping, and turning maneuvers. If this does not reproduce the failure, perform an ABS stop, on a low coefficient surface such as gravel, from approximately 30–50 mph (48–80 km/h) while triggering on any ABS code. If the failure is still not reproducible, use the enhanced diagnostic information found in CODE HISTORY to determine whether or not this failure should be further diagnosed.

5. Once all system failures have been corrected, clear the ABS codes. The Tech 1 and T-100, when plugged into the ALDL connector, becomes part of the vehicle's electronic system. The Tech 1 and T-100 can also perform the following functions on components linked by the Serial Data Link (SDL):

- Display ABS data
- Display and clear ABS trouble codes
- Control ABS components
- Perform extensive ABS diagnosis
- Provide diagnostic testing for "Intermittent" ABS conditions.

Each test mode has specific diagnosis capabilities which depend upon various keystrokes. In general, five (5) keys control sequencing: "YES," "NO," "EXIT," "UP" arrow and "DOWN" arrow. The FO through F9 keys select operating modes, perform functions within an operating mode, or enter trouble code or model year designations.

In general, the Tech 1 has five (5) test modes for diagnosing the antilock brake system. The five (5) test modes are as follows:

MODE FO: DATA LIST—In this test mode, the Tech 1 continuously monitors wheel speed data, brake switch status and other inputs and outputs.

MODE F1: CODE HISTORY—In this mode, fault code history data is displayed. This data includes how many ignition cycles since the fault code occurred, along with other ABS information. The first five (5) and last fault codes set are included in the ABS history data.

MODE F2: TROUBLE CODES—In this test mode, trouble codes stored by the EBCM, both current ignition cycle and history, may be displayed or cleared.

MODE F3: ABS SNAPSHOT—In this test mode, the Tech 1 captures ABS data before and after a fault occurrence or a forced manual trigger.

MODE F4: ABS TESTS—In this test mode, the Tech 1 performs hydraulic modulator functional tests to assist in problem isolation during troubleshooting. Included here is manual control of the motors which is used prior to bleeding the brake system.

Press F7 to covert from English to metric.

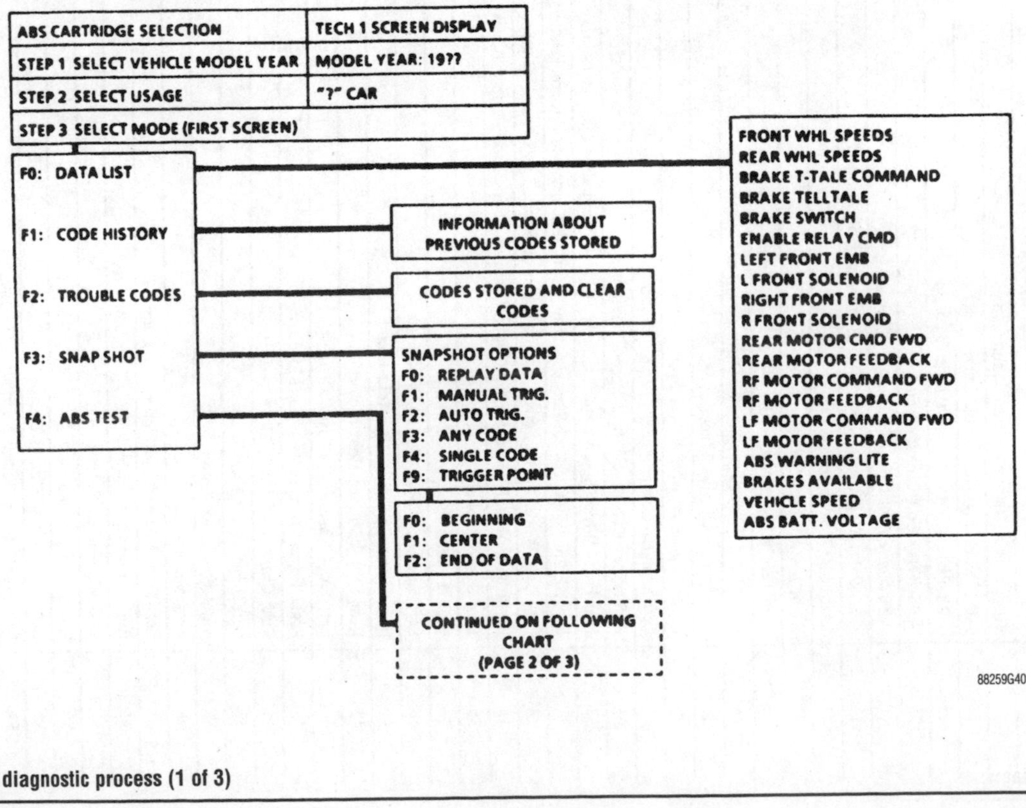

Fig. 42 TECH 1 diagnostic process (1 of 3)

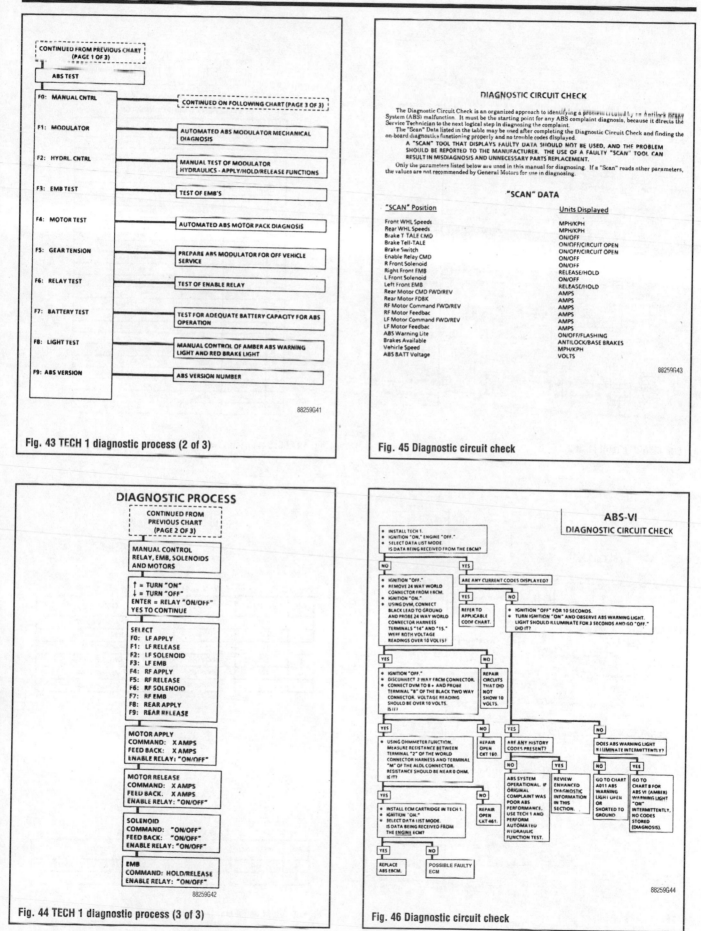

Fig. 43 TECH 1 diagnostic process (2 of 3)

CONTINUED FROM PREVIOUS CHART
(PAGE 1 OF 3)

ABS TEST

F0: MANUAL CNTRL	CONTINUED ON FOLLOWING CHART (PAGE 3 OF 3)
F1: MODULATOR	AUTOMATED ABS MODULATOR MECHANICAL DIAGNOSIS
F2: HYDRL. CNTRL	MANUAL TEST OF MODULATOR HYDRAULICS - APPLY/HOLD/RELEASE FUNCTIONS
F3: EMB TEST	TEST OF EMB'S
F4: MOTOR TEST	AUTOMATED ABS MOTOR PACK DIAGNOSIS
F5: GEAR TENSION	PREPARE ABS MODULATOR FOR OFF VEHICLE SERVICE
F6: RELAY TEST	TEST OF ENABLE RELAY
F7: BATTERY TEST	TEST FOR ADEQUATE BATTERY CAPACITY FOR ABS OPERATION
F8: LIGHT TEST	MANUAL CONTROL OF AMBER ABS WARNING LIGHT AND RED BRAKE LIGHT
F9: ABS VERSION	ABS VERSION NUMBER

88259G41

Fig. 45 Diagnostic circuit check

DIAGNOSTIC CIRCUIT CHECK

The Diagnostic Circuit Check is an organized approach to identifying a problem caused by an Antilock Brake System (ABS) malfunction. It must be the starting point for any ABS complaint diagnosis, because it directs the Service Technician to the next logical step in diagnosing the complaint.

The "Scan" Data listed in the table may be used after completing the Diagnostic Circuit Check and finding the on-board diagnostics functioning properly and no trouble codes displayed.

A "SCAN" TOOL THAT DISPLAYS FAULTY DATA SHOULD NOT BE USED, AND THE PROBLEM SHOULD BE REPORTED TO THE MANUFACTURER. THE USE OF A FAULTY "SCAN" TOOL CAN RESULT IN MISDIAGNOSIS AND UNNECESSARY PARTS REPLACEMENT.

Only the parameters listed below are used in this manual for diagnosing. If a "Scan" reads other parameters, the values are not recommended by General Motors for use in diagnosing.

"SCAN" DATA

"SCAN" Position	Units Displayed
Front WHL Speeds	MPH/KPH
Rear WHL Speeds	MPH/KPH
Brake T TALE CMD	ON/OFF
Brake Tell-TALE	ON/OFF/CIRCUIT OPEN
Brake Switch	ON/OFF/CIRCUIT OPEN
Enable Relay CMD	ON/OFF
R Front Solenoid	ON/OFF
Right Front EMB	RELEASE/HOLD
L Front Solenoid	ON/OFF
Left Front EMB	RELEASE/HOLD
Rear Motor CMD FWD/REV	AMPS
Rear Motor FDBK	AMPS
RF Motor Command FWD/REV	AMPS
RF Motor Feedbac	AMPS
LF Motor Command FWD/REV	AMPS
LF Motor Feedbac	AMPS
ABS Warning Lite	ON/OFF/FLASHING
Brakes Available	ANTILOCK/BASE BRAKES
Vehicle Speed	MPH/KPH
ABS BATT Voltage	VOLTS

88259G43

Fig. 44 TECH 1 diagnostic process (3 of 3)

DIAGNOSTIC PROCESS

CONTINUED FROM PREVIOUS CHART
(PAGE 2 OF 3)

MANUAL CONTROL RELAY, EMB, SOLENOIDS AND MOTORS

↑ = TURN "ON"
↓ = TURN "OFF"
ENTER = RELAY "ON/OFF"
YES TO CONTINUE

SELECT
F0: LF APPLY
F1: LF RELEASE
F2: LF SOLENOID
F3: LF EMB
F4: RF APPLY
F5: RF RELEASE
F6: RF SOLENOID
F7: RF EMB
F8: REAR APPLY
F9: REAR RELEASE

MOTOR APPLY
COMMAND: X AMPS
FEED BACK: X AMPS
ENABLE RELAY: "ON/OFF"

MOTOR RELEASE
COMMAND: X AMPS
FEED BACK: X AMPS
ENABLE RELAY: "ON/OFF"

SOLENOID
COMMAND: "ON/OFF"
FEED BACK: "ON/OFF"
ENABLE RELAY: "ON/OFF"

EMB
COMMAND: HOLD/RELEASE
ENABLE RELAY: "ON/OFF"

88259G42

Fig. 46 Diagnostic circuit check

ABS-VI DIAGNOSTIC CIRCUIT CHECK

- INSTALL TECH 1.
- IGNITION "ON," ENGINE "OFF."
- SELECT DATA LIST MODE
  IS DATA BEING RECEIVED FROM THE EBCM?

88259G44

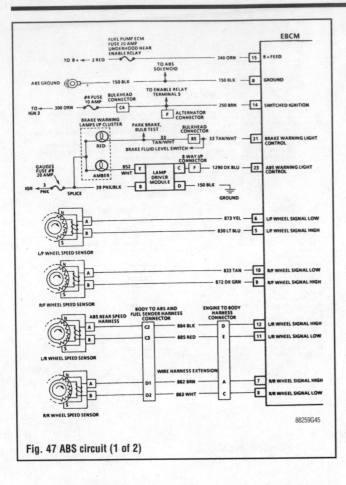

Fig. 47 ABS circuit (1 of 2)

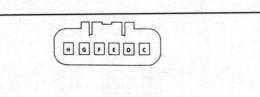

EBCM 24 PIN WORLD CONNECTOR

PIN	CIRCUIT NO.	COLOR	CIRCUIT
1	799	TAN/WHT	NOT USED
2	461	ORN	SERIAL DATA LINE
3	OPEN		NOT USED
4	1289	LT BLU/BLK	R/F ABS SOLENOID
5	830	LT BLU	L/F WHEEL SIGNAL HIGH
6	873	YEL	L/F WHEEL SIGNAL LOW
7	882	BRN	R/R WHEEL SIGNAL HIGH
8	883	WHT	R/R WHEEL SIGNAL LOW
9	872	DK GRN	R/F WHEEL SIGNAL HIGH
10	833	TAN	R/F WHEEL SIGNAL LOW
11	885	RED	L/R WHEEL SIGNAL LOW
12	884	BLK	L/R WHEEL SIGNAL HIGH
13	20	LT BLU	BRAKE SWITCH INPUT
14	250	BRN	SWITCH IGNITION
15	340	ORN	B + FEED
16	OPEN		NOT USED
17	OPEN		NOT USED
18	VENT TUBE	BLK	VENT TUBE
19	1286	LT GRN	L/F EMB
20	1287	GRY	R/F EMB
21	33	TAN/WHT	BRAKE TELLTALE
22	879	PPL/WHT	ENABLE RELAY CONTROL
23	1290	DK BLU	ABS WARNING LIGHT CONTROL
24	1288	DK GRN/YEL	L/F ABS SOLENOID

Fig. 49 EBCM connector face view (1 of 2)

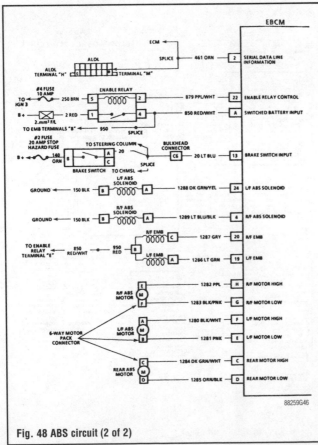

Fig. 48 ABS circuit (2 of 2)

6 WAY EBCM CONNECTOR

PIN	CIRCUIT NO.	COLOR	CIRCUIT
C	1284	DK GRN/WHT	REAR MOTOR HIGH
D	1285	ORN/BLK	REAR MOTOR LOW
E	1281	PNK	L/F MOTOR LOW
F	1280	BLK/WHT	L/F MOTOR HIGH
G	1283	BLK/PNK	R/F MOTOR LOW
H	1282	PPL	R/F MOTOR HIGH

2 WAY EBCM CONNECTOR

PIN	CIRCUIT NO.	COLOR	CIRCUIT
A	850	RED/WHT	SWITCHED BATTERY INPUT
B	150	BLK	GROUND

Fig. 50 EBCM connector face view (2 of 2)

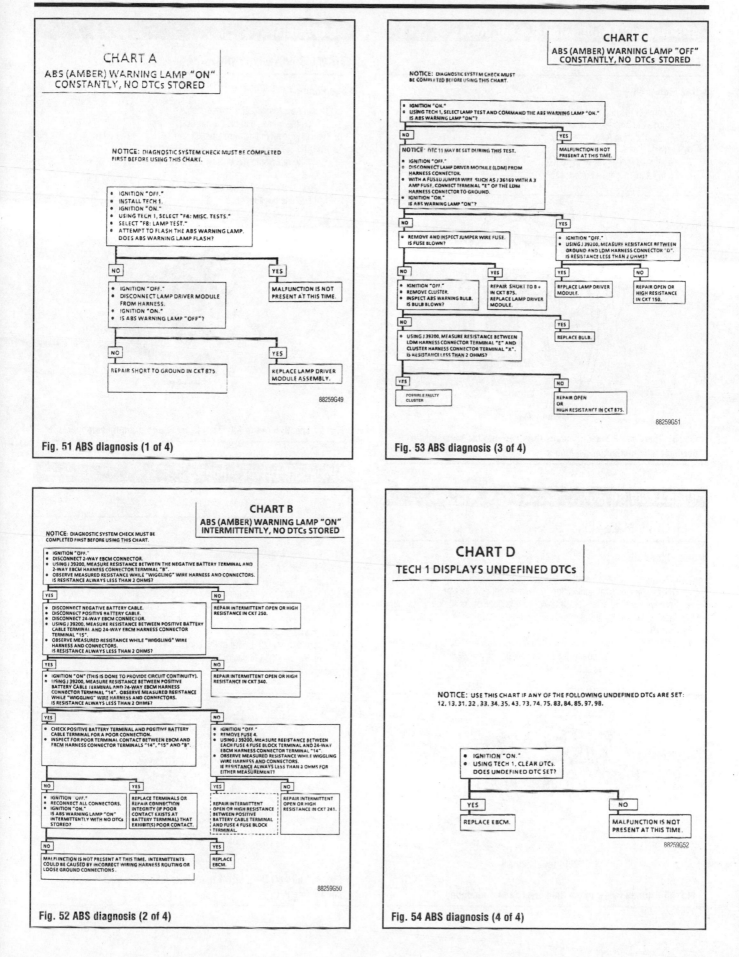

Fig. 51 ABS diagnosis (1 of 4)

Fig. 52 ABS diagnosis (2 of 4)

Fig. 53 ABS diagnosis (3 of 4)

Fig. 54 ABS diagnosis (4 of 4)

ABS Hydraulic Modulator Bleeder Valves

REMOVAL & INSTALLATION

♦ See Figure 55

1. Disconnect the negative battery cable.
2. Remove the bleeder valve or valves by unscrewing them from the master cylinder/hydraulic modulator assembly.

To install:

3. Install the bleeder valve and tighten to 65 inch lbs. (7 Nm).
4. Connect the negative battery cable.

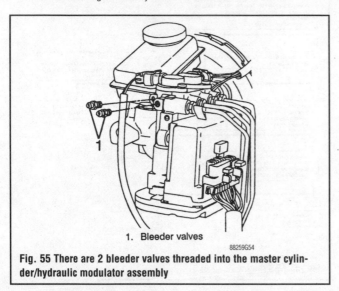

1. Bleeder valves

88259G54

Fig. 55 There are 2 bleeder valves threaded into the master cylinder/hydraulic modulator assembly

Fluid Level Sensor

REMOVAL & INSTALLATION

♦ See Figure 56

1. Disconnect the negative battery cable.
2. Detach the electrical connection from the fluid level sensor.
3. Remove the fluid level sensor using needle nose pliers to compress the switch locking tabs at the inboard side of the master cylinder.

To install:

4. Insert the fluid level sensor unit until the locking tabs snap in place.
5. Attach the electrical connector to the sensor.
6. Connect the negative battery cable.

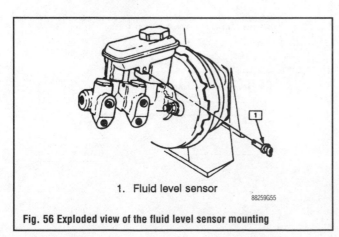

1. Fluid level sensor

88259G55

Fig. 56 Exploded view of the fluid level sensor mounting

Enable Relay

REMOVAL & INSTALLATION

♦ See Figure 57

1. Disconnect the negative battery cable.
2. Detach the relay electrical connection.
3. Release the retainer on the bracket and slide the relay off the bracket.

To install:

4. Slide the relay onto the bracket and make sure the retainer locks the relay to the bracket.
5. Attach the electrical connection.
6. Connect the negative battery cable.

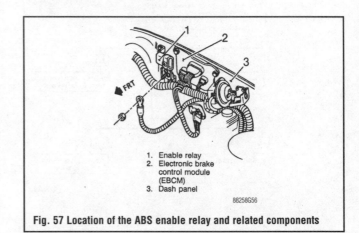

1. Enable relay
2. Electronic brake control module (EBCM)
3. Dash panel

88258G56

Fig. 57 Location of the ABS enable relay and related components

ABS Lamp Driver Module

REMOVAL & INSTALLATION

♦ See Figure 58

1. Disconnect the negative battery cable.
2. Remove the right side lower sound insulator panel.
3. Slide the glove box all the way out or remove it completely.
4. The lamp driver module is above the cruise control module taped to the instrument panel harness and is light green in color.
5. Open the connector and slide the circuit board out of the connector.

To install:

6. Install the circuit board to the connector.
7. Reposition the connector to the instrument panel harness and make sure it is retaped in place.

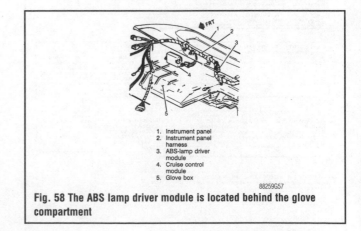

1. Instrument panel
2. Instrument panel harness
3. ABS-lamp driver module
4. Cruise control module
5. Glove box

88259G57

Fig. 58 The ABS lamp driver module is located behind the glove compartment

8. Slide the glove box back into the dash or reinstall the screws, if removed.
9. Install the right side lower sound insulator panel.
10. Connect the negative battery cable.

ABS Hydraulic Modulator Assembly

REMOVAL & INSTALLATION

♦ See Figure 59

❊❊❊ CAUTION

To avoid personal injury, use the Tech 1®, or equivalent scan tool to relieve the gear tension in the hydraulic modulator. This procedure must be performed prior to removal of the brake control and motor assembly.

1. Disconnect the negative battery cable.
2. Detach the 2 solenoid electrical connectors and the fluid level sensor connector.
3. Unplug the 6-pin and 3-pin motor pack electrical connectors.
4. Wrap a shop towel around the hydraulic brake lines and disconnect the 4 brake lines from the modulator.

➡Cap the disconnected lines to prevent the loss of fluid and the entry of moisture and contaminants.

5. Remove the 2 nuts attaching the ABS hydraulic modulator assembly to the vacuum booster.
6. Remove the ABS hydraulic modulator assembly from the vehicle.

To install:
7. Install the ABS hydraulic modulator assembly to the vehicle. Install the 2 attaching nuts and tighten to 20 ft. lbs. (27 Nm).
8. Uncap and connect the 4 brake pipes to the modulator assembly. Tighten to 13 ft. lbs. (17 Nm).
9. Attach the 6-pin and 3-pin electrical connectors and the fluid level sensor connector.
10. Properly bleed the brake system.
11. Connect the negative battery cable.

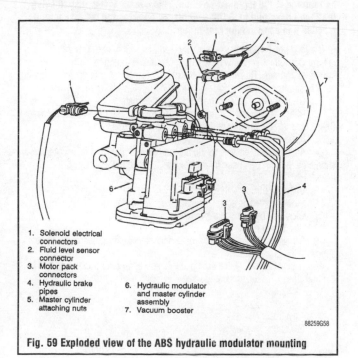

1. Solenoid electrical connectors
2. Fluid level sensor connector
3. Motor pack connectors
4. Hydraulic brake pipes
5. Master cylinder attaching nuts
6. Hydraulic modulator and master cylinder assembly
7. Vacuum booster

88259G58

Fig. 59 Exploded view of the ABS hydraulic modulator mounting

Hydraulic Modulator Solenoid Assembly

REMOVAL & INSTALLATION

♦ See Figure 60

1. Disconnect the negative battery cable.
2. Detach the solenoid electrical connector.
3. Remove the Torx® head bolts.
4. Remove the solenoid assembly.

To install:
5. Lubricate the O-rings on the new solenoid with clean brake fluid.
6. Position the solenoid so the connectors face each other.
7. Press down firmly by hand until the solenoid assembly flange seals on the modulator assembly.
8. Install the Torx® head bolts and tighten to 39 inch lbs. (5 Nm).
9. Attach the solenoid electrical connector.
10. Properly bleed the brake system.
11. Connect the negative battery cable.

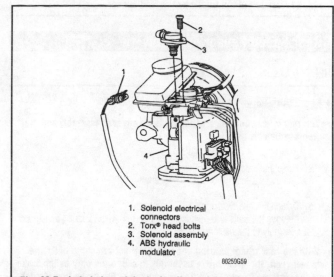

1. Solenoid electrical connectors
2. Torx® head bolts
3. Solenoid assembly
4. ABS hydraulic modulator

80259G59

Fig. 60 Exploded view of the hydraulic module solenoid mounting

Front Wheel Speed Sensor

REMOVAL & INSTALLATION

♦ See Figure 61

1. Disconnect the negative battery cable.
2. Raise and safely support the vehicle.
3. Detach the front sensor electrical connector.
4. Remove the Torx® bolt.
5. Remove the front wheel speed sensor.

To install:
6. Install the front wheel speed sensor on the mounting bracket.

➡Ensure the front wheel speed sensor is properly aligned and lays flat against the bracket bosses.

7. Install the Torx® bolt and tighten to 106 inch lbs. (12 Nm).
8. Attach the front sensor electrical connector.
9. Lower the vehicle.
10. Connect the negative battery cable.

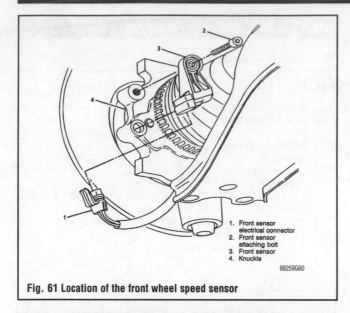

1. Front sensor electrical connector
2. Front sensor attaching bolt
3. Front sensor
4. Knuckle

88259G60

Fig. 61 Location of the front wheel speed sensor

Rear Speed Sensor Assembly

REMOVAL & INSTALLATION

▶ **See Figure 62**

➡ **The rear wheel bearing and sensor is an integral assembly and must be replaced as a unit.**

1. Disconnect the negative battery cable.
2. Raise and safely support the vehicle.
3. Remove the rear wheel and tire assembly.
4. Remove the brake drum.
5. Detach the rear sensor electrical connector.
6. Remove the bolts and nuts attaching the rear wheel bearing and speed sensor assembly to the backing plate.

➡ **With the rear wheel bearing and speed sensor attaching bolts and nuts removed, the drum brake assembly is supported only by the brake line connection. To avoid bending or damage to the brake line, do not bump or exert force on the assembly.**

7. Remove the rear wheel bearing and speed sensor assembly.
To install:
8. Install the rear wheel bearing and speed sensor assembly by aligning the bolt holes in the wheel bearing and speed sensor assembly, drum brake assembly and rear suspension bracket. Install the attaching bolts and nuts. Tighten to 38 ft. lbs. (52 Nm).
9. Attach the rear speed sensor electrical connector.
10. Install the brake drum.
11. Install the rear wheel and tire assembly.
12. Carefully lower the vehicle.
13. Connect the negative battery cable.

Bleeding the ABS System

BRAKE CONTROL ASSEMBLY

➡ **Only use brake fluid from a sealed container which meets DOT 3 specifications.**

1. Clean the area around the master cylinder cap.
2. Check fluid level in master cylinder reservoir and top-up, as necessary. Check fluid level frequently during bleeding procedure.

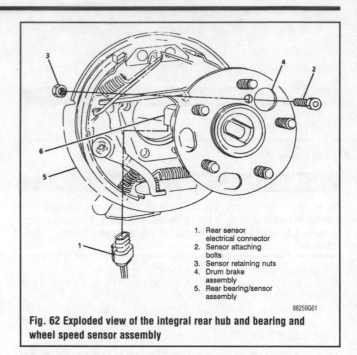

1. Rear sensor electrical connector
2. Sensor attaching bolts
3. Sensor retaining nuts
4. Drum brake assembly
5. Rear bearing/sensor assembly

88259G61

Fig. 62 Exploded view of the integral rear hub and bearing and wheel speed sensor assembly

3. Attach a bleeder hose to the rear bleeder valve on the brake control assembly. Slowly open the bleeder valve.
4. Depress the brake pedal slowly until fluid begins to flow.
5. Close the valve and release the brake pedal.
6. Repeat for the front bleeder valve on the brake control assembly.

➡ **When fluid flows from both bleeder valves, the brake control assembly is sufficiently full of fluid. However, it may not be completely purged of air. Bleed the individual wheel calipers/cylinders and return to the control assembly to purge the remaining air.**

Wheel Calipers/Cylinders

➡ **Prior to bleeding the rear brakes, the rear displacement cylinder must be returned to the top-most position. This can be accomplished using the Tech I Scan tool or T-100 (CAMS), by entering the manual control function and applying the rear motor.**

If a Tech I or T-100 are unavailable, bleed the front brakes. Ensure the pedal is firm. Carefully drive the vehicle to a speed above 4 mph to cause the ABS system to initialize. This will return the rear displacement cylinder to the top-most position.

1. Clean the area around the master cylinder cap.
2. Check fluid level in master cylinder reservoir and top-up, as necessary. Check fluid level frequently during bleeding procedure.
3. Raise and safely support the vehicle.
4. Attach a bleeder hose to the bleeder valve of the right rear wheel and submerge the opposite hose in a clean container partially filled with brake fluid.
5. Open the bleeder valve.
6. Slowly depress the brake pedal.
7. Close the bleeder valve and release the brake pedal.
8. Wait 5 seconds.
9. Repeat Steps 5–8 until the pedal begins to feel firm and no air bubbles appear in the bleeder hose.
10. Repeat Steps 5–9, until the pedal is firm and no air bubbles appear in the brake hose, for the remaining wheels in the following order:
    a. left rear
    b. right front
    c. left front.
11. Lower the vehicle.

BRAKE SPECIFICATIONS

All measurements in inches unless noted

Year	Model	Master Cylinder Bore	Brake Disc Original Thickness	Brake Disc Minimum Thickness	Brake Disc Maximum Runout	Brake Drum Diameter Original Inside Diameter	Brake Drum Diameter Max. Wear Limit	Brake Drum Diameter Maximum Machine Diameter	Wheel Cylinder or Caliper Bore Front	Wheel Cylinder or Caliper Bore Rear
1988	Corsica	0.945	0.885	0.830	0.004	7.879	7.929	7.899	NA	0.625
	Beretta	0.945	0.885	0.830	0.004	7.879	7.929	7.899	NA	0.748
1989	Corsica	0.945	0.885	0.830	0.004	7.879	7.929	7.899	NA	0.625
	Beretta	0.945	0.885	0.830	0.004	7.879	7.929	7.899	NA	0.748
1990	Corsica	0.875	0.885	0.830	0.004	7.879	7.929	7.899	NA	0.625
	Beretta	0.875	0.885	0.830	0.004	7.879	7.929	7.899	NA	0.748
1991	Corsica	0.875	0.885	0.830	0.004	7.879	7.929	7.899	NA	0.625
	Beretta	0.875	0.885	0.830	0.004	7.879	7.929	7.899	NA	0.748
1992	Corsica	0.875	0.885	0.830	0.004	7.879	7.929	7.899	NA	0.625
	Beretta	0.875	0.885	0.830	0.004	7.879	7.929	7.899	NA	0.748
1993	Corsica	0.875	0.885	0.830	0.004	7.879	7.929	7.899	NA	0.625
	Beretta	0.875	0.885	0.830	0.004	7.879	7.929	7.899	NA	0.748
1994	Corsica	0.875	0.885	0.830	0.004	7.879	7.929	7.899	NA	0.625
	Beretta	0.875	0.885	0.830	0.004	7.879	7.929	7.899	NA	0.748
1995	Corsica	0.875	0.885	0.830	0.004	7.879	7.929	7.899	NA	0.625
	Beretta	0.875	0.885	0.830	0.004	7.879	7.929	7.899	NA	0.748
1996	Corsica	0.875	0.885	0.830	0.004	7.879	7.929	7.899	NA	0.625
	Beretta	0.875	0.885	0.830	0.004	7.879	7.929	7.899	NA	0.748

88259C01

Troubleshooting the Brake System

Problem	Cause	Solution
Low brake pedal (excessive pedal travel required for braking action.)	· Excessive clearance between rear linings and drums caused by inoperative automatic adjusters	· Make 10 to 15 alternate forward and reverse brake stops to adjust brakes. If brake pedal does not come up, repair or replace adjuster parts as necessary.
	· Worn rear brakelining	· Inspect and replace lining if worn beyond minimum thickness specification
	· Bent, distorted brakeshoes, front or rear	· Replace brakeshoes in axle sets
	· Air in hydraulic system	· Remove air from system. Refer to Brake Bleeding.
Low brake pedal (pedal may go to floor with steady pressure applied.)	· Fluid leak in hydraulic system	· Fill master cylinder to fill line; have helper apply brakes and check calipers, wheel cylinders, differential valve tubes, hoses and fittings for leaks. Repair or replace as necessary.
	· Air in hydraulic system	· Remove air from system. Refer to Brake Bleeding.
	· Incorrect or non-recommended brake fluid (fluid evaporates at below normal temp).	· Flush hydraulic system with clean brake fluid. Refill with correct-type fluid.
	· Master cylinder piston seals worn, or master cylinder bore is scored, worn or corroded	· Repair or replace master cylinder
Low brake pedal (pedal goes to floor on first application—o.k. on subsequent applications.)	· Disc brake pads sticking on abutment surfaces of anchor plate. Caused by a build-up of dirt, rust, or corrosion on abutment surfaces	· Clean abutment surfaces
Fading brake pedal (pedal height decreases with steady pressure applied.)	· Fluid leak in hydraulic system	· Fill master cylinder reservoirs to fill mark, have helper apply brakes, check calipers, wheel cylinders, differential valve, tubes, hoses, and fittings for fluid leaks. Repair or replace parts as necessary.
	· Master cylinder piston seals worn, or master cylinder bore is scored, worn or corroded	· Repair or replace master cylinder
Decreasing brake pedal travel (pedal travel required for braking action decreases and may be accompanied by a hard pedal.)	· Caliper or wheel cylinder pistons sticking or seized	· Repair or replace the calipers, or wheel cylinders
	· Master cylinder compensator ports blocked (preventing fluid return to reservoirs) or pistons sticking or seized in master cylinder bore	· Repair or replace the master cylinder
	· Power brake unit binding internally	· Test unit according to the following procedure: (a) Shift transmission into neutral and start engine (b) Increase engine speed to 1500 rpm, close throttle and fully depress brake pedal (c) Slow release brake pedal and stop engine (d) Have helper remove vacuum check valve and hose from power unit. Observe for backward movement of brake pedal. (e) If the pedal moves backward, the power unit has an internal bind—replace power unit

TCCA9C01

10

BODY

EXTERIOR

Doses

ADJUSTMENT

▶ **See Figures 1 and 2**

The hinges are bolted to the door and to the body. The door side hinges have elongated holes which allow for some up and down and in and out adjustment by loosening the nuts. The nuts are tightened to 15–20 ft. lbs. (20–27 Nm). A floating cage plate inside the door also allows for adjustment. There is no fore and aft adjustment provision.

Hood

REMOVAL & INSTALLATION

1. Raise the hood and install protective coverings over the fender areas.
2. Disconnect the underhood lamp wiring.
3. Mark the position of the hinge to the hood to aid alignment upon installation.
4. While supporting the hood, remove the hinge to hood screws on each side of the hole.
5. Remove the hood assembly with the aid of a helper.
6. Installation is the reverse of removal. Align the hood properly and tighten the hinge-to-hood retaining screws to 24 ft. lbs. (33 Nm).

ALIGNMENT

The hood hinges are welded to the cowl assembly. Fore, aft and vertical adjustment may be made at the hinge to hood retaining screws. Vertical adjustment at the front may be made by adjusting the rubber bumpers up or down.

Rear Compartment Lid

REMOVAL & INSTALLATION

▶ **See Figure 3**

1. Place protective coverings along the adjacent body panels.
2. Detach all electrical connectors to electrical components attached to the lid.
3. Tie a string to the wiring harness assembly and pull the wiring harness out of the lid. Allow ample amount of string so that when the lid is removed there is enough string to allow for feeding the wiring harness back through the lid.
4. With the aid of a helper to support the lid, remove the lid to hinge screws and remove the lid.
   To install:
5. To install, with the aid of a helper, locate the lid to hinges, install the screws and tighten to 21 ft. lbs. (29 Nm).
6. Pull the string through the lid until the wiring harness is within the lid and attach the wiring connectors to the electrical components.

ALIGNMENT

1. To adjust the lid at the front corners, loosen the attaching bolts. Align as necessary, then tighten the bolts.
2. To adjust at the rear corners, loosen the rubber bumpers to raise the lid. Tighten the rubber bumpers to the lower lid.
3. Side to side adjustment can be performed as follows:
   a. Remove the rear seat cushion and back.
   b. Remove the quarter trim panels.
   c. Remove the center high mounted stop lamp.

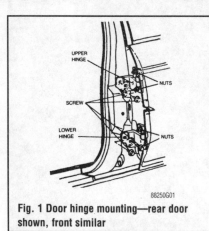

Fig. 1 Door hinge mounting—rear door shown, front similar

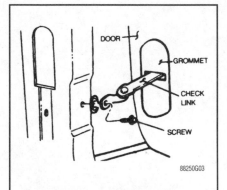

Fig. 2 Door check link-to-body attachment—rear door shown, front similar

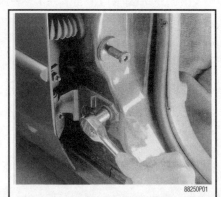

You can adjust the door at the hinges on the body or door

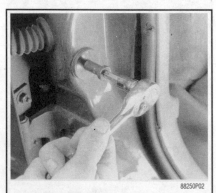

If necessary, the striker can be adjusted as well

Use a felt-tipped pen to matchmark the installed position of the hood hinges

Make sure you have the hood properly supported before removing the hinge bolts

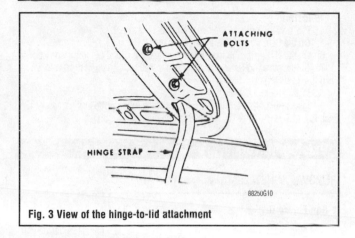

Fig. 3 View of the hinge-to-lid attachment

d. Remove the rear seat-to-back window foundation assembly.
e. Loosen the hinge-to-body screws and adjust the lid as necessary.
f. Reinstall all previously removed parts.

Lift Window (Hatchback)

REMOVAL & INSTALLATION

4-Door Hatchback Corsica

▶ See Figures 4, 5 and 6

1. Remove the lift window upper and side finish moldings.
2. Disconnect all electrical connectors to lamps, defogger etc.

➡ **The following step requires the help of an assistant so that the lift window does not fall down and cause personal injury.**

3. Remove the strut rod clips.
4. Mark the hinge outline on the lid if the lid is being reused. With the aid of a helper, remove the lift window-to-hinge bolts, then remove the lift window (hatchback) from the vehicle.

To install:
5. Position the lid on the hinge and loosely install the bolts.
6. Install the strut on the lid side.
7. Position the lid and align with mark or fit to opening.
8. Slightly tighten the bolts and check alignment and operation.
9. Tighten the bolts to 19 ft. lbs. (25 Nm).
10. Install the electrical connections and finish moldings.

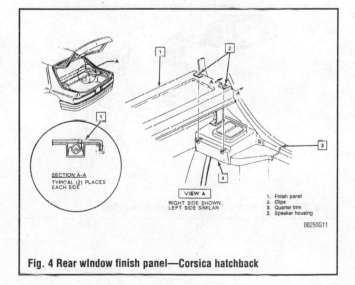

Fig. 4 Rear window finish panel—Corsica hatchback

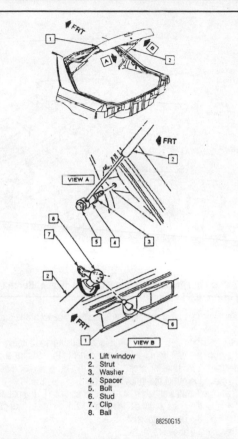

1. Lift window
2. Strut
3. Washer
4. Spacer
5. Bolt
6. Stud
7. Clip
8. Ball

Fig. 5 Exploded view of the lift window strut—Corsica hatchback

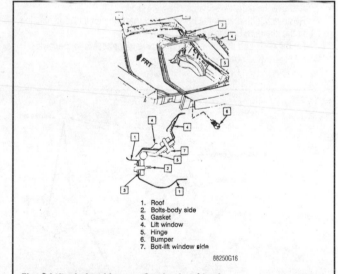

1. Roof
2. Bolts-body side
3. Gasket
4. Lift window
5. Hinge
6. Bumper
7. Bolt-lift window side

Fig. 6 Lift window hinges—Corsica hatchback

Front End Panel And Grille

REMOVAL & INSTALLATION

▶ See Figures 7 and 8

1988–89 Vehicles

1. Open the hood.
2. Remove the headlamp bezel screws.

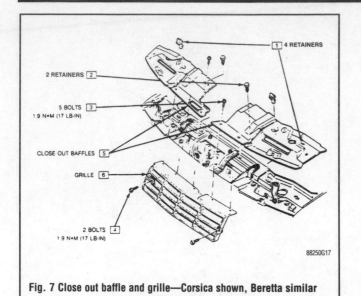

Fig. 7 Close out baffle and grille—Corsica shown, Beretta similar

3. Remove the bolt at each fender to front end panel at the upper corner at the headlamp.

4. Remove the screw at each turn signal housing and remove the housing.

5. Remove the bolt from the front end panel to the radiator support located below the turn signal housing area.

6. Remove the nut at the inner fender panel.

7. Remove the nuts attaching the bumper end cap to the panel at each side.

8. Remove the bolts at the baffles located at the radiator support.

9. Transfer the headlamps and grille.

10. Reverse the above to install.

1990–92 Vehicles

1. Remove the radiator air baffle.

2. Remove the bolts from the lower front corners to the headlamp housing panel on the standard Beretta and Corsica.

3. On the GTZ, pull the top of the grille forward for access to the lower retainer screw and remove the grille.

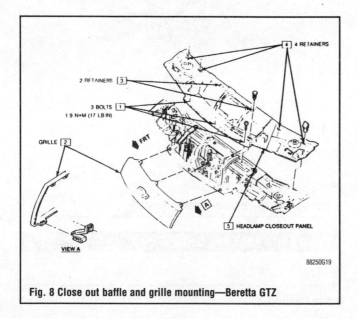

Fig. 8 Close out baffle and grille mounting—Beretta GTZ

To install:

4. Position the grille to the headlamp housing panel.

5. On the Beretta, install the lower retainer.

6. On the GTZ, press in the grille to engage the clip at the lower corners.

7. On the standard Beretta and Corsica install the bolts and tighten to 17 inch lbs. (1.9 Nm).

8. Install the radiator air baffle.

9. Install the bolts from the radiator air baffle to the grille and tighten to 17 inch lbs. (1.9 Nm). Three on the Beretta and five on the Corsica.

Outside Mirrors

REMOVAL & INSTALLATION

♦ **See Figure 9**

The door outside mirrors are stud mounted to the door filler. The mirror glass face may be replaced by placing a piece of tape over the glass then breaking the mirror face. Adhesive back mirror faces are available. Left side flat and right side convex mirror faces must be replaced with the same type mirror face when surfaced.

1. Remove the door trim panel.

2. Remove the upper trim panel.

3. Remove the sound absorber.

4. Remove the (3) nuts.

5. Remove the control cable from the upper trim panel.

6. Remove the filler and mirror.

To install:

7. Place the filler over the studs on the mirror.

8. Install the control cable through the filler and connect to the upper trim panel.

9. Install the (3) retaining nuts and tighten to 42–72 inch lbs. (4.7–8.1 Nm).

10. Install the sound absorber, upper trim panel and trim panel.

Antenna

REMOVAL & INSTALLATION

1. Unscrew the antenna mast, nut and bezel from on top of the fender.

2. Lift the hood and disconnect the antenna cable from the bottom of the antenna base.

3. Remove the two antenna retaining screws from inside the fender, then remove the antenna.

4. Reverse the above to install. Make sure all connections are tight.

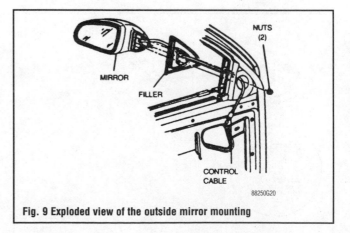

Fig. 9 Exploded view of the outside mirror mounting

INTERIOR

Instrument Panel and Pad Assembly

✳✳ CAUTION

Some vehicles are equipped with the Supplemental Inflatable Restraint (SIR) or air bag system. The SIR system must be disabled, as outlined in Section 6, before performing service on or around SIR system components, steering column, instrument panel components, wiring and sensors. Failure to follow safety and disabling procedures could result in accidental air bag deployment, possible personal injury and unnecessary SIR system repairs.

REMOVAL & INSTALLATION

1988–90 Vehicles

▶ See Figure 10

➠The instrument panel can be removed with some of its components left in place. Unless removal is necessary for component service, leave as much in place as possible. It may be easier to remove later on a workbench.

1. Disconnect the negative battery cable.
2. Remove the cluster assembly.
3. Detach the steering column electrical connectors.
4. Remove the accessory center, then remove the right sound insulator.
5. Remove the right instrument panel compartment.
6. Disconnect the electrical connectors behind the passengers side of the instrument panel by reaching through the glove compartment opening.
7. Disconnect the antenna by reaching through the glove compartment opening.
8. Remove the left compartment.
9. Detach the electrical connectors from the fuse block by reaching through the left compartment opening.
10. Remove the defroster grille.
11. Remove the speaker covers by prying gently with a suitable tool to release them from the 2 spring clips.
12. Reach under the driver's side of the instrument panel and remove the cover from the junction block.
13. From under the hood, remove the cover from the junction block on the driver's side of the cowl. Remove the 2 nuts from the junction block retainer and the 1 bolt from the center junction block retainer.
14. Remove the junction block from the cowl by reaching under the instrument panel.
15. Disconnect the electrical connector from the lower left side of the heater module.
16. Remove the 2 nuts holding the wiring harness and clutch neutral start switch at the cowl, on manual transaxle cars.

17. Remove the 2 bolts from the defroster opening and the bolt from each speaker opening.
18. Remove the 1 bolt at the lower front on each side of the instrument panel.
19. Remove the instrument panel.
20. Installation is the reverse of the removal procedure. Make sure all components are tightened securely and all connectors properly attached.

1991–96 Vehicles

▶ See Figures 11 and 12

Disable the Supplemental Inflatable Restraint (SIR) system, as outlined in Section 6 of this manual.

1. Remove the cluster bezel and cluster assembly, then remove the trim bezel.
2. Remove the heater, air conditioner and radio controls.
3. Remove the knee bolster panel, then lower the steering column.
4. Detach the Assembly line Diagnostic Link (ALDL) connector.
5. Remove the convenience center and bracket.
6. Remove the turn signal bracket.
7. Remove the left center brace bolt from the instrument panel.
8. Disconnect the left side window defogger hose from the heater module.
9. Remove the instrument panel compartment.
10. Remove the right sound insulator.
11. Remove the cruise control module mounting screws and move the module to one side.
12. Remove the wire harness retainer screw.
13. Remove the air distributor screws.
14. Remove the right side window defogger outlet duct.
15. Remove the right/center brace bolts and nuts from the instrument panel.
16. Remove the right and left pillar nuts.
17. Remove the windshield defroster grille.
18. Remove the upper instrument panel screws.
19. Disconnect the left side wire retainers and rotate the instrument panel to gain access to the right side.
20. Detach the cluster connection and wiring harness clips to the instrument panel.
21. Disconnect the knee bolster brace.
22. Disconnect the center wire harness retainer screws.
23. Disconnect the fuse block.
24. Disconnect the wire retainer on the right of the steering column.
25. Remove the instrument panel pad from the vehicle.
26. Disconnect the right and left window defogger outlets.
27. Disconnect the right and left defogger outlet nozzles.
28. Disconnect the left center air outlets.
29. Disconnect the right side outlet assembly (cup holder).
30. Remove the bracket from the right side of the instrument panel.
31. Remove the knee bolster reinforcement on the left side of the steering column.
32. Remove the pillar studs.
33. Installation is the reverse of the removal procedure. Make sure all components are tightened securely and all connectors properly attached.

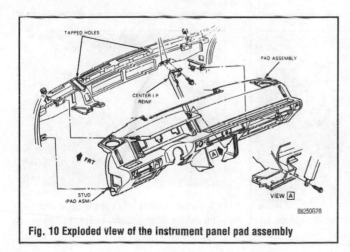

Fig. 10 Exploded view of the instrument panel pad assembly

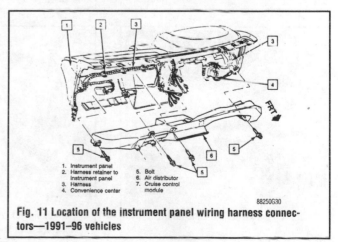

Fig. 11 Location of the instrument panel wiring harness connectors—1991–96 vehicles

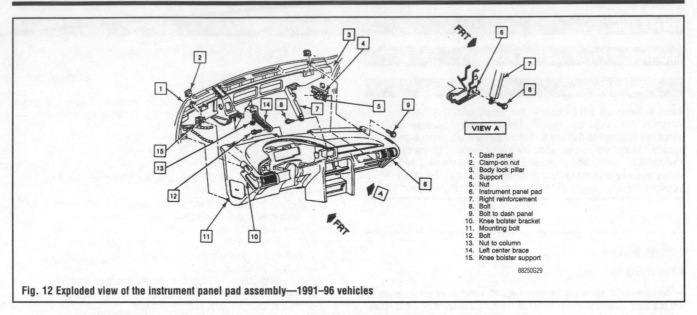

1. Dash panel
2. Clamp-on nut
3. Body lock pillar
4. Support
5. Nut
6. Instrument panel pad
7. Right reinforcement
8. Bolt
9. Bolt to dash panel
10. Knee bolster bracket
11. Mounting bolt
12. Bolt
13. Nut to column
14. Left center brace
15. Knee bolster support

88250G29

Fig. 12 Exploded view of the instrument panel pad assembly—1991–96 vehicles

34. Enable the SIR system as outlined in Section 6.
35. Install the right and left sound insulators.

Console

REMOVAL & INSTALLATION

Full-size and mini consoles are available depending on the model and options. The full-size includes a storage compartment at the rear. The mini console has a small compartment located at the front.

Full-Size Console

▶ **See Figure 13**

1. On the Beretta, remove the ashtray.
2. Remove the front compartment on the Corsica.
3. Remove the parking brake handle by removing the Phillips retaining screws.
4. Remove the shift lever handle/knob by removing the Torx® retaining screw or clip.
5. Remove the console trim plate by removing the 2 screws at the front of the trim plate and then lifting and pulling forward to release from the retainers at the rear. On manual transaxles, remove the 4 boot retainer screws.

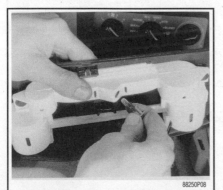

88250P05

Use an awl to remove the shift handle retaining clip . . .

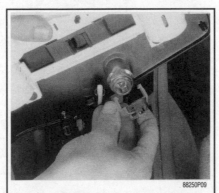

88250P06

. . . then remove the shift handle from the shaft

88250P07

Lift the console trim plate up and partially out

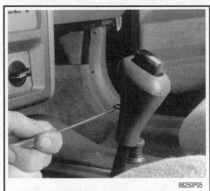

88250P08

Detach the bulb from the console trim plate . . .

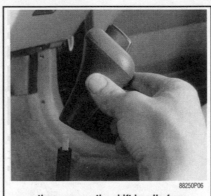

88250P09

. . . then detach any necessary electrical connectors from the plate

88250P10

Open the console rear compartment and lift out the liner, for access to the retaining screws

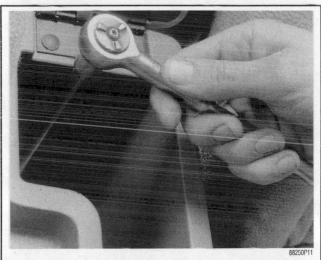

Unfasten the retaining bolts, then remove the console from the vehicle

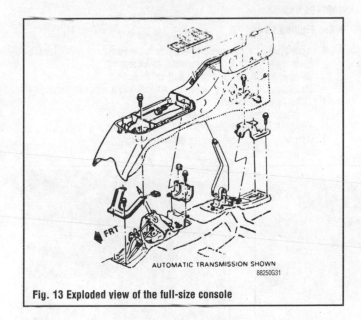

Fig. 13 Exploded view of the full-size console

6. Open the rear compartment of the console and remove the liner. Remove the trunk release switch by pulling out carefully and disconnecting the electrical connector. Remove the 2 bolts from the bottom of the compartment.

7. Remove the 2 bolts from the center, in the upper rear of the area covered by the trim plate.

8. Remove the 2 bolts at the front of the console.

9. Lift the console, then lift from underneath and push the power window switch out of the console.

10. Detach the electrical connector at the power window switch, then push the switch back into the console.

11. Remove the console.

12. Installation is the reverse of the removal procedure. Make sure all components are tightened securely.

Mini Console

◆ **See Figure 14**

1. Remove the liner from the front compartment.
2. Remove the 2 screws from the front compartment.
3. Remove the Torx screw holding the shift handle/knob.
4. Remove 1 screw from each side of the rear of the console.
5. Remove the console.

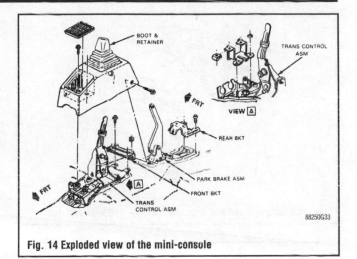

Fig. 14 Exploded view of the mini-console

6. On manual transaxles, remove the 4 boot retainer screws from inside the console.

7. Installation is the reverse of the removal procedure. Make sure all components are tightened securely.

Door Trim Panel

REMOVAL & INSTALLATION

1988–90 Vehicles

◆ **See Figures 15, 16, 17 and 18**

The armrest on the four door models is an integral part of the trim panel. The armrest on the two door models is retained by screws and inverted nuts from the back side of the trim panel and requires trim panel removal.

On models equipped with power window switches make sure the ignition is in the off position to eliminate the possibility of accidentally shorting out the switch with a metal tool.

1. Remove the door trim retaining screws on the two door models.
2. On the four door models, remove the armrest pull cups.
3. Remove the window regulator handle, if present.
4. Disconnect the switches if present.
5. Remove the trim panel using tool J-24595B or equivalent to disengage the fasteners on the trim panel from the holes in the door inner panel.

To install:

6. Insert the wiring harnesses, if present, through the openings in the trim panel.

7. Connect the switches to the wiring harnesses, if present.

8. Position the trim panel to the door by aligning the fasteners on the trim panel to the holes in the door inner panel and pressing the trim panel to the door until the fasteners are fully engaged.

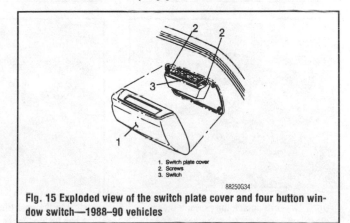

1. Switch plate cover
2. Screws
3. Switch

Fig. 15 Exploded view of the switch plate cover and four button window switch—1988–90 vehicles

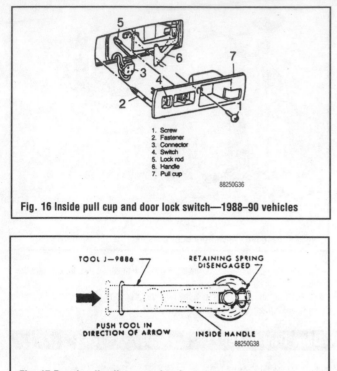

1. Screw
2. Fastener
3. Connector
4. Switch
5. Lock rod
6. Handle
7. Pull cup

88250G36

Fig. 16 Inside pull cup and door lock switch—1988–90 vehicles

Fig. 17 Door handle clip removal tool

9. Install the window regulator handle, if present.
10. Install the inside handle pull cups.
11. Install the armrest pull cups on the four door models.
12. Install the trim panel retaining screws on the two door models.

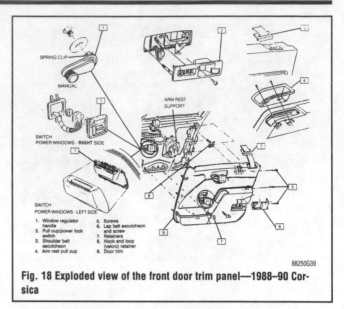

1. Window regulator handle
2. Pull cup/power lock switch
3. Shoulder belt escutcheon
4. Arm rest pull cup
5. Screws
6. Lap belt escutcheon and screw
7. Retainers
8. Hook and loop (velcro) retainer
9. Door trim

88250G39

Fig. 18 Exploded view of the front door trim panel—1988–90 Corsica

1991–96 Vehicles

♦ See Figures 19 and 20

1. If equipped with manual windows, remove the window regulator handle.
2. Remove the inside door handle and lock escutcheon.
3. Using Torx® No. 30, remove the pull handle screws.
4. Disengage the nine clips and velcro retainer with a door trim removal tool No. J 38778, or equivalent.
5. If necessary, remove the trim panel retaining screws.
6. Pull the trim upward and detach it from the inner sealing strip.
7. Remove the trim panel from the door.

88250P12

Unfasten the door handle escutcheon retaining screw

88250P13

Remove the remaining escutcheon retaining screw(s) . . .

88250P14

. . . then maneuver the door handle escutcheon around the handle and out of the vehicle

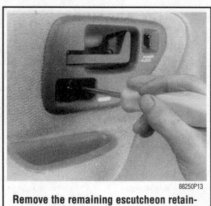

88250P15

Don't forget to detach the power window electrical connector from the escutcheon

88250P16

Unfasten the door trim panel retaining screws located in the pull handle

Remove the screws located on the outer side of the trim panel

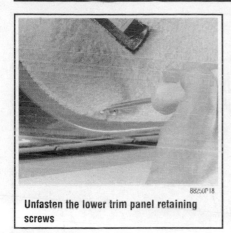

Unfasten the lower trim panel retaining screws

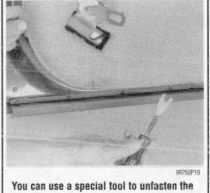

You can use a special tool to unfasten the trim panel retaining buttons

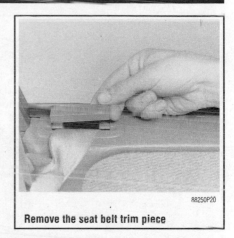

Remove the seat belt trim piece

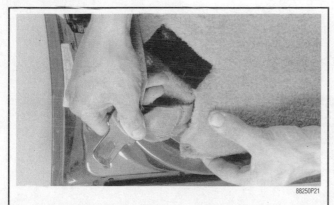

Feed the bottom of the seat belt through the door trim panel . . .

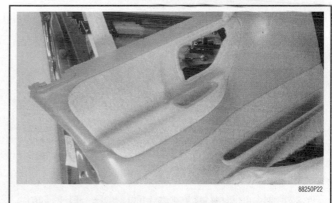

. . . then remove the door trim panel from the vehicle

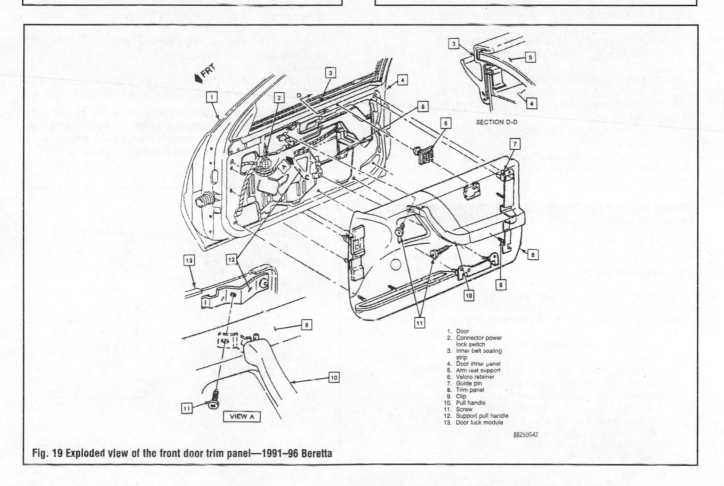

1. Door
2. Connector power lock switch
3. Inner belt sealing strip
4. Door inner panel
5. Arm rest support
6. Velcro retainer
7. Guide pin
8. Trim panel
9. Clip
10. Pull handle
11. Screw
12. Support pull handle
13. Door lock module

SECTION D-D

VIEW A

FRT

Fig. 19 Exploded view of the front door trim panel—1991–96 Beretta

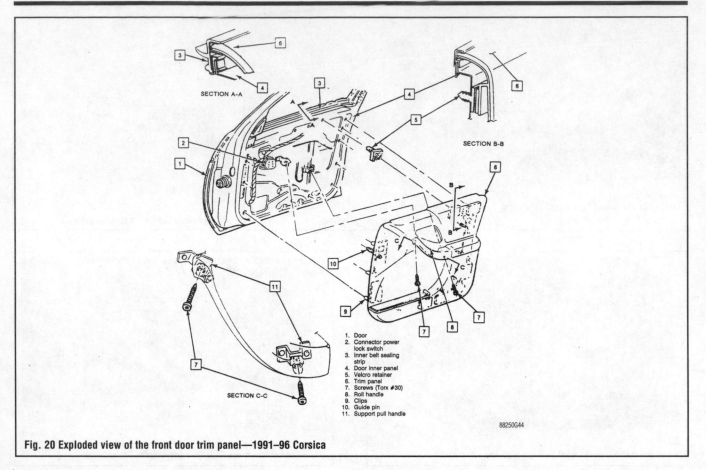

1. Door
2. Connector power lock switch
3. Inner belt sealing strip
4. Door inner panel
5. Velcro retainer
6. Trim panel
7. Screws (Torx #30)
8. Roll handle
9. Clips
10. Guide pin
11. Support pull handle

88250G44

Fig. 20 Exploded view of the front door trim panel—1991–96 Corsica

8. Remove the clips and velcro retainer from the trim panel.

To install:

9. Install the clips and velcro retainer to the trim panel.

10. Position the trim panel to the door and align the top edge to the inner sealing strip.

11. Press the trim panel into the sealing strip.

12. Route the door lock harness through the opening of the trim pad.

13. Install the trim panel to the door inner panel aligning the guide pins to the slots in the inner panel.

14. Position the clips against the holes in the door inner panel.

15. Apply pressure to secure to secure the velcro and engage the clips.

16. Using Torx® No. 30, install the pull handle screws.

17. Install the inside door handle and lock escutcheon.

18. Install the window regulator handle.

Door Lock Module

REMOVAL & INSTALLATION

▶ See Figures 21 and 22

All of the parts are contained in one unit, a module assembly. The entire module assembly is therefore removed when repair to any component is required except the power lock actuator and the inside handle which can be serviced on the vehicle.

1. Remove the trim panel as outlined earlier.

2. Loosen the water deflector.

3. Remove the front door lock pillar at the handle cover assembly.

4. Disconnect the lock cylinder at the lock rod.

5. Disconnect the outside handle at the lock rod.

6. If removing a rear door lock module, perform the following:

   a. Remove the inner and outer belt sealing strip.

   b. Remove the door glass.

   c. Remove the stationary vent glass.

7. Remove the lock retaining screws.

8. Remove the rivets by punching out the mandrel, then using a ³⁄₁₆ in. drill bit.

9. Disconnect the connector at the power lock system.

10. Remove the lock module assembly.

To install:

11. Place the lock module assembly in position through the access hole in the door inner panel. Align the module to the holes in the door facing.

➡**While performing the next step the lock assembly must be held tightly against the door facing while tightening the screws. All screws must be driven at a 90° angle to the door facing to prevent cross threading or stripping of screws. It is also required to tighten the screws to 62 inch lbs. (7 Nm).**

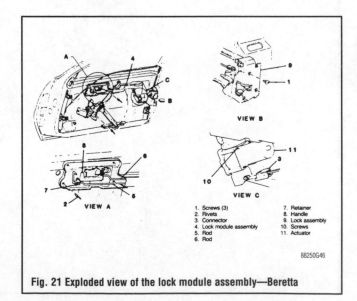

1. Screws (3)
2. Rivets
3. Connector
4. Lock module assembly
5. Rod
6. Rod
7. Retainer
8. Handle
9. Lock assembly
10. Screws
11. Actuator

88250G46

Fig. 21 Exploded view of the lock module assembly—Beretta

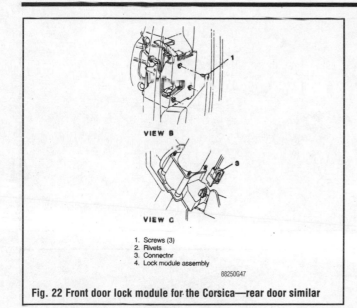

1. Screws (3)
2. Rivets
3. Connector
4. Lock module assembly

88250G47

Fig. 22 Front door lock module for the Corsica—rear door similar

12. Install and torque the retaining screws.
13. Install the connector to the power lock system.
14. Install new rivets using 3/16 in. x 1/4 in. peel type rivets.
15. For front door lock modules, perform the following:
    a. Connect the outside handle to the lock rod.
    b. Connect the lock cylinder to the lock rod.
Check the lock system for proper operation.
16. If installing a rear door lock module, perform the following:
17. Install the stationary vent glass.
18. Install the division channel.
19. Install the door glass.
20. Install the inner and outer belt sealing strip.
21. Install the cover assembly.
22. Install the water deflector and the trim panel.

Door Locks

REMOVAL & INSTALLATION

♦ **See Figures 23 and 24**

1. Remove the lock module assembly.
2. Disconnect all rods attached to the lock.
3. Remove the lock assembly from the module.

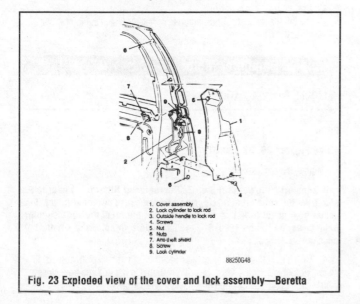

1. Cover assembly
2. Lock cylinder to lock rod
3. Outside handle to lock rod
4. Screws
5. Nut
6. Anti-theft shield
7. Screw
8. Lock cylinder
9. Lock cylinder

88250G48

Fig. 23 Exploded view of the cover and lock assembly—Beretta

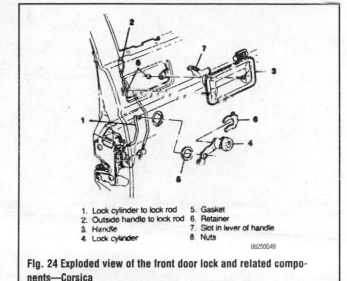

1. Lock cylinder to lock rod
2. Outside handle to lock rod
3. Handle
4. Lock cylinder
5. Gasket
6. Retainer
7. Slot in lever of handle
8. Nuts

88250G49

Fig. 24 Exploded view of the front door lock and related components—Corsica

➡A new service lock will have a block-out plug installed. Do not operate the lock or remove the plug until the lock is installed and the rod is connected to the lock.

4. Installation is the reverse of the removal procedure.

Rear Compartment Lid and Lift Window Lock

REMOVAL & INSTALLATION

♦ **See Figures 25, 26 and 27**

1. On the Corsica sedan, remove the rivets using a 1/4 in. (6mm) drill bit.
2. Remove the retaining screws on the Corsica hatchback and Beretta. On the Beretta the screws are located on the body end panel.
3. Remove the screws holding the release solenoid to the lock and remove the lock.
To install:
4. Position the lock and install the screws on the Corsica sedan and Beretta and the nuts on the Corsica hatchback. Tighten the screws to 53 inch lbs. (6 Nm). and the nuts to 124 inch lbs. (14 Nm).
5. Install the screws holding the release solenoid to the lock and tighten to 53 inch lbs. (6 Nm).

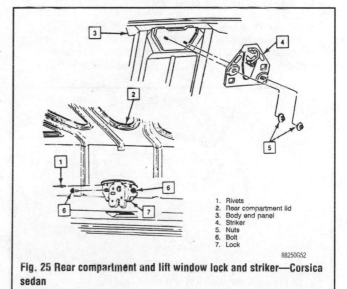

1. Rivets
2. Rear compartment lid
3. Body end panel
4. Striker
5. Nuts
6. Bolt
7. Lock

88250G52

Fig. 25 Rear compartment and lift window lock and striker—Corsica sedan

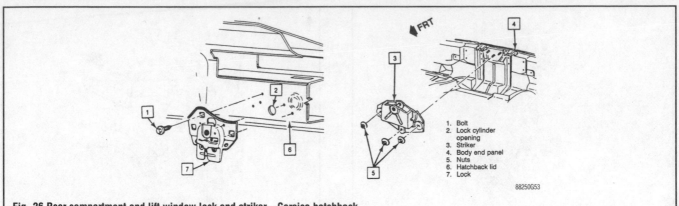

Fig. 26 Rear compartment and lift window lock and striker—Corsica hatchback

1. Bolt
2. Lock cylinder opening
3. Striker
4. Body end panel
5. Nuts
6. Hatchback lid
7. Lock

88250G53

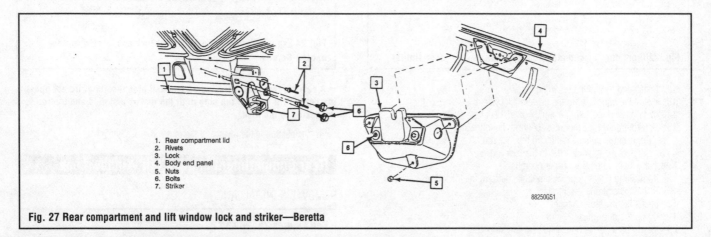

1. Rear compartment lid
2. Rivets
3. Lock
4. Body end panel
5. Nuts
6. Bolts
7. Striker

88250G51

Fig. 27 Rear compartment and lift window lock and striker—Beretta

Window Regulator

REMOVAL & INSTALLATION

♦ **See Figure 28**

1. Tape the glass in the full up position.
2. Remove the trim panel.
3. Remove the armrest support brackets or hanger plates. Drill out the hanger plate rivets using a ³⁄₁₆ in. drill bit.
4. Loosen the water deflector.
5. On all 1990–96 models, except 1990 Beretta, remove the lock module assembly as outlined earlier.
6. Drill out the four regulator retaining rivets using a ³⁄₁₆ in. drill bit.
7. Remove the regulator by disengaging the roller from the glass sash channel, disconnecting the electrical connector to the motor (power window systems) and removing the regulator through the door inner access hole.

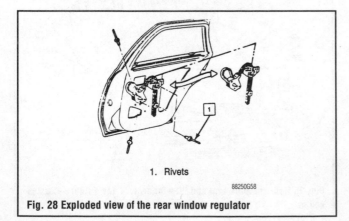

1. Rivets

88250G58

Fig. 28 Exploded view of the rear window regulator

➡ If you wish to remove the electric motor from the regulator, refer to the Electric Window Motor procedure. The regulator lift arm is under tension from the counterbalance spring and can cause personal injury if the sector gear is not locked in position.

To install:

8. Install the regulator through the door inner access hole and attach the roller to the sash channel.
9. Connect the electrical connector to the motor (power window systems).
10. Install the rivets using ¼ in. peel type.
11. On all 1990–96 models, except 1990 Beretta, install the lock module assembly as outlined earlier.
12. Install the water deflector.
13. Install the armrest support brackets or hanger plates using new rivets.
14. Install the trim panel.

Window Regulator Motor

REMOVAL & INSTALLATION

Front

♦ **See Figures 29, 30 and 31**

Remove the regulator.

➡ It is important to perform Step 2. The regulator lift arm is under tension from the counterbalance spring and can cause personal injury if the sector gear is not locked in position. Inspect the regulator for a counter balance spring. Some 1990–92 Corsica models do not use a counterbalance spring.

1. Drill a hole through the regulator sector gear and backplate and install a screw and nut to lock the sector gear in position. Do not drill the hole closer than ½ in. (13mm) to the edge of the sector gear or backplate.

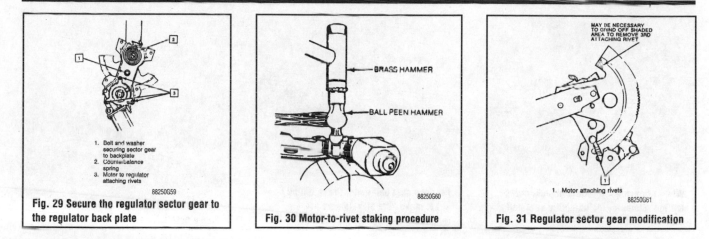

| Fig. 29 Secure the regulator sector gear to the regulator back plate | Fig. 30 Motor-to-rivet staking procedure | Fig. 31 Regulator sector gear modification |

1. Bolt and washer securing sector gear to backplate
2. Counterbalance spring
3. Motor to regulator attaching rivets

88250G59

BRASS HAMMER
BALL PEEN HAMMER

88250G60

MAY BE NECESSARY TO GRIND OFF SHADED AREA TO REMOVE 3RD ATTACHING RIVET

1. Motor attaching rivets

88250G61

2. Drill out the rivets using a ³⁄₁₆ in. drill bit.
3. Remove the motor.

➡ **Depending on the position of the regulator, it may be necessary to remove portions of one of the remaining rivets later.**

To install:

4. Attach the motor to the regulator using a ¼ in. x ³¹⁄₃₂ in. rivets.
5. Once at least 2 rivets are installed, remove the screw and nut locking the sector gear in the fixed position. Use an electric power source to rotate the regulator in the desired direction to provide access to the remaining rivet.

➡ **It may be necessary to grind a portion off the corner of the sector gear on some models to provide space to remove the remaining rivet.**

6. Once the remaining rivet can be removed install a new one.
7. Install the regulator and motor assembly to the door inner panel using ¼ in. x ½ in. peel type rivet.

Rear

1. Remove the regulator.
2. Remove the motor by drilling out the rivets holding the motor to the actuator using a ¼ in. (6mm) drill bit.

To install:

3. Attach the motor to the regulator using a ¼ in. x ³¹⁄₃₂ in. rivets.
4. Install the regulator.

Inside Rear View Mirror

REPLACEMENT

The rearview mirror head is attached to a support with a retaining screw. The support is secured to the windshield glass. This support is installed by the glass supplier using a plastic-polyvinyl butyl adhesive.

Service replacement windshield glass has the mirror support bonded to the glass assembly.

Service kits are available to replace a detached mirror support or install a new part. Follow the manufacturer's instructions for replacement.

Seats

REMOVAL & INSTALLATION

◗ **See Figures 32 and 33**

The front seat assemblies are secured to the floor at 3 points. The center, front of the seat is bolted to an adjuster which in turn is secured by 2 bolts that thread into weld nuts in the floor pan. Two rollers at the rear of the seat which are an integral part of the seat, travel in guide tracks. The inboard track is secured to the side of the inner rocker panel and the outboard track secures to the side of the floor pan tunnel. Removal and installation of both front and rear

seats are obvious upon inspection. When installing the seats and cushions the following torque specifications should be used:

1988–90 Vehicles:
- Seat adjuster to floor pan bolts—7–11 ft. lbs. (10–15 Nm).
- Recliner to seat frame bolts—15–21 ft. lbs. (20–28 Nm).
- Seat adjuster to seat frame nut—7–10 ft. lbs. (10–14 Nm).
- Track guide to floor pan bolt—7–10 ft. lbs. (10–14 Nm).

1991–92 Vehicles
- Seat adjuster to floor pan bolts—26 ft. lbs. (36 Nm)
- Recliner to seat frame bolts—18 ft. lbs. (24 Nm)
- Seat adjuster to seat frame nut—21 ft. lbs. (29 Nm)
- Rear seat cushion to floor pan bolts—11 ft. lbs. (15 Nm)
- Rear seat back anchor bolts—31 ft. lbs. (42 Nm)
- Foldown rear seat back bolts—18 ft. lbs. (25 Nm)

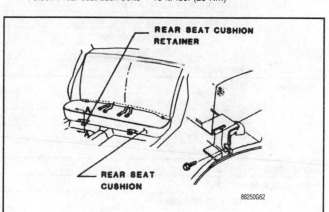

REAR SEAT CUSHION RETAINER

REAR SEAT CUSHION

88250G62

Fig. 32 Rear seat cushion attachment points

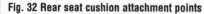

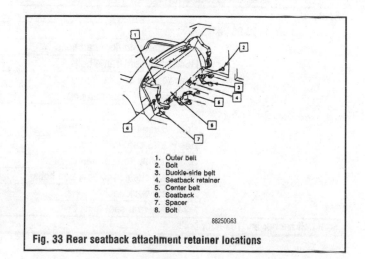

1. Outer belt
2. Bolt
3. Buckle-side belt
4. Seatback retainer
5. Center belt
6. Seatback
7. Spacer
8. Bolt

88250G63

Fig. 33 Rear seatback attachment retainer locations

When removing the rear seatback, unfasten the retainers, including the seat belt retaining bolt

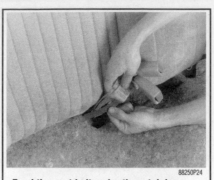
Feed the seat belt under the retaining strap, make sure all retainers are removed . . .

. . . then remove the rear seatback from the vehicle

TORQUE SPECIFICATIONS

Component			ft. lbs.	inch lbs.	Nm
Bumpers					
	Front bumper-to-absorber bolts		18-25		24-34
	Rear bumper-to-absorber bolts		18-25		24-34
Doors	Hinge-to-body				
		1988-90 vehicles	15-20		20-27
		1991-96 vehicles	18		25
	Check link screws		18		25
	Lock module retaining screws			62	7
	Front window channel retainer screws				
		1988-90 vehicles		80-106	9-12
		1991-96 vehicles		97	11
	Rear regulator-to-sash bolts			75	8.5
Hatchback lift window					
	Hinge-to-lift window bolts		19		25
	Lock retaining nuts			124	14
	Solenoid-to-lock screws			53	6
	Strut-to-body bolt		30		40
Hood hinge-to-hinge bolts			24		33
Rear compartment lid					
	Hinge-to-lid screws		21		29
	Lock retaining screws			53	6
	Solenoid-to-lock screws			53	6
Seats					
	1988-90 vehicles				
		Seat adjuster-to-floor pan bolts	10		14
		Recliner-to-seat frame bolts	18		25
		Seat adjuster-to-seat frame nut	10		14
		Track guide-to-floor pan bolt	10		14
	1991-96 vehicles				
		Seat adjuster-to-floor pan bolts	26		36
		Recliner-to-seat frame bolts	18		24
		Seat adjuster-to-seat frame nut	21		29
		Rear seat cushion-to-floor pan bolts	11		15
		Rear seat back anchor bolts	31		42
		Fold-down rear seat back bolts	18		25
Seat belt anchor and retractor bolts			31		42

88250C01

GLOSSARY

AIR/FUEL RATIO: The ratio of air-to-gasoline by weight in the fuel mixture drawn into the engine.

AIR INJECTION: One method of reducing harmful exhaust emissions by injecting air into each of the exhaust ports of an engine. The fresh air entering the hot exhaust manifold causes any remaining fuel to be burned before it can exit the tailpipe.

ALTERNATOR: A device used for converting mechanical energy into electrical energy.

AMMETER: An instrument, calibrated in amperes, used to measure the flow of an electrical current in a circuit. Ammeters are always connected in series with the circuit being tested.

AMPERE: The rate of flow of electrical current present when one volt of electrical pressure is applied against one ohm of electrical resistance.

ANALOG COMPUTER: Any microprocessor that uses similar (analogous) electrical signals to make its calculations.

ARMATURE: A laminated, soft iron core wrapped by a wire that converts electrical energy to mechanical energy as in a motor or relay. When rotated in a magnetic field, it changes mechanical energy into electrical energy as in a generator.

ATMOSPHERIC PRESSURE: The pressure on the Earth's surface caused by the weight of the air in the atmosphere. At sea level, this pressure is 14.7 psi at 32°F (101 kPa at 0°C).

ATOMIZATION: The breaking down of a liquid into a fine mist that can be suspended in air.

AXIAL PLAY: Movement parallel to a shaft or bearing bore.

BACKFIRE: The sudden combustion of gases in the intake or exhaust system that results in a loud explosion.

BACKLASH: The clearance or play between two parts, such as meshed gears.

BACKPRESSURE: Restrictions in the exhaust system that slow the exit of exhaust gases from the combustion chamber.

BAKELITE: A heat resistant, plastic insulator material commonly used in printed circuit boards and transistorized components.

BALL BEARING: A bearing made up of hardened inner and outer races between which hardened steel balls roll.

BALLAST RESISTOR: A resistor in the primary ignition circuit that lowers voltage after the engine is started to reduce wear on ignition components.

BEARING: A friction reducing, supportive device usually located between a stationary part and a moving part.

BIMETAL TEMPERATURE SENSOR: Any sensor or switch made of two dissimilar types of metal that bend when heated or cooled due to the different expansion rates of the alloys. These types of sensors usually function as an on/off switch.

BLOWBY: Combustion gases, composed of water vapor and unburned fuel, that leak past the piston rings into the crankcase during normal engine operation. These gases are removed by the PCV system to prevent the buildup of harmful acids in the crankcase.

BRAKE PAD: A brake shoe and lining assembly used with disc brakes.

BRAKE SHOE: The backing for the brake lining. The term is, however, usually applied to the assembly of the brake backing and lining.

BUSHING: A liner, usually removable, for a bearing; an anti-friction liner used in place of a bearing.

CALIPER: A hydraulically activated device in a disc brake system, which is mounted straddling the brake rotor (disc). The caliper contains at least one piston and two brake pads. Hydraulic pressure on the piston(s) forces the pads against the rotor.

CAMSHAFT: A shaft in the engine on which are the lobes (cams) which operate the valves. The camshaft is driven by the crankshaft, via a belt, chain or gears, at one half the crankshaft speed.

CAPACITOR: A device which stores an electrical charge.

CARBON MONOXIDE (CO): A colorless, odorless gas given off as a normal byproduct of combustion. It is poisonous and extremely dangerous in confined areas, building up slowly to toxic levels without warning if adequate ventilation is not available.

CARBURETOR: A device, usually mounted on the intake manifold of an engine, which mixes the air and fuel in the proper proportion to allow even combustion.

CATALYTIC CONVERTER: A device installed in the exhaust system, like a muffler, that converts harmful byproducts of combustion into carbon dioxide and water vapor by means of a heat-producing chemical reaction.

CENTRIFUGAL ADVANCE: A mechanical method of advancing the spark timing by using flyweights in the distributor that react to centrifugal force generated by the distributor shaft rotation.

CHECK VALVE: Any one-way valve installed to permit the flow of air, fuel or vacuum in one direction only.

CHOKE: A device, usually a moveable valve, placed in the intake path of a carburetor to restrict the flow of air.

CIRCUIT: Any unbroken path through which an electrical current can flow. Also used to describe fuel flow in some instances.

CIRCUIT BREAKER: A switch which protects an electrical circuit from overload by opening the circuit when the current flow exceeds a predetermined level. Some circuit breakers must be reset manually, while most reset automatically.

COIL (IGNITION): A transformer in the ignition circuit which steps up the voltage provided to the spark plugs.

COMBINATION MANIFOLD: An assembly which includes both the intake and exhaust manifolds in one casting.

COMBINATION VALVE: A device used in some fuel systems that routes fuel vapors to a charcoal storage canister instead of venting them into the atmosphere. The valve relieves fuel tank pressure and allows fresh air into the tank as the fuel level drops to prevent a vapor lock situation.

COMPRESSION RATIO: The comparison of the total volume of the cylinder and combustion chamber with the piston at BDC and the piston at TDC.

CONDENSER: 1. An electrical device which acts to store an electrical charge, preventing voltage surges. 2. A radiator-like device in the air conditioning system in which refrigerant gas condenses into a liquid, giving off heat.

CONDUCTOR: Any material through which an electrical current can be transmitted easily.

CONTINUITY: Continuous or complete circuit. Can be checked with an ohmmeter.

COUNTERSHAFT: An intermediate shaft which is rotated by a mainshaft and transmits, in turn, that rotation to a working part.

CRANKCASE: The lower part of an engine in which the crankshaft and related parts operate.

CRANKSHAFT: The main driving shaft of an engine which receives reciprocating motion from the pistons and converts it to rotary motion.

CYLINDER: In an engine, the round hole in the engine block in which the piston(s) ride.

CYLINDER BLOCK: The main structural member of an engine in which is found the cylinders, crankshaft and other principal parts.

CYLINDER HEAD: The detachable portion of the engine, usually fastened to the top of the cylinder block and containing all or most of the combustion chambers. On overhead valve engines, it contains the valves and their operating parts. On overhead cam engines, it contains the camshaft as well.

DEAD CENTER: The extreme top or bottom of the piston stroke.

DETONATION: An unwanted explosion of the air/fuel mixture in the combustion chamber caused by excess heat and compression, advanced timing, or an overly lean mixture. Also referred to as "ping".

DIAPHRAGM: A thin, flexible wall separating two cavities, such as in a vacuum advance unit.

DIESELING: A condition in which hot spots in the combustion chamber cause the engine to run on after the key is turned off.

DIFFERENTIAL: A geared assembly which allows the transmission of motion between drive axles, giving one axle the ability to turn faster than the other.

DIODE: An electrical device that will allow current to flow in one direction only.

DISC BRAKE: A hydraulic braking assembly consisting of a brake disc, or rotor, mounted on an axle, and a caliper assembly containing, usually two brake pads which are activated by hydraulic pressure. The pads are forced against the sides of the disc, creating friction which slows the vehicle.

DISTRIBUTOR: A mechanically driven device on an engine which is responsible for electrically firing the spark plug at a predetermined point of the piston stroke.

DOWEL PIN: A pin, inserted in mating holes in two different parts allowing those parts to maintain a fixed relationship.

DRUM BRAKE: A braking system which consists of two brake shoes and one or two wheel cylinders, mounted on a fixed backing plate, and a brake drum, mounted on an axle, which revolves around the assembly.

DWELL: The rate, measured in degrees of shaft rotation, at which an electrical circuit cycles on and off.

ELECTRONIC CONTROL UNIT (ECU): Ignition module, module, amplifier or igniter. See Module for definition.

ELECTRONIC IGNITION: A system in which the timing and firing of the spark plugs is controlled by an electronic control unit, usually called a module. These systems have no points or condenser.

END-PLAY: The measured amount of axial movement in a shaft.

ENGINE: A device that converts heat into mechanical energy.

EXHAUST MANIFOLD: A set of cast passages or pipes which conduct exhaust gases from the engine.

FEELER GAUGE: A blade, usually metal, or precisely predetermined thickness, used to measure the clearance between two parts.

FIRING ORDER: The order in which combustion occurs in the cylinders of an engine. Also the order in which spark is distributed to the plugs by the distributor.

FLOODING: The presence of too much fuel in the intake manifold and combustion chamber which prevents the air/fuel mixture from firing, thereby causing a no-start situation.

FLYWHEEL: A disc shaped part bolted to the rear end of the crankshaft. Around the outer perimeter is affixed the ring gear. The starter drive engages the ring gear, turning the flywheel, which rotates the crankshaft, imparting the initial starting motion to the engine.

FOOT POUND (ft. lbs. or sometimes, ft.lb.): The amount of energy or work needed to raise an item weighing one pound, a distance of one foot.

FUSE: A protective device in a circuit which prevents circuit overload by breaking the circuit when a specific amperage is present. The device is constructed around a strip or wire of a lower amperage rating than the circuit it is designed to protect. When an amperage higher than that stamped on the fuse is present in the circuit, the strip or wire melts, opening the circuit.

GEAR RATIO: The ratio between the number of teeth on meshing gears.

GENERATOR: A device which converts mechanical energy into electrical energy.

HEAT RANGE: The measure of a spark plug's ability to dissipate heat from its firing end. The higher the heat range, the hotter the plug fires.

HUB: The center part of a wheel or gear.

HYDROCARBON (HC): Any chemical compound made up of hydrogen and carbon. A major pollutant formed by the engine as a byproduct of combustion.

HYDROMETER: An instrument used to measure the specific gravity of a solution.

INCH POUND (inch lbs.; sometimes in.lb. or in. lbs.): One twelfth of a foot pound.

INDUCTION: A means of transferring electrical energy in the form of a magnetic field. Principle used in the ignition coil to increase voltage.

INJECTOR: A device which receives metered fuel under relatively low pressure and is activated to inject the fuel into the engine under relatively high pressure at a predetermined time.

INPUT SHAFT: The shaft to which torque is applied, usually carrying the driving gear or gears.

INTAKE MANIFOLD: A casting of passages or pipes used to conduct air or a fuel/air mixture to the cylinders.

JOURNAL: The bearing surface within which a shaft operates.

KEY: A small block usually fitted in a notch between a shaft and a hub to prevent slippage of the two parts.

MANIFOLD: A casting of passages or set of pipes which connect the cylinders to an inlet or outlet source.

MANIFOLD VACUUM: Low pressure in an engine intake manifold formed just below the throttle plates. Manifold vacuum is highest at idle and drops under acceleration.

MASTER CYLINDER: The primary fluid pressurizing device in a hydraulic system. In automotive use, it is found in brake and hydraulic clutch systems and is pedal activated, either directly or, in a power brake system, through the power booster.

MODULE: Electronic control unit, amplifier or igniter of solid state or integrated design which controls the current flow in the ignition primary circuit based on input from the pick-up coil. When the module opens the primary circuit, high secondary voltage is induced in the coil.

NEEDLE BEARING: A bearing which consists of a number (usually a large number) of long, thin rollers.

OHM: (Ω) The unit used to measure the resistance of conductor-to-electrical flow. One ohm is the amount of resistance that limits current flow to one ampere in a circuit with one volt of pressure.

OHMMETER: An instrument used for measuring the resistance, in ohms, in an electrical circuit.

OUTPUT SHAFT: The shaft which transmits torque from a device, such as a transmission.

OVERDRIVE: A gear assembly which produces more shaft revolutions than that transmitted to it.

OVERHEAD CAMSHAFT (OHC): An engine configuration in which the camshaft is mounted on top of the cylinder head and operates the valve either directly or by means of rocker arms.

OVERHEAD VALVE (OHV): An engine configuration in which all of the valves are located in the cylinder head and the camshaft is located in the cylinder block. The camshaft operates the valves via lifters and pushrods.

OXIDES OF NITROGEN (NOx): Chemical compounds of nitrogen produced as a byproduct of combustion. They combine with hydrocarbons to produce smog.

OXYGEN SENSOR: Use with the feedback system to sense the presence of oxygen in the exhaust gas and signal the computer which can reference the voltage signal to an air/fuel ratio.

PINION: The smaller of two meshing gears.

PISTON RING: An open-ended ring with fits into a groove on the outer diameter of the piston. Its chief function is to form a seal between the piston and cylinder wall. Most automotive pistons have three rings: two for compression sealing; one for oil sealing.

PRELOAD: A predetermined load placed on a bearing during assembly or by adjustment.

PRIMARY CIRCUIT: the low voltage side of the ignition system which consists of the ignition switch, ballast resistor or resistance wire, bypass, coil, electronic control unit and pick-up coil as well as the connecting wires and harnesses.

PRESS FIT: The mating of two parts under pressure, due to the inner diameter of one being smaller than the outer diameter of the other, or vice versa; an interference fit.

RACE: The surface on the inner or outer ring of a bearing on which the balls, needles or rollers move.

REGULATOR: A device which maintains the amperage and/or voltage levels of a circuit at predetermined values.

RELAY: A switch which automatically opens and/or closes a circuit.

RESISTANCE: The opposition to the flow of current through a circuit or electrical device, and is measured in ohms. Resistance is equal to the voltage divided by the amperage.

RESISTOR: A device, usually made of wire, which offers a preset amount of resistance in an electrical circuit.

RING GEAR: The name given to a ring-shaped gear attached to a differential case, or affixed to a flywheel or as part of a planetary gear set.

ROLLER BEARING: A bearing made up of hardened inner and outer races between which hardened steel rollers move.

ROTOR: 1. The disc-shaped part of a disc brake assembly, upon which the brake pads bear; also called, brake disc. 2. The device mounted atop the distributor shaft, which passes current to the distributor cap tower contacts.

SECONDARY CIRCUIT: The high voltage side of the ignition system, usually above 20,000 volts. The secondary includes the ignition coil, coil wire, distributor cap and rotor, spark plug wires and spark plugs.

SENDING UNIT: A mechanical, electrical, hydraulic or electro-magnetic device which transmits information to a gauge.

SENSOR: Any device designed to measure engine operating conditions or ambient pressures and temperatures. Usually electronic in nature and designed to send a voltage signal to an on-board computer, some sensors may operate as a simple on/off switch or they may provide a variable voltage signal (like a potentiometer) as conditions or measured parameters change.

SHIM: Spacers of precise, predetermined thickness used between parts to establish a proper working relationship.

SLAVE CYLINDER: In automotive use, a device in the hydraulic clutch system which is activated by hydraulic force, disengaging the clutch.

SOLENOID: A coil used to produce a magnetic field, the effect of which is to produce work.

SPARK PLUG: A device screwed into the combustion chamber of a spark ignition engine. The basic construction is a conductive core inside of a ceramic insulator, mounted in an outer conductive base. An electrical charge from the spark plug wire travels along the conductive core and jumps a preset air gap to a grounding point or points at the end of the conductive base. The resultant spark ignites the fuel/air mixture in the combustion chamber.

SPLINES: Ridges machined or cast onto the outer diameter of a shaft or inner diameter of a bore to enable parts to mate without rotation.

TACHOMETER: A device used to measure the rotary speed of an engine, shaft, gear, etc., usually in rotations per minute.

THERMOSTAT: A valve, located in the cooling system of an engine, which is closed when cold and opens gradually in response to engine heating, controlling the temperature of the coolant and rate of coolant flow.

TOP DEAD CENTER (TDC): The point at which the piston reaches the top of its travel on the compression stroke.

TORQUE: The twisting force applied to an object.

TORQUE CONVERTER: A turbine used to transmit power from a driving member to a driven member via hydraulic action, providing changes in drive ratio and torque. In automotive use, it links the driveplate at the rear of the engine to the automatic transmission.

TRANSDUCER: A device used to change a force into an electrical signal.

TRANSISTOR: A semi-conductor component which can be actuated by a small voltage to perform an electrical switching function.

TUNE-UP: A regular maintenance function, usually associated with the replacement and adjustment of parts and components in the electrical and fuel systems of a vehicle for the purpose of attaining optimum performance.

TURBOCHARGER: An exhaust driven pump which compresses intake air and forces it into the combustion chambers at higher than atmospheric pressures. The increased air pressure allows more fuel to be burned and results in increased horsepower being produced.

VACUUM ADVANCE: A device which advances the ignition timing in response to increased engine vacuum.

VACUUM GAUGE: An instrument used to measure the presence of vacuum in a chamber.

VALVE: A device which control the pressure, direction of flow or rate of flow of a liquid or gas.

VALVE CLEARANCE: The measured gap between the end of the valve stem and the rocker arm, cam lobe or follower that activates the valve.

VISCOSITY: The rating of a liquid's internal resistance to flow.

VOLTMETER: An instrument used for measuring electrical force in units called volts. Voltmeters are always connected parallel with the circuit being tested.

WHEEL CYLINDER: Found in the automotive drum brake assembly, it is a device, actuated by hydraulic pressure, which, through internal pistons, pushes the brake shoes outward against the drums.

MASTER

INDEX